The McGraw-Hill Guide to Acquiring and Divesting Businesses

The McGraw-Hill Guide to Acquiring and Divesting Businesses

Edward E. Shea

McGraw-Hill

New York San Francisco Washington, D.C. Auckland Bogotá
Caracas Lisbon London Madrid Mexico City Milan
Montreal New Delhi San Juan Singapore
Sydney Tokyo Toronto

Library of Congress Cataloging-in-Publication Data

Shea, Edward E.
The McGraw-Hill reference book on acquiring and divesting businesses / by Edward E. Shea
p. cm.
ISBN 0-07-058030-8
1. Consolidation and merger of corporations—United States. 2. Corporate divestiture—United States. I. Title.
KF1477.S53 1998
346.73′06626—dc21 98-13577
CIP

McGraw-Hill

A Division of The ***McGraw·Hill*** *Companies*

1 2 3 4 5 6 7 8 9 0 DOC/DOC 9 0 3 2 1 0 9 8

ISBN 0-07-058030-8

The sponsoring editor for this book was Roger Marsh and the production supervisor was Suzanne W. B. Rapcavage. It was set in Palatino by Inkwell Publishing Services.

Printed and bound by R.R. Donnelley & Sons Company.

This book is printed on acid-free paper.

CONTENTS

ACKNOWLEDGMENTS

The author wishes to thank friends who helped to create the *McGraw-Hill Guide to Acquiring and Divesting Businesses*. Thanks to Amy Gaber and Amy Ost, senior editors at Irwin Publishing, who sponsored the original project. Thanks to Roger Marsh, editor at McGraw-Hill, who completed the project.

Thanks to Dr. Edmund Mantell who commented on Chapter 4; Dr. Suzanne O'Callaghan who commented on Chapter 9; and my partner Jeffrey Levin who commented on Chapters 6, 7 and 8.

Thanks to lawyers at Simpson Thacher & Bartlett; Dykema Gossett; and Cadwalader Wickersham & Taft who years ago helped me to learn the craft skills of M&A transactions, especially Day Brigham, Brian Sullivan, Paul Trigg, Jerry Shelby, Jack Fritts and Bill Clarke.

Thanks to Henry Reichhold, the founder of Reichhold Chemicals, Inc. and its CEO for over 50 years. Henry made an acquisition, a joint venture, a licensing agreement or just a friendly customer or supplier in most of the commercially developed nations of this world. Henry provided to the author a remarkable opportunity to plan and implement transactions throughout the world and then to work with the acquired businesses.

Thanks to Sam Heyman, the principal shareholder and CEO of GAF Corporation. Sam included the author in the slate of directors for his successful proxy contest to acquire control of GAF Corporation and in some of the takeover activities underwritten by financing raised by Drexel Burnham Lambert Incorporated. Sam also taught the author and other managers some of his remarkably skilled business analysis and planning methods.

Thanks to my partners at Windels, Marx, Davies & Ives with whom I work daily on acquisitions, divestitures and financing transactions that never cease to present new and interesting challenges.

Thanks also to the faculty and students at Pace University's Graduate School of Business and the New York Institute of Finance. It was to answer their many good questions that I began writing this book.

Thanks also to Marilyn Gibbs who did most of the word processing and organized the overall text.

Finally, thanks to my friends, who often told me not to work too hard, although I did not always take their advice.

EDWARD E. SHEA

The McGraw-Hill Guide to Acquiring and Divesting Businesses

Chapter 1

INTRODUCTION TO THE M&A MARKET

A. A MARKET OF SELLERS, BUYERS AND FINANCIAL RESOURCE AND SERVICE PROVIDERS

Acquiring and divesting businesses has become a major activity in the United States and other developed commercial nations. There are so many merger and acquisition transactions involving such large exchanges of value that the term "M&A Market" has come into common use.

Mergers & Acquisitions, a leading periodical, reported 6,083 completed acquisitions in the United States for 1996. For acquisitions of known price, the total price for 1996 was $596 billion. *Mergers & Acquisitions* reports only transactions for which the price is $5 million or more, so the actual number of acquisitions was far higher.

For 1997, *Mergers & Acquisitions* reported 6,843 completed acquisitions, and known prices totaled $709 billion. In addition, *Mergers & Acquisitions* reported that U.S. companies acquired non-U.S. companies during 1997 in 1,094 transactions with a total value of $82 billion.

Of course, the M&A market is not a "market" of the kinds established for the trading of securities or commodities. There are no exchanges where auctions of entire businesses are held. There are no dealers who make markets by bidding or asking for quotations to buy or sell entire businesses. Businesses cannot be bought and sold quickly or on standard terms like securities and commodities.

Nevertheless, the "market" analogy is appropriate. Throughout the United States and in other commercial nations, there are numerous sellers and buyers whose needs are served by a large infrastructure of skilled providers of financial resources and services. These financial resource and service providers operate as a network that has many characteristics of a market. Most important, they provide extensive information about prices, terms and customs so that acquisitions and divestitures can be planned and completed with a level of reliability that is relatively high in relation to their complexity. Thus, the "market" consists of sellers, buyers and the extensive infrastructure of resource and service providers who help them to make satisfactory transactions.

B. Sellers and Buyers

Sellers and buyers and their objectives are discussed at length in Chapter 2. At this point, it is sufficient to say that the M&A market serves a remarkably diverse range of sellers and buyers. For example, sellers include large corporations divesting subsidiaries and divisions; owners divesting entire corporations and businesses; venture capital firms exiting from leveraged buyouts; owners selling to retire and raise funds for estate planning purposes; owners selling to participate in a larger organization; and management or trustees selling failing or bankrupt businesses. Buyers include corporate strategic buyers, management groups, venture capital firms and employee stock ownership plans.

C. Financial Resource and Service Providers

The major financial resource and service providers that maintain an M&A market for sellers and buyers are as follows:

Investment Banking Firms. Investment banking firms include the giant firms headquartered in New York's financial community such as CS First Boston, Goldman Sachs, Lehman Brothers, Merrill Lynch, Morgan Stanley and Paine Webber. They also include firms from other regions of the nation such as BT Alex Brown, Hambrecht & Quist and Montgomery Securities. As a relatively recent addition, they include M&A subsidiaries of banks such as J.P. Morgan and First Union. Investment banking firms offer a wide range of services and financial resources, although only some of them may be provided in any particular transaction. Their services include finding and introducing sellers and buyers; providing advice on strategies, structuring and financing; valuation analysis; conducting "auction" and other negotiations for sellers and buyers; acting as an agent to raise equity and debt financing through private placements and public offerings of securities; providing "fairness opinions" and solvency letters; direct investment in some transactions; making markets in over-the-counter securities; and arranging block sales and other sales of securities received in M&A transactions.

Business Brokers. Persons who wish to sell (or buy) small businesses often attempt to do so themselves, but learn that it is a difficult task. Some then hire a business broker to identify and screen candidates and to act as an intermediary in negotiations. There are numerous business brokers throughout the United States. Many began as licensed real estate brokers who found it necessary to sell businesses in order to realize full value in real estate transactions. Some business brokers began in other fields such as securities brokerage. See Chapter 3 for a discussion of licensing of business brokers and agreements with business brokers.

Finders. Finders are firms or individuals hired to find potential buyers and sellers and introduce them to each other. Experienced finders provide valuable services because they are in continuous touch with corporate executives and business development departments, investment bankers and others active in the M&A market. Some maintain relationships that enable them to open doors to key decision makers. Like Dolly Levy in *The Matchmaker,* they provide introductions and receive compensation if a marriage follows. Unlike business brokers, finders need not participate in negotiations or bring about an offer from a ready, willing and able buyer. Not surprisingly, finders make many efforts that go unrewarded. Thus, they must be well compensated for the transactions that succeed.

Business and Financial Consultants. Thousands of firms and individuals provide business and financial consulting services throughout the United States. Large firms, such as Arthur D. Little and McKinsey & Co., provide a wide range of services including strategic advice, management analysis and restructuring and surveys. Firms such as The Wyatt Company provide advice on employee compensation and benefits, including actuarial services. Investment bankers, consulting departments of accounting firms and other professionals provide advice on financial matters. Except in specialized areas, business and financial consulting is unregulated. Thus anyone with useful experience can offer some kinds of consulting services for M&A transactions. However, most services for M&A transactions are provided by licensed or regulated professionals such as investment bankers, accountants, lawyers and actuaries.

Valuation Analysts. Numerous firms provide valuation advice, a field that has grown rapidly in recent years as methods and technology have advanced. Firms such as American Appraisal, Marshall & Stevens and Cushman & Wakefield that have been engaged for many years in appraising property from art works to real estate using traditional comparable value methods have expanded their services to include business valuations. Investment banking firms have also provided valuation services for many years with a tendency to focus on market values and earnings multiples rather than so-called intrinsic values. With the development of the discounted future cash flow method for valuing businesses, firms such as Duff & Phelps, Willamette Management and Houlihan, Lokey, Howard & Zukin gained leading roles in valuation analysis. The consulting departments of accounting firms also provide valuation services.

Corporate Business Development Departments. In recent decades, many companies have established business development departments to handle on a full-time basis a group of activities once handled on a part-time basis by senior management and committees having other primary responsibilities. These departments systematically identify and analyze opportunities to enhance the corporate business, including internal development of new markets, products, technologies and facilities and restructuring or shutdown of unsuccessful operations. Especially when the department staff includes managers recruited from the financial community, acquisitions and divestitures are likely to be considered equal, and sometimes preferable, alternatives to internal development. Some corporate development departments have extensive resources, including their own carefully developed computer models for analyzing internal operations, capital expenditure proposals, acquisitions and divestitures. They also maintain contacts with investment bankers, business brokers, finders, business and financial consultants and others who may be sources of acquisition and divestiture opportunities, financial resources and information.

Lenders. A large part of the funds for acquisition prices paid in cash is borrowed from institutional and other lenders. The primary sources are insurers, banks, credit finance companies, venture capital funds, small business investment companies and government agencies that provide loans or loan guarantees. Many lending institutions maintain departments having special experience in M&A transactions. Insurers generally provide long-term loans that may be cash flow or asset based. Banks provide intermediate-term, revolving credit and line of credit loans that may be cash flow or asset based. Credit finance companies, such as CIT and Heller, provide intermediate term and line of credit loans that are generally asset based and secured by first mortgages, although the borrower's projected cash flows are also carefully evaluated. Venture capital funds are best known for providing "mezzanine" financing, which consists of loans in exchange for subordinated debt (or redeemable preferred stock) secured perhaps by second mortgages. Depending on the structure and perceived risk, "mezzanine" lenders typically require extra compensation, including stock options or other "equity sweetener" devices.

Venture Capital Funds. For many decades, a growing number of individuals made venture capital investments in M&A transactions that offered more risk, but also more reward, than traditional investments. Venture capital funds were then organized to provide investment management and allow larger numbers of individual investors to participate. Venture capital fund activities have become so important that Coopers & Lybrand publishes a quarterly survey of their investments. Venture capital funds typically provide "mezzanine" debt financing and, most important, equity financing for management buyouts, ESOP buyouts and other acquisitions for which the buyer lacks equity capital to provide support for senior debt. In recent years, many venture capital funds moved beyond investing in acquisitions originated by others to making their own acquisitions of businesses. Since their objectives are financial rather than strategic, venture capital funds typically limit their acquisitions to businesses that can be resold or taken public within about five years.

Accounting Firms. Accounting firms provide a wide range of services for M&A transactions. The most vital role is the audit function, because buy and sell decisions, price negotiations, business plans, valuation analysis and many other factors are based upon confidence in audited financial statements. Accounting firms also provide "agreed-upon procedures letters" describing the results of limited reviews in order to meet closing requirements for acquisition and financing transactions. Many accounting firms, such as Price Waterhouse, Coopers LLP and Arthur Andersen & Co., have M&A departments that offer consulting services. The services include financial and tax planning, valuation analysis and "due diligence" reviews. The role of accounting firms in developing generally accepted accounting principles (GAAP) and generally accepted auditing standards (GAAS) through participation in the proposals and programs of the Financial Accounting Standards Board (FASB) and the American Institute of Certified Public Accountants (AICPA) has a strong influence on the strategies and structures for M&A transactions.

Law Firms. Many law firms have departments specializing in M&A transactions. Large firms (such as Simpson Thatcher & Bartlett and Cadwalader, Wickersham & Taft) and middle-sized firms (such as the author's firm, Windels, Marx, Davies & Ives) are engaged continuously in acquisition-related activities in a wide variety of fields. Lawyers function as coordinators in M&A transactions and often also as negotiators or spokespersons for management. They prepare the acquisition and financing agreements and related documents. They participate in "due diligence" reviews and obtain clearances from government agencies. They advise management how to plan and implement an acquisition in a lawful manner and prepare disclosure documents and other communications. They render opinions on legal issues, including the validity and enforceability of agreements and financial instruments. They also represent the buyer, seller or other persons in lawsuits or proceedings seeking to prevent an acquisition or resulting from disputes after acquisitions.

Proxy and Tender Offer Solicitation Firms. When an acquisition is accomplished by a merger or sale of substantially all assets of a publicly owned company, a vote of the shareholders is required. A high percentage of favorable votes (and a low ratio of dissenting votes) must be obtained within a relatively short time period. When a tender offer, whether friendly or hostile, is made to public shareholders, a high percentage of tenders must be obtained within a relatively short period of time. Firms such as Georgeson & Company Inc. and Kissel Blake Inc. specialize in solicitation of proxies and tenders under these challenging circumstances.

Transfer Agents, Indenture Trustees and Depositaries. The work of transfer for agents for shares of stock and indenture trustees for debt instruments is usually performed routinely. However, M&A transactions involve major changes of outstanding stock and debt including new issues, redemptions, recapitalizations and exchanges. Thus, a large volume of transactions must be processed rapidly and accurately in a short time. The corporate trust departments of banks and firms such as Registrar and Transfer Company and American Stock Transfer & Trust Company perform these services. When given advance notice and the necessary information, they can assemble a team of managers and the necessary clerical help to accomplish the transfers and payments. The corporate trust departments of banks also serve as depositories for shares tendered in response to tender offers and as agents for the proration and payment of the price to the tendering shareholders. This depository work is also complex and time-sensitive, both because shares are usually tendered almost entirely during the last few days of a tender offer, often by brokers' guarantees of delivery, and because shareholders sometimes withdraw tendered shares to sell in the market or to tender to a competitive offer.

Public and Investor Relations Firms. Acquisitions and divestitures affect many groups of people in many different ways—shareholders, employees, labor unions, lenders, customers, suppliers and competitors. They attract the interest of the newsmedia, government agencies, consumer organizations, arbitrageurs and others in making a competitive offer to buy. Public and investor relations firms, such as Edelman Public Relations, advise buyer and seller managements about the steps they should take to maintain good relations with the diverse groups affected or interested. Their work is usually coordinated carefully with the work of law firms preparing required disclosure documents and communications.

Corporation Service Companies. Acquisitions and divestitures usually require the filing of numerous documents with government agencies. For example, merger agreements and certificates, charter amendments and other documents often must be filed simultaneously with the state departments in cities such as Dover, Delaware; Albany, New York; and Lansing, Michigan and sometimes also in overseas nations. Franchise and other tax payments often must also be made concurrently. Corporation service companies, such as the CT Corporation System and Prentice Hall, maintain offices in the capital cities and make it possible to complete these filings and payments in a correct and timely manner at relatively modest costs.

Title Insurers. Acquisitions and divestitures often require title, mortgage, deed of trust, security interest, tax and court docket searches as well as title insurance on real properties being sold. Title insurers (such as Chicago Title, Ticor and Lawyer's Title) provide both the searches and title insurance based on their searches. Corporation service companies provide some search services, but do not provide title insurance.

Financial Printers, Engravers and Rapid Delivery Services. M&A transactions involving buyers and sellers with publicly traded securities require the services of skilled financial printers who can produce proxy statements, registration statements and prospectuses, tender offer statements and related materials with high quality, speed and strict confidentiality. Firms such as Bowne & Co. Inc., Corporate Printing Co. and R.R. Donnelly & Sons Co. perform this work, which routinely requires night work and the need to respond to frequent changes as the work progresses. These firms must also adapt to new technologies affecting their field, such as the Electronic Data Gathering, Analysis and Retrieval (EDGAR) System of the Securities and Exchange Commission. Firms such as Merrill Corporation offer EDGAR assistance to medium-sized companies not having in-house capabilities.

Engravers such as Banknote Corporation of America, Inc. provide stock certificates, notes, debentures, bonds, warrants, options and other securities meeting stock exchange rules and other requirements. While securities are increasingly held in "street names" without issuance of certificates registered in the names of the beneficial owners, state corporation laws continue to require corporations to furnish certificates to holders who request them.

Because acquisitions and divestitures are so time-sensitive, rapid delivery services (such as Federal Express and DHL) have become vital to their success. These firms have gained a reputation for speed and reliability. They are sometimes used for packages sent within a city and sometimes even within the same building complex.

Arbitrageurs. When acquisition and divestiture transactions involve businesses with publicly traded securities, there is always a possibility that arbitrageurs will see opportunities for trades that earn profits and also narrow spreads in the trading prices. Firms such as Carl Marks & Co. and Wyser-Pratte & Co., Inc. have been known for years for their skills in arbitrage. The high volumes of securities that typically change hands in M&A transactions and the inherent uncertainty whether the transactions will be completed create unusual opportunities for arbitrage firms. In general, arbitrage can be divided into two categories. The first is fully hedged arbitrage, which is risk-free except for a counterparty default. The second is "risk" arbitrage in which the arbitrageur takes a position that relies on the success of the transaction. "Risk" arbitrage was a major activity during the M&A boom of the middle and late 1980s, but became associated in public perception with abuses such as insider trading and "parking" to avoid requirements of the securities and antitrust laws. Arbitrage activities have been conducted more conservatively in the 1990s.

Publications Covering M&A Transactions. Unlike most major business developments, acquisitions and divestitures receive attention in general media publications such as television news, national news services and newspapers. The media like acquisitions and divestitures because they create change and sometimes stir controversy. They create opportunities for stories about colorful individuals who can be portrayed as captains of industry, financial wizards, or villains. Of greater importance are the professional publications such as *Mergers & Acquisitions,* MRL Publishing; *M&A Database,* ADP Data Services; *Mergerstat Review,* Houlihan, Lokey, Howard & Zukin; *Valuing a Business* and the *Venture Capital Sourcebook,* McGraw-Hill; *Financial Valuation: Businesses and Business Interests,* Maxwell McMillan; *Acquisition Monthly* and *International Mergers and Acquisitions,* Euromoney Publications; *The Merger Yearbook* and *Pratt's Guide to Venture Capital Sources,* Securities Data Publishing; and numerous publications of The Practicing Law Institute. These professional publications play an essential role in the "market" because they provide a continuing flow of information about prices and terms and serve as a forum in which experts describe new techniques in finance, tax, accounting, law and other fields.

Regulatory and Other Indirect Services. A variety of other service providers play important roles in M&A transactions. They include the Internal Revenue Service and government regulatory organizations such as the Department of Justice's Antitrust Division, the Federal Trade Commission and the Securities and Exchange Commission. They also include The New York Stock Exchange, Inc. and other stock exchanges; the National Association of Securities Dealers, Inc. and its recently organized market and regulatory subsidiaries; the Financial Accounting Standards Board; and Moody's, Standard & Poor's and other nationally recognized securities rating organizations. They also include the federal and state courts that resolve disputed issues. The services of these organizations are often taken for granted. They may also be criticized if they delay or block an M&A transaction. However, their services are essential and their personnel often provide important expertise and dedicated effort enabling an M&A transaction to take place in a manner that is consistent with the public interests they protect.

D. Effects of the M&A Market

The M&A market can claim several accomplishments:

Liquidity and Risk Reduction for Business Owners. The M&A market provides an important avenue that many business owners can use to achieve liquidity. Thus, it reduces one of the important risks of business investment. The effect is to encourage organization of new businesses, an important function in a nation where new businesses regularly supplant older businesses through the processes of innovation and competition.

Strategic Opportunities for Businesses. The M&A market provides strategic opportunities for businesses. For some, the opportunities are modest, such as a chance for a "turnaround" leading to survival. For others, the opportunities are major and include growth, cost savings and avenues to new products and markets. The effects are preserved and increased employment and improved living standards.

Investment Opportunities for Financial Resource Providers. The M&A market provides highly remunerative opportunities for providers of debt and equity capital with necessary skills in investigation, evaluation and negotiation. The effect is the useful and remunerative employment of debt and equity capital.

Careers and Compensation for Service Providers. The M&A market provides challenging and rewarding careers for professionals and technicians who have the skills, experience and energy to provide services successfully in complex, result-oriented transactions. The effect is to provide well-compensated "white-collar" employment for a nation that is phasing out traditional "blue-collar" employment in response to the mandates of environmental laws and other social and economic forces.

Chapter 2

Strategies, Preparations and Negotiations

A. Introduction

Sellers have some common objectives in acquisition transactions. They want a generous price, a prompt and simple transaction and a buyer who will operate the business responsibly afterward. Buyers also have some common objectives. They want a modest price, a prompt and simple transaction, and a business they can operate successfully afterward.

Beyond such generalities, business sellers and buyers and their objectives differ greatly. As a result, their strategies, preparations and specific negotiating methods also vary greatly. Thus, it is best to discuss them in terms of sellers and buyers who have common circumstances and objectives.

Seller strategies and preparations are discussed under the following sections:

- Corporations divestiting subsidiaries and divisions
- Owners divesting entire corporations or businesses
- Venture capital firms exiting from leveraged buyouts
- Owners selling to retire and to raise funds for estate planning purposes
- Owners selling to participate in a larger organization as managers and perhaps as part owners
- Management or trustees of bankrupt companies selling businesses to obtain funds to pay creditors and administration expenses

Buyer strategies and preparations are discussed in the following sections:

- Acquisitions by corporate strategic buyers
- Acquisitions by management groups
- Acquisitions by venture capital firms
- Acquisitions by employee stock ownership plans
- Turnaround acquisitions

Negotiating methods are discussed in the last section.

B. Corporate Divestitures of Subsidiaries and Divisions

1. Divestiture Objectives

Many businesses sold in the M&A market during recent years were subsidiaries, divisions and other operations of large multioperation corporations. These divestitures can be grouped by their objectives:

- Divestitures of poorly performing businesses in order to salvage some value and avoid the losses and liabilities that usually result from a shutdown.
- Divestitures of sound businesses in order to raise cash to respond to a cash squeeze, pay down an excessive debt burden, or shore up other operations needing a capital infusion.
- Divestitures of sound businesses to avoid devoting effort and resources to businesses that do not fit management's plan for the overall corporate business.

Corporate management may refer to all of these divestitures as strategic. However, the first two categories are primarily reactive, although they may achieve worthwhile results. For example, in the mid-1990s Maytag Corp. divested businesses in Europe and Australia that it had acquired in the 1980s. The divestitures occurred after its earnings declined sharply, in part due to large losses in Europe. The third category is the result of corporate business planning to determine where the corporation should deploy its efforts and resources in future years. The decisions are usually made after management evaluates market trends and the corporation's strengths and weaknesses. Recent examples of divestitures of noncore businesses include sales by the Walt Disney Company of the *Institutional Investor* to Euromoney Publications, Chilton magazines to Reed Elsevier and four newspapers to Knight-Ridder. These businesses were, of course, outside of Disney's core entertainment businesses.

2. Divestitures to Simplify Diversified or Integrated Structures and Focus on Core Businesses

Today's leading business strategy is to focus on building core businesses, a specialization strategy. In industries such as computers and communications, the strategy may emphasize high technology. More often, however, the strategy is to build in one or more niche markets in which the businesses can achieve a leading market shares, special customer relationships, superior product or process technologies, or low raw material or labor costs. For example, there has been extensive development of customer–supplier relationships built on outsourcing of components and raw materials by major integrated manufacturers to suppliers who operate efficiently at significant cost savings and deliver on "just-in-time" schedules.

During the 1980s and 90s, large publicly owned corporations have deemphasized the previously favored strategy of diversification. Poor performance by a number of highly diversified corporations, called conglomerates, precipitated the trend. The hostile takeover campaigns of the 1980s and the shareholder activism that continued into the 1990s showed corporate executives that they should not undertake (or retain) diversified businesses that they cannot manage well. Thus, many corporations have been divesting businesses that provided diversification but were outside their core businesses.

The strategies of horizontal and vertical integration continue to be favored, but only so long as they obtain good results. These strategies can create real synergies such as enhancement of name recognition; growth of market shares; control of product quality; economies of scale in purchasing, warehousing and transportation; and development of technology. However, the benefits of horizontal and vertical integration are not automatic. For example, corporate managers whose careers were developed in industrial products sometimes make a serious error by integrating forward into retail products. Soon after doing so, they lose retail customers who will not buy from a supplier that has become a competitor. They may also find themselves unable to understand the opportunities and risks of style trends, imaginative advertising and customer relations involved in retail businesses. They may also find that their manufacturing operations perform less effectively for captive retail operations than they did when they competed for the business of independent customers.

For these reasons, some corporations have been divesting businesses that provided horizontal or vertical integration. At times, they have accomplished the divestitures by a spinoff distribution to shareholders rather than a sale. This strategic method does not allow the divesting corporation to maintain ownership or control of the spinoff corporation, but commercial relationships may last longer than they would after a sale. (See Chapter 7.)

3. Examples of Divestiture Programs

A remarkable strategic divestiture and acquisition program was accomplished over a period of three decades by Illinois Central Industries, Inc. (IC), now known as Whitman Corporation. IC recognized that its railroad businesses were doomed by government regulation and began to restructure in the 1960s. IC began by acquiring familiar industrial businesses such as an electrical equipment manufacturer and a foundry manufacturing precision castings and corrosion-resistant pumps. IC then acquired soft drink bottling and other food producers with strong consumer name recognition, such as PepsiCola, Pet and Whitman (which became its corporate name). IC also acquired Midas automotive services and Hussman refrigeration systems and equipment. Milestones were achieved in 1988 and 1989 when IC divested its industrial Pneumo-Abex subsidiaries for $1.2 billion cash and spun off its subsidiary, the Illinois Central Railroad Co. Thus, IC achieved a metamorphosis from a declining railroad business to a network of growing consumer-oriented businesses, i.e., soft drinks, auto repairs and refrigeration systems.

A more recent example of a major strategic acquisition and divestiture program was accomplished by Monsanto Company, a major manufacturer of chemicals and related products. In 1997, Monsanto divested by spinoff its $2.6-billion sales chemical business as Solutia, Inc., which instantly became a major producer of nylon and acrylic fibers, nylon resins, polyvinyl butyral interlayer, phosphates, specialty chemicals and herbicide chemicals. Monsanto also sold its styrenic plastics business for $580 million to BASF AG. Monsanto's strategy was to reposition itself as a market leader in biotechnology and pharmaceuticals, fields in which it made several acquisitions, including $1-billion acquisitions of Merck & Co.'s specialty chemicals division and Holden's Foundation Seeds and part or full ownership of Agracetus, Calgene Inc. and DeKalb Genetics Corp. Monsanto's dramatic strategy recognizes that the Environmental Protection Agency is rapidly deregistering and banning chemical pesticides and herbicides that are vital to worldwide food production. Thus, the design of genetically superior foods that can resist pests and viruses is growing in importance. In June 1998, Monsanto agreed to be acquired for $34-billion by American Home Products Corporation which also has a significant biotechnology business including its previous acquisition of American Cyanamid Corporation. If the acquisition receives the necessary government clearances, it will create one of the world's largest life sciences businesses while enabling Monsanto's shareholders to realize a significant return on their investment. Those shareholders who kept their shares of Solutia, Inc. have seen their price rise to $27 from $18 in 1997.

Other recent and dramatic acquisitions include the proposed acquisitions by the Travelers Group, Inc. of Citicorp and of Nikko Securities Company. Since Travelers already owns Salomon Smith Barney, the proposed combination of insurance, bank and securities businesses would be a landmark event and will require changes of existing laws and regulations.

4. Initial Preparations for Sale

To prepare a subsidiary, division or other operation for sale, a corporation should review the steps necessary to transform it into a stand-alone business. Most internal operations of large corporations share assets with other operations and provide and receive materials and services to and from other operations. For example, corporate headquarters usually provides administrative, financial, credit, legal and insurance services to subsidiaries and divisions in return for a simple general and administrative charge. If the business does not already have them, separate financial statements should be prepared. The financial statements should be adjusted to reflect assets, liabilities, income and expenses on a standalone basis. The corporation should also be ready to offer continuing arrangements to share facilities, purchase products, supply materials and furnish services for reasonable prices, at least during a transition period. These steps are necessary to enable the seller to determine a reasonable asking price. They are also necessary for buyers to evaluate the business, decide whether they can operate it successfully and determine an offering price.

During sale preparations, management should not allow the business to sink into apathy. It is important to maintain morale and take advantage of opportunities to improve sales and profits, if possible. Any successful efforts will ease the sale and improve the price for the business. Cost-cutting steps may also be appropriate, if they are not steps that a buyer will have to reverse after the closing. Buyers are alert during due diligence reviews to identify temporary "window-dressing" changes that create a misleading impression of improved profits. To respond to this cautious outlook, the author recommends that seller representatives be prepared to discuss with buyer representatives any operational and accounting changes that (favorably or unfavorably) affected the financial statements.

During the preparations, management should also consider the tax, accounting, legal, antitrust and other subjects discussed in later chapters of this book. For example, if the corporation is selling a subsidiary that is a member of its consolidated group for federal income tax purposes, its tax advisers should determine whether the corporation can agree to an election under Section 338(h)(10) of the Internal Revenue Code as described in Chapter 6. If so, a major tax saving may be available. If the divestiture is a spin-off, its tax advisers must carefully plan for compliance with Section 355 of the Code as described in Chapter 7. Management should discuss with its accountants how the transaction will be recorded in its financial statements, as described in Chapter 9. If the divestiture will result in a material profit or loss, management should be prepared to make a timely public announcement as described in Chapter 13.

5. Management-Conducted Private Sale Arrangements

Another important step is to decide whether the business should be sold by arrangements and negotiations conducted privately by management or by retaining an investment banking firm to conduct a private auction. Private sale arrangements can be handled confidentially, thus protecting the business from possible injuries that can result from premature disclosure to employees and customers. When successful, private sale arrangements can also be handled quickly and management can quietly terminate discussions with any buyer or buyers if the discussions do not appear to be productive. On the other hand, private sale arrangements cannot guarantee confidentiality and can seldom be conducted concurrently with more than one or two potential buyers. Thus, private sale arrangements sacrifice the opportunity to optimize the price and other terms that often results from an open, competitive bidding process.

6. Investment Banker–Conducted Private Auctions

An alternative to management-conducted private sale arrangements is the private auction method developed by investment banking firms into a familiar set of skillful techniques during the 1980s. Management hires an investment banking firm which performs a detailed review of the business to be sold and prepares a confidential offering memorandum, similar to a prospectus, containing descriptions of the business and its financial statements. Management notifies employees, customers and other key persons that the business will be offered for sale and makes arrangements to retain their confidence during the sale process. (For example, management may provide "stay" bonuses to key employees and assure them that they will have an opportunity to present themselves favorably for employment by the buyer.)

The investment banking firm then sends the memorandum to a relatively large number of potentially interested buyers together with an explanatory letter, a form of confidentiality agreement and instructions for submitting a first-round bid. A model form of acquisition contract is usually also enclosed. The bidding instructions invite each potential buyer to review the memorandum and a standard package of due diligence documents and to submit a non-binding, but serious, price offer together with any changes it wishes to make to the proposed acquisition contract. Since the first-round offers are non-binding, the potential buyers tend to submit large amounts in order to be selected for the second round.

Management and the investment banking firm then identify two or three potential buyers that have submitted the highest and best offers and invite them for a second round consisting of further due diligence and definitive negotiations. The potential buyers often hope to use the second-round, in-depth due diligence review and negotiations to drive down the high prices submitted during the first round. However, the investment banking firms are experienced in responding to these efforts and are able to sustain the price level by stimulating competition among the second-round potential buyers. Thus, for transactions where the selling corporation can live without confidentiality during the sale process, the private auction method can obtain a significantly higher price than could be obtained by management-conducted private sale arrangements.

Management considering use of the private auction method should not underestimate the risk of loss of confidentiality. Competitors will attempt to take away customers and key employees. They may succeed, especially if the highest bidder appears to be planning to downsize operations. If the sale falls through, the business may then be "damaged goods."

C. Divestitures of Entire Corporations or Businesses

When an entire corporation or business is sold or merged, the initial steps leading to the transaction may begin with the shareholder-owners rather than with corporate management. Even when the initial steps originate with management, the ultimate decisions will be made by the shareholders, who must decide whether to sell their shares or to approve a merger or sale of substantially all the corporate assets. Thus, the strategies relating to the sale of an entire corporation or business are quite different from the long-term strategic objectives of management that lead to divestitures of subsidiaries, divisions or other operations.

At times, an entire corporation or business must be sold or merged because of a business or financial crisis. Under those circumstances, there may be little time for strategic planning and preparations. A buyer must be found and negotiations undertaken as soon as possible. However, when a corporation and its business are operating successfully, there is usually time to develop strategies for a sale at the most favorable price and other terms.

When a corporation and its business are in good condition, the most important strategy is to time the sale skillfully. A corporation or business should be divested when the M&A market is strong and the corporation has a good recent earnings history and sound projections for the coming years. Both of these factors are important. During serious recessions in the

M&A market, buyers fade away and good businesses, if offered, can remain unsold or be sold for a disappointing price. However, even during a booming M&A market, the price will be disappointing if the earnings history and projections are weak.

When a corporation or its entire business will be sold, it may already be a stand-alone business. However, many privately owned corporations have important transactions with their shareholder-owners that were not negotiated on an arm's-length basis. For example, if the corporation leases property or purchases materials from its shareholders or their relatives, the arrangements should be either terminated or placed on terms that potential buyers would clearly recognize as fair to the corporation. During the preparations for sale, other problems should also be resolved, if possible. For example, if the corporation has pending lawsuits, efforts should be made to settle so that potential buyers will not fear possible liability for the amounts claimed, which are often overstated.

The corporation and its owner shareholders should decide at an early date whether to seek a price payable entirely in cash at the closing. If they are willing to be flexible, they should determine whether they would accept a partial deferral of the price which they would report for tax purposes as an installment sale, as described in Chapter 6. If the potential buyers include corporations with publicly traded shares, the corporation and its shareholders should also consider accepting the price in the form of the buyer's voting stock in order to gain the benefits of a tax-free reorganization, as described in Chapter 7.

When a privately owned corporation or its business is being sold, the owners may be surprised to find active bidding by a large corporation whose local division is a bitter competitor. The owners may be delighted to receive visits by senior executives from the competitor's corporate headquarters. They may receive compliments about their products and operations that the local division disparaged for years. Best of all, the competitor may offer a price that represents a substantial premium over prices offered by other potential buyers. Before going too far, the owners should consult with legal counsel and an economist familiar with antitrust analysis to determine whether a sale to the competitor may violate Section 7 of the Clayton Act. If so, the owners might go through a lengthy due diligence review, turn away other potential buyers and sign an acquisition contract, but then see the acquisition blocked by the U.S. Department of Justice or the Federal Trade Commission. (See Chapter 10.)

D. Venture Capital Firms Exiting from Leveraged Buyouts

Before venture capital firms invest in the equity capital of a corporation making a leveraged buyout (LBO) acquisition, their representatives review an "exit strategy" with the management group. They inform the management group that they are financial investors, not long-term business architects and that they have commitments to their fund investors to realize on investments on a time horizon of about five years. They explain that their targets for return on investment are high (e.g., 30 to 40 percent per annum) because they take both business risk and financial structure risk. They review the business plan to determine the feasibility of the exit strategy, perhaps by an initial public offering (often called a "reverse LBO") but more often by a sale to a strategic buyer. A management buyout may also be discussed. During the discussions, the venture capital firm's representatives also evaluate management's understanding and willingness to develop the business so that a successful exit can be achieved.

As with other divestitures of entire corporations or businesses, timing is important. A five-year exit horizon can be accelerated to three years if the business prospers, acquisition debt is rapidly reduced and the M&A market is strong. The exit can be deferred to seven or eight years if necessary to overcome unexpected problems and prepare the business for sale in a strong M&A market. For example, a leveraged buildup (which involves a series of LBO acquisitions) may take longer to prepare for sale than a single-acquisition LBO.

Preparations and timing typically include payment of much of the original acquisition debt and perhaps also a refinancing of the acquisition debt. The objective is to present to potential buyers a strong "track record," a business that is no longer heavily burdened with debt and extended debt payment schedules that can comfortably be met from cash flows. Refinancing of the original acquisition debt well before a sale also creates an opportunity to buy out warrants or other "equity sweeteners" of debtholders at an advantageous price. Of course, if the eventual sale is to a large corporation, the buyer may choose to prepay all outstanding debt because its own borrowing costs are lower. However, the reduction and refinancing of the original acquisition debt is still a good strategy because it maintains the business in sound financial condition and increases the range of potential buyers when the business is sold.

Venture capital firms are inclined to favor the investment banker–managed auction method of sale described earlier in this chapter because it optimizes the price. However, they usually do not object if management can arrange a favorable sale, either to a strategic buyer or to a management buyout corporation. Tension can develop, however, if such a sale favors the career objectives of management over a good return on investment for the venture capital firm.

Venture capital firms typically obtain "put," "call" or other contractual rights by which they can force a sale of the corporation if management or other shareholders do not wish to sell. However, every effort should be made to avoid the necessity to use these rights, so that unified presentations can be made to buyers.

Venture capital firms favor a sale for cash with a minimum of lingering obligations under the acquisition contract for representations, warranties, covenants or indemnities. To the extent they must undertake such obligations, they generally insist on time limits and "caps" on claims. This enables the firms to make distributions of the net price to fund investors (less escrow funds, if necessary) without concern about later claims. (See Chapters 12 and 13.)

Venture capital firms do not favor sales in tax-free reorganizations unless the advantages are sufficiently favorable to overcome the disadvantages from their point of view. One disadvantage is lack of liquidity of the buyer's stock resulting from the continuity of interest requirement (see Chapter 7). Another is lack of liquidity of the buyer's stock that results if it is not registered under the Securities Act of 1933 and is, therefore, restricted from resale (see Chapter 11).

E. Owners Selling to Retire and Raise Funds for Estate Planning

Many corporations or their businesses are sold every year to enable their owners to plan for retirement and to raise funds to plan their estates, including payment of estate and inheritance taxes.[1] Left to their own choices, some owners would presumably sell in order to liquify their assets for retirement years and to make gifts and bequests to family, friends and charities. Many other owners would answer liquidity needs by other means such as savings, annuities and insurance and would keep their business holdings. However, high federal tax rates preclude the second choice for many business owners.

Death and taxes are unpopular subjects for everyone. They are even less popular for entrepreneurial business owners, many of whom are founders whose whole lives are intertwined with their business activities. They make and break appointments with their advisors to discuss unpleasant subjects such as wills and plans to sell the business. However, some event, such as an unexpected illness, eventually leads them to begin making serious plans, although the planning often then continues over several years.

Owners, and especially founders, usually march to the beat of a different drum from other sellers. They would like a high price in order to show the value of the business that they built. However, price often becomes less important as planning and eventual negotiations proceed. Their real strategies often focus on finding a buyer that will preserve the business and provide continuing good employment opportunities for its managers and workers. For these reasons, retiring owners are often willing to consider leveraged buyouts led by management groups or employee stock ownership plans. They are cautious in dealing with large corporate strategic buyers, fearing that they may "clean house" and turn the business into "Plant No. 137" selling commodity products through a national distribution system. They are cautious in dealing with venture capital firms, fearing they may "clean house" and strip the assets for sale.

For these reasons, retiring owners prefer sales through private arrangements and they prefer negotiations to sales through investment banker–managed private auctions. They want to evaluate the buyers while the buyers evaluate the business. Buyers who demonstrate that they have constructive plans for the future of the business and its employees may still face challenging negotiations, but they will find the door open and they may receive concessions on key points that could be "deal breakers" for other buyers.

---

[1]The Taxpayer Relief Act of 1997 contains some provisions granting relief from the federal unified gift and estate tax. For example, the unified credit is increased gradually from $625,000 for decedents dying and gifts made in 1998 to $1,000,000 for 2006 and thereafter. A new section 2033A of the Internal Revenue Code allows an executor of an estate to elect to exclude up to $1,300,000 from the gross estate (including the unified credit) if the value of qualified family-owned business interests included in the estate (and certain other items) exceeds 50% of the decedent's adjusted gross estate.

Retiring owners considering a sale to a corporation with publicly traded shares can gain important advantages through a tax-free reorganization. Under the Internal Revenue Code, they do not recognize income upon the receipt of voting common stock from the acquiring corporation in a tax-free reorganization. Further, if they hold the stock until death, their estates or survivors obtain a step up of basis in the stock to its fair market on the date of death, or the alternate valuation date for federal estate tax purposes. (See Chapter 7.)

Section 1042 of the Internal Revenue Code allows owners to sell shares of stock to an ESOP without recognition of long-term capital gain if the proceeds are reinvested in "qualified replacement property." The shares sold must be "qualified securities" that meet several requirements, including a three-year holding period. The reinvestment of the proceeds must also meet the requirements for "qualified replacement property," but any broker can easily recommend a portfolio of stocks and bonds of domestic corporations that would fulfill the requirements. (See Chapter 15.)

F. Owners Selling to Participate in a Larger Organization

Owners (or management) of a corporation sometimes recognize that its business cannot succeed, or perhaps even survive, unless it can grow rapidly to respond to competitive pressures. This can happen in several situations:

- A business engaged in high technology may have developed a "state-of-the-art" product, process or system, but foresee that competitors with greater resources will soon match and exceed its present accomplishments.
- A business may have an unusual "window of opportunity" to obtain a major contract or customer, but may not have the resources to fulfill the performance requirements.
- A business may be in a declining industry in which customers are demanding price cuts, reducing purchase volume and imposing tighter quality and service requirements that are growing more and more difficult to meet.

In the first two situations, the owners are likely to be founders who work in the business. They usually will (and should) consider alternatives such as raising capital through a private placement or public offering of stock or other securities. However, as many "high-tech" companies have discovered, it can take a lot of time, effort and skill to turn financing proceeds into an aggressive sales and marketing organization or an efficient manufacturing capability. The owners may not have the time or know-how to develop them.

When owners sell a corporation or its business to participate in a larger organization, their most important strategies are to obtain contractual and other rights assuring that the participation will achieve their objectives. As a first objective, they may seek to obtain an equity investment in the buyer corporation and might use a tax-free reorganization to achieve that objective. (See Chapter 7.) If they can negotiate a substantial equity position, they should also seek representation on the board of directors of the buyer corporation. If these objectives are not feasible because the buyer corporation is much larger than the corporation or business being sold, the owners should then pursue secondary objectives. These objectives should include an employment contract providing sufficient time and authority to develop and demonstrate the value of the business within the buyer organization. The employment contract or related agreements should commit the necessary capital funds and other resources to develop the business. The employment contract should also contain commitments for stock options, bonuses, or other rewards that will compensate the owners fairly if they are successful. These contractual rights are very important because owners who sell corporations or businesses without such rights may encounter opposition at various levels within the buyer organization that can frustrate their ability to develop the business.

G. Sales of Bankrupt Businesses

1. Sales Pursuant to a Plan of Reorganization

Many business bankruptcies are initiated by management and seek reorganization (rather than liquidation) under Chapter 11 of the Bankruptcy Code. Under Chapter 11, the debtor's management has the exclusive right for an initial period of 120 days to propose a plan of reorganization, which usually includes restructuring of debt and equity and may also include sales of one or more of the businesses of the debtor. The exclusivity period is often extended by the bankruptcy court. However, if management fails to propose a plan of reorganization that can be confirmed, other parties may be authorized to propose a plan of reorganization. To obtain confirmation, a plan of reorganization must be accepted by each class of claims that is impaired under the plan, except that under some circumstances a dissenting class can be "crammed down" (or forced to accept the plan) after review and approval by the court.

The initial strategies of the debtor's management are usually to restructure the outstanding debt, obtain new financing, divest some businesses and retain others and continue on as directors and officers of the reorganized entity. However, shortly after the filing of the petition for reorganization, the creditors and stockholders usually appoint committees to represent their interests in the reorganization proceedings. The strategies of each of these committees frequently differ sharply from those of management and the other committees.

For example, the committee representing senior debtholders will often favor a rapid sale of businesses and assets for an amount that is sufficient to pay their senior debt. This committee is likely to oppose delay because continuing losses could impair the debtor's ability to pay their claims. The strategy of the committee representing mezzanine debtholders may also favor rapid sales of businesses if it appears that the sale proceeds would be sufficient to pay the senior debt and also the mezzanine debt. However, if the sale proceeds and any other available net assets will be insufficient to pay the mezzanine debt, the committee representing the mezzanine debtholders may support longer-term strategies in the hope of a better recovery over a period of time. Because rapid sales of businesses do not usually produce sufficient funds to make substantial payments to the unsecured creditors and equityholders, the committees representing these classes of claimants may support longer-term strategies for reorganization of the business.

The key to a successful reorganization is to propose a plan that includes compromise elements providing solutions acceptable to the debtor's management, the committees and the bankruptcy judge. When management cannot propose a satisfactory plan of reorganization, the judge may appoint an operating trustee to replace management and to develop a satisfactory plan of reorganization. There are professionals who have recognized skills in accomplishing those difficult tasks.

In developing a plan of reorganization, debtor management or an operating trustee can make use of powers provided in the Bankruptcy Code that ordinary sellers do not have. For example, burdensome executory contracts (including leases) can be rejected and beneficial executory contracts can be affirmed. Debts can be restructured. Properties can be sold free and clear of liens, provided that the lienholders are given adequate security to replace them, such as a lien on the sale proceeds. If the acquiring corporation wishes to issue securities to pay the purchase price, the securities can be issued without registration with the Securities and Exchange Commission based on the exemption provided in Section 1145 of the Bankruptcy Code. If the acquiring corporation wishes to preserve valuable tax characteristics of the debtor, such as net operating losses, by acquiring in tax-free reorganization, special tax benefits are available under Sections 368(a)(1)(G) and 382(l)(5) of the Internal Revenue Code.

Preparations for sale pursuant to a plan of reorganization require tireless efforts to preserve the businesses of the debtor that have value. Management or the operating trustee must fight efforts by competitors to take away customers and key employees. They must persuade environmental or other regulators to allow extra time to meet compliance schedules. They must persuade suppliers to continue to furnish raw material, components and services, although the suppliers are unhappy about previous unpaid invoices. If the business produces valuable inventories and accounts receivable, management can often obtain debtor-in-possession (DIP) financing to continue in operation.

Preparations for sale also require compliance with detailed legal requirements because bankruptcy proceedings are open and every significant action or expense requires court approval. However, the bankruptcy courts are equity courts with extensive administrative powers. Experienced bankruptcy judges can encourage a promising reorganization by expediting hearings and discouraging or denying groundless objections raised for tactical reasons.

During the last two decades, a strategic device called a "prepackaged bankruptcy" has frequently been used to save the time, effort and cost of extended court proceedings. The debtor negotiates a plan of reorganization with the claimants and then files a petition with the plan of reorganization and all supporting documents for approval by the bankruptcy court.

2. Other Sales of Businesses during Bankruptcy Proceedings

As described earlier, the debtor's management or an operating trustee can sell businesses and assets before approval of a plan of reorganization if the sale helps to preserve the value of the bankrupt estate. Title can be conveyed free and clear of mortgages, security interests, pledges, liens and encumbrances, provided that their holders are given adequate security to replace them. Adequate security is commonly provided by a court order subjecting the sale proceeds to the mortgages, security interests, pledges, liens and encumbrances. With careful preparation, it may even be possible to provide limited protection to the buyer against successor liability, at least for prepetition product and environmental liabilities.

The debtor's management or an operating trustee must overcome an important difficulty when negotiating sales. The Bankruptcy Code requires that all sales be approved by the court after an open notice and bidding process. Contracts for sale must, therefore, be conditional so that they can be terminated if a higher bid is received or the court does not approve. However, the debtor can agree to a reasonable termination fee if it must withdraw from the sale. The termination fee is also subject to court approval, but the approval can be obtained in the court order that initiates the notice and bidding process. Thus, the buyer can be afforded protection that is sufficient to cover its due diligence and other expenses. However, a bankruptcy court is unlikely to approve a termination fee that approaches the large "breakup fees" contained in acquisition contracts for companies involved in hostile takeover contests.

H. Acquisitions by Strategic Buyers

Strategic buyers are the foundation of the M&A market. While financial buyers add depth to the market, the opportunities and needs of strategic buyers are its backbone.

1. Corporate Development

Strategic buyers are usually corporations who make acquisitions as part of their overall corporate development program. Corporate development covers a wide variety of activities that can include market research, technology licensing, internal expansion, acquisitions and divestitures.

At small companies, corporate development activities are handled directly by management. Middle-sized companies may appoint a manager to handle corporate development activities. Large corporations often establish a corporate development department headed by an officer who manages the department.

Corporate development managers are closely involved with senior management in preparation and implementation of the corporate business plan. Among the key planning activities is the development of the business by internal expansion and acquisitions.

Corporate development departments usually maintain professional contacts, information resources and analytical capabilities that are valuable in their work. For example, they maintain contact with industry organizations and universities and with investment bankers and other intermediaries. They subscribe to industry publications of their own and other industries. They develop computer spreadsheet models for analyzing and evaluating internal expansion projects and acquisitions. The models enable the department to determine key ratios such as return on investment and internal rate of return. The models also include business valuation by discounted cash flow analysis using the debt-free and equity methods with sensitivity analysis. The New York Institute of Finance (2 World Trade Center, New York, NY 10048) offers courses in financial modeling (using Excel and Lotus 123) including valuation modeling for acquisitions.

2. Basic Growth Strategies

Internal expansion is the first alternative for business growth. Internal expansion begins simply when a corporation discovers that it is receiving more orders for its products or services than it has capacity to supply. The corporation responds by hiring employees and installing equipment and facilities. Internal expansion becomes strategic when the corporation decides to extend its products or services horizontally to add new territories or complementary products by hiring personnel and installing equipment and facilities. Horizontal integration can provide important synergies by increasing name recognition, expanding market shares, making "one-stop shopping" available to customers, sharing central warehousing facilities and obtaining volume discounts from suppliers and freight haulers.

If the business continues to grow, the corporation may extend the internal expansion vertically by establishing its own wholesale or retail distribution outlets or its own facilities to produce components and raw materials used in its products. Vertical integration can provide important synergies through improved quality control, shared technology and assured operation even during shortages. Vertical integration is a strong factor if most competitors in the industry are not vertically integrated. The nonintegrated customers and suppliers must deal at arm's length and each must earn a satisfactory profit. A vertically integrated competitor can, if it wishes, sacrifice all or part of its multilevel profitability in order to reduce prices and gain market share. As an alternative, a vertically integrated competitor can use its multilevel profits to fund research and product and process development, thus gaining market share through innovative or high quality, value-added products.

As a corporation's original products and services become widely accepted and competitors match them, they gradually become commodities that no longer command high profit margins and may become cyclically unprofitable. They may even become obsolete if competitors develop significant improvements or substitutes. Corporations use two strategies to protect themselves against the risks of cyclical unprofitability and obsolescence. Some diversify into unrelated products and services so that adverse events affecting a few products or services can be balanced by successes in other products or services. Others specialize so they can maintain their products and services at "state-of-the-art" levels by continually upgrading them and even replacing them with internally developed substitutes. For example, Intel reportedly replaces its own microprocessor chip products every three years.

During the 1980s and 1990s, diversification has declined as a strategic method and specialization has grown. Before that time, some directors and officers of conglomerates believed they could manage any kind of business by analysis of financial statements and operating and capital budgets and by setting return on investment thresholds. The conglomerates assembled businesses that were strange bedfellows, such as a combination of banks, hotels and oil and gas exploration ventures. The author recalls asking executives of conglomerates how often they visited the factories, sales offices and customers of their businesses. They responded that such "hands-on" management was unnecessary. The conglomerates did not perform well under such "ivory tower" management. Indeed, even corporations with diversification programs more cohesive than those of the conglomerates suffered from lack of knowledgeable management.

During the 1990s, growth strategy has focused on the development of core businesses characterized by leading market shares and products that command premium prices because they add value to customer products.

3. Acquisitions as an Alternative to Internal Expansion

From the point of view of corporate development, acquisitions are an alternative to internal expansion. Thus, it is useful to compare their relative advantages and disadvantages.

Internal expansion offers the significant advantage of business confidentiality during planning stages and until management decides that it should make a public announcement. Internal expansion also allows corporate development planners to have considerable freedom in selecting the size, scope, location, time schedule and cost of each project because they can make adjustments to meet forecasted needs and available resources. Corporate managements usually have return on investment or internal rate of return thresholds for internal expansion projects. Planners must present projects that meet these standards or terminate them if it becomes apparent that the standards cannot be met.

Internal expansion projects present an opportunity to design products, equipment or facilities that meet or surpass the "state of the art" in the industry and can become models for future expansion projects. Thus, internal expansion projects provide excellent experience to the managers and employees who participate in them. The value of the experience and skills gained through internal expansion projects was highlighted in a famous article titled "Managing as if Tomorrow Mattered" by Harvard University Professors Robert Hayes and David Garvin. They criticized the tendency of some corporate managers to favor acquisitions over internal investments by requiring high hurdle rates for internal investments while adopting more lenient standards for acquisitions.[2]

On the other hand, internal expansion has several potential disadvantages. Financing may be difficult to obtain because lenders must rely on the existing business "track record" which may not be matched by a proposed expansion project. Further, it is necessary to detach key managers and personnel from their regular duties to plan and implement each project. Out-

[2]*Harvard Business Review,* May-June 1982.

side contractors can be hired to perform much of the work, but the planning and supervision must be performed by trusted managers and personnel who may suffer from serious time problems and who may not be as effective at project management as they are in their regular duties. If the internal project managers lack time or skills, they tend to delegate and rely too heavily on the outside contractors who will attempt to "pinch hit" in order to maintain good customer relations. Mistakes can occur that lead to delays and cost overruns before the project is completed and ineffective operation after the project is completed.[3]

Acquisitions have several advantages over internal expansion. During the due diligence review, the buyer's management has an opportunity to evaluate all aspects of the businesses to be purchased before signing the acquisition contract. The buyer's management can also negotiate for a specific price and a definite closing date without concern about the cost overruns and delays that often occur during internal expansion projects. There is some need to divert management personnel to plan and implement acquisitions and to integrate the acquired businesses after a closing date. However, the time schedules are not likely to be as tight and the consequences of failing to meet the time schedules are not likely to be as severe as in the case of internal expansion projects. It may also be easier to obtain financing for acquisitions than for internal expansion projects if the business to be acquired has valuable assets, an established earnings history and reliable projected cash flows. Occasionally an opportunity exists to make an acquisition at a real bargain price from a seller who is under business or financial pressure or lacks negotiating skills.

Acquisitions have several disadvantages in comparison to internal expansion. Confidentiality is difficult to maintain. Negotiation of an acquisition can take months and can sometimes collapse, resulting in no transaction at all. If the due diligence review fails to detect contingent liabilities or other risks, the true cost of the acquisition could be much higher than the price intentionally negotiated. An acquisition can only obtain the seller's existing products, equipment and facilities and there is no opportunity to design technologically advanced products, equipment and facilities. An acquisition does not afford the same opportunity for management and employees to gain experience as an internal expansion project. After an acquisition, the acquired business must be integrated with the buyer's business, a process that can be difficult to accomplish if the management of the acquired company fights to maintain autonomy.

Management should weigh the advantages and disadvantages when deciding whether to fulfill a growth objective by internal expansion or by acquisition.

4. Examples of Strategic Acquisitions

Recent examples of horizontal acquisitions include the acquisition of Scott Paper Co. by Kimberly-Clark Corp. and Fort Howard Corporation by

[3]Henry Reichhold, the CEO of Reichhold Chemicals Inc., once recalled that he often cut a ribbon at a new plant opening ceremony, but the plant then had breakdowns for six months before it could be operated at capacity. He said that a big advantage of an acquisition is that the cash register starts ringing the day after the closing date.

James River Paper Co. These acquisitions resulted in a significant consolidation of the paper industry where overcapacity to produce some products has existed. Numerous horizontal acquisitions have also been made in the electric utility industry where federal regulation is replacing state regulation and electric power produced by utilities in rural areas is "wheeled" to large urban areas for local utilities to distribute to customers.

An example of an important vertical acquisition was the high-priced, but reportedly successful, acquisition of Medco Containment Services, Inc. by Merck & Co. Inc. Recognizing the growing government regulation of the distribution of pharmaceutical products, Merck, a major manufacturer that traditionally marketed directly to the medical profession, acquired Medco, a major distributor of pharmaceuticals to managed care suppliers.

Recent examples of acquisitions illustrating the trend away from diversification and toward concentration in core businesses are the purchase of the industrial chemicals business of Imperial Chemical Industries (ICI) by E.I. de Pont de Nemours & Company (du Pont) and ICI's purchase of the specialty chemicals business of Unilever N.V. Du Pont's acquisition strengthens its already leading position as producer of bulk chemicals, including titanium dioxide white pigment and provides entry into European markets. ICI's acquisition strengthens its position as a producer of specialty chemicals which are less cyclical and can earn higher profit margins than bulk chemicals.

5. A Strategic Buyer's Advantages and Disadvantages

A strategic buyer has several advantages over financial buyers when bidding to acquire a business. A strategic buyer may welcome, but does not need, a stand-alone business and does not need an exit strategy. A strategic buyer has more flexibility in buying turnaround or other businesses with cash flows that may be difficult to predict. A strategic buyer with a strong capital structure may be able to raise financing faster than a financial buyer who must satisfy its financing sources that each acquisition will pay for itself on a predictable time schedule.

A strategic buyer with publicly traded securities can offer them as acquisition currency, thus conserving its cash and borrowing power. A strategic buyer with publicly traded stock can also offer a tax-free transaction to sellers.

A strategic buyer may welcome, but does not always need, an acquired business with a strong existing management team. Indeed, a strategic buyer often wants a business that can be added to operations supervised by its existing management. On the other hand, if a strategic buyer needs key members of the seller's management, it can offer them long-term career opportunities and perhaps also more favorable stock option, pension and insurance benefits than financial buyers can readily provide.

A strategic buyer may also have some disadvantages. For example, a strategic buyer may be a large corporation that makes decisions slowly because any acquisition must be reviewed by several departments and levels of management. A strategic buyer will not usually offer significant equity participation to the acquired corporation's management, even when their skills are important. Indeed, seller's management often rightly fears that the buyer will terminate them after a brief transition period, unless they have strong contractual protection. Several examples of specific business improvements that can be implemented by a strategic buyer are provided in the discussion of post-closing integration methods on pages 547 to 551 of Chapter 18.

6. Preparations for Strategic Acquisitions

Preparations for strategic acquisitions potentially include the subjects covered by every chapter of this book. The preparations include at least financial planning, a due diligence review, tax planning, accounting treatment, antitrust compliance, securities registration or exemptions and listing, acquisition contract negotiation, closing arrangements and post-closing integration. For example, many recent acquisitions in the electric utility industry were carefully planned to qualify for accounting treatment as a "pooling of interests." (See Chapter 9.)

In strategic acquisitions, achievement of the business strategy may outweigh some other factors. During negotiation of the price and terms, a strategic buyer may be willing to offer more for a business that meets its strategic objectives than a financial buyer could justify. Some strategic buyers may even offer an initial premium bid designed to preempt other potential buyers. Strategic buyers may also forego tax benefits, assume liabilities and make other concessions in order to acquire a business that meets important strategic objectives.

A sound due diligence review assures that these decisions are made with knowledge of the consequences.

I. Acquisitions by Management Groups

Management groups use different strategies in buying businesses from those of strategic buyers because their objectives are career- as well as investment-oriented and their financial and other resources are much smaller.

The initial strategic objective of management groups is to persuade the owner or owners to decide to sell, a decision that may be difficult as was described earlier in this chapter. The second objective is to determine and negotiate a price. For small and middle-sized businesses, both the owner or owners and the management group will probably seek advice from a valuation analyst (see Chapter 4). The value is likely to be far higher than the managers can pay from their personal resources, so they will need to seek financing.

Management buyers often purchase in seller-financed acquisitions. Some transactions may be equivalent to leveraged buyouts because the deferred amount owed to the seller is a large part of the purchase price. However, the arrangements for small businesses are likely to be simpler than those described in Chapter 14 and elsewhere in this book. For example, owners of a small business corporation may agree to an installment sale of stock to the management group. As an alternative, the corporation may make an installment sale of its business and assets to a corporation organized by the management group.

Many owners are unwilling to provide seller financing to a management group, especially if they have opportunities to sell to other buyers who will pay the full price at the closing of the sale. The management group may then seek to obtain asset-based financing from a bank or finance company. If the business has readily marketed assets and reliable cash flows, the management group may be able to complete the purchase with the loan proceeds and operate the business with their own equity contributions and revolving credit loans. (See Chapter 3.)

Frequently, however, the lenders inform the management group that the equity investment they propose to contribute from their own resources is too small to support the debt financing needed. When that happens, the management group must seek more equity capital, a step that means sharing ownership. If the management group seeks equity investors, it must comply with the federal and state securities laws. (See Chapter 11.)

The management group usually sets a strategic goal to sell a minimal amount of equity to minimize dilution of its ownership. They organize a buyer corporation and purchase its shares for a small price per share. They plan, after the acquisition arrangements and other steps are taken, to sell shares to outside investors at higher prices that will allow the management group to retain most of the equity and voting control. If the management group has outstanding abilities and the business has excellent potential, they many be successful. However, many management groups find that the amount of risk capital they need to support debt financing requires additional financing from venture capital firms. These firms generally require a majority of the stock and voting control in return for the capital they provide. The negotiations to reach a financial structure can be very difficult. More often than not, the management group finds that it must accept the terms of the venture capital firms, although the managers may obtain concessions such as employment contracts and stock options or stock purchase rights that will eventually increase their share of the equity.

Once venture capital firms participate in an acquisition with a management group, the transaction is usually structured and planned in a manner that meets their requirements. The strategies and preparations for acquisitions by venture capital firms are discussed in the next section.

J. Acquisitions by Venture Capital Firms

Venture capital firms are financial buyers. Their strategies for acquisitions are significantly different from those of strategic buyers because the objectives and resources are different.

Venture capital firms typically purchase in leveraged buyout transactions. Their strategy is to seek stand-alone businesses with reliable projected cash flows. These characteristics are essential in order to obtain acquisition loans from insurers, banks, finance companies or other lenders. Venture capital firms also seek businesses for which they can develop a sound "exit strategy." An "exit strategy" is essential to realize upon the investment for the benefit of the venture capital funds they manage.

Venture capital firms seek to acquire businesses that have a strong and entrepreneurial existing management. They are often contacted by management groups looking for financing to buy a business from a retiring founder. They are also frequently contacted by management groups looking for financing to buy a subsidiary or division of a large corporation that is being divested because it does not fit with the corporation's overall plan for its core businesses. Venture capital firms evaluate the capability of the management groups and the soundness of their business plans and cash flow projections. They also evaluate the entrepreneurial instincts of the management groups to determine whether they will be sufficiently motivated by an equity investment opportunity to manage the business effectively while meeting the burdens of leveraged debt payments.

Some venture capital firms have developed a leveraged buildup strategy through which they acquire a series of small businesses that can be combined to achieve full stand-alone capability. Some financial buyers have associated themselves with experienced and entrepreneurial executives who can provide management for acquired businesses. These executives help financial buyers to evaluate candidate businesses, including businesses that may require a turnaround to achieve reliable cash flows.

A key strategic objective of venture capital firms acquiring in leveraged buyout transactions is to obtain favorable tax characteristics. The firms negotiate to obtain a stepped-up basis in the assets of an acquired business and to allocate the price to assets for which rapid depreciation and expense deductions can be obtained. If an acquired corporation is a Subchapter S corporation or a subsidiary included in a consolidated income tax return, the venture capital firms ask the seller to join in an election under Section 338(h)(10) of the Internal Revenue Code. The result can be tax deductions for the buyer corporation that will shelter it from income taxes for several years. The tax savings increase the buyer corporation's cash flows available to repay the acquisition debt.

Due diligence reviews and acquisition contract negotiations are especially important in preparing for leveraged-buyout acquisitions. Because the buyer corporation must have steady cash flows to pay the acquisition debt, it must minimize such risks as unexpected product or environmental liabilities. One reason venture capital firms welcome working with capable management groups is their ability to identify and evaluate potential liabilities. Venture capital firms typically negotiate with sellers for contractual indemnities against contingent liabilities and may require that part of the purchase price be held in escrow until contingent liabilities are resolved. (See Chapters 5, 16 and 17.)

K. Acquisitions by Employee Stock Ownership Plans

In recent years, many corporations have been acquired by their employees through Employee Stock Ownership Plans (ESOPs). A well-known example was the acquisition of Avis, Inc., the auto rental company. The initial arrangements are typically negotiated between the owners of the corporation, the management group and the labor union representing hourly paid employees. For example, the ESOP acquisition of Weirton Steel from national Steel Corporation was led by a management team and the unions representing the steelworkers and plant guards.

The primary strategic objectives of an ESOP acquisition are preservation of employment and an opportunity for employees to participate in the risks and rewards of equity ownership. The ESOP accomplishes a practical "worker capitalism."

At an early stage, the corporation adopts an ESOP for the benefit of its employees, including the trust that will acquire the stock of the corporation for the accounts of the employees participating in the ESOP. It is important to select a trustee, usually a bank, that will act independently on behalf of the employees to assure that the acquisition price is fair. As described in Chapter 15, the price paid by the ESOP trust must, among other requirements, meet regulations of the U.S. Department of Labor.

The typical ESOP acquisition is a leveraged buyout. The management group and the labor unions negotiate with lenders and perhaps also with venture capital firms to obtain financing secured by a pledge of the stock purchased by the ESOP trust. Thus, the strategies and preparations used in leveraged buyout transactions generally apply to ESOP acquisitions.

A major strategic objective is to structure the ESOP, the acquisition and the financing to obtain the generous tax benefits provided for ESOP-financed acquisitions by the Internal Revenue Code (See Chapter 15.) Another significant benefit is the exemption of ESOP acquisitions from the antitrust prenotification and reporting requirements of the U.S. Department of Justice and the Federal Trade Commission. (See Chapter 10.)

Preparations for an ESOP acquisition begin with the management group and the labor unions having extensive knowledge of the business. However, they should perform a due diligence review so that their knowledge is organized and complete. (See Chapter 5.) They will need the review for their own use and also to present information to potential lenders and perhaps also to potential equity investors.

Before commencing negotiations, the owners of the corporation, the management group, the union workers and the ESOP trustee should recognize that they have common objectives, but there are also some conflicting interests. When conflicting interests exist, each group should act independently and have independent advisers in the negotiations. (See Chapter 15 and the discussion of conflicts of interest in Chapter 14.)

L. Turnaround Acquisitions

Turnaround acquisitions offer unique opportunities for buyers who can perform knowledgeable due diligence reviews to identify and evaluate problems and provide solutions for them. Examples of businesses that can be turned around are as follows:

- Cyclical businesses being sold during a downturn period by a corporation experiencing a cash squeeze that prevents it from keeping the business until the next cyclical upturn.

- Subsidiaries or divisions of multi-operation corporations that have been neglected or used as "cash cows" because they did not fit the overall corporate business plan.
- Businesses burdened by needless expenses for owner or executive perquisites or by poorly planned expansion projects sponsored by management suffering from an "edifice complex."
- Businesses using outmoded manufacturing processes and equipment, if the buyer has the know-how and resources to upgrade them.
- Businesses burdened by a "millstone" operation that is an irreparable source of losses, but that can be shut down without excessive costs.
- Businesses that have become entangled in litigation or government regulatory problems that the buyer can resolve at reasonable cost.
- Businesses that have been headed by incompetent, corrupt or superannuated management, but have sound second-tier management who can replace them.
- Businesses that have suffered because their managers were frustrated by bureaucratic conditions within a large corporation that prevented them from making prompt and effective business decisions and burdened them with excessive costs.

Turnaround acquisitions range from corporations or businesses that are struggling but modestly profitable to the bankrupt businesses described earlier in this chapter. A buyer's major strategic objective is to obtain a price that reflects the risk and compensates for the cost and effort needed to achieve the turnaround. A strategic advantage for a buyer in a turnaround acquisition is that the existing management and employees of the acquired corporation are likely to support new business methods and austerity measures.

A successful turnaround acquisition can provide dramatic rewards. For example, the author once participated in the acquisition of a large multiproduct plant that had been closed by its owner. After reopening, the plant earned profits exceeding the purchase price for three years after the acquisition.

M. Negotiating Methods

1. Preparing for Negotiations

When discussing negotiating methods there is a tendency to think of chess or poker tactics by which a player seeks to outwit an opponent. Such tactics are occasionally used in acquisition negotiations. However, for the most part, the stakes are so high, the relationships so enduring, and the issues so numerous and complex that more serious methods are necessary.

Key prerequisites for successful acquisition negotiations are as follows:

- Collection and analysis of information to determine the entire economics of the acquisition.
- Establishing negotiating objectives.

- Designating priorities and values for the objectives, including probabilistic values to objectives that are subject to contingencies and present values to future values.
- Estimating the consequences of failure to obtain any or all of the objectives.
- Estimating the negotiating objectives of other persons involved in the negotiations or whose actions can affect the negotiations.
- Estimating the priorities and values of the other persons involved in the negotiations.
- Estimating the consequences to the other persons of failure to obtain any or all of their objectives.
- Applying "what-if" analysis to determine responses to positions that may be taken by other persons.

During preparations for negotiations, the negotiators should review all elements of the transaction, not just the amount designated as the "price." For example, if the seller offers to reduce the "price" by $800,000, the buyer is pleased. However, if the seller wants in return an assumption of sales tax payments, a lease with rents exceeding current market level and a two-year employment contract for the seller's present chief executive officer, the buyer must evaluate whether the three items are worth more or less than $800,000. In many transactions the federal income tax issues alone are worth millions of dollars. In some transactions, the liabilities assumed far exceed the amount paid as the "price" at the closing. In reality, the true price of an acquisition is its overall cost.

2. Negotiating Teams and Meetings

When a seller and a buyer are ready for negotiations, they should select a negotiating team. The members should usually be a senior officer or officers and one or more professional advisers who are familiar with the subjects to be discussed at particular meetings. The negotiating team should not usually include the person or persons with final approval authority such as the chief executive officer or the board of directors. Thus, the negotiators can reach constructive solutions to issues, but reserve commitments for review that may take more time and effort than is available during a negotiating session.

Appearances can be important during negotiations. The rank, number and authority of the persons attending negotiating sessions can convey unspoken messages. Even the places where meetings are held can have implications. For example, if a seller repeatedly agrees to hold meetings at the buyer's offices, it may be taken as a sign that the seller is eager and can be persuaded to make concessions.

Negotiators must recognize that negotiation is a give-and-take process. The seller and the buyer should each propose the price and terms they want, after enough review to assure that the proposals are "in the ballpark." It is a mistake to submit a proposal that asks for the "moon" because the other party may decide that the proposer is not serious and terminate the negotiations. It is also a mistake to make a proposal that is too generous because the other party will predictably try to improve it anyway.

Negotiations proceed best when they are conducted courteously. Each point should, of course, be proposed and answered clearly with supporting reasons. Tactics such as shouting, table pounding, bluffing, withholding of essential information, confrontation, sarcasm and staged walkouts are generally ineffective because the participants in acquisition negotiations are too experienced to be swayed by such conduct. The best negotiators receive proposals courteously, take time to study them and then respond with counterproposals. Each counterproposal should usually show movement toward compromise.

During negotiations, it is important to avoid an impasse. Negotiators for sellers and buyers sometimes reach an impasse by focusing unnecessarily on a narrow range of issues. Skilled negotiators maintain a sense of progress by moving from issues on which agreement cannot be reached to issues that can be resolved. Of course, the open issues must be revisited, but they may be solved more easily after a pattern of problem solving has been established.

As parties reach agreement on complex issues, it is important to be sure that the agreement extends to the subissues that are part of each of them. Otherwise, there may be subsequent disagreements and claims. For example, if a seller is persuaded to include additional properties in an assets acquisition, the parties should also agree who will pay the transfer taxes and expenses. If not, the seller may later say that it accommodated the buyer's request to add the properties and certainly should not be expected to make further concessions on transfer taxes and expenses. With equal logic, the buyer may say that the seller could hardly have promised to include the properties if it did not intend to pay the necessary costs to transfer them. Acquisition contracts should be prepared during negotiations because the lawyers can put verbal exchanges into writing in reasonable detail. As the acquisition contract is drafted, the lawyers for the seller and buyer usually identify subissues that have not been clearly addressed and recommend that they be clarified or further negotiated.[4]

[4]At times, lawyers are accused of "nit-picking" when they identify open points within issues on which a buyer and seller have reached broad agreement. However, the lawyers' function in identifying open points is vital because they may be important. If the points are unimportant, the negotiators can either clarify them quickly or inform the lawyers that neither the buyer nor the seller considers them sufficiently important to divert time from other matters.

N. Reference Materials

1. Books and Periodicals

Employee Stock Ownership Plans, Smiley, Prentice Hall

Mergers & Acquisitions, Rock, IDD Enterprises (bimonthly magazine)

The Mergers & Acquisitions Handbook, Rock, IDD Enterprises

Mergers & Acquisitions Report, Kollar, IDD Enterprises (newsletter)

Mergerstat Review, Houlihan, Lokey, Howard & Zukin

World M&A Network, International Executive Reports

2. Articles

"Are You Getting What You Pay for in an Acquisition?" Byczek, *Mergers & Acquisitions,* July-Aug 1997

"Avenues to Value in the Purchase of Troubled Companies," Koenig, *Mergers & Acquisitions,* Nov–Dec 1993

"Calculating the Value—Creation Potential of a Deal," Rappaport, *Mergers & Acquisitions,* Jul-Aug 1998

"Converting Merger Benefits to Shareholder Value," Rappaport, *Mergers & Acquisitions,* Mar–Apr 1987

"The Critical Line between Dealmakers and Dealbreakers," Gavai et al., *Mergers & Acquisitions,* Mar–Apr 1994

"Divesting in the 1990s," Greco, *CFO,* Sep 1994

"A Dose of Reality in the Business Plan for an Acquisition," Hartman, *Mergers & Acquisitions,* Mar–Apr 1993

"Evening Up the Odds in Negotiating a Deal of the 1990s," O'Donnell et al., *Mergers & Acquisitions,* Jan–Feb 1994

"Extricating a Division from Its Parent," *Mergers & Acquisitions,* Doran et al., Jul–Aug 1997

"Family Businesses: A Breed Apart in Crafting Deals," Gisser et al., *Mergers & Acquisitions,* Mar–Apr 1993

"Keeping Customers Satisfied While the Deal Proceeds," Clemente et al., *Mergers & Acquisitions,* Jul–Aug 1997

"Managing as if tomorrow mattered," Hayes and Garvin, *Harvard Business Review,* May–Jun 1982

"Mapping the Right Routes after the Decision to Sell," Foster, *Mergers & Acquisitions,* Jul–Aug 1994

"The master and the apprentice," Green, *Forbes,* Oct 6, 1997

"Monsanto v. Malthus," Lenzner et al., *Forbes,* Mar 10, 1997

"Paints and Coatings—Mergers Create an Altered Image," Fattah, D'Amico et al., *Chemical Week,* Oct 23, 1996

"Scouting the M&A Landscape for Quality Targets," Paul, *Mergers & Acquisitions,* Mar–Apr 1995

"Strategic Analysis for More Profitable Acquisitions," Rappaport, *Harvard Business Review,* Jul–Aug 1979

"Why Strategic Planning Goes Awry," Hayes, *The New York Times,* Apr 20, 1986

"You don't blow smoke at these guys," Hayes, *Forbes,* Oct 20, 1997

Chapter 3

ACQUISITION FINANCING

A. THREE BASIC METHODS OF PAYMENT

The basic "currencies" used to pay for acquisitions are cash, debt and equity. Each currency (and combinations of them) can be used regardless of whether the transaction is a merger, a stock purchase or an assets purchase.[1] Thus, the method of payment is decided by negotiation between the seller and buyer. Their ability to reach agreement depends on a multitude of factors including their financial resources, tax and accounting objectives, time availability and risk orientation.

1. Payment of the Price in Cash

Cash is the most common method of payment for a business. Cash is a high priority for sellers who are reluctant to take risk. Some sellers refuse to sell unless the price is payable in cash. Some will accept a lower price in cash than they would accept in debt or equity.

Cash is also preferred by some buyers. They like its simplicity and finality. A buyer who pays cash need not go through the delays and costs involved in payment with debt or stock and need not have the seller as a future creditor, stockholder or board member.[2]

Foreign companies acquiring businesses in the United States usually pay cash or a combination of cash and debt. They recognize that sellers in the U.S. may be hesitant to accept stock traded in a foreign nation. Foreign sellers likewise hesitate to accept stock of U.S. buyers, although their reluctance is somewhat less because of the relative liquidity, efficiency and strict regulation of the U.S. securities markets.

The most important disadvantage of a cash price to sellers is that the transaction is taxable. However, a mitigating factor is that the seller can use part of the cash to pay the taxes. In addition, the seller must also decide on appropriate investments or other uses for the cash. Some sellers who are

[1]For 1997, *Mergers & Acquisitions* reported 1,746 cash transactions, 1,120 stock transactions and 583 transactions for combinations of cash and securities. The data included transactions valued at $5,000,000 or more for which prices were disclosed.

[2]For example, difficulties between the management of General Motors Corporation and Ross Perot were reported during Perot's service as a director following the acquisition of Electronic Data Systems Corp., in part for Series E Common Stock of General Motors.

unaccustomed to managing financial assets do not reinvest the sale proceeds successfully.

When paying cash, buyers can sometimes obtain all or part of the cash from internal operations. That is common when the business acquired is small in relation to the size of the buyer's business. It also occurs when a buyer has accumulated significant amounts of cash from operations or sales of assets. Using internally generated cash offers the advantages of speed and simplicity. There is no need for the delay and complications involved in raising financing. A buyer who can pay with internally generated cash may have an advantage over other buyers who must make their offers contingent upon raising financing.

Cash buyers can also pay with cash borrowed from lenders or obtained by selling equity to investors. The most common method is borrowing from lenders because raising equity is relatively expensive, time-consuming and uncertain, except when the buyer can obtain equity investment from a parent corporation or a small group of existing stockholders who are familiar with the acquisition and believe it will enhance their investment. Methods for raising financing from lenders and equity investors are discussed later in this chapter.

2. Payment of the Price with Debt

Payment for a business wholly or partially with debt is very common and is often called "seller financing."

Sellers of businesses usually prefer to be paid in full when an acquisition is closed. However, willingness to provide seller financing is sometimes essential to achieve a sale of a business to a buyer who cannot obtain all or part of the necessary financing from lenders or equity investors. Even when not essential, a seller may decide to provide financing to obtain a better price or to enable a preferred buyer, such as an employee group, to purchase the business. Sellers usually consider a variety of factors in deciding whether to provide seller financing including the amount, interest rate, payment schedule and collateral. Sellers also consider judgmental factors such as confidence in the buyer, a factor that may be enhanced if the seller's existing management will continue in positions of responsibility after the acquisition.

Buyers generally welcome seller financing. Seller financing may save a buyer all or part of the difficult and time-consuming task of raising financing from outside sources. Strategically, seller financing enables the buyer to use cash generated from the acquired business to pay the purchase price. Seller financing also evidences the seller's confidence that the business will generate the necessary cash flows to pay the deferred part of the price.

A buyer who wants full independence from the seller after the acquisition will not prefer seller financing. However, a buyer who plans to retain seller's management to manage the acquired business is likely to see seller financing as a partial motivation for good management.

A buyer may agree to pay the seller by a contractual commitment to make installment payments. However, the buyer will usually deliver a promissory note (or notes) for the amount of the seller financing at the closing of the acquisition contract. When the acquired business is publicly owned, the buyer may deliver more elaborate debt instruments with features designed to be attractive to the public shareholders.

When all or part of the price is paid with debt, the transaction is taxable. However, the seller can ordinarily elect to report the installment payments and interest in the years when they are received. (See the discussion of installment sales in Chapter 6.)

Three recurring risks are associated with seller financing:

- A buyer receiving seller financing may hesitate to negotiate strongly as to the price and other terms. As a result, the buyer may overpay or may assume burdensome obligations that affect its ability to operate the business successfully.
- A seller who provides generous seller financing may enable a buyer to purchase too easily. Buyers who do not go through the rigorous tasks of obtaining financing from independent lenders and investors may be inadequately prepared to manage the acquired business from a financial point of view.
- A seller who provides partial seller financing is almost always asked to agree to subordinate its payment to financing of the price provided by banks or other institutional lenders. The seller will argue that the seller financing should have the same priority as other financing. However, banks and other institutional lenders believe that a seller who wants a price in excess of an amount they are willing to finance should take the risk of subordination. The lenders may allow the buyer to make payments to the seller so long as the buyer is not in default in its obligations to the lenders. However, if the buyer fails to meet financial ratio covenants or other commitments to the lenders, the buyer must cease payments on the seller financing until it cures all defaults.

If the buyer obtains satisfactory financing from lenders, then seller financing is not needed. A buyer who is unsuccessful in obtaining lender financing should ascertain the lenders' reasons and perhaps discuss them with the seller. Refusal to provide financing may mean that the lenders believe the business or the transaction is basically flawed, or that they believe the business and transaction are sound but should be restructured or renegotiated.

For example, if the lenders believe that the equity capital the buyer proposes to support the loans is inadequate, the buyer may have to raise additional equity capital. If the lenders believe that the values of net assets and projected cash flows will not support the loan financing requested, the buyer can go back to the seller to seek a price reduction. If the seller continues to insist on a price that exceeds the buyer's available financing, seller financing of the excess may become a compromise that saves the day. Under these circumstances, the seller should understand why the lenders will require that the seller accept subordination of the seller financing.

One form of seller financing is a contingent purchase price that depends partially on operating results after the sale. Contingent purchase prices are discussed in detail in Chapter 16.

3. Payment of the Price with Stock

Payment of the acquisition price with stock or other equity securities is common.[3] Buyers whose common stock is traded actively on a stock exchange or the NASDAQ National Market System often use their common stock as "acquisition currency." Further, the benefit of tax-free reorganization treatment under the Internal Revenue Code and the pooling of interests method under generally accepted accounting principles are available only if the price is paid with voting stock. (See the discussions of tax-free reorganizations in Chapter 7 and of pooling of interests accounting in Chapter 9.)

The stock used to pay for an acquisition can be common stock, preferred stock or a special stock. Common stock is the most widely used. However, a buyer can sometimes design a preferred stock with dividend, liquidation preference, redemption and possibly voting and conversion provisions satisfactory to a seller and may also agree to list the preferred stock for trading. A buyer can also sometimes design a "special stock," which is essentially a common stock with some special preferences added in order to make it attractive to a seller. For example, when General Motors Corporation acquired Electronic Data Systems Corp. (EDS), it used a Class E common stock with limited voting rights and other characteristics keyed partially to the performance of EDS after the acquisition.

Stock can seldom be used to pay for an acquisition unless the buyer's stock is traded on a stock exchange or in the over-the-counter (NASDAQ) market.[4] Even if the seller has no immediate plans to sell shares received from the buyer, the liquidity provided by the existence of a market for the shares is an important factor.

Buyers having stock traded at a relatively high price on a stock exchange or in the over-the-counter market and who wish to conserve cash and borrowing power may favor acquisitions for newly issued stock. However, the additional shares issued will dilute the percentage ownership of the buyer's existing shareholders. Thus, management must consider the effects of the dilution on voting control of the buyer. Management will not want to acquire for stock unless they are confident that the persons receiving the stock will vote in a manner friendly to management. Management must also consider the effects of the dilution on reported earnings and cash flows per share. For example, if a buyer issues stock to acquire a developmental "high-tech" business that will not soon be profitable, the buyer's shareholders may be displeased at the reduction of earnings and cash flows per share. However, if the acquired business is sufficiently profitable, the earnings and cash flows of the acquired business will increase the buyer's earnings per share and cash flow per share. Thus, the existing public shareholders will be pleased despite the dilution of their percentage ownership.

---

[3] *Mergers & Acquisitions* reported 1,120 acquisitions for stock in 1997 based on 3,449 transactions valued at $5 million or more for which prices were disclosed.

[4] When the owners of unincorporated businesses decide to incorporate, they receive stock that is not traded in any market. Further, privately owned corporations are often restructured in transactions involving exchanges of untraded stock. However, those transactions are not generally regarded as acquisitions because the "sellers" continue to control the businesses after the transactions.

Sellers of businesses are often reluctant to sell for stock. They worry about fluctuations in value and lack of liquidity that could deprive them of the full price negotiated for the sale of their businesses. Their concern increases if the stock is not registered with the Securities and Exchange Commission and must be held for a significant time period before sales in the public markets can be made. However, many sellers take stock to gain one or more advantages. One advantage is the benefit of a tax-free reorganization. Another advantage is acquiring a significant block of shares of the buyer that could mean a voice in the buyer's management after the acquisition. For example, the seller may negotiate for one or more board seats and executive positions. Still another advantage is that stock ownership permits the seller to benefit from growth and profitability of the buyer if the synergies that motivated the acquisition are obtained.

When a buyer issues stock to acquire a corporation whose shares are publicly owned, the buyer must register the offer and exchange of its stock with the Securities and Exchange Commission and applicable state securities commissions, a time-consuming and costly task. When a buyer issues stock to acquire a privately owned business, the stock can often be issued without registration because of the private offering exemptions in the securities laws. However, shares issued under these exemptions are restricted from resale to the public for up to two years unless they are subsequently registered for resale. Sellers concerned about restrictions on their freedom to resell stock received in an acquisition can negotiate for provisions in the acquisition contract requiring registration of the stock with the Securities and Exchange Commission. If the acquisition time schedule permits, the registration can be accomplished as part of the closing preparations and become effective on the closing date. Otherwise, the acquisition contract can entitle the sellers to registration of their stock at a future date. (See Chapter 11 for further information about registration of stock and other securities issued in acquisition transactions.)

B. Raising Debt Financing from Institutional Lenders

1. Sources of Debt Financing

Debt financing for business acquisitions is obtained from insurers, pension funds, banks, commercial credit companies, venture capital funds, wealthy individuals, small business investment companies (SBICs) and government agencies such as the Small Business Administration (SBA).

Insurers are a source of long-term financing. Life insurers are especially able to make long-term loans because they have continuous flows of premium income. Their actuaries can predict with reasonable accuracy the cash outflows required to pay death or annuity benefits. For example, life insurers lend for terms such as ten or twenty years. Property and casualty and liability insurers also lend for relatively long terms, but must be more conservative than life insurers because casualty and liability occurrences are difficult to predict.

Pension funds are also a source of long- and intermediate-term financing. Large pension funds receive relatively stable large inflows of contributions from employers. Actuaries can project with reasonable accuracy when employee benefits will become payable. Pension fund managers tend to be performance oriented and favor loans structured to provide favorable investment returns.

Banks, including commercial and savings institutions, are typically intermediate-term lenders. Their liabilities in excess of capital are demand deposits and relatively short-term certificates of deposit. A bank proposal for acquisition is likely to be a three-part package consisting of a five-year intermediate-term loan, a three-year revolving credit facility and a short-term line of credit facility. The package may also include a facility for capital expenditure borrowing. Recently, some banks have offered longer-term loans for which they purchase derivatives to hedge the risk.

Commercial credit companies also make intermediate- and short-term loans. Their liabilities in excess of capital consist of borrowings, including sales of commercial paper, at advantageous rates. They are also likely to provide a three-part package such as a five- or six-year intermediate-term loan, an intermediate term capital expenditure loan facility and a three-year revolving credit facility. Commercial credit companies typically require that the buyer pay interest and several kinds of fees in amounts substantially higher than those charged by insurers and banks. Their loans are also customarily secured by mortgages and other security interests that grant extensive powers to the lender, such as the right to collect the borrower's accounts receivable from customers.

Venture capital funds provide a wider and more imaginative range of loans than those available from other lenders. Their source of funds is typically a pool of capital raised by selling stock to wealthy or prosperous individuals. Their investments are made in accordance with the policies prescribed in the fund charter and the private placement memorandum used to raise the pool of capital. The most useful role of venture capital funds is to provide "mezzanine" financing. This financing consists of contractually subordinated debt, perhaps in two or more tiers, and preferred stock. "Mezzanine" financing is valuable, especially for buyers with a small equity capital base, because it supplements the equity capital to support senior debt borrowed from insurers, banks, commercial credit companies and other institutional lenders. Venture capital funds usually require a high return on investment in return for the risk they assume. They charge interest rates and fees in excess of those charged by conventional lenders. They almost always have additional requirements, including equity participation or "sweeteners" and participation in management by such means as membership in the borrower's board of directors.

Wealthy individuals who directly provide debt financing for business acquisitions use criteria similar to those used by venture capital funds. However, since they have not made commitments to investors who provided their pool of capital, they have greater flexibility. Wealthy individuals are most likely to provide financing when their business experience and participation in management are both valuable and welcome.

SBICs provide debt financing to small businesses under programs sponsored by federal legislation and regulated by the Small Business Administration (SBA) which may provide part of the financing through its participating securities program. SBICs are privately owned. Among other privileges, their licenses from the SBA allow SBICs to borrow from the Federal Financing Bank at advantageous rates. SBICs make intermediate-term loans of up to five to seven years and generally operate in a manner similar to venture capital funds. However, their lending and other activities are subject to regulation by the SBA.[5]

The SBA also provides loan guarantees of up to $1,250,000 to banks and other lenders who provide loans to small businesses and to other persons designated by the U.S. Congress. The SBA also provides some direct loan financing to eligible borrowers.[6]

2. Presentations to Obtain Debt Financing

To apply to a lender for acquisition financing, a buyer should submit at least the following:

- The buyer's financial statements, including cash flow statements and the related auditors' opinion.
- Financial statements for the business to be acquired, including cash flow statements, with the related auditors' opinion, if applicable.
- Business plan for the acquired business and the buyer's business after the acquisition.
- Cash flow projections for the acquired business and the combination or consolidation of the acquired business and the buyer's business, showing the entries to accomplish the combination or consolidation. These projections should be for the term of the proposed loan.
- Appraisals of the assets of the business to be acquired and perhaps also for all assets of the buyer.
- Other information including descriptions of management, products, raw materials, properties and credit rating.

In evaluating an application, lenders focus on liquidity as demonstrated by (1) future cash flows to be generated by the buyer and the acquired business and (2) future cash that could be realized from planned sales of assets by the buyer or, if necessary, by the lender through a foreclosure sale if a default should occur. If a lender emphasizes the first component, the loan is a "cash flow"–based loan. If a lender emphasizes the second component, the loan is an "asset"-based loan. In reality, all lenders consider both elements, but the relative weight assigned to each element in a lender's criteria can mean the difference between approval and rejection for some applications.

Lenders also review the soundness and reliability of management, products, manufacturing processes, technology liabilities and other important components of the business. This review is made to assure that cash flows and asset values can be expected to endure throughout the term of the loan.

---

[5]See 15 U.S.C. § 681 *et seq.* and 13 C.F.R. Part 107 (61 Fed. Reg. 3189, 1/31/96).

[6]See 15 U.S.C. § 636 *et seq.* and 13 C.F.R. Part 120 *et seq.* (61 Fed. Reg. 3235, 1/31/96).

Loan applicants, ranging from founders of new small businesses to experienced executives with large companies, frequently weaken their applications by presenting the wrong information. Some applicants focus on management credentials, market opportunities and technologies. Other applicants rely heavily on historical financial statements. Still other applicants describe exciting business development opportunities in uncharted new industries. Most lenders respond courteously to these presentations, but they range from only minimally helpful to disadvantageous to the loan application.

Many misfocused loan applications result from failure to understand a lender's function and priorities. A lender is a supplier of a commodity used to bridge a time difference from the time when a business must make cash expenditures to the time when cash receipts created by the expenditures are collected. A loan is repaid from future cash flow and that must be a lender's first priority. Cash flow–based loans are directly based on analysis of future cash receipts. Asset-based loans are also based on future cash receipts, both those expected from normal business operations and those that could be obtained from dispositions of assets after foreclosure.

Stated plainly, loans are not repaid with management credentials, technology or historical earnings. They are repaid from future cash flow. Thus, a loan applicant is not meeting a lender's first priority until it demonstrates that future cash flow will be reliably adequate to meet a realistic principal and interest payment schedule. Of course, a loan application can benefit from appropriate mention of key business strengths and good historical performance. Indeed, it may be necessary to explain operating problems or poor historical performance. However, these factors only get the applicant to first base. Demonstration of reliable future cash flows brings the applicant the rest of the way home.

Other misfocused loan applications result from failure to understand the difference between a lender and an investor. Lenders are legally obligated to make only those loans that their business judgment indicates will be repaid. Because business judgment about future events can never be perfect, lenders make some loans to borrowers that have modestly higher risk than borrowers with the highest credit ratings, and they charge an interest premium for them. However, a lender should never make a loan if there is serious doubt about ability to repay, except perhaps in some "workout" situations.

The lender's situation is very different from that of an investor. An investor is free to take risk and does so by purchasing equity. The investor expects to be rewarded both for the use of money and the assumption of risk. An equity investor also expects to be well rewarded for the risk element. On the other hand, a lender receives only its principal and interest payments. A lender receives no direct financial benefit if the borrower is highly successful and greatly overperforms its projections.

For these reasons, a loan applicant may be rejected if it presents a business plan and projections showing serious risk elements. Development of new business and technologies is an important subject in presentations to customers, employees and investors. However, discussions of these subjects in presentations to lenders must be accompanied by a demonstration that they will not impair the reliability of cash flows required to meet obligations to the lender.

3. Financial Covenants in Loan Agreements

Loan applicants must demonstrate not only ability to meet scheduled payments of principal and interest, but also ability to meet continuously during the term of the loan agreement several financial covenants requiring maintenance of financial condition and financial operating results that assure comfortable ability to pay. Some examples of restrictive financial covenants contained in loan agreements for acquisition financing are as follows:

> *Minimum net worth.* Total assets (perhaps excluding intangibles) less total liabilities will not be less than an agreed dollar amount.
>
> *Minimum leverage ratio.* The result obtained by dividing total assets by total liabilities will not exceed an agreed ratio, such as 3 to 1.
>
> *Minimum working capital.* Current assets less current liabilities will not be less than an agreed dollar amount.
>
> *Minimum working capital ratio.* The result obtained by dividing current assets by current liabilities will not be less than an agreed ratio, such as 1.5 to 1.
>
> *Interest coverage ratio.* The result obtained by dividing earnings before interest and taxes (EBIT) by interest charges will not be less than an agreed ratio, such as 2.0 to 1.
>
> *Fixed charges coverage ratio.* The result obtained by dividing EBIT by total fixed charges (i.e., interest, lease payments, installment purchases, etc.) will be not less than an agreed ratio, such as 1.5 to 1.
>
> *Limitation on borrowing.* The borrowers may not borrow money or guarantee any obligations except as allowed by the loan agreement.
>
> *Limitation on liens.* The borrower may not incur or allow liens to exist on its properties unless authorized by the loan agreement.
>
> *Limitation on certain payments.* The borrower may not pay dividends, redeem capital stock or make certain other payments except as allowed by the loan agreement.
>
> *Limitations on certain transactions.* The borrower may not sell or dispose of assets or merge with any other person except as allowed by the loan agreement.
>
> *Restrictions on transactions with affiliates.* The borrower may not engage in transactions with affiliated persons, such as payment of consulting fees to directors or major shareholders, except as allowed by the loan agreement.

Some examples of affirmative covenants contained in loan agreements for acquisition financing are as follows:

- Maintenance of corporate existence and good standing.
- Payment of taxes.

- Preparation of financial statements in accordance with GAAP, their audit by an independent auditor, and timely delivery of copies of the financial statements and audit reports to the lender.
- Maintenance of business lines.
- Maintenance of properties and insurance coverage.
- Compliance with laws and regulations.

In recent years, it has also become common, although far from universal, to include a "change of control" provision in loan agreements. This provision entitles the lender to declare the loan fully due and payable if certain events occur that materially change the management or ownership of the borrower. From a lender's viewpoint, such a provision can be valuable because the decision to make a loan assumes continuity of management and ownership of the borrower by persons in whom the lender has confidence. From the borrower's viewpoint, the provisions can be burdensome and, if accepted, should be carefully negotiated and drafted. However, some publicly owned borrowers welcome a "change of control" provision as part of their "shark-repellent" devices to deter a hostile takeover. An example of a "change of control" provision appears as Exhibit 3-1.

4. Limits on Debt Financing

Borrowers often wonder how much a bank or other institutional lender will be willing to lend. They wonder what internal criteria lenders use. Not surprisingly, criteria differ from lender to lender and are not published for competitive reasons. Further, lenders often make exceptions from criteria when they encounter special situations.

Borrowers can make some preliminary evaluations by considering several elements: asset values, cash flows, capital structure and borrowing costs. Small businesses and businesses in industries known for fluctuating cash flows are likely to find only "asset-based" financing available. If their cash flows appear to be sound for the foreseeable future, loans equal to the following percentages of asset values may be available:

Accounts receivable from reputable customers	70 to 80%
Raw material, work-in-process, and finished goods inventories	40 to 60%
Machinery and equipment	60 to 80% of appraised liquidation value
Land and buildings	60 to 80% of foreclosure value

Established businesses with reliable cash flows can estimate the amount of loan financing available by projecting cash flows available to repay principal and interest while maintaining compliance with financial covenants such as those described earlier in this chapter. However, if a proposed loan would result in a highly leveraged capital structure, a lender may reduce the amount of the loan to assure an adequate equity base. Lenders change their financial covenant and capital structure requirements in response to economic conditions, competition, available money supplies and credit experience; but they respond more favorably to questions about loan agreement covenants than to questions about internal loan application review criteria. Thus, the four factors can be used by borrowers for self-evaluation.

The remaining element in estimating borrowing limits is cost. In recent markets, senior debt of some borrowers has carried an interest cost of 7% to 10%. Subordinated debt, if needed, bears an interest cost in the range of 10% to 15%. In addition to interest, borrowers must expect to pay other costs that can be modest or very expensive. A borrower must expect to pay its own counsel, accountants and financial adviser (if any); to reimburse the lender for the fees of its counsel; and to pay closing costs for title insurance recordings, filing and taxes to the extent applicable. Commercial credit companies and some other lenders also require an array of other fees including closing fees, commitment fees for undrawn credit facilities, collateral management fees and prepayment fees. For "mezzanine" financing, they may require a warrant entitling them to purchase 10% to 15% of the borrower's equity for a nominal consideration.

5. Collateral for Loans

Lenders of "asset-based" financing can be expected to require a first mortgage and first priority security interests in all the borrower's assets. They will establish ongoing eligibility criteria for accounts receivable and inventories and old items will be dropped from the borrowing base. The asset values of machinery and equipment and of land and buildings should presume an orderly and reasonably prompt sale that is neither a "fire sale" nor a prolonged effort to obtain the highest price.

Lenders to closely held corporations often request that their shareholders sign personal guarantees of the loans. Lenders request personal guarantees not only to strengthen the credit status of the loans, but also to provide an incentive for the shareholders to support the corporate business during times of business or financial stress. Requests for personal guarantees can be a very sensitive subject. While some shareholders readily agree, many react with reluctance and some absolutely refuse.

6. A Comparison of Debt and Equity Financing

To the extent that it is feasible to use debt financing for an acquisition, that method usually results in a considerable cost advantage. The interest cost varies with the credit standing of the borrower and with economic conditions. However, whether the rate is 10% or 15%, the deductibility of interest for federal and state tax purposes reduces the net cost by about 40%. Further, existing shareholders do not incur the dilution of ownership that can add significantly to the cost of equity financing.

The transaction cost alone for selling equity is likely to range from 4% for large companies to over 15% for small companies. Dividends, if any, paid to shareholders cannot be deducted from corporate income for federal or state tax purposes. In addition, experienced equity investors, such as those who purchase in private placements, usually negotiate for a price and number of shares projected to provide an investment return far higher than the interest rates charged by lenders. For example, the investment return expected by venture capital investors in leveraged buyout transactions ranges from 30 to 40%.[7] The reason is that they assume both new business risk and financial structure risk.

Debt financing also has other advantages. It can usually be raised more rapidly and with more certainty than equity financing. If the interest cost is high, a borrower can usually negotiate for a right to refinance upon payment of a prepayment premium or after an agreed time period. Equity financing requires careful advance planning and can be difficult to obtain on reasonable terms, especially during periods when the stock markets are performing poorly. It can be very difficult and expensive to raise equity capital if there is any time pressure, such as exists when an acquisition is in progress. Thus, a company that is planning for expansion through acquisitions or internal growth should sell equity when its performance and market conditions are favorable rather than wait until specific opportunities arise. The equity base, or "war chest," obtained on favorable terms can then be augmented by debt financing as needed for acquisitions and other growth opportunities.

C. Raising Equity Financing

1. Sources of Equity Financing

Equity financing is a different world from debt financing, although some sources provide both kinds of financing. Sources of equity financing are as follows:

- Personal savings and other resources of the persons who plan to acquire a small business.
- Relatives, friends and business acquaintances of the persons who plan to acquire a small business.
- Wealthy or affluent individuals who invest in equity of promising companies.[8]
- Venture capital funds.
- Employees and employee stock ownership trusts.
- Purchasers in a public offering.

[7] Venture capital investors set high objectives for investment returns to compensate for risk. Their returns from successful investments must absorb the losses incurred when other investments fail.

[8] Investments in promising new companies can provide impressive returns. For a classic example, the Ford Motor Company was founded in 1903. Henry Ford received 51% of the stock in return for patent rights, machinery and equipment and other business assets. Four other investors received 5% of the stock for investments of $5,000 each: James Couzens, Horace and John Dodge, and Horace Rackham. Within less than ten years Ford Motor became one of the largest companies in the world and was declaring annual dividends of several million dollars. The Dodge brothers, whose interests were repurchased after litigation claiming that the dividends were inadequate, founded the Dodge Motor Company.

Investment bankers are not included in the list because they are intermediaries who arrange financing, but are not generally the source of the financing. Investment banking firms and their partners, officers and related funds make investments from time to time, but buyers hiring an investment banking firm to arrange financing should not assume that the firm will be the source of the funds. A description of intermediaries and the roles they play in arranging financing is provided later in this chapter.

2. Presentations to Obtain Equity Financing

To raise equity financing for an acquisition, the buyer should present the same basic information as is presented to prospective lenders, but with a considerably different emphasis.

- A business plan for the acquired business and the buyer's business after the acquisition.
- The buyer's financial statements, including cash flow statements and the related auditors' opinion.
- Financial statements for the business to be acquired, including cash flow statements, with the related auditors' opinion, if applicable.
- Cash flow projections for the acquired business and the combination or consolidation of the acquired business and the buyer's business, showing the entries to accomplish the combination or consolidation.
- Appraisals of the assets of the business to be acquired and perhaps also of all assets of the buyer.
- Other information including descriptions of management, products, raw materials, properties and credit rating.

Presentations to relatives, friends and business acquaintances to raise modest amounts of equity to acquire a small business generally are (and should be) kept straightforward and simple. Only limited paperwork is necessary in situations when the investors know the buyer and sometimes also the seller. Instead of detailed descriptions of management, products and properties, the buyer can arrange for the prospective investors to see them.

Presentations to professional equity investors, including venture capital funds, must be made more formally and in written documents. If they become actively interested, professional equity investors will probably also want to visit the business to be acquired, as part of a "due diligence" review. However, they will not reach a "due diligence" review if the initial documents presented by the buyer are not sufficiently sound and persuasive.

Unlike lenders, equity investors are not allergic to risk. While their interests and priorities vary greatly, equity investors know that good investment returns on equity are usually accompanied by some level of business and financial risk. For equity investors, the business plan, future cash flows, ownership and management control and "exit strategies" are the most important priorities. If the business plan is sound and shows potential for important growth prospective, equity investors may invest in a "turnaround" acquisition that presents considerable business risk. They may also invest in a leveraged buyout that presents considerable financial risk for an equity investor at the bottom of large layers of senior and subordinated debt. Needless to say, prospective equity investors want to verify that the business plan can actually achieve the "turnaround" and that future cash flows will meet the interest and principal requirements of the acquisition debt. They also want to see that the business plan and cash flows go beyond the "turnaround" and debt amortization period to achieve significant capital appreciation.

Assuming that prospective equity investors are satisfied with the business plan and future cash flows, two issues must be resolved that can be very difficult. The first is the percentage of ownership of the buyer that the investors will receive and the extent of their participation in the buyer's management. The second is the development of realistic "exit strategies." Founders seeking equity investment and prospective equity investors frequently have viewpoints that are almost polar opposites on these issues. It is sometimes prudent to have a preliminary discussion about percentage ownership and management participation before spending time on the business and financial aspects.

Some prospective buyers seeking equity financing to acquire a business begin with the objective of finding investors who will accept a small percentage of ownership, perhaps up to 20 percent and in no event a percentage that would amount to control. They look for passive investors who will be content to review quarterly and annual financial statements and provide support at annual stockholders' meetings. At most, they may be ready to offer a board membership to an investor representative. If a buyer is an established successful business with a strong business plan for the business to be acquired, these objectives may be achievable. However, if the purchase is a leveraged buyout or other startup venture, they may be far from reality.

Prospective equity investors, especially venture capital funds, often have objectives very different from those just described. Some want 80 percent ownership or more. In a leveraged buyout or startup venture, they may view the buyer's management as employees to be granted equity ownership only to the extent necessary to provide incentives for diligent work performance. Others are more flexible, but may have a policy that prohibits investment unless voting control of the stock is obtained. Others may accept minority ownership but require voting agreements enabling them to control the board of directors, at least if adverse events occur.

Differences of viewpoint on percentage ownership and management control cannot always be resolved. In many situations, however, especially if the acquisition opportunity is very attractive, buyer and investor representatives work to understand each other's viewpoints and the values to be contributed by the buyer and the equity investors. These efforts can produce mutually satisfactory compromises.

Prospective buyers seeking equity financing often underestimate the seriousness of the need to assure prospective equity investors of a viable exit strategy or strategies within a horizon of approximately five years. Buyer management is content to invest indefinitely and can have difficulty seeing the importance of an exit strategy. Management will readily talk of general plans to "go public" as a first alternative, but the business plan may lack information demonstrating that a public offering is an achievable exit strategy. Management may not welcome the second alternative, a sale of the acquired business. Management is usually more receptive to the third alternative, a buyout of the equity investors. However, the business plan may lack information demonstrating that a buyout is a viable exit strategy at a price likely to provide a satisfactory investment return to the equity investors.

To provide a credible exit strategy or strategies, management of the buyer should seriously study and evaluate the three alternatives. For example, they can consult with investment bankers to determine whether and how the buyer and the business to be acquired can be made a viable candidate for a public offering. If that alternative appears doubtful, they should consider how a sale could be achieved. For example, can the buyer and the business to be acquired be developed, perhaps including further acquisitions, to a level likely to attract buyers willing to pay a price providing a good investment return for the equity investors? Ironically, there are many businesses that operate steadily and meet all their obligations to lenders, customers, suppliers and employees, but are not good candidates to go public or to be sold to a strategic buyer willing to pay a premium price. If this is the case, the management buyout alternative should be explored. For example, can the buyer and the business to be acquired generate sufficient internal funds for a direct repurchase after meeting all other obligations? If not, will a management leveraged buyout be feasible based on projected future cash flows and asset values?

D. Financial Instruments Used as Acquisition Currency

The financial instruments used to finance acquisitions of some large public corporations and leveraged buyouts can be quite complex. However, a familiar range of financial instruments is used to finance the great majority of acquisitions:

- *Secured Notes.* Asset acquisitions are commonly financed by the issuance of a note secured by a mortgage and security interests in the acquired assets. The note often also contains financial covenants. The mortgage covers the assets that are real estate and fixtures and is recorded in the county or counties where the assets are located.[9] A security agreement (which may be part of the mortgage) creates security interests in other assets such as machinery and equipment, inventories, receivables, cash, intellectual properties and other intangibles. Brief financing statements on Form UCC-1 describing the collateral subject to the security interests are filed in the office of the secretary of state of each state where the collateral is located in order to perfect the security interests. The financing statements are usually also filed in the counties where the collateral is located.

[9]Mortgages and security interests are enforceable between the borrower and the lender when they are executed and delivered. Recording and filing are done to give notice to third parties that a mortgage or security interest is already outstanding and may have priority over rights the third parties seek to obtain.

Stock purchase acquisitions are commonly financed by the issuance of a note secured by a pledge of the stock as collateral. A pledge agreement creates the security interest in the stock. However, because stock certificates have the characteristic of negotiability, the security interest can be perfected only by obtaining possession or custody of the certificates.

- *Unsecured Notes.* Some acquisitions are financed by the issuance of unsecured notes. This form of financing may be appropriate when the borrower has strong credit standing and the amount of the loan is relatively small or the loan is based on strong cash flows generated by the acquiring and acquired businesses. A loan agreement or the note for unsecured financing typically contains covenants (called "negative pledge" covenants) restricting the borrower from granting any mortgage or security interest in the acquired assets so that the noteholder can have recourse to them if it must take legal action to enforce the note.

- *Subordinated Notes.* Subordinated notes are issued to persons providing part of the financing for many acquisitions. For example, they are issued to venture capital firms providing "mezzanine" financing. They are also issued to sellers in acquisitions when part of the financing is provided by a bank or institutional lender and part by the seller. A subordinated note contains provisions stating that the principal and interest are subordinate in right of payment to the prior payment in full of defined classes of senior debt, usually including all debt for money borrowed from banks and other lending institutions and usually excluding business accounts payable. Because of these provisions, holders of senior debt see subordinated notes as an augmentation of equity capital. On the other hand, trade creditors see subordinated notes as additional debt and may limit the amount and terms of the credit they extend if they decide that subordinated debt obligations create excessive risk of nonpayment of trade obligations.

Subordination provisions are usually written to match provisions of senior debt allowing payments of the principal and interest of the subordinated note so long as there is no event of default relating to the senior debt. If a subordinated note is secured by collateral, a second mortgage and a security agreement providing for junior or second priority security interests will be executed, recorded and filed in the state and counties where the collateral is located. Subordination provisions can be written briefly, but often become lengthy in order to provide specifically for future events that might occur. For example, senior lenders usually restrict the right of holders of subordinated debt to accelerate payments of principal and interest and to take foreclosure actions against collateral because those rights could impair the enforcement of the senior debt.

- *Junior Subordinated Notes.* Junior subordinated notes are usually issued to persons providing part of the "mezzanine" financing for leveraged buyouts or restructuring transactions. The subordination provisions state that principal and interest are subordinate in right of payment to the prior payment in full of defined classes of senior debt and senior subordinated debt. Otherwise, the subordination provisions parallel those of other kinds of subordinated debt.

• *Convertible Notes.* Convertible notes, sometimes called convertible debentures, are often issued to persons providing acquisition financing. These notes contain provisions authorizing the holder to surrender the note for conversion of the principal amount into common stock of the borrower at a specified conversion price. The conversion price is usually negotiated to be at a modest premium, such as 15 percent, over the fair market value of the borrower's common stock at the time the convertible note is issued. Borrowers who issue convertible notes usually include a "call" provision authorizing redemption of the notes after a specified time period. If the notes are "in the money" when called, the holders will be "forced" to convert or lose their bargain.[10] Convertible notes also contain antidilution provisions to protect the holder when stock splits and dividends are declared or other events affecting the conversion rights occur.

• *Preferred Stock.* Preferred stock is sometimes issued to persons providing acquisition financing, although it is less often used than debt instruments. Corporations usually prefer debt instruments because of the deductibility of interest expense for income tax purposes. Dividends on preferred stock are not deductible. On the other hand, some corporate investors favor preferred stock, partially because of the intercorporate dividends received deduction afforded by Section 243 of the Internal Revenue Code. The negotiated terms of a preferred stock are set forth in the issuer's certificate of incorporation, or in resolutions of its board of directors if the certificate of incorporation authorizes a "blank check" preferred stock. Terms typically include voting rights (if any), a dividend rate, a liquidation preference, redemption provisions, rights to participate in corporate earnings (if any) and conversion rights (if any).

• *Warrants.* Warrants are instruments that grant the holder a right to purchase common stock for a defined exercise price. They are commonly issued to lenders and investors who provide acquisition financing, especially to those who provide "mezzanine" financing in return for subordinated notes. Many lenders and investors prefer warrants to convertibility of their notes or preferred stock. The reason is that conversion is accomplished by surrendering the notes or preferred stock for cancellation, thus eliminating an instrument that might be providing a favorable interest or dividend return and might have other favorable features. A warrant, however, can be exercised while retaining the note or preferred stock. Warrants are issued for a definite term that may be either the same as the term of related notes or a fixed number of years. Warrants contain provisions stating the exercise price or prices which may, if negotiated, increase with the passage of time. They also state the exercise date or dates or state that exercise will be permitted at any time before the expiration date. Warrants contain antidilution provisions to protect the holder when stock splits or dividends are declared or other events occur affecting the exercise rights. See Chapter 6 for a description of original issue discount (OID) provisions that may apply to the issuance of warrants as "equity sweeteners" to lenders.

---

[10]The term "in the money" means that the market value of the common stock exceeds the conversion price.

E. Intermediaries

As described in Chapter 1, many acquisitions and divestitures happen in significant part because of the efforts of intermediaries who introduce potential buyers and sellers and may also arrange financing and provide financial advice and other services. Traditional intermediaries in the M&A field are investment banking firms, business brokers and finders. In recent years, M&A departments of commercial banks and accounting firms have also begun to act as intermediaries. Law firms sometimes provide introductions that lead to acquisitions and divestitures or to financing arrangements, but only a few law firms are likely to request separate compensation as an intermediary.

Many businesspeople fail to understand the value that a skilled intermediary can contribute to an acquisition. They see an intermediary as expensive and unnecessary and try with various degrees of success to work without one. When considering whether to retain an intermediary, it is useful to review the range of services that a skilled intermediary can provide:

- Experience with prior similar transactions.
- Advice on price and terms.
- Contacts with potential buyers, sellers, financing sources and skilled service providers.
- Ability to make confidential contacts for companies wishing to remain undisclosed.
- Screening of potential buyers or sellers to save management time.
- Advice during negotiations and, if requested, acting as a spokesperson to present proposals that can later be revised, if necessary.
- Experience in keeping a transaction focused on its goals and moving forward.

Investment bankers, business brokers and finders often say they add more value to a transaction than the amount of their compensation. That is not really a remarkable claim. It is and should be the normal standard of performance. The role of an intermediary is not needless "overload" unless the intermediary fails to perform with appropriate skill.

1. Investment Banking Firms

Investment banking firms are by far the most important intermediaries. For 1996, *Mergers & Acquisitions* reported that the leading firms in value of completed transactions were Goldman Sachs, Morgan Stanley, Merrill Lynch, Credit Suisse First Boston, J.P. Morgan, Lehman Brothers, Bear Stearns, Lazard, Salomon Brothers, Bankers Trust and Smith Barney. In numbers of completed transactions, the leaders were much the same firms, but Merrill Lynch led the list and Donaldson, Lufkin & Jenrette and Alex. Brown & Sons appeared in the top ten.

Buyers and sellers welcome the services of investment banking firms because of their wide array of business and financial contacts and their skilled and energetic services. Investment banking firms typically prefer to begin a relationship with analysis and advice on business strategy and financial structuring. Searches for potential sellers and buyers and arrangements for financing are then done to implement a plan, rather than opportunistically. As the plan progresses, the investment banking firm may also provide other services, including assistance in negotiations and "due diligence" investigations, "fairness opinions," and solvency letters.

Investment bankers charge a variety of fees for their services, all of which are negotiable to some extent. For finding a buyer or seller during the decades after World War II, negotiations often started with the so-called "Lehman Formula" which was based on a broad definition of the price and any other valuable consideration paid for the acquisition:

5% of the first $1,000,000, plus
4% of the second $1,000,000, plus
3% of the third $1,000,000, plus
2% of the fourth $1,000,000, plus
1% of the amount over $4,000,000.

Inflation and competition have rendered the "Lehman Formula" obsolete. Investment banking firms usually seek a front-end, nonrefundable fee, such as $50,000 or $100,000, plus expenses, to pay for research, analysis and networking efforts. Like accounting firms and law firms, investment banking firms must pay their professional and other employees, including numerous MBAs who work long hours to make deals happen. When assured of compensation that will cover internal costs and expenses, firms may agree to reduce their contingent compensation based on a percentage of a completed transaction. Investment banking firms also welcome arrangements under which they receive a fee for arranging financing and other services. The fees for these services and the potential for future business are also factors in negotiating compensation for acquisition services.

Buyers and sellers who have limited experience in working and negotiating with investment banking firms should be aware that members of that profession are trained to "think big." Meetings are likely to be arranged at prestigious restaurants. Partners or executives who have served in well-publicized government or industry positions may attend meetings briefly. These techniques stimulate customers to expansive thinking about transactions and the related fees and costs.

The best way to obtain favorable terms from investment bankers is to begin by comparison shopping. If more than one investment banking firm shows interest, the customer can use the competitive situation to advantage. Investment bankers sometimes say that they do not want to get into a "bidding war" and contend that certain compensation arrangements are sacrosanct. However, like all other businesspeople, investment bankers compete for business. Readers interested in competition in the investment banking industry as well as a very interesting history of the industry should read the opinion of Judge Harold Medina in *U.S. v. Morgan*, 118 Fed Supp. 621 (S.D.N.Y. 1953). In addition to the competitive factor, investment bankers are likely to provide favorable terms to companies with a reputation for credibility, successful performance and fairness in their dealings with investment bankers and other members of the financial community.

2. Business Brokers

Thousands of business brokers act as intermediaries in the sale of small and medium-sized businesses throughout the United States. The transactions range in size from a few hundred thousand dollars to a few million dollars.

Business brokers include experienced professionals with a variety of qualifications. Many are licensed real estate brokers. Others hold registrations, licenses or certifications in the securities industry or as financial planners. However, some business brokers have only limited qualifications and experience and some work in the field on a part-time basis. Thus, it is important for sellers and buyers to make inquiries and be satisfied that a business broker has appropriate qualifications and experience for the size and complexity of an acquisition.

Real estate brokers tend to become business brokers because sales of real estate frequently involve the businesses occupying the real estate being sold. An owner operating a business in real estate wants a sale price that includes the value of the business. An owner leasing real estate to business tenants wants a price that includes the value of the rents generated by the tenants' businesses. A tenant selling its business wants to include the lease among the assets sold if the rent and other terms are favorable.

In some situations, the businesses operated on real estate are worth far more than the land, buildings and improvements. In other situations, a business has little or no value beyond the real estate value. Thus, real estate brokers who work with commercial and industrial real estate must be reasonably familiar with the methods used to value and sell businesses in order to do their work successfully.

Owners of restaurants, clothing stores, groceries, metal working shops and taverns are examples of sellers who hire business brokers to obtain buyers. They usually negotiate and sign a written agreement hiring the broker as agent. The agreement generally covers at least the following items:

1. A description of the business to be sold and the items included and excluded.
2. The offering price, usually stated as a lump sum in cash.
3. The broker's compensation, usually stated as a percentage of the sale price.
4. The term of the agreement, including any initial exclusive period and later nonexclusive period.
5. The right of the broker to receive compensation if the business is sold within a certain period, such as year after the termination of the agreement, to a buyer introduced to the seller by the broker during the agreement term.

Business brokers are generally hired and compensated by sellers. Occasionally, a buyer hires a business broker to seek a business or help with negotiations. In either event, a legal relationship of agency is created. The broker has a fiduciary obligation as agent to act solely in the best interests and with reasonable prudence on behalf of its principal, i.e., the seller or buyer. The broker must refrain from such conduct as (1) acceptance of commissions from both the seller and buyer, (2) sale of a business in which the broker has an interest and (3) customer deposits with the broker's own funds. These duties are imposed by common law and reinforced by state statutes that contain some exceptions for transactions in which full disclosures of conflicting interests are made.

A business broker's objective is to procure a ready, willing and able buyer who accepts the seller's offering terms. Upon procuring such an acceptance, the broker is entitled to compensation, even if the seller then declines to make the sale. However, if the buyer unjustifiably refuses or fails to close, the broker is not entitled to compensation.[11]

In actual practice, few potential buyers simply accept a seller's offer. Instead, they submit a counteroffer of a lower price and other less favorable terms. This leads to a negotiation process during which the broker uses skill and experience to help achieve agreement on all significant terms, usually evidenced by a signed contract. When agreement is achieved, a sale usually follows. The broker attends the closing to receive the agreed compensation and participate in the goodwill of a successful transaction.

Under the laws of many states, business brokers are required to be licensed as real estate brokers and an unlicensed broker may be barred from enforcing a right to a commission for a business sale. If the business assets sold include real estate, many state courts have denied a commission claimed by an unlicensed business broker.[12] An unlicensed broker has even been denied compensation for procuring an offer to purchase all the stock of a supermarket corporation.[13] However, other courts have allowed unlicensed business brokers to recover a commission when the transaction was a sale of stock or when real estate was found to be incidental to the overall sale of a business.[14] In New Jersey, the courts allow an unlicensed business broker to recover compensation for a sale of the business, but subtract the portion attributable to real estate.[15]

The states also have so-called statutes of frauds that declare certain kinds of agreements to be unenforceable unless they are in writing and signed by the person against whom a claim for enforcement is made. Agreements to pay compensation for services in connection with sales of real estate and businesses are among the kinds of agreements subject to the statutes of frauds. For example, Section 5-701 (10) of the New York General Obligations Law reads as follows:

> *"Every agreement, promise or undertaking is void, unless it or some note or memorandum thereof be in writing, and subscribed by the party to be charged therewith, or by his lawful agent, if such agreement, promise or undertaking...*

---

[11]*Ellsworth Dobbs, Inc. v. Johnson,* 50 N.J. 528, 236 A.2d 843, 30 A.L.R. 3d 1370 (1967).

[12]*First Corporate Finance, Inc. v. Rogers,* 237 Neb. 727, 467 N.W. 2d 853 (1991).

[13]*Springer v. Rosauer,* 31 Wash. App. 418, 641 P.2d 1216 (1982). See also *Cardillo v. Canusa Extrusion Engineering,* 145 Mich. App. 361, 377 N.W. 2d 412 (1985); *All Points Traders, Inc. v. Barrington Associates,* 211 Cal. App. 3d 723, 259 Cal. Rptr. 780 (1989).

[14]*Business Brokers International Corp. v. Roderick,* 24 Mass. App. 957, 510 N.E.2d 301 (1987); *Flammia v. Mite Corp.* 401 F. Supp. 1121 (E.D.N.Y. 1975), aff'd 553 F.2d 93 (2d Cir. 1977). See also *Moody v. Hurricane Creek Lumber Co.,* 290 Ore. 729, 625 P.2d 1306 (1981).

[15]*Cooney v. Ritter,* 939 F.2d 81 (3d Cir. 1991).

> *10. Is a contract to pay compensation for services rendered in negotiating a loan, or in negotiating the purchase, sale exchange, renting or leasing of any real estate or interest therein, or of a business opportunity, business, its goodwill, inventory, fixtures or any interest therein, including a majority of the voting stock interest in a corporation and including the creating of a partnership interest. "Negotiating" includes procuring an introduction to a party to the transaction or assisting in the negotiation or consummation of the transaction. This provision shall apply to a contract implied in fact or in law to pay reasonable compensation but shall not apply to a contract to pay compensation to an auctioneer, an attorney at law, or a duly licensed real estate broker or real estate salesman."*

An effort to avoid the statutory language by commencing a common law action (called *"quantum meruit"*) to recover the fair value of services rendered performing an unenforceable agreement was rejected by the New York Court of Appeals.[16] Other state courts have also rejected such an "end run" around the statute of frauds.[17] The courts have also rejected theories such as unjust enrichment, estoppel, interference with contractual rights and fraud consisting of conduct no worse than refusal to pay a broker compensation based on an alleged verbal promise.[18]

The Federal Trade Commission (FTC) has adopted fair trade practice regulations governing the offer and sale of franchises and business opportunities. (16 C.F.R. Part 436). The regulations are subject to exceptions and exemptions. However, when applicable, they impose extensive disclosure requirements.

Over half of the states have adopted statutes regulating the offer and sale of franchises and business opportunities. They are consumer protection laws designed primarily to protect inexperienced persons from investing in franchises, marketing plans and other business opportunities without adequate disclosure of the risks. Many of the laws are based on three model laws: (1) the Uniform Franchise and Business Opportunities Act developed by the National Conference of Commissioners on Uniform State Laws; (2) the Model Business Opportunity Sales Act developed by the North American Securities Administrators Association ("NASAA"); and (3) the Model Franchise Investment Act developed by NASAA.

The business opportunity laws provide for registration of business opportunities and for extensive disclosure about the opportunities and the persons who offer them. They require that business opportunity sale contracts be in writing and meet other standards. They also require that business opportunity sellers meet minimum net worth or bond requirements. The laws contain a variety of exclusions and exemptions such as an offer or sale (1) by a seller or to a buyer meeting minimum net worth requirements; (2) of an entire ongoing business operated by a seller; or (3) of franchises or opportunities in compliance with the FTC's regulations at 16 C.F.R. Part 436 or the federal or state securities laws.

---

[16] *Minichiello v. Royal Business Funds Corp.*, 18 N.Y. 2d 521 (1966).

[17] *Beckham v. Klein*, 59 N.C. 52, 295 S.E. 2d 504 (1982).

[18] *Phillippe v. Shappell Industries*, 43 Cal. 3d 1247, 241 Cal. Rep. 22, 743 P.2d 1279 (1987).

3. Finders

Throughout the business and financial communities of the United States, a relatively small number of firms engage in business primarily as "finders" of acquisitions and loan and equity financing. A far larger number of firms and individuals provide finder services as part of their business or occasionally when an opportunity arises. They include investment banking firms, M&A consultants, financial consultants and other professionals.

As the name implies, a finder is a person employed to identify and introduce a buyer and a seller, a borrower and a lender, or other persons who can do business together. As a New York court said:

> *"Plaintiff was in nowise a broker. He merely was a finder of this piece of business. He was to receive his compensation for finding the business and bringing the same to the attention of Rogers Caldwell & Company and its associates. He claimed his compensation solely upon the ground that he was the originator of the business and had disclosed to Rogers Caldwell & Company and its associates the opportunity to engage in this financing."*[19]

Unlike a broker, a finder need not procure a ready, willing and able buyer for a business or participate in the negotiations. If a finder brings a buyer and seller together and their subsequent negotiations result in a sale, the finder is entitled to compensation.[20]

Professionals who engage in finding acquisitions or financing on a regular basis maintain extensive business contacts and other resources useful in performing their work successfully. They maintain extensive contacts with chief executive officers, chief financial officers, corporate development managers, loan officers, venture capital entrepreneurs and others active in the M&A field. They also maintain libraries and databases useful in search work. Thus, when they are hired, they can usually commence a search promptly and skillfully.

Experienced professionals who engage regularly in finder activities do not undertake assignments until their customer has signed a written agreement. The identities of their contacts and knowledge of potential matching interests are valuable intellectual properties that they cannot prudently disclose without contractual protection. They usually maintain standard agreement forms that outline in detail their proposed compensation and other arrangements. The proposed agreements are, of course, negotiable.

In New York, an agreement, promise or undertaking to pay compensation for a finder's services is void unless it is in writing and subscribed by the party charged therewith. (See Section 5-701 (10) of the New York General Obligations Law cited earlier in this chapter.) When New York law applies, a finder cannot enforce a claim for a finder's fee unless there is a writing evidencing the agreement subscribed by the person against whom the

[19] *Seckendorff v. Halsey, Stuart & Co., Inc.*, 254 N.Y. Supp. 250 (1931), see also *Business Development Services v. Field Container*, 96 Ill. App. 834, 422 N.E. 2d 86 (1981).

[20] *Morris Cohon & Company v. Russell*, 23 N.Y. 2d 569 (1969).

fee is claimed.[21] A finder cannot avoid this requirement by seeking to recover the reasonable value of the services.[22]

There are several court decisions determining what is a sufficient written agreement to support an enforceable claim for a finder's fee. References to a finder's fee in an acquisition contract signed by the buyer and seller can be sufficient.[23] However, a letter written by a broker (or finder) to a buyer or seller is insufficient.[24]

In other states, the courts have reached a variety of results in cases seeking to enforce alleged oral agreements to pay finder's fees. For example, an oral finder's fee agreement was found enforceable under Massachusetts law.[25] An oral agreement for a finder's fee was found unenforceable under California law.[26] A *quantum meruit* recovery for the value of services rendered was allowed under Illinois Law.[27]

Several lawsuits seeking to recover finder's fees have sought to avoid the requirements of Section 5-701 (10) by arguing that the laws of other states or nations should apply. Several leading court decisions discuss the choice of law issues and reject claims for finder's fees.[28] However, a finder's fee based on an oral agreement made during a telephone call between New York City and Boston was held to be govermed by Massachusetts law.[29]

---

[21]*Haskins v. Leob Rhoades & Co.*, 52 N.Y. 2d 523 (1981).

[22]*Minichiello v. Royal Business Finder Corp.*, 18 N.Y. 2d 521 (1966).

[23]*Morris Cohon & Company v. Russell*, supra; *Flammia v. Mite Corporation*, 401 F. Supp. 1121 (1975); affirmed 553 F.2d 93 (2d Cir. 1975); *Eaton v. Highland*, 81 App. Div. 2d 603 (N.Y. 1981); *Bottomley v. Coffin*, 399 A.2d 485 (R.I. 1979).

[24]*Ames v. Ideal Cement Co.*, 235 N.Y. Supp. 2d 622 (1962).

[25]*Bushkin Associates v. Ragtheon Co.*, 393 Mass. 622, 473 N.E. 2d 662 (1995).

[26]*Hasekian v. Krotz*, 268 Cal. App. 2d 311, 74 Cal. Rptr. 410.

[27]*Business Development Services v. Field Container Corp.*, 96 Ill. App. 3d 834, 422 N.E. 2d 86 (1981).

[28]*Intercontinental Planning v. Daystrom*, 24 N.Y. 2d 372 (1969); *Fort Howard Paper Co. v. William D. Witter, Inc.*, 787 F.2d 784 (2d Cir. 1986); and *Warshay v. Guinness PLC*, 750 F. Supp. 628 (S.D.N.Y. 1990).

[29]*Bushkin Associates, Inc. v. Raytheon Co.*, supra.

F. Reference Materials

Books

The Complete Handbook of Raising Capital, Tuller, McGraw-Hill, 1994
Directory of Venture Capital, Lister et al., John Wiley & Sons, 1996
The Venture Capital Sourcebook, Silver, Irwin Publishing, 1994

Securities Data Publishing issues several publications that provide information useful to persons seeking to raise financing for acquisitions:

Capital Market Analyst
Directory of Buyout Financing Sources
Directory of M&A Intermediates
European Venture Capital Journal

Pratt's Guide to Venture Capital Sources
UK Venture Capital Journal
Venture Capital Journal

Articles

Mergers & Acquisitions, published by MLR Publishing, frequently contains articles on acquisition financing by experienced authors. Some examples of these practical and informative articles are:

"How Lenders Tightened the Pursestrings for M&A," Torchen, *Mergers & Acquisitions,* Jul–Aug, 1991.

"The Surging Costs of Doing a Leveraged Deal," Vernick, *Mergers & Acquisitions,* Nov–Dec, 1991.

"A Prototype Deal for Cash-Flow Lending in Cautious Times," Dineen, *Mergers & Acquisitions,* Nov–Dec, 1992.

"Deal Financing by Suppliers and Customers," O'Donnell and Schulman, *Mergers & Acquisitions,* May–Jun, 1996.

G. Exhibits

3-1 A "Change of Control" Provision

EXHIBIT 3-1

A "CHANGE OF CONTROL" PROVISION

At its option and in its sole discretion, Lender may declare the full amount of the Loan immediately due and payable if a "change of control" or a "potential change of control" of the Borrower shall occur. For the purposes of this Agreement, a "change of control" shall mean a change of control of a nature that would be required to be reported in response to Item 5(f) of Schedule 14A promulgated under the Securities Exchange Act of 1934, as amended ("Exchange Act"); provided that, without limitation, such a change in control shall be deemed to have occurred:

(a) if any "person" (as such term is used in Section 13(d) and 14(d) of the Exchange Act), other than the Company who, as the result of acquisition(s) of the Borrower's stock, becomes directly or indirectly a "Beneficial Owner" (as defined in Rule 13d-3 of the Exchange Act) of more than 20% of the total outstanding voting stock of the Company; or

(b) if, within any period of two consecutive years, a majority of the individuals, who at the beginning of such period were members of the Board of Directors of the Borrower, cease for any reason to constitute at least a majority of the Board of Directors.

For purposes of this Agreement, a "potential change of control" shall have occurred if

(a) the Borrower enters into an agreement, the consummation of which would result in the occurrence of a change in control of the Borrower;

(b) any person publicly announces an intention to take actions which, if consummated, would constitute a change in control of the Borrower;

(c) any person becomes the beneficial owner, directly or indirectly, of securities of the Borrower representing 9.5% or more of the combined voting power of the Borrower's then outstanding securities; or

(d) the Board of Directors of the Borrower adopts a resolution to the effect that, for purposes of this Agreement, a potential change in control of the Borrower has occurred.

Chapter 4

Business Valuation from a Financial Point of View

A. Functions and Limits of Financial Valuation

Business valuation from a financial viewpoint is an important step in acquiring and divesting businesses. Under some circumstances, a financial valuation may even be a legal requirement. This chapter discusses financial valuations and the methods used to perform them.

A financial valuation estimates the price that a willing buyer would pay and a willing seller would accept for a business, assuming both to be equally informed and free of pressure to buy or sell. In actual practice, however, these conditions do not occur. Buyers and sellers are never equally informed or equally free of pressures. They also differ in business objectives, the priority they give to price and negotiating strength and skills.

A financial valuation necessarily measures value from a financial point of view. That point is always mentioned in the fairness opinions discussed later in this chapter. However, every business has important values that are "nonfinancial" because they cannot be adequately measured in financial statements and projections. In addition, all sellers and buyers bring to a transaction their own business values that cannot be found in the financial statements of the business to be acquired.

For these reasons, a financial valuation is a working tool that the managements of buyers and sellers can and should use in negotiating the price and other terms of a transaction. However, a negotiated price that differs from the valuation price does not necessarily indicate that the transaction is overpriced or underpriced. It may indicate that there are nonfinancial business values that were not reflected in the financial valuation.

In recent years, financial analysts have worked to develop methods designed to measure the financial effects of some nonfinancial values. This is one reason why future-oriented valuation methods have come into widespread use. To the extent that financial valuations can include and realistically measure the likely financial effects of nonfinancial business values, they become more valuable and useful. (See "Putting a Realistic Dollar Value on Acquisition Synergies," Bielinski, *Mergers & Acquisitions*, 1992.)

The author expresses appreciation to Dr. Edmund Mantell, a professor in the Finance Department of Pace University's Graduate School of Business and a valuation expert, who provided helpful comments on this chapter.

B. Valuation Professionals

Financial valuations of businesses are performed by a wide range of professionals. They include investment bankers, brokerage firms, banks, financial consulting firms, appraisal firms, financial consulting departments of accounting firms, professors in the finance departments of universities and others. The profession is not regulated, as such. Thus, qualifications of a valuation professional depend on individual education and experience, affiliation with an established firm or university and membership in such organizations as the American Society of Appraisers, the Institute of Chartered Financial Analysts and the Financial Analysts Federation.

In addition to the investment banking firms, some of the firms that are well known for business valuation expertise are Duff & Phelps; Houlihan, Lokey, Howard & Zukin; and Willamette Management. Kenneth Bodenstein of Duff & Phelps was the expert witness whose valuation of UOP Inc. led to the famous decision of the Delaware Supreme Court in *Weinberger v. UOP, Inc.* to free the law of dependency on the "Delaware Block" method and accept as evidence valuations based on the discounted future cash flow method. Howard Zukin of the Houlihan firm is the editor of *Financial Valuation: Businesses and Business Interests,* a leading book on financial valuation. Shannon Pratt of Willamette Management is the author of two well-written and useful classics: *Valuation of a Business* and *Valuing Small Businesses and Professional Practices.*

Several university professors have gained wide recognition for their business valuation expertise. The best known is Professor Alfred Rappaport of Northwestern University, whose famous article in the *Harvard Business Review* contributed to widespread use of the discounted future cash flow method and recognition of the extremely conservative nature of generally accepted accounting principles. Another well-known expert is Professor James Walter of the Wharton School at the University of Pennsylvania.

The American Society of Appraisers (ASA) was founded in 1952. The ASA certifies appraisers, including business valuation analysts, and has published *Standards for Business Valuation.* The Institute of Business Appraisers, Inc. (IBA) was founded in 1978 and also certifies business valuation analysts and has adopted business valuation standards. The Canadian Institute of Chartered Business Valuators was founded in 1971 and certifies business valuation professionals in Canada.

The Appraisal Foundation is an organization founded in 1987 by a number of member organizations including the ASA. The Foundation appoints the Appraisal Standards Board and the Appraisal Qualifications Board. In 1995, the Foundation published the *Uniform Standards of Professional Appraisal Practice* (USPAP) which must be followed by members of organizations such as the ASA and IBA. A copy of USPAP Statement SMT-2 on Discounted Cash Flow Analysis appears as Exhibit 4-1.

C. Primary Sources of Business Valuation Information

Many business valuations are performed under arrangements that are private and confidential. Thus, valuation professionals welcome information that becomes public from time to time. However, it is important to consider the nature and objectives of each valuation to determine its usefulness.

Sources of primary information about financial valuation methods include the following:

- Acquisition prices and fairness opinions filed with the SEC.
- Dissenting stockholder appraisal rights decisions of the state courts, published by West Publishing Company.
- Estate and gift tax decisions of the U.S. Tax Court under Revenue Procedure 59–60, published by Commerce Clearing House; and of the U.S. District Courts, published by West Publishing Company.
- The *IRS Valuation Guide for Income, Estate and Gift Taxes,* published by Commerce Clearing House.

D. Why Obtain a Financial Valuation?

Sellers can benefit from a financial valuation in several ways. A valuation can help a seller to decide whether or not to sell, especially if there are differences of opinion among its management or its owners. A valuation can help a seller to see where salable values exist in its business and where they do not, thus assisting its management with business planning. A valuation can help management or owners to set an asking price and strengthen their ability to interest and negotiate with potential buyers. A valuation can also lead to a decision to keep a business, either because it does not show a satisfactory sale value or because it shows more value than expected.

Buyers can also benefit from a financial valuation in several ways. A valuation can help buyers to decide whether to buy and to determine where values exist in the business to be acquired. A valuation can help to establish an offering price and information useful during negotiations. A valuation can be used to obtain financing and to evaluate alternative financing structures and methods. A valuation can be used in planning the tax and legal aspects of the acquisition. A valuation can be used in planning for post-acquisition integration of the acquired business. A valuation can also lead to a decision not to acquire a business.

E. Differences between Portfolio Valuation and Valuation for Acquisition Planning

Much of the information about financial valuation in leading books and articles describes methods used to value an existing business or a large or small equity investment in an existing business. That is also true of most information that can be gleaned from dissenters' appraisal decisions and tax decisions of the courts. Financial valuation for an acquisition requires important additional steps.

Financial valuations of existing businesses assume that the business will continue under the same management and with only such changes as management forecasts in its plans at the time of the valuation. An investment manager for a mutual fund or another institutional or private investor who plans to buy a few hundred or even a few thousand shares can seldom make any other assumption. Minority investors, especially those purchasing in the stock markets, do not expect to change the financial structure, the tax structure, the management, or the operations and properties of the business, unless they are investors who look for "turnaround" or "risk arbitrage" opportunities.

After an acquisition, the financial structure, tax structure, management and operations and properties always change. For example, the acquisition transaction creates a new capital structure and new financing sources for the acquired business that may be more or less generous than previous sources. A taxable purchase financed by debt creates important tax deductions that will augment cash flows in early post-acquisition years, but also creates cash flow obligations to amortize the acquisition debt. In addition, the buyer may decide to change the management and to build up, reduce or dispose of operations and properties. Financial valuation for an acquisition should take these changes into account and help management to evaluate whether and how the changes should be made.

Especially for a buyer, a financial valuation should be a planning tool. Valuation of the business as it is conducted by the seller is only the first step, one that is primarily useful in making the initial price offer and conducting early negotiations. The financial valuation becomes increasingly useful as it is revised to reflect changes as "due diligence" reviews, negotiations with the seller, arrangements for financing and other developments reveal opportunities and risks. In other words, a buyer's financial valuation should not be a static, one-time valuation, but an ongoing process that is revised as many times as significant new information makes it worthwhile to do so. Ultimately, the valuation should show the value of the business as it will be conducted by the buyer, not as it is conducted by the seller. The use of financial models in high-speed computers makes feasible such analysis and reanalysis.

The valuation process described is valuable to buyers, both in negotiations and in arranging financing. Needless to say, a buyer does not wish to pay a premium over the value of a business. However, if a seller is demanding a premium price, a financial valuation that shows value in the buyer's hands can show how much premium might be offered before the acquisition becomes unattractive. A clear demonstration of the financial value of an acquisition to the buyer is also very helpful in arranging financing because it will show how principal and interest on the debt will be amortized and how enhanced cash flows will build capital appreciation.

Of course, a seller cannot prepare a financial valuation of the business to be sold that will include the changes planned by the buyer. The buyer will keep many of its plans confidential in order to preserve its bargaining position during negotiations. However, alert sellers can usually obtain significant information during the negotiations, especially when the buyer proposes financial and tax structures and provides assurances about the sources and availability of financing. A seller may also obtain clues about a buyer's plans for future management, operations and properties from the focus of its "due diligence" reviews and its willingness or reluctance to make contractual commitments to employees, customers and suppliers. A seller can combine this information with knowledge of the buyer's existing businesses to estimate the value the buyer can obtain as a result of the acquisition. If the seller perceives that the added value will be important, the seller can then negotiate for a premium with some confidence, unless the buyer has other equivalent and available acquisition opportunities.

F. Business and Industry Data

In the early stages of preparing a financial valuation, the analyst should assemble information about the business itself and its industry. How does the business relate to its customers, suppliers and competitors in size, market shares, revenues, profits, growth trends and other factors? How does the industry compare to other industries in these factors? This information is necessary and useful in judging comparability, making realistic projections and selecting appropriate earnings multiples, growth rates and discount rates.

Industry data can be obtained from sources such as Standard & Poor's *Industry Surveys*, the *Value Line Investment Survey* and industry organizations that are usually glad to provide at least basic data about their industries insofar as they are available from their members. The data are quite helpful, but the analyst should realize that most industry surveys do not include all companies in the industry. For example, investment surveys often include only the companies whose shares are publicly traded. Industry surveys usually include only their members. Some organizations include only "independent" producers and do not include companies having internal capacity to produce the same products. A broader source of information is the industry surveys of the U.S. Census Bureau, such as the *Annual Survey of Manufacturers,* but they are not as readily available or as user friendly as surveys prepared for commercial sale.

G. Analysis and Adjustment of Financial Statements

As explained later in this chapter, modern financial valuation methods have turned away from direct use of historical financial statements prepared in accordance with generally accepted accounting principles (GAAP). However, those financial statements remain the foundation on which future-oriented projections can be developed with reasonable confidence. The reason is that GAAP has been developed and regulated for over 60 years by the SEC and by the Financial Accounting Standards Board (FASB) and its predecessor, the Accounting Principles Board (APB), together with generally accepted auditing standards (GAAS). While far from perfect, GAAP financial statements are generally reliable, consistent and well understood.

To use financial statements prepared in accordance with GAAP in valuation of a business, it is necessary to analyze and adjust them. The reason is that persons preparing financial statements in accordance with GAAP are allowed to elect among alternative accounting policies for recording many kinds of transactions. Their elections result in significantly different amounts in balance sheets and operating statements. For example, they can choose either the first-in, first-out (FIFO) method or the last-in, first-out (LIFO) method of valuing inventory. On the other hand, they are required to use some methods that are conservative and do not reflect economic reality. For example, land is recorded at cost and is not revalued as its value changes over years of ownership.

Thus, it is important to analyze and adjust financial statements in order to understand their significance and to assure that they are comparable to the financial statements of other businesses used in determining comparable values. Among the better-known adjustments that may be necessary are the following:

- Basic accounting methods—Standard cost, percentage of completion, etc.
- Capital structure choices resulting in debt expense costs, partially offset by tax savings.
- Consolidation or separate financial statements of affiliated companies, especially if they have transactions with each other.
- Timing of income and expense recognition.
- Inventories—FIFO, LIFO and writedown and writeoff policies.
- Receivables—Allowances for doubtful accounts and other reserves.
- Values assigned to purchased intangibles (such as intellectual property rights) and treatment of internal costs for development of intangible assets.
- Depreciation and depletion methods.
- Tax loss carrybacks and carryforwards.
- Treatment of leases as operating leases or as financing leases capitalized as assets and related debt.
- Treatment of minority interests in affiliated companies.
- Contingent liabilities and assets.
- Treatment of management compensation, particularly stock option or incentive compensation.
- Asset valuation methods.
- Treatment of extraordinary and nonrecurring items.
- Accrual of obligations for retiree medical and death benefits (FAS 106).
- Computation of book value and earnings per share to reflect dilution.

H. Asset-Based Valuation

1. Introduction

Asset-based valuation treats the value of a business as the sum of the values of its various assets, tangible and intangible, minus its various liabilities, fixed and contingent. Asset-based valuation includes all assets and liabilities, including goodwill, whether or not they appear on a balance sheet prepared in accordance with generally accepted accounting principles.

Asset-based methods are used to value investment companies, real estate investment vehicles and businesses that are in liquidation. They have also traditionally been used to value closely held middle-sized and small commercial and industrial businesses. For these businesses, the advantages of asset-based valuation are that the method is direct, simple and easily understood. If loan financing for the business is obtained from finance companies that provide asset-based loans, information about the values of specific assets and other useful information may be available. Disadvantages are that the method is very detailed and time-consuming and does not readily measure the overall fair market value or investment value of a going business engaged in commercial or industrial activities. The method also does not reflect the future profitability of the business.

2. Net Asset Value

Mutual funds value their shares daily at net asset value in compliance with Rule 22c-1 of the Securities and Exchange Commission under the Investment Company Act of 1940. The net asset value so determined is used as the redemption price of the shares and also as the offering price to which a sales "load" is added, unless the fund's shares are sold on a "no-load" basis.

3. Performing an Asset-Based Valuation

To prepare an "asset-based" valuation, the valuation professional must make a detailed due diligence review to identify all assets, regardless of whether they appear in the balance sheet. The reason is that businesses have numerous assets that were either (1) developed by costs that were expensed rather than capitalized or (2) fully written off by depreciation charges. Some examples are as follows:

- Internally developed intellectual properties such as customer lists, product design or formulation data and production process technology that never appeared on the balance sheet because the development costs were expensed as incurred.
- Favorable leases and customer and supplier contracts that provide economic advantages but the costs to obtain them were expensed as incurred. For example, a ten-year lease at $25 per square foot is a valuable asset when similar space commands $45 per square foot. A firm contract to buy natural gas at $0.21 per MCF is a valuable asset when natural gas is selling at $4.20 per MCF.
- Tools and dies that were expensed rather than capitalized.
- Reactors, heaters, boilers, generators, compressors and other equipment continuing in daily use after the depreciation periods applicable to their various lives under GAAP.

The valuation professional should also include "off-balance-sheet" liabilities. They may include, for example, burdensome leases and customer and supplier contracts. They may also include contingent liabilities such as claims and lawsuits that were not accrued under APB No. 5, but affect value.

The next step is to determine whether to value the assets on a "going-business" basis on the assumption that they will continue to be used together in the synergistic relationships of the existing business. If so, the intangible assets should perhaps include "goodwill," meaning value reflecting an investment return in excess of that attributable to the assets. However, if the business is a "going concern," the valuation professional should consider whether the business might better be valued by a method other than asset-based valuation.

If the business cannot be valued as a "going concern," the valuation will then proceed by methods similar to those used in determining liquidation value. The valuation professional should decide whether the assets should be valued for sale as a nonoperating entirety, or must be broken into pieces for sale. In practical business terms, this is an important issue. Even when a business is shut down, the assets as a whole retain some synergistic values that can be attractive to potential buyers who could reopen the business. For example, the author once participated in the acquisition of a large chemical plant near Portland, Oregon that had been closed for over six months due to low sales of its products to the agricultural industry. The buyer restarted the plant and operated successfully at full capacity by using and selling part of the production for wood adhesives.

If the business must be valued on the assumption of a sale in pieces, a time-consuming task of obtaining values for numerous assets must be performed. For example, receivables are evaluated for collectibility. Inventories must be evaluated for salability and then adjusted to market value from their recorded values in the balance sheet at the lower of cost or market value. Machinery and equipment values can be obtained from manufacturers and used equipment dealers. Land, building and fixture values can be obtained from real estate brokerage firms in the areas where real properties are located.

The valuation professional should also establish a time horizon for the assumed sale. In a few situations, it may be appropriate to assume there will be no time constraints limiting efforts to maximize sale prices. In some situations, it may be necessary to assume a rapid forced liquidation (or "fire sale") at which assets will be sold without time to plan and negotiate. In most situations, the assumption will be a prompt, but planned and orderly, liquidation.

Ultimately, the value of the business is the sum of the values of the assets determined by the methods described.

4. Liquidation Value

Businesses with operating or competitive problems sometimes find that the liquidation value of their assets is greater than their "going-business" value. That often happens during bankruptcy or other insolvency proceedings. Management often files in bankruptcy under Chapter 11 of the U.S. Bankruptcy Code in order to gain time to propose a plan of reorganization that will preserve what they perceive to be "going-business" value. However, management's efforts to prepare a plan that can obtain creditor approval sometimes demonstrate that the business is moribund and only its assets have value. If a business ceases to be a "going business," its financial statements must be prepared on a liquidation basis.

Liquidation values of assets are determined by traditional appraisal methods. The appraiser should first determine whether to assume that the assets will be sold together or separately. The appraiser should also determine whether to assume that the sale can be made with adequate time to realize full value by negotiated sales in the normal markets where the assets are sold, or whether assets must be sold under time pressure by such means as an auction. The appraiser should also determine whether to assume that liabilities and obligations related to the assets will be discharged, as happens in bankruptcy proceedings, or will continue in effect.

Liquidation values of some assets may be significantly less than the values at which they were previously carried on the balance sheet of a business. However, liquidation values of other assets may be substantially higher than the previous balance sheet values. Many businesses own land that has appreciated since its original purchase. Many businesses have assets that were fully depreciated and are no longer carried on the balance sheet, although they remain in active use and have value. Many businesses have assets, ranging from intellectual properties to small tools, that were expensed and never recorded on the balance sheet, but remain in use and have value. For example, if the assets will be sold together, a buyer usually also wants and is willing to pay for the related intellectual properties such as trademarks, product and manufacturing process information and customer lists, although they do not appear on the seller's balance sheet unless they were purchased.

If liabilities and obligations will continue in effect, the appraiser has a challenging task. In liquidation, some liabilities may decrease as creditors agree to reduce them in return for partial payments or continued business relationships. On the other hand, the liquidation may trigger contingent and other liabilities not previously appearing on the balance sheet.

When a business is in bankruptcy, a common perception among creditors unfamiliar with their rights in bankruptcy proceedings is that its assets must be sold at auction for "fire sale" prices. They ruefully assume recovery of only a fraction of the value of their claims. However, an active creditors' committee can require (and assist) a trustee to achieve asset sales at sound commercial prices. The power of the bankruptcy court to order sales free and clear of liens and contractual obligations is a strong advantage in arranging such sales.

Extra time and effort in liquidating assets is often rewarded. For example, assets with ready liquidation values can be an important plus factor in a "turnaround" acquisition. The author recalls an acquisition in which the proposed price was marginal based on operating history, and projections were difficult to prepare because of uncertain conditions in a highly competitive industry. However, the buyer learned during the "due diligence" review that the seller's assets included precious metals used in its manufacturing processes that could be sold promptly at any time for about half of the total acquisition price. This value was a key factor in the decision to make the acquisition because it put a limit on the downside risk if the "turnaround" could not be achieved.

5. "Going-Business" Values among Assets Being Liquidated

When a business is being sold on a liquidation basis, a seller may undervalue some assets if all assets are sold in bulk. The "going-business" value of the seller's business may be gone. However, some of the seller's assets may have "going-business" value for other businesses and such value should, if possible, be identified and realized.

For example, some years ago, a large manufacturer attempted to sell an old manufacturing facility in the northeastern United States. The buyer's managers learned during the "due diligence" review that the manufacturing facility and equipment were obsolete and unable to comply consistently with environmental laws. However, the buyer eventually agreed to purchase for a price of several million dollars the intellectual properties associated with two prestigious product lines that the seller had produced at the manufacturing facility. The assets consisted of product trademarks, product formulations and specifications, customer lists and applications technology. None of the assets sold had previously been carried on the seller's balance sheet.

Alert sellers sometimes retain the land and buildings when the assets of the business are sold. That is a good strategy when the land and buildings may have more eventual value as rental property than in their existing business use. For example, many industrial sites were founded years ago on undeveloped rural land distant from the nearest urban residential property. Residential neighborhoods developed near the industrial sites, populated by families attracted by industrial employment opportunities. But second- and third-generation dwellers in these areas have been generally less willing to work in industrial employment at competitive salaries and wages and more inclined to make environmental complaints. Eventually, industrial businesses in these sites must be sold or closed. However, the land and buildings may have important value if developed for modern light industry, a shopping center or an office complex. In some situations, an environmental cleanup can be combined with architectural and construction work that enable the seller to develop rentable or salable property with significant "going-business" value.

6. Replacement Value

Replacement value is determined by an appraisal survey to identify the amounts that would be paid to purchase or construct the assets of a business under present conditions.

Replacement value has become increasingly important in recent decades as environmental laws have made construction of new facilities in many industries a practical impossibility due to delay, uncertainty and the high design and construction costs required to obtain permits, if they can be obtained at all. Old industrial plants built before the early 1970s often sell at a premium because they have environmental permits that are difficult or impossible to obtain for new plants.

There is a practical limit to the usefulness of replacement value. A business in an industry that is declining or that is impacted by competition from foreign or domestic sources can often survive only by using older equipment that is fully depreciated because profit margins do not justify capital expenditures for modern equipment. These conditions have existed for several decades in many industries in the northeastern United States. For businesses operating under these conditions, replacement value becomes useful only for insurance purposes.

I. Valuation Methods Based on Historical Financial Statements

1. Book Value

Book value is an accounting concept that, for better or worse, has been used for many decades as a method of valuation. Its primary advantage is simplicity.

Book value is calculated by subtracting the liabilities from the assets shown on a balance sheet, as is done when calculating stockholders' equity.

Book value is commonly used as a valuation method in buy–sell agreements between small closely held corporations and their shareholders. A typical agreement provides for a purchase of shares at book value as of the end of the fiscal year or fiscal quarter immediately preceding a shareholder's death, termination of employment or other agreed events. The agreement usually also requires that the balance sheet be part of the financial statements, prepared in accordance with GAAP consistently applied.

For businesses with assets that are entirely or primarily financial and that are periodically revalued, an acquisition price equal to book value or a multiple of book value may approximate fair value. For example, it is common to use a multiple of book value as a factor in valuing bank stocks.

For most commercial and industrial businesses, including small closely held businesses, book value has no relation to fair market value, except by coincidence. The reason is that book value is based on accounting principles rather than valuation principles. For example, GAAP requires that land be recorded on a balance sheet at original cost and remain indefinitely at the original recorded amount, even though the land may appreciate greatly in value.

Depreciated values of buildings, machinery and equipment may also be understated if their fair market values have appreciated or their actual useful lives are longer than their depreciable lives. On the other hand, book values sometimes reflect overstated asset values. For example, in recent years, electric utilities with large generating facilities constructed at high costs required by environmental laws have been required by Congress to buy unneeded power from cogenerators and to "wheel" power to customers from utilities operating at lower costs in distant states. Thus, many utilities have costly plant, facilities and equipment that they are not allowed to utilize fully. The FASB recently adopted FAS No. 121 which, among other things, may require electric utilities to write off these "stranded costs" to the extent that their plant, equipment and related assets no longer reflect value recoverable in power rates.

2. Multiples of Earnings

Multiples of earnings have been used for several decades to value shares of common stock and also to value businesses. The method became popular in the 1960s, a decade when many companies made initial public offerings to investors who wanted to share in the industrial growth that followed World War II.

In the 1960s, owners of corporations that had grown steadily, or had good growth potential, still tended to perceive their value in terms of older methods such as book value. When investment bankers offered to underwrite sales to public investors based on earnings multiples, the result seemed magical to them. The corporation or the controlling shareholders could sell a minority interest in equity ownership to the public for a price they had previously regarded as more than the value of the whole business. Yet, they still retained majority ownership and control of the business. For true growth businesses, the valuation was not magical, but realistic and even conservative. Investors who were early purchasers of shares of Xerox Corporation, Polaroid Corporation and Hewlett-Packard at prices that were relatively high multiples of historical earnings were well-satisfied with their investments that had originally seemed risky to post-Depression investors.

Price–earnings multiples (or ratios) continue to be widely used. For example, *The Wall Street Journal* and other publications routinely include price-earnings ratios in their daily reports of trading on the exchanges and the NASDAQ markets. Even those valuation professionals who place primary emphasis on other methods often discuss price-earnings ratios in their reports.

To value a business by the price–earnings method, the first step is to select an appropriate period of earnings, such as the most recent year or an average of two or three years. The second step is to determine an appropriate multiple by comparison to the earnings multiples at which similar businesses were recently sold or to the earnings multiples of publicly traded shares of similar businesses. The third step is to analyze and adjust the earnings of the business being valued and the other businesses to eliminate nonrecurring items and assure that the earnings being compared are consistent. The multiple is then applied to the adjusted earnings to arrive at a value.

A disadvantage of the price–earnings method is the difficulty of obtaining multiples for businesses that are reasonably comparable to the business being valued. Full information about recent sales of businesses is not always publicly available. The available information about recent sales and about trading of shares of publicly owned businesses is usually about large companies. Some of the large companies have several lines of business. When valuing a small or medium-sized business, the use of multiples applicable to large and sometimes diversified, businesses can be questionable.

A second disadvantage of the price–earnings method is that it is based on GAAP. Congress originally prescribed GAAP in the federal securities laws to enhance consistency and accuracy in the presentation of financial statements so that investors could make better informed decisions. However, in recent years, the FASB has increasingly adopted standards that reduce reported earnings and assets when no actual reduction has occurred. The result is that earnings determined in accordance with GAAP may be substantially understated.

Another disadvantage of the price–earnings method is that it is usually based on historical earnings. Applying a multiple to a projection of earnings for the current year is only a partial answer. It is correct, of course, to observe that an earnings multiple derived by comparison to recent sales of similar businesses or publicly traded shares of similar businesses is future-oriented. However, the use of such a multiple assumes that the future of the business being valued will be the same as the similar businesses, although it may actually be better or worse. The price–earnings method does not compel a systematic effort to review the future prospects of the business being valued. This limits its usefulness in valuing acquisitions when the ability of the acquired businesses to repay acquisition debt and to provide a return on investment in future years is an important factor.

3. Multiples of Historical Cash Flows

In recent years, it has become common to use multiples of historical cash flows as a substitute for multiples of earnings. The most commonly used are earnings before interest and taxes (EBIT) and earnings before interest, taxes, depreciation and amortization (EBITDA). Use of these cash flows shows the earning power of a business without nonoperational charges related to its debt and tax situation and without noncash charges to depreciate or amortize capital expenditures.

4. Capitalization of Earnings

Capitalization of earnings has been used for many years to value shares of common stock and to value businesses. The method is somewhat similar to the price–earnings method, except that earnings are divided by a financially-oriented capitalization rate rather than multiplied by a market-oriented multiple.

To value a business by capitalization of earnings, the first step is to select the appropriate amount of earnings, such as the earnings for the most recent year or an average of the earnings for two or three years. The second step is to adjust the earnings to eliminate nonrecurring items. The third step is to develop an appropriate capitalization rate. The fourth step is to divide the earnings by the capitalization rate to arrive at a value.

The capitalization rate can be obtained from various sources. The cost of acquisition debt should not ordinarily be used because it does not reflect the true overall cost. A weighted average cost of capital can be used to capitalize cash flow. A capitalization rate for net income can also be constructed by adding a risk-free rate to an equity risk premium and perhaps a small business or unique risk premium. An internal rate of return, or "hurdle rate," can also be used. However, when future growth is anticipated, it should be reflected by reducing the capitalization rate because the earnings amount is static.

The capitalization of earnings method suffers from the tendency of GAAP to understate earnings as described under the price–earnings method. While the capitalization rate can be weighted to include an element of future orientation, the method does not require a systematic review of the future of the business being valued, a weakness it shares with the price–earnings method.

A capitalization rate differs from the discount rates described later in this chapter. A capitalization rate is applied in a single calculation to a selected annual or average earnings amount to arrive at a value, rather than to discount projected future earnings to present values. In the capitalization method, future growth is anticipated by reducing the capitalization rate used in the denominator. In the discounted future earnings or cash flows methods, anticipated future growth is reflected by adjustments to the amounts shown in the numerator for each year and in the final perpetuity discount calculation. Thus, in the discounted future cash flow method, no reduction for growth is applied to the discount rates used in the denominators.

J. Valuation Based on Market Prices of the Company Being Valued

1. General

The prices reported for sales of shares of companies with common stock traded on a stock exchange or in the over-the-counter (OTC) market have several uses in valuation. The reported trading prices can be used in valuing the company itself and also in valuing large and small blocks of shares of the common stock of the company. The reported trading prices can also be used as a guideline for the valuation of businesses owned by privately owned companies. Appraisers refer to the latter as a "comparable value" or "guideline company" approach.

2. Market Depth and Liquidity

There are wide differences in the extent of trading activity among shares traded on the stock exchanges and in the OTC market. Shares of large companies listed on The New York Stock Exchange are traded daily by the specialist firms and other firms in numerous transactions totaling large numbers of shares and many millions of dollars. Shares of "small-cap" companies with major growth potential also trade actively. Shares of "small-cap" companies in serious financial difficulty may also trade actively. However, shares of many "small-cap" companies with stable commodity businesses trade lightly, although they perform steadily from year to year.

In general, trading on the American Stock Exchange and the regional stock exchanges (Boston, Chicago, Philadelphia and Pacific) is much lighter than trading on The New York Stock Exchange. Some "small-cap" companies list their shares for trading on the nearest regional exchange, expecting to receive more attention than may be available on the New York Stock Exchange, but they do not always achieve that objective.

In the over-the-counter market, the trading variation is even wider. Shares of companies such as Microsoft are traded competitively in large daily volumes by dozens of market makers on the National Association of Securities Dealers Automated Quotation System's National Market. However, shares of some companies traded in the NASDAQ Small Cap Market may be traded lightly. In addition, shares of many middle-sized and small companies are traded only in the Electronic Bulletin Board, which succeeded to most of the shares formerly in the "pink sheets" distributed by the National Quotation Bureau, Inc. Intervals of hours, days, weeks and even months may occur between trades.[1] Thus, an assumption of liquidity

[1]The author once checked the trading history for a stock quoted daily in the OTC market and found that only three trades of a few hundred shares each had been made in a period of a year and a half before the valuation date.

used in valuation may be illusory unless the valuation professional determines the extent of activity represented by the prices (or quotations) reported in *The Wall Street Journal.*

Even though shares may be actively traded, valuation professionals must keep in mind that the stock exchange and NASDAQ markets are markets for minority interests. Their basic unit of trading is the 100-share "round lot." In recent decades, major broker-dealer firms have added the capability to handle relatively large transactions by block positioning, "twilight offerings," "in-house" crosses and other methods. Significant volumes of institutional trades are handled daily in "fourth-market" transactions on the Instinet and similar broker-sponsored trading facilities. However, even these trades are of securities evidencing minority interests.

3. Public Perception of Market Value

Valuation professionals should not give more weight to reported stock market prices than they deserve. However, when negotiating an acquisition or merger, the negotiators cannot simply ignore the reported prices. The public believes that the prices, or quotations, reported daily in the media are approximately the value of their shares. Even such sophisticated persons as chief executives, investment bankers and risk arbitrageurs watch the daily trading results and consider them in making decisions. For example, most acquisitions of publicly owned companies are made at a premium over market value, although a few are made at a so-called "negative premium."

If an acquisition price will be at a "negative premium," both the seller and the buyer should prepare to demonstrate to the public shareholders that arm's-length negotiations, supported by other generally accepted valuation methods, justify the agreed price. Otherwise, the public shareholders are likely to oppose the transaction by refusing to tender shares or by voting against a merger or sale of assets and exercising their dissenters' appraisal rights.

K. Valuation Based on Comparable Companies

1. Comparison to Companies with Publicly Traded Shares

Valuation of a closely held business based on comparison to the stock market prices of similar companies having publicly traded shares is a method regularly used by valuation professionals, especially those whose roots are in investment banking work.

The key to valid use of the comparable company method is the selection of companies with characteristics sufficiently similar to the business being valued. Once the selections are made, comparisons can be made by the methods described earlier in this chapter. For example, the multiples of earnings or cash flows at which shares of the comparable companies are traded can be used in valuing a privately owned business. In addition to valuations for acquisitions and divestitures, the comparable company method is commonly used in determining prices of shares for initial public offerings (IPOs) and in valuing shares for estate and gift tax purposes.

To use the comparable company method, valuation professionals seek companies in the same industry with the same or similar products or services sold to the same or similar markets. They also seek similarities in reputation, market share, maturity of business development, growth history and management. Similarities in sales, earnings and capital structure are also important.

The comparable company method is often used in pricing IPOs because investment bankers seek to underwrite offerings for growing companies in growing industries. In the IPO markets, companies welcome comparison to successful new companies, such as Netscape or Pixar. Any "me-too" perception is a minor disadvantage.

It is not an easy task to find comparable companies. First, companies with publicly traded shares tend to be larger and more diversified than most privately owned companies. Further, businesses generally seek to be different from each other. "Me-too" businesses are likely to succeed only in rapidly growing markets. In established markets, competition compels companies to distinguish themselves. Companies in the same industry offering similar products or services seek identity based on quality, price, service, territory or other factors.

The U.S. Tax Court has frequently rejected valuations based on a comparable company method because the companies selected were not sufficiently comparable (*The Northern Trust Company,* 87 U.S.T.C. 349 (1986); *Estate of Jung,* 101 U.S.T.C. 412 (1993)). However, the comparable company method has been accepted when the companies used for comparison were selected skillfully (*Estate of Mark S. Gallo,* 50 T.C.M. 470 (1985); *Estate of Joyce C. Hall,* 92 U.S.T.C. 312 (1989)). The decision in *Estate of Joyce C. Hall* is especially interesting because the Tax Court upheld a valuation by First Boston Corp. of shares of Hallmark Cards, Inc. based on comparison to its most proximate publicly held competitor, American Greetings Corp., and also to several other leading producers of brand name consumer goods with business and financial characteristics similar to Hallmark's, although their industries and products were different. The Tax Court rejected a valuation based only on comparison to American Greetings, a company with similar products but significant other differences.

When performing a valuation based on comparison to stock market prices of comparable companies, the valuation professional should keep in mind that the prices reported are for trades of minority interests. Further, as described earlier in this chapter, the reported prices may represent active, competitive trading or they may represent erratic trading in a thin market.

2. Comparison to Recent Acquisitions

Valuation of a business can also be based on comparisons to recent acquisitions of comparable companies or businesses. An advantage of this method is that the comparison is made to prices paid for whole companies or businesses rather than to sales of small minority interests such as occur in the stock markets.

There are two major tasks when performing a valuation using the comparable business acquisition method. The first is the selection of comparable companies, not an easy task as previously described. The second is to obtain full information about the structure and terms of the sale transaction in order to know all the elements affecting the price.

There are numerous sources from which information about business sales can be obtained. They include *Mergers & Acquisitions* which is published at two-month intervals by the Investment Dealers Digest and lists in M&A Rosters all acquisitions identified by the publisher and valued at $5,000,000 or more. The Rosters include a brief selection of information about the transaction, including the price if disclosed. Some details about the price may also be provided, such as whether payment was in cash or stock and perhaps also a related assumption of liabilities.

Annual publications containing more details are the *Mergerstat Review* published by Houlihan, Lokey, Howard & Zukin; the *Mergers & Acquisition Sourcebook* published by Quality Services Company; and the *Mergers Yearbook* published by Securities Data Company.

The information provided in the publications described is very interesting and helpful, but necessarily omits some elements that affect the prices of the transactions. However, once a transaction is identified, additional and relatively comprehensive information may be available from the SEC's files for the following transactions:

1. Acquisitions of companies with publicly traded shares.
2. Acquisitions that are of material significance to a buyer with publicly traded shares.
3. Divestitures that are of material significance to a seller with publicly traded shares.

In these situations, recent reports on Forms 8-K, 10-Q or 10-K, proxy statements, Schedules 13D and 14D-1 and other filings are likely to provide extensive information, including copies of the acquisition contracts.

When limited information is available, however, a valuation professional cannot place much weight on a reported price for the sale of a comparable company or business. The reason is that the price may be greatly affected by the transaction structure, the medium and timing of payment, the tax consequences, pre-sale distributions of assets, assumptions or retentions of liabilities, covenants not to compete, employment contracts and numerous other factors.

L. Valuation Based on Discounted Future Cash Flows

Methods for valuation of businesses based on discounted future cash flows were developed in the 1970s and 1980s in response to economic and business conditions. The methods have become the leading business valuation methods used today. A history of their development together with the leveraged buyout acquisition method is provided in Chapter 14.

1. The Basic Formulae

The basic mathematics used in a discounted future cash flow (DFCF) valuation are as follows:

$$PV = \sum \frac{PCF_t}{(1 + DR)^t} + \text{discounted residual (terminal) value*}$$

PV	=	Present value of the business
PCF	=	Projected cash flow of the business
DR	=	Discount rate
t	=	Years 1, 2, 3 ... n, the last year projected

In financing-neutral (debt-free) analysis, debt will be subtracted or excess cash added.

In the first calculation, future cash flows are projected for a period of years regarded as reasonable by the valuation professional. There is no prescribed period, but periods of five to seven years are commonly used and may coincide with the period of projections used to obtain loan financing for an acquisition. If possible, it is best to make a specific projection of cash flow for each year based on foreseeable future events. However, projections can be made by applying an annual percentage growth rate that seems appropriate for the business.

An example of the mathematics of the first calculation, using a 12% discount rate, is as follows:

$$PV = \frac{PCF_1}{(1 + .12)} + \frac{PCF_2}{(1 + .12)(1 + .12)} + \frac{PCF_3}{(1 + .12)(1 + .12)\ (1 + .12)}$$

$$(1.12) \qquad (1.25) \qquad (1.40)$$

In the second calculation, a residual value, often called a terminal value, is determined. In articles written in the early 1980s, valuation professionals sometimes suggested that residual value might be a projected book value at the end of the valuation period or an earnings multiple. However, a discount of cash flows to perpetuity has been recognized as the preferred method. The Gordon Growth Model is commonly used to make the calculation as follows:

$$RV = \frac{PCF\ (1+GR)}{(DR - GR)}$$

RV	=	Residual value
PCF	=	Projected cash flow for last year of projection period
GR	=	Growth rate
DR	=	Discount rate

The residual value is then discounted to present value by the same number of years as the years included in the projection period to reach the present value of the residual value:

$$\text{Present value of RV} = \frac{\text{RV}}{(1 + \text{DR})^n}$$

The present values of the cash flows for the projection period are then added to the present value of the residual value to reach the final value.

When calculating residual value, it is prudent to use a growth rate that is more conservative than the growth rate used during the projection period. If aggressive growth was assumed during the projection period, it is reasonable to presume that the growth may attract competition and reduce cash flows toward industry norms. It is also prudent to reevaluate the discount rate. Some authors suggest that the discount rate for the residual value should be more conservative than the discount rate for the projection period. However, if the discount rate for the projection period included a small stock premium or was based on a high weighted-average cost of capital, it may be reasonable to use a discount rate that reflects the accomplishments anticipated during the projection period. In any event, the discount rate must exceed the growth rate in the Gordon Growth Model.

2. Determination of Cash Flow

The determination of projected cash flows should be done carefully to include predictable changes, especially during the initial projection period.

The classic definition of cash flow is "reverse engineered" from the income statement of a business and defines cash flow as net income plus noncash charges such as depreciation, amortization and deferred taxes. Cash flow can also be determined according to Statement of Financial Accounting Standards (SFAS) No. 95.[2] However, neither can be used for acquisition analysis without further adjustment.

The components of cash flow depend on whether a valuation professional uses financing-neutral (debt-free) analysis or equity (leveraged) analysis.

Financing-Neutral Analysis. When using financing-neutral (debt-free) analysis, cash flow begins with earnings before interest, taxes, depreciation and amortization (EBITDA). EBITDA is then reduced by capital expenditures (CAPEX) and anticipated working capital changes (WCC), in other words, increases or decreases of cash needed to carry inventories and accounts receivable. The objective is to use in valuation the cash flows available to the entire capital structure. Although some valuation professionals suggest the contrary, the author believes that the proceeds of asset dispositions during the projection period should not be added to the operating cash flows to be discounted to present value, but applied to reduce debt in the final calculation.[3]

$$\text{CF} = \text{EBITDA} - \text{CAPEX} = \text{WCC}$$

[2]SFAS No. 95 prefers a "built-up" method for determining cash flows and includes flows from all sources including proceeds of financings.

[3]However, cash flows should be adjusted to reflect changes in operating revenues and costs that may result from dispositions of income-producing assets.

After a taxable acquisition financed primarily by debt, capital expenditures (CAPEX) will be kept at levels sufficient to maintain existing facilities and equipment in good operating condition during the projection period. However, few discretionary capital expenditures will be made unless they offer a rapid, sure and significant return on investment.

Equity Analysis. When using equity (leveraged) analysis, cash flow begins with net income after interest and taxes. Of course, interest and taxes are cash charges, although the amounts vary in response to capital structure choices. Noncash charges for depreciation, amortization and deferred taxes are added. Maintenance (nondiscretionary) capital expenditures are deducted. Working capital changes are added or subtracted. In this analysis, an addition for excess cash or a deduction for debt is not made. The objective is to use in valuation the cash flows of the business available to its equity holders.

Midyear Receipt of Cash Flows. Some valuation experts point out that businesses generate cash flows throughout each year, not on the last day of the year when their financial statements are prepared. Thus, they use an assumption that cash flows are received at midyear. The effect is to increase value because cash flows received earlier are not discounted for as long a period as later cash flows.

3. The Discount Rate

Like the elements of cash flow, selection of the discount rate depends on whether the valuation professional uses financing-neutral (debt-free) analysis or equity (leveraged) analysis.

Financing-Neutral Analysis. In financing-neutral (debt-free) analysis, the discount rate is determined by calculating a weighted average cost of capital (WACOC):

$$\text{WACOC} = \text{COE } (\% \text{ equity}) + \text{COD } (\% \text{ debt})$$

WACOC = Weighted average cost of capital
COE = Cost of equity
COD = Cost of debt

Some valuation professionals have written that an acquisition analyst should use the seller's cost of capital, not the buyer's cost of capital. They give two reasons. The first reason is that use of the seller's cost of capital results in fair market value of the seller's business based on its existing capital structure, but use of the buyer's cost of capital results in investment value to the buyer. The second reason is based on an assumption that the buyer's cost of capital is lower than the seller's cost of capital and the buyer should not enhance the value of the business by using a lower discount rate based on its own financial strength.

However, a buyer's capital cost is not always lower than the seller's capital cost, certainly not in a typical leveraged buyout. When a buyer's capital cost is higher, it becomes a realistic choice as a discount rate because a buyer should not pay more than the investment value. If the buyer has a lower capital cost, it makes practical sense to perform valuations using the capital costs of both the seller and the buyer. The negotiating team can make an offer based on the seller's existing fair market value, but will know that the offer can be increased to the buyer's investment value, if necessary.

Cost of equity can be the known actual cost of equity that the buyer has obtained to finance an acquisition. For a leveraged buyout, a buyer's cost of equity is generally in the 30 to 40 percent range, although it is a small percentage of the overall cost of capital.

A cost of equity capital can also be constructed according to the capital asset pricing model by adding a "risk-free rate," such as the current rate of a 10-year U.S. Treasury note and an equity risk premium derived from an equity market rate of return from a source such as Standard & Poor's multiplied by a "beta" volatility factor. For a small business, a small stock premium would also be added and perhaps also an unique risk premium.

An example is as follows:

$$\begin{aligned} COE &= RFR + Beta\ (ERP) + SSP \\ &\quad 7.0\% + 1.10\ (6\%) + 5\% \\ &\quad 7.0\% + 6.6\% + 5\% = 18.6\% \end{aligned}$$

COE = Cost of equity
RFR = Risk free rate
ERP = Equity risk premium (market rate – risk free rate)
SSP = Small stock premium

Cost of debt can be the actual cost of debt or a cost determined from public information. For a leveraged buyout, a buyer's cost of "mezzanine" debt may be a double-digit rate, especially if it includes high expense reimbursement, closing costs and "equity sweetener" compensation payable to the lenders. A formula for cost of debt is as follows:

$$\begin{aligned} &IR\ (1 - TR) = COD \\ &18\%\ (60\%) = 10.8\% \end{aligned}$$

IR = Interest rate
TR = Marginal corporate tax rate
COD = Cost of debt

4. Beta Factors

Beta is a volatility factor used to adjust the equity premium risk when calculating the cost of equity. The basic unit is 1.0 for stocks that rise and fall at the same rate as a general market index such as the S&P Index or the NYSE Composite Index. Stocks with a beta factor greater than 1.0 (i.e., 1.05 or 1.1) tend to rise or fall by a greater rate than the market. Stocks with a beta factor of less than 1.0 (0.95 or 0.9) tend to rise or fall at a lesser rate than the market.

Beta factors are published by several reporting services including CompuServe, Media General, Merrill Lynch, S&P Compustat and Value Line. When using beta factors, some adjustments may be needed. First, reported beta factors reflect the capital structure of the company for which they are assigned. When the leverage ratio for a company differs significantly from that assumed for the company to be valued, an adjustment should be made. Second, the various reporting services do not all use the same index or method to calculate beta factors, so there are differences in the beta factors shown for some companies. Third, the reporting services list beta factors for the major stocks followed by the general public. They do not list beta factors for stocks of small companies, such as those reported on the NASDAQ Electronic Bulletin Board.

The beta factors reported for publicly traded stocks are necessarily historical and reflect the capital structure of the companies from which they are derived. Thus, they are called leveraged beta factors because they reflect the extent of leverage in the capital structure of the respective companies. To obtain an unlevered beta factor, it is necessary to adjust the beta factor to the result that would exist if the company were debt free. In DFCF analysis, the unlevered beta factor is then adjusted to reflect the capital structure used in the valuation.

5. Residual (Terminal) Value

In DFCF valuation, much of the final result is in the residual (terminal) value. However, the calculation is necessarily for a future time beyond the period that the valuation professional can project with confidence on an annual basis. This dilemma led some valuation analysts to use residual values that were obviously conservative, such as book value, a low price–earnings multiple or a perpetuity discount with a zero growth assumption.

In recent years, use of a perpetual growth assumption in a residual value has gained acceptance for appropriate businesses and industries. However, even experts who favor assuming some level of perpetual growth warn that an unrealistic assumption could greatly overstate value.

In an interesting recent article, a valuation professional correctly observed that businesses do not continue to grow over long time periods without capital expenditures for the improvements needed to remain competitive. He recommended that the residual value formulae be modified to reflect anticipated need for new investment and the return on such investment ("A Real-World Focus in Calculating Terminal Values," Barnes, *Mergers & Acquisitions*, Jul-Aug 1996. See also, "Why Acquirers May Need to Rethink Terminal Values," Morris, *Mergers & Acquisitions*, 1994).

In his article, Barnes suggests debt-free analysis using residual (terminal) value formulae, which are modifications of the Gordon Growth Model described earlier. Barnes begins with a formula that he identifies as a Value Driver Formula:

$$RV = \frac{DFNI\,(1 - g/r)}{WACC - g}$$

RV	=	Residual value
DFNI	=	Debt-free net income
g	=	Expected growth rate of DFNI
r	=	Expected rate of return on new investment
WACC	=	Weighted average cost of capital

In the equation above, *r* must be greater than *g* and *WACC* must also be greater than *g*.

Barnes suggests that the Value Driver Formula and other techniques described in the article can be used to derive more realistic and internally consistent pricing conclusions. This author agrees with Barnes' observation that future investment is important to the continuing growth of a business, but doubts that the Value Driver Formula will always achieve more realistic valuation results. The Value Driver Formula achieves lower results by deleting the addition of growth from the numerator and substituting the subtraction of a ratio of growth to rate of return on new investment. Since growth is also achieved by means other than new investment, the mandatory subtraction might better be described as conservative than as inevitably realistic. Thus, the calculations suggested by Barnes are worth making for the insight they can provide, but the results should be weighed with other factors in acquisition price negotiations.

Finally, articles written by valuation professionals differ as to whether the cash flow to be used in residual value formulae should be the cash flow for the final year of the projection period or for the first year thereafter. This author believes that the professionals, including Shannon Pratt, who recommend using the cash flow for the final year of the projection period have a practical answer if the valuation professional assumes that cash flows in perpetuity will not change significantly, except for a selected growth rate. However, the author believes that the best choice is to follow the advice of Barnes and Morris to rethink cash flows for the perpetuity period and adjust them for factors such as future investment and return on such investment.

6. Sensitivity Analysis

DFCF valuation leads readily into sensitivity analysis, one of the most important and useful tools in planning and negotiating acquisitions. Relatively few articles have been written about sensitivity analysis by valuation professionals because they are usually hired to provide a definitive valuation rather than a strategic working tool. However, sensitivity analysis is regularly used by experienced managements to evaluate acquisitions and internal expansion projects. The reason is that sensitivity analysis helps not only with valuation, but also with identification of opportunities and risks and the related business planning.

To appreciate sensitivity analysis, some examples of business economics are helpful. Some businesses, such as the chemical industry, are very sensitive to changes of the cost of raw materials because they account for 60 to 80 percent of production costs. Other costs, such as labor and utilities, are modest. Other businesses, such as fiberglass production, have relatively low costs for sand and other raw materials, but high costs for utilities and personnel. Businesses like the hotel industry are sensitive to factors such as occupancy rates and room rental rates. Retail stores are sensitive to inventory turnover.

Sensitivity analysis involves the insertion of systematic changes in the parameters used in DFCF or other valuation methods in order to evaluate their effects. The changes should, of course, be within ranges that experience indicates are in the realm of realistic opportunity and risk. The analysis usually reveals a variety of useful information. For example, the analysis might show that the business is currently riding a crest based on cheap raw materials, and that a modest price increase by suppliers could slice cash flow sharply. The analysis might, on the other hand, show that the business is not sensitive to any likely material price changes, but is sensitive to power and other utility costs or to human resource costs. Thus, sensitivity analysis helps to refine a valuation by identifying and quantifying areas of risk and opportunity. The information is also useful to plan for post-acquisition integration and operation of the acquired business. In performing sensitivity analysis, a useful tool is an electronic spreadsheet provided by firms such as Lotus, QuattroPro and Excel. See also, "How to Sort Out the Premium Drivers of Post-Deal Value," Bielinski, *Mergers & Acquisitions*, 1993.

Computer models can be designed to allow two or more variables to be adjusted simultaneously. For example, the effects of a raw material cost increase partially offset by a price increase, and perhaps also a concurrent personnel cost increase can be programmed and evaluated.

7. Application to Leveraged Buyouts

When applying DFCF analysis to a leveraged buyout (LBO), a valuation analyst must consider several factors not usually present in other transactions. The buyer is typically a newly organized corporation. The buyer will raise capital for the acquisition using a leveraged structure consisting, for example, of 70% senior debt and subordinated (or "mezzanine") debt and 30% equity. The acquisition will be a taxable transaction so that the buyer can obtain a "stepped-up basis" in the assets acquired.

As a result, the buyer will have major cash flow obligations in order to pay interest and principal on the acquisition debt. However, these cash flow obligations will be partially counterbalanced by cash saved on income taxes as a result of large interest and depreciation deductions and deferral of discretionary capital expenditures. Buyers in LBO transactions usually pay only modest income taxes for several years. If the LBO is a management buyout or an ESOP transaction, other cash savings will probably also be realized as owner-managers find ways to control costs, including compensation payable in cash.

For the analyst, several steps should be taken to reflect the conditions likely to be present in LBO transactions:

- Debt-free (financing-neutral) analysis can be used as the initial method for planning the acquisition because it reflects intrinsic business value free of capital structure choices. The cash flows for the projection period should reflect the projected cash savings relevant to that method, including reduced operating expenses and capital expenditures.

- Equity (leveraged) analysis can then be used to determine fair market value based on the seller's capital structure and to determine investment value based on the buyer's proposed capital structure. The cash flows for the projection period should reflect the increased cash obligations for interest, but also the savings on taxes resulting from depreciation and interest deductions. Reduced operating expenses and capital expenditures should also be included.

M. Weighted Averages

When performing a business valuation, professionals seldom use a single method. They usually determine value by several methods and, within those methods, may determine several values based on different assumption or criteria. Having done so, they should then evaluate the several results and the weight, if any, that they should be assigned in reaching a final valuation decision.

The first step is selective. For example, book value should be assigned little or no weight in valuation of a business with significant off–balance sheet or understated assets and liabilities. Market value should be assigned little or no weight if trading in shares is very thin or distorted by unusual circumstances. Analysis using the DFCF method should perhaps be assigned little or no weight if future cash flows are too uncertain to forecast with reasonable confidence.

The next step is to assign weight percentages to the valuation results entitled to recognition. The valuation professional should carefully consider and explain why the several percentages were assigned. The last step is to multiply the assigned percentages by their respective values and add the results.

For many years, the Delaware courts used a "weighted average" method, called the "Delaware Block Method," to determine value in dissenters' appraisal rights proceedings. The Delaware Supreme Court authorized consideration of other generally accepted methods in *Weinberger v. UOP, Inc.*, 457 A.2d 701 (1983). The "Delaware Block Method" called for consideration of book value, market value and earnings multiples, but the courts did not assign similar weights to the component factors. For example, the courts sometimes assigned a weight of 5 percent or less to book value.

An interesting and practical article suggesting a simple weighted average method for valuing small closely held businesses is "Valuing the Closely Held Business," Faris *et al.*, *Mergers & Acquisitions*, 1983. The authors recommend the use of three factors likely to be available for small businesses: (1) effective liquidation value, (2) gross revenue capitalization value and (3) buyer's discretionary cash value. The article explains the three factors and how they should be weighted for different kinds of businesses.

N. Discounts for Lack of Marketability

There are thousands of well-established, successful privately owned businesses that cannot readily be sold or taken public. There are many reasons for this lack of marketability. For example, some businesses are so closely intertwined with the abilities of their owners that they would not have the same value without the owners. Others do not have technology, valuable intellectual properties, capital investment or other strengths that provide protection against easy entry by competitors. Most have simply not gone through the extensive planning and effort required to make them attractive to a buyer or to the public.

To reflect this lack of marketability, buy–sell agreements between privately owned corporations and their shareholders typically provide for deduction of a discount for lack of marketability when shares are valued for sale. A discount for lack of marketability is also allowed when valuing shares of a privately owned company for estate and gift tax purposes, except when the valuation method selected already includes the effects of the discount. (See the *IRS Valuation Guide for Income, Estate and Gift Taxes*.)

Experience has shown, however, that negotiations in acquisition and divestiture transactions seldom consider a discount for lack of marketability. The reason is that, when a seller has prepared a business for sale and attracted one or more willing potential buyers, the business is now presumably marketable and lack of marketability declines to a contingency.

A discount for lack of marketability may continue to be appropriate if there is only one potential buyer. It may also be appropriate if there will be only a limited number of alternate buyers if pending sale negotiations do not lead to a transaction. However, sellers seldom admit that they are under pressure to sell and usually try to create an impression that they have several potential buyers. Thus, open discussion of a discount for lack of marketability is rare. In some situations, both seller and buyer may be aware that the seller needs to sell and could not readily find another buyer. When that happens, the buyer may decide to offer a price that implicitly includes a substantial discount for lack of marketability. Faced with no good alternatives, the seller may not admit its quandary, but nevertheless may decide to accept the discounted price.

A discount for lack of marketability may also be appropriate when an acquisition involves a purchase of a half interest or minority interest. For example, the organization of a joint venture often involves the sale of such an interest to a buyer. In these negotiations, discussion of lack of marketability and its effects on valuation can be conducted openly together with discussion of a minority interest discount. The negotiations can also be combined with discussion of contractual rights of the buyer to participate in management and planning for "exit" strategies that could affect the discounts.

When a discount for lack of marketability is applicable, the percentage amount may be very significant. Studies by Robert W. Baird & Company and Willamette Management Associates have shown average differences between private transaction prices and public market prices well in excess of 40 percent. The U.S. Tax Court has historically allowed discounts for lack of marketability in estate and gift tax cases at lower rates, although gradually increasing as time passed. In recent years, however, the Tax

Court has frequently allowed discounts of over 30 percent. For example, in the *Gallo, Hall* and *Jung* cases described earlier, the Tax Court allowed discounts of 36 percent, 36 percent and 35 percent, respectively. Interested readers will find extensive information on discounts for lack of marketability in Chapter 15 of *Valuing a Business*, 3d ed., Pratt et al., Irwin Professional Publishing, 1995.

O. Control Premiums and Minority Discounts

When a company is owned by more than one person, an owner whose equity interest rights provide control of its management can often obtain benefits from exercise of the control that make the controlling interest worth more than a noncontrolling minority interest in the same company. The benefits may include employment in management positions and control of dividend policy and the timing of dividend payments. Thus, valuation professionals have long recognized that control shares are usually worth more than their simple proportionate ownership of the overall value of the corporation. They recognize this additional value by adding a control premium. Conversely, valuation professionals recognize that minority shares are worth less than their proportionate ownership of the overall value. They recognize this deficit by applying a minority discount.

The great majority of acquisition transactions involve a sale or merger of an entire corporation or its assets in which no distinction is made between the value of controlling shares and minority shares. In these transactions, management appointed by controlling shareholders negotiate for a price that will be paid or distributed equally to all shareholders. They do so for many reasons including their own concepts of fairness; the need for support in votes on mergers and sales of substantially all assets; a desire to minimize exercise of dissenters' appraisal rights; contractual provisions in shareholders' agreements providing specific rights for minority shareholders; and a desire to avoid potential controversies with minority shareholders.

Thus, in acquisition transactions, control premiums and minority discounts usually become relevant only when a transaction involves a sale of part of the shares of a corporation and the shares represent a controlling interest or a minority interest. If the shares represent control, the seller may seek and the buyer may be willing to pay a control premium, although they should first consider the legal principles applicable to sales of control, as discussed in Chapter 13. If the shares represent a minority interest and the corporation is privately owned, the buyer will probably insist on a minority discount and the seller will probably agree. If the shares represent a minority interest and are publicly traded, only a blockage discount would usually be appropriate.

Control of a corporation does not always result solely from share ownership. Control can also result from management skills and experience, contractual arrangements and other factors. For example, at many companies, management employees who own a very small percentage of the shares are able to exercise control because the other shareholders are passive investors. Further, even when majority shareholders exercise control, they must meet fiduciary obligations to the corporation and the minority shareholders. State corporation laws require that they meet the "business judgment" standard in the normal conduct of the business. They must meet the "entire fairness" standard for any transactions in which they have a self-interest. The corporation laws afford remedies to minority shareholders for breach of fiduciary obligations by controlling shareholders, including court orders enjoining unlawful transactions, awarding monetary damages and even ordering liquidation if a management "deadlock" exists. (See *Oppression of Minority Shareholders*, 2nd Ed., O'Neal et al., Callaghan & Co., 1985.) Thus, the powers and benefits of control and the disadvantages of minority status are sometimes overstated.

The applicability of a control premium or a minority discount varies with the valuation method used. If a valuation is based on the stock market trading price of shares of the corporation being sold or of comparable companies, the value determined is for a minority interest. Thus, if controlling shares are being sold, a control premium would be added. However, if minority shares are being sold, a minority discount would not be deducted. If the valuation is based on historical or future income or cash flows, a control premium or a minority discount may be appropriate. Based on the author's experience, if the valuation is based on asset values or recent sales of comparable corporations or their assets, a control premium or minority discount may also be appropriate.

Some valuation experts conclude that a control premium is not appropriate if a valuation is based on asset values or recent sales of comparable businesses. They reason that these transactions involve a transfer of control arranged by the controlling shareholders and, therefore, reflect the value of control. These experts do, however, consider that a minority discount is appropriate. Based on experience, this author does not agree and recommends close scrutiny in both situations. When valuation is based on asset sales, the author has seen asset transactions, including liquidations, in which controlling shareholders gained significant extra benefits and others in which they lost control or chose to forego the benefits of control. When valuation is based on recent sales of comparable businesses, the author recommends consideration of all aspects of those transactions, including payments to controlling shareholders and persons related to them pursuant to covenants not to compete, employment contracts, consulting contracts and other arrangements.

When a control premium is appropriate, it must then be quantified. A threshold question is the extent to which the shares being sold represent an effective power to exercise control. To answer, it is necessary to review the state corporation law, the certificate of incorporation and by-laws and any shareholders' agreements or voting trusts. In general, the state corporation laws require annual meetings of shareholders at which all directors are elected by a majority of a quorum, unless otherwise provided in the certificate of incorporation. The board then elects officers and acts on other matters by majority vote. However, board actions on certain matters must be approved by the shareholders, including mergers and sales of substantially all assets. In Delaware, the shareholder vote required to approve a merger or sale of substantially all assets is a majority. However, in other states, the required vote is two-thirds. In those states, a controlling shareholder could not arrange a merger or sale of substantially all assets without the approval of other shareholders unless the controlling shareholder owns or has the right to vote at least two-thirds of the outstanding shares. In addition, many corporations have provisions in their certificates of incorporation requiring supermajority votes for mergers and sales of substantially all assets. Many closely held corporations have shareholders agreements requiring supermajority, and sometimes even unanimous, votes for a list of corporate actions that typically includes mergers and sales of substantially all assets and may also include term loans, mortgages, major contracts, related-party transactions and other significant actions. To the extent applicable, these and other provisions (such as preemptive rights, cumulative voting, outstanding stock options and convertible securities) dilute the power of controlling shareholders to exercise control. They should be considered together with the always applicable fiduciary obligations of controlling shareholders in determining the amount of a control premium.

Chapter 14 of *Valuing a Business*, (Pratt *et al.*, Irwin Publishing, 1995) contains further useful information about control premiums, including a summary of information from the *Mergerstat Review* and studies by Houlihan, Lokey, Howard & Zukin. The information is very interesting. However, the premiums shown are based on comparison of acquisition prices of publicly owned companies to the previous trading prices of their shares before the announcement of an acquisition. The authors of *Valuing a Business* correctly caution readers that the price differences often reflect additional factors over the elements of control. In this author's experience, those factors probably account for a very significant part of the price differences.

Chapter 14 of *Valuing a Business* also contains helpful information on the determination of minority discounts. Of special interest is the discussion of whether a minority discount and a lack of marketability discount, when both are applicable, should be applied by sequential multiplication or by adding the two discount percentages and then multiplying. However, readers should review the decision of the U.S. Tax Court in *Estate of Jung*, 101 U.S.T.C. 412 (1993), refusing to allow a minority interest discount in addition to a 35 percent lack of marketability discount when the expert witnesses had used discounted future cash flow methods of valuation including a discount rate based on "small stock" equity risk premia for the smallest stocks traded on the New York Stock Exchange.

P. Valuation Standards and Reports

Valuation professionals customarily provide some discussion of valuation standards in their reports because value to one person frequently differs from value to another person. Valuation professionals frequently discuss fair market value, investment value and intrinsic value. They may also refer to fair value, although perhaps with some hesitancy because they perceive it to be a legal standard applicable to corporate governance obligations rather than a valuation standard.

Fair market value is defined in the *Standards for Business Valuation* of the American Society of Appraisers as the amount at which property would change hands between a willing seller and a willing buyer when neither is acting under compulsion and when both have reasonable knowledge of the relevant facts. The definition component that neither the seller nor the buyer is acting under compulsion implies that the transaction is at arm's length or steps have been taken in a transaction between affiliated persons to neutralize any compulsion resulting from the relationship. Thus, fair market value, as the term implies, approximates value in a hypothetically reasonable marketplace rather than value to a particular investor or value by fundamental methods of financial analysis that attempt to limit market-oriented influence.

Investment value, on the other hand, is an estimate of value from the point of view of a particular investor, or a hypothetical reasonable investor with identified objectives. An illustrative example is a corner lot in the downtown district of a city that is presently occupied by a restaurant and bar, but is needed by a developer who has acquired the rest of the block to build a high-rise office building. Investment value to the restaurant proprietor is quite different from the potential investment value to the developer.[4] In so-called "condemnation" cases, after real property is acquired through government eminent domain powers the courts resolve this difference by valuing properties, such as the corner lot coffee shop, at their "highest and best use," which may be a high-rise office building if there is adequate evidence that high rise development is a credible potential use.

Intrinsic value is an analytical estimate of value that attempts to use methods minimally affected by market influences and fluctuations and the investment objectives of particular investors. Some financial analysts who use the term intrinsic value are referring to a value obtained by a comprehensive, in-depth review of the capabilities of a business including management, technology, industry trends and other factors that lead them to believe that the business is undervalued or overvalued by current market prices or standards. Other financial analysts use the term to refer to value derived by cash flow-based valuation methods such as the discounted future cash flow method. Analysts who use cash flows as an indicator of intrinsic value assume, of course, that cash generated by a business is likely to be more consistently stable and widely useful than other indicators of value, such as either information contained in historical financial statements prepared in accordance with generally accepted accounting principles or market value.[5]

Fair value is a standard used primarily in valuing shares held by shareholders who have exercised statutory dissenters' appraisal rights and in other situations in which corporate governance issues are involved. The term is derived from the "entire fairness" standard that must be met by directors, officers and controlling shareholders in transactions in which they have self-interests (see Chapter 12). Since the fundamental issue is the fulfillment of fiduciary obligations, fair value is not limited to fair market

[4]The developer may be unable to achieve the potential value if restaurant proprietors, like the owners of P.J. Clarke's in Manhattan, refuse to sell.

[5]For several decades, monetary inflation has been a steady, but mild, factor in the United States and its dollar, although experiencing declines in relation to the currencies of some nations, continues to be a worldwide reserve currency. Under severe inflationary conditions, such as those experienced in this century in Brazil, Germany and Mexico, cash loses its meaning as an indicator of value.

value or any single method by the courts or the statutes that have codified the term. If that were so, directors, officers or controlling shareholders might use evidence of temporarily distorted market values to profit from breaches of fiduciary duties. Fair value has frequently been expressed as a range of prices that are fair. In lawsuits in which courts have found that two competing offers were within a range of fairness, they have allowed both to be made to shareholders.

Readers should be aware that the financial media, courts, government agencies and even valuation professionals are not uniformly consistent in their references to valuation standards or their use of other valuation terminology. However, close analysis of the facts under discussion will often show that there is a rough consistency in results reached. For example, the courts often reach decisions that are fair between the adversaries before them, but judges lacking technical background have difficulty explaining the decisions when they attempt to use the terminology of professionals in the field. Other judges may avoid use of technical terminology if they find it confining and likely to create troublesome precedents that would be broader or narrower than appropriate.

Q. The Internal Revenue Service and Valuation

Although not used directly in the negotiation or valuation of acquisitions, it is important for acquisitions planners to be familiar with the procedures of the Internal Revenue Service (IRS) for the valuation of business interests. The reason is that estate planning is a motive for many acquisition transactions.

The IRS is an organization within the U.S. Department of the Treasury that administers and enforces the Internal Revenue Code (26 U.S.C. § 1 *et seq.*). The IRS's regulations relating to valuation of business interests for estate tax purposes are at 26 C.F.R. § 20.2031-2 and 3, and for gift tax purposes at 26 C.F.R. § 25.2512-0.

The IRS's most significant guidance on the valuation of business interests is Revenue Ruling 59-60, 1959-1 C.B. 237. Written in a manner that seems quaint today, Revenue Ruling 59-60 approaches the valuation of stock of closely held corporations as though businesses are an aggregation of assets including tangible and intangible assets. The intangible assets include "goodwill" or "going-concern value," which represent earning capacity of the business in excess of a fair return attributable to its tangible assets. This circuitous approach resulted partially from the rudimentary valuation concepts existing several decades ago, but also from the IRS's preference for goodwill that would add to the taxable value of estates but was not deductible for income tax purposes.

In practice, the IRS uses, and allows taxpayers to use, modern generally accepted valuation methods, including methods based on multiples or capitalization of earnings, discounted future cash flows and comparable companies. Examples of the use of such methods by both the IRS and taxpayers are found in many court decisions, including the *Northern Trust, Jung, Gallo* and *Hall* decisions of the U.S. Tax Court cited earlier in this chapter. An interesting article that shows the gradual evolution from the basic concepts in Revenue Ruling 59-60 to the regular use of modern valuation methods is "Valuation of Goodwill and Going Concern Value," *Mergers & Acquisitions*, 1979.

The IRS supplemented Revenue Ruling 59-60 with several subsequent rulings. They include Revenue Ruling 65-192, 1965-2 C.B. 27; Revenue Ruling 1965-193, 1965-2 C.B. 370; Revenue Ruling 68-609, 1968-2 C.B. 237; Revenue Ruling 77-287, 1977-2 C.B. 319; Revenue Ruling 80-213, 1980-2 C.B. 101; Revenue Ruling 83-120, 1983-2 C.B. 120; and Revenue Ruling 93-12, 1993-1 C.B. 202.

The most important of the subsequent rulings are Revenue Ruling 77-287, discussing the relevance of studies of sales of restricted stock in determining discounts for lack of marketability; Revenue Ruling 83-120, discussing valuation of preferred stock; and Revenue Ruling 93-12, recognizing that minority interest discounts may be appropriate even for gifts of stock by members of a family that controls a closely held corporation.

The modern procedures used by the IRS are shown in the *IRS Valuation Training for Appeals Officers Coursebook*, Commerce Clearing House, 1998. It is noteworthy that the IRS's *Valuation Coursebook* regularly cites the methods described in *Valuation of a Business*, Pratt et al., Irwin Professional Publishers, 1989. However, the principle that the IRS is generally willing to recognize modern, sound valuation principles seems to be established.

R. The U.S. Department of Labor and Valuation

Section 3(18) of the Employee Retirement Income Security Act (ERISA), 29 U.S.C. § 1002(18), requires that the trust under an employee stock ownership plan (ESOP) receive "adequate consideration" when it acquires employers' securities. The U.S. Department of Labor (DOL) proposed regulations prescribing valuation methods to be used in determining "adequate consideration" under ERISA, but later withdrew the proposal. (See 53 Fed. Reg. 17632 (May 17, 1988) and 60 Fed. Reg. 23559 (May 8, 1995).) Further information on the use of ESOPs to finance acquisitions is provided in Chapter 15.

S. Fairness Opinions

As described in Chapter 12, directors, officers and controlling shareholders who direct the management of a corporation have fiduciary obligations to the corporation and its minority shareholders. In general, they can fulfill their obligations by using good faith or reasonable business judgment in managing the corporate business. However, if they elect to engage in transactions with the corporation or its minority shareholders in which they have a self-interest, they must meet a stricter, "entire fairness" standards. Examples of such transactions are management buyouts and "going-private" transactions. Further, management's response to tender offers and other unsolicited acquisition offers may be subjected to enhanced scrutiny that effectively requires them to meet an "entire fairness" standard. In addition, even under the "business judgment" standard, management has some risk of liability if it fails to obtain the advice of a valuation professional before making commitments to the price and terms of an acquisition.

Management's need to demonstrate that acquisition prices and terms are entirely fair led to the regular hiring of valuation professionals to prepare fairness opinions for management in buyouts, "going-private" transactions, tender offers and any other transactions in which class action lawyers can commence class actions on behalf of plaintiffs with nominal shareholdings.[6] The possible need for management to defend themselves against class action allegations of failure to use good faith or reasonable business judgment also led to the widespread use of fairness opinions.

When managements began to hire valuation professionals to prepare fairness opinions, some thought the objective was to select a professional who would furnish financial justification to reject offers unwanted by management and to support offers favored by management. Some valuation professionals saw the assignment in the same way and even combined preparation of a fairness opinion with tender offer defense work. When their fairness opinions were challenged in court, however, these firms suffered from lack of the credibility that comes with independence. For example, federal courts gave little weight to a fairness opinion finding inadequate a hostile offer by Dynamics Corp. written by Smith Barney & Co. for CTS Corporation. The trial court found that Smith Barney had furnished to CTS an unsolicited offer preparation program containing "poison pill" devices, was entitled to a $75,000 incentive fee if CTS prevailed in a proxy contest, and was entitled to large fees for arranging a merger with a "white knight" bidder. The appellate court commented that Smith Barney would not receive its fees if it found that Dynamics Corporation's offer was fair. In another case, the Delaware Chancery Court described as highly debatable a fairness opinion on a hostile offer by City Capital Associates written for Interco, Inc. by Wasserstein Perrella & Co., Inc. after finding that "Wasserella" had prepared an alternative plan for restructuring Interco, for which Wasserella would have received substantial compensation if successful.

Management whose own fairness or business judgment may be questioned should not obtain a fairness opinion from a valuation professional who lacks independence. That does not mean that management should not consult with its regular investment banker or other financial advisors on the price and terms involved in acquisitions, including unwanted offers, alternative offers and restructuring plans. Indeed, their advice is much needed and valuable. However, a fairness opinion is a separate matter that has little value if the preparer lacks independence.

Preparation of a fairness opinion should begin with a thorough due diligence review. While the objectives of a valuation analyst differ to some ex-

[6]Law firms specializing in class actions receive very large fees from these lawsuits, which have been filed within hours, and even minutes, after an acquisition is publicly announced. After filing the lawsuit, a law firm gains the right to represent the class of shareholders by mailing complex "negative option" letters approved by the courts. All shareholders who do not "opt out" by replying within a specified time period are represented by the law firm and bound by the results of the lawsuit. The amounts received by individual shareholders in these lawsuits are sometimes quite small but the legal fees are very large. On December 22, 1995, Congress adopted the Private Securities Litigation Reform Act of 1995 (P.L. 104-67), restricting some abusive practices in securities litigation, including class actions in that field.

tent from those of management investigating a potential acquisition candidate, the materials in Chapter 5 show the methods used in conducting due diligence reviews and the information to be reviewed. Valuation professionals will also find helpful the materials in Chapters 4 to 7 of *Valuing a Business* (Pratt, et al., Irwin Publishing Company, 1996), on gathering company data, site visits and interviews, researching economic and industry information and analyzing and adjusting financial statements.

Except in an emergency, a fairness opinion should not be limited by a need for hasty work (*Weinberger v. UOP, Inc.*, 457 A.2d 701 (Del. 1983)). Directors and officers must devote the necessary time and effort to review and become reasonably familiar with the basis for the fairness opinion, or they will not be entitled to rely on it (*Hanson Trust PLC v. ML SCM Acquisition, Inc.*, 781 F.2d 264 (2d Cir. 1986)). They should not underestimate the task because it requires reasonable familiarity with valuation methods and may include comparison of the "blended values" of competing offers (*Gelco Corp. v. Coniston Partners*, 652 F. Supp. 829 (D. Minn. 1986), *affirmed in part, vacated in part*, 811 F.2d 414 (8th Cir. 1987)).

Among the most difficult aspects of the valuation involved in a fairness opinion is the extent to which potential restructuring should be considered. In routine valuations, value reflecting changes in the business or financial structure will seldom arise unless management is planning the changes and demonstrates their feasibility. When preparing a fairness opinion, the valuation professional may find that persons opposed to management claim that changes in the business and financial structure should be made and that management disagrees entirely or partially. The valuation professional must face these issues squarely, decide whether and how they affect the fairness opinion and be prepared to respond to searching questions that may be asked if the fairness opinion is challenged in court. Indeed, the valuation professional may be named as a defendant.

Valuation professionals who prepare fairness opinions should assume that they may be challenged in court. They should also assume that counsel and experts for the opposition will have obtained and scrutinized their work papers and may challenge any or all of the data, assumptions and conclusions. When the challenge is made, the opposition will have the benefit of hindsight. For example, a valuation professional who wrote an opinion concluding that the price of a management buyout of Nutri/System, Inc. was fair was later named as a defendant in a lawsuit alleging that the proxy statement in which the fairness opinion was used was materially false and misleading. The plaintiff attorneys challenged numerous aspects of the fairness opinion, but the valuation professional was upheld on all points by the trial judge or the jury. On appeal, the court of appeals (in a two to one decision) upheld the district court on all except one point. The court of appeals granted a new trial in which a jury, rather than the trial judge, would decide whether use of a 46 percent income tax rate in preparing DFCF projections was correct (*Herskowitz v. Nutri/System, Inc.*, 857 F.2d 179 (3d Cir. 1988)).[7]

---

[7]The author's firm represented Nutri/System, Inc. and several management defendants in the lawsuit.

T. Solvency Letters

Solvency letters are provided to lenders financing a leveraged buyout transaction to assist them in determining that the borrower is solvent, has reasonably adequate capital and is able to meet its debts as they mature at the time when the transaction is consummated. Otherwise, the transaction may be a fraudulent conveyance (transfer) and creditors of the acquired corporation, or a trustee in bankruptcy, can seek to set it aside.

A solvency letter is not a valuation of the business acquired. However, the preparation of a solvency letter requires some of the same steps required to perform a DFCF valuation. To determine whether a corporation is solvent, the preparer must determine that the "present fair salable value" or the "fair value" of its assets exceed its liabilities. The courts have disagreed on the question of whether "present fair salable value" or "fair value" means orderly liquidation or "going-business" value.

To determine that a corporation has reasonably adequate capital and is able to meet its debts as they mature, the preparer must perform cash flow projections in a manner similar to those prepared for DFCF analysis. Further information on solvency letters is provided in Chapter 14.

U. Reference Materials

Books:

Business Valuation Review, American Society of Appraisers

Corporate Valuation, Cornell, Irwin Professional Publishing, 1993

Employee Stock Ownership Plans, Smiley and Gilbert, Maxwell McMillan, 1990 and annual updates

Financial Valuation: Business and Business Interests, Zukin, Maxwell McMillan, 1990 and annual updates

IRS Valuation Training for Appeals Officers Coursebook, Commerce Clearing House, January 1998

Mergers & Acquisitions, A Valuation Handbook, Marren, Irwin Professional Publishing, 1993

Valuing a Business, 3rd ed., Pratt et al., Irwin Professional Publishing, 1995

Valuing ESOP Shares, The ESOP Association, 1994

Articles:

"Confusing flows the cash flow," Lunzer, *Forbes*, April 2, 1986

"The Debt-Free DCF Model: A Fix on Intrinsic Values," Bielinski, *Mergers & Acquisitions*, 1989

"How to Capture Equity Value in Pricing a Target," Bielinski, *Mergers & Acquisitions*, 1991

"How to Sort Out the Premium Drivers of Post-Deal Value," Bielinski, *Mergers & Acquisitions*, 1993

"Managing as if Tomorrow Mattered," Hayes and Garvin, *Harvard Business Review*, 1982

"Putting a Realistic Dollar Value on Acquisition Synergies," Bielinski, *Mergers & Acquisitions*, 1992

"A Real-World Focus in Calculating Terminal Values" Barnes, *Mergers & Acquisitions*, Jul–Aug 1996

"Scenario Planning to Help Buyers in Dynamic Industries," McGillivray, *Mergers & Acquisitions*, 1995

"Strategic Analysis for More Profitable Acquisitions," Rappaport, *Harvard Business Review*, 1979

"The Valuation Process and Trends Affecting Valuations," Dolan, *The New Era of Investment Banking*, Probus Publishing, 1993

"Valuing the Closely Held Business," Faris *et al.*, *Mergers & Acquisitions*, 1993

"Why Acquirers May Need to Rethink Terminal Values," Morris, *Mergers & Acquisitions*, 1994

"The Comparable Company Approach," Bielinski, *Corporate Cash Flow Magazine*, Oct 1990

Standards:

Standards for Business Valuation, American Society of Appraisers

Uniform Standards of Professional Appraisal Practice, The Appraisal Foundation

V. Exhibits

4-1 USPAP Statement SMT-2 on Discounted Cash Flow Analysis

4-2 Example of a Fairness Opinion

STATEMENT ON APPRAISAL STANDARDS NO. 2 (SMT-2)

SUBJECT: Discounted Cash Flow Analysis

THE ISSUE:

Discounted cash flow (DCF) analysis is an accepted analytical tool and method of valuation within the income capitalization approach to value. DCF is not a new method, but it did not enjoy widespread use until modern computer technology enabled appraisers to automate the process. Because DCF analysis is profit oriented and dependent upon the analysis of uncertain future events, it is vulnerable to misuse. What steps can the appraiser take to avoid misuse of DCF analysis?

THE STATEMENT:

The acceptance of DCF analysis as a method of valuation began in the institutional real estate market and has spread to investment real estate in the general real estate market. DCF techniques may be applied in the valuation or analysis of proposed construction; land development; condominium development or conversion; rehabilitation development; and income-producing real estate of various types. DCF analysis is becoming a requirement of advisors, asset managers, fiduciaries, portfolio managers, syndicators, underwriters and others dealing in investment grade real estate. These users of appraisal services favor the inclusion of DCF analysis as a management tool in projecting cash flow and return expectations, capital requirements, refinancing opportunities and timing of future property dispositions. DCF analysis is regarded as one of the best methods of replicating steps taken to reach investor buy/sell/hold decisions, and is often a part of the exercise of due diligence in the evaluation of an investment.

DCF methodology is based on the principle of anticipation, i.e., value is created by the anticipation of future benefits. DCF analysis reflects investment criteria and requires the appraiser to make empirical and subjective assumptions. DCF analysis can be used for investment value and market value appraisals, as well as for other purposes such as sensitivity tests.

DCF analysis is an additional tool available to the appraiser and is best applied to value estimates in the context of one or more other approaches. This statement focuses on the criteria for proper DCF analysis and does not imply that DCF analysis is or should be the only method employed.

To avoid misuse or misunderstanding when DCF analysis is used in an appraisal assignment to estimate market value, it is the responsibility of the appraiser to ensure that the controlling input is consistent with market evidence and prevailing market attitudes. Market value DCF analyses should be supported by market derived data, and the assumptions should be both market and property specific. Market value DCF analyses are intended to reflect the expectations and perceptions of market participants along with available factual data. They should be judged on the market support for the forecasts when made, not whether specific items in the forecasts are realized. An appraisal report which includes the results of DCF analysis must clearly state the assumptions on which the analysis is based and must set forth the relevant data used in the analysis.

Standards Rule 1-1(b) states that the appraiser must not commit a substantial error of omission or commission that significantly affects the appraisal. Standards Rule 1-1(c) states that the appraiser must not render appraisal services in a careless or negligent manner, such as a series of errors that, considered individually, may not significantly affect the results of an appraisal but which, when considered in the aggregate would be misleading. These two rules are significant for DCF analysis because of the potential for the compounding effect of errors in the input, unrealistic assumptions, and programming errors.

Computer printouts showing the results of DCF analysis may be generated by commercial software or by software prepared by the appraiser. Either way, the appraiser is responsible for the entire analysis including the controlling input, the calculations, and the resulting output. The appraiser should cite the name and version of the software and provide a brief description of the methods and assumptions inherent in the software. Standards Rule 1-4(h) requires realistic forecasts in the appraisal of proposed improvements and development projects. Standards Rule 1-4(c) requires that estimates of anticipated future rent and expenses be based on reasonably clear and appropriate evidence. The explanatory comment to this rule makes specific reference to cash flow projections, the essence of DCF analysis.

SMT-2: Discounted Cash Flow Analysis (continued)

DCF accounts for and reflects those items and forces that affect the revenue, expenses and ultimate earning capacity of real estate and represents a forecast of events that would be considered likely within a specific market. For example, in the appraisal of a multi-tenant property, a lease-by-lease analysis addresses contract and market rents, specific escalations, operating expenses, pass-through provisions, market derived or specific concessions, capital expenditures, and any other measurable specific provisions applicable. Revenue growth rate or decline rate assumptions are premised upon analysis of supply/demand factors and other economic conditions and trends within the market area of the subject. Operating expense change rates should reflect both overall expense trends and the specific trend of significant expense items.

Discount rates applied to cash flows and estimates of reversion should be derived from data and information in the real estate and capital markets. Surveys of investor opinion and yield indices are also useful in the rate selection process, but only when the type of and market for the real estate being appraised is consistent with the type of and market for the real estate typically acquired by the investors interviewed in the survey. Considerations used in the selection of rates are risk, inflation, and real rates of return.

When reversion capitalization rates are used, they should reflect investor expectations considering the real estate type, age and condition, cash flow characteristics, and related factors. The projection period is a variable and should be set on the basis of the facts and circumstances of each analysis.

The results of DCF analysis should be tested and checked for errors and reasonableness. Because of the compounding effects in the projection of income and expenses, even slight input errors can be magnified and can produce unreasonable results. As examples, it is good practice to test whether cash flows are changing at reasonable rates, and to compare the reversion capitalization rate with the inferred entrance capitalization rate to see if the relationship between these rates is reasonable and explainable.

STANDARD 2 requires the appraiser to communicate each analysis, opinion and conclusion in a manner that is not misleading. Appraisals using the DCF method in the income capitalization approach may contain computerized projections of itemized future cash flow supported by exhaustive printouts that can be misleading. The seeming precision of computer generated projections may give the appearance of certainty to projections that are actually variable within a wide range. In DCF analysis, all of the assumptions (growth rates, decline rates, rental rates, discount rates, financing terms, expense trends, capitalization rates, etc.) directly affect the conclusion and must be clearly and accurately disclosed in the appraisal report.

Conclusions

— DCF analysis is an additional tool available to the appraiser and is best applied to value estimates in the context of one or more other approaches.

— It is the responsibility of the appraiser to ensure that the controlling input is consistent with market evidence and prevailing market attitudes.

— Market value DCF analyses should be supported by market derived data, and the assumptions should be both market and property specific.

— The appraiser should cite the name and version of the software and provide a brief description of the methods and assumptions inherent in the software.

— DCF accounts for and reflects those items and forces that affect the revenue, expenses and ultimate earning capacity of real estate and represents a forecast of events that would be considered likely within a specific market.

— The results of DCF analysis should be tested and checked for errors and reasonableness.

— Standards Rule 1-1(b) states that the appraiser must not commit a substantial error of omission or commission that significantly affects the appraisal.

SMT-2: Discounted Cash Flow Analysis (continued)

Adopted unanimously on July 8, 1991.

Appraisal Standards Board

John J. Leary, Chair
Sherwood Darington, Vice Chair
Charles B. Akerson
Daniel A. Dinote, Jr.
John L. Gadd

JAMES D. WOLFENSOHN
INCORPORATED

425 PARK AVENUE
NEW YORK, NEW YORK 10022
PHONE: (212) 909-8100
TELEX: 661830

May 22, 1986

Board of Directors
R. H. Macy & Co., Inc.
151 West 34th Street
New York, New York 10001

Members of the Board:

You have requested our opinion as investment bankers as to the fairness, from a financial point of view, of the consideration to be received by holders of the common shares, par value $.25 per share ("Common Shares"), of R. H. Macy & Co., Inc. ("Macy"), other than Macy Acquiring Corp. ("Acquiring Corp."), its subsidiaries and those shareholders of Macy who will be securityholders of Acquiring Corp., in connection with the proposed merger (the "Proposed Merger") of Macy Merger Corp. ("Merger Corp."), a subsidiary of Acquiring Corp., with and into Macy.

As more specifically set forth in the Agreement and Plan of Merger, dated as of January 15, 1986, by and among Acquiring Corp., Merger Corp. and Macy (the "Merger Agreement"), in the Proposed Merger each Common Share, other than treasury shares, shares held directly or indirectly by Acquiring Corp. and "Dissenting Shares" (as defined in the Merger Agreement), will be converted into the right to receive $68 in cash.

In arriving at our opinion as expressed herein, we have considered such financial and other factors as we have deemed appropriate and feasible in the circumstances, including, among others, the following: (i) the Proxy Statement being mailed to the shareholders of Macy in connection with the Proposed Merger; (ii) the Merger Agreement; (iii) Macy's Annual Reports to Shareholders for the five fiscal years ended August 3, 1985, and Macy's Quarterly Reports on Form 10-Q for the fiscal quarters ended November 2, 1985 and February 1, 1986; (iv) the current and historical financial position and results of operations of Macy; (v) the current and historical trading markets for the Common Shares and for the equity securities of certain other companies engaged in businesses that we believe to be comparable to the business of Macy; (vi) certain internal information (including forecasts and projections) relating to Macy and the industry segments in which it operates provided to us by the management of Macy; (vii) certain publicly available information concerning certain other companies engaged in businesses that we believe to be comparable to the business of Macy; and (viii) the terms and conditions of certain other business combinations that we believe to be relevant. We have also had discussions with management personnel of Macy with respect to the foregoing. We have also solicited proposals for the acquisition of Macy from prospective purchasers other than Acquiring Corp.

In arriving at our opinion, we have not conducted a physical inspection of the properties and facilities of Macy nor have we made or obtained any independent evaluation or appraisal of such properties and facilities. We have assumed the accuracy and completeness of, and have not independently verified, the financial and other information provided to us by Macy or otherwise available from public sources. We have also taken into account our assessment of general economic, market and financial conditions and our experience in business, asset and securities evaluations. Our opinion necessarily is based upon conditions as they exist and can be evaluated on the date hereof.

Based upon and subject to the foregoing, it is our opinion as investment bankers that the consideration to be received in the Proposed Merger by holders of the Common Shares of Macy (other than Acquiring Corp., its subsidiaries and those who will be securityholders of Acquiring Corp.) is fair, from a financial point of view, to such holders.

Very truly yours,

JAMES D. WOLFENSOHN INCORPORATED

Chapter 5

BUSINESS INVESTIGATION ("DUE DILIGENCE") REVIEWS

A. INTRODUCTION

A "due diligence" review is an investigation by a buyer of a business to be acquired. The review is important to verify the acquisition decision and also to negotiate the price and terms of the transaction. The review is also important to prepare for implementation of the acquisition and successful operation after the closing.

This chapter focuses primarily on the buyer's "due diligence" review. However, if the buyer plans to pay all or part of the price with debt or stock, the seller should perform a "due diligence" review of the buyer that includes some or all elements of a buyer's review.

B. PRECONDITIONS TO A "DUE DILIGENCE" REVIEW

Before a "due diligence" review is performed, both the seller and the buyer should be satisfied that the other is serious and capable of performing the proposed acquisition. No seller should undertake the risk and cost of a "due diligence" review without checking the credibility and feasibility of the buyer's proposal. Similarly, no buyer should undertake the cost of a "due diligence" review without assurance that the seller is willing and able to sell.

As described in Chapter 16, the negotiation and signing of a letter of intent is usually the formal step evidencing that the seller and buyer are ready to go forward and have reached a mutual understanding on the price and other major terms. However, even before a letter of intent is signed, several key points should be checked, formally or informally.

A seller should be satisfied about the following points:

- The buyer's reputation, not only for basic business integrity but also for other factors such as fairness in negotiations.
- The authority of the buyer's representatives. A seller can make a serious error by going far into an acquisition with middle-level buyer management before knowing whether senior executives of the buyer and its board of directors support the acquisition.
- The buyer's sources of funds and their likely availability.
- The government, lender and other approvals that the buyer must obtain for the acquisition and their likely availability.

- The buyer's objectives for the acquisition. If the buyer plans to liquidate the business or terminate significant numbers of employees, many sellers would prefer to find a buyer with affirmative plans for the business.
- The buyer is not merely shopping or gathering industrial intelligence.

A buyer should be satisfied about the following points:

- The seller's reputation for business integrity and fairness in negotiations.
- The authority of the seller's representatives. A buyer should not take it for granted that even senior management of a seller will have the support of the board of directors and shareholders.
- The government, lender and other approvals that the seller must obtain and their likely availability.
- The seller's objectives for the acquisition are realistic. For example, if the seller's management is seeking semi-autonomous status and support for growth when the buyer believes the business must be retrenched and contracted, the seller's management may learn the buyer's plans during later negotiations and withdraw from the transaction after considerable expense has been incurred.
- The seller is not simply "testing the market" or is likely to suffer "seller's remorse."

C. Responding to Seller Reluctance

Sellers are understandably cautious about "due diligence" reviews, even when they are willing to sell. One reason for caution is the need to protect the intellectual properties of the business. Another is that the review activities might result in premature disclosure of the acquisition transaction to customers, suppliers, employees and others. Still another is concern that the investigation will be costly, time-consuming or perhaps poorly performed. Finally, the seller may fear that the buyer will find unfavorable information.

Some sellers attempt to refuse or severely limit the scope of the buyer's "due diligence" review. When this happens, the buyer should respond to legitimate concerns of the seller, but should remain firm that the review will be performed. The buyer should sign a confidentiality agreement to assure the seller about protection of its intellectual properties. The confidentiality agreement can also contain provisions prohibiting premature disclosure and contacts with customers, suppliers and employees until arranged with mutual consent. A form of Confidentiality Agreement appears as Exhibit 5-1.

The buyer can furnish an outline and time schedule for the review and the identities and experience of the review team members in order to show that the review will be performed capably and efficiently. The buyer can also arrange to conduct the review in an unobtrusive manner so that employee morale will not be affected. For example, buyer visits to offices or plants can be handled by selected seller employees who are aware of the proposed acquisition. The visits can also be scheduled for evenings or weekends if necessary.

The buyer cannot, of course, assure the seller that the review will not reveal adverse information. That is one of the objectives of the review. However, the buyer can assure the seller that the review will be conducted courteously, efficiently and in a balanced manner. The buyer can explain that the review team has been instructed to look for both strengths and weaknesses. The buyer can also arrange for the team members to review the factual sections of their reports with seller personnel to minimize possible misinformation or misunderstanding. Most important, the buyer can emphasize that it is best to identify potential problems so that they can be resolved during negotiation of the acquisition contract.

Sellers should recognize that they can also benefit from the buyer's "due diligence" review. The review is an opportunity to reinforce the buyer's acquisition decision and to demonstrate that a favorable price and other terms are justified. The review is also an opportunity for seller and buyer personnel to meet and explore future working relationships. Seller personnel who demonstrate competence during a "due diligence" review improve their opportunity for responsible roles after the acquisition. The review is also an important opportunity to acquaint buyer personnel with problems of the business and how they can be managed or corrected. The problems can then be evaluated and adjustments can be made, if necessary, in the acquisition contract. These adjustments are usually much easier to negotiate than claims made by buyers who discover problems after the acquisition. Thus, the seller benefits from the "due diligence" review by reducing the potential for future claims.

Seller personnel will have the opportunity to observe how the buyer's representatives behave during the review and negotiations. If these observations reveal that there is a serious mismatch, the seller may wish to reconsider the sale to the buyer. For example, if the seller's personnel observe that the buyer's personnel are inexperienced and have an unrealistic business plan for the acquisition, the seller may reevaluate any buyer offer to pay with debt or stock. If buyer personnel are autocratic or bureaucratic, a seller whose personnel have achieved success through freedom to innovate may decide that the two organizations cannot work together. If it becomes apparent that the buyer is planning major changes in the business, a seller who feels moral obligations to employees, customers and suppliers who helped to build the business may decide not to sell to such a buyer. As Ted Stolberg of Stolberg Partners said: "Some owners just won't sell their pride and joy or friendships to some stranger who could turn out to be Attila the Hun."[1]

D. The Review Team

A "due diligence" review is usually performed by a team of people whose experience qualifies them to investigate one or more elements of the business to be acquired. The size and membership of the team should vary with the size and complexity of the business to be acquired.

[1]"Divesting in the 1990's, "Greco, *CFO*, Sep 1994.

There are several different viewpoints about who should lead the "due diligence" review and the methods to be used. Some investment bankers and some M&A departments of accounting firms offer "due diligence" reviews in their literature and some clients assume that their work fulfills the entire need for "due diligence" investigation. Needless to say, investment bankers and accounting firms work with skill and diligence in their own fields, but they cannot evaluate sales and marketing programs, manufacturing processes and equipment, research and development programs, insurance coverage and many other business elements. All too often, acquisitions are investigated and negotiated by a small team of senior executives, legal and financial managers and outside advisers. Thus, the buyer's experienced operating personnel only become involved after the closing when it is too late to identify developing business problems and opportunities and other issues that should have been evaluated and negotiated.

The author recommends that buyer management personnel lead and actively participate in the "due diligence" review. They should retain the experience and skills of outside firms as needed to supplement their own experience and skills. The buyer must operate the acquired business and live with the results after the acquisition and hired professionals can only occasionally help them as the years go by. Thus, the buyer's managers should, as much as possible, see the business at first hand. Some authors warn that internal managers may lack the experience and time to make an effective review. However, if internal managers cannot lead an effective investigation and evaluation with the help of experienced outside advisers, there is a serious question whether the buyer should be making the acquisition.

When hiring outside advisers to participate in a "due diligence" review, it is important to discuss the scope of their work with them. Most investment banking firms, accounting firms, law firms, environmental engineering firms and other advisers have developed checklists and procedures that they follow unless there are reasons to modify them. These checklists and procedures are valuable because they typically contain some items that buyer personnel might overlook. On the other hand, the checklists are usually lengthy and the professionals often overlap each other and duplicate tasks assigned to the buyer's own personnel. Buyer's management should outline for each of the outside advisers the work requested from them. If the work is less than the adviser customarily performs, the buyer or the adviser should confirm by letter the limited scope of the work assigned.

Helpful articles discussing due diligence reviews include "Putting the Right People on In-House M&A Teams," Bentley, *Mergers & Acquisitions*, May-Jun 1996, and "Meet the New M&A Masters," Barr, *CFO*, Jun 1996.

E. Preparing for the Review

Field trips to the seller's offices and plants and to important customers and suppliers are essential to effective "due diligence" reviews. However, team members should obtain and review as much publicly available information as possible before the field trips. Having absorbed this information, the team members will be able to investigate more effectively and to save scarce time during the field trips. Their knowledge will also make a good impression on managers and employees of the business being reviewed.

If the business to be acquired is all or part of a publicly owned corporation, extensive information can be obtained from the files of the Securities and Exchange Commission (SEC). For relatively modest photocopying charges, the review team can obtain within hours from the SEC's contractor, Disclosure Inc., copies of annual reports on Form 10-K, quarterly reports on Form 10-Q, current reports on Form 8-K, proxy statements for stockholders' meetings, annual reports to shareholders, registration statements for the sale of securities, Forms 3 and 4, Schedules 13D and 13G and the exhibits filed with all of them. The exhibits include copies of the certificate of incorporation, by-laws, securities sold, material loan agreements and indentures, executive employment contracts, employee benefit plans, material acquisition contracts and material business contracts. Documents filed with the SEC contain a wealth of information that took hundreds, and even thousands, of hours of careful preparation. Thus, review and analysis of the documents from the SEC's files can greatly expedite a "due diligence" review.

Some or all members of a "due diligence" team may find that the language, customs or technology of the business under review is unfamiliar. This unfamiliarity can often be remedied by obtaining literature and statistics from industry associations and by reading recent issues of industry publications. For almost all industries, there are also handbooks and encyclopedias that explain terminology.

F. Reviewing a Small Business

A "due diligence" review of a small business takes patience, courtesy and persistence. Small businesses may not have such items as a formal business plan or audited financial statements. The corporate minute book and stock book may have been left with a lawyer who has not been visited for years. Insurance policies may be at the office of an insurance agent who is behind in obtaining their issuance and may also resist delivering them. Leases and government permits may have expired without renewal. Contractual commitments, which the owner does not realize are enforceable, may have been made in exchanges of correspondence with customers, suppliers and employees.

The buyer's representatives should patiently insist that the seller take the necessary steps to put its business, financial and legal records in reasonable order. At times, a seller claims that "paperwork" is unimportant. Such a comment may be a harmless complaint, but it may also be an effort to divert the buyer from identifying a serious problem. The buyer should also keep the burden of taking the corrective actions on the seller in order to maintain an arm's-length relationship.

A practical checklist for review of a small business appears as Exhibit 5-2.

G. Reviewing a Large Business

A "due diligence" review of a large business is a challenging project, but may be easier in many ways than the review of a small business. Large businesses usually have experienced employees and written records in each significant business area. Thus, less time and effort are required to obtain meaningful information.

A detailed checklist for review of a large business appears as Exhibit 5-3.

H. Conducting the Review

Each important function of the seller's business should be reviewed by a team member with working experience and adequate time, resources and motivation to conduct a thorough review. A well-rounded team member may be able to handle more than one important function or even several functions of the seller's business that are not major or complex. However, the team members should not be overloaded or there will be a tendency just to "kick the tires."

After initial preparation, each team member should arrange the necessary field visit or visits. Field visits are essential because there is no substitute for meeting people and seeing facilities, equipment and original records at first hand. In the author's experience, field visits not only produce better information, but also save time and effort. A reviewer who can see a situation at first hand and review the relevant records will soon be able to decide whether a real problem or opportunity exists. The reviewer will also meet more of the seller's personnel who can contribute useful information.

Team members should plan for adequate time during field visits. Time must be allowed to get acquainted with seller personnel so that the work can proceed courteously and cordially. Time must also be allowed for some interruptions so that seller's personnel can handle important aspects of their regular responsibilities that cannot be postponed. There must be also time for meals, usually with seller personnel who often plan a special lunch or dinner during which the reviewer can meet personnel not directly participating in the review but having related responsibilities. There should also be time to visit off-site locations in the area.

During field reviews, a team member should politely and firmly insist on seeing all relevant facilities, meeting the personnel who actually operate them, reviewing original document files and arranging for photocopies of key documents for further review after the field visit. Otherwise, seller managers may provide a verbal overview and a whirlwind tour of facilities, assuming that nothing more is needed. It is best to describe the expected scope and degree of detail at an early point in the review by giving examples of facilities and equipment and records the reviewer wants to see. For example, if a reviewer merely mentions tax returns, the effect is not the same as a specific request to review Forms 1120 with all schedules including Form 5500. For another example, an environmental reviewer should state clearly the need to see the point sources of emissions, the discharge outfalls to rivers and streams and the related permits and monitoring records.

At times, seller personnel may feel that their credibility is being questioned when a reviewer closely inspects facilities and equipment and original document files. Several truthful and diplomatic responses can be given. First, the reviewer should express appreciation for the information provided, but should then explain that it is difficult to absorb a new situation as quickly as it can be explained by someone who has lived with it.

The reviewer can add that his or her report must contain a reasonable amount of detail to be read by other members of buyer's management who want to know that the reviewer personally saw the seller's facilities and equipment and reviewed its records. The reviewer should add that copies of documents will help readers to understand the report.

A reviewer can win the confidence of seller personnel by showing a balanced focus on both strengths and weaknesses identified during the review. When copies of documents are requested, they should be examples that fairly reflect the overall situation, not just the problems. When problems are identified, the reviewer should make it clear that corrective actions being taken will be described in the report. The reviewer can add, if appropriate, that buyer's management wants to know how seller personnel identify and respond to problems.

Finally, the management of the review team should cooperate with the seller by scheduling sensitive visits to major customers, key employees and labor unions for times late in the "due diligence" review so that both the seller and buyer can express confidence about the transaction, explain necessary changes and offer appropriate assurances.

I. Errors Frequently Made during Reviews

Errors frequently made during "due diligence" reviews are as follows:

- Limitation of the review to financial and legal matters.
- Delegation of review for performance solely by outside advisers and consultants.
- Use of the review only to make a "Go" or "No Go" decision on the transaction rather than to obtain information for use in negotiating and planning all aspects of the transaction, including post-transaction integration and operation.
- Appointment of team members who do not have sufficient experience, resources and time or who create a bad impression on seller personnel.
- Failure to arrange for team members to coordinate their work to avoid gaps and duplication and to share their work so that information found by one team member will be known by other members.
- Failure of management to make timely and effective use of information obtained during the review, often because of premature commitments made before the due diligence reports are received.

J. Making Strategic Use of the Review

The key to effective use of a "due diligence" review is to identify problems and opportunities and use the information to plan and negotiate a better acquisition than would be possible without the review. A timely and thorough "due diligence" review often allows a seller and buyer to find a mutually satisfactory solution to problems that could be "deal breakers" if discovered at the last minute or could lead to litigation if discovered after the acquisition is closed.

For example, a review may reveal that an important raw material supply contract cannot be assigned without the supplier's consent. Having identified the need, the seller and buyer can contact the supplier to request the consent. If the supplier decides to renegotiate the contract in return for the consent, the seller and buyer can determine whether to renegotiate and decide which of them will bear any additional costs. In some situations, the seller might agree to continue to purchase the raw materials and resupply them to the purchaser.

For another example, a review may show that the Internal Revenue Service has issued a deficiency assessment notice to the seller after an audit of its income tax return for a recent year, but the seller plans to contest the assessment. When this happens, the seller may agree to indemnify the buyer against loss, liability, cost and expense related to the assessment. However, if the seller's assets also include meritorious tax refund claims or usable tax loss carryforwards, the buyer may agree to assume the risk.

For still another example, a review may identify that an underground storage tank at one of the seller's properties leaked gasoline into the soil and groundwater. When this happens, the seller and buyer can investigate further to determine the extent of the contaminant plume and whether the concentrations of BTEX and MTBE components exceed applicable cleanup guidelines. If a cleanup is necessary, they can develop a cleanup plan and negotiate for its performance and costs, including indemnification arrangements.

K. Acquisition Checklists

Acquisition checklists are useful for team members planning to perform a "due diligence" review. The author recommends that they be adapted for each transaction because no two businesses are the same. The adaptation is especially important if the list will be sent to seller personnel preparing for the review. If the seller is anxious that the review may be lengthy, costly or poorly performed, it is a mistake for buyer representatives to send a lengthy checklist that includes items that are irrelevant to the business being sold.

The author has occasionally worked with buyers who developed questionnaires to be answered by seller personnel. The author recommends against the use of questionnaires for several reasons. Seller personnel tend to react negatively to questionnaires, especially when they arrive before a field visit. Inevitably, some of the questions are not on point and seller personnel become frustrated at the perceived need to answer them in writing. In addition, seller management tends to prepare brief favorable answers to the questions that can become an obstacle during the field visits when seller's operating personnel are reluctant to provide in-depth information that might seem inconsistent with the answers to the questionnaire.

L. Exhibits

5-1 Confidentiality Agreement
5-2 Checklist for Review of a Small Business
5-3 General Checklist for a Due Diligence Review

EXHIBIT 5-1

CONFIDENTIALITY AGREEMENT

Dear ____________________:

We have been engaged in preliminary negotiation of your proposed acquisition of the assets and business of Acme Manufacturing Company ("Acme") as described in a Letter of Intent dated _____, 199__. You have requested authorization to perform a due diligence review of Acme's assets, business and financial condition. In consideration for authorization of the due diligence review, including examination of documents and visits by your employees to Acme's facilities, you agree as follows:

1. You will treat all information received from Acme as confidential proprietary trade secret information of Acme and will neither disclose such information to any third party nor use such information for any purpose other than evaluation of its proposed acquisition.

2. Your obligations in paragraph 1 do not apply to any information you can show (1) was known by you before it was received from Acme; (2) was when received or is in the public domain other than as a result of a disclosure for which you are responsible; (3) was obtained by you from a third party lawfully entitled to provide the information to you free of obligations to Acme; or (4) was developed in your organization by personnel who did not have access to Acme's information.

3. You agree to restrict access to Acme's information within your organization to employees who need to know and who have signed an Employee Confidentiality Agreement in the form attached as *Annex A* hereto. You agree to furnish copies of each signed Employee Confidentiality Agreement to us. You agree to enforce the Employee Confidentiality Agreements so as to protect our information.

4. When you receive documents from us containing information marked as confidential, you agree to notify us promptly if the information was already known by you or generally available to the public and to furnish information showing your prior knowledge or the sources where the information is generally available to the public.

5. If you do not acquire Acme on or before _______, 199____, you agree to discontinue all use of Acme's information and to return all written information promptly to us without retaining any copies.

6. This Agreement shall continue in effect for a period of ______ years after completion of the due diligence review.

Please indicate your agreement by signing and returning a copy of this Agreement.

Very truly yours,

AGREED:

____
Company Name

ACME MANUFACTURING COMPANY

By ____________________
Signature and Title

By ____________________

____
Date

____
Date

EXHIBIT 5-1 (CONT.)

EMPLOYEE CONFIDENTIALITY AGREEMENT

Gentlemen:

Annex A

As an employee of Acme Manufacturing Company ("Acme") selected to participate in its due diligence review of your business, I agree *individually* to the obligations stated in the attached Confidentiality Agreement. I agree that my obligations shall continue in effect for the time provided in the Confidentiality Agreement even if I should cease to be employed by Acme.

____
Signature of Employee

____
Printed Name of Employee

____
Name of Company

____
Date

EXHIBIT 5-2

Checklist for Review of a Small Business

Small businesses do not generally prepare or retain extensive records and those they have are usually informal. They retain lawyers, accountants and other professionals only occasionally and for minimal services. Yet, they may be very sound and successful. The following checklist includes items that a small business may have or be able to obtain.

- Business plan, formal or informal.
- Extent of dependency of the business on the present owners and managers and their plans for the future.
- Financial statements and accountants' reports. While small businesses do not always ask accountants to audit their financial statements, they may hire accountants to provide a review or to help with a compilation.
- Federal and state tax returns and information about any audits of the returns by the Internal Revenue Service and state tax authorities. Even the smallest businesses must prepare and file tax returns. They usually hire an accountant to prepare them. For some businesses, tax returns may be the only comprehensive and consistent record of financial results and financial condition.
- Organization papers. For a corporation, the certificate of incorporation, by-laws, minute book and stock book should be reviewed, even if they have not been maintained in good order. Any shareholders' agreements should also be reviewed including those contained in letters and other informal documents. For a partnership, any formal agreement or correspondence about ownership and management.
- Governmental permits and licenses to operate the business and any registrations of the business and its products.
- Product specifications and quality control methods.
- Physical condition and operating efficiency of facilities and equipment.
- Property and liability insurance coverage and claims history.
- List of existing and potential competitors, direct and indirect.
- Franchise or dealership agreements; valuable memberships in an industry organization such as a stock exchange or the NASD; product certifications by a testing organization such as Underwriters Laboratories; approved supplier status with significant customers.
- A list of employees and job descriptions.
- Employment agreements, formal or informal.
- Workers compensation, health insurance and any other employee benefits and claims history.
- Loan agreements.
- Purchase agreements and purchase orders with suppliers including credit terms.
- Customer agreements and sales orders including credit terms.
- Leases of real property and equipment.
- Deeds, title policies and mortgages or security agreements for owned real property and equipment.
- Lawsuits or any other serious claims or disputes not covered by insurance.
- Any indications of unlawful or risk-oriented conduct such as employment discrimination, failure to pay withholding or income taxes, sale of defective products or deceptive sales tactics.
- Any indications of environmental or health problems.

Exhibit 5-3

General Checklist for a Due Diligence Review

I. General Information

A. Corporations with Publicly Traded Shares

- 10-K, 10Q and 8-K reports, annual reports to shareholders, proxy statements, registration statements, Forms 3 and 4, Schedules 13D and 13G, other SEC filings and exhibits filed with all of them. **Note:** It is usually necessary to request selected filings over a period of years to obtain all exhibits including the certificate of incorporation, shareholder agreements, loan agreements, employee benefits plans, material contracts and other documents.
- Recent stock trading history. Identify prices and volumes if traded on a stock exchange or NASDAQ market. Identify market makers if the shares are traded in the NASDAQ market, Electronic Bulletin Board or "Pink Sheets."
- Research reports by investment firms on the seller and its industry and competitors.

B. Closely Held Corporations

- Ownership and shareholder agreements.
- Subsidiaries, affiliates and unincorporated divisions.
- Management.
- Descriptions and locations of all businesses and properties.
- Business plans.

C. Both Publicly Traded and Closely Held Corporations

- Professional relationships including accounting firm, law firm, bank, actuarial firm, technical consultants and investment banking firm, if applicable. Who are the officers, partners and other personnel at these firms maintaining the relationship?

II. Management Information

- Resumes and position descriptions of management. **Note**: If these items do not exist or are not current, request that they be prepared with a focus on functional responsibilities and reporting relationships, direct and advisory.
- Relationships between officers and the board of directors and its committees.
- Relationships between management (directors and officers) and controlling shareholders including founders.
- Shareholders' agreements and other corporate control devices.
- Employment contracts and management perquisites.
- Management information systems.
- Recent and anticipated management changes.
- Management methods and attitudes including delegation of authority, decision -making processes and participation in decisions; orientation toward risk, and supervisory systems and accountability.
- Key middle- and junior-level employees and their potential.
- Compensation amounts and systems as compared to similar businesses and their effectiveness in achieving performance and objectives.
- Any serious internal management disputes.
- Any transactions between the corporation and its management and shareholders, whether or not disclosed and authorized.
- Evidence of understaffing or overstaffing.
- Any dependency on outside consultants or others to perform responsibilities usually performed internally.

III. Financial iInformation

- Consolidated financial statements and audit reports of accounting firm.
- Consolidating financial statements and accountants' work papers.
- Management letters from accounting firm on internal financial controls.
- Internal financial statements (monthly) for operating units.
- Operating budgets and modifications.
- Capital budgets including recent proposals and modifications.
- Cash flow projections and debt repayment schedule.
- Cash and bank accounts.

EXHIBIT 5-3 (CONT.)

- Short-term investments.
- Inventories (raw materials, work-in-process and finished goods) and their age and quality.
- Receivables and their age and collectibility.
- Prepaid expenses.
- Property accounts including off-balance sheet assets and depreciation and amortization deductions.
- Goodwill including history of the related businesses and write-off policies.
- Accounts payable and supplier credit terms.
- Deferred liabilities.
- Loan agreements and lines of credit including any recent payment or covenant defaults.
- Debt and equity securities and their financial characteristics including senior debt, subordinated debt, preferred stock and common stock. **Note:** Debt collateral and convertible securities, options and warrants should be identified as well as any innovative securities.
- Off-balance sheet, noncontingent liabilities such as operating leases.
- Contingent liabilities including guarantees, contractual indemnities, purchase and other contractual obligations, claims and lawsuits, gaps in insurance coverage, environmental compliance obligations and obligations for employee pension, profit sharing, stock option or purchase, medical, life, disability, vacation and severance benefits.
- Federal, state and local income tax returns and status of audits and open unaudited returns for recent years.
- Tax audit reports and any deficiency assessments and any refunds claimed or allowed.
- Asset appraisals.
- Payroll taxes and sales, use, property and other excise taxes.
- Tax incentives.
- Potential tax opportunities or problems such as loss carryforwards and assets that will support a stepped-up basis or aggressive positions on income recognition or deductions that may be challenged.
- Reports analyzing financial performance including trends, internal rate of return, return on investment, return on assets, gross operating margins, backlogs, inventory turnover and other operating ratios and break-even points.
- Qualifications and performance of financial personnel.
- Financial facilities and equipment (condition, performance and cost).

IV. Marketing and Sales

- Product lines: gross sales and profits.
- Product lines: domestic, export and foreign sales.
- Product lines: market shares by nation and region.
- Product lines: backlog, inventory turnover and other ratios.
- Product lines: sales forecasts, market trends and strategies.
- Product lines: analysis of vertical integration through production of components and raw materials and horizontal integration through production of complementary products.
- Service lines: data and analysis corresponding to product lines.
- Major customers: volume and profitability; customer contracts and purchase orders; discounts; consignment sales; etc.
- Marketing and sales staff and structure.
- Order processing system and coordination with manufacturing.
- Distributors and agents and their relation to the internal marketing and sales staff including the extent of dependency on distributors and agents.
- Market surveys prepared internally or by outside firms.
- Major competitors, direct and indirect. Identify relative advantages and disadvantages such as technology, control of raw materials and economies of scale at production facilities.
- Dependency on franchise, distributorship or licensing agreements authorizing and supporting product sales including the annual royalties and other costs of these agreements.
- Technical service and research support.
- Product design and packaging; product specifications and formulations.
- Advertising, sales literature and technical literature.

Exhibit 5-3 (Cont.)

- Price decision processes including trends and volume sensitivity.
- Bid estimating capability and performance history.
- Sales terms: credit, returns, freight absorption, deposits, customs duties, etc.
- Quality control, warranties and claims.
- Intellectual properties: patents, trademarks, trade secrets and copyrights. **Note:** Identify patents nearing issuance and expiration and the potential effects on revenues.
- Regulatory status: registrations, permits and other clearances by the EPA, FDA and other government agencies; compliance with labelling, MSDS and other requirements and their effects on revenues and costs.

V. Production

A. Manufacturing Operations

- Plant facilities and equipment and their condition, capacities, ages, technologies and performance. How do they compare to the "state of the art?" Have ISO 9000 qualifications been achieved?
- Components and raw materials and their suppliers and the suppliers' sources; internally produced components and raw materials and the related transfer pricing.
- Use of subcontractors, toll converters or equivalent suppliers; "outsourcing;" "just in time deliveries."
- Utilities: electricity, natural gas, fuel oil, water, pipeline industrial gases and liquids and other utilities.
- On-site materials handling and storage facilities.
- Off-site facilities for warehousing and processing.
- Production processes and yields; quality control programs; maintenance history including turnarounds; shut-down history; scrap and waste; coproducts and recycling; waste disposal.
- Capacity surpluses or shortages.
- Inbound and outbound freight; ship, barge, rail, truck, aircraft.
- Salaried and labor workforces, union and nonunion.
- Analysis of fixed and variable costs.
- Capital expenditures: recent and proposed.
- Safety and environmental compliance (see later checklist).
- Insurance (see later checklist).

B. Service Operations

- Facilities and equipment.

VI. Purchasing

- Coordination with manufacturing and transportation managers to establish component and raw material specifications and cost objectives and to monitor inventory levels and supplier performance.
- Coordination with research and technical personnel to obtain acceptable new or substitute components and raw materials.
- Coordination with marketing and sales personnel to monitor sales trends and resale opportunities.
- Coordination with transportation personnel to monitor shipping, in-transit and receiving arrangements.
- Major suppliers and their locations and sources of materials; economic trends affecting suppliers.
- Bid and negotiation policies and procedures; ISO 9000 policies.
- Long- and short-term contracts and purchase orders.
- Credit terms of suppliers.
- Policies and evaluation methods for use of internally produced components and raw materials.
- Use of cost-saving methods such as arrangements with suppliers to reclaim and recycle containers, scrap and residues; "just-in-time" deliveries; "baseload" contracts; "toll" manufacture contracts; and "backhaul" transportation arrangements and opportunities.

VII. Transportation

- Ships, barges, rail equipment, tractor and trailer units and other transportation equipment: condition, maintenance history and performance, whether owned or leased.
- Charter and lease agreements.

EXHIBIT 5-3 (*CONT.*)

- Maintenance and repair facilities and equipment.
- Materials loading and unloading facilities including weigh scales.
- Private carriage and other permits and licenses.
- On-site transportation equipment including fork trucks.
- Spurtrack and safety signal agreements.
- Off-site warehouse and terminal facilities.
- Common carrier agreements including mileage credits, demurrage costs and indemnities.
- Conference and association memberships.
- In-transit insurance and relation to risk transfer sale terms such as FOB, CIF and FAS.
- Compliance with the labeling, marking and packaging and other safety regulations of the U.S. Department of Transportation (RSPA, Coast Guard, FAA, FRA, FHWA).
- Cost -saving opportunities such as "backhauling," customer pickup arrangements, and pipeline transportation.

V.III Properties (Tangible)

A. Land and Buildings (Owned and Leased)

- Area maps, surveys, plot plans, aerial photographs and layout drawings of buildings and facilities.
- Title policies including descriptions of mortgages and other encumbrances; easements, rights of way and encroachments; and zoning restrictions (owned properties).
- Leases and any purchase options (leased properties).
- Buildings, facilities and equipment: uses; capacities; performance; conditions; replacement cost; obsolescence (if any); access to utilities; etc.
- Land and facilities available for expansion or for sale as surplus.
- Property appraisals.
- Property assessed valuations and taxes.
- Neighboring properties and their uses.
- Government or other non-owned equipment used.
- Fully depreciated facilities and equipment and expensed tools, dies and maintenance inventories in active use.
- Inactive facilities and equipment and potential for sale or cost of removal.
- Environmental compliance and possible existence of environmental hazards or contamination.
- Out-of-service facilities including requirements and costs to restart, sell, or disassemble, remove and dispose, including safety and environmental costs.

B. Equipment

- Locations; capacities; performance capabilities; condition, including scheduled major maintenance; ages; and manufacturers.
- Maintenance inventories of tools and replacement parts.

IX. Research and Development

- Qualifications and experience of personnel.
- Research programs: objectives, status, feasibility and costs.
- Development and technical service support programs: objectives, status, feasibility and costs.
- Facilities and equipment: condition, utilization and comparison to the state of the art.
- Allocation of research facilities and services among other corporate activities such as marketing and sales, manufacturing, quality control, safety and environmental.
- Implementation of invention and confidentiality agreements, laboratory notebooks, and invention disclosure and patent prosecution procedures.
- Government, customer and supplier sponsored research programs.
- History of utilization of research to develop successful products, processes and equipment.

X. Intellectual and Other Intangible Properties

- Corporate names, trade names and brand names.
- Corporate reputation.

EXHIBIT 5-3 (CONT.)

- Customer lists including contact persons, product application information, product specifications, delivery requirements and schedules.
- Franchise and distributorship agreements.
- License agreements.
- Business opportunities.
- Long-term sale and supply contracts.
- Government permits, registrations, licenses and other clearances including demonstrated ability to meet government standards.
- Approved supplier standing with customers.
- Certifications by rating organizations and demonstrated ability to meet standards set by standards organizations such as ANSI, ASTM, UL, NACE, AICHE, ICBO, NFPA, Factory Mutual, Kosher and ISO 9000 and 14000.
- Laboratory notebooks.
- Patents and patent applications.
- Trademarks and trademark registration applications.
- Trade secrets and systems to prevent their wrongful disclosure and use, including confidentiality agreements.
- Copyrights.

XI. Insurance Coverage

Property and Casualty Coverage (Current Policies)

- Fire and extended coverage policies.
- "All risks" coverage policies.
- Motor vehicle collision policies.
- Flood coverage.
- Premiums.
- Coverage limits and basis for reimbursement, i.e., depreciated value or replacement value.
- Coinsurance provisions including those applicable to underinsurance.
- Deductibles.
- Coverage of off-site property located at warehouses, customer facilities or in common carrier vehicles.
- Insurers and their reputability, solvency and claims handling capabilities.
- Agents and their reputability and capability.
- Status of pending claims, if any.
- Status of coverage disputes, if any.
- Status of renewal negotiations, if in progress.

Liability Coverage (Current and Historical Policies)

- Comprehensive general liability policies.
- Public liability policies.
- Product liability policies, if separate.
- Environmental liability policies, if separate.
- Motor vehicle liability policies.
- Bases of coverage, i.e., "occurrence" or "claims made."
- Coverage limits, aggregate and per occurrence and the extent of claims exhausting the limits to date.
- Endorsements covering directors, officers, subsidiaries, etc.
- Coverage exclusions, such as named insured's products, pollution, asbestos, lead, etc.
- Deductibles and self-insured retentions.
- Premiums, including any retrospective adjustment provisions.
- Insurance archeology efforts in progress, if any.
- Status of pending claims including effectiveness of investigation and defense arrangements.
- Status of coverage disputes.
- Status of renewal negotiations, if in progress.

EXHIBIT 5-3 (CONT.)

- Excess insurance policies and their relation to the primary policies, including "drop-down" provisions, if any.
- Insurers and their reputability, solvency and claims handling capability.
- Agents and their reputability and capability.

Special Coverages[1]

- Fidelity.
- Errors and omissions (E&O) liability.
- Directors' and officers' (D&O) liability[2].
- Employee Retirement Income Security Act (ERISA) liability.
- Employment discrimination liability.
- "Builder's Risk" coverage if construction is in progress.
- Marine insurance for any barges or other watercraft and for products and raw materials in transit as cargo.
- Workers compensation, in states where this risk is insured.

Insurer Reports

- Inspection reports of property and casualty insurers.
- Claims reports by liability insurers.
- Workers compensation "loss run" reports.

XII. Personnel Matters

- Obtain or prepare an organization chart with functional descriptions of responsibilities and direct and indirect reporting relationships.
- Obtain compensation list including benefits and compare to industry norms.
- Identify key officers and managers with essential skills or relationships.
- Review policies on hiring, promotion, compensation adjustments, transfers and terminations.
- Review the general employment conditions in the areas where seller's offices and plant facilities are located. Is there an ample supply of qualified workers? Are living conditions and costs satisfactory? Is there competition for employees from competitors in other industries? What training programs does the seller offer? Are there any incentive programs related to employment?
- Review employment contracts.
- Review pension, 401(K), stock option, health and life insurance plans, how they are funded and how the benefits and costs compare to industry norms. **Note:** Is there a significant unfunded liability for pension benefits or for retiree health benefits? What are the vacation and severance pay policies and are they a potential contingent liability? Are HMO's or PPO's involved in providing health programs? What controls exist for reimbursement of employee expenses?
- Obtain or prepare data reflecting employee morale and effectiveness including productivity data, turnover, attendance, workers compensation and other claims, arbitrations, strikes and work stoppages and labor union activities.
- Review collective bargaining contracts including reserved management rights, wage and benefit scales, expiration dates and reopeners and restrictive practices. **Note:** Which labor unions represent the hourly employees? Who handles negotiations? Are any organization or decertification campaigns in progress?
- Determine how fair employment practices programs are handled regarding race, religion, color, national origin, age, sex, disabilities, military service and other groups entitled to special protected status under law. Review EEO-1 reports and affirmative action programs. Review the procedures for handling complaints and any existing complaints.
- Review any drug and alcohol testing programs and compliance with no-smoking ordinances.

XIII. Employee Benefit Plans

- Determine who are the plan administrators for each plan.
- Review tax returns, reports, determination letters and other forms and communications to and from the Internal Revenue Service, Department of Labor and Pension Benefit Guaranty Corporation (PBGC) including Form 5500, Annual Return/Report of Employee Benefit Plan. Identify any reportable event, accumulated funding deficiency, prohibited transaction or funding surplus.

---

[1]To the extent applicable, these policies should be reviewed for the same items as the property and casualty and the liability policies, i.e., coverage exclusions and limits, deductibles, premiums, claims, etc.

[2]Serious review of D&O liability coverage should be undertaken to determine whether it should be retained after an acquisition. D&O policies have numerous exclusions and may not cover any risk that is a serious exposure for directors and officers of privately owned companies.

EXHIBIT 5-3 (CONT.)

- Review plan documents including amendments, trust agreements, group annuity contracts, pension commitments in collective bargaining or other agreements, summary plan descriptions and plan booklets.
- Review financial statements of each plan and any related audit reports with special attention to the quality of assets and their liquidity in relation to cash flow obligations for benefits and expenses.
- Review any investment management contracts and the record of performance of the investment managers.
- Review actuarial reports including the actuarial methods and assumptions and any recent and proposed changes. Determine the amount of all benefit liabilities (not only vested benefits) and how they compare to plan assets.
- Determine whether there are any liabilities for failure to meet minimum funding obligations under defined benefit pension plans including any failure to notify participants and government agencies of such failure.
- Determine the amount of any potential termination liability under the Single Employer Pension Plan Amendments Act and the Multiemployer Pension Plan Amendments Act.
- Determine the amount of any overfunding of defined pension plans and the related future potential cost savings.
- Identify any transactions between any employee benefit plan and the seller or its affiliates and any issues relating to compliance with fiduciary obligations under the Employee Retirement Income Security Act.
- Compare the benefits and costs under seller's employee benefit plans with those of the buyer. Should the seller's plans be continued separately, frozen or terminated, or merged into buyer's plans?

XIV. Legal Matters

- Review the corporate minute books including the following documents, whether or not contained in the minute books: certificate of incorporation and amendments; by-laws and amendments; qualifications to do business; and minutes of board, committee and shareholders' meetings. **Note:** Identify any "supermajority" or other special voting rights and restrictions, preemptive rights and other provisions affecting the proposed transaction and any material business transactions, contracts, liabilities and other matters discussed at meetings.
- Outline the capital structure including the characteristics of senior debt, subordinated debt, preferred stock, special stock, common stock, options, warrants, rights and other exchangeable or convertible securities. **Note:** For debt, describe any collateral and all prepayment obligations including any "poison debt" provisions. For stock, describe all voting rights and obligations and also any preemptive rights. What are the rights of option holders and warrant holders in an acquisition transaction? Are any "poison pill" rights issuable and in what events?
- Review the stock certificate book and ledger, if the corporation is privately owned. Review the outstanding stock certificates. Have any been pledged to lenders? Are any certificates missing?
- Review any shareholders' agreements or voting trust agreements.
- Review the same books and records for subsidiaries and affiliates and prepare memoranda summarizing the important information.
- Review existing title insurance policies and commence real estate title searches, surveys and searches for security interests, tax liens, etc. **Note:** Identify any easements, rights of way, restrictions, structures and conditions that may affect the proposed use of the property.
- Identify and review employee benefit plans and agreements, especially any "handbook" or similar inadvertent commitments to employees.
- Identify and obtain copies of significant regulatory permits and licenses. **Note:** Be sure to identify all permits and licenses for which a consent to transfer will be needed.
- Review compliance with applicable regulatory laws including antitrust, environmental, fair employment practices, foreign corrupt practices, safety, political contributions, etc.
- Review claims, lawsuits and administrative proceedings and the related primary and excess insurance coverage. **Note:** In reviewing insurance, check the aggregate and occurrence limits, exclusions, deductibles, self-insured retentions and the extent to which policy limits may have been exhausted. In addition, determine whether disclaimers or reservations of rights have been issued.
- Review potential product liability exposure including express and implied warranties; product hazards, labels and warnings; hazardous uses of products by customers; procedures for handling claims including comparison to retained samples and goodwill settlement policies; etc.
- Identify other potential liabilities including contractual indemnities; agreements to provide insurance coverage; on-site contractors and subcontractors; financial guarantees.
- Identify and review significant contracts including loan agreements and indentures and related mortgage and security agreements; distributorship and franchise agreements; customer agreements including important "blanket" purchase orders; supplier agreements including raw materials and utilities; leases and warehousing and terminating agreements, etc. **Note:** Be sure to identify all contracts for which a consent to the acquisition will be needed.

EXHIBIT 5-3 (CONT.)

- Identify actions that will be necessary to complete the acquisition as structured and how they may be affected by matters found during the review:
  - What corporate approvals will be needed? Is it necessary and feasible to obtain shareholder approval? What governance and other issues may arise? Will waivers of rights of first refusal or preemptive rights be needed? Should a limit be placed on exercise of dissenters' appraisal rights?
  - Will a notification and report under the Hart-Scott-Rodino provisions of the Clayton Act be required? Will there be significant antitrust issues?
  - Will tax rulings or opinions be needed? How will they be coordinated with other contract conditions?
  - Will it be necessary to delist and deregister any securities issued by the seller? Will it be necessary to list and register any securities to be issued by the buyer? If so, how will these steps be coordinated with other contract conditions?
  - Will consents of lenders, customers and suppliers be needed? If so, how and when should they be obtained?
  - What other government clearances may be needed and what steps will be necessary to obtain them?
  - Will it be necessary to unwind any transactions with officers, directors, shareholders or other related persons or to continue them on a negotiated basis?
  - What confidentiality and noncompetiton agreements may be needed?
  - What obligations to employees may be triggered by the acquisition? Will there be obligations for severance pay or to recognize a labor union or assign a collective bargaining contract? Must a WARN notice be given?
  - Should bulk transfer procedures be used or waived?
  - Will any transfer, sales, use or other excise taxes be payable as a result of the acquisition? Are any "bulk sale" or other exemptions available?
  - Is there any potential liability to brokers or finders?
  - What fairness opinions and solvency opinions will be needed and have appropriate arrangements been made to obtain them?
  - Will any environmental liabilities be triggered by the acquisition under environmental laws including "super-lien" laws or responsible property transfer laws such as those in Connecticut, Illinois, Indiana and New Jersey? What steps must be taken to transfer (or reissue) environmental permits?
  - Should part of the purchase price be held in escrow? If so, what will be the escrow arrangements and terms?
  - What legal opinions will be needed?

XV. Environmental Matters

1. Environmental Reviews Limited to Site Contamination

If a business to be acquired is conducted entirely in office buildings or other commercial real estate and does not involve manufacturing or processing of materials, a full environmental "due diligence" review may be unnecessary.

During recent years, environmental professionals have developed a two-phase method to investigate commercial real estate for contamination. The investigation begins with a phase I environmental site assessment which consists of the development of a site description; performance of a records review; site reconnaissance and interviews; and preparation of a report showing findings and conclusions. The assessment focuses on contamination of structures, soil, surfacewater and groundwater with hazardous substances or petroleum products that may have leaked or spilled from underground storage tanks, containers, electrical equipment and other sources. The assessment usually also includes investigation for asbestos-containing materials and lead-based paint, although these materials are not hazardous if properly maintained. The assessment may also include other materials, such as polychlorinated biphenyls (PCBs), fluids formerly sold for use in electrical equipment, and radon, a radioactive gas that occurs naturally in some areas. The American Society for Testing and Materials, Inc. has published Standard Practice E 1527-97 defining good commercial and customary practice for conducting a phase I environmental site assessment.

A phase I environmental site assessment can usually be obtained at modest cost, approximately $2,500 to $7,500, from a large number of environmental consulting firms. If the firm reports recognized environmental conditions involving the presence or likely presence of hazardous substances or petroleum products under conditions indicating an existing, past or threatened release into structures, ground, groundwater or surfacewater, the firm will recommend a phase II environmental assessment.

A phase II environmental site assessment involves sampling and testing of the structure, containers, soil, surfacewater or groundwater where recognized environmental conditions were found in order to determine whether hazardous substances, petroleum products and other substances such as asbestos or lead are present and, if so, where and at what concentrations. Depending on the results of this assessment, remedial action may be necessary or prudent. In addition, there may be reporting obligations to the U.S. Environmental Protection Agency and state and local environmental agencies who will then regulate further investigation and remediation.

EXHIBIT 5-3 (CONT.)

2. "Due Diligence" Reviews of Environmental Compliance and Conditions including Effects on Operations

If the business to be acquired is engaged in manufacturing, processing, mining or other industrial operations, phase I and phase II environmental site assessments are not adequate to evaluate environmental compliance and a "due diligence" review is needed. The review team should use care in hiring an environmental professional for the review because many firms that perform phase I and II assessments do not have enough experience to perform a "due diligence" review which has much more extensive scope.

A checklist for an environmental "due diligence" review is as follows:

Clean Air

- Identify point source emissions and fugitive emissions and the hazardous substances and pollutants emitted.
- Identify the control equipment for the emissions.
- Review construction permits for the point sources and control equipment.
- Review operating permits including the emission limits and monitoring and reporting requirements.
- Determine whether compliance is based on standards for sources existing in 1972 or new source performance standards.
- Review monitoring records and reports.
- Review history of excursions over permit limits and any violation proceedings and corrective actions.
- Review adverse effects, if any, on capacity and operating rates of any inability to meet permit limits and the capital operating costs to upgrade facilities to achieve compliance at higher capacity and operating rates.
- Review the capital and operating costs of upgrading facilities to meet new source performance standards if they are not being met.
- Review permits and controls on fugitive emissions.
- Review effects of "no significant deterioration" rules if the plant is in a nonattainment area.
- Review compliance with any applicable national emission standards for hazardous air pollutants (NESHAPs), if applicable, such as the carbon monoxide or the nitrogen oxides standard.
- Review compliance with the acid deposition control (acid rain) and stratospheric ozone (Montreal Protocol) regulations and the proposed accidental release regulations.

Clean Water

- Identify direct point source discharges of pollutants to an ocean, lake, river or stream.
- Identify indirect discharges of pollutants to sewer systems leading to publicly owned treatment works (POTWs).
- Identify stormwater discharges.
- Identify equipment and facilities used to control and pretreat direct and indirect discharges. Does the business have collection and treatment systems? What are the capabilities of the systems? Do they neutralize acid or caustic effluent? Do they skim or filter solids? Do they treat and biodegrade organics?
- Review national pollution discharge elimination system (NPDES) permits including the pollutant limits and monitoring and reporting requirements. Review monitoring records and reports.
- Determine whether there are other dischargers to the receiving water and the effects of their discharges.
- Review permits, ordinances or regulations of POTWs restricting discharges to sewers and imposing sewer charges and pretreatment requirements.
- Determine whether the POTW is complying with its NPDES permit and, if not, whether it plans to tighten restrictions on any indirect dischargers.
- Review stormwater permits.
- Review the Spill Control Program.
- Identify any tidal or freshwater wetlands and transition areas on the seller's properties.
- Review exceedances over permit limits and any violation proceedings.
- Review processes and equipment and the capital and operating costs required to achieve compliance.

Waste Management

- Identify solid wastes generated, both hazardous and nonhazardous and test procedures used to characterize waste.
- Obtain EPA generator identification number.
- Review any treatment, storage and disposal (TSD) facilities located on seller's properties. If any exist, except for storage less than 90 days, review the TSD permit and compliance history. Has the seller complied with "corrective action" requirements for the entire facility?

EXHIBIT 5-3 (*CONT.*)

- Review the TSD facilities for compliance such as secondary containment, labeling, etc. Review the closure and postclosure plan and estimated costs.
- Review registrations and records relating to underground storage tanks (USTs). What are and were the contents? Are the USTs registered? Are the USTs active or inactive? Have the inactive USTs been properly closed? Have active USTs been tightness tested and upgraded to meet RCRA requirements?
- Review aboveground storage tanks. What are their contents? Are they properly constructed, including adequate secondary containment?
- Review arrangements for off-site disposal of hazardous waste and compliance with manifest and labeling requirements. Identify present and former waste transporters and disposal sites. Are any of the disposal sites listed in the National Priority List (NPL) or the CERCLIS database or any state "mini-superfund" or other cleanup list? How costly are the disposal arrangements? What methods are used at the present disposal sites? What is their capacity and how long will they remain available?
- Review arrangements for off-site disposal of nonhazardous waste. Identify present and former transporters and disposal sites. Are any of the disposal facilities listed on any federal, state or local list for cleanup? What disposal methods are used at the disposal facilities? Are any of the disposal sites nearing capacity and planning to close or to adopt stricter specifications for acceptable wastes? How costly are the disposal arrangements?
- Review waste minimization and recycling activities. Can raw materials and intermediates not fully converted to products be returned to early stages of the process and blended with similar materials? Does the process produce coproducts or by-products? Are any wastes reclaimed or recycled? If wastes are transported for reclamation or recycling at off-site locations, identify the transporters and the locations. How do they accomplish the reclamation or recycling? Does it involve land application or use as fuel? Obtain copies of permits and beneficial use determinations.
- If application, verify compliance with small generator regulations, if applicable.

Community Right-to-Know

- Review any history of releases of hazardous chemicals and compliance with requirements for notification of state and local emergency response officials, including continuous releases.
- Review compliance with supplier notification requirements.
- Review material safety data sheets (MSDS) of hazardous chemicals from suppliers and evidence of their delivery to state and local officials.
- Review Tier One/Tier Two reports to state and local officials.
- Review Form R—Toxic Chemical Release Inventory Forms and their filing with state and local officials including the inventory of hazardous chemicals and any reported releases.
- Review compliance with record keeping requirements.

Waste Cleanup

- Review the National Priority List (NPL) and the CERCLIS database for the properties of the business to be acquired and properties near them. Review state "mini-superfund" and other property cleanup lists for the same purpose.
- Walk through the seller's properties to understand its present and historical manufacturing processes including raw materials, finished products and intermediates and onsite and off-site disposal practices.
- Perform a "windshield" review of neighboring properties to learn about their manufacturing processes and products.
- Review available aerial photographs, Sanborn maps and other data showing the history of properties.
- Obtain lists of present and former waste haulers and disposal sites for hazardous and nonhazardous wastes.
- Determine whether the seller has received any CERCLA § 104 letters from the EPA or has been named as a potentially responsible party (PRP) at any site listed or under review by the EPA or a state or local environmental agency.
- If the seller is responsible for any remedial activity, what are the levels of the soil, surfacewater, groundwater or other contamination? How do the levels compare to the residential and nonresidential cleanup guidelines? What progress has been made to accomplish the cleanup? What are the estimated cleanup costs? What share of the cleanup costs is likely to be allocated to the seller and any successors to the seller's obligations?
- Will the transaction trigger cleanup obligations under responsible property transfer laws such as those in Connecticut, Illinois, Indiana and New Jersey? Are the seller's properties subject to any lien or superlien under the environmental laws?

EXHIBIT 5-3 (CONT.)

Toxic Substances Control (TSCA)

- Determine whether all chemical substances produced or used appear on the TSCA inventory.
- Review compliance with premanufacturing notice (PMN) requirements for any new chemical substances and any consent orders or significant new use regulations (SNURs) under which they are being manufactured, used or sold.
- Determine whether any products are or may be subject to testing orders by the EPA.
- Determine whether any chemical substances are or may be applied to significant new uses and, if so, whether seller is in compliance with the EPA's regulations.
- Determine whether seller is in compliance with Section 8(e) reporting requirements.
- Determine whether seller's properties have any transformers, capacitors or other electrical equipment containing polychlorinated biphenyl (PCB) dielectric fluid and, if so, whether seller is in compliance with applicable regulations. If the equipment is owned by a public utility, verify the status with the utility.

Asbestos; Lead; Radioactive Materials

- Determine whether the seller's properties may have asbestos containing materials (ACMs). Are they hazardous (i.e., friable) or nonhazardous (i.e., nonfriable)? Does the seller have an operations and maintenance program? Are there any plans for demolition, renovation or remodeling that may disturb ACMs?
- Determine whether seller historically manufactured or used ACMs. Is there any history of worker exposure or claims?
- Determine whether seller's properties may have lead-based paint (LBP). Are they intact or in deteriorated condition? Does the seller have an operations and maintenance program? Are there any plans for demolition, renovation or remodeling that may disturb LBP? Does the drinking water contain lead at a concentration in excess of the EPA's "action level" of 15 parts per billion.
- Determine whether seller historically manufactured products containing lead or used lead in its processes. Is there any history of worker exposure or claims?
- Determine whether seller's properties have any radioactive materials, equipment or wastes. Does seller have a license from the Nuclear Regulatory Commission (NRC) or a state having a regulatory agreement with the NRC?
- Determine whether seller historically manufactured radioactive materials or equipment or used radioactive materials in its processes. Is there any history of worker exposure or claims?

Worker Safety

- OSHA 200 Log.
- OSHA (or state agency) inspection reports.
- Insurer inspection reports.
- Safety committee minutes and reports.
- Workers compensation "loss runs."
- Compliance with OSHA's hazard communication system including MSDS and labeling requirements.
- Compliance with OSHA's process safety management (PSM) regulations including "lockout/tagout" and "confined space entry" rules, if applicable.
- Air test results if manufacturing processes result in workplace air emissions.
- Repetitive stress injuries, i.e., carpal tunnel syndrome.
- Equipment for the engineering control of health hazards.
- Personal protective equipment including respirators.

Chapter 6

FEDERAL TAXATION OF TAXABLE ACQUISITIONS

A. INTRODUCTION

Federal taxation is one of the most important elements that must be considered when planning an acquisition or divestiture. There are several fundamental reasons:

- The Internal Revenue Code (the "Code") taxes the income of corporations at graduated rates up to 35 percent. When a corporation then distributes its post-tax income as dividends to its shareholders, the Code taxes the income again to the shareholders. A corporation may not deduct dividends from its income as it deducts interest and other business expenses. Thus, corporate income is taxed twice, unless the corporation is a small business corporation that has elected to be taxed under Subchapter S of the Code or some other provision that shelters it from taxation. Indeed, when a corporation distributes income to corporate shareholders, it can be taxed three times, although the Code provides a variety of methods to avoid or limit triple taxation such as consolidated returns and the intercorporate dividends received deduction of 70 to 100 percent, depending on the ownership interest. In acquisition planning, it is important, when possible, to structure the transactions to minimize the number of levels at which corporate income will be taxed. Increasingly, partnerships and limited liability companies are used in acquisitions to eliminate one level of taxation.
- The Code taxes income from many sources, including compensation from services, dividends, interest, sales of inventories and sales of capital assets. The Code imposes tax on most sources of income at ordinary income rates up to 39.6 percent for individuals and up to 35 percent for corporations. For individuals, the Code taxes gains from sales of most capital assets at rates not exceeding 20 percent for assets held more than one year. In acquisition planning, it is important, when possible, to structure the transactions so that the price will be allocable to sources of income taxed at lower rates.
- The Code taxes a wide range of transactions, but provides for nonrecognition of income or loss realized in some transactions. The Code also provides numerous deductions, limitations, exemptions, credits and defer-

---

The author expresses appreciation to Jeffrey S. Levin, his tax partner at Windels, Marx, Davies & Ives, for helpful comments on this chapter.

rals that can be used in determining income, taxable income and income tax payable. In acquisition planning, it is important, when possible, to structure the transactions to take advantage of opportunities for whole or partial nonrecognition of income as well as exemptions, credits and deferrals.

• The Code typically links tax-saving opportunities to requirements designed to assure that the savings can be obtained only as intended by the U.S. Congress. Acquisition planners must determine whether and how they can structure acquisition transactions to meet Code requirements for tax savings. Planners must also determine whether structuring to achieve tax savings will have adverse side effects on other aspects of the acquisitions. If there are adverse side effects, planners must weigh the importance of the tax savings against the adverse side effects.

As described in earlier chapters, acquisitions can be accomplished by numerous methods. For many years, acquisition planners have structured acquisition transactions to minimize federal taxes, insofar as they could do so without sacrificing other objectives of equal or greater importance. This chapter describes how the Code taxes corporate acquisition transactions, the major steps that can be taken to minimize federal taxes, and some of the side effects that should be weighed against tax-saving opportunities.[1]

B. Some Fundamental Concepts

1. Corporate Organization and Liquidation

In general, a corporation can be organized and can obtain equity capital by selling stock without recognition of income by either the corporation or its shareholders.[2]

Until 1987, it was also possible to liquidate a corporation without recognition of income at the corporate level by several methods. However, the present general rule is that distributions to shareholders in complete liquidation of a corporation are treated as payment in exchange for stock, a taxable transaction at both the corporate and shareholder levels.[3] However, nonrecognition continues to be available for distributions to a parent corporation upon complete liquidation of a subsidiary if the parent owns 80 percent or more of the voting power and total value of the subsidiary's stock.[4]

2. Deductions from Corporate Income

Section 161 and subsequent sections of the Code allow corporate and individual taxpayers to deduct numerous items in computing taxable income.

---

[1]The famous Judge Learned Hand wrote: "Anyone may so arrange his affairs that his taxes shall be as low as possible; he is not bound to choose that pattern which will best pay the Treasury; there is not even a patriotic duty to increase one's taxes." *Helvering v. Gregory,* 69 F.2d 809 (1934); affirmed 293 U.S. 465 (1935).

[2]Sections 351 and 1032 of the Code. See the IRS "Check the Box" regulations at Reg. Sec. 301.7701-1(a) through (e) and Reg. Sec 301.7701-3(a) through (f).

[3]Sections 331 and 336 of the Code.

[4]Sections 332 and 337 of the Code.

For example, Section 162 allows deduction of all ordinary and necessary trade or business expenses. Section 165 allows deduction of losses with some exceptions. Section 172 allows net operating losses (NOLs) that exceed the amount usable in a taxable year to be carried back 2 taxable years and forward 20 taxable years, subject to numerous exceptions. NOL carryovers are valuable intangible assets because they can partially shelter future income from tax.

While double taxation of corporate income has come to be the norm, a variety of provisions continue to prevent or limit triple taxation. Among them is the deduction allowed to corporations for various items including dividends received from a domestic corporation.[5]

3. Basis

Each shareholder of a corporation has a basis in his, her or its stock. Basis in stock is adjusted from time to time for contributions to capital by shareholders and distributions to shareholders constituting a return of capital. Basis in stock is also adjusted for various items including stock splits, stock dividends and stock recapitalizations.

Each corporation has a basis in its assets. Basis in assets is adjusted for numerous items including capital improvements and depreciation.

Basis is used in determining the amount of gain or loss that results upon a taxable sale or exchange of assets. The type of gain or loss depends on the nature of the asset. Sales of some assets (such as inventory held for sale to customers) result in ordinary income or loss. Sales of capital assets (such as land and goodwill) result in capital gain or loss. Under Code Section 1231, property used in a trade or business (machinery and equipment) is taxed as a capital gain, if sold for a price in excess of adjusted basis, and as an ordinary loss, if sold at a loss. The characterization is based on the aggregation of all Section 1231 assets each tax year. Intangibles (such as patents, trademarks, trade secrets and customer lists) were for many years generally classified as capital assets, but were difficult to identify and value. Since 1993, many intangible assets are grouped and treated under Code Section 197 as depreciable property and are taxable upon sale as Section 1231 assets.

Gain or loss on the sale of each asset is measured by the difference between its sale price (less expenses) and the seller's adjusted basis in the asset. However, if the asset is depreciable, the sale triggers "recapture" of the depreciation. In essence, gain on the sale is taxed as ordinary income to the full extent of the depreciation claimed on machinery and equipment and other assets constituting "Section 1245 Property" and to the extent of depreciation claimed in excess of straight-line depreciation on buildings, fixtures and other property constituting "Section 1250 Property." Gain, if any, in excess of basis recomputed to include the recaptured depreciation is treated as capital gain.

A buyer of business assets obtains a basis in the assets equal to cost, which is the purchase price plus liabilities assumed and related expenses.

---

[5]Sections 243 *et seq.* of the Code.

If the asset is of a nature eligible for depreciation or amortization deductions, the buyer will claim such deductions measured by the new basis. When the purchase price is higher than the seller's adjusted basis prior to the sale, the "stepped-up" basis provides increased deductions that help the buyer recover the purchase price for tax purposes. This improves the buyer's cash flow after the purchase of assets.

4. Depreciation and Amortization

Section 167(a) of the Code allows as a depreciation deduction a reasonable allowance for exhaustion, wear and tear (including a reasonable allowance for obsolescence) of (1) property used in a trade or business and (2) property held for production of income. For decades, the allowance was based on the useful life of the property, rather than its actual life, and took into account a salvage value remaining at the end of the useful life.

For most property placed in service after 1970, a new method was established, called the Class Life Asset Depreciation Range (ADR) system. Tangible properties were assigned class lives, i.e., asset guideline periods. Each class was assigned an ADR extending about 20 percent above and below the class life. Taxpayers were allowed to select a depreciation period within the ADR, except for buildings and land improvements. Some companies still own properties placed in service in the 1970s under the ADR system.

For most property placed in service after 1980, another new method was adopted, called the Accelerated Cost Recovery System (ACRS). For property placed in service after 1986, Section 168 of the Code was amended to modify ACRS and the modified system was called MACRS. Like the ACRS provisions, the MACRS provisions assign definite recovery periods to properties based on their class lives and provide for 100 percent recovery without regard to salvage value. The MACRS provisions do not apply, or apply only with modifications, to certain kinds of property. For example, Section 169 of the Code provides for amortization of certified pollution control equipment over a 60-month period. For another example, Section 168 of the Code limits the use of the MACRS provisions for public utility property, property used by tax-exempt organizations or property financed by the exempt securities and property used outside the United States.

Section 168 of the Code implements MACRS by providing that the depreciation deduction provided by Section 167(a) shall be determined by using applicable depreciation methods, recovery periods and conventions for determining when property is placed in service:

Depreciation Methods. Section 168(b) provides that the applicable depreciation method for most properties is the 200 percent declining balance method, switching to the straight-line method for the first taxable year when that method will yield a larger allowance. However, the applicable method is the 150 percent declining method for 15 and 20 year property and property used in a farming business and may be used for other property pursuant to an irrevocable election. The straight-line method is the applicable depreciation method for nonresidential and residential property, certain railroad and agricultural properties and any other property if the taxpayer makes an irrevocable election of the straight-line method.

Applicable Recovery Periods. Section 168(c) provides applicable recovery periods ranging from 3 years to 50 years for various classifications of properties. Section 168(e) provides for the classification of properties, except where otherwise specified, based on their class lives. Class lives and recovery periods for most properties can be found in Revenue Procedure 87-56, 1987-2 C.B. 647, as amended by Revenue Procedure 88-22, 1988-1 C.B. 785. In general, the recovery periods for machinery and equipment range from 3 to 7 years, but the recovery periods for some large durable plant facilities and fixtures are longer periods, such as 10, 15 and 20 years. Section 168(e) directly specifies the treatment of certain properties. For example, it specifies that 5-year property includes any automobile, light general purpose truck, semiconductor manufacturing equipment and certain other properties. It also defines the residential rental and nonresidential real properties that are assigned 27.5 year and 39 year recovery periods. MACRS depreciation tables can be found in Revenue Procedure 87-57, 1987-2 C.B. 687.

Applicable Conventions. Section 168(d) prescribes the conventions to be used in determining when property is placed in service. They are the half year convention, the mid-month convention and the mid-quarter convention.

As depreciation deductions are claimed, taxpayers reduce their basis in the assets being depreciated. If additions or improvements are made to property in service, depreciation deductions based on the cost of the additions or improvements should be claimed from when they are placed in service.

5. Distributions of Property and Stock by Corporations

a. Distributions of Money and Other Property. In general, Section 301 of the Code provides that a distribution of property, including cash, made by a corporation to a shareholder with respect to its stock is taxed as follows:

1. The portion which is a dividend under Section 316 is included in the shareholder's income. Section 316 treats as a dividend any distribution out of current or accumulated earnings and profits of the distributing corporation.
2. The portion which is not a dividend is applied to reduce the adjusted basis of the shareholder's stock.
3. The portion, if any, which is not a dividend and exceeds the adjusted basis of the stock is treated as gain from the sale or exchange of property.

The distributing corporation is not entitled to any trade or business deduction under Section 162 with respect to the distribution. No gain or loss is recognized by the corporation on a distribution (not a complete liquidation) with respect to its sale of (i) its stock or rights to acquire its stock or (ii) property. However, if a corporation distributes appreciated property (i.e., property with a fair market value exceeding its adjusted basis), then gain is recognized by the distributing corporation as if such property were sold to the distributee at its fair market value.[6] The effects of distributions on the earnings and profits of the distributing corporation are provided in Section 312.

b. Distributions of Stock. For the purposes of determining the tax consequences of distributions, the term "property" means money, securities or any other property, but does not include stock in the corporation making the distribution or rights to acquire such stocks.[7]

In general, shareholders do not include in gross income the amount of any distribution of stock of a corporation made by such corporation to its shareholders with respect to its stock.[8] However, certain distributions which allow a shareholder to elect stock or property, disproportionate distributions among all shareholders and certain distributions including or consisting of preferred stock may be treated as distributions of property and, thus, subject to dividend treatment.[9]

c. Redemptions of Stock. Under Section 302(a) of the Code, if a corporation redeems its stock and certain conditions apply, the redemption is treated as a distribution in part or full payment in exchange for stock rather than as a dividend. Section 302(b) provides that Section 302(a) applies if:

1. The redemption is not essentially equivalent to a dividend.
2. The redemption is substantially disproportionate with respect to the shareholder, as measured by specific tests.
3. The redemption is in complete redemption of all stock of the corporation owned by the shareholder.
4. The redemption is a distribution in redemption of stock for a shareholder who is not a corporation and is made in partial liquidation of the distributing corporation.

Detailed rules on constructive ownership of stock must be applied in determining the ownership of stock for the purposes of Section 302.[10] Rules on redemption of stock through the use of related corporations also limit the applicability of Section 302(a). If the distribution does not qualify as a redemption, then the transaction is treated as a distribution of money or other property subject to dividend treatment.

d. Corporate Liquidations. Section 331 of the Code provides that amounts received by a shareholder in a distribution in complete liquidation of a corporation are treated as in full payment in exchange for the shareholder's stock. The dividend treatment prescribed by Section 301 does not apply to a distribution in complete liquidation of a corporation.

Section 332 provides that no gain or loss shall be recognized on receipt by a corporation of property distributed in complete liquidation of another corporation.

---

[6]Section 311.

[7]Section 317(a).

[8]Section 305(a).

[9]Section 305(b).

[10]Sections 302(c) and 318.

C. Taxation at Corporate and Shareholder Levels

A taxable corporate acquisition can be accomplished by three basic methods: (1) a stock sale, (2) an assets sale, or (3) a merger including a two-party merger or a three-party merger For each of the three methods, the price can be paid with cash, debt, assumption of liabilities, stock, or combinations of cash, debt, assumption of liabilities or stock.[11] For each method, acquisition planners should consider the potential effects on the corporate seller and buyer and their shareholders.

Historically, the Code accepted the basic concepts of the corporation and contract laws. However, as the years have passed, the Code has often been amended to impose tax or to provide tax relief in ways that override corporate structures and contractual arrangements. A well-known example is the right of small business corporations and their stockholders to elect under Subchapter S of the Code not to be taxed generally at the corporate level, with the result that corporate income is taxed only at the shareholder level in a manner similar to a partnership or sole proprietorship.

Brief examples of the basic acquisition methods and their tax effects on the corporations and shareholders involved are as follows:

1. *A Stock Sale.* The shareholders of the corporation being sold deliver their stock certificates directly to the buyer corporation in return for payment of the price to them. The corporation sold becomes a subsidiary of the buyer corporation. The selling shareholders realize capital gain or loss on the stock sale to the extent the price is more or less than their respective bases in the stock sold. No tax is imposed on the corporation sold which retains the previous basis in its assets and other tax characteristics. The buyer obtains a basis in the purchased stock equal to its cost, consisting of the price plus acquisition expenses. The buyer corporation may continue the existence of its new subsidiary and may elect to include it in a consolidated return. The buyer corporation may also liquidate the subsidiary or merge the subsidiary into itself or another subsidiary with the effects described later in this chapter.

2. *An Assets Sale and Corporate Liquidation.* The seller corporation sells assets to the buyer corporation which pays the price to the seller corporation. The assets sold are then owned by the buyer corporation and, if the buyer wishes, can be operated as an unincorporated division. The seller corporation is taxed on the sale of the assets according to the Code provisions applicable to the particular assets sold. If the seller corporation has sold substantially all of its operating assets, it will probably liquidate by paying its taxes and other debts, distributing the remaining balance of the purchase price to its shareholders in a complete liquidation and dissolving its corporate existence. The shareholders will be taxed on the liquidation distribution as capital gain or loss to the extent the distribution is more or less than their respective bases in their stock. The buyer corporation will obtain a basis in the assets equal to its cost, consisting of the purchase price plus liabilities assumed and acquisition expenses. The buyer corporation will allocate its cost among the assets to establish its bases in the respective assets.

[11]Any acquisition that fails to qualify as a tax free reorganization is taxable.

3. *A Corporate Liquidation and Assets Sale.* The seller corporation liquidates and distributes its assets to its shareholders who then sell them to the buyer corporation. The seller corporation is taxed on the assets distributed to its shareholders as if it sold the property to the shareholders at fair market value. The shareholders will be taxed on the liquidation distribution as capital gain or loss to the extent the fair market value of the assets distributed is more or less than their respective bases in their stock. The shareholders obtain a basis equal to the fair market value of the assets distributed. The shareholders then sell the assets to the buyer corporation, are taxed again on the sale, but benefit from the stepped-up bases in the assets sold. The buyer corporation obtains a basis in the assets equal to its cost and allocates the cost among the assets as described previously. This method is a cumbersome means to sell assets and is not used frequently.

4. *Taxable Mergers.* The seller corporation is merged into the buyer corporation or a subsidiary of the buyer corporation. The separate corporate existence of the seller corporation ceases and the buyer corporation (or subsidiary) survives as the successor to the seller corporation. The shareholders of the seller corporation surrender their stock certificates for cancellation in return for the purchase price paid by the buyer corporation or its subsidiary. This so-called "forward merger" transaction is treated as a sale of the seller corporation's assets followed by a complete liquidation of the seller corporation.[12] As an alternative, the buyer corporation can contribute the price to a transitory subsidiary and merge the subsidiary into the seller corporation, which would then become a subsidiary of the buyer corporation. This so-called "reverse merger" transaction is treated as a stock purchase.[13]

D. Structure Diagrams

Structure diagrams of the basic acquisition methods described in the preceding section are as follows:

1. A Stock Sale

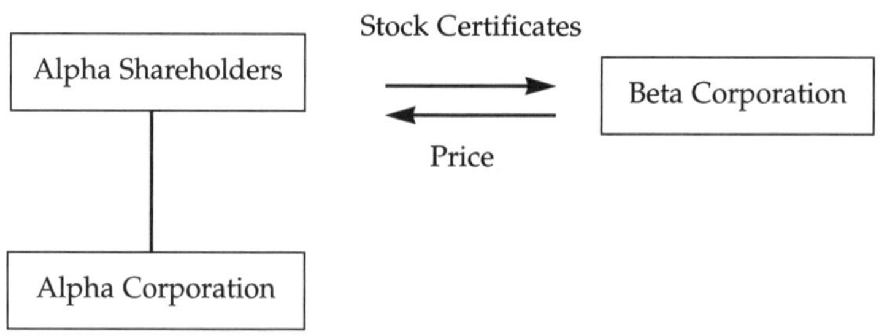

[12]Rev. Rul. 69-6, 1969-1 C.B. 104.

[13]Rev. Rul. 73-427, 1973-2 C.B. 301; Rev. Rul. 79-273, 1979-2 C.B. 125; Rev. Rul. 90-95, 1990-2 C.B. 57. To the extent that the price is paid by the seller corporation or from the proceeds of indebtedness incurred by the seller corporation, the transaction is treated as a redemption of stock by the seller corporation rather than a purchase by the buyer corporation.

2. An Assets Sale and Corporate Liquidation

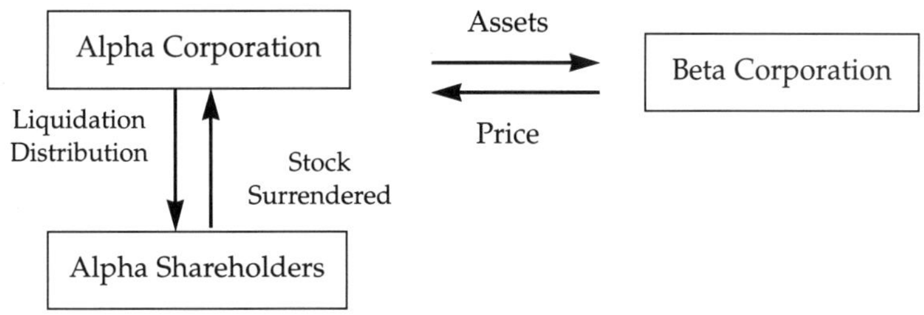

3. A Corporate Liquidation and Assets Sale

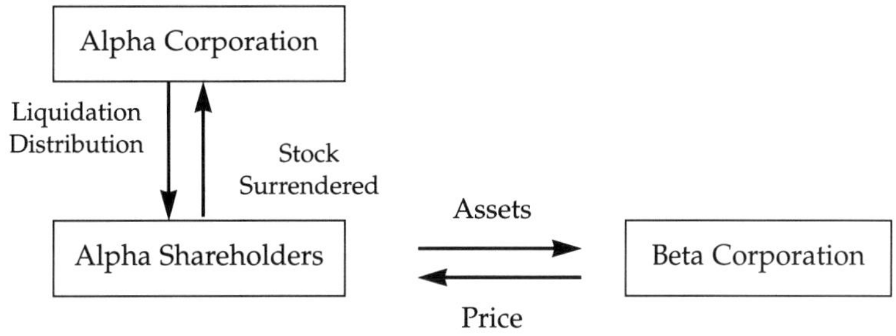

4. A Two-Party Merger

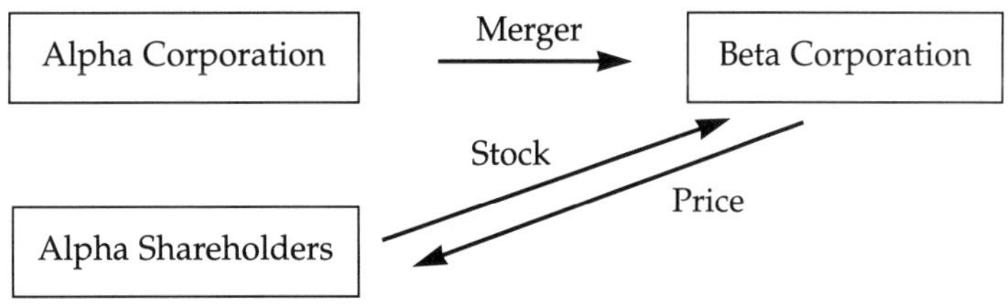

5. A Triangular "Forward Merger"

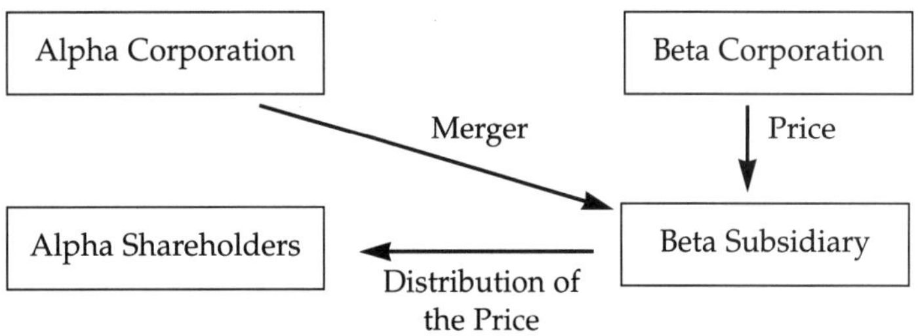

6. A Triangular "Reverse Merger"

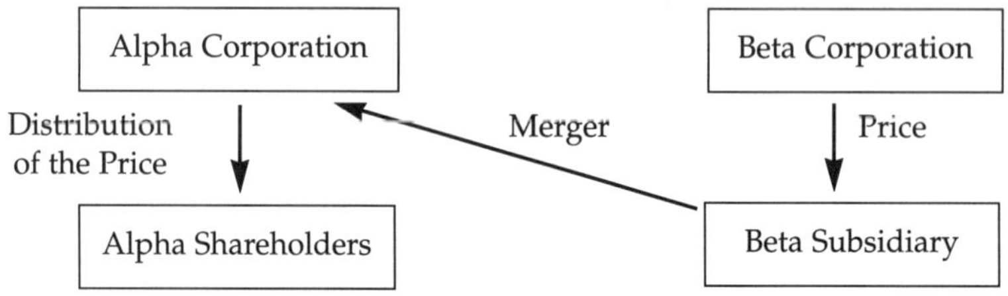

E. Two-Level Taxation of Acquisition Transactions

Until the early 1980s, the Code contained several provisions enabling corporations and their shareholders to obtain relief from taxation in acquisition transactions both at the corporate level and the shareholder level. These provisions were important because most capital gain income does not result from real capital appreciation, but from inflation fostered by government policies. However, during the 1980s, Congress was seeking new revenue sources to replace revenues from reductions of individual taxes and to pay for major environmental and other rapidly growing government programs. Thus, Congress amended the Code to repeal the relief provisions:

- *Former Section 336.* Under the former Section 336, a corporation could distribute its assets in kind to its shareholders in a complete liquidation and did not recognize any gain on the distribution.[14] Thus, after such a liquidation, the shareholders could sell the assets and tax would be paid only at the shareholder level.[15]
- *Former Section 337.* Under the former Section 337, a corporation could adopt a plan of complete liquidation and sell its assets and distribute the net proceeds to its shareholders within 12 months pursuant to the plan without recognizing any gain or loss at the corporate level.[16]
- *Former Section 334(b)(2).* Under the former Section 334(b)(2), a buyer corporation could acquire a corporation by a taxable stock purchase and then liquidate it according to a plan adopted within two years. The result was that the buyer corporation could step up to cost (fair market value) its basis in the assets of the acquired corporation.[17] The stepped-up basis was allowed although no tax was imposed on the acquired corporation with respect to the appreciation that resulted in the increased fair market value.

[14]Section 336 implemented a principle obtained from a decision of the U.S. Supreme Court in *General Utilities & Operating Co. v. Helvering,* 296 U.S. 200 (1935).

[15]*U.S. v. Cumberland Public Service Co.,* 338 U.S. 451 (1950).

[16]Section 337 provided relief from the decision of the U.S. Supreme Court in *Commissioner v. Court Holding Co.,* 324 U.S. 331 (1945).

[17]See also the decision of the U.S. Tax Court in *Kimbell-Diamond Milling Co. v. Commissioner,* 14 T.C. 74 (1950); affirmed 187 F.2d 718 (5th Cir. 1951); cert den. 342 U.S. 827 (1951).

As described later in this chapter, Section 338 of the Code continues to provide a mechanism by which a buyer corporation can use the stock purchase method, but elect to obtain a stepped-up basis in the assets of the acquired subsidiary. However, a Section 338 election creates a "deemed sale" of the acquired corporation's assets at fair market value after the stock purchase, resulting in recognition of gain or loss that cannot easily be offset by other deductions or credits. Thus, the Section 338 election is seldom used because a buyer corporation will not elect to trigger a current tax obligation, only to obtain later deductions of lesser value. An important benefit under Section 338 is the exception in subsection 338(h)(10) that provides more favorable treatment when an acquired corporation has been a member of an affiliated group's consolidated return.

F. Allocation of Cost among Assets

Code Section 1060 requires that the consideration (purchase price) received for assets constituting a trade or business be allocated among the assets in accordance with the Internal Revenue Service ("IRS") regulations for purposes of determining both:

1. the transferee's basis in the assets, and
2. the gain or loss of the transferor.

In other words, an allocation of the purchase price is made to determine the buyer's basis in each acquired asset and the seller's gain or loss on the transfer of each asset.

If the transferee and transferor agree in writing as to the allocation of any consideration or the fair market value of any assets, the agreement is binding unless the IRS determines otherwise. See the standards for rejection of such an agreement in *Commissioner v. C.L. Danielson,* 378 F.2d 771 (3d Cir. 1967); *Ullman v. Commissioner,* 264 F.2d 305 (2d Cir. 1959); and *Freres Lumber Co., Inc., v. Commissioner,* 70 TCM (CCH) 1549 (1995).

Under Section 1060, the seller and buyer must each file a Form 8594 with the IRS if assets that constitute a trade or business are acquired and the buyer's basis in the assets is determined only by the amount paid for the assets. The buyer's consideration is the cost of the assets. The seller's consideration is the amount realized.

Under IRS Temporary Regulation §1.1060-1T, cost is allocated among asset classes as follows:

Class I Assets. Cash and cash equivalents (dollar for dollar).

Class II Assets. Certificates of deposit, U.S. government securities, foreign currency, readily marketable securities and similar items.

Class III Assets. All tangible and intangible assets that are not Class I,II or IV assets such as furniture, equipment, buildings, accounts receivable and covenants not to compete.

Class IV Assets. All Section 197 intangibles except those in the nature of goodwill and going-concern value.

Class V Assets. Section 197 intangibles in the nature of goodwill and going-concern value.

Under Temporary Regulation § 1.1060-1T(d), the residual method is used to allocate the price among the assets. The amount allocated to an asset, other than a Class V asset, cannot exceed its fair market value on the purchase date. Fair market value is gross fair market value, unreduced by mortgages, liens, pledges or other liabilities. Fair market values are usually obtained by appraisal. (**Note:** The IRS has not yet updated Form 8594 to show certain Section 197 intangibles as separate Class V Assets).

The price is allocated in the following order:

a. Reduce the consideration by the amount of Class I assets transferred.

b. Allocate the remaining consideration to Class II assets in proportion to their fair market values on the purchase date.

c. Allocate to Class III and IV assets respectively, in proportion to their fair market values on the purchase date.

d. Allocate to Class V assets.

The IRS regulations provide for reallocation of the purchase price if it is subsequently increased or decreased. For example, the price may be increased if a contingent additional amount becomes payable. It may be decreased if the seller must repay part of the price based on the results of an audit or because of breaches of representations and warranties in the acquisition agreement. If the increase or decrease occurs in the same tax year as the purchase date, the increase or decrease is considered to have occurred on the purchase date. If it occurs in a later tax year, the increase or decrease is considered in the year when it occurs.

An example selected from IRS Regulation Section 1.1060-1T(g) illustrates the basic methods for allocating a purchase price among the classes of assets:

Example

(i) On January 1, 1987, S, a sole proprietor, sells to P, a corporation, a group of assets that constitute a trade or business under paragraph (b)(2) of this section. P pays S $2,000 in cash and assumes $1,000 in liabilities. Thus, the total consideration is $3,000.

(ii) Assume that P acquires no Class I assets and that on the purchase date, the fair market values of the Class II and III assets S sold to P are as follows:

Asset Class	Asset	Fair Market Value
II	Portfolio of marketable securities	$ 400
	Total Class II	$ 400
III	Furniture and Fixtures	$ 800
	Building	800
	Land	200
	Equipment	400
	Accounts receivable	100
	Total Class III	$2,300
IV	Covenant not to compete	$ 100
	Total Class IV	$ 100

(iii) Under paragraphs (d)(1) and (d)(2) of this section, the amount of consideration allocable to the Class II, III, IV and V assets is the total consideration reduced by the amount of any Class I assets. Since P acquired no Class I assets, the total consideration of $3,000 is next allocated first to Class II, then to Class III, and then to Class IV assets. Since the fair market value of the Class II asset is $400, $400 of consideration is allocated to the Class II assets. Since the remaining amount of consideration is $2,600 (i.e., $3,000 - $400), an amount that exceeds the sum of the fair market values of the Class III assets ($2,300), the amount allocated to each Class III asset is its fair market value. Since, after allocation to Class III assets, the remaining amount of consideration is $300 ($3,000 - ($400 + $2,300)), an amount which exceeds the fair market value of the Class IV asset ($100), the amount allocated to the Class IV asset is its fair market value. Thus, the total amount allocated to the Class II assets is $400, the total amount allocated to the Class III assets is $2,300, and the total amount allocated to the Class IV asset is $100.

(iv) The amount allocated to the Class V assets (assets in the nature of goodwill and going-concern value) is $200 (i.e., $3,000 – ($400 + $2,300 + $100).

The Code does not require sellers and buyers to agree contractually on the allocation of the purchase price among assets sold. However, it is prudent and customary to do so. An allocation bargained at arm's length on the basis of independent appraisals is be more likely to be accepted by the IRS. However, Section 1060 authorizes the IRS to allocate differently and to determine different values. The IRS is likely to exercise this authority when an allocation is not made at arm's length or not supported by independent appraisals. (*Freres Lumber Co., Inc. v. Commissioner,* supra).

An example of a contractual allocation of a purchase price of $5,000,000 among assets in which the seller had an aggregate basis of $3,000,000, and the related effects on the seller and buyer, is as follows:

Asset	Seller's Basis	Allocated Value
Cash	$100,000	$ 100,000
Accounts receivable	600,000	600,000
Inventories	600,000	650,000(1)
Prepaid items	100,000	100,000
Equipment	1,000,000	1,800,000(2)
Buildings	500,000	700,000(3)
Land	100,000	300,000(4)
Class IV §197 Intangibles	–	200,000(5)
Class V §197 Intangibles	–	550,000(6)
	$3,000,000	$5,000,000

1. Seller has $50,000 gain taxable as ordinary income. Buyer has increased basis in the inventories.
2. Seller has § 1231 capital gain, subject to § 1245 recapture. Buyer has increased basis in the equipment, usable for MACRS deductions.
3. Seller has § 1231 capital gain, subject to § 1250 recapture. Buyer has increased basis in the building, usable for MACRS deductions.
4. Seller has § 1231 capital gain. Buyer has increased basis, but no depreciation deductions.

5. Seller has capital gain (see Section 1235). Buyer has amortizable § 197 intangible.
6. Seller has § 1231 gain. Buyer has amortizable § 197 intangible.

Buyers have a strong incentive to allocate as much of the price as possible to assets that can be expensed, depreciated or amortized over the shortest times. Such an allocation results in deductions that save income tax and, therefore, enhance the buyer's cash flow. Thus, buyers favor allocation to inventories or to equipment that can be written down quickly under MACRS. Buyers have a lesser incentive to allocate to assets such as buildings and Section 197 intangibles that are depreciated or amortized over longer periods.

During times when long-term capital gain rates are lower than ordinary income rates, sellers have an incentive to resist allocation to the assets favored by buyers because the seller will be taxed at ordinary income rates on the excess of the allocated amounts over their bases.[18] During times when corporate long-term capital gain income and ordinary income are taxed at the same rates, corporate sellers do not have that incentive.

During times when long-term gains are taxed at reduced rates, sellers have an incentive to allocate the price to capital assets such as land. Buyers have an incentive to minimize the allocation to land because the amount allocated cannot be used for depreciation or amortization deductions. At times when corporate sellers pay the same tax rate for long-term capital gain income and ordinary income, they are not strongly inclined to resist buyer efforts to minimize an allocation to land.

Notwithstanding such general principles, a seller or buyer may have unique tax characteristics that might motivate a different purchase price allocation.

G. Section 197 Intangibles

For decades, allocation of the price among purchased assets was a major source of controversy. Goodwill or going-concern value could not be amortized and deducted for income tax purposes. Thus, buyers sought to allocate the price to assets other than goodwill or going-concern value. To the extent that buyers could not obtain appraisals supporting allocation to tangible assets eligible for depreciation or amortization, they often allocated part of the price to intangible assets arguably eligible for amortization. Common examples of such assets were 1) intellectual properties such as patents, trade secrets, trademarks and copyrights; 2) covenants not to compete; 3) franchise or distributorship agreements; 4) government permits; 5) advantageous contracts with customers or suppliers; and 6) advantageous contracts with employees such as athletes or entertainers. The IRS often challenged these allocations by contending that the intangibles were either nonexistent or overvalued and that all or most of the amounts allocated to them should have been allocated to goodwill or going-concern value.

The Omnibus Budget Reconciliation Act of 1993 amended the Code to add a new Section 197. It allows an amortization deduction for intangible

[18] A seller could realize capital gain to the extent that the allocated amount excceds the amounts recaptured under Sections 1245 to 1250.

assets called "Section 197 Intangibles" acquired by a taxpayer after August 10, 1993 if acquired in connection with an acquisition of assets constituting a trade or business or a substantial portion thereof. The deduction is taken by amortizing the adjusted basis ratably over a 15-year period from the month when the intangibles are acquired.

From the seller's point of view, Section 197(f)(7) provides that any amortizable Section 197 Intangible be treated as property that is of a character subject to the allowance for depreciation provided in Code Section 167. The House Committee report explains that this means that an amortizable Section 197 Intangible is not a capital asset for purposes of Section 1221, but, if held for more than one year, will generally qualify as property used in a trade or business for purposes of Code Section 1231.

Stated briefly, a Section 197 Intangible means: (A) goodwill; (B) going-concern value; (C) workforce in place including contracts with them; (D) information bases such as customer lists or operating systems; (E) any patent, copyright, formula, process or other similar item; (F) any customer-based intangible; (G) any supplier-based intangible; (H) licenses, permits or other rights granted by the government; (I) a covenant not to compete; and (J) a franchise, trademark or trade name. There are several exclusions from the definition, including financial interests, land, certain kinds of computer software, interests under existing leases and debt instruments, sports franchises, mortgage servicing rights and certain transaction costs.

Section 197 provides that the amortization deduction is exclusive and no other depreciation or amortization deduction is allowable for any amortizable Section 197 Intangible. The deduction is not allowed for any self-created amortizable Section 197 Intangible. Section 197 also contains anti-churning and anti-abuse provisions.

No loss is recognized if any Section 197 Intangible is disposed of, or becomes worthless, while any one or more Section 197 Intangibles acquired in the same transaction or series of transactions are retained. Instead, adjustments to the adjusted bases of the retained intangibles are to be made for the unrecognized loss.

Section 197 should reduce the economic motivations that led to many disputes between taxpayers and the IRS over amortization deductions for intangible assets and their classification as goodwill or going-business value for which deductions were not allowed. It will not eliminate the need to allocate the price paid for an acquisition of business assets pursuant to Section 338(b)(5) or Section 1060 of the Code. Further, taxpayers will continue to seek advantageous allocations. For example, an allocation to machinery and equipment supported by sound evidence would result in deductions over periods shorter than 15 years. In contrast, an amount allocated to land would not result in any deduction until such time as the land is sold. Further, buyers may continue to provide employment or consulting contracts to seller personnel, resulting in compensation deductions over periods shorter than 15 years.

H. Depreciation Recapture

During times when long-term capital gains are taxed at lower rates than ordinary income, the accelerated depreciation deductions provided by Section 168 and the amortization deductions allowed by other sections of the Code could provide windfall profits to persons, including speculators, unless their use is subject to limitations. Taxpayers could buy depreciable or amortizable property and obtain deductions from ordinary income. They could then sell the property for a price exceeding the adjusted basis and report the profit as long-term capital gain, thus arbitraging the rate differential.

The Code contains two sections designed to restrict taxpayers from obtaining capital gain income as a result of depreciation and amortization deductions. The first is Section 1245, which applies to personal property and certain other properties called "Section 1245 property" depreciable under Section 167 or amortizable under Section 197. The second is Section 1250, which applies to real property depreciable under Section 167 and called "Section 1250 property." Both sections contain exceptions for gifts, certain transfers at death, certain tax-free transactions, certain like-kind exchanges and involuntary conversions and certain other transactions. Sections 1245 and 1250 are commonly called "depreciation recapture" provisions. However, readers should understand that they do not retroactively deny any depreciation deductions as the word *recapture* might seem to imply. Rather, they simply convert some or all of the gain on a sale or disposition of Section 1245 property and Section 1250 property from capital gain to ordinary income.

Section 1245 converts gain that would otherwise be capital gain to ordinary income by requiring a recomputation of the basis of "Section 1245 property" upon any sale or other disposition. The amount by which the lower of:

A. the recomputed basis, or

B. **i.** the amount realized in the case of a sale, exchange or involuntary conversion, or

ii. the fair market value in the case of any other disposition,

exceeds the adjusted basis of the property is ordinary income.

IRS Regulation §1.1245-1(b)(2) provides examples of the computation:

Example 1.

On January 1, 1964, Brown purchases Section 1245 property for use in his manufacturing business. The property has a basis for depreciation of $3,300. After taking depreciation deductions of $1,300 (the amount allowable), Brown realizes after selling expenses the amount of $2,900 upon sale of the property on January 1, 1969. Brown's gain is $900 ($2,900 amount realized minus $2,000 adjusted basis). Since the amount realized upon disposition of property ($2,900) is lower than its recomputed basis ($3,300, i.e., $2,000 adjusted basis plus $1,300 in depreciation deductions), the entire gain is treated as ordinary income under Section 1245(a)(1) and not as gain.

Example (2).

Assume the same facts as in Example 1 except that Brown exchanges the Section 1245 property for land that has a fair market value of $3,700, thereby realizing a gain of $1,700; the recomputed basis ($3,300) is lower than the amount realized upon its disposition ($3,700); the excess of recomputed basis over adjusted basis, or $1,300, is treated as ordinary income under Section 1245(a)(1). The remaining $400 of the gain may be treated as Section 1231 gain.

Section 1250 accomplishes a similar result, but uses different methods. Upon a disposition of "Section 1250 property," gain is recognized and treated as ordinary income to the extent that depreciation deductions after 1969 exceeded the amounts available if the straight-line method had been used. Thus, Section 1250 allows capital gain treatment to the extent of depreciation deductions allowable under the straight-line method, except that all depreciation is converted to ordinary income if the disposition is of property held for one year or less. However, the portion of the gain attributable to straight-line depreciation that can be treated as ordinary income is reduced by 20 percent upon disposition of Section 1250 property (other than a certified pollution control facility) by a corporation other than a Subchapter S corporation.

The Taxpayer Relief Act of 1997 provides that any long-term (more than 18 months) gain from a sale or exchange of Section 1250 property that would be treated as ordinary income if it were Section 1245 property shall be taxed at a maximum rate of 25 percent.

I. Complete Liquidation of Subsidiaries

If a parent corporation completely liquidates a subsidiary, Section 332 of the Code provides for different treatment than the treatment under Section 336 described earlier. Under Sections 332 and 337, no gain or loss is recognized on the receipt by a corporation of property distributed in complete liquidation of another corporation, provided that:

- The corporation receiving the property owns stock of the liquidated corporation that meets an 80 percent or more voting power and total value test, and either,
- the distribution by the liquidating corporation is in complete liquidation or redemption of all its stock and the transfer of all the property occurs within the taxable year, or
- the distribution is one of a series of distributions by the liquidating corporation in complete liquidation or redemption of all its stock in accordance with a plan of liquidation under which the transfer of all property is to be completed within 3 years.

Under Section 381(a), the parent corporation receiving a distribution to which Section 332 applies succeeds to the tax characteristics of the liquidated subsidiary. The parent corporation, if it wishes, can then sell the assets received in the distribution and will be taxed on the gain or loss, measured by the bases in the assets obtained by succession from the liquidated subsidiary. An effect of Section 332 is to eliminate the triple taxation of corporate income that could otherwise occur upon a sale of the assets of a subsidiary.

A corporation receiving distributions under Section 332 must keep permanent records and meet the filing requirements of IRS Regulation Section 1.332-6.

If a subsidiary has minority shareholders who receive distributions, they are not entitled to the nonrecognition treatment afforded to the parent corporation.

J. Section 338 Elections

Section 338 of the Code allows certain acquisitions by the stock purchase method to be treated as asset purchases. This treatment is available only if the purchasing corporation elects such treatment and acquires, within a 12-month acquisition period, stock of another corporation (called the "target corporation") meeting 80 percent or more voting power and total value tests.

Section 338 is quite complex. Using its own terminology, if a purchasing corporation makes a qualified purchase of the stock of a target corporation and a required election, the target corporation is treated as having sold and purchased all of its assets in a fictional sale called a "deemed sale." The target corporation is taxed on the sale and is treated as having a basis in the assets equal to the purchasing corporation's basis in the stock of the target corporation. The basis is allocated among the assets of the target corporation under IRS regulations using the same residual allocation method used under Section 1060 discussed previously (see Temp. Regulation § 1.338(b)-2T). The stepped-up values allocated to the assets support increased depreciation and amortization deductions. Since the "deemed sale" takes place after the stock purchase, the seller is unaffected by the election and treats the transaction as a stock sale.

A qualified stock purchase is any transaction or series of transactions in which a purchasing corporation acquires 80 percent or more of the voting power and total value of the stock of another corporation by purchase during a 12-month acquisition period. The required election by the purchasing corporation is made by filing a Form 8023-A with the IRS within 9 months and 15 days after the acquisition date. The election is irrevocable.

Section 338 has not been used extensively because the immediate tax generated by the "deemed sale" outweighs the tax savings that result over years from the stepped-up basis of the assets. However, a section 338 election can be valuable if:

- The target corporation has NOL carryforwards sufficient to offset all or most of the income from the "deemed sale."
- The target corporation is a member of a consolidated group that has NOL carryforwards sufficient to offset all or most of the income from the "deemed sale" and the election is made under Section 338(h)(10) by both the buyer and seller.
- The target corporation is a member subsidiary of a consolidated group or an affiliated group filing separate returns, the outside basis in the target's stock and the inside basis in its assets are approximately equal and the election is made under Section 338(h)(10).
- The target corporation is a Subchapter S corporation not subject to the penalty tax on built-in gains under Section 1374 and an election is made under Section 338(h)(10).

An election under Section 338(h)(10) is a valuable exception to the general rules under Section 338. The Form 8023-A must be signed by the purchasing corporation and also by the common parent of a selling consolidated group, or the selling affiliate, or the shareholders of a Subchapter S corporation.

When a Section 338(h)(10) election is made for a consolidated group, the "deemed sale" is treated as made by the target corporation, when it is a member of the consolidated group, for an amount equal to the price paid by the purchasing corporation for the target corporation. The target corporation is treated as liquidated in a tax-free liquidation under Section 332. The consolidated group recognizes no gain or loss on its sale of stock of the target corporation. Thus, only a single tax is paid with respect to the "deemed sale." As described earlier, a parent corporation could accomplish a similar result (i.e., a single tax) by completely liquidating the subsidiary under Section 332 and selling its assets to the buyer corporation.

When a Section 338(h)(10) election is made for a target corporation that is a Subchapter S corporation, the purchasing corporation and the shareholders of the target corporation must sign the Form 8023-A. The effect of the election is that the target corporation is deemed to be liquidated under Section 331, a taxable transaction and no gain or loss is recognized on the sale of stock to the purchasing corporation. Thus, double tax is avoided. However, the shareholders should consider the extent to which 1) ordinary income rather than capital gain will result from the "deemed sale;" 2) differences in the target corporation's basis in its assets and their basis in the stock may increase their tax burden; and 3) the tax on built-in gains under Section 1274 may apply.

A purchasing corporation that has not voluntarily made a Section 338 election will be treated as having made an election if it acquires any asset of the target corporation (or a target affiliate) within a time period called the "consistency period." This period consists of 1) the 1-year period before the beginning of the 12-month acquisition period, 2) the acquisition period through the acquisition date and 3) and the 1-year period after the acquisition date. This "deemed election" treatment does not apply if the asset acquired is pursuant to a sale by the target corporation in the ordinary course of business or if certain other exceptions apply.

Section 269(b) of the Code provides that if an election under Section 338 is not made with respect to a qualified stock purchase by a corporation and the acquired corporation is liquidated pursuant to a plan of liquidation adopted more than two years after the acquisition date, and if the principal purpose for the liquidation is the evasion or avoidance of federal income tax by securing the benefit of a deduction, credit or other allowance the acquiring corporation would not otherwise enjoy, then the IRS may disallow such deduction, credit or other allowance.

K. Deferred Payment of the Price

1. Installment Sales

As a general rule, Section 453 of the Code provides that the income from an installment sale be taken into account by the installment method. An installment sale is a disposition of property in which at least one payment is to be received after the taxable year in which the disposition occurs. However, it does not include dispositions by dealers or of inventories of personal property.

The installment method recognizes income in any taxable year as payments are received. The amount of income is the proportion of the payments received in that year that the gross profit bears to the contract price. Sellers who wish to use the installment method must prepare and file IRS Form 6252, a copy of which appears as Exhibit 6-3. A seller who does not want installment treatment can elect not to use the installment method by so indicating on IRS Form 4797, Sales of Business Property.

Most sellers prefer to report income by the installment method because it enables them to match their tax obligations with receipt of installment payments that can be used to pay the taxes.

The installment method can be illustrated by assuming a sale of stock for a net cash price of $1,000,000. Of this amount, $500,000 is payable at the closing and the balance is payable in five equal $100,000 installments on the next five anniversary dates of the closing. The seller's basis in the stock is $500,000. Based on these assumptions, the proportion that gross profit bears to the contract price is 50 percent. Thus, 50 percent of the closing payment and 50 percent of each of the $100,000 installment payments is taxable in the year received. However, if depreciable assets are sold, an amount equal to any recapture income under Sections 1245 and 1250 must be fully recognized in the year of disposition under Section 453(i).

In applying Section 453, the term *payment* does not include the receipt of notes or other evidence of indebtedness of the buyer of the property, whether or not payment of the indebtedness is guaranteed by another person. However, receipt of a bond or other evidence of indebtedness is treated as payment if it is payable on demand or is issued by a corporation or a government or political subdivision thereof and is readily tradable. The term *readily tradable* means a bond or other evidence of indebtedness that is readily tradable in an established securities market. A bond or other evidence of indebtedness with interest coupons attached or in registered form is considered to be readily tradable unless the taxpayer establishes to the contrary.

If a seller elects not to use the installment method, the installment obligation will be taxed in the current taxable year. The value will ordinarily be the "issue price" determined in the manner provided in Section 1274.

Section 453A of the Code provides that interest must be paid to the IRS on the so-called deferred tax liability resulting from use of the installment method. Section 453A applies only if the sales price of property exceeds $150,000. The interest obligation arises only if the face amount of all obligations that arose during, and are outstanding at the close of, the taxable year exceed $5,000,000. Exceptions are provided for installment obligations arising from dispositions of personal use property and property used in the trade or business of farming.

2. Imputed Interest Under Section 483

When payment of all or part of the price for a sale or exchange of property is deferred, the seller and buyer usually negotiate for payment of interest by the buyer on the amount deferred. A seller who expects to pay tax at reduced rates on capital gains has an incentive to bargain for a higher price in exchange for a lower interest rate that would be taxed at ordinary income rates. Section 483 of the Code reduces the incentive by treating part of the price as interest if the seller and buyer contract for an interest rate below rates published by the IRS.

Using its own terminology, Section 483 provides that a payment under any contract for the sale or exchange of property shall be treated as interest in proportion to the total unstated interest under such contract. Unstated interest means the excess of:

1. the sum of the payments due under the contract, over
2. the sum of the present values of such payments and the present values of any interest payments due under the contract.

The present values of payments are determined by using discount rates published monthly by the IRS.

The imputed interest provisions of Section 483 were largely superseded when Section 1274 on original issue discount was adopted for sales or exchanges after 1984. Since then, Section 483 has applied only to transactions that occurred prior to its effective date and to small transactions within the exceptions to Section 1274.

3. Original Issue Discount

Sections 1271 to 1275 of the Code contain rules for the determination and inclusion in income of original issue discount (OID) on debt instruments. The rules are not limited to acquisition transactions, but apply generally (with some exceptions) to debt instruments that have a maturity date over one year.

The OID rules focus on understated interest, like the imputed interest rules of the older Section 483. However, the OID rules are far more complex and also focus on the times when imputed interest must be recognized. In essence, the OID rules require taxpayers to recognize and to include in income by an accrual method both stated interest and imputed interest, regardless of their usual accounting methods, including the cash receipts method. In general, OID must be accrued by a constant yield to maturity method that compounds semiannually. Since the OID rules supervene the contractual terms of debt instruments, an understanding of their requirements and effects is important for acquisition planners.

Recharacterization of Certain Debt Payments: Section 1271 provides that amounts received by a holder on retirement of a debt instrument shall be received in exchange therefor.[19] Thus, the retirement of a debt instrument results in capital gain or loss. However, if at the time of original issue there was an intention to call a debt instrument before maturity, any gain realized on the sale or exchange that does not exceed the OID (reduced by certain amounts) is treated as ordinary income.

Current Inclusion of OID in Income: Section 1272 requires current inclusion in the income of the holder of a debt instrument having OID an amount equal to the OID for each day during the taxable year in which the holder holds the debt instrument, regardless of actual cash receipt of interest.

[19]This treatment applies to the holder, not the issuer. The issuer's payments are deductible to the extent allowed by Code Section 163 which contains, among other things, its own provisions governing deduction of OID.

Amount of OID: Section 1273 determines the amount of OID, which is the excess, if any, of

A. the stated redemption price at maturity, over
B. the issue price[20]

The stated redemption price at maturity includes interest and other amounts payable at that time other than interest based on a fixed rate and payable unconditionally at fixed periodic intervals of one year or less during the entire term of the debt instrument.

The issue price of debt instruments not issued for property or issued for publicly traded property is as follows:

• Publicly offered debt not issued for property[21]	The initial offering price to the public
• Other debt instruments not issued for property	The price paid by the first buyer
• Debt instruments issued for property where there is public trading	The fair market value of the property

The issue price of certain debt instruments issued for property is determined by different rules contained in Section 1274. These rules are important for acquisition planners because they affect acquisition negotiations and financing costs. If Section 1274 applies to a debt instrument, the issue price is (A) the stated principal amount if there is adequate stated interest, or (B) an imputed principal amount in any other case.

Section 1274 applies if

A. the stated redemption price at maturity exceeds
  i. the stated principal amount, if there is adequate stated interest, or
  ii. the imputed principal amount, in any other case, and
B. some or all payments are due more than six months after the exchange, and
C. neither the debt instrument nor the property for which it is issued are publicly traded.[22]

There is adequate stated interest if the stated principal amount is less than or equal to the imputed principal amount of the debt instrument.

The imputed principal amount is equal to the sum of the present values of all payments due under the debt instrument. The present value of a

[20]OID is treated as zero if it is less than a *de minimis* amount, i.e., (A) 1/4 of 1% of the stated redemption price at maturity, multiplied by (B). the number of complete years to maturity.

[21]For this purpose, the term "property" includes services and the right to use property, but such term does not include money. In general, debt instruments not issued for property are sold for money.

[22]Section 1274 contains other exceptions for small transactions such as sales for $1,000,000 or less of farms by individuals or small businesses; sales of principal residences; sales involving payments of $250,000 or less; certain sales of patents; and certain land transfers between related persons.

payment is calculated as of the date of the sale or exchange using a discount rate equal to the applicable federal rate (AFR):

Debt Instrument Term	*Federal Rate*
Not over 3 years	Short-term rate
Over 3 years, but not over 9 years	Mid-term rate
Over 9 years	Long-term rate

The IRS publishes AFRs monthly in the Internal Revenue Bulletin.

The practical effect of the issue price rules is that the amount of OID on debt instruments that are publicly traded or are issued for publicly traded property is derived from fair market value and reflects the yield to maturity indicated by the market. The amount of OID on other debt instruments is based on imputed AFR rates that are likely to be lower than the yields on debt instruments issued by large, privately owned companies.

Section 1274A provides special rules for certain transactions in which the stated principal amount does not exceed $2,800,000. The first rule allows the use of a discount rate not exceeding 9 percent, compounded semiannually, with respect to a debt instrument if its stated principal amount does not exceed $2,800,000. The second rule allows a joint election by a borrower and a lender to use the cash method if the stated principal amount of a cash method debt instrument does not exceed $2,000,000. To be allowed to make the election, the lender must not use an accrual method of accounting and may not be a dealer in the property sold or exchanged.

4. Contingent Payments

Many acquisition contracts do not provide for a definite purchase price, but for an agreed amount that will be increased by additional payments if certain business or financial objectives are achieved. For example, a buyer may commit to pay a seller a percentage of earnings in excess of agreed levels. The commitment is usually limited to a period of years or by a "cap" on the total payments, or both.

For many years, it was recognized that the fair value of many kinds of contingent payment rights could not readily be determined. If a portion of a price was unascertainable, selling shareholders using either the accrual or the cash method could defer taxation of the unascertainable portion under the "open transaction" concept described by the U.S. Supreme Court in *Burnet v. Logan.*[23]

A seller could elect not to use the installment method and claim that the value of contingent payments is so uncertain that the "open transaction" doctrine of *Burnet v. Logan*, supra, should apply. The IRS is likely to challenge such a claim and contend that Code Section 1001 requires recognition of the entire gain or loss except as provided in specific sections authorizing deferral, such as the installment sale provisions of Section 453.

A seller who has contracted for contingent payments can use the installment method provided in Section 453 and be taxed on the payments in

[23]283 U.S. 404 (1931).

the year received. Under this method, the seller's basis must be allocated among the payments, although their amount is unknown. If the contingent payments are subject to a "cap," the IRS regulations require that basis be allocated on the assumption that the full amount allowed by the "cap" will be received.[24] The effect is to defer the seller's recovery of basis. If the contingent payments are not limited by a "cap," basis is allocated and recovered over the time period during which the contingent payments may be received.[25] No loss can be recognized, but the basis is carried forward to the next year. If the contingent payments are not limited by a "cap" or a time period, the IRS will review them to determine whether the arrangement should be recharacterized as rent or royalty income. If the payments continue to be characterized as debt, basis is recovered in equal increments over 15 years.[26]

A seller who has contracted for contingent payments must also consider the OID rules and particularly IRS Regulation § 1.1275-4.[27]

5. Escrow Retentions

Acquisition contracts commonly provide that part of the price will be retained in escrow for some time period as security to protect the buyer if any seller representations and warranties or covenants are breached. Escrow arrangements differ from other arrangements involving contingencies because the amount of the price is known and the seller will receive the escrow retention if its representations and warranties are accurate and it performs its covenants. On the other hand, buyers often negotiate for representations and warranties and covenants that are difficult to meet and are quick to submit claims. Thus, a seller's eventual receipt of an escrow retention may be far from a certainty.

A seller should ordinarily be allowed to treat the amount retained in escrow as an installment payment taxable in the year received under Section 453 of the Code and to allocate basis in accordance with that method.[28] In drafting the escrow arrangements, counsel for the seller and buyer should review the IRS regulations on constructive receipt of income.[29]

Acquisition agreements typically provide that the escrow agent must invest retained funds in short-term investments such as bank certificates of deposit or U.S. Treasury securities. For many years, buyers and sellers provided that the interest from these investments would follow the funds paid wholly or partially to each of them when any claims were resolved and distributions made. However, since 1986, Section 468B of the Code has implied that the interest income is subject to current income tax. Section 468B

---

[24]IRS Reg. § 15A.453-1(c) (2).

[25]IRS Reg. § 15A.453-1(c) (3).

[26]IRS Reg. § 15A.453-1(c) (4).

[27]The IRS can recharacterize contingency payment arrangements even when they are subject to a "cap" or time limit (IRS Reg. § 15A.453-1(c)(1)). However, typical contingent payments of a reasonable percentage of earnings (or excess earnings) for two or three years to compromise price negotiations should not be recharacterized.

[28]*Granneman v. U.S.*, 649 F. Supp. 949 (E.D. Mo. 1986); 97-1 USTC (CCH) § 9287 and cases cited therein.

[29]IRS Reg. 1.451-2.

directs the IRS to prescribe regulations for taxation as a grantor trust or otherwise, but the IRS has not done so. Nevertheless, the parties should address this issue in the controlling escrow agreement or consider investing in an otherwise exempt obligation.

L. Loss of Interest Deductions for Acquisition Debt

1. Recharacterization of Debt As Equity

A simple debt instrument provides for payment of a definite amount of money on a specific date with interest at a stated rate approximating currently prevailing rates. The instrument confers no rights to elect the management or share in the profits of the issuer. Upon default, the holder is entitled to enforce payment. In bankruptcy, the holder is entitled to payment with other creditors before any payment is made to stockholders.

By contrast, simple common stock represents ownership, including the right to elect directors and to benefit through dividends and capital appreciation in the profits of the issuer. However, the holder has no commitment for repayment of the amount invested or dividends. In bankruptcy, the holder is not entitled to payment until all creditors are paid in full.

For both debt instruments and stock, the basic characteristics are often modified to increase or reduce the rights of their holders. For example, a debt instrument can be subordinated to the rights of other creditors or made convertible into stock. A class of stock can be issued with preferences including dividend and redemption commitments and a right to be paid a specified amount in bankruptcy before any amounts are paid on common stock. The modifications sometimes create a hybrid instrument that is labeled as debt or stock, but has few characteristics indicated by the label. When that happens, the IRS may seek to impose tax based on the predominant characteristics of the instrument rather than its label.[30]

Section 385 of the Code has for many years authorized the IRS to prescribe regulations to determine whether an interest in a corporation is stock or indebtedness. However, IRS regulations adopted in 1980 were withdrawn in 1983 and none have been adopted since then. The IRS may believe that it can act more successfully on a case-by-case basis. However, the absence of regulations leaves taxpayers with limited guidance on the factors that distinguish debt from equity.

Section 385 lists five factors that the IRS may include in its regulations among other factors:

1. Whether there is a written unconditional promise to pay on demand or on a specified date a sum certain in money in return for an adequate consideration in money or money's worth, and to pay a fixed rate of interest.
2. Whether there is subordination to or preference over any indebtedness of the corporation.

[30]See IRS Notices 94-47 and 94-48, 1994-1 C.B. 347.

3. The ratio of debt to equity of the corporation.
4. Whether there is convertibility into the stock of the corporation.
5. The relationship between holdings of stock in the corporation and holdings of the interest in question.

The IRS has also said that it will consider the intent of the parties.[31] A list of eleven factors was used by the U.S. Court of Appeals for the Ninth Circuit to conclude that the IRS had improperly recharacterized a debt obligation arising from a sale as an equity interest arising from a capital contribution.[32] The eleven factors were as follows:

1. The names given to the certificates evidencing the indebtedness.
2. The presence or absence of a maturity date.
3. The source of the payments.
4. The right to enforce payment of principal and interest.
5. Participation in management.
6. A status equal to or inferior to that of regular corporate creditors.
7. The intent of the parties.
8. "Thin" or adequate capitalization.
9. Identity of interest between creditor and stockholder.
10. Payment of interest only out of "dividend" money.
11. The ability of the corporation to obtain loans from outside lending institutions.

In addition, in order to prevent taxpayers from taking inconsistent positions that favor each taxpayer (for example, the issuer claims it is interest and the holder claims it is equity), Section 385(3) requires that the characterization by the issuer will be binding on all holders, but not on the IRS. There is an exception for any seller who notifies the IRS of an inconsistent reporting position.

2. Disallowance of Deductions for Interest Paid on Corporate Acquisition Indebtedness

Section 279 of the Code provides that no deduction shall be allowed for interest paid or incurred by a corporation during a taxable year for corporate acquisition indebtedness exceeding (1) $5,000,000 reduced by (2) interest paid or incurred on certain other acquisition-related obligations. Corporate acquisition indebtedness means any obligation evidenced by a bond, debenture, note or other evidence of indebtedness issued by a corporation and meeting all of the following four conditions:

1. The obligation is issued to provide consideration for (A) the acquisition of stock in another corporation, or (B) the assets of another cor-

---

[31]Rev Rul. 83-98, 1983-2 C.B. 40.

[32]*Hardman v. U.S.*, 827 F.2d 1409 (9th Cir. 1987); 87-2 USTC (CCH) § 9523. See *R.W. Lease*, 66 T.C. Memo. (CCH) 1121 for a decision using 13 factors.

poration pursuant to a plan to acquire at least two-thirds (in value) of all assets (excluding money) used in its trades and businesses.

2. The obligation is either (A) subordinated to the claims of trade creditors of the issuing corporation, or (B) expressly subordinated in right of payment to any substantial amount of present or future unsecured indebtedness of the issuing corporation.
3. The evidence of indebtedness is either (A) convertible directly or indirectly into stock of the issuing corporation, or (B) part of an investment unit or other arrangement that includes an option to acquire, directly or indirectly, stock in the issuing corporation.
4. On the last day of any taxable year when the issuing corporation issues any obligation to acquire stock or assets as described above, either (A) its debt-to-equity ratio exceeds 2 to 1, or (B) its projected earnings do not exceed 3 times the annual interest to be paid or incurred.

Corporations paying less than $5,000,000 of interest on corporate acquisition indebtedness are not limited by Section 279. However, they should consider its effects if they have plans for future acquisition financing that could result in interest costs exceeding $5,000,000.

Skillful acquisition planners do not usually have great difficulty designing acquisition debt that avoids the risk of loss of interest deductions under Section 279. For example, the first condition does not apply to debt issued by the acquired corporation. The second condition does not apply if subordination is limited to secured indebtedness of the issuing corporation. The third condition does not apply if the obligation is not convertible and does not include any option to acquire stock in the issuing corporation. The fourth condition does not apply if neither of the specified ratios are exceeded on the applicable date, although this can be difficult to accomplish if a buyer is making effective use of leverage in its financial structure.

In the fourth condition, the ratio of debt to equity is the ratio of total indebtedness of the issuing corporation to the sum of its money and other assets. Projected earnings means the average annual earnings of the issuing corporation for a three-year period ending with the taxable year when it issues any obligation to provide consideration for an acquisition of stock or assets. However, if the issuing corporation has acquired 80 percent or more voting control or substantially all the properties of the acquired corporation, projected earnings must also include the average annual earnings of the acquired corporation. In either case, the earnings are computed without reduction for (i) interest paid or accrued, (ii) depreciation or amortization, (iii) federal income tax and (iv) dividends other than any dividends from the acquired to the issuing corporation. If the average annual earnings of the issuing corporation and the acquiring corporation must be combined, the annual interest to be paid or incurred by both corporations must also be combined in calculating the ratio.

Examples contained in the IRS regulations showing the calculation of the ratios prescribed in the fourth condition are as follows:

Example 1

On June 1, 1971, X Corporation, which files its federal income tax returns on a calendar year basis, issues an obligation for $45 million to the shareholders of Y Corporation to provide consideration for the acquisition of all of the stock of Y Corporation. Such obligation has the characteristics of corporate acquisition indebtedness described in Section 279(b)(2) and (3). The projected earnings of X Corporation and Y Corporation exceed 3 times the annual interest to be paid or incurred by those corporations and, accordingly, the condition described in Section 279(b)(4)(B) is not present. Also, on December 31, 1971, X Corporation has total assets with an adjusted basis of $150 million (including the newly acquired stock of Y Corporation having a basis of $45 million) and total indebtedness of $90 million. Hence, X Corporation's equity is $60 million, computed by subtracting its $90 million of total indebtedness from its $150 million of total assets. Since X Corporation's ratio of debt to equity of 1.5 to 1 ($90 million of total indebtedness over $60 million equity) does not exceed 2 to 1, the condition described in section 279(b)(4)(A) is not present. Therefore, X Corporation's obligation for $45 million is not corporate acquisition indebtedness because on December 31, 1971, neither of the conditions specified in Section 279(b)(4) existed.

Example 2

Corporation X's earnings and profits calculated in accordance with Section 279(c)(3)(B) for 1972, 1971 and 1970 respectively were $29 million, $23 million and $20 million. The interest to be paid or incurred during the calendar year of 1973 as determined by reference to the issuing corporation's total outstanding indebtedness as of December 31, 1972, was $10 million. By dividing the sum of the earnings and profits for the three years by 36 (the number of whole calendar months in the 3-year period) and multiplying the quotient by 12, the average annual earnings for X Corporation is $24 million. Since the projected earnings of X Corporation do not exceed by 3 times the annual interest to be paid or incurred (they exceed by only 2.4 times), one of the circumstances described in Section 279(b)(4) is present.

Acquisition planners usually avoid the application of Section 279 by assuring that either the second or third conditions are not met. In planning for the second condition, they should confirm that the amount and payment schedule for the acquisition indebtedness will not be perceived as a problem by trade creditors and other unsecured lenders. In planning for the third condition, they should compare the interest yield payable on acquisition indebtedness without a conversion feature to the yield that could be obtained with a conversion feature. In the author's experience, lenders like a conversion (or option) feature, but are reluctant to sacrifice much interest yield in return for it.

3. Partial Disallowance of Deductions of OID on High-Yield Discount Obligations

Section 163(e) of the Code allows an issuer to deduct OID with some exceptions for debt instruments held by related foreign persons. However, if a corporation issues an applicable high-yield discount obligation (HYDO), no deduction is allowed for a disqualified portion of the OID and the remainder of the OID may not be deducted until paid.

An applicable HYDO is any debt instrument if (A) its maturity date is more than 5 years from its issue date; (B) its yield to maturity equals or exceeds the applicable federal rate (AFR) under Section 1274(d) for the calendar month when issued plus 5 percent; and (C) it has significant OID as defined. A debt instrument has significant OID if the aggregate amount includible in income by a holder before the close of any accrual period ending more than 5 years after its issue date exceeds the sum of (i) the aggregate interest paid before the close of such period, and (ii) the product of its issue multiplied by its yield to maturity.

The disqualified portion of OID is the lesser of (1) the amount of OID, or (2) the portion of the total return that bears to the yield to maturity. The disqualified yield is the excess of the yield to maturity over the AFR plus 6 percent, which is 1 percent more lenient than the test used in defining an applicable HYDO.

Acquisition planners can avoid the disallowance and deferral imposed by Section 163(e) by negotiating for a yield below the level for disqualification or by providing for payment of sufficient interest before the end of the accrual period.

Section 163(e) is, in essence, a complex technique for denying an interest deduction to the extent that "deep discount" obligations are more characteristic of stock than debt. Consistent with this rationale, Section 163(e)(5)(B) allows a dividends received deduction for the dividend equivalent portion of the OID on a HYDO.

4. Disallowance of Deductions of Interest on Certain Obligations Not in Registered Form

Section 163(f) of the Code disallows interest deductions on any registration-required obligation unless it is in registered form. A registration-required obligation is any obligation except one that (i) is issued by a natural person, (ii) is not of a type offered to the public, (iii) has a maturity at issue of not more than a year, or (iv) is sold under certain arrangements to persons who are not U.S. persons. The effect is that publicly offered debt instruments for a term of more than one year must be in registered form if sold to U.S. persons.

M. Loss of Capital Gain Treatment in Certain Transactions

The Code contains a variety of provisions designed to treat transactions as ordinary income that might otherwise be treated as capital gain.

1. Depreciation Recapture

The depreciation recapture requirements of Sections 1245 and 1250 are an important example of provisions that convert income otherwise eligible for capital gain treatment to ordinary income.

2. Section 306 Stock

The provisions of Section 306 of the Code are designed to convert to ordinary income a portion or all of the income realized upon a sale of preferred stock defined as "Section 306 stock."

3. Collapsible Corporations

Section 341 of the Code provides that gain from the sale or exchange of stock of a collapsible corporation shall be considered as ordinary income. Section 341 also provides that a distribution in complete or partial liquidation of a collapsible corporation or a nondividend distribution of property of a collapsible corporation in excess of a stockholder's adjusted basis will be treated as ordinary income. The treatment does not apply to a shareholder who owns, directly or indirectly, 5 percent or less of the stock of a collapsible corporation.

A collapsible corporation is a relatively rare entity. It is defined as a corporation formed or availed of principally for the manufacture, construction, or production of property called "Section 341 assets," or for the holding of stock in a corporation so formed or availed of, with a view to (1) a sale or exchange of the stock by its shareholders or distribution to its shareholders before realization by the corporation of two-thirds of the taxable income to be derived from such property and (2) the realization by such shareholders of gain attributable to such property. "Section 341 assets" are the following properties if held by the corporation for less than three years:

A. Stock in trade or other property of a kind that could properly be included in its inventory if on hand at the close of the taxable year.

B. Property held primarily for sale to customers in the ordinary course of its trade or business.

C. Unrealized receivables or fees, except receivables from property other than property described in A and B.

D. Property described in Section 1231(b), without regard to the holding period therein, except property used in the manufacture, construction, production or sale of property described in A or B.

As indicated by the list of Section 341 assets, Section 341 is intended to prevent the use of a corporation to accumulate properties that generate ordinary income and then to realize their appreciated value as capital gain through a stock sale, liquidation or other distribution before the corporation has operated long enough to realize ordinary income from the assets.

Section 341 does not apply to a sale of stock of a corporation if it consents to recognition of gain with respect to certain assets. Section 341 also does not apply to certain tax-free transactions in which the basis of assets in the hands of a transferee is determined by reference to the basis in the hands of the transferor under Section 332, 351 or 361 of the Code.

N. Loss or Limitation of Net Operating Losses

A buyer who acquires a corporation or its assets in a taxable transaction does not succeed to its net operating loss (NOL) carryforwards and other tax characteristics under Section 381 of the Code. However, the buyer of a corporation wants the acquired corporation, if possible, to be able to continue to use its own NOL carryforwards.

Section 269 of the Code provides for the disallowance of NOL carryforwards after certain taxable acquisitions the principal purpose was evasion or avoidance of federal income tax. Section 382 provides for total loss of NOL carryforwards if the business enterprise is not continued. Section 382 also limits the amount of NOL carryforwards that can be used to offset taxable income after an ownership change occurs. See Chapter 7 for discussion of Sections 269 and 382. In addition, the consolidated tax return regulations have provisions that could apply to limit or preclude the use of any target company NOLs.

Section 172(b)(1)(E) was enacted to limit the use of NOL carrybacks as a partial financing source for leveraged buyout and leveraged restructuring transactions. Section 172(b)(1)(E) accomplishes this result by limiting the use of NOL carrybacks to offset certain losses incurred in taxable years after a corporate equity reduction transaction. Section 172(h) defines a corporate equity reduction transaction as a major stock acquisition or an excess distribution. The losses limited are those resulting from interest attributable to the corporate equity reduction transaction. Section 172 should be carefully considered before completing any acquisition or restructuring transaction that will rely on leveraging the acquired or restructured corporation.

O. Reference Materials

1. Books

CCH Standard Federal Tax Reporter (16 volumes)

Federal Taxation of Corporations and Shareholders, Bittker et al., Warren, Gorham & Lamont, 1996

Mergers, Acquisitions & Buyouts, Ginsburg et al., Little, Brown & Company, 1998

Tax Management Portfolio (BNA):

Structuring Corporate Acquisitions—Tax Aspects

Corporate Liquidations—Planning

Stock Purchases Treated as Asset Acquisitions—Section 338

Tax Strategies for Corporate Acquisitions, Dispositions, Spin-Offs, Joint Ventures, Financings, Reorganizations and Restructurings—1998, Freeman, Practicing Law Institute (11 volumes)

2. Articles

"Proposed Regs Would Treat Stock Redemptions as Extraordinary Dividends," *Tax Notes,* June 24, 1996.

P. Exhibits

6-1 Form 8594, Asset Acquisition Statement under Section 1060

6-2 Form 8023-A, Corporate Qualified Stock Purchases (Section 338)

6-3 Form 6252, Installment Sale Income (Section 453)

EXHIBIT 6-1

Form **8594**
(Rev. Jan. 1996)
Department of the Treasury
Internal Revenue Service

Asset Acquisition Statement
Under Section 1060

▶ Attach to your Federal income tax return.

OMB No. 1545-1021

Attachment Sequence No. 61

Name as shown on return | Identification number as shown on return

Check the box that identifies you: ☐ Buyer ☐ Seller

Part I **General Information**—To be completed by all filers.

1 Name of other party to the transaction | Other party's identification number

Address (number, street, and room or suite no.)

City or town, state, and ZIP code

2 Date of sale | 3 Total sales price

Part II **Assets Transferred**—To be completed by all filers of an original statement.

4 Assets	Aggregate Fair Market Value (Actual Amount for Class I)	Allocation of Sales Price
Class I	$	$
Class II	$	$
Class III	$	$
Class IV	$	$
Total	$	$

5 Did the buyer and seller provide for an allocation of the sales price in the sales contract or in another written document signed by both parties? . . . . ☐ Yes ☐ No
If "Yes," are the aggregate fair market values listed for each of asset Classes I, II, III, and IV the amounts agreed upon in your sales contract or in a separate written document? . . . . ☐ Yes ☐ No

6 In connection with the purchase of the group of assets, did the buyer also purchase a license or a covenant not to compete, or enter into a lease agreement, employment contract, management contract, or similar arrangement with the seller (or managers, directors, owners, or employees of the seller)? . . . . ☐ Yes ☐ No
If "Yes," specify (a) the type of agreement, and (b) the maximum amount of consideration (not including interest) paid or to be paid under the agreement. See the instructions for line 6.

For Paperwork Reduction Act Notice, see instructions. Cat. No. 63768Z Form **8594** (Rev. 1-96)

Form 8594 (Rev. 1-96) Page 2

Part III **Supplemental Statement**—To be completed only if amending an original statement or previously filed supplemental statement because of an increase or decrease in consideration.

7 Assets	Allocation of Sales Price as Previously Reported	Increase or (Decrease)	Redetermined Allocation of Sales Price
Class I	$	$	$
Class II	$	$	$
Class III	$	$	$
Class IV	$	$	$
Total	$		$

8 Reason(s) for increase or decrease. Attach additional sheets if more space is needed.

9 Tax year and tax return form number with which the original Form 8594 and any supplemental statements were filed.

EXHIBIT 6-2

Department of the Treasury
Internal Revenue Service

Instructions for Form 8023-A

(May 1994)

Corporate Qualified Stock Purchases

Paperwork Reduction Act Notice

We ask for the information on this form to carry out the Internal Revenue laws of the United States. You are required to give us the information. We need it to ensure that you are complying with these laws and to allow us to figure and collect the right amount of tax.

The time needed to complete and file this tax form will vary depending on individual circumstances. The estimated average time is:

Recordkeeping . . . . .9 hr., 34 min.

Learning about the law or the form . . . . .1 hr., 23 min.

Preparing and sending the form to the IRS . . .1 hr., 36 min.

If you have comments concerning the accuracy of these time estimates or suggestions for making this form more simple, we would be happy to hear from you. You can write to both the **Internal Revenue Service,** Attention: Reports Clearance Officer, PC:FP, Washington, D.C. 20224, and the **Office of Management and Budget,** (Paperwork Reduction Project 1545-1428), Washington, D.C. 20503. Do not send this form to either of these offices. Instead, see **When and Where To File** on this page.

General Instructions

Section references are to the Internal Revenue Code unless otherwise noted.

Purpose of Form

To make elections under section 338 and to implement the consistency rules of section 338, Form 8023-A must be filed when the purchasing corporation makes a qualified stock purchase (QSP) of another corporation (the "target" corporation). The form must be filed whether or not a section 338 election is made for the target.

If a section 338 election is made for the target, the target is treated for purposes of Subtitle A of the Code as having sold all of its assets on the acquisition date and then as having purchased the assets as a new corporation ("new" target) on the day after the acquisition date. (For periods on or before the acquisition date, the target is sometimes referred to as the "old" target.) In addition, the target must recognize gain or loss on the deemed sale of its assets (the "deemed sale gain").

If a section 338(h)(10) election is made for the target, the target generally is treated as making the deemed sale and liquidating. The treatment of the target shareholders generally is consistent with the sale and liquidation treatment. A section 338(h)(10) election cannot be made for a target corporation unless it is acquired from a selling consolidated group, a selling affiliate, or an S corporation shareholder.

Who Must File

The purchasing corporation must file Form 8023-A for the target. In certain cases, however, a United States shareholder of a foreign purchasing corporation may file Form 8023-A on behalf of the purchasing corporation. See Regulations section 1.338-1(g)(3). If a section 338(h)(10) election is made for a target, Form 8023-A must be filed jointly by the purchasing corporation and the common parent of the selling consolidated group (or selling affiliate or S corporation shareholder).

One Form 8023-A (rather than multiple Forms 8023-A) may be used for targets that each have the same acquisition date, were members of the same affiliated group immediately before the acquisition date, and are members of the same affiliated group immediately after the acquisition date. All of the information that would be required for the additional target if a separate Form 8023-A were filed must be provided for that target in schedules attached to the form.

When and Where To File

To make a section 338 election for the target corporation, file Form 8023-A with the Internal Revenue Service Center where the Federal income tax return that includes the deemed sale gain is or will be filed. File Form 8023-A by the 15th day of the 9th month beginning after the month that includes the acquisition date. Form 8023-A must be attached to the final income tax return for the old target and the first return of the new target.

Whether or not a section 338 election is made for the target, the purchasing corporation must attach Form 8023-A to its Federal income tax return for the tax year that includes the acquisition date.

Special rules may apply to foreign purchasing corporations or foreign targets. The time during which a qualifying foreign purchasing corporation may make a section 338 election for a qualifying foreign target is described in Regulations section 1.338-1(g)(1)(iii). A foreign purchasing corporation that does not file a Federal income tax return must file Form 8023-A with the Office of Assistant Commissioner (International), Attention: Chief of Examination, 950 L'Enfant Plaza South S.W., Washington, DC 20024. In addition, if a section 338 election is made for a foreign target for which a **Form 5471,** Information Return of U.S. Persons With Respect To Certain Foreign Corporations, is filed, Form 8023-A must be attached to the last Form 5471 for the old target and the first Form 5471 for the new target.

Definitions

Acquisition date.—The acquisition date is the first day on which a QSP has occurred.

Qualified stock purchase.—A QSP is the purchase of at least 80% of the total voting power and value of the stock of a corporation by another corporation during a 12-month acquisition period. Preferred stock (as described in section 1504(a)(4)) is not included in computing voting power or value. See section 338(h)(1) for the definition of "12-month acquisition period" and section 338(h)(3) for the definition of "purchase."

Specific Instructions

Employer identification number.—An employer identification number (EIN) must be included for each corporation identified in Section A, B, or C, or on attached schedules. An EIN is not required if the corporation does not have, and is not otherwise required to have, an EIN.

Country of incorporation.—When identifying the country of incorporation, include political subdivisions, if any.

Tax year ending.—The tax year ending date of any corporation is determined without regard to any QSP.

Attachments.—Attach a schedule identifying any assets to which the carryover basis rules of Regulations section 1.338-4 apply, the consideration paid for each asset, and the basis for each asset as determined under the carryover basis rules. Also, provide the name of each corporation buying or selling such an asset.

Attach a schedule listing the date of each purchase of foreign target stock, the purchaser's name, and the purchased percentage, the place of incorporation of the target, the name and place of incorporation of any selling entities, and whether any affirmative answer was indicated in any part of question 6 of Section D in regard to the target.

Section A—Purchasing Corporation

If more than one purchasing corporation acquires the stock of a target corporation listed in Section B or identified in an attached schedule, attach a schedule that lists which target stock was acquired by each purchasing corporation. The schedule should also provide the information requested on this Form 8023-A and instructions for each purchasing corporation (other than the purchasing corporation listed in Section A).

Section B—Target Corporation

Note: *If an election is made for a controlled foreign corporation, a passive foreign investment company, or a foreign personal holding company, the purchasing corporation must send written notice of the election to affected U.S. shareholders of the foreign target. See Regulations section 1.338-1(g)(4). Attach a schedule containing the name, address, and employer identification number or social security number of each such shareholder.*

If Form 8023-A is filed for more than one target, attach a schedule providing for each target corporation the information requested in Sections B, C, and D.

Line 2e.—Enter the Internal Revenue Service Center where the return was filed for the period immediately preceding the acquisition date.

Section C—Selling Shareholders

If Form 8023-A is filed for a target corporation that is an S corporation and a section 338(h)(10) election is made for that target, the information requested in Section C must be provided for each shareholder who sells target stock in the QSP in Section C and, if necessary, in an attached schedule.

Line 3b—Identifying number.—Enter the social security number to identify an individual. Enter the employer identification number to identify a corporation.

Section E—Elections under Section 338

Lines 7 and 8—Section 338 elections.—If a section 338 election is made for the target corporation listed in Section B, attach a schedule as appropriate listing the amount of **(a)** the consideration paid for the target stock in the QSP, **(b)** the liabilities of the target corporation on the acquisition date, and **(c)** the tax liability on the deemed sale (if a section 338(h)(10) election is not filed). In addition, describe any other relevant items and list the aggregate fair market value by class of the Class II and Class III assets of the target corporation on the acquisition date. Also, identify each intangible amortizable Class III asset, specifying its fair market value and useful life. Do not file **Form 8594,** Asset Acquisition Statement under Section 1060, for the deemed sale.

Line 9—Gain recognition election.—If a gain recognition election is made, it applies to any "P" group member. If a section 338(h)(10) election is made for a target, a gain recognition election is deemed made by each P group member. A "P" group member is any corporation that, on the acquisition date, is a member of the affiliated group that includes the purchasing corporation and holds nonrecently purchased target stock. See Regulations section 1.338(b)-1(e)(2). If a gain recognition election is made or deemed made for a target corporation, attach a schedule providing the target corporation's name, and the name, address, and EIN of each P group member. The schedule must also contain the following declaration (or a substantially similar declaration): "EACH CORPORATION HOLDING STOCK SUBJECT TO THIS GAIN RECOGNITION ELECTION AGREES TO REPORT ANY GAIN UNDER THE GAIN RECOGNITION ELECTION IN ITS FEDERAL INCOME TAX RETURN (INCLUDING AN AMENDED RETURN, IF NECESSARY) FOR THE TAX YEAR IN WHICH THE ACQUISITION DATE OF TARGET OCCURS." The schedule must be signed on behalf of each P group member by a person who states under penalties of perjury that he or she is authorized to act on behalf of the corporation.

A gain recognition election for the target also applies to any target affiliate having the same acquisition date as the target. Attach a schedule with the information requested above for each target affiliate.

Line 10.—If Form 8023-A is filed to make an election under section 338 for any corporation other than the target listed in Section B, attach a schedule stating which elections are made for each target and providing the information requested on lines 7, 8, and 9, Section E. Include appropriate signatures (or signature attachments), for each target.

Special Rules for Elections Made By United States Shareholders of Certain Controlled Foreign Purchasing Corporations

U.S. shareholders of certain controlled foreign purchasing corporations may make the section 338 election for the corporation. To do so, complete Form 8023-A and attach a statement to the form showing the name, address, identifying number, and stock interest of each U.S. shareholder. Instead of signing Form 8023-A, place a reference in the signature space to the attached statement. The statement must be signed by each U.S. shareholder. When signing the statement, each U.S. shareholder must state under penalties of perjury that the stock interest for that shareholder specified in the statement is correct. As an alternative to a jointly signed statement, the shareholder signatures may be shown on separate statements attached to Form 8023-A. If a U.S. shareholder is not an individual or does not have delegated authority to sign the statement, the person signing must state under penalties of perjury that he or she is authorized to sign the statement for the U.S. shareholder.

Each U.S. shareholder making the election must attach a copy of Form 8023-A and its required attachments to Form 5471, and file the forms for the foreign purchasing corporation's tax year that includes the acquisition date. See Regulations section 1.338-1(g)(3).

Signature

If a QSP of a target corporation is made by two or more corporations that are members of the same affiliated group, Form 8023-A must be signed by a person authorized to act on behalf of each corporation. Also, if a section 338(h)(10) election is made for an S corporation, Form 8023-A must be signed by each S corporation shareholder who sells target stock in the QSP. The signatures, dates, and titles (if applicable) of those persons must be provided in a "SIGNATURE ATTACHMENT" to Form 8023-A under a heading containing the sentence printed immediately above the signature line on the form. You must place a reference to the signature attachment in the signature space on Form 8023-A.

If the common parent of a consolidated group is the agent of the purchasing corporation under Regulations section 1.1502-77, the person authorized to sign the statement of section 338 election is the person authorized to act on behalf of that common parent.

Form **8023-A**
(Rev. May 1994)
Department of the Treasury
Internal Revenue Service

Corporate Qualified Stock Purchases

► See separate instructions.

OMB No. 1545-1428
Expires 4-30-97

Section A—Purchasing Corporation

1a Name and address of purchasing corporation	1b Employer identification number (see instructions)	
	1c Tax year ending	1d State or country of incorporation

Section B—Target Corporation

2a Name and address of target corporation	2b Employer identification number	
	2c Tax year ending	2d Acquisition date
	2e Service Center where income tax return filed and date filed (see instructions)	
	2f State or country of incorporation	

Section C—Common Parent, Selling Affiliate, or S Corporation Shareholder (Complete only for a section 338(h)(10) election.)

3a Name and address of common parent, selling affiliate, or S corporation shareholder	3b Identifiying number
	3c Tax year ending
	3d Service Center where income tax return filed and date filed

Section D—General Information

		Yes	No
4	Was the purchasing corporation listed in Section A, above, a member of an affiliated group of corporations before the acquisition date?		
5	Was the target corporation listed in Section B, above, before the acquisition date:		
a	A member of an affiliated group?		
b	A member of a consolidated group?		
6	Is the target corporation or any target affiliate:		
a	A controlled foreign corporation?		
b	A foreign corporation with income, gain, or loss effectively connected with the conduct of a trade or business within the United States (including U.S. real property interests)?		
c	A qualifying foreign target?		
d	A corporation to which section 936 applies?		
e	A corporation electing under section 1504(d) or section 953(d)?		
f	A domestic international sales corporation (DISC)?		
g	A passive foreign investment company (PFIC)?		
h	If the answer to item 6g is "Yes," is the PFIC a pedigreed qualified electing fund?		

For Paperwork Reduction Act Notice, see separate instructions.

Form **8023-A** (Rev. 5-94)

Form 8023-A (Rev. 5-94) Page **2**

Section E—Elections under section 338

7	Check here to make a section 338(h)(10) election for the target corporation listed in Section B on page 1 . . . . ▶	☐
8	Check here to make a section 338 election (other than a section 338(h)(10) election) for the target corporation listed in Section B on page 1 . . . . ▶	☐
9	If the box on line 8 is checked for the target corporation listed in Section B on page 1, check here to make a gain recognition election for that corporation. . . . . ▶	☐
10	Check here if this form is filed to make a section 338 election for any target corporation, in addition to the one listed in Section B on page 1 . . . . ▶	☐

Under penalties of perjury, I state and declare that I am authorized to make the election(s) on line 7, 8, 9 or 10 on behalf of the purchasing corporation(s).

▶ ______________________________ | ________ ▶ ______________________

Signature of Authorized Person for Purchasing Corporation(s) — Date — Title

Under penalties of perjury, I state and declare that I am authorized to make the section 338(h)(10) election on line 7 on behalf of the common parent of the selling group, the selling affiliate, or S corporation shareholder.

▶ ______________________________ | ________ ▶ ______________________

Signature of Authorized Person for the Common Parent, selling affiliate, or S corporation shareholder. — Date — Title

(Applicable only if a section 338(h)(10) election is made.)

EXHIBIT 6-3

1997

Department of the Treasury
Internal Revenue Service

Instructions for Form 6252

Installment Sale Income

Section references are to the Internal Revenue Code unless otherwise noted.

General Instructions

Purpose of Form

Use Form 6252 to report income from casual sales of real or personal property (other than inventory) if you will receive any payments in a tax year after the year of sale.

Do not use Form 6252 to report sales after 1986 of stock or securities traded on an established securities market. Treat all payments from these sales as received in the year you sold the stock.

Do not use Form 6252 if you elect not to report the sale on the installment method. To elect out, report the full amount of the gain on a timely filed return (including extensions), using **Form 4797,** Sales of Business Property, or the **Schedule D** for your return, whichever applies.

Note: *Generally, once you file Form 6252, you cannot later elect out of the installment method. However, if your original return was filed on time, you may make the election on an amended return filed no later than 6 months after the due date of your return, excluding extensions. See Temporary Regulations section 301.9100-2T for more details.*

Which Parts To Complete

For the year of sale. Complete lines 1 through 26.

For years after the year of sale. Complete lines 1 through 4, and Part II, for any year you receive a payment from an installment sale.

Related party sales. If you sold marketable securities to a related party (defined below), complete Form 6252 for each year of the installment agreement, even if you did not receive a payment. For any year after the year of sale, complete lines 1 through 4, and Part III. If you received a payment, also complete Part II.

If you sold property other than marketable securities to a related party, complete Form 6252 for the year of sale and for 2 years after the year of sale even if you did not receive a payment. If during this 2-year period you did not receive an actual or deemed payment, complete lines 1 through 4, and Part III. After this 2-year period, see **For years after the year of sale** above.

Special Rules

Interest. If any part of an installment payment you received is for interest, report that interest on the appropriate form or schedule. **Do not** report interest received, carrying charges received, or unstated interest on Form 6252. Get **Pub. 537,** Installment Sales, for details on unstated interest.

Installment sales to related party. A special rule applies to a first disposition (sale or exchange) of property under the installment method to a related party who then makes a second disposition (sale, exchange, gift, or cancellation of installment note) before making all payments on the first disposition. For this purpose, a **related party** includes your spouse, child, grandchild, parent, brother, sister, or a related corporation, S corporation, partnership, estate, or trust. See section 453(f)(1) for more details.

Under this rule, treat part or all of the amount the related party realized (or the fair market value (FMV) if the disposed property is not sold or exchanged) from the second disposition as if you received it from the first disposition at the time of the second disposition. Figure the gain, if any, on lines 30 through 37. This rule does not apply if any of the conditions listed on line 29 are met.

Sale of depreciable property to related person. Generally, if you sell depreciable property to a related person (as defined in section 453(g)(3)), you may not report the sale using the installment method. For this purpose, depreciable property is any property that can be depreciated by the person or entity to whom you transfer it.

However, you may use the installment method if you can show to the satisfaction of the IRS that avoidance of Federal income taxes was not one of the principal purposes of the sale (e.g., no significant tax deferral benefits will result from the sale).

If the installment method does not apply, report the sale on Schedule D or Form 4797, whichever applies. Treat all payments you will receive as if they were received in the year of sale. Use FMV for any payment that is contingent as to amount. If the FMV cannot be readily determined, basis is recovered ratably.

Pledge rule. If an installment obligation from a nondealer disposition of real property used in a trade or business or held for the production of rental income with a sales price over $150,000 is pledged as security on debt after December 17, 1987, treat the net proceeds of the secured debt as a payment on the installment obligation. This rule applies to the disposition of any property under the installment method after 1988 with a sales price over $150,000, except for farm property and personal use property disposed of by an individual. The amount treated as a payment cannot exceed the excess of the total contract price over any payments received under the contract before the secured debt was obtained.

The pledge rule does not apply to pledges made after December 17, 1987, if the debt is incurred to refinance the principal amount of a debt that was outstanding on December 17, 1987, AND was secured by nondealer real property installment obligations on that date and at all times after that date until the refinancing occurred. However, this exception does not apply to the extent that the principal amount of the debt resulting from the refinancing exceeds the principal amount of the refinanced debt immediately before the refinancing. Also, the pledge rule does not affect refinancing due to the calling of a debt by the creditor as long as the debt is then refinanced by a person other than this creditor or someone related to the creditor.

Interest on deferred tax. Generally, interest must be paid on the deferred tax related to any obligation that arises during a tax year from the disposition of property under the installment method if:

- The property had a sales price over $150,000, AND
- The aggregate balance of all nondealer installment obligations arising during, and outstanding at the close of, the tax year is more than $5 million.

Interest must be paid in subsequent years if installment obligations, which originally required interest to be paid, are still outstanding at the close of a tax year.

These rules **do not** apply to dispositions of:

- Farm property,
- Personal use property by an individual,
- Real property in tax years beginning before 1988, or
- Personal property before 1989.

How to report the interest. The interest is not figured on Form 6252. See section 453A to figure the interest. Enter the interest as an additional tax on your tax return. Include it in the amount to be entered on the total tax line after credits and other taxes. For individuals, this is line 53 of the 1997 Form 1040. For corporations, it is line 10 of Schedule J (Form 1120). Write "Section 453A(c) interest" to the left of the amount.

Corporations may deduct the interest in the year it is paid or accrued. For individuals and other taxpayers, this interest is not deductible.

Additional Information

See Pub. 537 for additional information, including details about reductions in selling price, the single sale of several assets, like-kind exchanges, dispositions of installment obligations, and repossessions.

Specific Instructions

Part I—Gross Profit and Contract Price

Line 5. Enter the total of any money, face amount of the installment obligation, and the FMV of other property that you received or will receive in exchange for the property sold. Include on line 5 any existing mortgage or other debt the buyer assumed or took the property subject to.

If there is no stated maximum selling price, such as in a contingent sale, attach a schedule showing the computation of gain. Enter the taxable part on line 24 and also on line 35 if Part III applies. See Temporary Regulations section 15A.453.

Line 6. Enter only mortgages or other debts the buyer assumed from the seller or took the property subject to. **Do not** include new mortgages the buyer gets from a bank, the seller, or other sources.

Line 8. Enter the original cost and other expenses you incurred in buying the property. Add the cost of improvements, etc., and subtract any qualified electric vehicle credit, diesel-powered highway vehicle credit, enhanced oil recovery credit, disabled access credit, or casualty losses previously allowed. For more details, get **Pub. 551**, Basis of Assets.

Line 9. Enter all depreciation or amortization you deducted or should have deducted from the date of purchase until the date of sale. Add any section 179 expense deduction; the downward basis adjustment under section 50(c) (or the corresponding provision of prior law); the deduction for qualified clean-fuel vehicle property or refueling property; and deductions claimed under section 190, 193, or 1253(d)(2) or (3) (as in effect before the enactment of P.L. 103-66). Subtract any investment tax credit recapture amount if the basis of the property was reduced under section 50(c) (or the corresponding provision of prior law); any section 179 or 280F recapture amount included in gross income in a prior tax year; and any qualified clean-fuel vehicle property or refueling property deduction you were required to recapture because the property ceased to be eligible for the deduction. **Do not** include on this line any section 179 expense deduction for a partnership or an S corporation that passed through the deduction to its partners or shareholders.

Line 11. Enter sales commissions, advertising expenses, attorney and legal fees, etc., in selling the property.

Line 12. Any ordinary income recapture under section 1245 or 1250 (including sections 179 and 291) is fully taxable in the year of sale even if no payments were received. To figure the recapture, complete Form 4797, Part III. The ordinary income recapture is the amount on line 31 of Form 4797. Enter it on line 12 of Form 6252 and also on line 13 of Form 4797. **Do not** enter any gain for this property on line 32 of Form 4797. If you used Form 4797 only to figure the recapture on line 12 of Form 6252, enter "N/A" on line 32 of Form 4797.

Part II—Installment Sale Income

Line 19. Enter the gross profit percentage determined for the year of sale even if you did not file Form 6252 for that year.

Line 21. Enter all money and the FMV of any property you received in 1997. Include as payments any amount withheld to pay off a mortgage or other debt, such as broker and legal fees. **Do not** include the buyer's note, any mortgage, or other liability assumed by the buyer. If you did not receive any payments in 1997, enter zero.

If in prior years an amount was entered on the equivalent of line 32 of the 1997 form, **do not** include it on this line. Instead, enter it on line 23.

See **Pledge rule** on page 1 for details about proceeds of debt secured by installment obligations that must be treated as payments on installment obligations.

Line 23. Enter all money and the FMV of property you received before 1997 from the sale. Include allocable installment income and any other deemed payments from prior years.

Line 25. Enter here and on Form 4797, line 15, any ordinary income recapture on section 1252, 1254, or 1255 property. This includes recapture for the year of sale or any remaining recapture from a prior year sale. **Do not** enter ordinary income from a section 179 expense deduction. If this is the year of sale, complete Form 4797, Part III. The amount from line 27c, 28b, or 29b of Form 4797 is the ordinary income recapture. **Do not** enter any gain for this property on line 31 or 32 of Form 4797. If you used Form 4797 only to figure the recapture on line 25 or 36, enter "N/A" on lines 31 and 32 of Form 4797.

Also report on this line any ordinary income recapture remaining from prior years on section 1245 or 1250 property sold **before** June 7, 1984.

Do not enter on line 25 more than the amount shown on line 24. The excess **must** be reported in future years on Form 6252 up to the taxable part of the installment sale until all of the recapture has been reported.

Line 26. For trade or business property held more than 1 year, enter this amount on Form 4797, line 4, column (g), and if applicable, column (h). If the property was held 1 year or less, or if you have an ordinary gain from a noncapital asset (even if the holding period is more than 1 year), enter this amount on Form 4797, line 10, and write "From Form 6252."

For capital assets, enter this amount on Schedule D as a short- or long-term gain. Use the lines identified as from Form 6252.

Part III—Related Party Installment Sale Income

Line 29. If one of the conditions is met, check the appropriate box. Skip lines 30 through 37. If you checked box 29e, attach an explanation. Generally, the nontax avoidance exception will apply to the second disposition if:

- The disposition was involuntary (e.g., a creditor of the related person foreclosed on the property, or the related person declared bankruptcy), or
- The disposition was an installment sale under which the terms of payment were substantially equal to or longer than those for the first sale. However, the resale terms must not permit significant deferral of recognition of gain from the first sale (e.g., amounts from the resale are being collected sooner).

Line 30. If the related party sold all or part of the property from the original sale in 1997, enter the selling price of the part resold. If part was sold in an earlier year and part was sold this year, enter the cumulative amount of the selling price.

Line 33. If you completed Part II, enter the sum of lines 22 and 23. Otherwise, enter all money and the FMV of property you received before 1997 from the sale. Include allocable installment income and any other deemed payments from prior years. **Do not** include interest whether stated or unstated.

Line 36. See the instructions for line 25 above. **Do not** enter on line 36 more than the amount shown on line 35. The excess **must** be reported in future years on Form 6252 up to the taxable part of the installment sale until all of the recapture has been reported.

Line 37. See the instructions for line 26 above.

Paperwork Reduction Act Notice. We ask for the information on this form to carry out the Internal Revenue laws of the United States. You are required to give us the information. We need it to ensure that you are complying with these laws and to allow us to figure and collect the right amount of tax.

You are not required to provide the information requested on a form that is subject to the Paperwork Reduction Act unless the form displays a valid OMB control number. Books or records relating to a form or its instructions must be retained as long as their contents may become material in the administration of any Internal Revenue law. Generally, tax returns and return information are confidential, as required by section 6103.

The time needed to complete and file this form will vary depending on individual circumstances. The estimated average time is:

Recordkeeping	1 hr., 25 min.
Learning about the law or the form	40 min.
Preparing the form	56 min.
Copying, assembling, and sending the form to the IRS	20 min.

If you have comments concerning the accuracy of these time estimates or suggestions for making this form simpler, we would be happy to hear from you. See the instructions for the tax return with which this form is filed.

Form **6252**

Department of the Treasury
Internal Revenue Service

Installment Sale Income

▶ See separate instructions. ▶ Attach to your tax return.
▶ Use a separate form for each sale or other disposition of property on the installment method.

OMB No. 1545-0228

1997

Attachment Sequence No. **79**

Name(s) shown on return | Identifying number

1 Description of property ▶ ....

2a Date acquired (month, day, year) ▶ ___/___/___ **b** Date sold (month, day, year) ▶ ___/___/___

3 Was the property sold to a related party after May 14, 1980? See instructions. If "No," skip line 4 . . . ☐ Yes ☐ No

4 Was the property you sold to a related party a marketable security? If "Yes," complete Part III. If "No," complete Part III for the year of sale and the 2 years after the year of sale . . . ☐ Yes ☐ No

Part I Gross Profit and Contract Price. Complete this part for the year of sale only.

5	Selling price including mortgages and other debts. **Do not** include interest whether stated or unstated		5
6	Mortgages and other debts the buyer assumed or took the property subject to, but not new mortgages the buyer got from a bank or other source	6	
7	Subtract line 6 from line 5	7	
8	Cost or other basis of property sold	8	
9	Depreciation allowed or allowable	9	
10	Adjusted basis. Subtract line 9 from line 8	10	
11	Commissions and other expenses of sale	11	
12	Income recapture from Form 4797, Part III. See instructions	12	
13	Add lines 10, 11, and 12		13
14	Subtract line 13 from line 5. If zero or less, **stop here. Do not** complete the rest of this form		14
15	If the property described on line 1 above was your main home, enter from Form 2119 the total of lines 14 and 22, or the amount from line 27, whichever applies. Otherwise, enter -0-		15
16	**Gross profit.** Subtract line 15 from line 14		16
17	Subtract line 13 from line 6. If zero or less, enter -0-		17
18	**Contract price.** Add line 7 and line 17		18

Part II Installment Sale Income. Complete this part for the year of sale **and** any year you receive a payment or have certain debts you must treat as a payment on installment obligations.

19	Gross profit percentage. Divide line 16 by line 18. For years after the year of sale, see instructions		19
20	**For year of sale only:** Enter amount from line 17 above; otherwise, enter -0-		20
21	Payments received during year. See instructions. **Do not** include interest whether stated or unstated		21
22	Add lines 20 and 21		22
23	Payments received in prior years. See instructions. **Do not** include interest whether stated or unstated	23	
24	**Installment sale income.** Multiply line 22 by line 19		24
25	Part of line 24 that is ordinary income under recapture rules. See instructions		25
26	Subtract line 25 from line 24. Enter here and on Schedule D or Form 4797. See instructions		26

Part III Related Party Installment Sale Income. Do not complete if you received the final payment this tax year.

27 Name, address, and taxpayer identifying number of related party ....

28 Did the related party, during this tax year, resell or dispose of the property ("second disposition")? . . . ☐ Yes ☐ No

29 **If the answer to question 28 is "Yes," complete lines 30 through 37 below unless one of the following conditions is met. Check only the box that applies.**

- **a** ☐ The second disposition was more than 2 years after the first disposition (other than dispositions of marketable securities). If this box is checked, enter the date of disposition (month, day, year) ▶ ___/___/___
- **b** ☐ The first disposition was a sale or exchange of stock to the issuing corporation.
- **c** ☐ The second disposition was an involuntary conversion where the threat of conversion occurred after the first disposition.
- **d** ☐ The second disposition occurred after the death of the original seller or buyer.
- **e** ☐ It can be established to the satisfaction of the Internal Revenue Service that tax avoidance was not a principal purpose for either of the dispositions. If this box is checked, attach an explanation. See instructions.

30	Selling price of property sold by related party	30
31	Enter contract price from line 18 for year of first sale	31
32	Enter the **smaller** of line 30 or line 31	32
33	Total payments received by the end of your 1997 tax year. See instructions	33
34	Subtract line 33 from line 32. If zero or less, enter -0-	34
35	Multiply line 34 by the gross profit percentage on line 19 for year of first sale	35
36	Part of line 35 that is ordinary income under recapture rules. See instructions	36
37	Subtract line 36 from line 35. Enter here and on Schedule D or Form 4797. See instructions	37

For Paperwork Reduction Act Notice, see separate instructions.

Form 6252 (1997)

Chapter 7

TAX FREE ORGANIZATIONS, REORGANIZATIONS AND DIVISIONS

A. INTRODUCTION

In general, the Internal Revenue Code allows corporations to be organized, combined and subdivided without taxation, if the parties to the transaction are not "cashing out" their investment. Thus, the Code enables corporations to organize, reorganize and divide without imposing taxes on transactions that do not generate cash to pay the taxes. State and local tax laws may vary from the Code treatment and should be reviewed carefully.

B. CORPORATE ORGANIZATIONS

1. Organization of New Corporations

So many corporations are routinely organized every year that few think of the transactions as acquisitions or of their tax effects as anything unusual. However, a brief review of the principles applicable to corporate organizations provides a good practical introduction to the principles involved in tax free reorganizations.

Section 351 of the Code provides that no gain or loss shall be recognized if property is transferred to a corporation by one or more persons solely in exchange for stock in such corporation and immediately after the exchange such person or persons are in control of the corporation. For this purpose, *control* means ownership of stock possessing at least 80 percent of (1) the total combined voting power of all classes of stock and (2) the total number of shares of all other classes of stock.[1] In most corporate organizations, the founding shareholders receive all of the stock and are not concerned about the 80 percent stock ownership tests.

If the shareholders receive other money or property in addition to stock, gain is recognized, but not in excess of the money received plus the fair market value of the property received.[2] However, no loss, if any, is recognized.

The author expresses appreciation to Jeffrey S. Levin, a tax partner at Windels, Marx, Davies & Ives, for his helpful comments on this chapter.

[1]Section 368(c).

[2]Section 351(b). Note that receipt of money or property from the corporation does not prevent tax free treatment of the rest of the transaction.

The tax free treatment does not apply to stock issued for services or for indebtedness of the transferee corporation not evidenced by a security.[3]

A corporation does not have any gain or loss on the receipt of money or other property in exchange for its stock, whether newly issued shares or treasury shares.[4]

For example, assume that Mary Jones and Peter Smith organize ABC Consultants, Inc. Mary contributes to ABC a computer that she has been using in an existing consulting business. Peter contributes $20,000 in cash. The corporation issues 100 shares of its common stock to Mary and 100 shares of its common stock to Peter in exchange for their contributions. Mary and Peter are in control of ABC and do not recognize any gain or loss upon receipt of ABC's stock. ABC does not recognize any gain or loss upon receipt of the computer or the cash. If ABC issued shares to Mary or Peter for services rather than property, however, Section 351 would not shield the exchange from recognition of gain or loss.

Under Section 362 of the Code, the corporation obtains a basis in property received without recognition of gain or loss that is the same as that of the transferor.[5] The same treatment is afforded to subsequent capital contributions. However, if gain were recognized because, for example, money or property were received in addition to stock, the corporation's basis would be increased in the amount of the gain recognized by the transferor on such transfer.[6] Section 362 does not require any reduction of basis because the corporation assumed a liability of the transferor.

Under Section 358 of the Code, shareholders who receive stock under Section 351 obtain a basis in the stock received that is the same as that of the property they exchanged for the stock.[7] If the corporation also paid money or property, the shareholders' basis in the stock is decreased by the money received, the fair market value of other property received and any loss to the shareholder recognized on the exchange.[8] The shareholders' basis is increased by any amount treated as a dividend and any gain recognized on the exchange.[9]

If the corporation assumes a liability of the shareholders as part of the consideration, or acquires property subject to a liability from them, such assumption or acquisition is not treated as money or other property and does not prevent the exchange from being tax free under Section 351.[10] However, any such assumption or acquisition is treated as money or other property received by the shareholders for the purpose of determining basis under Section 358.[11]

In the earlier example, assume that Mary's basis in the computer is $18,000. After the exchange, ABC's basis in the computer will be $18,000

---

[3]Section 351(c).

[4]Section 1032.

[5]Section 362(a).

[6]Section 362.

[7]Section 358(a)(1)

[8]Section 358(a)(1)(A).

[9]Section 358(a)(1)(B).

[10]Section 357. This treatment is subject to exceptions if the transaction was for tax avoidance purposes or the liabilities exceed the shareholders' basis in the property.

[11]Section 358(d).

and Mary's basis in her stock will be $18,000. The corporation's basis in the money received from Peter will, of course, be $20,000 and Peter's basis in his stock will be $20,000. If ABC agreed to pay a $4,000 balance owed by Mary on the computer, the assumption would not prevent tax free treatment, but ABC's basis in the computer and Mary's basis in her stock would be adjusted to reflect the $4,000 liability assumed.

Basis received by corporations and shareholders under Sections 362 and 358 is commonly called a "substituted basis" or a "carryover basis." It is a customary side effect of tax free treatment and applies generally throughout the Code. As readers saw in Chapter 6, when a taxpayer must recognize gain or loss in a taxable transaction, the Code provides for an adjustment of the taxpayer's basis to the amount used in determining the gain or loss. When the taxpayer need not recognize gain or loss, the basis of the property acquired is the same as its adjusted basis in the hands of the transferor. This retention of basis at the same level, of course, means that so-called "tax free" corporate organizations and reorganizations are really only tax deferrals. The organization or reorganization event is not taxed, but the event also provides no increase of basis usable to reduce gain or increase a loss upon a future sale or exchange.

Finally, anyone organizing limited liability companies, partnerships or other unincorporated legal entities should be familiar with the "Check the Box" regulations issued by the IRS in December 1996 effective January 1, 1997 and appearing at Reg. Sec. 301.7701-1(a) through (e) and Reg. Sec. 301.7701-3(a) through (f). Moreover, analogous nonrecognition and basis principles apply to the formation of partnerships, although the assumption of liabilities is somewhat more complicated. See Sections 721 to 723 and 752 of the Code.

2. Acquisitions Using Section 351

Section 351 can be used in corporate acquisition transactions, although such use is not widespread.

For example, two corporations sometimes identify important advantages that could be gained by combining their efforts under common ownership, but each wishes to retain its identity and is unwilling to be "acquired" by the other. These obstacles may be overcome in some situations by organizing a holding company to acquire both corporations in exchange for its stock pursuant to Section 351, thus allowing the two corporations to maintain their separate identities and existing management structures. Before the transaction, the corporations and their shareholders negotiate a shareholders' agreement to govern the ownership and management of the holding company, including identification of the persons who will serve as directors and officers of the holding company. **Note:** If the holding company acquires the two corporations solely for voting stock, the transaction may also qualify as a B Reorganization.

For another example, the organization of a joint venture subsidiary by two corporations can be accomplished tax free by using Section 351. To illustrate, a corporation may have a division with underutilized manufacturing capacity. Another corporation may have a division in the same line of business with strong marketing and technical capabilities, but lacking manufacturing facilities. If neither corporation wishes to sell its division, the two corporations may decide to organize a joint venture. They can do so by organizing a corporation and contributing the assets of their respective divisions to it in exchange for stock. Before the transfers, the two corporations negotiate a shareholders' agreement providing for the ownership and management of the joint venture corporation. (A joint venture arrangement could also be structured as a partnership, depending upon the preferences of the parties.)

For still another example, the author's first corporate organization assignment as a young lawyer was to form a new high-technology corporation. The corporation later made a public offering of its common stock, which was thereafter publicly traded on the American Stock Exchange. Eventually, much of the high-technology corporation's business consisted of supplying products and technology to the electronic equipment manufacturing division of a very large customer whose shares were traded on the New York Stock Exchange. The high-technology corporation and the customer agreed to a combination of assets and operations using Section 351. The customer transferred its electronic equipment manufacturing division to the high-technology corporation in exchange for newly issued shares of its common stock that would provide the customer with 83 percent ownership of the high technology corporation after the transaction. Thus, the high-technology corporation acquired a large new division and the customer acquired "control" of the high-technology corporation as required by Section 351. The previously issued shares of the high technology corporation remained outstanding, although diluted to 17 percent of total ownership. The shares of the high technology corporation rose sharply in market value on the American Stock Exchange.

C. The Repeal of tax free Liquidations

Before reviewing tax free reorganizations, it is helpful to recall that corporate liquidations were tax free events for many decades. Under the *General Utilities* doctrine,[12] prior versions of Sections 311, 336 and 337 of the Code allowed a corporation to be liquidated by various methods without recognition of gain or loss at the corporate level on the distribution of appreciated property.

In the extensive amendments that made up the Internal Revenue Code of 1986, Congress imposed an exit toll on doing business as a corporation by renouncing the *General Utilities* doctrine and making fundamental amendments to Sections 311, 336 and 337. For example, Section 311(b) now illustrates the revised doctrines by providing that, if a corporation distributes property (other than its own obligations) to a shareholder, and the fair market value of such property exceeds its basis, then the corporation recognizes gain as if the property were sold to the distributee at its fair market value. Section 336 imposes similar treatment upon a distribution in complete liquidation by requiring the liquidating corporation, other than certain subsidiary corporations, to recognize gain or loss as if the property were sold to the distributee at its fair market value. A significant difference between the two provisions is that Section 331 prescribes recognition of

[12] *General Utilities & Operating Co. v. Helvering*, 296 U.S. 200 (1935).

gain, but not loss. Section 336 prescribes recognition of both gain and loss, although it disallows recognition of loss in certain distributions to related persons.

The 1986 amendments also repealed the former 12-month liquidation provisions of Section 337, except for nonrecognition of gain or loss by a liquidating subsidiary upon a distribution of property in a complete liquidation under Section 332(b) to an "80-percent distributee," i.e., a parent corporation that owns at least 80 percent of the voting power and value of the subsidiary's stock. The amended Section 337 does not prevent double taxation of corporate income, but shelters it from triple taxation.

D. Tax Free Reorganizations—The Operative Code Sections

1. Effects on Shareholders and Securityholders

Section 354(a)(1) provides that no gain or loss shall be recognized by shareholders or securityholders if stock or securities in a corporation that is a party to a reorganization are, in pursuance to a plan of reorganization, exchanged solely for stock or securities in such corporation or another party to the reorganization. However, nonrecognition treatment does not apply if (1) the principal amount of securities received exceeds the principal amount of securities surrendered or (2) securities are received and no securities are surrendered.

For example, if ABC Corporation issues its stock to the shareholders of XYZ Corporation solely for stock in XYZ Corporation pursuant to a plan of reorganization, no gain or loss is recognized by the shareholders on the exchanges of stock. If, as part of the plan of reorganization, ABC Corporation also issues $1,000,000 principal amount of its ten year subordinated notes to XYZ Corporation's securityholders in exchange for $1,000,000 of six year subordinated notes of XYZ Corporation, no gain or loss is recognized on the exchanges of securities. However, if the principal amount of the notes issued by ABC Corporation is $1,500,000, gain will be recognized. Further, if notes are issued by ABC in exchange for stock, rather than securities, of XYZ Corporation, gain will be recognized.

The term *security* in Section 354 and other sections involving tax free reorganizations is much narrower than the broad definitions used in federal and state securities laws. The term is not actually defined in the Code. However, the federal courts have interpreted the term to mean a debt obligation of a corporation of a nature that constitutes an investment in the corporation by its holder. An unsecured, long-term subordinated note is an obvious example. Some courts have been willing to treat other unsecured debt instruments as securities.[13]

Section 358 of the Code provides that the basis of property received without recognition of gain or loss by distributees under Section 354 (and certain other Code sections) shall be the same as that of the property exchanged, subject to certain increases and decreases if other property or money is received in addition to the nonrecognition property. Thus,

[13]*U.S. v. Mills*, 399 F.2d 944 (5th Cir. 1968) and *U.S. v. Hertwig*, 398 F.2d 452 (5th Cir. 1968); *Bradshaw v. U.S.*, 683 F.2d 365 (Ct.Cl. 1982) and cases cited therein.

shareholders and securityholders obtain a substituted basis in the nonrecognition property.

The taxation of money and property other than stock and securities received pursuant to a plan of reorganization is discussed later in this chapter in the section on "Taxation of 'Boot.'"

2. Effects on Corporations

Section 361(a) provides that no gain or loss shall be recognized by a corporation if such corporation is a party to a reorganization and exchanges property, in pursuance of the plan of reorganization, solely for stock or securities in another corporation that is a party to the reorganization. For example, if, in connection with a plan of reorganization, ABC Corporation transfers its assets to XYZ Corporation solely in exchange for voting stock of XYZ Corporation, no gain or loss is recognized by ABC Corporation.

If Section 361(a) would apply except that the exchange is not solely for stock or securities, but also for other property or money, no gain is recognized to the corporation upon their receipt if it distributes the other property or money pursuant to the plan of reorganization. Otherwise, any gain (but not loss) to the corporation is recognized, but not exceeding the amount of money and the fair market value of the other property received and not distributed.[14] For example, if ABC Corporation transfers its assets to XYZ Corporation pursuant to a plan of reorganization and receives in exchange stock and $1,000,000 cash, ABC Corporation does not recognize any gain if it distributes the cash to its shareholders.

The general nonrecognition rule described above does not apply, however, if a corporate party distributes, pursuant to a plan of reorganization, appreciated property other than "qualified property," i.e., stock (or rights to acquire stock) or obligations of the distribution corporation or of another corporate party to the reorganization. Appreciated property is property with a fair market value exceeding its basis. A transfer of appreciated property to creditors is treated as a distribution to shareholders pursuant to the plan of reorganization.[15]

Section 362(b) of the Code provides that the basis of property acquired by a corporation in a reorganization is the same as in the hands of the transferor, increased by the amount of any gain recognized by the transferor on the transfer. Thus, the corporation obtains a substituted basis in the property transferred without recognition of gain or loss pursuant to the reorganization.

3. Adjustment of Basis on Death

Because the Code provides for a substituted basis in stock, securities and property received without recognition of gain or loss pursuant to a reorganization, the term tax free reorganization is a slight overstatement. Indeed, no tax is imposed at the time of the reorganization, but a tax will be imposed if and when the stock, securities or property are subsequently

[14]Section 361(b). ABC Corporation can also use the cash to pay creditors.

[15]Section 361(c)(3).

sold or otherwise disposed of in a taxable transaction. Because of the substituted basis, the full amount of any deferred gain will then be taxed. Thus, a tax free reorganization defers taxation, but does not create a permanent freedom from taxation.

For example, assume that June Smith owns 100 shares of Alpha Corporation in which she has a basis of $8 per share. Alpha is acquired in a tax free reorganization by Beta Corporation which issues one of its shares to Alpha's shareholders for each share held by them. June Smith will receive 100 Beta shares and will have a basis of $8 in each share. If June Smith then sells the Beta shares for $12 per share, she will realize a taxable gain of $4 per share.

Acquisition planners should be aware, however, that if an individual shareholder or securityholder does not sell, exchange or dispose of stock or securities received without recognition of gain or loss pursuant to a reorganization before his or her death, the stock or securities will obtain a new basis in the hands of heirs or other persons acquiring them that could be much higher than the substituted basis. Under Section 1014 of the Code, the new basis is equal to the fair market value of the stock or securities on the date of death, or the alternate valuation date allowed by the estate tax provisions of the Code. Alternatively, if the date of death value is less than the basis, the new basis is reduced to the value used for estate tax purposes. The new basis applies regardless of whether the estate of the shareholder or securityholder must actually pay federal estate taxes.

For example, if June Smith dies while still holding the 100 Beta shares and their fair market value on the date of death is $20, her heirs who inherit the shares will have a basis of $20 per share. If June Smith's estate elects an alternate valuation date and the shares have a fair market value of $19 on that date, the heirs will have a basis of $19 per share.

The income tax savings available under Section 1014 are an important estate planning factor and an incentive for the choice of a tax free reorganization when elderly shareholders (and securityholders) are planning to sell a corporate business.

E. Tax Free Reorganizations—Definitions of Reorganizations

As described, the nonrecognition (tax free) treatment of gain or loss provided in both Sections 354 and 361 is linked to a plan of reorganization. Without a reorganization, the nonrecognition treatment is unavailable.

Section 368(a)(1) provides that any one of several alternate transactions can qualify as a "reorganization:"

(A) a statutory merger or consolidation.

(B) the acquisition by one corporation, in exchange solely for all or a part of its voting stock (or in exchange solely for all or a part of the voting stock of a corporation which is in control of the acquiring corporation) of stock of another corporation if, immediately after the acquisition, the acquiring corporation has control of such other corporation (whether or not such acquiring corporation had control immediately before the acquisition).

(C) the acquisition by one corporation, in exchange solely for all or a part of its voting stock (or in exchange solely for all or a part of the voting stock of a corporation which is in control of the acquiring corporation), of substantially all of the properties of another corporation, but in determining whether the exchange is solely for stock the assumption by the acquiring corporation of a liability of the other, or the fact that property acquired is subject to a liability, shall be disregarded.

(D) a transfer by a corporation of all or a part of its assets to another corporation if immediately after the transfer the transferor, or one or more of its shareholders (including persons who were shareholders immediately before the transfer), or any combination thereof, is in control[16] of the corporation to which the assets are transferred; but only if, in pursuance of the plan, stock or securities of the corporation to which the assets are transferred are distributed in a transaction which qualifies under Section 354, 355 or 356.

(E) a recapitalization.

(F) a mere change in identify, form, or place of organization of one corporation, however effected.

(G) a transfer by a corporation of all or part of its assets to another corporation in a title 11 or similar case[17]; but only if, in pursuance of the plan, stock or securities of the corporation to which the assets are transferred are distributed in a transaction which qualifies under Section 354, 355 or 356.

Tax practitioners commonly refer to reorganizations by the subparagraphs that define their basic requirements, such as an "A Reorganization," a "B Reorganization" or a "C Reorganization." Although relatively complex, the requirements are so important that the basic elements are widely known to M&A professionals as well as to tax specialists.

In general, the IRS acts as a strict gatekeeper for the definitions in Section 368(a)(1). Attempted reorganizations that fail to meet one of the definitions cannot obtain nonrecognition of gain or loss under Sections 354 and 361.

Several matters should be considered in planning reorganizations:

- An A Reorganization has minimal requirements at the definition stage. Only a statutory merger or consolidation is required. Under IRS regulations, a valid merger or consolidation under the laws of the United States, a state, a territory of the United States, or the District of Columbia is required.[18] Otherwise, there is considerable freedom in deciding what to acquire and the forms of payment, if they meet the requirements of Sections 354 and 361.

[16]*Control* is defined in Section 368(c) as ownership of stock possessing at least 80 percent of the total combined voting power of all classes entitled to vote and at least 80 percent of the total number of shares of all other classes.

[17]"Title 11 or similar case" refers to a bankruptcy reorganization proceeding under Title 11 of the U.S. Code or a receivership, foreclosure or similar proceeding in a federal or state court. Section 368(a)(3)(A).

[18]IRS Reg.§ 1.368-2(b)(1).

• A B Reorganization requires that payment be solely in voting stock. Cash, securities and nonvoting stock cannot be used.[19] Even limitations on voting rights may raise troublesome issues.[20] The acquiring corporation must also be in "control" of the acquired corporation immediately after the acquisition. This means meeting the 80 percent tests in Section 368(c).[21] Payment of a dividend or redemption of its stock by the acquired corporation does not disqualify a B Reorganization.[22] The IRS has ruled that employment agreements and certain other incidental arrangements also do not disqualify a B Reorganization.

• A C Reorganization requires the acquisition by one corporation of substantially all the properties of another corporation. In its requirements for a favorable ruling, the IRS has said it requires an acquisition of at least 70 percent of gross assets and 90 percent of net assets to fulfill this requirement.[23] In an actual case, however, both the IRS and the courts are likely to focus on the extent to which operating assets were transferred and to be disinclined to disqualify a reorganization because nonoperating assets were retained for payment of liabilities.[24] A C Reorganization also requires that the acquisition be solely for voting stock except that liabilities may be assumed and assets subject to liabilities may be acquired. However, as described earlier, Section 368(a)(2)(B) modifies this requirement to allow payment of money and other property if at least 80 percent of the fair market value of all property of the other corporation is acquired solely for voting stock. In effect, this allows 20 percent of the acquisition price to be paid with money or other property, but the amount allowable under the 20 percent limit is reduced by liabilities assumed and liabilities to which any acquired property is subject.[25] As in a B Reorganization, if the acquiring corporation previously owned stock of the other corporation that was not acquired for voting stock, careful planning is required to avoid disqualification.[26] Further, as in a B Reorganization, the other corporation may pay dividends and redeem part of its stock without disqualifying a C Reorganization.

• A D Reorganization is a complex transaction and can be used to accomplish a divisive reorganization or a nondivisive reorganization. Its requirements are discussed later in the section titled Tax Free Divisions of Corporate Businesses.

• An E Reorganization is a transaction that involves "the reshuffling of a capital structure within the framework of an existing corporation"

---

[19]Previous stock ownership in the acquired corporation can disqualify a B Reorganization if it was not acquired for voting stock, unless the previously-owned stock is "old and cold." It may be feasible for the acquired corporation to redeem any such previously-owned stock before the B Reorganization.

[20]See Rev. Rul. 69-126, 1969-1 Cum. Bull. 218.

[21]Eighty percent of **each** class of voting and nonvoting stock must be acquired. Rev. Rul. 59-259, 1959-2 Cum. Bull. 115.

[22]Rev. Rul. 68-435, 1968-2 Cum. Bull. 155; Rev. Rul. 69-443, 1969-2 Cum. Bull. 54; Rev. Rul. 70-172, 1970-1 Cum. Bull. 77; Rev. Rul. 68-285, 1968-1 Cum. Bull. 147.

[23]Rev. Proc. 77-37, 1977-2 Cum. Bull. 568.

[24]Rev. Rul. 57-518, 1957-2 Cum. Bull. 253; *Commissioner v. First National Bank of Altoona*, 104 F.2d 865 (3d Cir. 1939); *Smith v. Commissioner*, 34 B.T.A. 702 (1936).

[25]Section 368(a)(2)(B).

[26]*Bausch & Lomb Optical Corporation v. Commissioner*, 267 F.2d 75 (2d Cir. 1959).

(*Southwest Consolidated Corp.*, 315 U.S. 194 (1942); 42-1 USTC (CCH) § 9248). A recapitalization, such as an exchange of preferred stock for bonds or an exchange of common stock for preferred stock, is a financial rather than an acquisition transaction.

• An F Reorganization is most commonly used to reincorporate an existing corporation in another jurisdiction. For example, corporations organized in states with disadvantageous corporation laws that are planning initial public offerings (IPOs) often migrate to Delaware by organizing a new corporation under the Delaware General Corporation Law and merging into it. Thus, an F Reorganization is not a substantive acquisition or divestiture transaction. See Revenue Rulings 75-250 and 96-29 for further guidance on F Reorganizations.

• A G Reorganization is a complex transaction with several important advantages designed to enhance the opportunity for debtor corporations to reorganize under Chapter 11 of the Bankruptcy Code.

F. Tax Free Reorganizations—Special Rules

Section 368(a)(2) contains several special rules, some facilitating and others limiting the ability of corporations to meet the reorganization definitions. Examples of these special rules are as follows:

- A transaction that meets both the requirements of a C Reorganization and a D Reorganization is treated as a D Reorganization.[27]
- In a C Reorganization, the acquiring corporation may exchange money or property in addition to voting stock, if it acquires solely for voting stock property of the other corporation having a fair market value of at least 80 percent of the fair market value of all its property.[28]
- An A, B or C Reorganization is not disqualified because part or all of the assets or stock acquired are transferred to a controlled subsidiary by the acquiring corporation. A G Reorganization is also not disqualified by such a transfer if additional requirements are met.[29]
- An A or G Reorganization is not disqualified if the acquiring corporation is a subsidiary using stock of a controlling corporation to acquire substantially all the properties of another corporation, if (1) no stock of the acquiring corporation is used and (2) in the case of an A Reorganization, the transaction would have qualified as an A Reorganization if the merger had been into the controlling corporation.[30] (**Note:** This provision facilitates forward triangular mergers).
- An A Reorganization is not disqualified if the merged corporation is a subsidiary using voting stock of a corporation that before the merger was in control of the merged corporation, if (1) after the

[27]Section 368(a)(2)(A)

[28]Section 368(a)(2)(B).

[29]Section 368(a)(2)(C).

[30]Section 368(a)(2)(D).

transaction, the surviving corporation holds substantially all of its properties and the merged corporation's properties other than stock of the controlling corporation distributed in the transaction and (2) in the transaction, former shareholders of the surviving corporations exchanged for an amount of voting stock of the controlling corporations an amount of the surviving corporation's stock that constitutes control of the surviving corporation.[31] (**Note:** This provision facilitates reverse triangular mergers).

- A transaction fails to qualify as a C Reorganization unless the acquired corporation distributes the stock, securities and other properties it receives, as well as its other properties, pursuant to the plan of reorganization. If the acquired corporation is liquidated pursuant to the plan of reorganization, a distribution to creditors in connection with the liquidation is treated as pursuant to the plan of reorganization.[32]

G. Tax Free Reorganizations—Triangular Transactions

1. Background

During recent decades, two-party mergers have been used with growing caution as the courts, the U.S. Congress and state legislatures have created new tort, environmental and other liabilities and imposed them retroactively on industry. For example, GAF Corporation acquired the Ruberoid Company by merger on May 1, 1967, automatically succeeding to Ruberoid's liabilities. A decade later, GAF found itself engulfed in asbestos litigation resulting from Ruberoid's sales of asbestos insulation products manufactured and sold over many decades.

As a result, triangular transactions in which a subsidiary is used to accomplish the acquisition have come to be customary. For example, triangular mergers can be structured to qualify as A, B or C Reorganizations. The Code and the IRS regulations have provided special rules that enable, and also restrict, tax free reorganizations accomplished by triangular transactions.

2. Forward Triangular

As described earlier, the special rule in Section 368(a)(2)(D) facilitates the use of a subsidiary to acquire by merger substantially all the properties of another corporation. The parent contributes its stock to a subsidiary which then acquires by merger the acquired corporation. The subsidiary is the surviving corporation and the separate existence of the acquired corporation is merged into the subsidiary. In effect, the subsidiary acquires the properties of the acquired corporation and assumes its liabilities by operation of law.

A forward triangular transaction can be used to accomplish an A Reorganization. However, no stock of the subsidiary should be used as part of the acquisition currency. Further, the transaction must otherwise meet the

[31]Section 368(a)(2)(E).

[32]Section 368(a)(2)(G).

requirements for an A Reorganization applicable to two-party transactions, such as business purpose, continuity of interest and continuity of business enterprise, discussed in the next section.

3. Reverse Triangular

As described earlier, the special rule in Section 368(a)(2)(E) facilitates the use by a parent corporation of a transitory subsidiary to acquire another corporation. The parent corporation contributes its stock to the transitory subsidiary, which is then merged into the acquired corporation which survives the merger. The parent's stock is distributed to the shareholders of the acquired corporation.

A reverse triangular transaction may qualify as a B Reorganization, provided that it meets the applicable requirements. If the transaction will be an A Reorganization in reliance on Section 368(a)(2)(E), some requirements in addition to those required for a B Reorganization must be met. After the transaction, the acquired corporation that survives the merger must (1) continue to hold substantially all of its properties and (2) hold substantially all of the properties of the merged transitory subsidiary other than the parent's stock distributed in the transaction. In addition, the IRS has interpreted the requirements for acquisition of "control" in exchange for voting stock more strictly than those applicable to B Reorganizations.

H. Tax Free Reorganizations—Structural Diagrams

1. An "A" Reorganization—Two Corporations

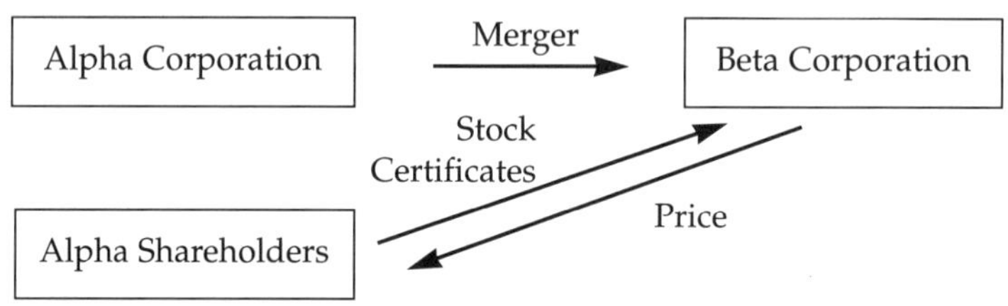

2. A "B" Reorganization

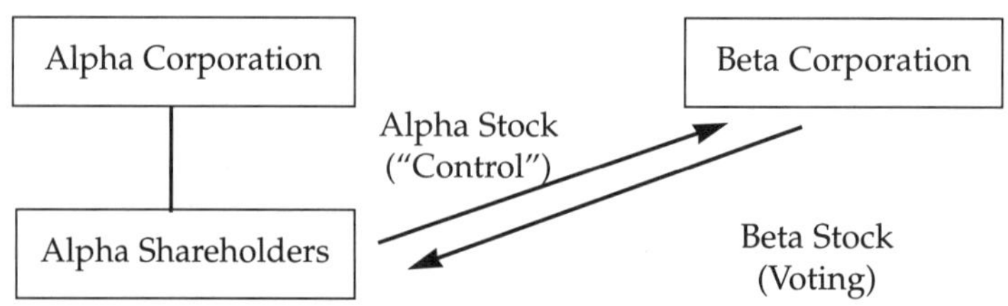

3. A "C" Reorganization

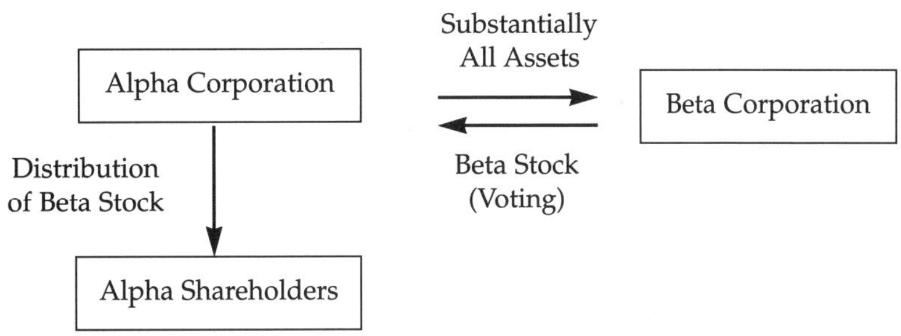

4. A "Forward" Triangular Merger

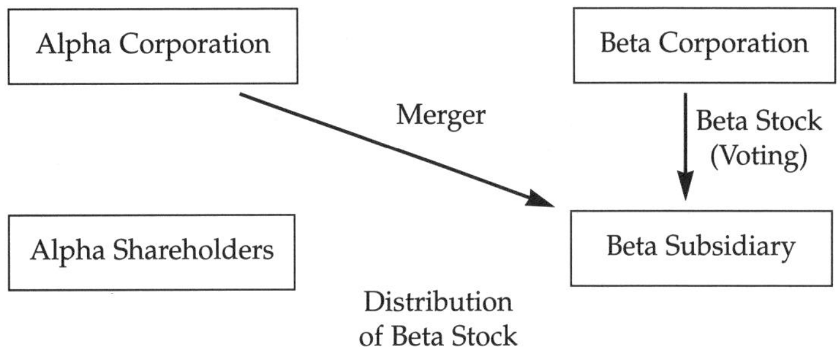

5. A "Reverse" Triangular Merger

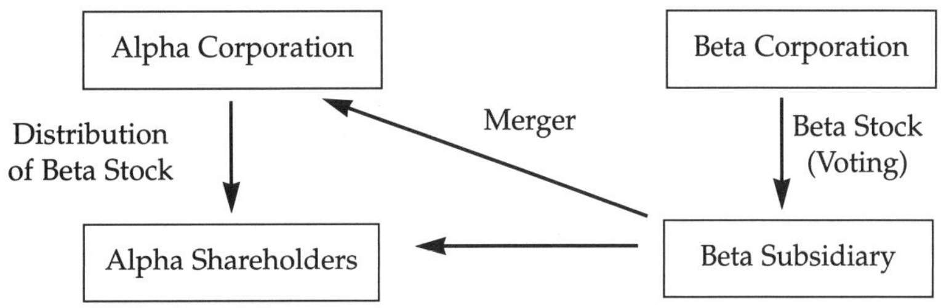

I. Tax Free Reorganizations—Court Imposed Requirements

Using their powers to interpret the Code, the courts have created some requirements not found in the statutory provisions of Section 368 and its related sections. The Tax Court and other federal courts may deny tax free treatment under the business purpose, step transaction, continuity of interest and continuity of business doctrines. Not surprisingly, the IRS has adopted those doctrines in its regulations and rulings and seeks to enforce them when opportunities arise.

1. Business Purpose

A transaction that has the form of a reorganization, but lacks a valid corporate or business purpose, is likely to be scrutinized by the IRS to determine whether it is a scheme or mere device to avoid income tax. If found to be a scheme or mere device, the transaction will not be treated as a plan of reorganization even though the definitions in Section 368 are met.[33]

The business purpose doctrine is not a serious obstacle for most tax free reorganizations. They are negotiated between unrelated persons and have one or more valid business purposes that can readily be demonstrated. A variety of business purposes have been found to be sufficient, such as maintenance of corporate control,[34] solving problems of divided control,[35] cost savings,[36] diversification[37] and preservation of assets from nationalization.[38] A purpose to obtain a net operating loss carryforward has not been recognized as a valid business purpose.

2. Step Transactions

If corporations and their shareholders take a series of steps that appear to be separate, the courts may combine them and treat them as a single transaction if they were parts of a single plan. Thus, if a plan of reorganization may be linked to other past, present or future transactions, there is risk that the other transaction or transactions may be found to be part of the plan, which may then no longer fulfill the requirements of Section 368. However, the IRS will treat steps as separate if each has an independent economic significance other than mere tax avoidance.[39]

The courts use various tests to determine whether transactions that appear to be separate should be treated as parts of a single plan. The courts will inquire whether there was a mutual interdependence between the steps and whether they were intended to achieve a preplanned ultimate result.[40] If the parties to a reorganization make binding contractual commitments to take subsequent steps, those steps will be deemed part of the plan.[41]

3. Continuity of Interest

The former shareholders of a corporation acquired in a tax free reorganization must maintain continuity of interest by receiving a significant amount of the stock of the acquiring corporation issued pursuant to the

---

[33] Reg. Sec. § 1.368-1(c); *Gregory v. Helvering*, 293 U.S. 465 (1935).

[34] *Dean v. Commissioner*, 10 T.C. 19 (1948).

[35] *Cannahan v. U.S.*, 1960-2 USTC (CCH) § 9773; 188 F.Supp. 461 (D.C. Mont. 1960).

[36] *American Bronze Corporation v. Commissioner*, 64 T.C. 1111 (1975).

[37] Rev. Rul. 74-155, 1974-1 Com. Bull. 86.

[38] *Wortham Machinery Company v. U.S.*, 1975-2 USTC (CCH) § 9665; 521 F.2d 160 (10th Cir. 1975).

[39] Rev. Rul. 79-250, 1979-2 Cum. Bull 156 (1979).

[40] *Penrod v. Commissioner*, 88 T.C. 1415 (1987); *Tandy Corporation v. Commissioner*, 92 T.C. 1165 (1989).

[41] *McDonald's Restaurants of Illinois v. Commissioner*, 688 F.2d 520, 1982-2 USTC (CCH) § 9581 (7th Cir. 1982).

plan of reorganization. This continuity of interest requirement was originally developed by the courts, but is now prescribed in the IRS regulations.[42] The reason for the requirement is that the various Code requirements relating to the issuance of stock pursuant to a plan of reorganization would arguably become meaningless if the former shareholders of the acquired corporation could cash out their investment by reselling the stock promptly after the reorganization in a transaction where the cash is provided directly or indirectly by the acquiring corporation.

As a condition for a favorable ruling, the IRS requires that the former shareholders of the acquired corporation have a continuing interest equal in value to at least 50 percent of the value of all the formerly outstanding stock of the acquired corporation as of the effective date of the reorganization.[43] The courts have been satisfied with somewhat lower percentages.[44]

The continuity of interest requirements have their greatest significance in A Reorganizations that do not require payment solely in voting stock as is required in a B Reorganization or C Reorganization.

Recent controversies concerning the continuity of interest requirement have focussed on contractual provisions for registration under the federal securities laws and resales of stock of the acquiring corporation by former shareholders of the acquired corporation. Contractual provisions for resales that destroy continuity of interest may disqualify a reorganization,[45] but resales as a result of events and decisions made after the reorganization do not disqualify it.[46] However, new regulations adopted January 23, 1998 now permit more flexibility for the acquired corporation shareholders.

When an opinion of tax counsel is delivered at the closing of a tax free reorganization, counsel usually obtains certificates from the shareholders stating that they have no intention to dispose of their shares. The representations in these certificates amount to commitments to hold the stock for a period that verifies the representation. Thus, the certificates and the underlying provisions of the Code reduce the immediate liquidity of the stock received in the reorganization.

4. Continuity of Business Enterprise

Another nonstatutory requirement for a tax free reorganization is continuity of business enterprise.[47] To achieve continuity of business enterprise requires that the acquiring corporation either (1) continue the acquired corporation's historic business, or (2) use a significant portion of the acquired corporation's assets in a business.[48]

---

[42]Reg. Sec. 1.368-1(e) and Reg. Sec. 1.368-IT(e).

[43]Rev. Proc. 77-37, 1977-2 Com. Bull. 568 (1977).

[44]*Nelson v. Helvering,* 296 U.S. 374 (1935) and *Miller v. Commissioner,* 84 F.2d 415 (6th Cir. 1936). However, see *Kass v. Commissioner,* 60 T.C. 218 (1973), aff'd 491 F.2d 749 (3d Cir. 1974).

[45]*McDonald's Restaurants of Illinois v. Commissioner,* 688 F.2d 520 (7th Cir. 1982). However, see 61 Fed. Reg. 67513 (Dec. 23, 1996).

[46]*Penrod v. Commissioner,* 88 T.C. 1415 (1987).

[47]Reg. Sec. 1.368-1(b).

[48]Reg. Sec. 1.368-1(d)(1).

As to business continuity, the fact that an acquiring corporation is in the same line of business as the acquired corporation tends to establish the requisite continuity, but is not alone sufficient. If the acquired corporation has more than one line of business, only one significant line of business must be continued. A corporation's historic business is the one it conducted most recently, but not one that it enters into as part of the plan of reorganization.[49]

As to asset continuity, continued use of historic business assets may include stock and securities and intangible operating assets such as goodwill, patents and trademarks, whether or not they have a tax basis. Whether the portion of the assets is "significant" is based on their relative importance to the operation of the business, but other facts and circumstances, such as their net fair market value, will be considered.[50]

Examples from the regulations are as follows:

Example (1)

T conducts three lines of business: manufacture of synthetic resins, manufacture of chemicals for the textile industry and distribution of chemicals. The three lines of business are approximately equal in value. On July 1, 1981, T sells the synthetic resin and chemical distribution businesses to a third party for cash and marketable securities. On December 31, 1981, T transfers all of its assets to P solely for P voting stock. P continues the chemical manufacturing business without interruption. The continuity of business enterprise requirement is met. Continuity of business enterprise requires only that P continue one of T's three significant lines of business.

Example (2)

P manufactures computers and T manufactures components for computers. T sells all of its output to P. On January 1, 1981, P decides to buy imported components but retains T's equipment as a backup source of supply. The use of the equipment as a backup source of supply constitutes use of a significant portion of T's historic business assets, thus establishing continuity of business enterprise. P is not required to continue T's business.

Example (5)

T manufactures farm machinery and P operates a lumber mill. T merges into P. P disposes of T's assets immediately after the merger as part of the plan of reorganization. P does not continue T's farm machinery manufacturing business. Continuity of business enterprise is lacking. [Reg. § 1.368-1(d)(5).]

The acquiring corporation need not continue its own business enterprise or business assets in order to meet the continuity of business enterprise requirement.[51] A temporary lull in business caused by financial distress does not necessarily mean that continuity of business enterprise is lacking if the business assets are retained and the business is then resumed.

---

[49]Reg. Sec. 1.368-1(d)(2); Rev. Rul. 81-247, 1981-2 Com. Bull. 235.

[50]Reg. Sec. 1.368-1(d)(3).

[51]Rev. Rul. 81-25, 1981-1 Cum. Bull. 132.

J. Tax Free Divisions of Corporate Businesses

5. Introduction

Section 355 of the Code allows tax free divisions of corporate businesses, subject to several restrictions developed over decades by the IRS. Despite the restrictions, spin-offs are important tools used in strategic restructuring of corporate businesses. For example, in 1996, Union Pacific Corporation spun off its oil and gas subsidiary, Union Pacific Resources. In 1993 and 1995, Marriott Corporation divided itself into three corporations: Marriott International, Inc., Host Marriott Corporation and Host Marriott Services Corporation. Monsanto Company, a pioneer in the chemical industry, recently spun off its chemical businesses as Solutia, Inc. in order to concentrate on its formulated agricultural products businesses. Some shareholders of Philip Morris Companies, Inc. have recently been campaigning to compel management to spin-off its tobacco products businesses. AT&T Corporation recently completed a spin-off of NCR Corporation, which experienced several years of disappointing results after it was acquired in a hostile takeover by AT&T in 1991.

A spin-off is the typical transaction accomplished under Section 355. A parent corporation distributes pro rata to its shareholders the stock (and perhaps securities) of an existing or newly organized subsidiary. Thus, the parent and subsidiary relationship ceases and the two corporations are, immediately after the distribution, owned by the same shareholders. In a spin-off, the parent corporation's shareholders do not surrender stock of the parent corporation in exchange for the stock of the subsidiary. For example, in 1993, Eastman Kodak Co. spun off its major chemical subsidiary, Eastman Chemical Company, by distributing one share of Eastman Chemical for each four shares of Eastman Kodak.

A split-off of a controlled subsidiary is another transaction that can be accomplished tax free under Section 355. In a split-off, the parent corporation makes a non–pro rata distribution of the stock of the controlled subsidiary to selected shareholders in exchange for their stock in the parent corporation. The shareholders who receive the distribution then own the former subsidiary, but surrender their stock in redemption and cease to be shareholders of the parent corporation. A split-off allows a dissident shareholder or shareholder group to separate from the parent corporation and take a corporate subsidiary with them without imposition of income tax. For example, a split-off can be used to resolve an internal management dispute or to reverse an acquisition that has proven to be a misfit.

A split-up of a parent corporation and its subsidiaries is still another transaction that can be accomplished tax free under Section 355. In a split-up, the parent corporation is completely liquidated by making non-pro rata distributions of all of its controlled subsidiaries to different shareholder groups. The shareholders receiving the distributions then own the respective corporations, but surrender their stock in the parent corporation as part of the liquidation.

As discussed in the following paragraphs, the eligibility for tax free treatment under Section 355 is not always clear. Consequently, it is quite common for corporations intending to take advantage of this provision to obtain a favorable ruling from the IRS before making distributions under Section 355.

6. Taxation of Stockholders and Securityholders

Section 355(a) contains the general rule for taxation of stockholders and securityholders who receive a distribution of stock of a controlled subsidiary. If a corporation distributes solely stock or securities of a corporation that it controls immediately before the distribution to (1) a shareholder with respect to its stock, or (2) a securityholder in exchange for its securities, then no gain or loss is recognized by (and no amount is includible in the income of) such shareholder or securityholder on receipt of such stock or securities.

The general rule applies whether or not (1) the distribution is pro rata to shareholders, (2) the shareholders surrender stock, or (3) the distribution is pursuant to a plan of reorganization as defined in Section 368(a)(1)(D).[52]

The general rule is, however, subject to several requirements and limitations:

- The controlled corporation and, if applicable, the distributing corporation must meet requirements for being engaged in the active conduct of a trade or business.[53]
- The transaction must not be used principally as a device for distribution of earnings and profits of the distributing corporation or the controlled corporation, or both.[54]
- The distributing corporation must distribute either (1) all its stock or securities in the controlled corporation, or (2) an amount of stock in the controlled corporation constituting control. The distributing corporation must establish that any retention of stock (or stock and securities) was not pursuant to a plan having as one of its principal purposes the avoidance of federal income tax.[55]
- The principal amount of the securities in the controlled corporation received must not exceed the principal amount of the securities, if any, surrendered in connection with the distribution.[56]
- If the stock distributed was acquired by the distributing corporation within 5 years of the distribution in transactions in which gain was recognized, in whole or part, such stock is treated as "boot." Any cash or property distributed other than stock or securities of the controlled corporation is also treated as "boot."[57]
- The transaction must meet business purpose, continuity of business enterprise and continuity of interest requirements.[58]

---

[52] Section 355(a) (2).

[53] At least 80 percent of the total combined voting power of all classes of stock and 80 percent of the total number of shares of all other classes.

[54] Section 355(a)(1)(B).

[55] Section 355(a)(1)(D).

[56] Section 355(a)(3)(A).

[57] Section 355(a)(3)(B).

[58] Reg. Sec. § 1.355-2(c).

7. Taxation of Corporations

Section 355(c) provides the general rule for taxability of a distributing corporation on any distribution of stock or securities of a controlled corporation pursuant to Section 355 and that is **not** pursuant to a plan of reorganization. The general rule is that the distributing corporation does not recognize any gain or loss.

After 1990, the IRS became concerned that Section 355 was one of the few methods remaining after the *General Utilities* repeal by which a corporation could distribute some kinds of property without gain at the corporate level. This raised the specter of a step transaction in which a purchaser that wished to buy for cash a subsidiary of another corporation could instead buy stock of the parent corporation equal to the value of the subsidiary. The parent could then redeem the stock by distributing the stock of the subsidiary to the purchaser in a tax free split-off pursuant to Section 355.

In 1990, Section 355(c) was clarified to limit the general rule of nonrecognition to "qualified property," in other words, stock or securities in the controlled corporation. If any other property is distributed and its fair market value exceeds its adjusted basis, the distributing corporation must recognize gain as if the property had been sold to the distributee at fair market value.

A new Section 355(d) was also added providing that even a distribution of "qualified property" will not be entitled to nonrecognition treatment if the distribution is a "disqualified distribution." There is a "disqualified distribution" if, immediately after the distribution, any person holds 50 percent or greater interest (by voting power or total value) in all shares of all classes of stock of either the distributing or the controlled corporation and such stock was acquired by purchase after October 9, 1990 and during the 5-year period ending on the distribution date. Aggregation and attribution rules are used, among other things, to give full effect to the amendment.

The Taxpayer Relief Act of 1997 added a new Section 355(e) providing, in effect, that gain will be recognized by the distributing corporation upon the distribution if either the distributing corporation or the controlled corporation is acquired pursuant to a plan or arrangement existing on the distribution date. The intent of Section 355(e) is to limit so-called "Morris Trust" transactions which the IRS perceived as allowing transfers of assets without taxation at the corporate level. Under Section 355(e), a plan or arrangement is presumed to exist unless the shareholders control 50 percent of the voting power and total value of both the distributing corporation and the controlled corporation for two years after the distribution.

8. The Active Business Requirements

A corporation is engaged in the active conduct of a trade or business if it is directly so engaged or is a holding company whose assets consist substantially entirely of stock and securities of controlled subsidiaries so engaged.

The trade or business must have been actively conducted during the 5-year period ending on the distribution date and must not have been acquired during that period in a taxable transaction. Further, control of any corporation conducting such a trade or business must not have been acquired during the 5-year period in a taxable transaction by the distributing corporation or any distributee corporation.[59]

The IRS has provided regulations illustrating when a trade or business will be treated as actively conducted, including the direct performance of its active and substantial management and operational functions. Passive activities, such as holding of property for investment, will not fulfill the active business requirements.[60]

9. The Denial of Effect to "Devices"

As described earlier, Section 355 denies nonrecognition treatment to any transaction used principally as a device for the distribution of the earnings and profits of the distributing corporation or the controlled corporation, or both.[61] To provide guidance, the IRS has identified in its regulations some factors that it regards as "device factors" and "nondevice factors." The presence or absence of such factors will be considered by the IRS together with other facts and circumstances in determining whether nonrecognition is appropriate.

The "device factors" are (1) a pro rata distribution; (2) a sale or exchange of stock after the distribution, especially if negotiated or agreed upon before the distribution or made within a relatively short time after the distribution; and (3) the nature, kind, amount and use of the assets of the distributing and the controlled corporations immediately after the transaction.[62]

The "nondevice factors" are whether (1) there is a corporate business purpose; (2) the distributing corporation is publicly traded and widely held; and (3) distribution to domestic corporate shareholders is entitled to the dividends received deductions provided by Sections 243(a) or 245(b) of the Code.

K. Taxation of "Boot"

For some reorganizations, Section 368 of the Code requires that the acquisition price consist solely of voting stock. For A Reorganizations and other reorganizations, the acquisition price may include securities, money or other property, subject to various limitations including those in Section 354. Taxation of the money and other property, commonly called "boot," is governed by Section 356 of the Code.

In corporate divisions, Section 355(a) provides for nonrecognition treatment of certain distributions of stock and securities of controlled subsidiary corporations. If any "boot" is received, its treatment is governed by Section 356.

Section 356(a) provides that any gain on the exchange of money or other property in an exchange to which Section 354 or 355 otherwise ap-

[59]Section 355(b).

[60]IRS Reg. Sec. 1.355-3(b)(2).

[61]Section 355(a)(1)(B).

[62]Reg. Sec. 1.355-2(d)(2).

plies shall be recognized, but not in excess of the money and the fair market value of the other property. However, if the exchange has the effect of the distribution of a dividend, then the gain will be taxed as a dividend. Section 356(b) provides similar treatment for money or other property received in distributions to which Section 355 otherwise applies and specifically refers to Section 301.

Under Section 356, securities are treated as "other property" subject to taxation with three exceptions. The first exception is for securities to the extent entitled to nonrecognition under Sections 354 and 355. The second and third exceptions apply to transactions in which the principal amount of securities received exceeds the principal amount surrendered.

Section 356 is a one-way street. When it applies, gain is recognized upon the receipt of "boot," but no loss is recognized.[63]

L. Carryovers of Tax Characteristics

10. Introduction

Section 381(a) of the Code provides that an acquiring corporation will succeed to certain tax characteristics of the acquired corporation after a liquidation distribution under Section 332 or a transfer under Section 361 in connection with an A, C, D, F or G Reorganization. Such a succession does not apply to a B Reorganization because the acquired corporation continues its own separate existence. Succession to tax characteristics also does not apply to divisive reorganizations, E Reorganizations and transfers to controlled corporations pursuant to Section 351.

Except for an F Reorganization, the tax year of the distributor or transferor ends on the distribution or transfer date. The acquiring corporation is not entitled to carry back any net operating or net capital loss for any taxable year after that date to any taxable year of the distributor or transferor.

The acquiring corporation succeeds to numerous tax characteristics, subject to various limitations. A nonexhaustive list of over 20 of such characteristics is contained in Section 381(c). Among the most important items are net operating loss carryovers, earnings and profits, capital loss carryovers, accounting method, inventory method, depreciation method, installment method, bond discount or premium method and methods of accounting for contributions to employee benefit plans.

11. Limitations on Net Operating Loss Carryforwards

a. Section 269 Disallowance. If a corporation has accumulated a significant net operating loss (NOL) carryforward, it is a valuable asset that can be used, subject to various limitations discussed below, to shelter future income from taxation. The carryforward recognizes the fairness of allowing business taxpayers to recover losses before they must pay tax on income. Otherwise, income tax would be a burden for businesses attempting to recover from setbacks that resulted in losses.

[63]Section 356(c).

As described earlier, Section 381 provides that an acquiring corporation will succeed to NOL carryforwards after certain tax free liquidations and reorganizations. This carryover of NOLs can be helpful to the acquiring business in achieving a turnaround of the acquired business. A few decades ago, however, when the Code had few restrictions on succession to NOLs, speculators began trading in "shell corporations" with NOL carryforwards. Advertisements were published in the financial pages of newspapers offering to sell shell corporations that typically had no valid business.

Section 269 of the Code inhibits speculation in NOL carryforwards by authorizing the IRS to disallow them under some circumstances. However, the language of Section 269 is not limited to speculative transactions. Thus, any corporation acquiring any other corporation with an NOL carryforward must proceed cautiously or risk its loss.

Section 269 applies to the acquisition (1) by any person or persons of control[64] of a corporation, or (2) by a corporation of property of another corporation not controlled by the acquiring corporation or its shareholders when the basis of such property in the hands of the acquiring corporation is determined by reference to its basis in the hands of the transferor corporation. If the principal purpose of the acquisition is evasion or avoidance of federal income tax by securing the benefit of a deduction, credit or other allowance that such person would not otherwise enjoy, the IRS may disallow such deduction, credit or other allowance.

Under Section 269, the IRS has disallowance and also distribution, apportionment and allocation powers if (1) a corporation makes a qualified stock purchase of another corporation as defined in Section 338, (2) a Section 338 election is not made for such purchase, (3) the acquired corporation is liquidated pursuant to a plan of liquidation adopted within 2 years after the acquisition date and (4) the principal purpose for such liquidation is evasion or avoidance of federal income tax by securing the benefit of a deduction, credit or other allowance that the acquiring corporation would not otherwise enjoy.

Section 269 does not limit the disallowance of losses to those that occurred prior to the acquisition. If a corporation acquires another corporation with a history of losses and the acquisition is motivated principally to avoid federal income taxes, the IRS can disallow a deduction even if those losses occur after the acquisition.[65] The Tax Court and two U.S. Circuit Courts of Appeal have held that the IRS can even disallow deductions and other tax benefits claimed by the acquired corporation if the principal purpose of the acquisition was tax avoidance or evasion.[66]

The IRS does not issue rulings or determination letters as to whether an acquisition is within the meaning of Section 269.[67]

---

[64]The first part of Section 269 applies to any acquisition of control, whether taxable or tax free. Section 269 defines *control* as ownership of stock with at least 50 percent of the voting power and value of all classes. See *Hermes Consolidated, Inc. v. U.S.*, 88-1 USTC (CCH) § 9220 (U.S. Claims Court, 1988). The second part of Section 269 applies to transactions such as Section 332 liquidations and A, C, D, F and G Reorganizations.

[65]*Hall Paving Company v. U.S.*, 74-2 USTC (CCH) § 9539 (D.C. Fla., 1973).

[66]*Coastal Oil Storage Co.*, 57-1 USTC (CCH) § 9518, 242 F.2d 396 (4 Cir. 1957); *Jones Realty Co.*, 60-2 USTC (CCH) § 9600, 280 F.2d 394 (8 Cir. 1960); *Concord Supply Corp.*, 37 T.C. 919 (1962).

[67]Rev. Proc. 98-3, 1998–1 IRB 100 (Jan. 5, 1998)

b. Limitation of NOL Carryforwards After an Ownership Change. Section 382 of the Code contains provisions that disallow or limit the use of NOL carryforwards following an ownership change. These provisions apply to ownership changes resulting from acquisitions as well as other transactions that result in an ownership change.

To understand the terminology of Section 382, it helps to begin with its use of the terms "old loss corporation" and "new loss corporation." An "old loss corporation" is any corporation that has an ownership change and was a loss corporation before the ownership change. A "new loss corporation" is any corporation that is a loss corporation after an ownership change. A "loss corporation" is any corporation entitled to use an NOL carryover or having an NOL for the taxable year in which an ownership change occurs. The "old loss corporation" and the "new loss corporation" may be the same corporation continuing in existence after an ownership change.

Section 382(a) provides that the taxable income of any new loss corporation for any post-change year may not be offset by pre-change losses exceeding the Section 382 limitation for the year.

If the new loss corporation does not continue the business enterprise of the old loss corporation at all times during the 2-year period beginning on the change date, the Section 382 limitation for any post-change year, with certain exceptions, is zero. In other words, the NOL carryforward is lost entirely if the continuity of business enterprise requirements are not met.

If the continuation of business enterprise requirements are met, the Section 382 limitation is determined by a formula. The limit for any post-change year equals:

(A) the value of the old loss corporation, multiplied by

(B) the long-term tax exempt rate.

Thus, if the value of the old loss corporation was $5,000,000 and the long-term tax-exempt rate is 7%, the annual Section 382 limit is $350,000. If the Section 382 limit for any post-change year exceeds the taxable income of the new loss corporation offset by pre-change losses, the Section 382 limitation for the next post-change year is increased by the amount of the excess.

The value of the old loss corporation is the value of its stock immediately before the ownership change. The long-term tax-exempt rate is the highest of the adjusted federal long-term rates in effect for any month in the three calendar month period ending with the calendar month when the change date occurs. (The IRS announces these rates every month.)

At this point, readers will have observed that the Section 382 limits have been described, but the "ownership change" that triggers them has not yet been described. The author's reason for leaving this concept for last is that most acquisitions result in an ownership change. Thus, acquisition planners should give priority to planning for the Section 382 limits rather than analyzing the complex provisions defining an "ownership change." Nevertheless, a brief discussion of the shifts that constitute an "ownership change" is appropriate.

The definition of an "ownership change" is quite technical. As defined in Section 382(g), it involves two concepts:

(A) An ownership shift involving a 5 percent shareholder.

(B) An equity structure shift.

An ownership shift involving a 5 percent shareholder occurs if any change in the respective ownership of stock of a corporation affects the percentage of such stock owned by any person who is a 5 percent shareholder before or after such change. An equity structure shift includes any reorganization defined in Section 368 (except certain D or G Reorganizations), all F Reorganizations and also certain taxable reorganization-type transactions.

Using these concepts, Section 382(g) provides that an ownership change occurs if, immediately after any owner shift involving a 5 percent shareholder or any equity structure shift:

(A) the percentage of stock of the loss corporation owned by one or more 5 percent shareholders has increased by more than 50 percentage points in value over

(B) the lowest percentage of stock of the loss corporation owned by such shareholders during a 3-year test period.

The IRS has issued extensive regulations interpreting Section 382.[68]

12. Limitation on Offsets to Built-In Gains

Section 384 of the Code limits the use of preacquisition losses to offset recognized built-in gains other than preacquisition losses of the gain corporation. A built-in gain is the excess of the fair market value of an asset over its adjusted basis on the acquisition date.

13. Consolidated Returns

No deduction is allowed for any loss recognized by a member of a consolidated group with respect to the disposition of the stock of a subsidiary. (IRS Reg. Sec. 1.1502-20(a)(1))

For information about the use of NOLs in consolidated returns, see the temporary consolidated return change of ownership regulations issued by the IRS effective January 1, 1997 at Reg. Sec. 1.1502-1(g) and the earlier separate return limitation year (SRLY) regulations.[69]

M. Section 306 Stock

Section 306 of the Code was enacted several decades ago in response to a transaction known as the "preferred stock bailout." A corporation with accumulated earnings and profits would make tax free distributions of preferred stock to its shareholders. The shareholders would later sell the preferred stocks to unrelated investors, thus realizing long-term capital gain income rather than ordinary income. The corporation would later redeem

[68]See IRS Reg. Section 1.382-1 *et seq.*

[69]Section 1.1502-1(f) and *Libson Shops, Inc. v. Koehler,* 353 U.S. 382 (1957).

the preferred stock from the investors, using its accumulated earnings and profits. However, the redemption was not treated as a dividend because the redemption completely terminated the interest of the investors in the corporation. Thus, the preferred stock distribution, disposition and redemption were a circuitous method to "bail out" earnings and profits without dividend treatment.

Section 306 is of concern to acquisition planners because its provisions go beyond those needed to deny effect to the classic "preferred stock bailout." Section 306 can be a trap for persons insufficiently familiar with its provisions.

Section 306 provides that, if a shareholder sells or otherwise disposes of "Section 306 Stock", the shareholder shall be taxed as follows:

1. If the disposition is a redemption, the amount realized is treated as a distribution of property to which Section 301 applies. In effect, this means treatment as a dividend to the extent required by Section 301.
2. If the distribution is not a redemption, the amount realized is treated as ordinary income with certain exceptions. No loss is recognized.

In view of this unfavorable treatment of redemptions and other dispositions of Section 306 Stock, it is important to be able to identify stock that is or may be Section 306 Stock as defined in Section 306(a). First, Section 306 Stock is not necessarily preferred stock. It can be any stock other than common stock, meaning that some innovative special stocks may be Section 306 Stock. Second, Section 306 Stock is stock (other than common stock) held by a shareholder distributed in any of the following tax free transactions:

1. A distribution of stock not included in the shareholder's gross income pursuant to Section 305.
2. A distribution of stock received pursuant to a plan of reorganization pursuant to Section 368(a) or in a distribution or exchange pursuant to Section 355 with respect to which gain or loss to the shareholder was not recognized, but only to the extent that either (a) the effect was substantially the same as the receipt of a stock dividend or (b) the stock received was in exchange for Section 306 Stock.
3. A distribution of stock having a transferred or substituted basis.
4. A distribution of stock in an exchange pursuant to which Section 351 applied if receipt of money (in lieu of the stock) would have been treated as a dividend.

Nevertheless, Section 306 Stock does not include any stock if no part of the distribution would have been a dividend if money had been distributed in lieu of the stock because the corporation did not have current or accumulated earnings and profits. See Section 306(c)(2).

The adverse treatment of Section 306 Stock does not apply to some dispositions and redemptions:

1. A disposition that is not a redemption that terminates a shareholder's entire stock interest in the corporation or a redemption that either completely redeems all of the shareholder's stock in the corporation or is made to a shareholder who is not a corporation in partial liquidation of the corporation. See Sections 306(b)(1) and 302(b)(3) and (4). The attribution rules of Section 318 apply to these transactions.
2. A redemption in complete liquidation pursuant to Sections 331 or 332. See Section 306(b)(2).
3. A disposition in a transaction in which gain or loss is not recognized. See Section 306(b)(3).
4. A distribution, disposition or redemption that is established to the satisfaction of the IRS as not in pursuance of a plan having as one of its principal purposes the avoidance of federal income tax. See Section 306(b)(4).

N. Foreign Corporations

14. Pre-1985 Background

As described earlier in this chapter, the sections of the Code allowing tax free organizations, reorganizations and divisions of corporations and tax free liquidations of 80 percent owned subsidiaries provide for nonrecognition of gain or loss upon those events. However, those sections are linked to sections providing for succession to tax characteristics and substitution of bases that assure the nonrecognition is a mere deferral of taxation and not a means to avoid permanently the taxation of gain or loss on the property, stock or securities involved.

The IRS and the U.S. Congress have for decades been concerned that deferral could become permanent avoidance if tax free treatment were allowed without restrictions for transactions involving foreign corporations. For example, appreciated property could be transferred in a tax free transaction beyond the effective taxing power of the United States. Accordingly, before 1985, Section 367 of the Code denied tax free treatment to exchanges described in Sections 332, 352, 354, 355, 356 and 361 unless a ruling was obtained from the IRS that the exchange was not in pursuance of a plan having as one of its principal purposes the avoidance of federal income taxes. Section 367 accomplished the denial of tax free treatment by providing that a foreign corporation was not a corporation within the meaning of Sections 332, 351, 354, 355, 356 or 361.

15. Overview of the 1985 Amendments

Effective January 1, 1985, Section 367 was amended to eliminate the general requirement that a ruling be obtained from the IRS. In place of the ruling requirement, several rules and exceptions were added that allow tax free treatment of some transactions involving foreign corporations, but impose tax on other transactions that would be tax free for domestic corporations.

Section 367 covers a wide range of transactions, using a variety of techniques. The IRS has supplemented Section 367 with lengthy and complex regulations, temporary regulations and proposed regulations. To begin with an overview, the provisions of Section 367 are grouped in five subsections:

- Exchanges involving transfers of property by a U.S. person to a foreign corporation.
- Exchanges not involving any transfer of property to a foreign corporation including sales or exchanges of stock or securities in a foreign corporation by a U.S. person.
- Transactions to be treated as exchanges whether or not they would otherwise be treated as exchanges, in other words, distributions under Section 355 and the provisions of Section 356 relating to Section 355 and transfers of property as capital contributions to 80 percent controlled foreign corporations.
- Transfers of intangible property by a U.S. person to a foreign corporation in an exchange described in Sections 351 or 361 of the Code.
- Distributions by domestic corporations to non–U.S. persons pursuant to Section 355 and liquidations of 80 percent owned subsidiaries under Sections 332 and 337 of the Code.

16. Exchanges Transferring Property to Foreign Corporations

The general rule contained in Section 367(a)(1) provides that a foreign corporation is not a corporation for the purposes of determining the extent to which gain or loss is recognized if a U.S. person transfers property to a foreign corporation in an exchange described in Sections 332, 351, 354, 356 or 361 of the Code. In simpler terms, the general rule is that outbound transfers of property by U.S. persons to foreign corporations are taxable even though made by exchanges that would be tax free if they involved domestic corporations.

The general rule has two important exceptions that allow tax free treatment of certain exchanges:

(a) The transfer of stock or securities of a foreign corporation which is a party to an exchange or reorganization, except as provided in IRS regulations.

(b) The transfer of property to a foreign corporation for use by such foreign corporation in the active conduct of a trade or business, except for certain transfers of inventories, installment obligations, receivables, foreign currency, intangibles, leased property and other assets, commonly called "tainted assets." The active trade or business exception also does not apply to certain transfers of foreign branch assets of U.S. persons.

A special rule applies to transfers of partnership interests that are treated as the transfer of a pro rata share of the assets of the partnership, except as provided in IRS regulations. The two exceptions to the general rule do not apply to certain exchanges described in Section 361.

17. Exchanges Not Involving Transfers of Property to a Foreign Corporation

Section 367(b)(1) provides that a foreign corporation shall be considered to be a corporation in the case of any exchange described in Sections 332, 352, 354, 355, 356 or 361 if there is no transfer property described in the Section 367(a)(1) general rule, except as provided in IRS regulations. In other words, an exchange may be tax free if it does not involve an outbound transfer of property from a U.S. person to a foreign corporation. The IRS is authorized to adopt regulations providing exceptions to the tax free treatment. The regulations may include sales or exchanges of stock in a foreign corporation by a U.S. person.

18. Transactions to be Treated as Exchanges

Section 367(c)(1) provides that any distribution described in Section 355 (or so much of Section 356 as relates to Section 355) shall be treated as an exchange whether or not it is an exchange. See the later discussion of Section 367(e)(1) which provides that, in any such distribution by a domestic corporation to a person who is not a U.S. person, gain shall be recognized to the extent provided in IRS regulations.

Section 367(c)(2) provides that any transfer of property to a foreign corporation as a contribution to its capital by one or more persons who, immediately after the transfer, own stock with 80 percent of the total combined voting power of all classes of stock shall be treated as an exchange of such property for stock of the foreign corporation equal in value to the fair market value of the property transferred. This treatment as a taxable exchange is in sharp contrast to the tax free treatment provided by Section 351 for contributions of property to the capital of an 80 percent controlled corporation. The effect is that persons who contribute appreciated property as capital to a foreign corporation will be taxed to the extent that the fair market value of the property exceeds their adjusted basis in the property.

19. Exchanges Involving Transfers of Intangible Property to a Foreign Corporation

Section 367(d) provides rules applicable to exchanges involving transfers of intangible property to a foreign corporation as described in Section 351 (capital contributions) or Section 361 (reorganizations). The rules begin by providing that the general rule of Section 367(a) does not apply to such transfers and that the provisions of Section 367(d) will apply. As will be described, the provisions of Section 367(d) are unusually strict.

Section 367(d) provides that any transfer of intangible property to a foreign corporation in a Section 351 exchange shall be treated as a sale of the property in exchange for payments contingent on the productivity, use or disposition of such property. The U.S. person is treated as receiving as ordinary income amounts that reasonably reflect the amounts that would have been received (1) annually as payments over the useful life of the property or (2) at the time of any disposition made after the transfer. This "pay tax now, earn income later" treatment is, of course, a deterrent to transfers of intangible property to foreign corporations.

20. Distributions under Section 355 and Liquidations under Section 332

Section 367(e)(1) provides that gain shall be recognized upon any distribution described in Section 355 (or so much of Section 356 as relates to Section 355) by a domestic corporation to a person who is not a U.S. person to the extent provided in IRS regulations.

Section 367(e)(2) provides that the nonrecognition of gain or loss in a liquidation distribution to an 80 percent distributee pursuant to Sections 332 and 337 shall not apply when the distributee is a foreign corporation, except as provided in IRS regulations. Thus, the protection from triple taxation afforded to domestic corporations by Section 337 is not available to foreign corporations.

O. Reference Materials

1. Books

CCH Standard Federal Tax Reporter (16 volumes)

Federal Taxation of Corporations and Shareholders, Bittker et al., Warren, Gorham & Lamont, 1996

Mergers, Acquisitions & Buyouts, Ginsburg *et al.*, Little, Brown & Company, 1998

Tax Management Portfolios:

Corporate Acquisitions—(A), (B) and (C) Reorganizations

Corporate Acquisitions—D Reorganizations

Single-Entity Reorganizations: Recapitalizations and F Reorganizations

Tax Strategies for Corporate Acquisitions, Dispositions, Spin-Offs, Joint Ventures, Financings, Reorganizations and Restructurings—1998, Freeman, Practicing Law Institute (11 volumes)

2. Articles

"IRS Issues Final 954 A Rules on Controlled Foreign Corporation Income," *BNA*, G-3, June 2, 1997

"IRS Overhauls Spin-Off Ruling Guidelines," Finkelstein et al., *Taxes*, 366, June 1996

"IRS Rules in Favor of Viacom, Ignoring Its Own Guidelines," *Tax Notes*, 1728, June 24, 1996

"New Temporary Regs on Stock Transfers to Foreign Corporations," Ruckelman et al., *Tax Notes*, 1537, June 10, 1996

Chapter 8

STATE TAXATION

A. INTRODUCTION

The subject of state taxation includes a numerous and diverse array of laws existing throughout the United States. This chapter provides an overview of the principles common to state taxation and then a discussion of selected tax issues that frequently affect acquisition and divestiture transactions.

B. TAXES FREQUENTLY AFFECTING ACQUISITIONS AND DIVESTITURES

The state taxes that most frequently and significantly affect acquisition and divestiture transactions are as follows: (1) franchise and income taxes; (2) sales, use and gross receipts taxes; (3) real property transfer and gain taxes; and (4) mortgage recording and security interest filing taxes; and (5) ad Valorem taxes imposed annually on assessed property values.

Over forty states (and several municipalities) impose on corporations a franchise tax measured by net income or a direct net income tax. In legal theory, a franchise tax is imposed on the privilege of doing business in the state. A direct net income tax is imposed without regard to the privilege of doing business. Some states impose a tax based on both theories.

A sales tax is imposed on retail sales of tangible personal property and is separately stated as an addition to the sale price. In some states, a sales tax is also imposed on leases and specified services. A sales tax is accompanied by a complementary use tax that is imposed on the use of tangible personal property in a state, but grants credits for sales tax paid on its purchase. These taxes are based on consumption and their burden is intended to be borne by retail purchasers. However, sales and use tax laws require sellers to collect and remit the sales tax to the state taxing authority. Some states impose a gross receipts tax that may be effectively equivalent, but the tax is imposed upon the person generating the receipts and is perceived as a tax on the privilege of engaging in business. Some gross receipts taxes apply to receipts from all sources, but others apply only to receipts from particular businesses. A gross receipts tax is not usually stated separately as an addition to a sales price, although the burden is passed on to customers like other costs of doing business.

The author expresses appreciation to Jeffrey S. Levin, his tax partner at Windels, Marx, Davies & Ives, for his helpful comments on this chapter.

Real property transfer taxes are excise taxes imposed on the transfer of real property and are based on the price or value at the time of the transfer. They are typically collected in connection with the recording of a deed or other transfer document. They may apply in transactions that are otherwise considered "tax free." A gain tax is also imposed on the transfer of real property, but allows the transferor to deduct the price paid for the property from the sale price. New York's unpopular "Cuomotax" was an example of such a tax, but it has been repealed. In a few states, transfer taxes are also imposed upon transactions such as mergers or sales of stock that indirectly transfer control of real property.

Mortgage recording taxes and taxes on the filing of financing statements to perfect a security interest are sometimes modest fees imposed by the states to help to defray the costs of the related governmental services. In New York, however, the 1% mortgage tax adds significantly to the cost of buying real property for purchasers who must borrow part of the purchase price. In Maryland, a surprisingly high tax is imposed on the filing of a financing statement on Form UCC-1 with the Secretary of State.

The states impose, or authorize counties or other municipalities to impose, annual taxes on the value of real property and perhaps also on the value of personal or intangible property. These taxes are commonly called "ad valorem" taxes. The laws imposing these taxes provide a variety of methods to determine the assessable value of property that may be assessed at 100 percent of its value or at a lesser percentage.

The states cooperate with each other in tax administration and enforcement through various arrangements including the Uniform Exchange of Information Agreement.

C. State Authority to Impose Taxes

1. Basic Jurisdictional Principles

The power of the states to impose taxes is subject to constitutional and statutory limitations. If state tax authorities attempt to impose taxes beyond these limitations, the courts may declare the tax assessments invalid.

A state has the power to tax any corporation organized under its own corporation law on the corporation's entire income, whether the source of the income is inside or outside of the state. A state also has full authority to tax any corporation having a "commercial domicile" in the state, even though it is incorporated in another state.[1]

A state that imposes unduly burdensome taxes on corporations organized under its laws or having commercial domiciles within its borders will encourage them to relocate to another state. Most states attempt to tax their domestic corporations in a manner that does not place them at a disadvantage in competition with foreign corporations. Thus, the states do not exercise their full power when taxing domestic and domiciliary corporations.

The states have authority to exclude corporations organized under the laws of other states and nations (both called "foreign corporations") from doing business other than solely interstate or foreign business within their

[1] *Memphis Natural Gas v. Beeker,* 315 U.S. 649 (1942).

borders. All the states, therefore, place conditions on the right of foreign corporations to do intrastate business within their borders. They require a foreign corporation to file an application for qualification to do business that includes a consent to pay the state franchise, income and other applicable taxes and an agreement to accept service of process issued by the state courts. Qualification confers power upon the state to tax the income of the foreign corporation, regardless of source. However, the states recognize that imposition of unduly burdensome taxes on foreign corporations would discourage them from qualifying to do business. Thus, they allow qualified corporations to account separately or to allocate or apportion their income to reduce duplicative taxation of the same income by several states.

2. Constitutional and Statutory Limitations

A state's power to impose tax beyond its borders is subject to provisions of the U.S. Constitution commonly called the "commerce clause" and the "due process clause." The commerce clause bars any state tax that discriminates against or constitutes an undue burden on interstate commerce.[2] The due process clause bars any state tax that does not meet minimum standards for due process of law.[3]

The states do not have constitutional authority to impose direct income, sales and other taxes on foreign corporations whose activities within their borders are solely in interstate commerce and do not create a sufficient contact (or "nexus") to support taxing jurisdiction. The U.S. Supreme Court ruled in 1959 that very modest activities are sufficient to create such a nexus.[4] Dismayed by this interpretation, which retreated from previous interpretations, Congress adopted the Interstate Income Law (IIL).[5] The IIL prohibits any state from taxing the net income of foreign corporations from sources within its borders if the only business activities within such state by or on behalf of a person during a taxable year are either, or both, of the following activities:

> *(i) The solicitation of orders by such person, or his representative, in such State for sales of tangible personal property, which orders are sent outside the State for approval or rejection, and, if approved, are filled by shipment or delivery from a point outside the State; and*
>
> *(ii) The solicitation of orders by such person, or his representative, in such State in the name of or for the benefit of a prospective customer of such person, if orders by such customer to such person to enable such customer to fill orders resulting from such solicitation are orders described in paragraph (1).*[6]

---

[2]*U.S. Constitution,* Article 1, Section 8. Section 8 also includes the so-called "foreign commerce clause" which grants the U.S. Congress the power to regulate commerce with foreign nations and bars any state tax that discriminates against foreign commerce.

[3]*U.S. Constitution,* Amendment XIV, Section 1. The Fourteenth Amendment also contains the so-called "equal protection" clause.

[4]*Northwest States Portland Cement Co. v. Minnesota,* 358 U.S. 450 (1959); *Wisconsin Dept. of Revenue v. William Wrigley, Jr. Co.,* 505 U.S. 214 (1992).

[5]15 U.S.C. § 381 *et seq.*

[6]15 U.S.C. § 381 (a). See *Massachusetts Commissioner of Revenue v. National Private Truck Council, Inc.,* ____ Mass. ____; cert.den. ____ U.S. ____ (No. 97-1570, May 26, 1998).

The IIL provides that the foregoing provisions do not prohibit, however, a net income tax imposed by a state (or municipality) upon any corporation incorporated under the laws of such state or any individual domiciled in or a resident of such state.[7]

The power of states to require foreign corporations to pay or collect its sales or use taxes is also limited by the U.S. Constitution. For businesses such as mail order houses, even if there are activities sufficient to meet the "minimum contacts" test of the "due process" clause of the Constitution, a state does not have the power to require collection or payment of its sales or use taxes unless the activities also meet the "substantial nexus" test of the "commerce" clause of the Constitution.[8]

3. Allocating and Apportioning Income

Assuming that a state has jurisdiction to tax the income of a foreign (nondomiciliary) corporation, it is not free to tax income earned outside its borders unless there is a "minimal connection" between the interstate activities and the taxing state. Further, there must be a rational relation between the income attributed to the taxing state and the intrastate value of the corporate business. A state may tax an apportioned sum of the corporation's multistate business if the business is unitary. A state may not tax a nondomiciliary corporation's income, however, if it is derived from an unrelated business activity that constitutes a discrete business enterprise.[9]

To the extent that a nondomiciliary corporation is engaged in a unitary business, a state can impose its income tax on the entire income of the unitary business, both inside and outside its borders, provided that state applies a fair apportionment formula.[10] However, a state is not entitled to tax income from corporate businesses outside the state that are unrelated and not a part of the unitary business done in the state.[11] The U.S. Supreme Court has identified three indicia of a unitary business: functional integration, centralization of management and economies of scale.[12]

The states use a variety of methods to comply with the constitutional requirement that income be apportioned. A state may authorize a corporation to determine income derived within its borders by separate accounting if performed accurately. A state may require that certain kinds of income, such as capital gains and losses from real or tangible personal property that are nonbusiness income, be allocated based on the situs of the property.

---

[7]15 U.S.C. § 381 (b).

[8]*Quill Corp. v. North Dakota*, 504 U.S. 298 (1992).

[9]*Allied-Signal, Inc. v. Director, Div. of Taxation*, 504 U.S. 768 (1992); *Mobil Oil Corp. v. Commissioner of Taxes*, 445 U.S. 425 (1980); *ASARCO Inc. v. Idaho Tax Commission*, 458 U.S. 307 (1982); *Exxon Corp. v. Dept. of Revenue*, 447 U.S. 207 (1980).

[10]*Container Corporation of America v. California Franchise Tax Board*, 463 U.S. 159 (1983); *Mobil Oil Corp. v. Commissioner of Taxes*, supra.

[11]*Allied-Signal, Inc. v. Director, Div. of Taxation*, supra; *ASARCO Inc. v. Idaho Tax Commission*, supra; *F.W. Woolworth Co. v. Taxation and Revenue Department*, 458 U.S. 354 (1982).

[12]*Allied Signal, Inc. v. Director, Div. of Taxation*, supra; *F.W. Woolworth Co. v. Taxation and Revenue Dept.*, 458 U.S. 354 (1982); *Container Corporation of America v. California Franchise Tax Board*, supra. Another test is to measure the extent to which various parts of a business contribute to, and depend upon, each other.

It is difficult to allocate business income of a multistate unitary business when activities such as purchasing, manufacturing and sales are conducted in different states. Arguments can be made that business income is earned at each of these levels of economic activity. Thus, most states have adopted statutes apportioning business income according to a three-factor formula based on property, payroll and sales in the state as compared to those of the entire multistate unitary business. Some states use variations such as a three-factor formula with double weight for sales. Iowa has an unusual single-factor formula based on gross sales.[13]

Many states have adopted all or part of a model law called the Uniform Disposition of Income for Tax Purposes Act (UDITPA) or the Multistate Tax Compact (MTC), both of which contain standard methods for allocating nonbusiness income and apportioning business income. The UDITPA, which has been adopted in substance by over half the states, apportions business income based on a three-factor formula, after allocating nonbusiness income based on other factors. The three factors are property, payroll and sales. The Multistate Tax Commission established by the MTC has issued allocation and apportionment regulations.

D. State Taxes Based on Income

1. Introduction

Most states have incorporated by reference the U.S. Internal Revenue Code (the "Code") as the starting point for their corporate taxes based on income. Some states incorporate the Code as it existed on a prior date, such as December 31, 1992, and periodically revise the date. Other states incorporate the Code as it exists in the current taxable year.

All the states (except Alabama, Arkansas, Mississippi and Utah) use income as defined by the Code as the starting point for determining corporate income. The state laws then make a variety of changes from the Code to reach taxable income. For example, California and New Jersey do not allow use of the modified accelerated cost recovery system (MACRS) provided by the Code. For another example, many states modify the net operating loss (NOL) deduction provided by the Code to allow only an NOL carryforward, but no carryback. Thus, it is possible for a corporation with a net operating loss (and no tax liability) on its federal return to owe a substantial state corporate tax.

The states do not provide for consolidated tax returns in the same manner as the Code. However, some states allow, and others require, combined tax returns by affiliated corporations engaged in a unitary business. Other states require each corporate entity in a group to file a separate return.

Corporate income tax rates vary considerably from state to state, some being flat and others graduated. The rates are generally below 10%, but a few states impose rates of 10% or more: Connecticut (11.5%); District of Columbia (10.5%); Iowa (graduated up to 12%); North Dakota (graduated up to 10.5%); and Pennsylvania (12.25%). Some states also impose surtaxes,

---

[13]See *Moorman Mfg. Co. v. Bair,* 437 U.S. 267 (1978) and *Kraft General Foods, Inc. v. Iowa Department of Revenue and Finance,* 505 U.S. 71 (1992).

surcharges and additional taxes. In New York, the annual tax is the greater of (i) a percentage of taxable income, (ii) a significantly lower percentage of net worth, or (iii) a minimum amount. Thus, a corporation that has no federal income tax liability may owe a significant state tax in New York.

2. "Nexus" in Acquisition and Divestiture Transactions

An acquisition of assets can create a "nexus" to a state that would subject the acquiring corporation to income tax on a unitary business that was not previously subject to income tax in that state.[14] Conversely, a divestiture can break the "nexus" to a state that is subjecting the selling corporation to a state tax on a multistate or worldwide unitary business. An acquisition of assets can also change the way the business income of a unitary business is allocated and apportioned under state tax laws such as the UDITPA.

An acquisition of stock resulting in a new subsidiary subject to taxation of its business income in a state may create a requirement for combined reporting of the multistate or worldwide income of a unitary business. Conversely, a divestiture of a subsidiary can eliminate the requirement of combined reporting.

3. Differences in Treatment of Gain or Loss from Treatment under the Internal Revenue Code

In general, gain or loss on a taxable acquisition or divestiture transaction is taxed under state law in a manner similar to its taxation by the Code, except in the states that have not incorporated the Code by reference into the state tax law. However, differences exist in states that do not use MACRS deductions, limit NOL deductions, or have other variations from the Code.[15] Differences will also arise when affiliated corporations file consolidated returns under the Code, but do not file on a combined basis in one or more states.

A sale of stock of a subsidiary is also usually taxed under state law in a manner similar to its taxation under the Code. However, New York exempts gain from the sale of stock of a subsidiary.[16] Most states accept a Section 338 election to have a stock acquisition treated as an assets acquisition by the acquired subsidiary of the buyer corporation. However, some states have not accepted a Section 338(h)(10) election. New Jersey and New York were once among the states that declined to accept a Section 338(h)(10) election, but both have changed their positions[17] with respect to a sale of a subsidiary that is part of an affiliated group filing a combined return for a unitary business. However, even those states that recognize a Section 338(h)(10) election will not do so if the selling consolidated or affiliated group does not file a combined return with the state.

---

[14] *Reuters Limited v. Tax Appeals Tribunal*, 82 N.Y.2d 112, 623 N.G. 2d 112 (1993).

[15] For example, the State of New York partially disallows interest expense for acquisition debt that increases leverage in excess of specified levels. *New York Tax Law*, § 208.9(b). New York also limits NOL carryovers. *New York Tax Law*, § 208.9(f).

[16] *New York Tax Law*, § 208.9(a)(1).

[17] In New York, a Section 338(h)(10) election can create a tax for a seller consolidated or affiliated group that would not otherwise be payable because of the exemption for sale of stock of a subsidiary.

4. Business or Nonbusiness Income

Important state income tax issues can arise from the characterization of income (or loss) from a sale of assets. Under state laws, nonbusiness income (or loss) from the sale of property is generally allocated under situs principles. For example, states that have adopted the UDITPA allocate gain from sales of real property and tangible personal property to the states where the property is located.[18] Gain from the sale of intellectual property is allocated to the state of the corporation's commercial domicile. On the other hand, business income (or loss) from a sale of property is apportioned by the methods provided in the UDITPA or other applicable state apportionment formulae. Thus, it is important to determine whether income (or loss) from a sale of assets will be treated as nonbusiness or business income.

In states that have adopted the UDITPA, and especially those that have also adopted the MTC, income (or loss) from a sale of the assets of a business will usually be characterized as business income unless the assets were not being used in the regular course of its business.[19] In states that have not adopted the UDITPA, characterization depends on whether the state applies a transactional test or a functional test to determine business income. Under the transactional test, income from a sale of assets is business income if the corporation makes such asset sales in the regular course of its business. Under the functional test, income from a sale of assets is business income if the assets were being used in the corporation's business to produce business income, regardless of the extraordinary nature and infrequency of the transaction.[20]

Under the transactional test, sales of assets will result in business income if they occur with some frequency, even if they are not the corporation's daily business activity.[21] However, when a Pennsylvania construction contractor made a sale of 21.5 acres of a 24.5-acre property in New Jersey, the Pennsylvania Supreme Court found that the gain was nonbusiness income. Three acres of the property were fenced, improved with a building, and used for the storage of construction equipment and materials. The 21.5 acres sold were heavily wooded and unimproved and had never produced any income. The Court found the sale was not subject to Pennsylvania's corporate net income tax, but was allocable to New Jersey.[22]

Under the functional test, gain from a sale of assets has often been held to be business income.[23] However, gain from the sale of a pipeline that had

---

[18]If the tangible personal property was located in a state not having jurisdiction to tax the divesting corporation, nonbusiness income is allocated to the corporation's commercial domicile.

[19]This interpretation is based on the definition of "business income" in Section 1(a) of the UDITPA. However, see *Union Carbide Corporation v. Huddleston,* 854 S.W.2d 87 (Tenn. 1993) for a contrary interpretation of the UDITPA in an unusual case involving divestitures by Union Carbide to finance potential liabilities resulting from the accident at Bhopal, India and a major repurchase of its shares to defeat a tender offer by GAF Corporation. See also *Appeal of Chief Industries, Inc.,* 875 P.2d 278 (Kansas, 1994). However, see *General Care Corporation v. Olson,* 705 S.W.2d 642 (Tenn. 1986).

[20]*Union Carbide Corporation v. Huddleston,* supra.

[21]*Atlantic Richfield v. State of Colorado,* 601 P.2d 628 (Col. 1979); *Welded Tube Co. v. Commonwealth of Pennsylvania,* 515 A.2d 988 (Pa. 1986).

[22]*Ross-Araco Corp. v. Commonwealth of Pennsylvania,* 674 A.2d 691 (Pa. 1996). The Court held that the sale produced nonbusiness income under both the transactional and functional tests.

[23]*Pledger v. Getty Oil Exploration Co.,* 831 S.W. 121 (Ark. 1992); *Welded Tube Co. v. Commonwealth of Pennsylvania,* supra; *National Realty v. Department of Revenue,* 494 N.E.2d 924 (Ill. 1986).

been shut down for three years was held to be nonbusiness income under both the functional test and the transactional test when the proceeds were not reinvested in the business, but distributed to shareholders.[24]

Some corporations have avoided the controversy over the transactional and functional tests by seeking authorization to account separately for gain from a sale of real estate.[25]

5. Tax Free Reorganizations

The states generally follow the Code in determining whether to allow tax free reorganization treatment to transactions qualifying as such under the Code. However, the states modify the treatment to some extent. For example, as described earlier, some states limit carryovers of tax characteristics such as NOLs.

Like other acquisitions, a tax free reorganization may create a "nexus" between one or more states and those businesses of all corporate parties to the reorganization that can be brought within the scope of a unitary business. The result may be state tax burdens exceeding the levels projected in planning and valuing the acquisition.

Some transactions are also accorded tax free treatment under the Code because they involve members of a consolidated group. However, these transactions may be taxable under state law.

6. Spinoffs, Splitoffs and Splitups

The states generally follow the Code in determining whether to accord nonrecognition (tax free) treatment to spinoff, splitoff and splitup transactions. These transactions may remove a corporation from the jurisdiction of some states to impose taxes on unitary business activities. For example, if all of the divesting corporation's manufacturing plants, warehouses, sales offices and other activities creating a "nexus" to a state are included in a subsidiary being spun off, the state will no longer have the power to impose its taxes on the divesting corporation.

7. Entities Not Taxed as Corporations

This chapter focuses on state taxes as they apply to corporations taxable under Subchapter C of the Code. Under Subchapter S of the Code, a small business corporation and its shareholders may elect that the corporation not be subject to corporate income taxes, provided that a series of conditions are met. The effect of the election is that the income of a Subchapter S corporation is taxed to its shareholders. However, tax planners should keep in mind that some states and municipalities refuse such treatment. For example, the City of New York does not recognize an election to be taxed under Subchapter S and the States of New Jersey and New York impose the corporate income taxes on the income of Subchapter S corporations, although both states apply reduced tax rates to the income taxed.

---

[24] *Laurel Pipe Line Co. v. Commonwealth of Pennsylvania,* 642 A2d 472 (Pa. 1994).

[25] *British Land (Maryland), Inc. v. Tax Appeals Tribunal,* 85 N.Y.2d 139, 647 N.E. 2d 1280 (1995).

Under the "check the box" regulations adopted by the Internal Revenue Service effective January 1, 1997, entities such as limited liability companies can elect to be taxed either as a corporation or as a partnership without concern about classification according to entity characteristics. However, a few states impose corporate income taxes on limited liability companies. Many states have followed the federal treatment of LLCs.

E. Sales, Use and Gross Receipts Taxes

The application of state sales or use taxes to acquisitions and divestitures depends initially on the structure of the transaction. If a transaction is structured as a sale of stock or securities or as a merger, sales and use taxes will generally not apply because sales and use taxes are imposed on transfers of tangible personal property. Some states have statutory exclusions or exemptions for sales of stock or securities, mergers and consolidations.

If a transaction is structured as a sale of assets, some of the assets are usually tangible personal property. Thus, it is important to review the potentially applicable state sales and use tax laws to determine whether they may apply.

Most sales and use taxes are intended to apply to retail sales transactions and should not ordinarily apply to acquisition and divestiture transactions. Many state tax laws have express provisions that exclude or exempt the following: (1) inventories held for resale[26]; (2) manufacturing machinery and equipment and research and development equipment[27]; and (3) bulk sales or casual sales.[28]

In general, the states provide the same exclusions and exemptions from both sales and use tax, but some states have different exclusions and exemptions from the two taxes. Thus, tax planners should review the statutes and regulations applicable to both taxes.

Special sales taxes may apply to certain types of property such as motor vehicles. It may be possible to locate movable property, such as aircraft, in a state such as Oregon that does not have a sales tax, thus achieving a significant saving.

State tax laws often require that sellers who wish to claim a sale for resale exemption obtain a certificate from the buyer that the sale is for resale.[29] New York requires that the resale certificate be obtained within 90 days and in good faith.[30]

Some states impose general sales taxes that are not limited to retail sales. Some states impose gross receipts taxes and others impose gross income taxes that allow certain deductions in calculating gross income.

---

[26]For example, see *Conn. Gen. Stat. Annot.* §§ 12-407(3); *New Jersey Stat. Annot.* § 54:32B-(2)(e)(1); *New York Tax Law,* § 1101(b)(4)(A).

[27]For example, see *Connecticut Gen. Stat. Annot.,* §§ 12-412(34) and 12-412i and *New Jersey Stat. Annot.,* §§ 54:32B-8.13 and 8.14 and *New York Tax Law,* § 1115(a)(12). Some states use a narrow interpretation of manufacturing that does not include all the activities that industry regards as manufacturing. For example, see *Marweg v. Pennsylvania,* 513 Atl.2d 525 (Pa. 1986).

[28]For example, see *New Jersey Stat. Annot.,* § 54:32B-8.6. The definition of a "casual sale" varies from state to state.

[29]For example, see *Conn. Gen. Stat. Annot.,* § 12-410; New York Tax Law, § 1141.

[30]NYSRR § 522.4(b)(2).

Some state tax laws require advance written notification to the state of proposed bulk sales of assets.[31] The state then notifies the buyer of a specific amount that must be deducted from the purchase price until the state determines that the seller has paid its full tax liability to the state. The seller and the buyer usually agree that the amount withheld will be held in escrow. When the state is satisfied, it will notify the person serving as escrow agent that the amount in the escrow fund can be paid to the seller. A buyer who fails to negotiate contractual arrangements to comply with the bulk sale notification and withholding requirements risks liability for any tax that may be left unpaid by the seller.

Sales and use tax laws may designate certain officers of corporations and other persons as personally responsible for the collection and payment of sales taxes.[32] These obligations are quite serious because the state will hold such persons personally liable if they fail to perform their obligations.

Sellers and buyers should be alert to the possibility that a state might seek to impose its sales or use tax on the "deemed sale" of assets that constructively results from an election to treat a sale of stock as a sale of assets under Section 338 of the Internal Revenue Code.

F. Real Property Transfer Taxes

Many states impose real property transfer taxes. These taxes apply when deeds or other instruments transferring interests in real property are recorded. Some states implement the tax by requiring that persons recording deeds and other instruments purchase and affix documentary stamps to them. Other states require that a return be filed with the recording official or a state agency.

The transfer tax rate is based on the consideration for the transfer and is usually stated as a dollar amount of tax per dollar amount of consideration. For example, the basic real property transfer tax imposed by the State of New York is $2 for each $500 fraction of consideration, or 0.4%.

Exemptions from real property transfer taxes may be available for transfers upon the organization, reorganization, merger or liquidation of a corporation. However, some states (such as Connecticut) do not exempt such transactions.

G. Mortgage Recording and Security Interest Filing Taxes

Many states have a mortgage recording tax and a tax upon the filing of a financing statement to perfect a security interest in personal property. For example, the State of New York imposes mortgage recording taxes that total $1 per $100 of principal debt or obligation that is, or under any contingency may be, secured by the mortgage.[33] Thus, the tax applies to the

[31]For example, see *Conn. Gen. Stat. Annot.* § 12-424(1); *New Jersey Stat. Annot.*, § 54:32B-22(c); *New York Tax Law*, § 1141(c).

[32]For example, see *New Jersey Stat. Annot.*, § 54:32B-2(w) and *New York Tax Law*, § 1138(3)(B).

amount of future advances that may be secured by the mortgage as well as the original principal amount of the loan.

H. Taxes Imposed on Assessed Values of Property

All states impose ad valorem taxes annually on the value of real property as assessed by state or local officials. Some states also impose taxes on the assessed value of tangible personal property. A few states impose a tax on intangible property. However, most states are reluctant to impose intangibles taxes because of enforcement difficulties.

Ad valorem taxes are typically stated as an amount per dollar unit of the assessed property value which may be set at 100 percent or a lesser percentage of its actual value. State or local officials issue annual invoices for the tax which is secured by a statutory lien on the property that can be foreclosed if the tax is not paid.

Tax assessors tend to make increases gradually. Thus, if a property is held by one owner for a long time period, the assessed value may become considerably less than the value for which the property could be sold. If property is then sold or transferred in an acquisition or divestiture transaction, the tax assessor will reassess the value of the property, often to a much higher value that increases the annual property tax.[34]

Tax assessors are also slow to reduce assessed values of old properties located in urban areas with declining economies. Thus, a buyer of old urban property in an acquisition transaction has an opportunity to seek a reduction of its assessed value if the price paid for the property is lower than the assessed value.

I. Reference Materials

State Taxation, Hellerstein, Warren Gorham Lamont.

State Taxation of Mergers and Acquisitions, Stern, BNA Tax Management Portfolio No. 73.

State Tax Guide, Commerce Clearing House

---

[33] *New York Tax Law,* § 253.

[34] This method of assessment was found in violation of the New Jersey Constitution in *Township of West Milford v. Van Decker,* 120 N.J. 354, 576 A.2d 881 (1990). See also *Allegheny Pittsburgh Coal v. Webster County,* 488 U.S. 336 (1989).

Chapter 9

ACCOUNTING METHODS

A. INTRODUCTION

Accounting treatment is an important element of acquisition planning and strategy. Managements of corporations with public shareholders want to make acquisitions and divestitures that enhance the business, but recognize that shareholders may not perceive the improvement unless reported earnings also increase. Managements of privately owned corporations seeking to use debt to finance growth through acquisitions want accounting treatment that reflects increased asset values in the corporate balance sheet. Thus, acquisition planners must be familiar with the methods used to account for acquisitions and their effects on the corporate financial statements at the time of the acquisition and thereafter.

For example, in early 1996, First Bank Systems, Inc. withdrew from a planned merger with First Interstate Bancorp when the Securities and Exchange Commission took a position that plans to repurchase shares after the merger could prevent use of the pooling of interests method to account for the transaction. (Wells Fargo & Co. later acquired First Interstate.) Later in 1996, threatened loss of pooling of interests treatment was reported to be a deterrent to an acquisition of ADT Ltd. by Republic Industries in an article that appeared in *The New York Times*, July 9, 1996.

Accountants use generally accepted accounting principles to prepare financial statements. These principles are regulated and conventional. They measure financial condition and operating results. They are not intended to measure other business factors (such as management skills or technology) unless and until they affect financial condition and operating results. They differ significantly from the asset values and cash flows used by valuation analysts to determine the value of a business. Thus, this chapter begins with some basic information about generally accepted accounting principles.

B. GENERALLY ACCEPTED ACCOUNTING PRINCIPLES

Since the adoption of the Securities Act of 1933 and the Securities Exchange Act of 1934, companies offering securities to the public or having securities traded in public markets have been required to file registration statements,

The author thanks Dr. Suzanne O'Callaghan, a Professor in the Accounting Department of Pace University's Graduate School of Business, for her helpful comments on this chapter.

periodic reports and other disclosure documents with the Securities and Exchange Commission (SEC). Those laws and the SEC's Regulation S-X on the Form and Content of Financial Statements require that the financial statements in the disclosure documents be prepared in accordance with generally accepted accounting principles (GAAP). The objective is to provide stockholders and other investors a fair and consistent presentation of financial statements.

There are several sources of GAAP:

The Financial Accounting Standards Board. In recent decades, the primary source of GAAP has been the Financial Accounting Standards Board (FASB) which is located in Norwalk, Connecticut. The members of the FASB are appointed by the Financial Accounting Foundation, a nonprofit organization, whose Board of Trustees includes nominees from accounting, investment, financial, federal and state government and securities industries organizations. The FASB succeeded to roles previously performed by the American Institute of Certified Public Accountants (AICPA) from 1936 to 1959 and the Accounting Principles Board (APB) from 1959 to 1973.

The American Institute of Certified Public Accountants. The American Institute of Certified Public Accountants (AICPA), headquartered at the Harborside Financial Center, Jersey City, New Jersey, is a membership organization of certified public accountants (CPAs). The AICPA defers to the FASB in the development of GAAP, but the AICPA issues, from time to time, Standard Operating Procedures (SOPs) that provide useful guidance to members and also assists in the development of GAAP.

The Securities and Exchange Commission. The SEC and its office of the Chief Accountant, a federal government agency created by the U.S. Congress, play a limited direct role in the development of GAAP, but is indirectly a driving force behind the development of GAAP.

The FASB, AICPA and SEC produce GAAP in several forms of work product:

The FASB. The primary work products of the FASB are its Statements of Financial Accounting Standards (SFASs) which, as of June 1, 1997, totaled 129. They include such well-known standards as FAS No. 95 which first required statements of cash flows, FAS No. 106 on accounting for retiree health benefits and FAS No. 119 on derivatives. The FASB also develops and issues statements of financial accounting concepts, interpretations and technical bulletins. The Emerging Issues Task Force of the FASB serves as a group that can identify emerging issues before they become widespread and the subject of divergent practices, so that consensus positions can be developed and issued. Finally, some opinions of the APB, the FASB's predecessor, remain in effect, such as APB No. 16, which is discussed later in this chapter.

The AICPA. The AICPA issues Statements of Position (SOPs) on issues that it believes need clarification for the benefit of its members. The SOPs are coordinated with the FASB.

The SEC. The SEC's Regulation S-X governing the form and content of financial statements filed with the SEC and the qualifications of independent accountants is a very important basic document in the accounting field. The SEC also issues Accounting Series Releases (ASRs) and Staff Accounting Bulletins (SABs). ASRs and SABs apply to the financial statements of companies with securities registered with the SEC under the federal securities laws. However, they also influence the thinking of other companies and their accountants.

Freedom under GAAP to Elect Different Accounting Policies. GAAP does not mandate absolute uniformity. From industry to industry and company to company, there is freedom to use alternative methods that have come to be generally accepted. For example, the construction industry is well known for its use of the percentage of completion method. Manufacturing companies can use either the first-in, first-out (FIFO) or the last-in, first-out (LIFO) method to account for inventories. These choices of accounting policies must be consistently applied, once selected and are disclosed in notes to financial statements prepared in compliance with GAAP.

Conservative Orientation of GAAP. The foundations of GAAP are in the federal securities laws and the ultimate enforcement agency for noncompliance is the SEC. The FASB, AICPA and SEC correctly view their responsibilities as primarily to foster full disclosure for the protection of public investors. As discussed in Chapter 11, nothing in the federal securities laws requires that full disclosure be conservative. Indeed, full and prompt disclosure of material information of a favorable nature is mandatory. However, regulatory organizations tend to believe they can best protect the public by encouraging disclosure on a conservative basis. Companies and the professionals who prepare disclosure documents tend to believe that conservative disclosure policies can best protect them from liability because optimistic disclosures that do not materialize can easily be second-guessed.

For example, land is valued under GAAP at original cost unless and until it is sold. Companies must treat future retiree medical benefits as a present liability even in situations where an obligation to pay is not clear. Research and development (including software development costs) must be expensed, even though a work product is created that has long-term value similar to that of a machine or facility. Companies must treat as expense the bargain purchase element of "cheap stock," although the actual burden is in dilution of shareholder ownership. Readers interested in further discussion of the conservative bias of GAAP should read *Creating Shareholder Value,* Rappaport, Free Press, 1986.

The conservative orientation of GAAP has important effects in acquisition transactions. The most important effect is that the financial statements of well-established, successful companies are likely to understate both assets and income in relation to the values that would be assigned by a valuation professional or an economist. On the other hand, overstatement of assets or income may occur among small, inexperienced companies that do not understand GAAP and, therefore, apply the rules incorrectly. Overstatements may also be made by financially precarious companies that do not comply with GAAP in the hope that recognition of their difficulties can be deferred long enough to save the business.

As discussed in Chapter 12, many hostile tender offers are made because the offerors have investigated the target company and found values not reported under GAAP. "Going private" and management buyout transactions also frequently result from situations in which GAAP financial statements and stock market prices undervalue a company. However, the SEC's rules for "going private" and management buyout transactions call for disclosure of fairness opinions and other information designed to provide information about values not found in the GAAP financial statements.

C. Generally Accepted Auditing Standards

The AICPA issues statements on auditing standards that establish a body of generally accepted auditing standards (GAAS).

GAAS includes general standards on the competence and independence of auditors, the care they must use in their examination of financial statements and the preparation of their reports on audited financial statements.

In addition, GAAS includes field work standards on planning and supervision of audit work, evaluation of internal controls and obtaining evidential matter to afford a reasonable basis for the opinions expressed in an audit report.

GAAS also contains reporting standards. An auditor's report must include several statements. The title must indicate that the auditor is independent. The text must state that the financial statements were audited and explain that the company's management is responsible for the financial statements and the auditor is responsible to express an opinion on them based on the audit. The text must state that the audit was conducted according to GAAS and explain that GAAS requires that the auditor plan and perform the audit to obtain reasonable assurance that the financial statements are free of material misstatements. The text must explain that an audit includes (1) examining, on a test basis, evidence supporting the amounts and disclosures in the financial statements; (2) assessing the accounting principles used and significant estimates made by management; and (3) evaluating the overall financial statement presentation. The text must also include a statement that the auditor believes that the audit provides a reasonable basis for its opinion.

Further, GAAS requires that the text of an auditor's report include an opinion as to whether the financial statements present fairly, in all material respects, the financial position of the company as of the balance sheet date and the results of its operations and cash flows for the period then ended in conformity with GAAP. Under GAAS, the opinion may be qualified or unqualified, but a qualified opinion may be unacceptable in documents filed with the Securities and Exchange Commission. An unqualified opinion may require explanatory language if, for example, there is substantial doubt about the company's ability to continue as a going concern or there has been a material change between periods in accounting principles or the methods of their application. An example of an independent auditor's report appears as Exhibit 9-1.

D. Tax Accounting Principles

The extensive accounting principles that compose GAAP must be distinguished from the income tax accounting principles contained in the U.S. Internal Revenue Code (the "Code") and in state and local tax laws. The tax accounting principles in the Code are a product of political processes.

They are adopted by the U.S. Congress and are interpreted in regulations adopted by the Internal Revenue Service, an organization within the U.S. Department of the Treasury.

The tax accounting principles contained in the Code are less comprehensive than GAAP. When particular methods are not provided, companies are allowed and required by the Code to use methods that accurately reflect income and expenses. Many companies use the same methods for shareholder reporting and income tax reporting except when the Code mandates a different method or provides a tax benefit linked to the use of a different method.

To the extent that accounting methods and tax methods differ, GAAP requires that the effects be reflected by such methods as the creation of deferred tax accounts and disclosures in notes to the financial statements.

E. The Basic Methods of Accounting for Acquisitions

Under APB No. 16, there are two basic methods to account for acquisitions, the purchase method and the pooling of interests method. These methods are not alternatives that can be elected by choice. Acquisitions that meet detailed criteria described later in this chapter are eligible for the pooling of interests method. All other acquisitions must use the purchase method.

Some articles have recently referred to a third method used for certain leveraged buyouts (LBOs) based on FASB's EITF 88-16 and related EITF publications. However, accounting for LBOs is essentially a combination of purchase and pooling concepts designed to present financial statements resulting from LBOs in a conservative manner.

Since the SEC issued its SAB No. 54 in 1983, many corporations have been required to use the "push down" accounting method after the acquisition of a subsidiary by a purchase of common stock. To do so, the subsidiary adjusts its assets and liabilities to current fair market values including goodwill, if applicable, thus causing the subsidiary's net assets to equal the parent's investment in the acquired common stock. Accumulated depreciation is eliminated. Accumulated earnings accounts are transferred to paid-in capital. The result is that the subsidiary has new bases in its assets and liabilities in a manner similar to the status that would have existed if the parent had purchased the subsidiary's assets rather than its common stock. "Push down" accounting is an important extension of the purchase method, but not a different method.

As described in Chapter 15, several special methods have been developed by the AICPA and the FASB to account for acquisitions by an Employee Stock Ownership Plan (ESOP). However, these methods are special applications of the purchase method to ESOP transactions intended to reflect the special benefits and restrictions applied to ESOPs by the Code and the Employee Retirement Income Security Act (ERISA).

F. The Purchase Method

Description of the Method. APB No. 16, paragraph 11, describes the purchase method as follows:

The purchase method accounts for a business combination as the acquisition of one company by another. The acquiring corporation records at its cost the acquired assets less liabilities assumed. A difference between the cost of an acquired company and the sum of the fair values of tangible and identifiable intangible assets less liabilities is recorded as goodwill. The reported income of an acquiring corporation includes the operations of the acquired company after acquisition, based on the cost to the acquiring corporation.

Determination of Cost. APB No. 16, paragraph 67, indicates that the cost to the acquiring corporation depends on the nature of the transaction:

- An asset acquired by exchanging cash or other assets is recorded at cost—that is, at the amount of cash disbursed or the fair value of other assets distributed.
- An asset acquired by incurring liabilities is recorded at cost—that is, at the present value of the amounts to be paid.
- An asset acquired by issuing shares of stock of the acquiring corporation is recorded at the fair value of the asset—that is, shares of stock issued are recorded at the fair value of the consideration received for the stock.

Paragraph 67 goes on to recognize that, when assets are acquired for other than cash, fair value may not be reliably determinable in some circumstances. Accordingly, cost may be determined either by the fair value of the consideration given or of the property acquired, whichever is more clearly evident.

The cost of an acquired company includes direct acquisition costs such as finder's fees and legal fees. The costs of issuance and registration of equity securities are treated as a reduction of the determinable fair value of those securities. Indirect acquisition costs and general expenditures are deducted as incurred in determining net income.

Amortization of Goodwill. Goodwill recorded when using the purchase method should be amortized over its economic life, but not longer than 40 years. The amortization should be deducted by the straight-line method unless it is demonstrated that an accelerated method is more appropriate (APB No. 16, paragraph 90 and APB No. 17, Intangible Assets, paragraphs 27 to 31).

Election of a period of less than 40 years for amortization of goodwill is often appropriate. APB No. 17 describes a number of factors that should be considered in estimating the life of goodwill:

- Legal, regulatory, or contractual provisions may limit the maximum useful life.
- Provisions for renewal or extension may alter a specified limit on useful life.
- Effects of obsolescence, demand, competition and other economic factors may reduce a useful life.
- A useful life may parallel the service life expectancies of individuals or groups of employees.

- Expected actions of competitors and others may restrict present competitive advantages.
- An apparently unlimited useful life may in fact be indefinite and benefits cannot be reasonably projected.
- An intangible asset may be a composite of many individual factors with varying lives.

The SEC has said that companies in high tech, health care and banking industries should amortize goodwill over periods of substantially less than 40 years. During 1998, the FASB has been reviewing goodwill and is considering changes that would require management to identify the discernible elements of core goodwill and to demonstrate why it paid for each element and the useful economic life during which the company expects to benefit from the element. If management cannot determine a useful economic life, the goodwill should be reviewed for impairment.

Some acquiring corporations in high tech industries prefer to write off goodwill soon after an acquisition. This "big bath" technique can be explained to shareholders as a nonrecurring event and subsequent earnings will not be reduced by charges to amortize goodwill. The claimed justification for the writeoff is that all or part of the goodwill is not as valuable as originally determined. However, especially for a company with publicly traded shares, this technique can raise questions as to whether management overpaid for the acquisition or, if not, is simply seeking to overstate earnings.

Allocation of Cost to Assets. Customary practice in negotiating an acquisition is to agree to acquire a corporation or its assets for a price stated as a lump sum. In an assets acquisition, the acquisition contract may contain provisions allocating the price to certain major groups of assets having tax significance, but the contract rarely allocates to individual assets. Thus, a detailed allocation is a task that must be accomplished after the acquisition contract is closed. APB No. 16, paragraph 67 prescribes allocation of cost to individual assets on the basis of fair value. Any difference between the sum of the costs of tangible and identifiable intangible assets acquired, less liabilities assumed and the total cost is evidence of unspecified intangible values.

APB No. 16, paragraph 87 prescribes the methods to be followed in recording the allocated costs of the assets acquired and liabilities assumed:

> *First, all identifiable assets acquired, either individually or by type and liabilities assumed in a business combination, whether or not shown in the financial statements of the acquired company, should be assigned a portion of the cost of the acquired company, normally equal to their fair values at date of acquisition.*
>
> *Second, the excess of the cost of the acquired company over the sum of the amounts assigned to identifiable assets acquired less liabilities assumed should be recorded as goodwill.*

Independent appraisals may be used as an aid in determining the fair values of some assets and liabilities. Subsequent sales of assets may also provide evidence of values. The effect of taxes may be a factor in assigning amounts to identifiable assets and liabilities (APB No. 16, paragraph 87).

General Allocation Guides. APB No. 16, paragraph 88 provides general guides for assigning amounts to individual assets acquired and liabilities assumed as follows:

> *(a) Marketable securities at current net realizable values;*
>
> *(b) Receivables at present values of amounts to be received determined at appropriate current interest rates, less allowances for uncollectibility and collection costs, if necessary.*
>
> *(c) Inventories:*
>
> > *1. Finished goods and merchandise at estimated selling prices less the sum of (a) costs of disposal and (b) a reasonable profit allowance for the selling effort of the acquiring corporation.*
> >
> > *2. Work in process at estimated selling prices of finished goods less the sum of (a) costs to complete, (b) costs of disposal and (c) a reasonable profit allowance for the completing and selling effort of the acquiring corporation based on profit for similar finished goods.*
> >
> > *3. Raw materials at current replacement costs.*
>
> *(d) Plant and equipment: (1) to be used, at current replacement costs for similar capacity unless the expected future use of the assets indicates a lower value to the acquirer, (2) to be sold or held for later sale rather than used, at current net realizable value and (3) to be used temporarily, at current net realizable value recognizing future depreciation for the expected period of use.*
>
> *(e) Intangible assets which can be identified and named, including contracts, patents, franchises, customer and supplier lists and favorable leases, at appraised values.*
>
> *(f) Other assets, including land, natural resources and nonmarketable securities, at appraised values.*
>
> *(g) Accounts and notes payable, long-term debt and other claims payable, at present values of amounts to be paid determined at appropriate current interest rates.*
>
> *(h) Liabilities and accruals—for example, accruals for pension cost, warranties, vacation pay, deferred compensation—at present values of amounts to be paid determined at appropriate current interest rates.*
>
> *(i) Other liabilities and commitments, including unfavorable leases, contracts and commitments and plant closing expense incident to the acquisition, at present values of amounts to be paid determined at appropriate current interest rates.*

"Negative Goodwill". After a bargain purchase, the market and appraisal values of the assets acquired, less liabilities assumed, may exceed the cost of the acquired company. If so, the excess should be allocated to reduce the values assigned to noncurrent assets other than long-term investments in marketable securities. If the allocation reduces the noncurrent assets to zero value, any remainder of the excess should be classified as a deferred credit (often called "negative goodwill") and amortized to income over a period not more than 40 years (APB No. 16, paragraphs 87 and 91).

The reason for requiring the allocation of the excess to reduce the values of noncurrent assets is to act as a check on the use of optimistic appraisals to create "negative goodwill" that could be amortized to income.

As a result of this requirement, "negative goodwill" arises only after the values of noncurrent assets are reduced to zero.

Contingent Consideration. Contingent consideration is sometimes included in an acquisition contract when a buyer and a seller agree that the price should be adjusted if certain favorable or unfavorable events occur after the closing date. For example, part of the price may be deferred or held in escrow for a specified time period for payment to the buyer in the event of breaches of representations and warranties, but for payment to the seller to the extent such breaches do not occur. For another example, a buyer using its securities as acquisition currency may agree to protect the seller against a decline in value of the securities for a specified time period by committing to issue additional securities at the end of the period to make the total value of the securities equal to the original agreed value.

Contingent consideration deferred for payment at the end of a contingency period or held in escrow pending the outcome of a contingency should be disclosed in a note to the financial statements, but not recorded as a liability unless the outcome of the contingency is determinable beyond reasonable doubt. The contingent consideration is then recorded as additional cost, if and when it becomes payable when the contingency is resolved (APB No. 16, paragraphs 79 and 80). On the other hand, the issuance of additional securities or distribution of other consideration based on security prices should not change the recorded cost of an acquired company. The issuance of additional securities or other consideration is recorded, but the value of the previously issued securities is reduced to the current lower value (APB No. 16, paragraphs 81 and 82).

Restructuring Costs. Acquiring corporations sometimes plan to restructure an acquired company to achieve a variety of business and financial objectives. They often prefer to accrue the restructuring costs as liabilities assumed in the acquisition transaction rather than to charge them as expenses reducing earnings for some time after the acquisition. Restructuring costs to (1) sell or close a plant, dispose of a subsidiary or otherwise close a facility or (2) terminate or relocate employees can be accrued as assumed liabilities, subject to several conditions. The conditions require that management begin as of the closing to assess and formulate a plan and commit to the plan within a year thereafter. For employee terminations or relocations, the plan must also be communicated to employees in considerable detail. The plan must specifically identify the significant actions to be taken and must be detailed for employee terminations and relocations. Actions to implement the plan must begin as soon as possible and significant changes must be unlikely. The accrual of restructuring costs as assumed liabilities must, of course, be limited to the acquired company and cannot be used for costs to restructure the acquiring corporation (EITF 95-3).

Preacquisition Contingencies. During recent decades, rapidly growing government regulation and liabilities created by legislation and court decisions have resulted in a situation such that few, if any, acquired companies are free of preacquisition contingencies. Some of them are so-called "long-tail" contingencies that endure for decades so long as plaintiff attorneys and environmental advocates focus on particular subjects and cannot be evaluated by any objective criteria. However, GAAP requires that preacquisition contingencies be resolved within an allocation period that should usually not exceed one year from the consummation of a business combination. They may be treated as assumed liabilities if accrued within the allocation period, but must be charged to income thereafter (FAS No. 38).

Application to Results of Operations. The acquiring corporation begins to include in its results of operations the operations of the acquired business from the closing of the acquisition. The results of operations of the acquired business are based on the acquiring corporation's costs as determined by the revaluation methods described previously. When the asset values have been significantly increased, the effect is to reduce earnings of the acquired business.

Acquisitions of Subsidiaries; Push-Down Accounting; Consolidation. Thus far, the discussion of the purchase method has been presented in terms of an acquisition of assets. That presentation helps to illustrate the method and follows the presentation in APB No. 16.

When a corporation purchases all or a majority of the stock of another corporation, the acquired corporation becomes a subsidiary of the acquiring corporation. The parent may elect to record the cost of the acquisition as "investment in subsidiary." If so, the subsidiary will continue to account for its assets, liabilities and results of operations as it did in the past and without any change of recorded values of assets and liabilities.

However, as described earlier in this chapter, if a subsidiary subject to the reporting requirements of the federal securities laws issues separate financial statements, the "push-down" accounting requirements of the SEC's SAB No. 54 apply with some exceptions. The subsidiary must adjust its assets and liabilities to their fair values on the acquisition date and, if necessary, record goodwill. The subsidiary should also make appropriate adjustments to its depreciation, retained earnings and capital accounts. The SEC encourages, and may require, "push-down" accounting when a parent owns 80 percent or more of a subsidiary.

The parent corporation may also consolidate the subsidiary into the parent's financial statements. If so, the parent separates its investment costs in the subsidiary into three elements: book value of the subsidiary's net assets, the increased value of the subsidiary's net assets and goodwill. The parent then charges amortization of these assets against consolidation income. The effect is similar to push-down accounting.

Disclosures. When the purchase method is used, several disclosures are required in the notes to the consolidated financial statements. They include the name and a brief description of the acquired company; the use of the purchase method; the period for which operating results of the acquired company are included in the acquiring company's income statement; the cost to the acquired company; the method and period for goodwill amortization; and any contingent payments, options or commitments in the acquisition agreement and their accounting treatment. The notes should also contain pro forma results of operations for the current period and the immediately preceding period as though the companies had combined at the beginning of that period (APB No. 16, paragraphs 95 and 96).

G. Example of the Purchase Method

As an example of the purchase method, assume that a buyer agrees to purchase a seller's assets for $500,000 cash plus an assumption of all liabilities. The balance sheets of Seller and Buyer are as follows:

Assets	Seller	Buyer
Cash and investments	$25,000	$625,000
Accounts receivable, net	125,000	225,000
Inventories	125,000	250,000
Prepaid items	10,000	25,000
Machinery & equipment, net	165,000	300,000
Buildings & fixtures, net	150,000	225,000
Land	50,000	150,000
Trademarks & trade secrets	–	–
	$650,000	$1,800,000

Liabilities and Shareholders' Equity		
Accounts payable	$100,000	$210,000
Accrued G & A	50,000	115,000
Accrued taxes	25,000	75,000
Loans payable	125,000	200,000
Common stock	100,000	300,000
Retained earnings	250,000	900,000
	$650,000	$1,800,000

The reader will observe that the seller's book value is $350,000. Thus, the $500,000 cash price is $150,000 over the seller's book value. The liabilities assumed total $300,000.

Appraisals show that the current fair value of some of seller's assets is higher than their book value, as follows:

Assets	Book Value	Fair Value	Increases
Machinery & equipment	$165,000	$200,000	$35,000
Buildings & fixtures	150,000	200,000	50,000
Land	50,000	70,000	20,000
Trademarks & trade secrets	–	20,000	20,000
			$125,000

Thus, $125,000 of the $150,000 purchase price premium over the seller's net book value can be attributed to the revalued assets. The remaining $25,000 is goodwill. (**Note:** For simplicity, the example does not assume that seller provided a covenant not to compete for which value should be determined and recorded.)

The buyer's balance sheet after the acquisition, reflecting the increased asset values, is as follows:

Assets		
Cash and investments	–	$ 150,000
Accounts receivable, net	–	350,000
Inventories	–	375,000
Prepaid items	–	35,000
Machinery & equipment, net	–	500,000
Buildings & fixtures, net	–	425,000
Land	–	220,000
Trademarks & secrets	–	20,000
Goodwill	–	25,000
		$2,100,000

Liabilities and Shareholders' Equity		
Accounts payable	–	$310,000
Accrued G & A	–	165,000
Accrued taxes	–	100,000
Loans payable	–	325,000
Common stock	–	300,000
Retained earnings	–	900,000
		$2,100,000

H. The Pooling of Interests Method

Description of the Method. APB No. 16, paragraph 12 describes the pooling of interests method as follows:

> *The pooling of interests method accounts for a business combination as the uniting of the ownership interests of two or more companies by exchange of equity securities. No acquisition is recognized because the combination is accomplished without disbursing resources of the constituents. Ownership interests continue and the former bases of accounting are retained. The recorded assets and liabilities of the constituents are carried forward to the combined corporation at their recorded amounts. Income of the combined corporation includes income of the constituents for the entire fiscal period in which the combination occurs. The reported income of the constituents for prior periods is combined and restated as income of the combined corporation.*

Criteria for Use of the Method. APB No. 16 imposes strict conditions, all of which must be fulfilled, on use of the pooling of interests method. The purpose of the conditions is to limit use of the method to combinations of previously independent stockholder interests and the combined rights and risks represented by those interests. The conditions require that stockholder groups neither withdraw nor invest assets, but in effect exchange voting common stock in a ratio that determines their respective interests in the combined corporation. The conditions are 12 in number and are grouped in three classifications:

- attributes of the combining companies,
- manner of combining interests, and
- absence of planned transactions.

Attributes of the Combining Companies. Each of the combining companies must meet two conditions:

- Each must have been autonomous and not a subsidiary or division of another corporation within 2 years before the plan of combination was initiated.
- Each must be independent of the other combining companies.

As to the condition requiring autonomy, a plan of combination is initiated on the earlier of (1) the date that the major terms of a plan, including the ratio of exchange of stock, are announced publicly or otherwise formally made known to the stockholders of any one of the combining companies or (2) the date that stockholders of a combining company are notified in writing of an exchange offer. Therefore, a plan of combination is often initiated even though consummation is subject to the approval of stockholders and others. A transitory subsidiary in a triangular merger transaction distributing voting common stock of a parent that would have met the condition if it issued its stock directly is also considered an autonomous company. If a divestiture of assets is made to comply with an order of a government authority or judicial body, either a subsidiary divested or a new company that acquires assets is deemed autonomous.

As to the condition requiring independence, none of the combining companies may hold as intercorporate investments more than 10 percent of the outstanding voting common stock of any combining company.

Combining of Interests. The exchanges to combine the companies must meet seven conditions:

- The combination is effected in a single transaction or is completed in accordance with a specific plan within 1 year after the plan is initiated.
- A corporation offers and issues only common stock with rights identical to those of the majority of its outstanding voting common stock in exchange for substantially all the voting common stock in-

terest of another company at the date the plan of combination is consummated.

- None of the combining companies changes the equity interest of the voting common stock in contemplation of effecting the combination either within 2 years before the plan of combination is initiated or between the dates the combination is initiated and consummated; changes in contemplation of effecting the combination may include distributions to stockholders and additional issuances, exchanges and retirements of securities.
- Each of the combining companies reacquires shares of voting common stock only for purposes other than business combinations and no company reacquires more than a normal number of shares between the dates the plan of combination is initiated and consummated.
- The ratio of the interest of an individual common stockholder to those of other common stockholders in a combining company remains the same as a result of the exchange of stock to effect the combination.
- The voting rights to which the common stock ownership interests in the resulting combined corporation are entitled are exercisable by the stockholders; the stockholders are neither deprived of nor restricted in exercising those rights for a period.
- The combination is resolved at the date the plan is consummated and no provisions of the plan relating to the issue of securities or other consideration are pending.

For purposes of the condition requiring a single plan completed within 1 year, an alteration of the terms of an exchange of stock initiates a new plan unless earlier exchanges are adjusted to the new terms. Delay beyond the control of combining companies because governmental proceedings or litigation prevents completing a combination within a year is excused.

For purposes of the exchange of stock condition, a wholly-owned subsidiary may distribute the voting common stock of its parent corporation if the parent would have met the conditions if it issued the stock directly. Distribution of cash or other consideration for fractional shares or shares held by dissenting shareholders is permissible, but not a pro rata distribution of cash or other consideration. Substantially all the voting common stock interest means 90 percent or more. The number of shares exchanged excludes certain shares previously acquired, shares acquired after the plan is initiated for other than voting common stock and shares outstanding after the combination is consummated. The condition is not met if shares and warrants or contingent shares are issued. However, restrictions from public sale without registration under federal and state securities laws are permissible. Further, certain assumptions of debt securities and exchanges with, or distributions to, holders of debt securities are permissible. The condition can also be satisfied by an acquisition of all net assets in exchange for voting common stock. In an assets transaction, cash, receivables or marketable securities may be retained to settle liabilities, contingencies or disputes, but the assets remaining after settlement must be transferred to the corporation issuing stock to effect the combination.

For purposes of the condition restricting equity interest changes, distributions of normal dividends to shareholders are not considered changes.

For purposes of the condition restricting reacquisitions of voting common stock, certain systematic acquisitions of treasury stock for option and compensation plans are permissible. In 1996, the SEC issued an SAB indicating that a significant repurchase of shares within 6 months after consummation of a combination will be presumed to be for the purpose of the combination.

For purposes of the ratio of interest condition, each individual common stockholder who exchanges stock must receive voting common stock in exact proportion to the voting common stock interest before the combination.

For purposes of the voting rights condition, for example, shares of common stock issued to effect the combination may not be transferred to a voting trust. The reason is that a voting trust would deprive or restrict the exercise of voting rights for some time period.

For purposes of the condition requiring resolution of the combination at the consummation date, the issuance of contingent shares or other consideration at a later date is not allowed. The issuance of shares or other consideration to an escrow agent for resolution of a contingency is also not allowed. However, an acquisition agreement may provide for a revision of the number of shares upon later settlement of a contingency. Reasonable employment, consulting or deferred compensation contracts or plans are permissible, but not if granted to former shareholders of a combining company who were not or will not be active.

Corporations considering "breakup" fees and "standstill" agreements should consider their possible effects on ability to participate in a transaction that will meet the criteria for the pooling-of interests method. "Lock-up" and "Crown Jewel" agreements and options undertaken in connection with hostile takeovers should also be reviewed for the same purpose.

Absence of Planned Transactions. The combined corporation must refrain from three kinds of planned transactions that would be inconsistent with the combining of entire interests of common stockholders and must be careful after the combination to avoid transactions that could be perceived as one of the three planned transactions:

- The combined corporation does not agree directly or indirectly to retire or reacquire all or part of the common stock issued to effect the combination.
- The combined corporation does not enter into other financial arrangements for the benefit of the former stockholders of a combining company, such as a guaranty of loans secured by stock issued in the combination, which in effect negates the exchange of equity securities.
- The combined corporation does not intend or plan to dispose of a significant part of the assets of the combining companies within 2 years after the combination other than disposals in the ordinary course of business of the formerly separate companies and to eliminate duplicate facilities or excess capacity.

SEC Restrictions on Affiliates. For companies with securities registered under the federal securities laws, the SEC has imposed an additional condition upon use of the pooling of interests method. The condition applies to "affiliates", meaning all persons who control, are controlled by, or are under common control with either combining company. No affiliate may reduce the risk of his, her or its common stock holding from a date 30 days before the consummation of the business combination to the subsequent publication of results of operations of the combined corporation including a period of at least 30 days after consummation of the business combination. However, an affiliate may sell up to 1 percent of the total outstanding common stock without triggering the condition, provided that all sales by affiliates do not aggregate more than 10 percent of the total outstanding common stock of their corporation. It is important for corporations planning to use the pooling of interests method to coordinate and control sales by affiliates that could exceed the amounts allowed by the SEC.

Application to the Balance Sheet. To apply the pooling of interests method to an assets acquisition or merger transition, the recorded assets and liabilities of the combining companies are combined to become the assets and liabilities recorded in the balance sheet of the combined corporation at the date of consummation. The existing basis of accounting continues without changes of the recorded values of assets and liabilities to reflect current fair value such as are made under the purchase method. However, if the two corporations have recorded assets and liabilities under different accounting methods, appropriate retroactive adjustments may be made to the same basis of accounting. The stockholders' equities of the separate corporations are also combined. The combined corporation records as capital the capital stock and capital in excess of par or stated value of outstanding stock of the separate combining companies. The retained earnings or deficits are also combined. If the outstanding shares of stock of the combined corporation exceed the total capital stock, the excess should be deducted first from the other contributed capital and then from the combined other contributed capital and then from the combined retained earnings (APB No. 16, paragraphs 51-63). Since assets and liabilities are not revalued, no goodwill is created by use of the pooling of interests method.

Application to Results of Operations. The results of operations of the combining companies for the current period should be reported as though they had been combined as of the beginning of the period, including elimination of intercompany transactions. The results of operations and other financial statements of the separate combining companies for prior years should also be restated on a combined basis to furnish comparative information. Expenses incurred to effect the combination should not be capitalized, but should be deducted from the net income of the combined corporation for the period when incurred (APB No. 16, paragraphs 56-58). Since there is no revaluation of asset values or creation of goodwill, such as occurs when the purchase method is used, reported earnings are not reduced by increased charges for depreciation and amortization. Thus, reported earnings after use of the pooling of interests method are often higher than they would be if the purchase method were used. However, earnings per share may be reduced because of dilution resulting from the issuance of new shares of common stock by the combined corporation.

Consolidated Financial Statements. If the combination was accomplished by a purchase of stock, the combined corporation will be a parent owning the stock of the combined company. The parent can prepare consolidated financial statements by recording its investment at book value as of the combination date and adjusting for its equity in net income (less dividends) thereafter by using the equity method of accounting or the cost method. In either event, the investment is eliminated in consolidation.

Disclosures. When the pooling of interests method is used, several disclosures are required in the notes to the financial statements of the combined corporation. The disclosures include the names and descriptions of the companies combined; the use of the pooling of interests method; the description and number of shares of stock issued in the combination; details of the results of operations of the previously separate companies for the period before the combination that are included in the current combined net income; a description of the adjustments of net assets made to adopt the same accounting practices and their effects on net income reported previously and now presented in comparative financial statements; details of any increase or decrease of retained earnings from any change of the fiscal year of a combining company; and reconciliations of amounts of revenues and earnings previously reported by the corporation that issues the stock to achieve the combination (APB No. 16, paragraphs 63-64).

I. Example of the Pooling of Interests Method

As an example of the pooling of interests method, assume that S Co. and B Co. agree to a combination in which B Co. will be the combined corporation which will survive a merger of S Co. into B Co. B Co. will issue 800 shares of its voting common stock in a transaction that meets all conditions of APB No. 16. The preacquisition balance sheets of S Co. and B Co. are as follows:

Assets	S Co.	B Co.
Current assets	$200,000	$300,000
Other assets	300,000	500,000
	$500,000	$800,000

Liabilities and Shareholders' Equity	S Co.	B Co.
Current liabilities	$120,000	$200,000
Long-term debt	130,000	200,000
Common stock $1 per share (1,000 shares outstanding)	1,000	1,000
Paid-in surplus	99,000	149,000
Retained earnings	150,000	250,000
	$500,000	$800,000

The fair value of the assets of S Co. on the consummation date is irrelevant to the pooling of interests method. The market value of the 800 shares issued by B Co. to acquire S Co. is also irrelevant to the pooling of interests method.

The resulting balance sheet of B-S Co., the combined corporation, is as follows:

Assets	
Current assets	$500,000
Other assets	800,000
	$1,300,000

Liabilities and Shareholders' Equity	
Current liabilities	$320,000
Long-term debt	330,000
Common stock $1 per share (1,800 shares outstanding)	1,800
Paid-in surplus	248,200
Retained earnings	400,000
	$1,300,000

The reader will observe that most of the recorded amounts are simple additions of the amounts shown in the balance sheets of S Co. and B Co. However, paid-in surplus is adjusted to reflect the change resulting from the issuance of 800 additional shares with a nominal par value of $1 per share.

The reader will also observe the absence of increased asset values and of goodwill or other intangibles.

J. Comparison of the Effects of the Purchase and Pooling of Interests Methods

1. The Purchase Method

Balance Sheet. The purchase method typically results in the recording on the acquirer's balance sheet of asset values increased from the values recorded in the seller's balance sheet. The additional asset values often include goodwill and other intangibles. The acquirer's capital stock, paid-in surplus and accumulated earnings accounts are not usually reduced by the entries to record the acquisition of assets and liabilities.

Earnings Statement. The purchase method requires that the reported income of the acquiring corporation include the acquired operations commencing from and after the acquisition, based on the cost to the acquiring corporation. Depreciation and amortization charges resulting from the increased asset values recorded on the acquirer's balance sheet reduce the earnings realized by the acquirer from the acquired business. However, if the acquired business continues to realize net earnings, the acquirer's earnings per share will increase, especially if the buyer paid cash or debt. If the acquiring corporation paid the acquisition price wholly or partially with common stock, earnings per share may also increase, but will be reduced to some extent by dilution resulting from the issuance of additional shares.

2. The Pooling of Interests Method

Balance Sheet. The pooling of interests method results in the recording on the books of the combined corporation of asset values that are the same as the values on the books of the combining companies. No increased asset values, such as goodwill or other intangibles, are added to the balance sheet. The capital stock, paid-in surplus and retained earnings accounts are also combined.

Earnings Statement. The results of operations of the combining companies are reported as though they had been combined from the beginning of the period in which the acquisition is consummated. The results of operations of the combining companies for prior years are restated on a combined basis to furnish comparative information. Since no increased asset values resulting from the acquisition must be depreciated or amortized, no decrease of earnings of the combined corporation results from the acquisition except that acquisition expenses are charged to income. Since the purchase price must be paid with common stock, earnings per share of the combined company may be reduced to some extent by dilution resulting from the issuance of shares.

The foregoing summary comparison is, of course, intended to contrast the basic effects of the purchase and pooling of interests methods in simple, relatively typical acquisitions. In particular transactions, there can be many variations, such as the recording of "negative goodwill" as described under the purchase method.

K. Controversies about the Basic Methods

Prior to the issuance in 1970 of APB No. 16, the pooling of interests method was very controversial. During the 1960s, there was serious concern about the pooling of interests method for several reasons. Prior to APB No. 16, there were only a limited number of general criteria for use of the method. Many companies made expansive interpretations of the criteria in order to use the pooling of interests method in situations that had predominant characteristics of a purchase transaction in order to be able to avoid the reduction of earnings that resulted from use of the purchase method. Critics also pointed out that the method does not reflect (1) the transactional bargaining in which current asset values influence the number and value of the shares to be issued or (2) the value of the shares issued.

In addition, some high-technology companies that had sold stock to the public based on the anticipation of rapid growth of earnings made acquisitions of profitable low-technology businesses whose results of operations were pooled with those of the high-technology businesses in order to obscure the fact that the high-technology businesses were only minimally profitable and perhaps even unprofitable. This reason for concern was alleviated by the issuance in December 1976 of FAS No. 14, Financial Reporting for Segments of a Business Enterprise. FAS No. 14 requires that companies present separate information in their financial statements for reportable industry segments and also about foreign operations, export sales and major customers. Thus, the ability of companies to obscure their sources of revenues and earnings was considerably reduced together with the motivation to use the pooling of interests method for such a purpose.

Criticism of the pooling of interests method continues today because the method generally allows an acquiring corporation to report higher earnings after an acquisition than the purchase method. In August 1996, the FASB announced that it would reexamine use of the pooling of interests method because of the difference that exists between the United States and other countries that use only or primarily the purchase method. Prodded by the SEC, which prefers methods that reduce corporate income, the FASB plans a report during 1998.

Critics of the pooling of interests method fail to recognize that investors buy stock based on earnings per share, not total corporate earnings. If an acquiring corporation overpays by issuing too many shares, investors will see the effects reflected in reduced earnings per share.

There are also critics of the purchase method. They are concerned about the higher recorded asset values that usually result from that method. They point to the difficulty of valuation of stock when it is the "acquisition currency" used to pay for an acquisition. They also point to the difficulty of valuing and determining the life of goodwill and the inconsistency in reporting of results of operations from company to company that results from their decisions relating to goodwill. They are also concerned about negative goodwill which, on rare occasions, enhances the earnings of acquiring corporations using the purchase method.

L. Leveraged Buyouts

APB No. 16, paragraph 1, describes a business combination as follows:

> *"A business combination occurs when a corporation and one or more incorporated or unincorporated businesses are brought together into one accounting entity. The entity carries on the activities of the previously separate, independent enterprises."*

Many acquisitions that use borrowed money to finance the purchase price do not meet this definition in a strict sense. In a typical leveraged buyout ("LBO"), a "shell" corporation with no active business operations is organized and used to finance and acquire a company with active business operations. The only activities of the acquiring corporation in a typical LBO are those related to the financing and the acquisition. The question arose whether, in economic substance, the methods prescribed in APB No. 16 should be used to account for LBOs.

There was never any question whether LBOs could qualify for the pooling of interests method. LBOs meet few, if any, of the criteria for use of that method. Thus, the serious question was whether all aspects of the purchase method should be applied to LBOs. If the acquiring corporation is owned after the acquisition by shareholders who are unrelated to the shareholders of the acquired corporation, the purchase method is appropriate. However, if shareholders who were in control of the acquired corporation purchase or otherwise obtain shares constituting control of the acquiring corporation, the economic substance of the transaction may be viewed as essentially a restructuring of the ownership and the financial structure of the acquired corporation, rather than as a purchase.

The issue was raised whether an LBO transaction that does not result in a change of control should be entitled to increase the recorded values of assets to current fair values. Strategically, such an increase is important in an LBO. Otherwise, the acquiring corporation, which has typically paid a premium price primarily financed by debt constituting 70 percent to 90 percent of its capital structure, could be made to appear insolvent or lacking in adequate capital. As described in Chapter 13, adverse legal consequences may result if the acquiring corporation is insolvent or lacks adequate capital. While the conventions of GAAP do not determine the legal issues, financial statements prepared in accordance with GAAP may be presented as evidence in court proceedings. Since there were many controversies associated with LBOs in the 1980s, it became important for the Emerging Issues Task Force (EITF) of the FASB to review the methods used to account for LBOs.

Notwithstanding concern about the write-up of asset values resulting from use of the purchase method for LBOs, the EITF could not lose sight of the fact that the purchase method is generally regarded as conservative. Depreciation and amortization charges based on the increased asset values reduce earnings for years after an acquisition.

After its review, the EITF published EITF No. 88-16, *Basis in Leveraged Buyout Transactions,* which restricts, but does not eliminate, the use of the purchase method to account for LBO transactions. EITF 88-16 applies to LBOs using a holding company (called "Newco") with no substantive operations that acquires a company with business operations (called "Oldco") in a single, highly leveraged transaction or a series of transactions that result in the acquisition by Newco of all previously outstanding equity interests in Oldco. The accounting treatment depends on whether a change in control of the voting equity interests has occurred:

- If there is a change in control, EITF 88-16 treats the LBO transaction as a recapitalization and prescribes the use of predecessor basis to the extent that Oldco shareholders become Newco shareholders with equity interests equal to or in excess of specified percentage levels. The remainder of the investment by Newco in Oldco is stepped up to fair value, subject to a limitation based on the extent to which the consideration paid to the Oldco shareholders is monetary.
- If there is no change in control, EITF 88-16 treats the entire LBO transaction as a recapitalization and prescribes the use of predecessor basis for the entire transaction.

EITF 88-16 requires that one of the following conditions be met for a change of control to occur:

- *New Shareholders.* A single shareholder (or group of shareholders) who had no previous equity interest in Oldco obtains unilateral control of more than a 50 percent voting equity interest in Newco. These new shareholders may include management and there is a rebuttable presumption that all management shareholders, as a group, constitute a single shareholder.
- *Oldco Management.* A single member (or group of members) of Oldco's management who did not have unilateral control of Oldco obtains unilateral control of more than 50 percent voting equity interest in Newco.
- *Oldco Nonmanagement Shareholders.* The Newco control group acquiring unilateral control of Newco has no subset that had unilateral control of Oldco.
- *Combinations of the First Three Conditions.* Combinations of the previous three conditions may also achieve a change in control of the voting equity interests.

In determining whether a change of control has occurred, the effects of dilutive securities (other than options or warrants) should be considered. Dilutive securities are securities substantially equivalent to voting interests in Newco that are held by investors who are not members of the Newco controlling shareholder group. There is a *presumption* that options and warrants held by such investors are equivalent to voting interests.

The change in control must be genuine, substantive and nontemporary. The new shareholders controlling Newco must be able to implement major operating and financial policies, such as selling or acquiring assets or refinancing debt. If the provisions of nonvoting securities issued to former Oldco shareholders allow them to regain control or to restrict the ability of the new controlling shareholders of Newco to implement its major operating and financial policies, then a change in control may not have occurred.

Three tests are used to determine the shareholders including the Newco control group:

- *Management.* There is a rebuttable presumption that the management group shareholders are part of the control group. Management is identified by reference to the SEC's Regulation S-X, Item 401.
- *Increasing Equity Interests.* Shareholders who obtain a greater equity interest in Newco than they held in Oldco (called "Bulls") and whose residual interest in Newco is 5 percent or more are included in the Newco control group. Shareholders who obtain less than a 5 percent equity interest in Newco are excluded.
- *Decreasing Equity Interests.* Shareholders who obtain the same or a lesser equity interest in Newco than they held in Oldco (called "Bears") may also be included in the Newco control group if they meet either a voting-interest test or a capital-at-risk test. If neither test is met, a shareholder is excluded. A Bear who holds 20 percent or more of the voting interest (including dilutive securities)

or the fair value of the cumulative capital-at-risk (including all equity and debt securities) of Newco is included in the Newco control group.

The investment of Newco in Oldco is then valued as follows:

- If there is a change of control and no carryover of shareholders from Oldco to Newco, then Newco's entire investment in Oldco is revalued to current fair values.
- If there is no change of control, none of Newco's investment in Oldco is revalued and Newco must use predecessor basis.
- If there is a change of control and a carryover of shareholders from Oldco to Newco, predecessor basis must be used proportional to the equity interests of the carryover shareholders included in the Newco control group plus Bears not included in the control group that have individual equity interests of 5 percent or more and aggregate interests of 20 percent or more. The remaining proportionate amount of the investment should be revalued based on current fair values, provided that at least 80 percent of the consideration paid to the Oldco shareholders was monetary including cash, debt and debt-type instruments such as mandatorily redeemable preferred stock. If less than 80 percent of the consideration was monetary, the percentage of Newco's investment in Oldco that is revalued to current fair value should not exceed the percentage of the consideration that was monetary.

M. Leveraged Recapitalizations

As described in the previous section, a leveraged buyout by a Newco that does not result in a change of control is treated as a recapitalization and EITF 88-16 prescribes the use of predecessor basis.

An acquiring corporation can also structure a leveraged recapitalization by a direct purchase of shares from the acquired company or a purchase of shares from its existing shareholders. The purchase is accompanied by major borrowing by the acquired company and a distribution of the borrowing proceeds to the acquired company's shareholders. The direct investment, if any, increases the capital of the acquired company, but the distribution of the borrowing proceeds reduces its capital significantly. So long as a substantive percentage of the previous shareholders continue to own their shares, there is no requirement to revalue the assets of the acquired corporation and add goodwill and other intangibles with the effect of reducing future earnings. Thus, a leveraged recapitalization is an alternative that may be used by acquirers planning to use an initial public offering (IPO) as an exit strategy. However, when the acquired corporation files a registration statement for its IPO, the SEC may require "push-down" accounting according to SAB No. 54 if the acquiring corporation owns 80 percent or more of the acquired corporation's common stock.

N. Push-Down Accounting

Brief descriptions of "push-down" accounting appear on pages 209 and 214 of this chapter. Readers interested in further information about push-down accounting should refer to the SEC's SAB No. 54 and the SEC's Topic 5—Miscellaneous Accounting; Section J.

In Topic 5J, the SEC provided several interpretations of push-down accounting. Among other things, the SEC's staff recognized that the existence of outstanding public debt, preferred stock or a significant minority interest might impact the parent's ability to control the form of ownership of a subsidiary acquired by purchase of substantially all common stock in purchase transactions. In these circumstances, the SEC's staff encourages, but does not require, push-down accounting.

However, when a subsidiary files a registration statement for an IPO after its acquisition by a parent in an LBO, the SEC's staff believes that the parent's debt, related interest expense and debt issue costs should be included in the subsidiary's financial statements if: (1) the subsidiary will assume the parent's debt, (2) the proceeds of a debt or equity offering by the subsidiary will be used to retire the parent's debt, or (3) the subsidiary guarantees or pledges its assets as collateral for the parent's debt (SEC Topic 5J).

O. Accounting for Acquisitions by Employee Stock Ownership Plans

A variety of special issues arise in accounting for acquisitions by employee stock ownership plans (ESOPs). These issues have become the subject of standard operating practices published by the AICPA and issue summaries published by the Emerging Issues Task Force of the FASB. See Chapter 15.

P. Reference Materials

AICPA Codification of Statements on Auditing Standards, Commerce Clearing House.

Financial Accounting Standards Board, Original Pronouncements, Accounting Standards, John Wiley & Sons, Inc.

Q. Exhibit

9-1 Example of a report of independent auditors

EXHIBIT 9-1

REPORT OF INDEPENDENT AUDITORS

To the Stockholder of Lucent Technologies Inc.:

We have audited the consolidated financial statements of Lucent Technologies Inc. and subsidiaries (the "Company") listed in the index on page F-1 of this Form S-1. We have also audited the financial statement schedule of the Company appearing on page S-1 of this Form S-1. These financial statements and financial statement schedule are the responsibility of the Company's management. Our responsibility is to express an opinion on these financial statements and financial statement schedule based on our audits.

We conducted our audits in accordance with generally accepted auditing standards. Those standards require that we plan and perform the audit to obtain reasonable assurance about whether the financial statements are free of material misstatement. An audit includes examining, on a test basis, evidence supporting the amounts and disclosures in the financial statements. An audit also includes assessing the accounting principles used and significant estimates made by management, as well as evaluating the overall financial statement presentation. We believe that our audits provide a reasonable basis for our opinion.

In our opinion, the financial statements referred to above present fairly, in all material respects, the consolidated financial position of Lucent Technologies Inc. and subsidiaries at December 31, 1995 and 1994, and the consolidated results of their operations, changes in their stockholder's equity and their cash flows for each of the three years in the period ended December 31, 1995, in conformity with generally accepted accounting principles. In addition, in our opinion the financial statement schedule referred to above, when considered in relation to the basic financial statements taken as a whole, presents fairly, in all material respects, the information required to be included therein.

As discussed in Note 3 to the consolidated financial statements, in 1993 the Company changed its methods of accounting for postretirement benefits, postemployment benefits and income taxes.

Coopers & Lybrand L.L.P.
1301 Avenue of the Americas
New York, New York
January 25, 1996
(Note 14 is dated February 1, 1996)

Chapter 10

ANTITRUST LAW REQUIREMENTS

A. THE ANTITRUST LAWS

Competition between persons who sell products or services is an essential element of a market- or consumer-oriented economy. There are several federal laws designed to protect competition. The most important are the Sherman Act, the Clayton Act, the Federal Trade Commission Act and the Robinson-Patman Act.

The principal federal antitrust law applicable to acquisition transactions is the Clayton Act, particularly Sections 7 and 7A found at 15 U.S.C., §§18 and 18a. Section 7 prohibits acquisitions that may substantially lessen competition in any line of commerce in any section of the country. Section 7A contains the premerger notification and reporting requirements added by the Hart-Scott-Rodino Federal Trade Commission Improvement Act. The prohibitions of Section 7 apply to all acquisitions including those below the notification and reporting thresholds of Section 7A.

The federal antitrust laws are enforced by the Antitrust Division of the Department of Justice (DOJ) and the Federal Trade Commission (FTC) whose jurisdiction overlaps and is shared on a basis of prior experience, available resources and other factors.

B. SECTION 7 OF THE CLAYTON ACT

Section 7 of the Clayton Act reads as follows:

> *"That no person engaged in commerce or in any activity affecting commerce shall acquire, directly or indirectly, the whole or any part of the stock or other share capital and no person subject to the jurisdiction of the Federal Trade Commission shall acquire the whole or any part of the assets of another person engaged also in commerce or in any activity affecting commerce, where in any line of commerce or in any activity affecting commerce in any section of the country, the effect of such acquisition may be substantially to lessen competition, or to tend to create a monopoly."*

To prepare an analysis determining whether an acquisition is lawful, it is necessary to identify:

- the line of commerce;
- the applicable section or sections of the country; and
- the effects of the acquisition on competition.

1. Line of Commerce

The first step of the analysis is to identify any lines of commerce in which the businesses of the acquiring company and the acquired company overlap. To do so, the relevant product market must be identified. In 1962, the U.S. Supreme Court held that the product market could also include a "submarket" that met the characteristics of a market.

In *Brown Shoe Co. v. United States,* 370 U.S. 294 (1962), the U.S. Supreme Court ruled as follows:

> *"[t]he outer boundaries of a product market are determined by the reasonable interchangeability of use and crosselasticity of demand between the product itself and substitutes for it. However, within this broad market, well-defined submarkets may exist which in themselves, constitute product markets for antitrust purposes. [*Id. *at 325, citing* United States v. E.I. du Pont de Nemours & Co., *353 U.S. 586, 593-95 (1957).]"*

The Supreme Court identified "practical indicia" which have been widely used to identify a product market or submarket: (1) public recognition; (2) peculiar product characteristics and uses; (3) unique production facilities; (4) distinct customers; (5) distinct prices; (6) sensitivity to price changes; and (7) specialized vendors. These practical indicia are not exclusive and not all of them need to be proven to establish the product market (*Brown Shoe Co. v. United States,* supra; *United States v. Aluminum Company of America,* 377 U.S. 271 (1964); *Abex Corp. v. FTC,* 420 F.2d 928 (6th Cir. 1970), *cert. den.* 400 U.S. 865 (1970)).

The legal standing of an acquisition often depends on the determination of the relevant product market. For example, E.I. du Pont was ordered to divest its shares of General Motors Corporation once automotive coatings were found to be a separate product market, although there may have been no substantial adverse effect on the overall coatings market (*U.S. v. E I. du Pont de Nemours & Co.,* supra). For a more recent example, in 1993, a federal district court upheld the FTC's determination of a product market carefully constructed to include two swimming pool dry sanitizer product lines (isocyanurates and hypochlorites), but to exclude liquid pool bleach, thus supporting a divestiture order (*Olin Corp. v F.T.C.,* 986 F.2d 1295 (9th Cir. 1993)). In 1995, a federal district court denied an injunction after finding that sales of products and services to large form-intensive customers was not a separate submarket of the broad market for the manufacture and sale of business forms (*Moore Corp., Ltd. v. Wallace Computer Services, Inc.,* 1996-1 CCH Trade Cases, § 71,287 (D. Del. 1995)).

2. Sections of the Country

The second step of the analysis is to determine the section or sections of the country in which the product market exists. For example, in what areas of the country are sales made by each company and by each of their plants and sales offices? How far can a product be shipped before transportation cost reduces and eventually eliminates its salability?

For computers, the product market is likely to be national. For businesses such as cement and beer, the product market may be regional or even local. An interesting case in which a U.S. Court of Appeals reversed a finding of a national market by the FTC and found that a regional market existed is *Jim Walter Corp. v. Federal Trade Commission,* 1980-2 CCH Fed. Trade Reg. Rep. § 63,535 (5 Cir. 1980).

The term *relevant market* is used to refer to an identified product market and its geographical territory. Criteria currently used to determine relevant markets under the Merger Guidelines adopted by the DOJ and the FTC are described later in this chapter. The courts sometimes consider the Merger Guidelines in Section 7 cases, but need not do so (*Olin Corp. v. F.T.C.,* supra; *Moore Corp. Ltd. v. Wallace Computer,* supra).

3. Effects on Competition

The third step of the analysis is to determine whether the effect of the acquisition may be substantially to lessen competition in the relevant market. For many years, the DOJ and FTC regarded antitrust analysis of acquisitions and mergers as almost entirely a matter of market shares and concentration. The DOJ's 1968 Merger Guidelines applied to horizonal, vertical and conglomerate acquisitions and were permeated by a "big is bad" theory. The DOJ and FTC sought to prevent any acquisition involving firms with significant market shares. Even relatively big was considered bad as the FTC successfully challenged some very small (under $1 million) acquisitions after defining the relevant market as a small product submarket. The "failing company" defense was strictly limited and procompetitive efficiencies were considered only in exceptional circumstances.

For decades, when the DOJ or the FTC instituted a lawsuit, the federal courts agreed with whatever position the government advocated. The DOJ and FTC had consistent success in defining relevant markets in a manner that resulted in excessive market shares and concentration. The courts gave little weight to economic evidence about other competitive effects, including procompetitive effects. Indeed, the U.S. Supreme Court established a presumption of illegality based on market concentration in *United States v. Philadelphia National Bank,* 374 U.S. 321 (1963).

In the middle 1970s, the courts began to react against mechanistic application of market share and concentration ratios to determine the fate of acquisitions. In *United States v. General Dynamics Corp.,* 415 U.S. 486 (1974), the U.S. Supreme Court held that a prima facie case built on market concentration and market shares in the coal industry could be rebutted by showing an insubstantial effect on competition because the coal reserves of the acquired company, United Electric Coal Company, were largely depleted or subject to long-term supply contracts and it did not have sufficient remaining reserves to compete effectively.

The federal courts, particularly the U.S. Circuit Court of Appeals for the Seventh Circuit led by Judge Richard Posner, a lawyer-economist, welcomed the new freedom to consider a broader range of procompetitive and anticompetitive evidence. In *Kaiser Aluminum & Chemical Corporation v. FTC*, 652 F.2d 1324 (7th Cir. 1981), the Court of Appeals listed a series of decisions following the *General Dynamics* precedent. See also *FTC v. Great Lakes Chemical Corporation*, 528 F. Supp. 84 (1981).

C. Merger Guidelines

Since 1968, the DOJ has issued guidelines to its enforcement policies under Section 7 of the Clayton Act so that firms considering acquisitions could evaluate whether the DOJ might challenge them. In 1992, the FTC joined the DOJ in issuing joint guidelines. The guidelines do not have the force of law and are not binding on the courts. However, they contain extensive information and are widely used by acquisition planners. The courts also use them from time to time, although they are not bound to do so (*Olin Corp. v. F.T.C.*, supra; *Moore Corp. Ltd. v. Wallace Computer Services, Inc.*, supra, footnote 27).

1. The 1982 and 1984 Merger Guidelines

In 1982, the DOJ issued new guidelines under the supervision of William Baxter, the first Assistant Attorney General responsible for the Antitrust Division who was also an economist. The 1982 Merger Guidelines superseded the 1968 Guidelines and began to make fundamental changes in antitrust analysis and enforcement.

In 1984, the DOJ issued new Merger Guidelines revising the 1982 Guidelines in five areas: (1) market definition and measurement; (2) factors affecting the significance of concentration and market share data in evaluating horizontal acquisitions; (3) foreign competition; (4) procompetitive efficiencies; and (5) failing divisions of healthy firms. Market concentration and shares became one of four major standards, together with ease of entry, other factors and procompetitive efficiencies. Further, a new standard was added to list factors that might limit the significance of market concentration and share data: (1) changing market conditions, (2) financial condition of firms in the relevant market; and (3) special factors affecting foreign firms.

The introduction of procompetitive efficiencies as a standard was a major element of the 1984 Guidelines. The DOJ indicated that it would consider clear and convincing evidence of efficiencies such as economies of scale, integration of production facilities, lower transportation costs and reductions in general selling, administrative and overhead costs. However, if the same or similar efficiencies could be achieved independently, they would not be considered. Further, the DOJ cautioned that the more significant the competitive risks, the greater the level of efficiencies that must be established to outweigh them.

The new Guidelines improved methods for defining relevant markets so that it became unnecessary to resort to the sometimes troublesome concept of a "submarket" meeting the characteristics of a market. The new Guidelines also introduced the use of the Herfindahl-Hirschman Index (the "HHI Index") as an improved tool for measuring market share concentration. A description of the HHI Index appears later in this chapter.

The 1984 Guidelines reflected an evolving policy to analyze vertical acquisitions differently from horizontal acquisitions. Alerted by economic research by "Chicago School" economists, the DOJ and FTC recognized that the initial adverse effects of vertical acquisitions are often short-lived because customers and suppliers reposition themselves. When a supplier acquires a customer, the supplier gains a captive customer who may thereafter decline to buy from competing suppliers. However, competitors of the captive customer often react by refusing to buy from the acquiring supplier, whom they now see as an opponent. This creates new sales opportunities for the competing suppliers who lost sales to the acquired customer. The DOJ and FTC also recognized that vertical acquisitions often bring procompetitive efficiencies. Thus, the 1984 Guidelines focused on the horizontal effects of vertical acquisitions, such as elimination of potential market entrants.

In discussing competitive problems of vertical acquisitions, Section 4 of the 1984 Guidelines indicated that competitively objectionable barriers to market entry could result when three conditions exist.

> *"First, vertical integration must be so extensive that entrants to one market (the "primary market") must enter the other market (the "secondary market") simultaneously. This condition does not exist if there is sufficient unintegrated capacity in the secondary market.*
>
> *Second, the requirement of entry at the secondary level must make entry at the primary level significantly more difficult and less likely. This condition does not exist solely because more capital is required to enter two markets, but exists if overall costs and risks of secondary market entry are significant.*
>
> *Third, the structure and characteristics of the primary market must be otherwise so conducive to non-competitive performance that the increased difficulty of entry is likely to affect its performance. Barriers to performance are unlikely to affect performance unless the structure of the primary market is conducive to collusion. Thus, the DOJ is unlikely to challenge an acquisition unless the overall concentration of the primary market is above 1800 HHI."*

In analyzing vertical acquisitions, the DOJ also considers factors that might facilitate collusion, such as (1) vertical integration to the retail level where price monitoring is relatively easy, (2) elimination of a disruptive buyer in a downstream market and (3) potential evasion of rate regulation.

2. The 1985 Vertical Restraint Guidelines

Continuing its reassessment of vertical conduct, the DOJ issued Vertical Restraints Guidelines on January 23, 1985. Of broader application than acquisition and merger transactions, the Vertical Restraints Guidelines focused on vertical restraints that have horizontal effects. In particular, they focused on territorial and customer restraints and on exclusive dealing arrangements.

During the 1990s, the pendulum began to swing back again as some economists and lawyers wrote articles criticizing the policy of the DOJ and FTC on vertical acquisitions. The DOJ withdrew the Vertical Restraints Guidelines on August 10, 1993 and has not indicated whether or when any replacement guidelines may be issued.

3. The 1992 Horizontal Merger Guidelines

In 1992, the DOJ and the FTC, acting jointly for the first time, issued revisions titled Horizontal Merger Guidelines. The primary purpose was to clarify the guidance to reflect advances in legal and economic thought as well as experience in applying the 1982 and 1984 Guidelines. The DOJ and FTC stated that neither agency had changed its policy on non-horizontal mergers and referred interested persons to Section 4 of the 1984 Guidelines for guidance on non-horizontal mergers.

D. Analysis of Acquisitions under the 1992 Merger Guidelines

1. Introduction

The Table of Contents for the 1992 Guidelines illustrates the revised analytical focus of economic analysis. The major headings are titled as follows:

1. Market Definition, Measurement and Concentration
2. The Potential Adverse Competitive Effects of Mergers
3. Entry Analysis
4. Efficiencies
5. Failure and Exiting Assets

The formerly predominant elements of market definition, measurement and concentration continue to be important, but are only the first phase of a five-step analysis. The 1992 Guidelines caution, however, that the burden of proof of procompetitive efficiencies or of a failing business or division is on the proponents of an acquisition.

The 1992 Guidelines focus on "market power." For a seller, market power is the ability profitably to maintain prices above competitive levels for a significant time period. This power can sometimes be exercised unilaterally by a single seller. It can also sometimes be exercised by several firms explicitly or implicitly coordinating their actions. A buyer, or a coordinating group of buyers, can also exercise market power to depress prices to a level below a competitive price that will eventually depress output.

The 1992 Guidelines indicate that the DOJ and FTC will challenge competitively harmful acquisitions, but will seek to avoid unnecessary interference with the larger universe of acquisitions that are competitively beneficial or neutral. However, the traditional enforcement policy to interdict competitive problems in their incipiency continues.

The 1992 Guidelines remind acquisition planners of two other basic concepts. The economic analysis is future-oriented and will consider evidence of change from past conditions. References to profitability mean economic profits rather than accounting profits. Economic profits are the excess of revenues over costs, when costs include the opportunity cost of invested capital.

2. Market Definition, Measurement and Concentration

The 1992 Guidelines state that an acquisition is unlikely to create or enhance market power or facilitate its exercise unless it significantly increases concentration and results in a concentrated market. Thus, analysis begins with market definition and measurement of market shares and concentration.

Market definition focuses solely on demand substitution factors, in other words, possible consumer responses. A market is defined as a product (or group of products) and a geographic area where it is produced or sold such that a hypothetical profit-maximizing firm that is the only producer or seller could impose a "small but significant and nontransitory" price increase up to 5 percent ("SSN price increase"). The determination is then based on evaluation of the likely reactions of consumers to such a price increase. The price increase could be made unprofitable by consumers switching to other products or to the same products produced by other firms at other locations. If such switching is likely, so that reductions of sales volume would render the price increase unprofitable, the tentatively identified market is too narrow. The determination is then repeated by adding to the product (or product group) the next best substitute products. The relevant market eventually becomes the smallest product and geographic market where the SSN price increase could profitably be imposed.

In considering buyers' likely reactions, the DOJ and FTC consider evidence of their actual or planned shifting of product purchases, the competition which buyers face in their downstream customer markets and the time and costs of shifting products. If there is evidence that sellers charge different prices for the same product to different buyer groups, in other words, price discrimination, the DOT and FTC will consider whether those groups should be evaluated separately using SSN price increase analysis.

To identify firms that participate in the relevant market, the DOJ and FTC begin with all current producers and sellers and may include foreign firms and firms producing and selling used, reconditioned and recycled goods. The DOJ and FTC may also include firms that are not current participants if they would be likely to enter the market within a year in response to an SSN price increase and could do so without significant sunk costs of entry and exit. These firms are called "uncommitted entrants" because they could enter and exit opportunistically without significant risk. The DOJ and FTC also consider other potential entrants in the later entry analysis, but not during the first-step analysis of market shares and concentration. An example of an uncommitted entrant is a firm with equipment capable of stamping a variety of light metal products that is not currently producing a particular metal product but could readily do so if the price became attractive.

Market shares are calculated using the best indicator of a firm's future competitive significance. Dollar sales or shipments generally are used if firms are distinguished by differentiation of their products. Unit sales are generally used if firms are distinguished by their advantages in serving different buyers or buyer groups. Physical capacity or reserves are generally used for undifferentiated products, in other words, products that are essentially identical commodities as produced by all market participants. However, a firm's sales or capacity will not be included to the extent it is committed outside the relevant market and unavailable to respond to a price increase in the market.

Once the number of firms in the relevant product and geographic market and their respective market shares are determined, the DOJ and FTC use the HHI Index of market concentration as an aid to interpreting the market data. The HHI Index is calculated by summing the squares of the market shares of all the relevant market participants. For example, a market with five equal participants would be calculated as follows:

$$20^2 + 20^2 + 20^2 + 20^2 + 20^2 = 2{,}000$$

The DOT and FTC divide the spectrum of market concentration, as measured by the HHI Index, into three regions. The likelihood that an acquisition will require further analysis for potential adverse competitive effects depends on the market concentration and the change of concentration that would result from the acquisition.

Post-Merger HHI	Market Concentration	Likely Action
<1,000	Unconcentrated	No further analysis
>1,000, but <1,800	Moderately concentrated	If <100 increase, no further analysis; If >100 increase, further analysis of competitive concerns
>1,800	Highly concentrated	If <50 increase, no further analysis; If >50 increase, further analysis; If <100 increase; presumption of challenge unless overcome by further analysis

The increase of concentration resulting from an acquisition can be calculated by doubling the product of the market shares of the firms. For example, an acquisition of a firm with a market share of 6 percent by a firm with a market share of 8 percent would increase the HHI Index by 96, or $6 \times 8 \times 2 = 96$.

The DOJ and FTC comment, however, that some factors can affect the significance of market shares and concentration and are necessarily based on historical evidence. One factor is changing technology and other competitive conditions. Another is the degree of the difference between products and locations in the market and substitutes outside the market.

3. Potential Adverse Competitive Effects

The 1992 Guidelines point out that the potential adverse competitive effects of an acquisition can arise through coordinated interaction, tacit or express, between firms selling in a market. They can also arise through unilateral action. Thus, the question is whether the acquisition is likely to create or enhance market power or facilitate its exercise by coordinated interaction or unilateral action.

The 1992 Guidelines discuss the possibility of collusion, including conditions that facilitate collusion and the likelihood that participants in coordinated interaction can detect and punish deviations. Product heterogeneity and ready availability of information are among the factors that can contribute to coordinated interaction. The role of maverick firms and of excess capacity in the hands of maverick and non-maverick firms is also frankly discussed. If there has been a history of express collusion in a market, the DOJ and FTC will consider market conditions to be conducive to collusion unless they have changed appreciably since the last such incident.

The 1992 Guidelines also discuss lessening of competition through unilateral effects. Here, the analysis is divided into markets for differentiated products (products that are not perfect substitutes for one another) and undifferentiated products (products that are readily substitutable).

When the acquisition proponents have differentiated products, the DOJ and FTC will consider the first and second choices of consumers, as shown by market surveys or other evidence, and their relative closeness. If the market concentration data fall outside the safe harbor regions determined by the HHI Index, the merging firms have a combined market share of at least 35 percent and a significant share of purchasers of one merging firm's product consider the other firm's product as their second choice, then market share data may be relied upon to show there is a significant share of sales in the market accounted for by consumers who would be adversely affected. However, potential for unilateral elevation of prices of differentiated products is unlikely if either of the merging firms is likely to be replaced by rival sellers who will reposition their product lines. The likelihood of such repositioning is evaluated by the same methods described in the following section. The cost for buyers to evaluate the quality of the repositioned products is also evaluated.

When the acquisition proponents have products that are relatively undifferentiated and capacity primarily distinguishes them and their competition, a combined market share of at least 35 percent may result in unilateral ability profitably to raise prices and reduce output. This unilateral effect is unlikely if competitors are likely to increase output in response to a price increase. However, if the competitors face capacity constraints or excess capacity would be significantly more costly to operate, their expansion will be considered unlikely.

4. Entry Analysis

The 1992 Merger Guidelines state that a merger is not likely to create or enhance market power or to facilitate its exercise, if entry into the market is so easy that market participants, after the merger, either collectively or unilaterally, could not profitably maintain a price increase above premerger levels. Entry is that easy if it would be timely, likely and sufficient in its magnitude, character and scope to deter or counteract the competitive effects of concern.

The DOJ and FTC use a three-step methodology to determine whether committed entry would deter or counteract a competitive effect. First, would the committed entry achieve significant market impact within a timely period? Second, would the committed entry be profitable at premerger prices and, hence, a likely response? Third, would the committed entry be sufficient to return prices to premerger levels?

The DOJ and FTC will consider all entry alternatives including recent examples of entry, successful or unsuccessful. They will generally consider to be timely only those committed entry alternatives that can be achieved within 2 years from initial planning to significant market impact. The DOJ and FTC recognize that a new entrant will not be profitable if its output would be excessive and would depress prices to levels below profitability. Thus, they will consider entry to be unlikely if the minimum viable scale that a committed entrant must persistently achieve for profitability at premerger prices is larger than the likely sales opportunity. The DOJ and FTC will consider a likely entry to be sufficient only if the entrant has the tangible and intangible assets to respond fully to sales opportunities, including localized opportunities resulting from output reduction. If the effect of concern is unilateral price elevation involving differentiated products, the entry must involve a product so close to the products of the merging firms that a price increase would be rendered unprofitable.

5. Efficiencies

The 1992 Merger Guidelines recognize that acquisitions can benefit the economy by their efficiency-enhancing potential, which can increase competition and result in lower prices to consumers. Thus, some acquisitions that might be challenged may be reasonably necessary to achieve significant net efficiencies.

The DOJ and FTC will consider efficiencies such as economies of scale, better integration of production facilities, plant specialization and lower transportation costs. They may also consider efficiencies resulting from reductions of GS&A expenses, although they may be difficult to demonstrate. To validate an acquisition, the expected net efficiencies must outweigh the identified competitive risks. The burden of proof of procompetitive efficiencies is on the acquisition proponents.

On April 8, 1997 the FTC and DOJ released an Efficiency Guideline amending the 1992 Merger Guidelines. The Efficiency Guideline states that the FTC and DOJ will consider only efficiencies shown to be acquisitions-specific and cognizable. They must also be verifiable by reasonable means, likely to be accomplished by the aqcuisition and unlikely to be accomplished without the acquisition or another means having comparable anticompetitive effects. The Guideline prescribes criteria for showing that efficiencies are cognizable. The Guideline indicates that criteria for showing that efficiencies from shifting production are more likely to be verifiable than those relating to research and development.

6. Failure and Exiting Assets

The 1992 Merger Guidelines recognize that an acquisition is unlikely to create or enhance market power or facilitate its exercise if imminent failure of one of the firms would cause the assets of that firm to exit the relevant market.

To establish a "failing firm" defense, the acquisition proponents must show four elements: (1) the failing firm would be unable to meet its financial obligations in the near future; (2) it would not be able to reorganize successfully under Chapter 11 of the Bankruptcy Act; (3) it has made unsuccessful efforts to obtain reasonable alternative offers that pose less severe danger to competition; and (4) its assets would exit the relevant market in the absence of the proposed acquisition.

A "failing division" defense can be made by showing essentially the same elements. However, to demonstrate inability to meet financial obligations, the division must have a negative cash flow on an operating basis after applying appropriate cost allocation rules. The DOJ or FTC require evidence of negative cash flows and the prospect of exit from the relevant market that is not based solely on management plans prepared to justify the acquisition.

E. Enforcement by the DOJ and the FTC

The willingness of the DOJ and FTC to consider a wider range of economic factors in acquisition analysis contributed to the growth of merger and acquisition activity in the 1980s. The courts also considered a wider range of factors. For example, changing technology was considered in reaching a conclusion that acquisition in the oilfield drilling services business did not violate the Clayton Act (*Gearhart Industries, Inc. v. Smith International, Inc.*, 592 F.Supp. 203 (N.D. Tex 1984); partially affirmed, modified and reversed on other issues 741 F.2d 707 (7th Cir. 1984)). After the DOJ's definition of the market for plastic pump sprayers and dispensers was rejected in *U.S. v. Calmar, Inc.*, 612 F. Supp. 1298 (D.N.J. 1985), ease of entry and availability of alternative products became the basis for denial of a preliminary injunction. Ease of entry was also considered in a decision upholding an acquisition in the waste collection market (*U.S. v. Waste Management Inc.*, 743 F.2d 976 (2d Cir. 1984)). Lack of evidence that an acquisition was likely to have significant anticompetitive effects in the ready-to-eat cereal market (because the acquiring firm manufactured Grape Nuts and the acquired firm manufactured Shredded Wheat) led to a denial of divestiture order in *State of New York v. Kraft General Foods, Inc.*, 1995-1 Trade Cases, § 70,911 (S.D.N.Y. 1995).

The DOJ and FTC have responded to the need for improved economic analysis and have continued to enforce Section 7 of the Clayton Act actively and strictly. A few examples of the many cases involving acquisitions found to be wholly or partially unlawful in recent years include *FTC v. Bass Brothers Enterprises, Inc.*, 1984-1 CCH Trade Cases § 66,041 (N.D. Ohio 1984) (carbon black); *Christian Schmidt Brewing Co., Inc. v. G. Heileman Brewing Co., Inc.*, 753 F.2d 1354 (6th Cir. 1985) (beer brewing); *FTC v. PPG Industries, Inc.*, 1986-2 *CCH Trade Cases*, § 67,235 (D.C. 1986) (glass and acrylic transparencies for aircraft); *FTC v. Elders Grain*, 868 F.2d 901 (7th Cir. 1989) (industrial dry corn); *Owens-Illinois, Inc.*, CCH Trade Reg. Rep § 22,731 (FTC 1989) (glass containers); *Emerson Electric Co.*, CCH Trade Reg. Rep. § 22,786 (FTC 1990) (mounted ball bearings); *Imo Industries, Inc.*, 1992-2 CCH Trade Cases § 69,943 (D.C. 1992) (25-millimeter image intensifier tubes); *Rhone-Poulenc S.A.*, CCH Trade Reg. Rep. § 22,796 (FTC 1990) (dairy culture products); *U.S. v. Pacific Dunlop Holdings, Inc.*, 1990-1 CCH Trade Cases § 69,087 (ED Pa. 1990) (industrial gloves); *Promedes, S.A.*, 1990-1 CCH Trade Reg. Rep. § 22,800 (FTC 1990) (grocery stores); and *Olin Corporation v. F.T.C.*, 986 F.2d 1295 (9th Cir. 1993) (swimming pool sanitizers).

Examples of recent consent decrees requiring whole or partial divestitures of acquired assets are *U.S. v. Georgia-Pacific Corp.*, CCH Trade Reg. Rep. § 50,798 (D.C., Del. 1996); *U.S. v. American Skiing Co.*, CCH Trade Reg.

Rep. § 50,802 (D.C.,D.C. 1996); *U.S. v. Interstate Bakeries Corp.*, 1996-1 CCH Trade Cases § 71,271 (N.D., Ill. 1995); *U.S. v. Kimberly-Clark Corp.*, 60 Fed. Reg. 66557 (Dec. 22, 1995); and *U.S. v. Tele-Communications, Inc.*, 59 Fed. Reg. 24723 (May 12, 1994).

In recent years, the FTC and DOJ have become increasingly concerned about the effects of acquisitions on innovation markets when a firm may foreclose potential competition by acquiring companies engaged in inventing and developing future generations of technology. These concerns apply especially to rapidly changing fields such as communications, computers and pharmaceuticals. Several consent decrees have been negotiated that use mandatory licensing as a remedy. See *The Dow Chemical Company*, 59 Fed. Reg. 34625 (July 6, 1994); *American Home Products Corp.*, 59 Fed. Reg. 60807 (Nov. 28, 1994); *Montedison S.p.A., HIMONT Incorporated and Shell Petroleum N.V.*, 60 Fed. Reg. 5414 (Jan. 27, 1995); and *Boston Scientific Corp.*, 60 Fed. Reg. 12948 (March 9, 1995).

These consent decrees impose severe and costly obligations and could not be obtained except for the reputation of the DOJ and FTC for strong and skillful enforcement.

F. Private Antitrust Enforcement

It has long been clear that private citizens are entitled to commence lawsuits under Section 7 of the Clayton Act. In a recent successful example, a department store company seeking entry to the market in northeastern New York joined with the State Attorney General to obtain an injunction against an acquisition of department stores by May Department Stores (*Bon-Ton, Inc. v. May Dept. Stores Co.*, 881 F.Supp. 860 (W.D.N.Y. 1994)).

The elements that must be shown to obtain treble damages for business injury under Section 4 of the Clayton Act as a result of a violation of Section 7 are far less clear (*Brunswick Corp. v. Pueblo Bowl-O-Mat, Inc.*, 429 U.S. 477, 97 S. Ct. 690 (1977)).

Several court decisions denied standing to initiate private antitrust lawsuits to takeover target companies and to competitors, both of whom are likely to have motives other than to protect competition (*Carter-Hawley Hale Stores Inc. v. Limited, Inc.*, 587 F.Supp. 246 (C.D. Cal. 1984) (1986); *Cargill, Inc. v. Monfort of Colorado, Inc.*, 761 F.2d 570 (10 Cir. 1985); 479 U.S. 104 (1986); and *Moore Corp. Ltd. v. Wallace Computer Services, Inc.*, supra). However, the courts have granted standing when unusually strong cases were alleged. A competitor was granted standing based on allegations that an acquisition would result in an 84 percent share of the herbal tea market (*R.C. Bigelow, Inc. v. Unilever N.V.*, 867 F.2d 102 (2d Cir. 1989)). A tender offer target was granted standing in *Consolidated Gold Fields PLC v. Minorco, S.A.*, 871 F.2d 252 (2d Cir. 1989).

G. State Antitrust Enforcement

As the DOJ and FTC instituted more extensive analysis of economic effects before taking enforcement action, more issues were resolved by voluntary corrective measures and settlements rather than by lawsuits. The trend led to layoffs at the major law firms that had specialized in antitrust lawsuits for many years. Many of these attorneys began to work in other litigation fields. However, some devoted themselves to opposing the new DOJ and FTC policies and augmenting state law enforcement. They gained support in the academic community from scholars who are rivals to the "Chicago School" economists whose economic analysis is reflected in the merger guidelines. See "Challenges to the Chicago School Approach," 40 *Antitrust Law Journal* 629 (1989) and "Why the States are Stepping Up Attacks on Large Mergers," *Mergers and Acquisitions*, Lewis, July-August, 1990.

In 1987, the National Association of Attorneys General (NAAG), a group of state law enforcement attorneys, issued Horizontal Merger Guidelines to be used in enforcing state antitrust laws. They also adopted preclearance procedures.

The state attorneys generally advocate simpler industry or market concentration tests to measure legality of acquisitions. They reject defenses based on efficiencies and give lesser weight to factors such as ease of entry. They emphasize protection of regional and local businesses. Although they would not state it so simply, the "big is bad" concept underlies their policies. The policies also favor litigation based on adverse effects that can be argued by imaginative lawyers rather than evaluated by systematic economic analysis to determine whether the effects are real and likely to occur.

In April 1990, the U.S. Supreme Court ruled that state governments (and other private parties) have standing to seek divestiture of businesses acquired in violation of Section 7 of the Clayton Act. Unlike the DOJ and FTC, they must show threatened loss or damage to their own interests. They are also subject to equitable defenses such as undue delay or unclean hands (*California v. American Stores Co.*, 1990-1 CCH Trade Cases § 69,003 (1990)).

In view of the decision in *American Stores*, antitrust enforcement of Section 7 of the Clayton Act has become a federal and state function. Among recent state enforcement actions, the Attorney General of the State of New York joined with Bon-Ton Stores, Inc. to obtain a preliminary injunction against an acquisition of department stores in northwestern New York by the May Department Stores Co. (*Bon-Ton, Inc. v. May Dept. Stores, Co.*, 881 F.Supp. 860 (W.D.N.Y. 1994)). The lawsuit was later settled by an agreement for the sale of four stores to the plaintiff, Bon-Ton Stores, Inc. See *1995-1 CCH Trade Cases*, § 70,917. The result was a victory for Bon-Ton Stores. Whether it will benefit competition in northeastern New York remains to be seen.

On the other hand, the New York Attorney General failed to persuade a U.S. District Court to enjoin a sale of the ready-to-eat cereal assets of RJR Nabisco, Inc. to Kraft General Foods, Inc. (*New York v. Kraft General Foods, Inc. et al.*, 1995-1 CCH Trade Cases, § 70,911). The Attorney General commenced the lawsuit after the sale had been reviewed without challenge by the FTC under the Hart-Scott-Rodino provisions of the Clayton Act, and had been closed. The District Court reviewed the relevant products (Grape Nuts and Shredded Wheat) and markets and concluded that the Attorney General had not shown that the acquisition was likely to have the effect of substantially diminishing competition.

In 1995, because of their perception that the DOJ and FTC do not take a sufficiently strict enforcement stance regarding vertical acquisitions and other vertical restraints, the NAAG adopted Vertical Restraints Guidelines.

(See 4 CCH Trade Reg. Rep., § 13,400.) Since the DOJ's Vertical Restraints Guidelines were withdrawn in 1993, the NAAG sees the states as now having the primary role in protecting competition against unlawful vertical restraints.

Public concern has been expressed about the effects of multiple enforcement actions, some by states whose interests may be narrowly focused. For example, one reason why federal antitrust policies were reconsidered was to permit the formation of companies large enough to compete with large multinational companies from Europe and Japan demonstrating higher levels of competitive efficiencies in production of automobiles, electronic equipment and other products. Congress may eventually be required to consider full or partial preemption of the state antitrust laws in order to protect employment in those industries.

H. Premerger Notification and Waiting Periods

1. Statutory Requirements and Size Tests

Section 7A of the Clayton Act imposes prenotification and reporting requirements and waiting periods on larger mergers and acquisitions affecting interstate commerce if:

- **(a)** Any voting securities or assets of a person engaged in manufacturing which has annual net sales or total assets of $10 million or more are being acquired by any person which has total assets or annual net sales of $100 million or more;
- **(b)** any voting securities or assets of a person not engaged in manufacturing which has total assets of $10 million or more are being acquired by any person which has total assets or annual net sales of $100 million or more; or
- **(c)** any voting securities or assets of a person with annual net sales or total assets of $100 million or more are being acquired by any person with total assets or annual net sales of $10 million or more; and

as a result of such acquisition, the acquiring person would hold:

- **(a)** 15 percent or more of the voting securities or assets of the acquired person, or
- **(b)** an aggregate total amount of the voting securities and assets of the acquired person in excess of $15 million.

Thus, the notification and reporting requirements are based on "size of person" and "size of transaction" tests.

2. FTC Regulations

The premerger notification rules of the FTC are found at 16 CFR, Parts 801-803 and CCH Fed. Trade Reg. Rep. § 42,000.

3. Exemptions

A variety of exemptions are provided in Section 7A(c) of the Clayton Act and 16 CFR, Part 802.

Regulation Section 802.20 provides that acquisitions of 15 percent or more of voting securities or assets need not be notified and reported if (1) assets are acquired which do not have a total value greater than $15 million; or (2) voting securities are acquired which do not confer control of a company which, together with all entities it controls, has annual net sales or total assets of $25 million or more. In general, control means 50 percent or more of the outstanding securities.

Some other important exemptions are as follows:

- Acquisitions, solely for investment by banks and certain other financial institutions, of voting securities pursuant to a plan of reorganization or dissolution or of assets in the ordinary course of business.
- Certain acquisitions by foreign persons.
- Certain acquisitions by creditors and insurers.
- Acquisitions of convertible voting securities, but not their later conversion.
- Acquisitions by gift, intestate succession or devise, or irrevocable trust.
- Acquisitions of voting securities solely for investment if the acquiring person would hold 10 percent or less of the outstanding voting securities of the issuer, regardless of the dollar value involved.
- Acquisitions of voting securities by underwriters in the ordinary course of business and in the process of underwriting.
- Acquisitions by newly formed entities not controlled by another entity that have not yet drawn up a regular balance sheet and have assets consisting only of cash that will be used to make an acquisition and securities of the entity it is acquiring.
- Acquisitions by an employee stock ownership trust qualified under Section 401 of the Internal Revenue Code (IRC) of voting securities of the employer that organized the trust.

The last two exemptions are specially significant in leveraged buyout (LBO) transactions. In effect, they exempt the typical management buyout using a "shell" corporation as the buyer and the typical employee buyout financed through an employee stock ownership plan (ESOP).[1]

[1]The LBO "exemption" is actually part of Section 801.11, which defines annual net sales and total assets. Subsection (e) allows an acquiring person that does not have a regularly prepared balance sheet to exclude all cash that will be used in the acquisition (including incidental expenses) and all securities of the acquired person.

For many years, the notification and reporting requirements were not applied to certain acquisitions by persons using a partnership as the acquisition vehicle, although the requirements applied if a corporation was used as the vehicle. That distinction was partially terminated by amendments adopted in 1987 (52 Fed. Reg. 20058, May 29, 1987).

4. Waiting Periods

Persons subject to the notification and reporting requirements are subject to a 30-calendar-day waiting period before the acquisition can be made. The DOJ or FTC can extend the waiting period an additional 20 days. For a cash tender offer the waiting period is 15 days, extendable by 10 days.

The waiting periods run from the time when the completed notification is filed or when an incomplete notification is filed with a statement of reasons for noncompliance. (16 CFR, §803.10). As a practical matter, this means that the waiting periods can be significantly longer than the stated numbers of days, as will be explained.

5. The Reports and Fees

A notification and report must be filed by both parties to a voluntary acquisition and by the acquiring person in a tender offer. The acquired person in a tender offer is also required to file in response to DOJ and FTC rules, and it usually cooperates eagerly in an effort to persuade the DOJ and FTC that the tender offer should be enjoined.

An acquiring person who files a notification and report must pay a filing fee of $20,000. In a consolidation or joint venture, if there is more than one acquiring person, each must pay a full fee (54 Fed. Reg. 48726, November 24, 1989).

The report forms require the filing of extensive information about the businesses of the acquiring person and the acquired person, including documents obtained or prepared to evaluate the acquisition. Because the information usually includes trade secrets, Section 7A(h) of the Clayton Act prohibits their disclosure.

Products are reported by the Standard Industrial Code (SIC) system, and the heart of each report is the section that lists overlapping products of the two companies. In their requests for information, the DOJ and FTC focus inquiry on the overlapping products, requiring further detail about sales volumes and territories, pricing, plant capacities, competitors, substitute products, recent acquisitions and divestitures in the industry, foreign and potential competition, uses of the products by customers, capital and technology required by potential new entrants and numerous other matters.

The current Notification and Report Form for Certain Mergers and Acquisitions (FTC Form C4)can be found at 16 C.F.R. Part 803, Appendix, and in the CCH *Federal Trade Regulation Reporter*.

6. Enforcement of the Reporting Requirements

In early 1996, the DOJ and FTC settled a lawsuit against Sara Lee Corporation alleging wrongful failure to report a 1991 acquisition of shoe care assets from Reckitt & Colman P.L.C., a United Kingdom company. The settlement required Sara Lee to pay a civil penalty of $3.1 million without admitting a violation of Section 7A. Sara Lee, the owner of Kiwi Brands, Inc., acquired from Reckitt & Colman its Meltonian, Griffin and Magix product lines for $25,800,000. The issue was whether the assets in the U.S. were worth more than the $15,000,000 exemption, based on an allocation of the price between U.S. and U.K. assets. In an earlier related action, Sara Lee settled proceedings by the FTC by agreeing to sell the assets related to its Griffin and Esquire products (1996-1 CCH Trade Cases § 71,301 (D.C. Dist. Col. 1996)). Shortly thereafter, civil penalties of $130,000 were imposed by consent decree on *Titan Wheel International, Inc. U.S. v. Titan Wheel International, Inc.*, 1996-1 CCH Trade Cases § 71,406 (D.C. Dist. Col. 1996).

7. Answering the Questions

Item 4(c) of Form C4 requiring studies, surveys, analyses and reports must not be taken lightly. Officers and directors should be contacted and asked to think and review their files before answering. When an acquisition has been planned over an extended time period, they may have more documents than they realize.

Item 1(e) requires a listing of the "ultimate parent entities" of the acquiring person and acquired person. This term is defined in 16 CFR, Section 801.1(3), and this item must be answered with care, especially by foreign companies whose ownership structure may be complex and indirect.

Some companies become bewildered in their efforts to answer the questions in Items 5 and 7 of Form C4. Their products, services and other activities do not match the classifications shown in the SIC codes. This is normal because the Standard Industrial Code Manual uses a limited system and cannot possibly include all the variations that occur in actual business operations.

When SIC codes create mismatches or overlaps, the author recommends that the reporting person select the most nearly applicable SIC code and report the revenues under it. Reasons for the choice among alternatives can be explained in an attached sheet or letter. The FTC and DOJ generally appreciate a candid explanation that saves time and effort for both the reporting person and the reviewing staff.

Items 7, 8 and 9 receive the most attention from the FTC and DOJ and, accordingly, should receive the most care in preparation. For example, Item 7(a) uses broad, four-digit SIC codes. The reports of both the acquired person and the acquiring person may show revenues within a SIC code although their products or activities are quite different and noncompetitive. A concise explanation in an attached sheet or letter will save time and effort. Similarly, if the reports show revenues in the same states but the persons cannot actually compete for reasons such as location and freight costs, brief explanations of the facts may be helpful.

In recommending explanations of factual data, the author does not suggest that the notification and report form be used to argue the economic and legal merits of the acquisition or merger. Separate reports or memoranda analyzing the economic and legal issues can be submitted with the notification and report. However, if there are no obvious issues at the time of submission, it may be best to wait and see what issues will be raised by the FTC or DOJ before undertaking the cost and effort of an economic report or legal memorandum.

8. How the Waiting Periods Work; Second Requests

When the notification and report forms are filed, the DOJ or FTC reviews them. If the lawyers for the acquiring and acquired person have requested early termination of the waiting period and no serious issues are presented, a staff representative calls the lawyers to advise them that the requests have been granted. Confirmatory letters are sent and the acquisition can proceed to closing.

When the staff is considering early termination, a staff representative may call and request specific additional information to clarify the facts. Needless to say, the information should be obtained, evaluated and furnished promptly.

When potentially serious issues are presented, the DOJ or FTC undertake more extensive investigation. Of course, staff representatives review the historical information and experience within their own libraries and files. They can contact persons in the industry for information. They may receive unsolicited information from persons in the industry and other persons who feel their interests are affected by the proposed acquisition. They may serve lengthy civil investigative demands (mandatory questionnaires) on competitors, customers and suppliers who will furnish information on sales, production capacities and recent acquisitions, as well as other information.

The DOJ or FTC may also send a second request for additional information to the acquiring person and acquired person. These requests have often been extremely lengthy and detailed. However, the staff representatives remind the firms that the waiting periods do not commence running until all required information is furnished. See 16 C.F.R. § 803.20(c).

Frustrated lawyers and company personnel often tell the staff representatives that it might take weeks to assemble the information if the broad scope of a second request is taken literally. Further, much of the information requested is likely to be of little or no value. At this point, it is usually possible to review the list with the staff representatives and identify a shorter list of relevant information. Although the staff representatives will probably not withdraw their requests, they will agree to review the information sent and determine its adequacy. They will preserve the right to request more, if the additional information is insufficient or raises new questions. As a practical matter, the needs of the staff representatives for information can usually be met without furnishing the "kitchen sink" in response to the standard second request.

When problems are serious, it may be necessary to arrange a meeting with the staff at the DOJ or FTC. The meeting can be attended by company officers and managers who can explain matters such as products, manufacturing processes and the state of competition. Economists and other experts can also attend. In turn, the DOJ or FTC may arrange for its own economists, engineers, or other specialists to attend. It is important to prepare carefully for such a meeting and to emphasize orderly presentation within the time available. Efforts to be argumentative will waste time and seldom be as effective as clarification and supplementation of the factual data. Indeed, both analysis and argument are more effectively presented in memoranda that can be reviewed, researched and circulated among government staff personnel.

When the staff is satisfied that all necessary information has been furnished, a representative advises the lawyers that the waiting period has commenced. If the government does not object to the acquisition, termination of the waiting period may also be granted.

On March 23, 1995, the DOJ and FTC announced premerger program improvements, including a model request form and procedures to appeal second requests when acquisition proponents believe that staff personnel are requesting excessive documentation. This step may alleviate some of the problems in responding to second requests.

9. Solving Substantive Objections

At times, the DOJ or FTC may find potential adverse effects on competition of a nature critical to the objectives, structure or financing of the acquisition. If so, the seller and buyer must face a choice either to terminate the acquisition or to defend the lawsuit by the DOJ or FTC.

More often, the DOJ or FTC may identify adverse effects on competition of a limited nature. The adverse effects may impact only a single product or subproduct line. They may affect competition only in one section of the country where both buyer and seller have manufacturing plants accounting for important market shares. These limited problems can sometimes be resolved by negotiating a consent decree that permits the acquisition to proceed followed by "hold separate" and divestiture arrangements designed to preserve competition.

Before discussion of a consent decree requiring divestiture, the buyer must clearly understand that the DOJ and FTC are absolutely serious about the divestiture. They will require that the decree contain realistic steps to hold separate and preserve the business to be divested and to accomplish the divestiture with the time scheduled. The buyer must understand that the DOJ or the FTC will not excuse the divestiture because bids are few and prices are disappointing. Failure to accomplish a divestiture can result in civil penalties, appointment of a trustee to operate the business and even instructions to make capital and operating expenditures to make the business more attractive to potential buyers. For a case in which both the DOJ and a federal district afforded considerable cooperation and leniency, but eventually imposed a $1,000,000 penalty, see *U.S. Work Wear Corp.*, 602 F.2d 110 (6th Cir. 1979).

An example of a recent consent decree is *U.S. v. Kimberly-Clark Corporation*, U.S.D.C., N.D., Texas, Civil No. 3, 3:95 CV 3055-P, as published at 60 Fed. Reg. 66557, Dec. 22, 1995. Another example of a recent consent decree is *F.T.C. v. Boston Scientific Corp.*, 60 Fed. Reg. 12948 (March 9, 1995). Of special interest, the *Boston Scientific* decree contains "hold separate" and technology licensing provisions.

I. Recent Developments

The FTC published amendments to its premerger notification rules in early 1996 in order to clarify them and to simplify their compliance requirements. The amendments that may be the most useful are those that exempt acquisitions of voting securities of issuers holding assets, the direct acquisition of which is exempt (see 16 C.F.R. § 802.4). The exemptions also include additional purchases of goods in the ordinary course of business, certain real estate acquisitions, certain acquisitions of carbon-based mineral reserves and certain acquisitions of investment rental property assets (61 Fed. Reg. 13666 (March 28, 1996)).

J. Planning to Meet the Requirements of the Clayton Act

Planning for compliance with the requirements of the Clayton Act is an important part of acquisition planning.

For large acquisitions that present no serious competitive issues, the notification and report forms must nevertheless be prepared, a task that is detailed and time-consuming. Time must also be allowed for the DOJ and FTC to complete the review and terminate the waiting period. There can be no assurance that the termination will occur rapidly, because a competitor or customer may decide to complain about the acquisition, thus creating a delay in the review process while the merits of the complaint are evaluated. The DOJ and FTC will not reveal complainants. Thus, when they ask for information about an issue that seems far-fetched, the best response is to overcome any initial feeling of frustration at the delay and provide prompt and factual information demonstrating that the issue is not valid.

For large acquisitions that involve competitive overlaps, acquisition planners should obtain both legal and economic advice. There are many law firms with one or more lawyers who have experience in antitrust work. Economists specializing in antitrust work are less plentiful, but acquisition planners can retain a firm such as National Economic Research Associates, Inc. (NERA) in White Plains, New York or an econometrics professor with experience in antitrust work. Working as a team, these advisers can help acquisition planners to decide whether a proposed acquisition can be justified as proposed or can be restructured to achieve compliance. These advisers can prepare materials for consideration by the DOJ or FTC and can assist in the negotiation of any necessary restructuring or divestiture arrangements.

For small acquisitions, the first task is to determine whether the notification and reporting requirements apply. This is a serious question in view of the large penalties imposed for noncompliance. If the notification and reporting requirements do not apply, the second task is to resist the urge to assume without a serious review that there are no issues under Section 7 of the Clayton Act. As described earlier, acquisitions are subject to Section 7 whether or not the notification and reporting requirements of Section 7A apply. Further, there is no statute of limitations for enforcement of Section 7, so the DOJ, the FTC or a private party can initiate action to challenge an acquisition when the acquisition or its effects come to their attention several years later.

A small acquisition may obviously have no effect on competition in any broad national market, no matter how it is analyzed. However, Section 7 also protects competition in more narrowly defined product and geographical markets. The author recommends that acquisition planners apply the concepts of the 1992 Merger Guidelines to a proposed small acquisition to see whether there may be relevant regional or local product markets in which competition may be significantly and adversely impacted. If questions arise, it is best to consult with experienced legal and economic advisers before making an acquisition that might later have to be divested.

K. Reference Materials

Books

Acquisitions under the Hart-Scott-Rodino Antitrust Improvements Act, Axinn et al., Law Journal Seminars-Press

Antitrust Laws and Trade Regulation, Von Kalinowski, Matthew Bender (multivolume set)

Federal Trade Regulation Reporter, Commerce Clearing House (seven-volume set)

Articles

"Advances of the 1992 Horizontal Merger Guidelines in the Analysis of Competitive Effects," Denis, 36 *Antitrust Bulletin* 473, 1993.

"Evaluating Vertical Mergers: A Post-Chicago Approach," Riordan et al., 63 *Antitrust Law Journal* 513, ABA, 1995.

"The FTC's Use of Innovative Merger Remedies," Steptoe et al., *Antitrust*, ABA, Fall 1995.

"The Goals of Antitrust: A Dialogue on Policy," Bork et al., 65 *Columbia L.R.* 363, 1965.

"Market Power in Antitrust Cases," Landes and Posner, 94 *Harvard L. Rev.* 937, 1981.

"Mergers with Differentiated Products," Shapiro, *Antitrust*, ABA, Spring 1996.

"The Role of Third Parties in Agency Merger Reviews," Fullerton, *Antitrust*, ABA, Spring 1995.

"The Shape of Things to Come: Innovation Market Analysis in Merger Cases," Dahdouh et al., 64 *Antitrust Law Journal* 405, ABA, 1996.

"Thirty-One Merger Policy Questions Still Lingering After the 1992 Guidelines," 38 *Antitrust Bulletin* 593, 1993.

"What Makes Mergers Anticompetitive?: 'Unilateral Effects' Analysis under the 1992 Merger Guidelines," Starek et al., 63 *Antitrust Law Journal* 801, ABA, 1995.

Chapter 11

The Securities Regulation Laws—Overview, Public Offerings and Private Placements

A. How the Securities Laws Affect Acquisitions and Divestitures

The federal securities regulation laws apply to acquisition and divestiture transactions in many ways. For example, if an acquisition price will be paid in stock, notes or other securities, the acquiring corporation must register the securities by preparing and filing a registration statement with the Securities and Exchange Commission (SEC) under the Securities Act of 1933 (the "1933 Act") unless an exemption applies. The acquisition price may not be paid until the SEC orders the registration statement effective. Registration is an expensive and time-consuming process and must be planned as part of the schedule for the acquisition.

If the acquisition price will be a cash price financed by a sale of stock, notes or other securities, the securities to be sold to investors must be registered with the SEC under the 1933 Act unless an exemption applies. Here also, the sale of the securities may not commence until the SEC has ordered the registration statement effective.

An acquiring corporation can sometimes save the cost and time involved in registration of securities by offering and selling securities pursuant to an exemption. However, if it makes a private placement of the securities in reliance on the private offering exemption in the 1933 Act or the SEC's Regulation D, the securities must be offered only to persons qualifying under those exemptions. The securities sold will be restricted from resale in the public markets for up to 2 years unless the resale is registered with the SEC or the resales are made within applicable exemptions such as the SEC's Rules 144 or 144A. These restrictions have important effects on the sale of the securities.

This chapter describes how the registration and exemption requirements of the 1933 Act affect sales of securities to pay or finance the purchase price of acquisitions. Chapter 12 discusses the many requirements of the Securities Exchange Act of 1934 (the "1934 Act") that affect acquisitions. They include registration of securities under the 1934 Act so that they can be traded on a stock exchange or quoted in the NASDAQ stock market. They also include solicitation of proxies for votes on mergers and sales of substantially all assets and regulation of tender offers, "going private" transactions and proxy contests.

B. The Securities Laws

The federal securities laws having broad application are as follows:

- The Securities Act of 1933[1]
- The Securities Exchange Act of 1934[2]
- The Trust Indenture Act of 1939[3]
- The Investment Company Act of 1940[4]
- The Investment Advisers Act of 1940[5]
- The Glass-Steagall Act[6]

The two federal securities laws that have by far the greatest impact on acquisition and divestiture transactions are the 1933 Act and the 1934 Act. This chapter will focus primarily on their requirements.

Readers will often see or hear references to the popular names of laws adopted over the years as amendments and additions to the 1934 Act which is a lengthy, multipurpose law. An example is the Williams Act which amended the 1934 Act to provide for regulation of tender offers. Another example is the Foreign Corrupt Practices Act which required registered companies to establish internal financial control systems. In the discussions throughout the chapter, the text will refer to the 1934 Act.

All the states have some form of securities regulation law, generally called a "blue sky" law. The state laws range from brief laws focusing primarily on licensing of broker-dealers to elaborate laws requiring registration of securities and granting to state securities regulatory authorities the authority to impose "merit" regulation beyond the authority of the SEC. However, while this book was being written, the U.S. Congress adopted the Capital Markets Efficiency Act of 1996 that contains provisions preempting much of the authority of the states to require registration of securities.[7] Thus, the discussion will focus on the "blue sky" laws as a group and on transactions, such as tender offers, on which the state laws have a significant impact.

C. How the Securities Laws Accomplish Their Objectives

Before the twentieth century, securities were sold to companies and wealthy individuals who generally, if not always, had knowledge and resources to

---

[1]15 U.S.C. § 77a *et seq.*

[2]15 U.S.C. § 78a *et seq.*

[3]15 U.S.C. § 77aaa *et seq.*

[4]15 U.S.C. § 80a-1 *et seq.*

[5]15 U.S.C. § 80b-1 *et seq.*

[6]12 U.S.C. §§ 24, 78, 377 and 378

[7]15 U.S.C. § 77r. This Act is part of the National Securities Markets Improvement Act of 1996.

protect their interests. Early in the twentieth century, Henry Ford and other industrial entrepreneurs recognized that steady employment of large numbers of workers at increased salary and wage levels was essential to the expansion of markets for industrial products as well as for improved living standards. As work became steady and workers accumulated savings, investment bankers and brokers recognized that workers as a whole were a major potential source of capital. As described by Judge Harold Medina in *U.S. v. Morgan*,[8] investment banking and investment by the public grew significantly during the early part of the twentieth century.

During the first three decades of the century, only a few state laws and no federal laws were adopted to regulate securities or the investment bankers and brokers who sold them. However, after the severe market crash on "Black Friday" in 1929 and the arrival of the "Great Depression," it became apparent that workers who purchased securities lacked the knowledge and resources to protect themselves. As workers lost their savings and unemployment rose, a concerned public supported President Franklin Roosevelt and the U.S. Congress in adopting federal laws to regulate industry, including the securities industry.

While planning and debating the 1933 Act and the 1934 Act, Congress made policy decisions so fundamental that they created a new commercial and financial culture in the United States. It is helpful to identify these fundamental decisions because they are critical to understanding the securities laws.

Congress decided that the government should not directly control the securities industry, but should maintain an investor-oriented market. This decision meant that the new securities laws would rely on the principle of full disclosure to enable investors to make their own investment decisions with knowledge of the material risks. Congress granted broad authority to the SEC to prescribe and enforce disclosure standards, but did not grant it authority to approve or rate securities or to prevent the sale of securities when the disclosure standards were met.

The 1933 Act and the 1934 Act were pioneering laws that introduced new regulatory principles that continue in effect today:

- Full disclosure to prospective investors by issuers and others offering securities for sale to the public.
- Self-regulation of the securities industry, supervised by a strong government agency, the SEC, having authority to regulate both the industry and the self-regulatory organizations.
- Improvement of financial statements of securities issuers by requiring their preparation in accordance with generally accepted accounting principles (GAAP) and their certification by an independent accountant.
- Imposition of strict liability on issuers for failure to comply with the new disclosure standards and, with some limitations, on other persons including directors and officers, controlling persons, un-

[8] 118 F. Supp. 621 (S.D.N.Y. 1953). Judge Medina's description of the syndicated sales in 1906 of shares of Sears Roebuck & Co. and United Cigar Corporation by Lehman Brothers and Goldman Sachs & Co. is of special interest.

derwriters, broker-dealers, accountants, lawyers and other professionals participating in distributions of securities.

In effect, the 1933 Act and the 1934 Act shifted the legal principle allocating the risk of uninformed investment decisions from "*caveat emptor*" to "*caveat vendor,*" but left the securities industry free to function and its customers free to buy and sell. The two laws allowed and encouraged the game to continue, but leveled the playing field.

Because the securities laws operate in an innovative and rapidly changing industry, both the laws and the SEC's regulations have become extensive and complex. However, there is a widespread consensus that they have been, and continue to be, remarkably effective. Efforts in recent years to eliminate obsolete or duplicative regulatory programs and to simplify compliance methods are providing some relief from excessive compliance burdens.

D. Registration under the 1933 Act: A Brief Introduction

Briefly, the Securities Act requires that issuers (and certain other persons) who wish to offer and sell securities to the public must prepare and file a registration statement with the SEC before offering the securities, and wait until it has become effective before selling the securities. The registration statement must include the proposed prospectus to be used in offering and selling the securities. The use of communications other than the prospectus is prohibited with a few exceptions such as "tombstone" advertisements.

The prospectus must contain extensive information including descriptions of the issuer and its business, the securities and the issuer's financial statements prepared in accordance with GAAP and certified by an independent accountant. The SEC may review and furnish comments to the issuer on the registration statement.[9] If it does so, the issuer responds by filing one or more amendments to the registration statement until the SEC agrees to order it effective. The issuer (and certain others participating in the distribution of the securities) must then deliver the final prospectus to the persons to whom the securities are offered before or concurrently with sales of the securities.

The 1933 Act imposes liability on issuers (and certain other persons) for (1) failure to register securities; (2) failure to deliver required prospectuses; (3) any untrue statement of a material fact or omission of a material fact required or necessary to make statements in a registration statement not misleading; and (4) any untrue statement of material fact or omission of a material fact required to make statements not misleading in a prospectus or communication in connection with the offer or sale of a security. The liability imposed by the 1933 Act is strictly enforced by the SEC and the courts.

---

[9]The SEC undertakes a full review of about one-fifth of the total registration statements filed, but fully reviews a substantial majority of the registration statements for initial public offerings ("IPOs"). After a full review, the SEC may furnish its comments in a lengthy and detailed comment letter. Registration statements filed by seasoned companies that have demonstrated their familiarity and compliance with the disclosure requirements are likely to receive a limited review and comments, if any, may be furnished by telephone.

The Securities Act allows only a few defenses to liability. Most significantly, persons other than the issuer are allowed under some circumstances a "due diligence" defense, which requires that they prove that, after reasonable investigation, they had reasonable grounds to believe and did believe that the statements in the registration statement were true and there was no omission to state a material fact required to be stated therein or necessary to make the statements therein not misleading.

The SEC has adopted detailed regulations prescribing requirements for the preparation of registration statements.[10] They include forms such as the S-1 series for domestic issuers, the F-1 series for foreign issuers, the SB-1 series for small business issuers and the N-1 series for investment companies. The S-1 and S-B forms refer to central disclosure regulations for specific instructions, requirements and guidance:

- Regulation S-B for small businesses,[11]
- Regulation S-K for most domestic issuers, and[12]
- Regulation S-X on form and content of financial statements.[13]

The SEC emphasizes that compliance with the requirements in its forms does not excuse issuers and others from their overall disclosure obligations under the 1933 Act, nor do any review and comments of the SEC. Indeed, prospectuses state on their cover that it is a criminal offense to represent that the SEC has approved or disapproved securities or passed upon the accuracy or adequacy of the prospectus.

Since 1996, registration statements must be filed electronically with the SEC using the Electronic Data Gathering, Analysis and Retrieval (EDGAR) system prescribed by Regulation S-T.[14]

E. Registration of Exchange Offers to Public Securityholders

Acquiring corporations that can use their stock, notes or other securities as acquisition currency usually have well-established businesses and outstanding securities that are already traded on a stock exchange or the National Association of Securities Dealers Automated Quotation System (the "NASDAQ System"). They commit to list the securities to be issued in an acquisition for trading on the exchange or in the NASDAQ System, thus providing market liquidity for the securities.

If the acquiring corporation plans to offer its securities in exchange for the shares (and perhaps other securities) of the acquired corporation, the

[10]See Regulation C., 17 C.F.R. § 210.400 *et seq.*

[11]17 C.F.R. Part 228.

[12]17 C.F.R. Part 229.

[13]17 C.F.R. Part 210. Regulation S-X also contains rules on the qualifications and reports of accountants. For example, accountants must meet independence requirements. Their reports must address specific points including the scope of their audit and conformity of the financial statements to generally accepted accounting principles. An example of an independent auditor's report appears as Exhibit 11-1.

[14]17 C.F.R. Part 232.

offer is called an "exchange offer." If the acquired corporation has public shareholders to whom the exchange offer will be made, the acquiring corporation must register the securities with the SEC under the 1933 Act.

The acquiring corporation registers the exchange offer using Form S-3, if it meets the applicable eligibility requirements, or may use Form S-1. The prospectus describes the acquisition and the acquisition contract appears as an exhibit to the registration statement. Financial statements of the acquiring corporation and the corporation to be acquired are included in the prospectus. The shareholders of the corporation to be acquired can then use the prospectus to decide whether they wish to accept the exchange offer.

To accomplish the exchange offer, the acquiring corporation sends transmittal letter forms to the shareholders of the corporation to be acquired. Those shareholders who wish to accept the exchange offer list their stock certificates on the transmittal letter forms and send them to the depository bank designated by the acquiring corporation. The transmittal letter forms customarily require signature guarantees and evidence of authority of executors and other persons who submit shares in a representative capacity. If and when the minimum percentage of shares is submitted and any other conditions are met, the acquiring corporation accepts the shares submitted to the depositary. The depositary then sends the securities of the acquiring corporation to the shareholders whose shares were accepted.

F. Registration of Securities Issued in Mergers and Asset Acquisitions Approved by a Vote of Shareholders

When an acquiring corporation uses its shares, notes or other securities to acquire another corporation by merger or to acquire substantially all the assets of another corporation, the acquiring corporation does not offer the securities directly to the shareholders of the corporation to be acquired. The securities are offered in negotiations between the managements of the two corporations. The negotiations result in a merger agreement or an assets purchase agreement in which the acquiring corporation commits to issue the securities to the acquiring corporation. In both transactions, a meeting of the shareholders of the acquired corporation is called and the shareholders vote to approve or disapprove the merger or assets sale. If the shareholders vote to approve by the required percentage, all shareholders are bound by the vote.

In a merger, merger certificates are then filed with state corporate officials and the merger becomes effective. The distribution of securities of the acquiring corporation to the shareholders of the acquired corporation follows by operation of law. In an assets acquisition, the acquiring corporation issues the securities to the seller corporation in exchange for its assets. The seller corporation usually then winds up its affairs and distributes the securities pro rata to its shareholders.

For many years, the SEC's Rule 133 treated issues of securities in shareholder-approved merger and asset sale transactions as "no sale" transactions that need not be registered under the 1933 Act. The SEC took comfort in the fact that the votes of the public shareholders of the acquired corporation were solicited by a proxy statement pursuant to its proxy rules.

As time passed, however, the SEC became concerned that Rule 133 was being used to create public markets for shares without adequate disclosure. The SEC was also concerned that structuring choices should not dictate the disclosure to be furnished in acquisition transactions. In 1972, the SEC rescinded Rule 133 and adopted a new Rule 145.[15]

Rule 145 requires registration of securities offered or sold if a corporation submits for the vote or consent of its securityholders a plan or agreement for:

- A statutory merger or consolidation or similar plan or acquisition in which securities of the corporation or other person held by its securityholders will become or be exchanged for securities of any other person, unless the sole purpose of the transaction is to change an issuer's domicile solely within the United States.
- A transfer of assets of such corporation or other person to another person for securities of such other person or any of its affiliates, if the plan or agreement provides for the dissolution of the corporation or other person or for a pro rata or similar distribution of such securities to the securityholders voting or consenting. If the agreement or plan does not provide for such a dissolution or distribution, registration is nevertheless required if the board of directors or similar representatives of the corporation adopt resolutions relating to such a dissolution or distribution within a year after the vote or consent or the transfer of assets was part of a pre-existing plan for distribution of the securities.[16]

To ease the burden of compliance, the SEC allows the use of a simplified registration statement form, Form S-4, for the registration of securities in transactions covered by Rule 145 and similar transactions. An S-4 registration statement can also be used for public offers or resales of the securities covered by the registration statement by affiliated persons, provided that post-effective amendments are filed to keep the information up to date. The prospectus in an S-4 registration is wrapped around the proxy statement used to solicit the vote on the merger or sale of assets. This "wraparound" technique saves time and cost because the prospectus often requires only a few pages of information in addition to the information in the proxy statement. Form S-4 appears as Exhibit 11-2 to this chapter.

The expansion in 1982 of the periodic reporting obligations of corporations registered under the 1934 Act was a more fundamental method than Rule 145 for providing information to the trading markets after mergers and sales of assets. However, Rule 145 continues to place acquisition methods in a relatively equal status with regard to registration obligations and provides a simplified means for registration under the 1933 Act of securities to be resold by persons affiliated with a corporation being acquired.

---

[15] 17 C.F.R. § 230.145.

[16] Rule 145 also requires registration of securities offered or sold if a corporation submits for the vote or consent of its securityholders a plan or agreement for a reclassification of its securities, other than a stock split, reverse stock split, or change in par value, which involves substitution of a security for another security.

G. Registration of Securities Sold to Raise Acquisition Financing

An acquiring corporation that plans to pay cash to acquire another corporation by a purchase of its stock or by a merger or by a purchase of its assets often obtains the funds by a public sale of stock, notes or other securities. If the securities are offered to the public, the corporation registers them with the SEC under the 1933 Act by the same methods it would use to sell securities to raise capital for other purposes. Most corporations whose securities can readily be sold to raise acquisition financing are eligible to use Form S-3 and may also have effective "shelf" registration statements that can quickly be updated by post-effective amendments under the SEC's Rule 415 to raise acquisition financing. However, Forms SB-1 and SB-2 can be used by small business issuers.

For strategic and legal reasons, it is usually better to raise capital to be used for acquisition financing well in advance of negotiations for a specific acquisition. For example, corporations often make a large offering of securities at a time when market conditions are favorable and disclose that the proceeds will be used for several purposes including internal expansion and possible acquisition opportunities. The SEC typically reminds the corporation of its obligation to disclose any material expansion plans or acquisitions in progress, but the corporation should already have done so.

A strategic advantage of raising advance acquisition financing is the ability to move more quickly than competitive acquirers and to bargain effectively with cash-oriented sellers. The mind-set of many sellers seeking a cash price is also to obtain payment at the earliest practical time. These sellers sometimes accept a reduced price from a buyer who can commit to pay cash without any financing condition. These sellers may be reluctant to sign a conditional acquisition contract, even when the buyer plans to borrow privately from a bank or another readily accessible source. Such sellers are likely to walk away from any buyer who proposes to raise the price from a source as time-consuming and difficult as a public offering of securities, although strong support from an established investment banking firm can sometimes save the day.[17]

H. Acquisitions for Unregistered Securities

1. Registration Exemptions in the 1933 Act.

Acquiring corporations planning to use stock, notes or other securities as acquisition currency can often issue them without the time and expense of registration with the SEC under the 1933 Act. The 1933 Act contains several exemptions from registration, most importantly the private offering exemption. However, the conditions for use of the exemptions are strict and have important side-effects. Planners for both buyers and sellers must weigh the advantages and disadvantages.

[17] While cash is the payment medium favored by most sellers, there are, of course, many sellers who want or will accept stock or debt and will agree to financing and other conditions that take time and effort to fulfill. These sellers have different objectives or a different mind-set. For example, a seller who wants to benefit from a tax free reorganization will accept payment in voting stock and will agree to conditions that require significant time and effort to fulfill, such as government clearances, shareholder approvals and tax rulings.

To understand the private offering exemption and its effects, it is necessary to review some basic provisions of the 1933 Act. Section 5 of the 1933 Act begins with a broad prohibition against the offer or sale of securities by "any person" without their registration with the SEC. However, Sections 3 and 4 contain numerous exemptions of securities and transactions. Two transaction exemptions in Section 4 are especially important in acquisition transactions:

- Section 4(1) exempts transactions by any person other than an issuer, underwriter or dealer. The definition of an underwriter also excludes from this exemption persons who control the issuer.
- Section 4(2) exempts transactions by an issuer not involving any public offering.

It is important to understand that the transaction exemptions excuse only the registration and prospectus delivery requirements of the 1933 Act. The strict liability standards of the 1933 Act continue to apply to any material misstatements or omissions in connection with the offer and sale of securities.

2. The Section 4(1) Exemption.

The practical effect of the Section 4(1) exemption is to limit the obligation to register securities to issuers, persons who control issuers, underwriters and dealers. Whenever these persons wish to offer or sell securities, they must either register them or find an exemption from registration that they can demonstrate is available. The burden of proof that an exemption applies rests on the person claiming it.

3. The Section 4(2) Private Offering Exemption.

The most important transaction exemption is the Section 4(2) private offering exemption. Under this exemption, an acquiring corporation may issue securities as the price for an acquisition if the transaction does not involve any public offering. The SEC and the courts have interpreted the private offering exemption strictly so that its use would not deprive public investors of the information provided by the registration process, including the delivery of prospectuses to them.

In determining whether an offer is public or private, several criteria are considered. Important first phase criteria include the number of offerees, their business experience and their financial resources. Absence of any public advertising or general solicitation of investors is also important. Other significant criteria include the relationship between the issuer and the offerees and their access to information about the issuer. A classic analysis of the private offering exemption was provided by the U.S. Supreme Court in *Securities and Exchange Commission v. Ralston Purina Co.*[18] A detailed and strict analysis of the criteria used in determining whether the private offering exemption applies was provided in *Doran v. Petroleum Management Corp.*[19]

---

[18]346 U.S. 119, 73 S. Ct. 981, 97 L.Ed 1494 (1953).

[19]545 F.2d 893 (5th Cir. 1977); later proceedings 576 F.2d 91 (5th Cir. 1978).

The private offering exemption is often used by an acquiring corporation to issue unregistered securities in payment for a closely held corporation or its assets. The acquiring corporation can often show that the owner-shareholders of the business to be acquired are few in number and have ample business experience and financial resources as well as advice from their lawyers, accountants and financial advisers. The acquisition negotiations, including the offer of securities, are conducted privately. The acquiring corporation furnishes information about its business and financial affairs, including its annual, quarterly and current reports under the 1934 Act, to the owner-shareholders. In many transactions, the owner-shareholders have had prior business relationships with the acquired corporation. The owner-shareholders often continue in employment as managers of the acquired business operations. In some transactions, they may even become officers or directors of the acquiring corporation. Thus, the first phase criteria for the private offering exemption are often clearly met.

4. Restrictions on Resale and Other Transfers.

The availability of the private offering exemption also depends on meeting second phase criteria. An issuer cannot claim that an offer of securities does not involve a public offering if the persons who receive them intend to resell or distribute them to the public. A purported private placement with investors who plan to resell in the public markets is a sham and the investors are mere conduits in a public offering. Thus, acquiring corporations and other issuers have long taken practical steps to restrict resales and other transfers of securities issued in reliance on the private offering exemption by the persons who receive the securities. While the restrictions reduce the liquidity of the securities, the securityholders agree to them in order to establish that they are not "underwriters" who, as explained earlier, are among the persons required to register securities under the 1933 Act.[20]

By custom, an acquiring corporation issuing securities in reliance on the private offering exemption obtains representations and warranties in the acquisition contract from each person who will receive the securities, that he, she or it is acquiring the securities for investment and without any intent to resell or otherwise distribute them to the public. The acquisition contract also authorizes the acquiring corporation to endorse a restrictive legend on the face of the securities stating that they may be transferred only upon receipt of an opinion of counsel acceptable to the acquiring corporation or a "no action" letter from the SEC confirming that the transfer is lawful.[21] An example of such a legend appears as Exhibit 11-3.

As will be explained shortly, the transfer restrictions on securities endure for up to 2 years. During the restricted period, a securityholder may sell the securities only if they are registered or are sold pursuant to an ex-

---

[20]Stated briefly, Section 2(11) includes in its definition of an underwriter any person who acquires securities from an issuer with a view to, or for resale in connection with, a (public) distribution of the securities.

[21]The acquiring corporation may also require each person to deliver a letter at the closing acknowledging his, her or its business and investment experience and financial resources and confirming his, her or its investment intent and understanding of the nature of the restrictions on transfer of the securities. An example of such an investment letter appears as Exhibit 11-4, Subscription Agreement.

emption from registration. The transfer restrictions increase the investment risk of the securities.[22] The restrictions also limit the liquidity of the securities and reduce their value.[23] Thus, owner-shareholders selling a business in exchange for unregistered securities often insist on a provision in the acquisition contract entitling them to require the acquiring corporation to register the shares for resale. Examples of contractual registration rights provisions appear as Exhibit 11-5.

5. Resales of Restricted Securities.

In the early decades of its enforcement of the 1933 Act, the SEC would issue a "no action" letter allowing resale of restricted securities in the public markets only after a holding period such as 5 (later 3) years or the occurrence of an unforeseeable change of circumstances that did not cast doubt on the veracity of a securityholder's representations given when the securities were issued. The SEC did not recognize foreseeable events, such as fluctuations in market value or adverse developments in the issuer's business, as sufficient to justify resales. However, an unexpected, serious and costly illness or personal injury might be sufficient.

The uncertainty resulting from the SEC's interpretations led to public requests that the SEC clarify the circumstances under which restricted securities could be resold. After several efforts, the SEC adopted Rule 144,[24] which it has modified from time to time. Rule 144 provides relatively clear standards for determining when and how restricted securities can lawfully be resold in the public markets. Rule 144 is described later in this chapter.

Restricted securities can also lawfully be resold in other transactions that are exempt under the 1933 Act. Examples are sales pursuant to the so-called Section 4($1^1/_2$) exemption and sales pursuant to Rule 144A.[25] These exemptions are discussed in more detail later in this chapter.

6. Contractual Provisions to Register Securities.

Because of the disadvantages of restricted securities, business sellers who agree to accept shares of stock or other securities in payment of the purchase price frequently negotiate provisions in the acquisition contract that will entitle them to require the purchaser to register the shares or securities with the SEC so that they can lawfully be sold without restriction. A common provision entitles the seller (or sellers) to make one request that a registration statement be prepared and filed with the SEC at the expense of the purchaser. The request is usually limited to a time during the purchaser's fiscal year when its audited financial statements are current. In addition,

---

[22]A former acquaintance of the author sold his business to a public corporation some years ago in return for unregistered restricted stock and without contractual registration rights. Before the restrictions expired, the public corporation became bankrupt and the stock became worthless. This example is unusual, but dramatically illustrates the investment risk of restricted securities.

[23]Valuation discounts for lack of marketability of restricted stock vary considerably. However, several studies have shown discounts in the 30 percent range. See Chapter 15 of *Valuing a Business*, Pratt *et al.*, Irwin Publishing, 1996.

[24]17 C.F.R. § 230.144.

[25]17 C.F.R. § 230.144A.

the seller (or sellers) may be entitled to request that their shares be included in a registration statement that the purchaser has decided to file for other reasons.

The contractual provision usually contemplates a registration statement for any offering method, including an offering underwritten by an investment banking firm. However, business sellers who request that a registration statement be filed usually plan a "shelf offering" under which they will sell their shares from time to time at prices prevailing on the stock exchange, the NASDAQ Stock Market or other over-the-counter market where the shares are traded.

I. Private Placements to Raise Acquisition Financing

1. Introduction to Private Placements.

Acquiring corporations often sell stock, notes or other securities in private placements to raise acquisition financing. The sales are made without registration under the 1933 Act in reliance upon the Section 4(2) private offering exemption. The sales may also be made in reliance on the SEC's optional "safe harbor" regulation, Regulation D.[26]

Very large amounts of acquisition financing are raised by sales of debt instruments to banks, insurers, pension funds and other institutional investors. They are sometimes accompanied by warrants and other "equity sweeteners." Sales of subordinated (mezzanine) debt and of equity instruments are also made in large amounts to venture capital funds and wealthy individuals.

Sales of securities to institutional investors usually meet the requirements of the Section 4(2) private offering exemption with little reason for concern. There may be no need to follow the procedures in Regulation D if offers of securities are made only to well-established institutional investors. However, if offers will be made to individuals, small businesses or small investment funds, compliance with Regulation D may be a prudent choice. The formal procedures of Regulation D not only protect investors, but can also protect the issuer and its management from unjustified claims by investors who may regret their investment after it is made and seek to recover their money.[27]

2. Regulation D.

The SEC adopted Regulation D as an optional "safe harbor" regulation to clarify and simplify the standards that issuers can use in making private placements and certain other limited offerings of securities. Regulation D consists of the SEC's Rules 501 through 508 under the 1933 Act.

Regulation D contains three exemptions:

[26] 17 C.F.R. § 230.501 to 508

[27] When enthused about a private placement, potential investors gladly present themselves as experienced, affluent and well-informed. When seeking a refund, they portray themselves as inexperienced, financially needy and easily misled by misstatements and omissions allegedly made by the issuer's representatives.

- *Rule 504.* An issuer may offer and sell securities for an aggregate offering price not exceeding $1,000,000 within a 12-month period in compliance with Rule 504. However, the exemption is not available to any issuer that is (1) required to file reports under the Exchange Act, (2) an investment company, or (3) a development stage company that either has no business plan or has a business plan to engage in a merger or acquisition with an unidentified company or companies. Because of its limitations, Rule 504 is seldom used to raise acquisition financing.
- *Rule 505.* An issuer that is not an investment company may offer and sell securities for an aggregate offering price not exceeding $5,000,000 within a 12 month period in compliance with Rule 505. The issuer may not use any general solicitation or advertising and may sell only to accredited investors and 35 other purchasers. A purchaser who is not an accredited investor must (alone or with a purchaser representative) have such knowledge or experience in financial and business matters that he or she is capable of evaluating the merits and risks of the prospective investment. The issuer must furnish specified information to purchasers who are not accredited investors and must file a notice on Form D with the SEC pursuant to Rule 503 within 15 days after the first sale of securities. Rule 505 is less restrictive and more useful than Rule 504, but is also used only occasionally to raise acquisition financing.
- *Rule 506.* Any issuer may offer and sell securities without any dollar limit in compliance with Rule 506. The issuer may not use any general solicitation or advertising and may sell only to accredited investors and 35 other persons. The issuer must furnish specified information to purchasers who are not accredited investors and must file a notice on Form D with the SEC. A purchaser who is not an accredited investor must (alone or with a purchaser representative) have such knowledge or experience in financial and business matters that he or she is capable of evaluating the merits and risks of the prospective investment. Rule 506 is by far the most important exemptive rule in Regulation D and is often used to raise acquisition financing.

Many issuers limit offerings under Regulation D to accredited investors because the requirements to furnish specific information to prospective investors do not apply to accredited investors. Regulation D contains a detailed definition of an accredited investor that includes institutional investors such as banks, registered broker-dealers, registered investment companies, insurance companies and certain employee benefit plans and charitable organizations. The definition also includes any natural person:

- whose individual net worth, or joint net worth with that person's spouse, at the time of purchase exceeds $1,000,000, or
- who had an individual net income in excess of $200,000 in each of the two most recent years or joint income with that person's spouse in excess of $300,000 in each of those years and reasonably expects the same income in the current year.

A short form of Investor Questionnaire designed for compliance with Regulation D appears as Exhibit 11-6.

Regulation D provides an exemption only from the registration provisions of the 1933 Act and not from the strict antifraud provisions that impose liability for material misstatements and omissions. The fact that Regulation D does not prescribe specific information to be furnished to accredited investors does not excuse this liability. Issuers who limit disclosure to accredited investors risk liability for material omissions. Issuers who furnish overoptimistic business plans and financial projections to accredited investors risk liability for untrue or misleading statements.

Rule 502 prescribes the information that must be furnished to purchasers who are not accredited investors in offerings under Rules 505 and 506. An issuer required to file reports under the Exchange Act must furnish its most recent annual report to shareholders and proxy statement, its annual report on Form 10-K or 10-KSB and other materials filed under the 1933 Act and the 1934 Act as well as a description of the securities offered, the use of proceeds and any material changes in its affairs not disclosed in the documents furnished. An issuer not subject to reporting under the 1934 Act must furnish the same kind of nonfinancial statement information as is required by Regulation A, if applicable, or by the registration statement form for which the issuer is eligible. The financial statement information required varies with the size of the offering. For offerings up to $2,000,000, the financial statements must correspond to Regulation SB, Item 310, but the balance sheet must be audited. For offerings over $2,000,000 and up to $7,500,000, the financial statements must be those required by Form SB-2 with certain exceptions from the audit requirements. For offerings over $7,500,000, the financial statements must be those required by the registration form that the issuer would be eligible to use with certain exceptions from the audit requirements.

Rule 502(d) provides that securities acquired in a transaction under Regulation D cannot be resold without registration under the 1933 Act or an exemption therefrom.[28] The issuer must exercise reasonable care to assure that purchasers are not underwriters within the meaning of Section 2(11) of the 1933 Act. Reasonable care may be demonstrated by the following steps:

1. Reasonable inquiry to determine whether the purchaser is acquiring the securities for itself or for other persons;
2. Written disclosure to each purchaser prior to sale that the securities have not been registered under the Act and, therefore, cannot be resold unless they are registered under the Act or unless an exemption from registration is available; and
3. Placement of a legend on the certificate or other document that evidences the securities stating that the securities have not been registered under the Act and setting forth or referring to the restrictions on transferability and sale of the securities.

In addition, Rules 502 and 504 require the delivery of written disclosure of the resale limitations to investors in certain instances.

---

[28] Certain securities sold under Rule 504 are not subject to the resale restrictions, but see the change proposed in Securities Act Release 7541, May 21, 1998.

3. Contractual Provisions to Register Securities.

Because of the nonliquidity of restricted securities, investors who agree to purchase unregistered shares of stock or other securities frequently negotiate provisions in the private placement agreement that will entitle them to require the issuer to register the shares or securities with the SEC so that they can lawfully be sold without restriction. A common provision entitles the shareholders to make one request that a registration statement be prepared and filed with the SEC at the expense of the issuer. The request is usually limited to a time during the issuer's fiscal year when its audited financial statements are current. In addition, the purchaser (or purchasers) may be entitled to request that their shares be included in a registration statement that the issuer has decided to file for other reasons, for example, a "piggyback" registration right.

The contractual provision usually contemplates a registration statement for any offering method including an offering underwritten by an investment banking firm. However, shareholders who request that a registration statement be filed usually plan a "shelf offering" under which they will sell their shares from time to time at prices prevailing on the stock exchange, the NASDAQ Stock Market or other over-the-counter market where the shares are traded.

An example of contractual registration rights provisions appears as Exhibit 11-5.

4. Rule 144.

The SEC's Rule 144 allows limited resales of securities restricted from resale because they were acquired in transactions exempt under the private offering exemption in Section 4(2) of the 1933 Act and under Regulation D.[29] Any person making such resales must assure that several conditions are met:

- *Current Public Information.* Adequate current public information about the issuer must be available. For example, if the issuer has securities registered under the 1934 Act, it must be in compliance with its reporting requirements.
- *Holding Period.* Restricted securities must generally be held for 1 year before resales can be made within the limits of Rule 144. The resale restrictions terminate at the end of 2 years for persons who are not an affiliate of the issuer at the time of the sale or within 3 months prior to the sale. Rule 144 contains detailed provisions for calculation of the applicable holding periods. For example, they include provisions by which donees, pledgees and others can "tack" the holding period of the person from whom they acquired the securities to their own holding period.
- *Limitation on Amount of Securities Sold.* After a 1 year minimum holding period, holders of restricted securities are entitled to sell them in limited amounts. A holder may sell in a 3 month period an amount not exceeding the greater of (1) 1 percent of the shares

[29]Rule 144 also allows certain other resales including resales by controlling persons and other issuer affiliates.

or other units of the class outstanding as shown in the issuer's most recently published report, (2) the average weekly trading volume in the securities on all national securities exchanges and the NASDAQ System during the 4 weeks preceding the notice to the SEC of the sales, or (3) the average weekly volume of trading in such securities reported in the consolidated reporting system established under the 1934 Act during the same 4 week period. As described above, the restrictions terminate for persons not affiliated with the issuer at the end of 2 years. Affiliates must continue to sell within the limits so long as the affiliate relationship continues. Thus, for example, if a person who receives restricted shares in an acquisition transaction becomes the chief executive officer or controlling shareholder of the acquiring corporation, he or she will continue to be subject to the limitations of Rule 144. Rule 144 contains detailed provisions for calculation of the amounts of securities that may be sold.

- *Manner of Sale.* Resales of securities pursuant to Rule 144 must be made in unsolicited brokers' transactions or in transactions directly with a "market maker" for the securities, except for securities sold for a decedent's estate or a beneficiary of such an estate. Rule 144 contains detailed provisions prescribing the methods to be used in making unsolicited brokers' transactions.[30]
- *Notice of Proposed Sale.* A notice on Form 144 must be filed with the SEC and, if the securities are listed on an exchange or exchanges, with the principal exchange upon which the securities are listed for trading, if the securities sold in reliance on Rule 144 exceed in any 3 month period either 500 shares or other units or an aggregate sale price of $10,000. The notice must be transmitted concurrently with the placing of the order with a broker or the execution of a sale directly with a market maker. A copy of Form 144 appears as Exhibit 11-7.
- *Bona Fide Intention to Sell.* A person filing a notice on Form 144 must have a bona fide intention to sell the securities described in the notice within a reasonable time thereafter.

To summarize, restricted securities received in an acquisition transaction must be held for at least 1 year. During the second year, they may be resold within the limits and according to the procedures prescribed in Rule 144. After 2 years, the restrictions terminate for persons unaffiliated with the issuer, but affiliates must continue to resell in compliance with the limits and procedures of Rule 144 for so long as the affiliate relationship continues.

5. The So-Called Section 4(1 $^1/_2$) Exemption.

A careful reading of the exemptions provided by Sections 4(1) and 4(2) of the 1933 Act links them to transactions that do not involve an unregistered

[30] In releases published in February, 1997, the SEC proposed to amend the manner of sale and notice of sale provisions and make other changes to Rule 144. 62 Fed. Reg. 9246 (Feb. 28, 1997).

public distribution of securities, either by issuers or by persons whose intent makes them an underwriter. While the language of the two Sections does not expressly so state, a reasonable implication is that resales of privately placed securities that do not involve a public distribution do not violate the 1933 Act.

Investors in privately placed securities began years ago to request "no action" letters from the SEC allowing them to resell restricted securities to institutional or other investors who met the SEC's sophistication and other criteria for the private offering exemption. In its "no action" letters, the SEC recognized that such resales were consistent with the policies underlying Sections 4(1) and 4(2), provided that the resale purchasers also acquired without any intent to make a public distribution of the securities. In some letters, the SEC required that restrictive legends be placed on the securities issued to the purchaser and it became customary to do so.[31]

As the right to make private resales became widely recognized, securities lawyers began to refer to the justifying analysis as an imaginary Section 4(1½) exemption. An important practical advantage of this "exemption" is that restricted securities can be resold without any waiting period and can thereafter be resold again repeatedly, so long as they are not resold to the public. During the 1980s and 1990s, broker-dealers began to make high-volume, relatively active markets in restricted securities among institutional investors, especially in debt securities. These markets provided some liquidity for institutional investors while preserving the obligation to register securities if they are sold to the public.

6. Rule 144A.

Although investors welcomed the liquidity provided by the so-called Section 4(1½) exemption, uncertainty about its interpretation and the necessity to document the purchaser's qualifications and intentions and continue to use restrictive legends limited the liquidity of restricted securities in institutional markets. Urged by investors, the securities industry and Congress, the SEC sought to develop a rule that would allow efficient resales of restricted securities in institutional markets under procedures that would nevertheless assure against their distribution to the public. The loss of significant shares of the securities markets in the U.S. to less restrictive markets in Europe and Asia was also an incentive to clarify and modernize the SEC's rules and "no action" letters on resales of restricted securities.

In 1990, the SEC adopted Rule 144A, a "safe harbor" rule designed to facilitate private resales of securities to institutions. As an exemption for resales, Rule 144A is not available to issuers. Resales under Rule 144A must meet several conditions:

1. Offers and sales must be made only to qualified institutional buyers (QIBs).

[31]See also *Value Line Income Fund v. Marcus*, 1964-66 CCH Fed. Sec. L. Rep. §§ 91,523 (S.D.N.Y. 1965).

2. The seller and anyone acting on its behalf must take reasonable steps to assure that the purchaser is aware that the seller may rely on the Rule 144A exemption.
3. The securities must not be of the same class as any of the issuer's securities listed on a national stock exchange or quoted in the NASDAQ System, except that securities convertible or exchangeable for securities so listed or quoted may be permissible under certain circumstances.
4. Specified reasonably current information about the issuer must be furnished to prospective purchasers if the issuer is not subject to the reporting requirements of the Exchange Act or exempt from the reporting requirements pursuant to Rule 12g3-2(b).[32]

A seller who complies with the four conditions is not deemed to be engaged in a distribution of securities. Therefore, the seller is not an underwriter of the securities and is not obligated to register their offer and sale.

A definition of a QIB includes any of several entities that, acting for its own account or the accounts of other QIBs, in the aggregate owns or invests on a discretionary basis at least $100 million in securities of issuers with which it is not affiliated. These entities include insurance companies; investment companies registered under the Investment Company Act of 1990; small business investment companies licensed by the U.S. Small Business Administration; state and municipal employee benefit plans; employee benefit plans as defined in the Employee Retirement Income Security Act; trust funds for certain plans other than H.R. 10 plans; business development companies; investment advisers registered under the Investment Advisers Act of 1940; and any bank, savings and loan institution, foreign bank or savings and loan association or equivalent institution that also has an audited net worth of at least $25,000,000.

A definition of a QIB also includes any dealer registered under the 1934 Act, acting for its own account or the accounts of other QIBs, that in the aggregate invests on a discretionary basis at least $10,000,000 of securities of issuers with which it is not affiliated. If a registered dealer does not meet this test, it may nevertheless act in riskless principal transactions on behalf of a QIB or act as an agent on a nondiscretionary basis in a transaction with a QIB.

A QIB also includes certain investment companies that are part of a family of investment companies that own in the aggregate at least $100 million in securities of issuers unaffiliated with the family of investment companies.

Rule 144A is widely used in private placements to raise financing for acquisitions and many other purposes. Although the exemption does not apply to issuers,[33] cooperation of issuers is necessary because they must issue a specially designed security that is not of the same class as the is-

[32]Rule 12g3-2 (b) exempts foreign private issuers from the annual, quarterly and other periodic reporting requirements of the 1934 Act if they furnish to the SEC certain information consisting primarily of the information they are required to make public pursuant to the laws of their own nation or are required to file with a stock exchange or distribute to their securityholders.

[33]Issuers usually rely on Section 4(2), Regulatino D or Regulation S.

suer's securities listed on a stock exchange or quoted in the NASDAQ System. Thus, an issuer usually works with an investment banking firm to design the security and the term of sale. The private placement agreement, among other things, requires the issuer to comply with the reporting requirements of the 1934 Act or Rule 12g3-2(b) or to furnish other documents sufficient to enable the purchaser to fulfill the information requirements of Rule 144A.[34]

7. Regulation S.

For jurisdictional and policy reasons, the SEC enforces the 1933 Act for the protection of U.S. citizens and residents and does not require registration by persons offering and selling securities in good faith outside the United States. Over the years, however, the SEC encountered a variety of schemes in which securities were sold in sham transactions outside the United States and were quickly resold in the United States without registration under the 1933 Act. Civil and criminal proceedings were brought against the persons who engaged in these transactions.

Citizens and residents of the U.S. are, of course, free to purchase securities traded in foreign markets and some securities sold in legitimate offerings outside the United States eventually find their way into the United States. Publicity surrounding the civil and criminal proceedings against persons who had evaded the registration requirements of the 1933 Act through sham sales of securities outside the United States created concern for issuers, investment bankers and others participating in legitimate offerings outside the United States.

Over the years, issuers and investment banking firms requested "no action" letters from the SEC that would distinguish good faith offerings outside the United States from those that might be challenged by the SEC. The SEC issued a number of "no action" letters identifying procedures to be implemented that would evidence good faith and inhibit a flow of the securities into the United States. The procedures included verification that purchasers were foreign citizens or residents, delayed issuance of certificates for securities and transfer restrictions. However, it was difficult to derive general guidance from the "no action" letters because they were directed to particular offerings and did not always prescribe the same procedures.

In 1990, the SEC adopted Regulation S, a "safe harbor" rule designed to clarify the procedures that should be followed by issuers and other persons to establish that an offer and sale of securities is legitimately made outside the United States. In its preliminary notes to Regulation S, the SEC warns that Regulation S is not available for any transaction or series of transactions that, although in technical compliance, is part of a plan or scheme to evade registration under the 1933 Act.

Until 1998, Regulation S was composed of Rules 901 through 904. Rule 901 clarifies that the registration requirements of Section 5 of the 1933 Act apply to offers and sales that occur in the United States and do not apply

[34]Rule 144A does not prevent issuers from selling securities designed for compliance with Rule 144A directly to to institutional investors. However, investment banking firms have played a leading role in developing Rule 144A offerings and are active in the resale markets.

to offers and sales that occur outside the United States. Rule 902 contains definitions.

Rule 903 provides that an offer or sale of securities by an issuer (or certain other persons) will be deemed to occur outside the United States if it is made in an offshore transaction, no directed selling efforts are made in the United States and certain additional conditions are fulfilled to assure that the securities are sold to non-U.S. persons and cannot readily be resold to U.S. persons.

Rule 904 provides that resales of securities will also be deemed to occur outside the United States if they are made in an offshore transactions, no directed selling efforts are made in the United States and certain additional conditions are fulfilled.

To be recognized as an offshore transaction, an offering must not be made to any person in the United States. In addition, either (A) each buyer must be outside the United States when the buy order is originated or (B) the transaction must be executed at certain foreign securities exchanges or in certain offshore securities markets designated by the SEC without any knowledge that the transaction has been prearranged with a buyer in the United States.

The prohibition of directed selling efforts in the United States means that the issuer (and certain other persons including resellers) must refrain from any activity that could condition the market in the United States for resales of the securities sold under Regulation S. No advertisement may be placed in a publication with a general circulation in the United States. Exceptions are made for "tombstone ads" and advertisements in foreign publications with limited circulation in the United States.

The additional conditions required by Rule 903 are as follows:

(A) Each distributor must agree in writing that all offers and sales during the restricted period (described in C. and D.) will be made in accordance with Rule 903 or 904 unless the securities are registered or another exemption is available.

(B) All offering materials and documents (other than press releases) used during the restricted period (described in C. and D.) must state that the securities were not registered under the 1933 Act and may not be offered or sold in the United States or to U.S. persons (other than distributors) unless registered or an exemption is available.

(C) For debt securities, offers and sales may not be made to or for the account or benefit of a U.S. person during a 40-day restricted period. In addition, the securities may be issued only as a temporary global security until the expiration of the 40-day restricted period and, for persons other than distributors, until certification of their beneficial ownership by a non-U.S. person or a U.S. person who purchased in a transaction not requiring registration under the 1933 Act.

(D) For equity securities, offers and sales may not be made to or for the account or benefit of a U.S. person during a 1-year restricted period. In addition, the purchaser (other than a distributor) must certify that it is not a U.S. person and is not acquiring the securities for a U.S. person, or is a U.S. person who purchased in a transaction not requiring registration. The purchaser must also agree to resell only in accordance with Regulation S or pursuant to registration or an available exemption under the 1933 Act. A domestic issuer must place a legend on the securities prohibiting transfer except in accordance with Regulation S. The issuer must be required by contract or a provision in its articles, bylaws or other comparable document to refuse to register a transfer not made in accordance with Regulation S.

The conditions are less extensive for an issuer reporting under the 1934 Act or a foreign issuer offering debt securities. They are required to comply with conditions (1), (2) and 3(A) and (B) above, but not (3)(C) and (D). Further, offers and sales may not be made to or for the account or benefit of a U.S. person for a 40-day restricted period. In addition, each distributor selling securities to a distributor, dealer or person receiving remuneration related to the securities sold must, during the 40-day restricted period, send confirmations or other notices to each purchaser that it is subject to the same restrictions that apply to a distributor. Essentially the same conditions apply to non-reporting foreign issuers offering and selling nonparticipating preferred stock and asset-backed securities.

The following offers and sales may be made by complying only with conditions (1) and (2) above, but not condition (3):

- Foreign issuers that reasonably believe there is no substantial U.S. market interest in the class of equity securities or the debt securities to be offered or sold, including any securities issuable upon their exercise or conversion.
- Securities sold in an overseas directed offering, for example, an offering by (1) a foreign issuer of securities directed into a single country other than the U.S. to the residents thereof in accordance with the laws, customary practices and documentation of such country, or (2) a domestic issuer of nonconvertible debt securities made in the same manner, provided that the principal and interest are denominated in foreign currency and are neither convertible into U.S. dollar-denominated securities nor linked to U.S. dollars other than through currency or interest rate swap transactions.
- Securities backed by the full faith and credit of a foreign government.
- Securities offered and sold to employees of the issuer or its affiliates pursuant to an employee benefit plan established and administered under the laws of a foreign nation, provided that several conditions are met.

With appropriate procedures, offerings pursuant to Regulation S and Regulation D can be made concurrently and it has become common to do so.

Rule 904 establishes simpler conditions for resales than the conditions prescribed by Rule 903. An offer or sale occurs outside the United States if made in an offshore transaction and without any directed selling efforts in the United States. Additional conditions apply to dealers and persons receiving selling concessions and to certain officers and directors of the issuer or a distributor.

During the 1990s, the SEC commenced proceedings against issuers and other persons who had participated in several offerings outside the United States that the SEC alleged were sham transactions designed to avoid registration under the 1933 Act. These proceedings were followed by public criticism of Regulation S as too lenient. In February, 1998, the SEC adopted extensive amendments to Regulation S that make its requirements stricter.[35]

8. The NASD's PORTAL Market.

In 1990, the NASD established an automated quotation and communications system to facilitate private offerings, resales, trading, clearance and settlement of designated domestic and foreign securities by its participants. The system is called the PORTAL Market, a name that is an acronym for "Private Offerings, Resales and Trading through Automated Linkages." The NASD's PORTAL Market Rules are found in the *NASD Manual* (CCH), Rule 5300 *et seq.*

The purpose of the PORTAL Market is to provide an efficient market for the trading of restricted securities as defined in Rule 144 and other securities that upon issuance and continually thereafter can only be sold under Rule 144, Rule 144A, Regulation S or a transaction exempt under Section 4 of the 1933 Act and not involving any public offering. If a security is sold pursuant to Rule 144, including Rule 144(k), it ceases to be a PORTAL security.

A broker or dealer who wishes to participate in the PORTAL Market must register with the NASD as a PORTAL broker or a PORTAL dealer by demonstrating its eligibility. An investor who wishes to participate in the PORTAL Market, directly or indirectly, must also register, execute a subscriber agreement and demonstrate it is a "qualified institutional buyer" or "qualified buyer" under Rule 144A.

PORTAL participants may apply to the NASD to designate PORTAL securities that meet prescribed qualification requirements. The application can be filed with or without the concurrence of the issuer.

The advantage of the PORTAL Market is that qualified securities can be traded by the participants without the delays and paperwork usually required for sales of securities subject to Rule 144, Rule 144A, Regulation S or the Section 4 transaction exemptions because the participants and the securities have been precleared. If a PORTAL security is sold outside the PORTAL Market, the usual requirements again apply.

J. Liability for Sale of a Business by the Stock Purchase Method

As discussed in other chapters, when a business is sold by a merger, sale of stock or sale of assets, the buyer usually performs a due diligence review

[35]See 63 Fed. Reg. 9632 (Feb. 25, 1998) for amendments that, among other things, classify securities sold by domestic issuers under Regulation S as "restricted securities" under Rule 144. However, they must be held for a 1 year "distribution compliance period" rather than the 2 year period required by Rule 144. Issuers must report the issuance of securities under Regulation S in their next report on Form 10-Q or 10-K.

and the buyer and the seller negotiate and sign an extensive and detailed acquisition contract. The acquisition contract typically contains representations and warranties, covenants, conditions and indemnities for the protection of the buyer and seller that are negotiated in give-and-take bargaining. In lawsuits for breach of acquisition contracts, the courts decide issues of contract interpretation. However, having done so, the courts typically hold the buyer and seller to the rights and remedies they negotiated in the absence of proof of fraud, including its traditional elements such as *scienter* and reliance. This is appropriate because both the buyer and the seller are usually experienced in business and are advised by counsel, accountants, financial advisers and other consultants.

For decades, plaintiff attorneys, faced with losing cases under acquisition contracts, sought to persuade the federal courts to allow them to assert claims under the 1933 Act and the 1934 Act if the method used to sell a business was a sale of stock. Their objective was to bypass the acquisition contracts their clients negotiated and subject the seller to liability under laws enacted to protect the general public, which necessarily buys securities without any opportunity to perform due diligence or to negotiate a contract protecting their rights.

Recognizing the opportunistic nature of such claims, the federal courts developed a "sale of a business" doctrine that treated stock transactions in the same manner as mergers and asset sales and denied the one-sided remedies of the federal securities laws to buyers who privately negotiated the acquisition of a business by the stock purchase method. Leading decisions by the U.S. Supreme Court emphasizing substance over form provided ample support for the "sale of a business" doctrine.[36]

In 1985, the U.S. Supreme court turned away from its previous emphasis on substance over form. In *Landreth Lumber Company v. Landreth*,[37] the Supreme Court rejected the "sale of a business" doctrine and held that the buyer of a sawmill business could sue under the federal securities laws because the business was sold by the stock purchase method.[38] The Supreme Court reached its decision in *Landreth* although the transaction was a private acquisition of an entire business, the buyer had an audit and an inspection of the business conducted and a stock purchase agreement was negotiated.

In response to the *Landreth* decision, sellers of businesses by the stock purchase method often prepare a memorandum similar to a private placement memorandum containing a full description of the business and its financial statements. The memorandum is prepared to function as a disclosure document, so that the plaintiff attorneys cannot later readily claim that material misstatements or omissions were made by the seller during the transaction.

---

[36]*SEC v. W.J. Howey Co.*, 328 U.S. 293 (1946); *United Housing v. Forman*, 421 U.S. 837 (1975).

[37]471 U.S. 681 (1985), Justice Stevens dissenting. See also *Gould v. Ruefenacht*, 471 U.S. 701 (1985).

[38]The *Landreth* decision may be reconciled with the prior decisions by observing that the *Howey* decision was in favor of the SEC, a federal government agency, and the *United Housing* decision was in favor of a popular federal government program. In *Landreth*, the parties seeking a similar interpretation were private businesspeople, perceived as "deep pockets."

K. Blue Sky Laws

For decades, corporations selling securities to raise acquisition financing were required to consider registration or available exemptions under the blue sky laws of the states where the securities would be offered. Many states have exemptions for listed securities and other securities meeting quality standards, as well as various kinds of private offering exemptions. It has been customary to obtain an opinion of counsel, called a Blue Sky Survey, to determine the applicable state requirements and the states where securities can lawfully be offered and sold.

In 1996, the U.S. Congress adopted the Capital Markets Efficiency Act (CMEA) as Title I of the National Securities Markets Improvement Act of 1996. The CMEA amended Section 18 of the 1934 Act to prohibit the states from requiring registration of, and imposing conditions on, offers of "covered securities," except that the states may continue to require notices and impose fees on such offerings. "Covered securities" are (1) securities listed on the NYSE or AMEX or quoted in the NASDAQ, NMS and securities of the same issuer that are equal in seniority or senior to such securities; (2) securities issued by an investment company registered under the Investment Company Act of 1940; (3) securities offered and sold to "qualified purchasers"; and (4) certain securities that are exempt or are offered and sold in exempt transactions under the 1933 Act. The SEC is instructed to define the term "qualified purchaser" by rule, but had not yet done so when this book was written.

The CMEA created national securities markets and made a fundamental change in the historical shared regulation of securities offerings by federal and state authorities. The effect is that state authorities will in the future regulate only public offerings made by small issuers. However, the states continue to retain jurisdiction to investigate and bring enforcement actions for fraud or deceit, or for unlawful conduct by a broker or dealer, in connection with securities or securities transactions.

L. Reference Materials

1. Books

AICPA Statements of Auditing Standards, Commerce Clearing House

American Stock Exchange Guide, Commerce Clearing House

Blue-Sky Law Reporter, Commerce Clearing House

Blue-Sky Practice, Fass, Clark Boardman Callaghan

Company Guide, American Stock Exchange

Exempted Transactions under the Securities Act of 1933, Hicks, Clark Boardman Callaghan

Federal Securities Law Reporter, Commerce Clearing House

Financial Accounting Standards Board, Original Pronouncements, Accounting Standards, John Wiley & Sons, Inc.

Going Public Handbook, Bloomenthal, Clark Boardman Callaghan

How to Prepare an Initial Public Offering, Practicing Law Institute

The Limited Offering Exemptions: Regulation D, Hicks, Clark Boardman Callaghan

Listed Company Manual, New York Stock Exchange

Mechanics of Underwriting, Practicing Law Institute

NASAA Reports, Commerce Clearing House

NASD Manual, Commerce Clearing House

New York Stock Exchange Guide, Commerce Clearing House

Resales of Restricted Securities, Hicks, Clark Boardman Callaghan

Securities Law Handbook, Bloomenthal, Clark Boardman Callaghan

Securities Regulation, Jennings, Marsh, Coffee and Seligman, Foundation Press, 1998

Article

"SEC Registration of Public Offerings under the Securities Act of 1933," Barker, *The Business Lawyer*, 1996

M. Exhibits

11-1. Example of an Independent Auditor's Report
11-2. Registration Statement Form S-4
11-3. Legend Restricting Transfer of Restricted Securities
11-4. Form of Subscription Agreement
11-5. Example of Contractual Registration Rights Provisions
11-6. Form of Accredited Investor Questionnaire

EXHIBIT 11-1

REPORT OF INDEPENDENT PUBLIC ACCOUNTANTS

To Guangshen Railway Company Limited,

We have audited the accompanying Combined Balance Sheets of Guangshen Railway Company Limited and its subsidiaries (Note 1) (established in the People's Republic of China—"PRC") as of December 31, 1994 and 1995, and the related Combined Statements of Income and Cash Flows for the years ended December 31, 1993, 1994 and 1995, expressed in PRC Renminbi. These financial statements are the responsibility of the management of Guangshen Railway Company Limited and its subsidiaries. Our responsibility is to express an opinion on these Combined Financial Statements based on our audit.

We conducted our audit in accordance with auditing standards established by the Hong Kong Society of Accountants, which are substantially similar to generally accepted auditing standards in the United States of America. Those standards require that we plan and perform the audit to obtain reasonable assurance about whether the financial statements are free of material misstatement. An audit includes examining, on a test basis, evidence supporting the amounts and disclosures in the financial statements. An audit also includes assessing the accounting principles used and significant estimates made by management, as well as evaluating the overall financial statement presentation. We believe that our audit provides a reasonable basis for our opinion.

In our opinion, the Combined Financial Statements referred to above present fairly, in all material respects, the financial position of Guangshen Railway Company Limited and its subsidiaries as of December 31, 1994 and 1995, and the results of their operations and their cash flows for the years ended December 31, 1993, 1994 and 1995 in conformity with International Accounting Standards.

Arthur Andersen & Co.

Hong Kong
April 11, 1996

EXHIBIT 11-2

OMB APPROVAL	
OMB Number:	3235-0324
Expires:	June 30, 1997
Estimated average burden hours per response . . .	1472

UNITED STATES
SECURITIES AND EXCHANGE COMMISSION
Washington, D.C. 20549

FORM S-4

REGISTRATION STATEMENT UNDER THE SECURITIES ACT OF 1933

____
(Exact name of registrant as specified in its charter)

____
(State or other jurisdiction of incorporation or organization)

____
(Primary Standard Industrial Classification Code Number)

____
(I.R.S. Employer Identification Number)

____
(Address, including zip code, and telephone number, including area code, of registrant's principal executive offices)

____
(Name, address, including zip code, and telephone number, including area code, of agent for service)

Approximate date of commencement of proposed sale of the securities to the public: ____________________

If the securities being registered on this Form are being offered in connection with the formation of a holding company and there is compliance with General Instruction G, check the following box ☐

CALCULATION OF REGISTRATION FEE

Title of each class of securities to be registered	Amount to be registered	Proposed maximum offering price per unit	Proposed maximum aggregate offering price	Amount of registration fee

Note: Specific details relating to the fee calculation shall be furnished in notes to the table, including references to provisions of Rule 457 (§230.457 of this chapter) relied upon, if the basis of the calculation is not otherwise evident from the information presented in the table.

GENERAL INSTRUCTIONS

A. **Rule as to Use of Form S-4.**

1. This Form may be used for registration under the Securities Act of 1933 ("Securities Act") of securities to be issued (1) in a transaction of the type specified in paragraph (a) of Rule 145 (§230.145 of this chapter); (2) in a merger in which the applicable state law would not require the solicitation of the votes or consents of all of the security holders of the company being acquired; (3) in an exchange offer for securities of the issuer or another entity; (4) in a public reoffering or resale of any such securities acquired pursuant to this registration statement; or (5) in more than one of the kinds of transaction listed in (1) through (4) registered on one registration statement.

2. If the registrant meets the requirements of and elects to comply with the provisions in any item of this Form or Form F-4 (§239.34 of this chapter) that provides for incorporation by reference of information about the registrant or the company being acquired, the prospectus must be sent to the security holders no later than 20 business days prior to the date on which the meeting of such security holders is held or, if no meeting is held, the earlier of 20 business days

EXHIBIT 11-2

prior to (1) the date of such vote, consent or authorization, or (2) the date the transaction is consummated or the votes, consents or authorizations may be used to effect the transaction. Attention is directed to Sections 13(e), 14(d) and 14(e) of the Securities Exchange Act of 1934 ("Exchange Act") the rules and regulations thereunder regarding other time periods in connection with exchange offers and going private transactions.

3. This Form shall not be used if the registrant is a registered investment company or a business development company as defined in Section 2(a)(48) of the Investment Company Act of 1940.

B. Information with Respect to the Registrant.

1. Information with respect to the registrant shall be provided in accordance with the items referenced in one of the following subparagraphs:

   a. Items 10 and 11 of this Form, if the registrant elects this alternative and meets the following requirements of Form S-3 (§239.13 of this chapter) (hereinafter, with respect to the registrant, "meets the requirements for use of Form S-3") for this offering of securities:

      (i) the registrant meets the requirements of General Instructions I.A. of Form S-3; and

      (ii) one of the following is met:

         A. The registrant meets the aggregate market value requirement of General Instruction I.B.1. of Form S-3; or

         B. Non-convertible debt or preferred securities are to be offered pursuant to this registration statement and are "investment grade securities" as defined in General Instruction I.B.2. of Form S-3; or

         C. The registrant is a majority-owned subsidiary and one of the conditions of General Instruction I.C. of Form S-3 is met.

   b. Items 12 and 13 of this Form, if the registrant meets the requirements for use of Form S-2 (§239.12 of this chapter) or Form S-3 and elects this alternative; or

   c. Item 14 of this Form, if the registrant does not meet the requirements for use of Form S-2 or S-3, or if it otherwise elects this alternative.

2. If the registrant is a real estate entity of the type described in General Instruction A to Form S-11 (§239.18 of this chapter), the information prescribed by Items 12, 13, 14, 15 and 16 of Form S-11 shall be furnished about the registrant in addition to the information provided pursuant to Items 10 through 14 of this Form. The information prescribed by such Items of Form S-11 may be incorporated by reference into the prospectus if (a) a registrant qualifies for and elects to provide information pursuant to alternative 1.a. or 1.b. of this instruction and (b) the documents incorporated by reference pursuant to such elected alternative contain such information.

C. Information With Respect to the Company Being Acquired.

1. Information with respect to the company whose securities are being acquired (hereinafter including, where securities of the registrant are being offered in exchange for securities of another company, such other company) shall be provided in accordance with the items referenced in one of the following subparagraphs:

   a. Item 15 of this Form, if the company being acquired meets the requirements of General Instructions I.A. and I.B.1. of Form S-3 (hereinafter, with respect to the company being acquired, "meets the requirements for use of Form S-3") of Form S-3 and this alternative is elected;

   b. Item 16 of this Form, if the company being acquired meets the requirements for use of Form S-2 or S-3 and this alternative is elected; or

   c. Item 17 of this Form, if the company being acquired does not meet the requirements for use of Form S-2 or S-3 or if this alternative is otherwise elected.

EXHIBIT 11-2

2. If the company being acquired is a real estate entity of the type described in General Instruction A to Form S-11, the information that would be required by Items 13, 14, 15 and 16(a) of Form S-11 if securities of such company were being registered shall be furnished about such company being acquired in addition to the information provided pursuant to this Form. The information prescribed by such Items of Form S-11 may be incorporated by reference into the prospectus if (a) the company being acquired would qualify for use of the level of disclosure prescribed by alternative 1.a. or 1.b. of this instruction and such alternative is elected and (b) the documents incorporated by reference pursuant to such elected alternative contain such information.

D. Application of General Rules and Regulations.

1. Attention is directed to the General Rules and Regulations under the Securities Act, particularly those comprising Regulation C thereunder (§230.400 et seq. of this chapter). That Regulation contains general requirements regarding the preparation and filing of registration statements.

2. Attention is directed to Regulation S-K (Part 229 of this chapter) for the requirements applicable to the content of nonfinancial statement portions of registration statements under the Securities Act. Where this Form directs the registrant to furnish information required by Regulation S-K and the item of Regulation S-K so provides, information need only be furnished to the extent appropriate.

3. A "small business issuer," defined in §230.405, shall refer to the disclosure items in Regulation S-B (17 CFR 228.10 *et seq.*) and not Regulation S-K except with respect to disclosure called for by subpart 900 of Regulation S-K. Small business issuers shall provide or incorporate by reference the information called for by Item 310 of Regulation S-B.

4. (a) Registrants and Companies to be Acquired that are eligible to use Form SB-1 may rely upon Part (b) or (c), as applicable, of this instruction in lieu of the narrative disclosure items set forth in this Form. These Registrants and Companies to be Acquired should look to Part F/S of Form SB-1 with respect to their financial statement requirements.

   (b) Registrants and Companies to be Acquired which relied upon Alternative 1 in their most recent Form 10-KSB:

      (i) Part 1.A. — furnish the information required by Part 1.A. of this Form;

      (ii) Part I.B. — in lieu of the information required in Item 14, furnish the information required in (a) Questions 3, 4, 11, 43 and 47 – 50 of Model A of Form 1-A, and (b) Item 14(d) and 14(i) of this Form;

      (iii) Part 1.C. — in lieu of the information required in Item 17, furnish the information required in (a) Item 17(a), 17(b)(1), 17(b)(2), 17(b)(6), 17(b)(7) and 17(b)(8) of this Form, and (b) Questions 4, 11 and 47 – 50 of Model A of Form 1-A;

      (iv) Part 1.D. — (*1*) in lieu of providing the information required in Item 18, furnish the information required in (a) Items 18(a)(1) – 18(a)(6) and (b) Questions 29 – 36 and 39 – 42 of Model A of Form 1-A; and (*2*) in lieu of providing the information required in Item 19(a), furnish the information required in (a) Items 19(a)(1) – 19(a)(6) of this Form and Questions 29 – 36 and 39 – 42 of Model A of Form 1-A; (*3*) in lieu of providing the information required in Item 19(b), furnish the information required in (a) Items 19(a)(4) – 19(a) (6) of this Form and Questions 29 – 36 and 39 – 42 of Model A of Form 1-A.

      (v) Part II — in lieu of the exhibits required by Item 21(a) and 21(b), furnish the exhibits required in Part II of Form SB-1.

   (c) Registrants and Companies to be Acquired which relied upon Alternative 2 in their most recent Form 10-KSB:

      (i) Part 1.A. — furnish the information required by Part 1.A. of this Form;

      (ii) Part 1.B. — in lieu of the information required in Item 14, furnish the information required in (a) Items 6 and 7 of Model B of Form 1-A, and (b) Items 14(c), (d), and (i) of this Form;

      (iii) Part 1.C. — in lieu of the information required in Item 17, furnish the information required in (a) Item 17(a), 17(b)(1), 17(b)(2), 17(b)(6), 17(b)(7) and 17(b)(8) of this Form, and (b) Item 6(a)(3)(i) of Model B of Form 1-A;

EXHIBIT 11-2

(iv) Part 1.D. — *(1)* in lieu of providing the information required in Item 18, furnish the information required in (a) Items 18(a)(1) – 18(a)(6) and (b) Items 8, 9 and 11 of Model B of Form 1-A; (2) in lieu of providing the information required in Item 19(a), furnish the information required in (a) Items 19(a)(1) – 19(a)(6) of this Form and Items 8, 9 and 11 of Model B of Form 1-A; and *(3)* in lieu of providing the information required in Item 19(b), furnish the information required in (a) Items 19(a)(4) – 19(a)(6) of this Form and Questions Items 8, 9 and 11 of Model B of Form 1-A.

(v) Part II — in lieu of the exhibits required by Item 21(a) and 21(b), furnish the exhibits required in Part II of Form SB-1.

E. Compliance with Exchange Act Rules.

1. If a corporation or other person submits a proposal to its security holders entitled to vote on, or consent to, the transaction in which the securities being registered are to be issued, and such person's submission to its security holders is subject to Regulation 14A (§§240.14a-1) through 14b-1 of this chapter) or 14C (§§240.14c-1 through 14c-101 of this chapter) under the Exchange Act, then the provisions of such Regulations shall apply in all respects to such person's submission, except that (a) the prospectus may be in the form of a proxy or information statement and may contain the information required by this Form in lieu of that required by Schedule 14A (§240.14a-101) or 14C (§240.14c-101) of Regulation 14A or 14C under the Exchange Act; and (b) copies of the preliminary and definitive proxy or information statement, form of proxy or other material filed as a part of the registration statement shall be deemed filed pursuant to such person's obligations under such Regulations.

2. If the proxy or information material sent to security holders is not subject to Regulation 14A or 14C, all such material shall be filed as a part of the registration statement at the time the statement is filed or as an amendment thereto prior to the use of such material.

3. If the transaction in which the securities being registered are to be issued is subject to Section 13(e), 14(d) or 14(e) of the Exchange Act, the provisions of those sections and the rules and regulations thereunder shall apply to the transaction in addition to the provisions of this Form.

F. Transactions Involving Foreign Private Issuers.

If a U.S. registrant is acquiring a foreign private issuer, as defined by Rule 405 (§230.405 of this chapter), such registrant may use this Form and may present information about the foreign private issuer pursuant to Form F-4. If the registrant is a foreign private issuer, such registrant may use Form F-4 and

1. If the company being acquired is a foreign private issuer, may present information about such foreign company pursuant to Form F-4 or

2. If the company being acquired is a U.S. company, may present information about such company pursuant to this Form.

G. Filing and Effectiveness of Registration Statement Involving Formation of Hold-Companies; Requests for Confidential Treatment; Number of Copies

Original registration statements on this Form S-4 will become effective automatically on the twentieth day after the date of filing (Rule 456, §230.456 of this chapter), pursuant to the provisions of Section 8(a) of the Act (Rule 459, §230.459 of this chapter) provided:

1. The transaction in connection with which securities are being registered involves the organization of a bank or savings and loan holding company for the sole purpose of issuing common stock to acquire all of the common stock of the company that is organizing the holding company; and

2. The following conditions are met:

   a. the financial institution furnishes its security holders with an annual report that includes financial statements prepared on the basis of generally accepted accounting principles;

EXHIBIT 11-2

b. there are no anticipated changes in the security holders' relative equity ownership interest in the underlying company's assets except for redemption of no more than a nominal number of shares of unaffiliated persons who dissent;

c. in the aggregate, only nominal borrowings are to be incurred for such purposes as organizing the holding company to pay non-affiliated persons who dissent, or to meet minimum capital requirements;

d. there are no new classes of stock authorized other than those corresponding to the stock of the company being acquired immediately prior to the reorganization;

e. there are no plans or arrangements to issue any additional shares to acquire any business other than the company being acquired; and

f. there has been no material adverse change in the financial condition of the company being acquired since the latest fiscal year end included in the annual report to security holders.

Pre-effective amendments with respect to such a registration statement may be filed prior to effectiveness, and such amendments will be deemed to have been filed with the consent of the Commission (Rule 475a, §230.475 of this chapter). Accordingly, the filing of a pre-effective amendment to such a registration statement will not commence a new twenty-day period. Post-effective amendments to such a registration statement on this Form shall become effective upon the date of filing (Rule 464, §230.464 of this chapter). Delaying amendments are not permitted in connection with either original filings or amendments on such a registration statement (Rule 473(d) §230.473(d) of this chapter), and any attempt to interpose a delaying amendment of any kind will be ineffective. All filings made on or in connection with this Form pursuant to this instruction become public upon filing with the Commission. As a result, requests for confidential treatment made under Rule 406 (§230.406 of this chapter) must be processed by the Commission's staff prior to the filing of such a registration statement. The number of copies of such a registration statement and of each amendment required by Rules 402 and 472 (§§230.402, 472 of this chapter) shall be filed with the Commission; *provided, however,* that the number of additional copies referred to in Rule 402(b) may be reduced from ten to three and the number of additional copies referred to in Rule 472(a) may be reduced from eight to three, one of which shall be marked to clearly and precisely indicate changes.

H. Registration Statements Subject to Rule 415(a)(1)(viii) (§230.415(a)(1)(viii) of this chapter)

If the registration statement relates to offerings of securities pursuant to Rule 415(a)(1)(viii), required information about the type of contemplated transaction or the company to be acquired only need be furnished as of the date of initial effectiveness of the registration statement to the extent practicable. The required information about the specific transaction and the particular company being acquired, however, must be included in the prospectus by means of a post-effective amendment: *Provided, however,* that where the transaction in which the securities are being offered pursuant to a registration statement under the Securities Act of 1933 would itself qualify for an exemption from Section 5 of the Act, absent the existence of other similar (prior or subsequent) transactions, a prospectus supplement could be used to furnish the information necessary in connection with such transaction.

I. Roll-Up Transactions.

1. If securities to be registered on this Form will be issued in a roll-up transaction as defined in Item 901(c) of Regulation S-K (17 CFR 229.901(c)), then the disclosure provisions of Subpart 229.900 of Regulation S-K (17 CFR 229.900) shall apply to the transaction in addition to the provisions of this Form. To the extent that the disclosure requirements of Subpart 229.900 are inconsistent with the disclosure requirements of any other applicable forms or schedules, the requirements of Subpart 229.900 are controlling.

2. If securities to be registered on this Form will be issued in a roll-up transaction as defined in Item 901(c) of Regulation S-K (17 CFR 229.901(c)), the prospectus must be distributed to security holders no later than the lesser of 60 calendar days prior to the date on which action is to be taken or the maximum number of days permitted for giving notice under applicable state law.

J. Where two or more classes of securities being registered on the form are to be offered on a delayed or continuous basis pursuant to §230.415(a)(1)(viii), §230.457(*o*) under the Securities Act permits the registration fee to be calculated on the basis of the maximum offering price of all the securities listed in the "Calculation of Registration Fee" Table ("Fee

EXHIBIT 11-2

Table"). In this event, while the Fee Table would list each of the classes of securities being registered and the aggregate proceeds to be raised, the Fee Table need not specify by each class information as to the amount to be registered, proposed maximum offering price per unit, and proposed maximum aggregate offering price.

PART I
INFORMATION REQUIRED IN THE PROSPECTUS

A. INFORMATION ABOUT THE TRANSACTION

Item 1. Forepart of Registration Statement and Outside Front Cover Page of Prospectus.

Set forth in the forepart of the registration statement and on the outside front cover page of the prospectus the information required by Item 501 of Regulation S-K (§229.501 of this chapter).

Item 2. Inside Front and Outside Back Cover Pages of Prospectus.

Set forth on the inside front cover page of the prospectus or, where permitted, on the outside back cover page. the information required by Item 502 of Regulation S-K (§229.502 of this chapter). In addition, on the inside front cover page include the following statement in bold face type, where applicable:

> This prospectus incorporates documents by reference which are not presented herein or delivered herewith. These documents are available upon request from (name, address and telephone number to which a request is to be directed). In order to ensure timely delivery of the documents, any request should be made by (date five business days prior to the date on which the final investment decision must be made.)

Item 3. Risk Factors, Ratio of Earnings to Fixed Charges and Other Information.

Provide in the forepart of the prospectus a summary containing the information required by Item 503 of Regulation S-K (§229.503 of this chapter) and the following:

(a) The name, complete mailing address (including the Zip Code), and telephone number (including the area code) of the principal executive offices of the registrant and the company being acquired;

(b) A brief description of the general nature of the business conducted by the registrant and by the company being acquired;

(c) A brief description of the transaction in which the securities being registered are to be offered;

(d) The information required by Item 301 of Regulation S-K (§229.301 of this chapter) (selected financial data) for (i) the registrant; (ii) the company being acquired; and (iii) if material, the registrant, on a pro forma basis, giving effect to the transaction. To the extent the information is required to be presented in the prospectus pursuant to Items 12, 14, 16 or 17, it need not be repeated pursuant to this Item;

(e) If material, the information required by Item 301 of Regulation S-K for the registrant on a pro forma basis, giving effect to the transaction. To the extent the information is required to be presented in the prospectus pursuant to Items 12 or 14, it need not be repeated pursuant to this Item.

(f) In comparative columnar form, historical and pro forma per share data of the registrant and historical and equivalent pro forma per share data of the company being acquired for the following items:

  (1) book value per share as of the date financial data is presented pursuant to Item 301 of Regulation S-K (§229.301 of this chapter) (selected financial data);

  (2) Cash dividends declared per share for the periods for which financial data is presented pursuant to Item 301 of Regulation S-K (§229.301 of this chapter) (selected financial data);

EXHIBIT 11-2

(3) income (loss) per share from continuing operations for the periods for which financial data is presented pursuant to Item 301 of Regulation S-K (§229.301 of this chapter) (selected financial data).

Instruction to paragraph (e) and (f).

For a business combination accounted for as a purchase, the financial information required by paragraphs (e) and (f) shall be presented only for the most recent fiscal year and interim period. For a business combination accounted for as a pooling, the financial information required by paragraphs (e) and (f) (except for information with regard to book value) shall be presented for the most recent three fiscal years and interim period. For a business combination accounted for as a pooling, information with regard to book value shall be presented as of the end of the most recent fiscal year and interim period. Equivalent pro forma per share amounts shall be calculated by multiplying the pro forma income (loss) per share before nonrecurring charges or credits directly attributable to the transaction, pro forma book value per share, and the pro forma dividends per share of the registrant by the exchange ratio so that the per share amounts are equated to the respective values for one share of the company being acquired.

(g) In comparative columnar form, the market value of securities of the company being acquired (on an historical and equivalent per share basis) and the market value of the securities of the registrant (on an historical basis) as of the date preceding public announcement of the proposed transaction, or, if no such public announcement was made, as of the day preceding the day the agreement with respect to the transaction was entered into;

(h) With respect to the registrant and the company being acquired, a brief statement comparing the percentage of outstanding shares entitled to vote held by directors, executive officers and their affiliates and the vote required for approval of the proposed transaction;

(i) A statement as to whether any federal or state regulatory requirements must be complied with or approval must be obtained in connection with the transaction, and if so, the status of such compliance or approval;

(j) A statement about whether or not dissenters' rights of appraisal exist, including a cross-reference to the information provided pursuant to Item 18 or 19 of this Form; and

(k) A brief statement about the tax consequences of the transaction, or if appropriate, consisting of a cross-reference to the information provided pursuant to Item 4 of this Form.

Item 4. Terms of the Transaction.

(a) Furnish a summary of the material features of the proposed transaction. The summary shall include, where applicable:

(1) A brief summary of the terms of the acquisition agreement;

(2) The reasons of the registrant and of the company being acquired for engaging in the transaction;

(3) The information required by Item 202 of Regulation S-K (§229.202 of this chapter), description of registrant's securities, unless: (i) the registrant would meet the requirements for use of Form S-3, (ii) capital stock is to be registered and (iii) securities of the same class are registered under Section 12 of the Exchange Act and (i) listed for trading or admitted to unlisted trading privileges on a national securities exchange; or (ii) are securities for which bid and offer quotations are reported in an automated quotations system operated by a national securities association;

(4) An explanation of any material differences between the rights of security holders of the company being acquired and the rights of holders of the securities being offered;

(5) A brief statement as to the accounting treatment the transaction; and

(6) The federal income tax consequences of the transaction.

(b) If a report, opinion or appraisal materially relating to the transaction has been received from an outside party, and such report, opinion or appraisal is referred to in the prospectus, furnish the same information as would be required by Item 9(b)(1) through (6) of Schedule 13E-3 (§240.Be-100 of this chapter).

Exhibit 11-2

(c) Incorporate the acquisition agreement by reference into the prospectus by means of a statement to that effect.

Item 5. Pro Forma Financial Information.

Furnish financial information required by Article 11 of Regulation S-X (§210.11-01 et. sq. of this chapter) with respect to this transaction.

Instruction.

1. Any other Article 11 information that is presented (rather than incorporated by reference) pursuant to other Items of this Form shall be presented together with the information provided pursuant to Item 5, but the presentation shall clearly distinguish between this transaction and any other.

2. If pro forma financial information with respect to all other transactions is incorporated by reference pursuant to Item 11 or 15 of this Form only the pro forma results need be presented as part of the pro forma financial information required by this Item.

Item 6. Material Contracts with the Company Being Acquired.

Describe any past, present or proposed material contracts, arrangements, understandings, relationships, negotiations or transactions during the periods for which financial statements are presented or incorporated by reference pursuant to Part I.B. or C. of this Form between the company being acquired or its affiliates and the registrant or its affiliates, such as those concerning: a merger, consolidation or acquisition; a tender offer or other acquisition of securities; an election of directors; or a sale or other transfer of a material amount of assets.

Item 7. Additional Information Required for Reoffering by Persons and Parties Deemed to Be Underwriters.

If any of the securities are to be reoffered to the public by any person or party who is deemed to be an underwriter thereof, furnish the following information in the prospectus, at the time it is being used for the reoffer of the securities to the extent it is not already furnished therein:

(a) The information required by Item 507 of Regulation S-K (§229.507 of this chapter), selling security holders; and

(b) Information with respect to the consummation of the transaction pursuant to which the securities were acquired and any material change in the registrant's affairs subsequent to the transaction.

Item 8. Interests of Named Experts and Counsel.

Furnish the information required by Item 509 of Regulation S-K (§229.509 of this chapter).

Item 9. Disclosure of Commission Position on Indemnification for Securities Act Liabilities.

Furnish the information required by Item 510 of Regulation S-K (§229.510 of this chapter).

B. INFORMATION ABOUT THE REGISTRANT

Item 10. Information with Respect to S-3 Registrants.

If the registrant meets the requirements for use of Form S-3 and elects to furnish information in accordance with the provisions of this Item, furnish information as required below:

(a) Describe any and all material changes in the registrant's affairs that have occurred since the end of the latest fiscal year for which audited financial statements were included in the latest annual report to security holders and that have not beer described in a report on Form 10-Q (§249.308a of this chapter) or Form 8-K (§249.308 of this chapter) filed under the Exchange Act.

(b) Include in the prospectus, if not incorporated by reference from the reports filed under the Exchange Act specified in Item 11 of this Form, a proxy or information statement filed pursuant to Section 14 of the Exchange Act, a prospectus

EXHIBIT 11-2

previously filed pursuant to Rule 424 under the Securities Act (§230.424 of this chapter), or a Form 8-K filed during either of the two preceding fiscal years:

(1) Financial information required by Rule 3-05 (§210.3-05 of this chapter) and Article 11 of Regulation S-X with respect to transactions other than that pursuant to which the securities being registered are to be issued;

(2) Restated financial statements prepared in accordance with Regulation S-X (Part 210 of this chapter), if there has been a change in accounting principles or a correction of an error where such change or correction requires a material retroactive restatement of financial statements;

(3) Restated financial statements prepared in accordance with Regulation S-X where one or more business combinations accounted for by the pooling of interest method of accounting have been consummated subsequent to the most recent fiscal year and the acquired businesses, considered in the aggregate, are significant pursuant to Rule 11-01(b) of Regulation S-X (§210.11-01(b) of this chapter); or

(4) Any financial information required because of a material disposition of assets outside the normal course of business.

Item 11. Incorporation of Certain Information by Reference.

If the registrant meets the requirements of Form S-3 and elects to furnish information in accordance with the provisions of Item 10 of this Form:

(a) Incorporate by reference into the prospectus, by means of a statement to that effect listing all documents so incorporated, the documents listed in paragraphs (1), (2) and, if applicable, (3) below.

(1) The registrant's latest annual report on Form 10-K (§249.310 of this chapter) filed pursuant to Section 13(a) or 15(d) of the Exchange Act which contains financial statements for the registrant's latest fiscal year for which a Form 10-K was required to be filed;

(2) All other reports filed pursuant to Section 13(a) or 15(d) of the Exchange Act since the end of the fiscal year covered by the annual report referred to in Item 11(a)(1) of this Form; and

(3) If capital stock is to be registered and securities of the same class are registered under Section 12 of the Exchange Act and: (i) listed for trading or admitted to unlisted trading privileges on a national securities exchange; or (ii) are securities for which bid and offer quotations are reported in an automated quotations system operated by a national securities association, the description of such class of securities which is contained in a registration statement filed under the Exchange Act, including any amendment or reports filed for the purpose of updating such description.

(b) The prospectus also shall state that all documents subsequently filed by the registrant pursuant to Sections 13(a), 13(c), 14 or 15(d) of the Exchange Act, prior to one of the following dates, whichever is applicable, shall be deemed to be incorporated by reference into the prospectus:

(1) If a meeting of security holders is to be held, the date on which such meeting is held;

(2) If a meeting of security holders is not to be held, the date on which the transaction is consummated;

(3) If securities of the registrant are being offered in exchange for securities of any other issuer, the date the offering is terminated; or

(4) If securities are being offered in a reoffering or resale of securities acquired pursuant to this registration statement, the date the reoffering is terminated.

Instruction.

Attention is directed to Rule 439 (§230.439 of this chapter) regarding consent to the use of material incorporated by reference.

EXHIBIT 11-2

Item 12. Information with Respect to S-2 or S-3 Registrants.

If the registrant meets the requirements for use of Form S-2 or S-3 and elects to comply with this Item, furnish the information required by either paragraph (a) or paragraph (b) of this Item. The information required by paragraph (b) shall be furnished if the registrant satisfies the conditions of paragraph (c) of this Item.

(a) If the registrant elects to deliver this prospectus together with a copy of either its latest Form 10-K or Form 10-KSB filed pursuant to Sections 13(a) or 15(d) of the Exchange Act or its latest annual report to security holders, which at the time of original preparation met the requirements of either Rule 14a-3 or Rule 14c-3:

(1) Indicate that the prospectus is accompanied by either a copy of the registrant's latest Form 10-K or Form 10-KSB or a copy of its latest annual report to security holders, whichever the registrant elects to deliver pursuant to paragraph (a) of this Item.

(2) Provide financial and other information with respect to the registrant in the form required by Part I of Form 10-Q or 10-QSB as of the end of the most recent fiscal quarter which ended after the end of the latest fiscal year for which certified financial statements were included in the latest Form 10-K or Form 10-KSB or the latest report to security holders (whichever the registrant elects to deliver pursuant to paragraph (a) of this Item), and more than forty-five days prior to the effective date of this registration statement (or as of a more recent date) by one of the following means:

(i) including such information in the prospectus;

(ii) providing without charge to each person to whom a prospectus is delivered a copy of the registrant's latest Form 10-Q or Form 10-QSB; or

(iii) providing without charge to each person to whom a prospectus is delivered a copy of the registrant's latest quarterly report that was delivered to its security holders and which included the required financial information.

(3) If not reflected in the registrant's latest Form 10-K or Form 10-KSB or its latest annual report to security holders (whichever the registrant elects to deliver pursuant to paragraph (a) of this Item) provide information required by Rule 3-05 (§210.3-05 of this chapter) and Article 11 (§210.11-01 through §210.11.03 of this chapter) of Regulation S-X.

(4) Describe any and all material changes in the registrant's affairs which have occurred since the end of the latest fiscal year for which audited financial statements were included in the latest Form 10-K or 10-KSB or the latest annual report to security holders (whichever the registrant elects to deliver pursuant to paragraph (a) of this Item) and that were not described in a Form 10-Q, Form 10-QSB or quarterly report delivered with the prospectus in accordance with paragraphs (a)(2)(ii) or (iii) of this Item.

Instruction.

Where the registrant elects to deliver the documents identified in paragraph (a) with a preliminary prospectus, such documents need not be redelivered with the final prospectus.

(b) If the registrant does not elect to deliver its latest Form 10-K or Form 10-KSB or its latest annual report to security holders:

(1) Furnish a brief description of the business done by the registrant and its subsidiaries during the most recent fiscal year as required by Rule 14a-3 to be included in an annual report to security holders. The description also should take into account changes in the registrant's business that have occurred between the end of the latest fiscal year and the effective date of the registration statement.

(2) Include financial statements and information as required by Rule 14a-3(b)(1) (240.14a-3(b)(1) of this chapter) to be included in an annual report to security holders. In addition, provide:

(1) the interim financial information required by Rule 10-01 of Regulation S-X (§210.10-01 of this chapter) for a filing on Form 10-Q;

EXHIBIT 11-2

(ii) financial information required by Rule 3-05 and Article 11 of Regulation S-X with respect to transactions other than that pursuant to which the securities being registered are to be issued;

(iii) restated financial statements prepared in accordance with Regulation S-X if there has been a change in accounting principles or a correction of an error where such change or correction requires a material retroactive restatement of financial statements;

(iv) Restated financial statements prepared in accordance with Regulation S-X where one or more business combinations accounted for by the pooling of interest method of accounting have been consummated subsequent to the most recent fiscal year and the acquired businesses, considered in the aggregate, are significant pursuant to Rule 11-01(b) of Regulation S-X; and

(v) Any financial information required because of a material disposition of assets outside of the normal course of business.

(3) Furnish the information required by the following:

(i) Item 101(b), (c)(1)(i) and (d) of Regulation S-K (§229.101 of this chapter), industry segments, classes of similar products or services, foreign and domestic operations and export sales;

(ii) where common equity securities are being offered, Item 201 of Regulation S-K (§229.201 of this chapter), market price of and dividends on the registrant's common equity and related stockholder matters;

(iii) Item 301 of Regulation S-K (§229.301 of this chapter), selected financial data;

(iv) Item 302 of Regulation S-K (§229.302 of this chapter), supplementary financial information;

(v) Item 303 of Regulation S-K (§229.303 of this chapter), management's discussion and analysis of financial condition and results of operations; and

(vi) Item 304 of Regulation S-K (§229.304 of this chapter), changes in and disagreements with accountants on accounting and financial disclosure.

(c) The registrant shall furnish the information required by paragraph (b) of this Item if;

(1) the registrant was required to make a material retroactive restatement of financial statements because of

(i) a change in accounting principles; or

(ii) a correction of an error; or

(iii) a consummation of one or more business combinations accounted for by the pooling of interest method of accounting was effected subsequent to the most recent fiscal year and the acquired businesses considered in the aggregate meet the test of a significant subsidiary; OR

(2) the registrant engaged in a material disposition of assets outside the normal course of business; AND

(3) such restatement of financial statements or disposition of assets was not reflected in the registrant's latest annual report to security holders and/or its latest Form 10-K or Form 10-KSB filed pursuant to Sections 13(a) or 15(d) of the Exchange Act.

Item 13. Incorporation of Certain Information by Reference.

If the registrant meets the requirements of Form S-2 or S-3 and elects to furnish information in accordance with the provisions of Item 12 of this Form:

(a) Incorporate by reference into the prospectus, means of a statement to that effect in the prospectus listing all documents so incorporated, the documents listed in paragraphs (1) and (2) of this Item and, if applicable, the portions of the documents listed in paragraphs (3) and (4) thereof.

EXHIBIT 11-2

(1) The registrant's latest annual report on Form 10-K filed pursuant to Section 13(a) or 15(d) of the Exchange Act which contains audited financial statements for the registrant's latest fiscal year for which a Form 10-K was required to be filed.

(2) All other reports filed pursuant to Section 13(a) or 15(d) of the Exchange Act since the end of the fiscal year covered by the annual report referred to in paragraph (a)(1) of this Item.

(3) If the registrant elects to deliver its latest annual report to security holders pursuant to Item 12 of this Form, the information furnished in accordance with the following:

(i) Item 101(b), (c)(1)(i) and (d) of Regulation S-K, segments, classes of similar products or services, foreign and domestic operations and export sales;

(ii) Where common equity securities are being issued, Item 201 of Regulation S-K, market price of and dividends on the registrant's common equity and related stockholder matters;

(iii) Item 301 of Regulation S-K, selected financial data;

(iv) Item 302 of Regulation S-K, supplementary financial information;

(v) Item 303 of Regulation S-K, management's discussion and analysis of financial condition and results of operations; and

(vi) Item 304 of Regulation S-K, changes in and disagreements with accountants on accounting and financial disclosure.

(4) If the registrant elects, pursuant to Item 12(a)(2)(iii) of this Form, to provide a copy of its latest quarterly report which was delivered to security holders, financial information equivalent to that required to be presented in Part I of Form 10-Q.

Instruction.

Attention is directed to Rule 439 regarding consent to the use of material incorporated by reference.

(b) The registrant also may state, if it so chooses, that specifically described portions of its annual or quarterly report to security holders, other than those portions required to be incorporated by reference pursuant to paragraphs (a)(3) and (4) of this Item, are not part of the registration statement. In such case, the description of portions that are not incorporated by reference or that are excluded shall be made with clarity and in reasonable detail.

(c) *Electronic filings.* Electronic filers electing to deliver and incorporate by reference all, or any portion, of the quarterly or annual report to security holders pursuant to this Item shall file as an exhibit such quarterly or annual report to security holders, or such portion thereof that is incorporated by reference, in electronic format.

Item 14. Information with Respect to Registrants Other Than S-3 or S-2 Registrants.

If the registrant does not meet the requirements for use of Form S-2 or S-3, or otherwise elects to comply with this Item in lieu of Item 10 or 12, furnish the information required by:

(a) Item 101 of Regulation S-K, description of business;

(b) Item 102 of Regulation S-K, description of property;

(c) Item 103 of Regulation S-K, legal proceedings;

(d) Where common equity securities are being issued, Item 201 of Regulation S-K, market price of and dividends on the registrant's common equity and related stockholder matters;

(e) Financial statements meeting the requirements of Regulation S-X, (schedules required by Regulation S-X shall be filed as "Financial Statement Schedules" pursuant to Item 21 of this Form), as well as financial information required

EXHIBIT 11-2

by Rule 3-05 and Article 11 of Regulation S-X with respect to transactions other than that pursuant to which the securities being registered are to be issued.

(f) Item 301 of Regulation S-K, selected financial data;

(g) Item 302 of Regulation S-K, supplementary financial information;

(h) Item 303 of Regulation S-K, management's discussion and analysis of financial condition and results of operations; and

(i) Item 304 of Regulation S-K, changes in and disagreements with accountants on accounting and financial disclosure.

C. INFORMATION ABOUT THE COMPANY BEING ACQUIRED

Item 15. Information with Respect to S-3 Companies.

If the company being acquired meets the requirements for use of Form S-3 and compliance with this Item is elected, furnish the information that would be required by Items 10 and 11 of this Form if securities of such company were being registered.

Item 16. Information with Respect to S-2 or S-3 Companies.

(a) If the company being acquired meets the requirements for use of Form S-2 or S-3 and compliance with this Item is elected, furnish the information that would be required by Items 12 and 13 of this Form if securities of such company were being registered.

(b) *Electronic filings.* In addition to satisfying the requirements of paragraph (a) of this Item, electronic filers that elect to deliver and incorporate by reference all, or any portion, of the quarterly or annual report to security holders of a company being acquired pursuant to this Item shall file as an exhibit such quarterly or annual report to security holders, or such portion thereof that is incorporated by reference, in electronic format.

Item 17. Information with Respect to Companies Other Than S-3 or S-2 Companies.

If the company being acquired does not meet the requirements for use of Form S-2 or S-3, or compliance with this Item is otherwise elected in lieu of Item 15 or 16, furnish the information required by paragraph (a) or (b) of this Item, whichever is applicable.

(a) If the company being acquired is subject to the reporting requirements of Section 13(a) or 15(d) of the Exchange Act, or compliance with this subparagraph in lieu of subparagraph (b) of this Item is selected, furnish the information that would be required by Item 14 of this Form if the securities of such company were being registered; *however*, only those schedules required by Rules 12-15, 28 and 29 of Regulation S-X (§210.12-15, 28, 29 of this chapter) need be provided with respect to the company being acquired.

(b) If the company being acquired is not subject to the reporting requirements of either Section 13(a) or 15(d) of the Exchange Act; or, because of Section 12(i) of the Exchange Act, has not furnished an annual report to security holders pursuant to Rule 14a-3 (§240.14a-3 of this chapter) or Rule 14c-3 (§240.14c-3 of this chapter) for its latest fiscal year; furnish the information that would be required by the following if securities of such company were being registered:

(1) a brief description of the business done by the company which indicates the general nature and scope of the business;

(2) Item 201 of Regulation S-K, market price of and dividends on the registrant's common equity and related stockholder matters;

(3) Item 301 of Regulation S-K, selected financial data;

(4) Item 302 of Regulation S-K, supplementary financial information;

EXHIBIT 11-2

(5) Item 303 of Regulation S-K, management's discussion and analysis of financial condition and results of operations:

(6) Item 304(b) of Regulation S-K (§229.304 of this chapter), changes in and disagreements with accountants on accounting and financial disclosure;

(7) financial statements as would have been required to be included in an annual report furnished to security holders pursuant to Rules 14a-3(b)(1) and (b)(2) (§240.14a-3 of this chapter) or Rules 14c-3(a)(1) and (a)(2) (§240.14c-3 of this chapter), had the company being acquired been required to prepare such a report; *Provided, however,* that the balance sheet for the year preceding the latest full fiscal year and the income statements for the two years preceding the latest full fiscal year need not be audited if they have not previously been audited. In any case, such financial statements need only be audited to the extent practicable. If this Form is used for resales to the public by any person who with regard to the securities being reoffered is deemed to be an underwriter within the meaning of Rule 145(c), the financial statements of such companies must be audited for the periods required to be presented pursuant to Rule 3-05.

(8) the quarterly financial and other information as would have been required had the company being acquired been required to file Part I of Form 10-Q (§249.308a) for the most recent quarter for which such a report would have been on file at the time the registration statement becomes effective or for a period ending as of a more recent date.

(9) schedules required by Rules 12-15, 28 and 29 of Regulation S-X.

D. VOTING AND MANAGEMENT INFORMATION

Item 18. Information if Proxies, Consents or Authorizations are to be Solicited.

(a) If proxies, consents or authorizations are to be solicited, furnish the following information, except as provided by paragraph (b) of this Item:

(1) The information required by Item 1 of Schedule 14A, date, time and place information;

(2) The information required by Item 2 of Schedule 14A, revocability of proxy;

(3) The information required by Item 3 of Schedule 14A, dissenters' rights of appraisal;

(4) The information required by Item 4 of Schedule 14A, persons making the solicitation;

(5) With respect to both the registrant and the company being acquired, the information required by:

(i) Item 5 of Schedule 14A, interest of certain persons in matters to be acted upon; and

(ii) Item 6 of Schedule 14A, voting securities and principal holders thereof;

(6) The information required by Item 21 of Schedule 14A, vote required for approval; and

(7) With respect to each person who will serve as a director or an executive officer of the surviving or acquiring company, the information required by:

(i) Item 401 of Regulation S-K (§229.401 of this chapter), directors and executive officers;

(ii) Item 402 of Regulation S-K (§229.402 of this chapter), executive compensation; and

(iii) Item 404 of Regulation S-K (§229.404 of this chapter), certain relationships and related transactions.

(b) If the registrant or the company being acquired meets the requirements for use of Form S-2 or S-3, any information required by paragraphs (a)(5)(ii) and (7) of this Item with respect to such company may be incorporated by reference from its latest annual report on Form 10-K.

EXHIBIT 11-2

Item 19. Information if Proxies, Consents or Authorizations are not to be Solicited or in an Exchange Offer.

(a) If the transaction is an exchange offer or if proxies, consents or authorizations are not to be solicited, furnish, where applicable, the following information, except as provided by paragraph (c) of this item;

(1) The information required by Item 2 of Schedule 14C, statement that proxies are not to be solicited;

(2) The date, time and place of the meeting of security holders, unless such information is otherwise disclosed in material furnished to security holders with the prospectus.

(3) The information required by Item 3 of Schedule 14A, dissenters' rights of appraisal;

(4) With respect to both the registrant and the company being acquired, a brief description of any material interest, direct or indirect, by security holdings or otherwise, of affiliates of the registrant and of the company being acquired, in the proposed transaction;

Instruction.

This subparagraph shall not apply to any interest arising from the ownership of securities of the registrant where the security holder receives no extra or special benefit not shared on a pro rata basis by all other holders of the same class.

(5) With respect to both the registrant and the company being acquired, the information required by Item 6 of Schedule 14A, voting securities and principal holders thereof;

(6) The information required by Item 21 of Schedule 14A, vote required for approval;

(7) With respect to each person who will serve as a director or an executive officer of the surviving or acquiring company the information required by:

(i) Item 401 of Regulation S-K, directors and executive officers;

(ii) Item 402 of Regulation S-K, executive compensation; and

(iii) Item 404 of Regulation S-K, certain relationships and related transactions.

(b) If the transaction is an exchange offer, furnish the information required by paragraphs (a)(4), (a)(5), and (a)(7) of this Item, except as provided by paragraph (c) of this Item.

(c) If the registrant or the company being acquired meets the requirements for use of Form S-2 or S-3, any information required by paragraphs (a)(5) and (7) of this Item with respect to such company may be incorporated by reference from its latest annual report on Form 10-K.

PART II
INFORMATION NOT REQUIRED IN PROSPECTUS

Item 20. Indemnification of Directors and Officers.

Furnish the information required by Item 702 of Regulation S-K (§229.702 of this chapter).

Item 21. Exhibits and Financial Statement Schedules.

(a) Subject to the rules regarding incorporation by reference, furnish the exhibits as required by Item 601 of Regulation S-K (§229.601 of this chapter).

(b) Furnish the financial statement schedules required by Regulation S-X and Item 14(e), Item 17(a) or Item 17(b)(9) of this Form. These schedules should be lettered or numbered in the manner described for exhibits in paragraph (a) of this Item.

Exhibit 11-2

statement. Attention is directed to Rule 402 (§230.402 of his chapter) concerning manual signatures and Item 601 concerning signatures pursuant to powers of attorney.

3. If the securities to be offered are those of a corporation not yet in existence at the time the registration statement is filed which will be a party to a consolidation involving two or more existing corporations, then each such existing corporation shall be deemed a registrant and shall be so designated on the cover page of this Form, and the registration statement shall be signed by each such existing corporation and by the officers and directors of each such existing corporation as if each such existing corporation were the registrant.

11-7. Form 144

EXHIBIT 11-3

RESTRICTIVE LEGEND

The shares of Common Stock represented by this certificate have not been registered under the Securities Act of 1933 or any state securities law and were issued under an exemption that depends, among other things, on the holder's acquisition of the shares for investment and without any view to, or resale in connection with, any public distribution of the shares. The shares represented by this certificate may not be sold or transferred except pursuant to a registration statement ordered effective by the Securities and Exchange Commission or after delivery to the Company of either a "no action" letter of the

SUBSCRIPTION AGREEMENT
(U.S. Persons)

THIS SUBSCRIPTION AGREEMENT is made between __________________, a Delaware corporation (the "Corporation"), and the person executing this Subscription Agreement as the Investor ("Investor").

1. General. This Subscription Agreement states the terms under which Investor will subscribe for and purchase shares of Common Stock, par value $.01 (the "Shares") of the Corporation offered by the Confidential Private Offering Memorandum dated __________ __, 19__ (the "Memorandum"), receipt of which is hereby acknowledged by Investor.

This subscription is one of a limited number of subscriptions for Shares of the Corporation. Execution of this Subscription Agreement by the Investor is an offer by the Investor to the Corporation to subscribe. The Corporation may accept such offer by executing and delivering a copy of this Subscription Agreement to Investor.

2. Subscription Amount and Payment. Investor hereby subscribes for _____ Shares at a price of $______ per Share. A check in the amount of $_______ for the full subscription price is enclosed or such amount is being wire transferred concurrently.

3. Investor's Representations and Warranties. Investor represents and warrants to the Corporation that (a) Investor is acquiring the Shares for his own account for investment and not with a view to public resale or other distribution; (b) Investor is an "accredited investor" as defined in the regulations of the Securities and Exchange Commission ("SEC") under the Securities Act of 1933 (the "Act"); (c) Investor has consulted with financial and legal advisors to the extent Investor regards appropriate; and (d) Investor is able to bear the substantial economic risk of investment in the Shares and at the present time could afford a complete loss of such investment if that should occur.

Investor understands that he or she must bear the economic risk of this investment for an indefinite period of time because the Shares are not registered under the Act or the securities laws of any state. Investor agrees that the Shares shall not be resold or transferred unless subsequently registered under the Act and any applicable state laws requiring registration or unless exemptions from such registration are available. Investor

EXHIBIT 11-4

agrees that the Corporation may endorse and maintain the following legend on all certificates representing his or her Shares:

> "THE SHARES REPRESENTED BY THIS CERTIFICATE HAVE BEEN ISSUED WITHOUT REGISTRATION UNDER THE SECURITIES ACT OF 1933 OR ANY STATE SECURITIES LAW AND WERE ACQUIRED FOR INVESTMENT AND NOT WITH A VIEW TO, OR IN CONNECTION WITH, THE SALE OR DISTRIBUTION THEREOF. NO SALE OR TRANSFER OF SUCH SHARES MAY BE EFFECTED IN THE ABSENCE OF AN EFFECTIVE REGISTRATION STATEMENT OR AN OPINION OF COUNSEL SATISFACTORY IN FORM AND SUBSTANCE TO THE CORPORATION THAT SUCH REGISTRATION IS NOT REQUIRED UNDER THE SECURITIES ACT OF 1933 OR ANY STATE LAW"

Investor represents and warrants that the Shares will be purchased solely for his own account and with his own funds and not, wholly or partially, for any other person or persons. If Investor is a partnership, Investor further represents it was not organized for the purpose of acquiring the Shares.

Investor represents and warrants that the address set forth below is the true and correct residence of Investor. Investor has no present intention of becoming a resident of any other state or jurisdiction.

Investor represents and warrants that he or she has reviewed the Memorandum and Investor acknowledges that no person is authorized to give any information or to make any statement inconsistent with the information contained in the Memorandum and that any such information or statement must not be relied upon as having been authorized by the Corporation.

Investor acknowledges that he or she had the opportunity to ask questions and receive answers from the Corporation to the extent they desired. Investor further acknowledges that he or she were invited to review documents, records and books pertaining to this investment at the offices of the Corporation, ____________________, New York, New York.

Investor acknowledges that the Shares have not been approved or disapproved by the Securities and Exchange Commission, or any other federal or state agency, nor has such agency passed upon the accuracy or adequacy of the Memorandum.

Investor represents and warrants that:

(a) He or she has not entered into any agreement or arrangement with any other person or entity regarding:

EXHIBIT 11-4

(i) the acquisition, voting, or disposition of the Shares;

(ii) the election of directors of the Corporation;

(iii) the management or operations of the Corporation;

(iv) the acquisition of additional shares of the Corporation; or

(v) the appointment of officers of the Corporation.

(b) His or her investment in the Shares is not conditioned upon the acquisition of Shares by any other person or entity.

(c) He or she is not acquiring the Shares in concert with any other person or entity.

4. Responsibility, Indemnification. Investor shall indemnify and hold harmless the Corporation and its directors, officers, advisers and affiliates, any professional advisors thereto, from and against any and all loss, damage, liability and expense, including reasonable attorneys' fees, which each of them may incur in connection with any misrepresentation made by Investor or his failure to fulfill any of his agreements in this Subscription Agreement.

5. Miscellaneous.

(a) This Subscription Agreement shall be governed by the laws of New York.

(b) This Subscription Agreement contains the entire agreement between the parties with respect to the purchase of the Shares by Investor. The provisions of this Subscription Agreement may not be modified or waived except in writing.

(c) This Subscription Agreement shall, except as set forth herein, bind and inure to the benefit of the heirs, executors, administrators, legal representatives, successors and assigns of the parties hereto. Investor may not assign any of Investor's rights or interests in and under this Subscription Agreement

EXHIBIT 11-4

without the prior written consent of the Corporation and any attempted assignment without such written consent shall be void and without effect.

____

________________, Witness

____
Signature of Investor

____
Social Security or Federal I.D. Number
(Please Print)

ACCEPTED:

By:______________________
President

____
Name of Investor's Attorney
(Please print)

____
Name of Investor's Other Advisers with respect to this Investment (Please print)

Commission or an opinion of counsel in form or substance acceptable to the Company that the proposed transfer is lawful in the absence of such registration.

Exhibit 11-4

Exhibit 11-5

Registration Rights

INTRODUCTORY COMMENT: Registration rights for unregistered securities issued to sellers in acquisition transactions and to investors in private placements need not be as extensive as those contained in underwriter's warrants for an initial public offering. Shares issuable upon exercise of underwriter's warrants are deemed to be acquired with a view to distribution and must be sold pursuant to a registration statement without regard to the holding period of the warrants and/or the shares. On the other hand, unless issued to a person who becomes an affiliate of the issuer, unregistered shares issued in acquisition transactions and in private placements by issuers registered under the Securities Exchange Act of 1934 can be sold in limited amounts after one year and without restriction after two years. They can also be sold pursuant to Rule 144A to qualified institutional buyers.

* * *

Section 9. Registration Rights

A. Rights upon Written Demand. For a Period of Two Years after the Closing Date. Shareholders holding at least 51% of the Shares shall be entitled to furnish a written notice to the Corporation demanding registration of their Shares under the Securities Act of 1933, as amended (the "Securities Act"). Subject to the limitations stated hereinafter, upon receipt of such notice, the Corporation shall prepare and file as soon as practicable a registration statement with the Securities and Exchange Commission ("SEC") with respect to such Shares and shall use its best efforts to cause such registration statement to become effective. The Shareholders shall be entitled to only one registration statement under this Section 10A. The Corporation shall not be required to file any registration statement hereunder if it will then be required by the SEC to include audited financial statements as of any date or dates other than its fiscal year end dates.

B. Piggyback Registration Rights. For a period of two years after the Closing Date, if the Corporation shall plan to file a registration statement on Form S-1 or S-3 with the SEC for a primary or secondary offering of its securities, it shall give prompt written notice to each of the Shareholders describing the offering and the proposed registration statement and offering to include the Shares held by such Shareholder in the registration statement. To the extent that the Shareholders shall furnish written acceptance of such offers to the Corporation within 15 days thereafter, the Corporation shall include their Shares in the registration statement and shall use its best efforts to cause it to become effective. Any such offer and its acceptance shall not, however, obligate the Corporation to file the registration statement or prevent the Corporation from withdrawing the registration statement if it shall decide for any reason to discontinue the offering of its securities for which the registration statement was planned. Further, if the managing underwriter for such offering shall furnish written advice to the Corporation that the member of Shares requested for inclusion in the registration statement would adversely affect its ability to make the offering, the Corporation shall be entitled to reduce the number of Shares so included on a pro rata basis among the Shareholders.

C. Other Obligations of the Corporation. In addition to the obligations in subsections A and B of this Section, the Corporation shall perform the following obligations:

(1) Prepare and file applications to register or qualify the Shares included in the registration statement under the Blue Sky Laws of such states and other jurisdictions as the Shareholders reasonably request and use its best efforts to cause such applications to become effective, but such applications shall not be required when the Corporation must qualify to do business or file a general consent to service of process in connection therewith.

(2) Furnish to the Shareholders reasonable numbers of the prospectus included in the registration statement and file such prospectus with the SEC and the NASDAQ Stock Market, Inc.

(3) Prepare and file with the SEC and state securities authorities such post-effective amendments to the registration statement as shall be required from time to time in order to maintain it in effect and in compliance with all applicable requirements of the Securities Act and the rules and regulations of the SEC thereunder until the Shareholders whose Shares were included in the registration statement have completed their distribution thereof.

(4) Provide reasonable cooperation with the due diligence and other requirements of the managing underwriter of any underwritten offering by the Shareholders of Shares included in the registration statement including, without limitation, becoming a party to the underwriting agreement in order to assure the managing underwriter of such corporation.

(5) Pay all expenses relating to its registration and other obligations under this Section other than any underwriting discounts or commissions, documentary or transfer taxes, and fees and disbursements of counsel for the Shareholders.

D. Obligations of the Shareholders. The Shareholders who request that their Shares be included in a registration statement pursuant to this Section shall perform the following obligations:

(1) Furnish to the Corporation for inclusion in the registration statement such information about themselves, the Shares held by them, and the proposed method of distribution of their Shares as shall be required by the Securities Act and the rules and regulations of the SEC.

(2) If the distribution of the Shares will be made by a "shelf offering" from time to time at prices prevailing in the NASDAQ Steels Market, the Shareholder, will retain a coordinating broker-dealer and shall comply with all laws and regulations applicable to the distribution including, without limitation, Regulation M.

(3) Notify the Corporation promptly when each Shareholder completes the distribution of his or her Shares included in the registration statement.

* * *

Note: The foregoing provisions are typically followed by standard cross-indemnity provisions against liabilities related to the registration statement and the sale of the securities to the extent that such indemnities may be valid under the Securities Act.

EXHIBIT 11-6

Accredited Investor Questionnaire

Number of Shares ____________________

Total Investment ____________________

1. Name: ____________________ Age: ____________________

   Number of Dependents: ____________________

   Social Security Number: ____________________

   Name of Spouse: ____________________

2. Home Address (Include Street, City,

   State and Zip Code: ____________________

   ____

3. Name of Employer: ____________________

   Nature of Business: ____________________

   Position: ____________________

   Length of Time in Present Position: ____________________

   Business Telephone Number: (Area Code) ____________________

   Business Address (Include Street, City,

   State and Zip Code): ____________________

   ____

4. List Each Employment Position or Business Occupation during Last 10 Years, Giving Dates and Description of Principal Responsibilities: ____________________

   ____

   ____

5. List Business or Professional Education, Indicating Degrees Received: ____________________

   ____

   ____

   ____

6. Please Identify Each Company Which You Serve or Have Served as a Member of the Board of Directors or General Partner during the Last Ten (10) Years and the Term of Service: ____________________

   ____

   ____

   ____

7. My Net Worth is in Excess of $1,000,000 including my Home, Furnishings and Automobiles.

   Yes ____________________ No ____________________

8. My Income* for 19— and 19— Exceeded $200,000 in Each Year and I Reasonably Expect Income in 19— Exceeding $200,000.

   Yes ____________________ No ____________________

*Income under this test is defined as adjusted gross income for federal income tax purposes plus (i) deductions for depletion under § 611 *et seq.* of the Internal Revenue Code; (ii) any exclusion for interest under § 103 of the Internal Revenue Code; and (iii) any deductible losses of a partnership allocated to the individual limited partners of the partnership as reported on Schedule E of Form 1040.

9. My Income* with the Income of My Spouse for 19— and 19— Exceeded $300,000 in Each Year and I Reasonably Expect My Income with the Income of My Spouse in 19— to Exceed $300,000.

Yes ____________ No ____________

10. I Have Previously Participated in Other Private Placements of Securities.

Yes ____________ No ____________

If Yes, Which of the Following Types of Investments:

Banking	Yes ____	No ____
Industrial	Yes ____	No ____
Oil & Gas	Yes ____	No ____
Real Estate	Yes ____	No ____
Other	Yes ____	No ____

11. Please List the Names of Any Financial Advisers, Accountants or Attorneys with Whom You Have Reviewed the Proposed Investment:

Name: ____________

Firm: ____________

Profession or Occupation: ____________

Address (Including Street, City, State & Zip Code): ____________

____

Telephone No: (Area Code) ____________

Name: ____________

Firm: ____________

Profession or Occupation ____________

Address (Including Street, City, State & Zip Code): ____________

____

Telephone No.: (Area Code) ____________

12. Do You Have Any Other Investments or Contingent Liabilities Which You Can Reasonably Anticipate Could Cause the Need for Sudden Cash Requirements in Excess of Cash Readily Available to You?

Yes ____________ No ____________

13. I Acknowledge Receipt of the Confidential Private Placement Memorandum Dated ________, 19__ Offering ________ Shares of ________ Common Stock (the "Shares") of ____________. I Acknowledge That the Shares Have Not Been Registered under the Securities Act of 1933 or the Securities Act of Any State and That the Corporation is Relying upon Exemptions which Depend, In Part, on the Accuracy and Completeness of the Information Contained in this Questionnaire.

14. I Represent and Warrant as Follows:

a) I am acquiring the shares for my own account for investment, and not with a view toward resale or other distribution;

b) I have sufficient knowledge and experience in business, tax and financial matters to evaluate the merits and risks of an investment in the shares and have consulted with the advisers listed above in connection with my decision to purchase the shares, and;

c) I am able to bear the economic risk of investment in the shares at the present time, and could afford a complete loss of the investment;

d) The answers to the above questions are complete and correct and may be relied upon by the Corporation in determining whether the offering of the shares is exempt from registration under the Securities Act of 1933 and in complying with applicable state securities laws;

e) I will notify the Corporation immediately of any material change in any statement made herein occurring prior to my purchase of the shares.

____________ ____________

Signature of Witness Signature of Investor

____________ ____________

Print Name of Witness Print Name of Investor

EXHIBIT 11-7

OMB APPROVAL
OMB Number: 3235-0101
Expires: September 30, 1998
Estimated average burden hours per response 2.0

SEC USE ONLY
DOCUMENT SEQUENCE NO.
CUSIP NUMBER
WORK LOCATION

UNITED STATES
SECURITIES AND EXCHANGE COMMISSION
Washington, D.C. 20549

FORM 144

NOTICE OF PROPOSED SALE OF SECURITIES PURSUANT TO RULE 144 UNDER THE SECURITIES ACT OF 1933

ATTENTION: *Transmit for filing 3 copies of this form concurrently with either placing an order with a broker to execute sale or executing a sale directly with a market maker.*

1 *(a)* NAME OF ISSUER *(Please type or print)*	*(b)* IRS IDENT. NO.	*(c)* S.E.C. FILE NO.

1 *(d)* ADDRESS OF ISSUER	STREET	CITY	STATE	ZIP CODE	*(e)* TELEPHONE NO. AREA CODE	NUMBER

2 *(a)* NAME OF PERSON FOR WHOSE ACCOUNT THE SECURITIES ARE TO BE SOLD	*(b)* SOCIAL SECURITY NO. OR IRS IDENT. NO.	*(c)* RELATIONSHIP TO ISSUER	*(d)* ADDRESS STREET	CITY	STATE	ZIP CODE

INSTRUCTION: The person filing this notice should contact the issuer to obtain the I.R.S. Identification Number and the S.E.C. File Number.

3 *(a)* Title of the Class of Securities To Be Sold	*(b)* Name and Address of Each Broker Through Whom the Securities are to be Offered or Each Market Maker who is Acquiring the Securities	SEC USE ONLY Broker-Dealer File Number	*(c)* Number of Shares or Other Units To Be Sold *(See instr. 3(c))*	*(d)* Aggregate Market Value *(See instr. 3(d))*	*(e)* Number of Shares or Other Units Outstanding *(See instr. 3(e))*	*(f)* Approximate Date of Sale *(See instr. 3(f))* (MO. DAY YR.)	*(g)* Name of Each Securities Exchange *(See instr. 3(g))*

INSTRUCTIONS:

1. (a) Name of issuer
   (b) Issuer's I.R.S. Identification Number
   (c) Issuer's S.E.C. file number, if any
   (d) Issuer's address, including zip code
   (e) Issuer's telephone number, including area code

2. (a) Name of person for whose account the securities are to be sold
   (b) Such person's Social Security or I.R.S. identification number
   (c) Such person's relationship to the issuer (e.g., officer, director, 10% stockholder, or member of immediate family of any of the foregoing)
   (d) Such person's address, including zip code

3. (a) Title of the class of securities to be sold
   (b) Name and address of each broker through whom the securities are intended to be sold
   (c) Number of shares or other units to be sold (if debt securities, give the aggregate face amount)
   (d) Aggregate market value of the securities to be sold as of a specified date within 10 days prior to the filing of this notice
   (e) Number of shares or other units of the class outstanding, or if debt securities the face amount thereof outstanding, as shown by the most recent report or statement published by the issuer
   (f) Approximate date on which the securities are to be sold
   (g) Name of each securities exchange, if any, on which the securities are intended to be sold

SEC 1147 (5-96)

EXHIBIT 11-7

TABLE I — SECURITIES TO BE SOLD

Furnish the following information with respect to the acquisition of the securities to be sold and with respect to the payment of all or any part of the purchase price or other consideration therefor:

Title of the Class	Date you Acquired	Nature of Acquisition Transaction	Name of Person from Whom Acquired *(If gift, also give date donor acquired)*	Amount of Securities Acquired	Date of Payment	Nature of Payment

INSTRUCTIONS:

1. If the securities were purchased and full payment therefor was not made in cash at the time of purchase, explain in the table or in a note thereto the nature of the consideration given. If the consideration consisted of any note or other obligation, or if payment was made in installments describe the arrangement and state when the note or other obligation was discharged in full or the last installment paid.
2. If within two years after the acquisition of the securities the person for whose account they are to be sold had any short positions, put or other option to dispose of securities referred to in paragraph (d)(3) of Rule 144, furnish full information with respect thereto.

TABLE II — SECURITIES SOLD DURING THE PAST 3 MONTHS

Furnish the following information as to all securities of the issuer sold during the past 3 months by the person for whose account the securities are to be sold.

Name and Address of Seller	Title of Securities Sold	Date of Sale	Amount of Securities Sold	Gross Proceeds

REMARKS:

INSTRUCTIONS:
See the definition of "person" in paragraph (a) of Rule 144. Information is to be given not only as to the person for whose account the securities are to be sold but also as to all other persons included in that definition. In addition, information shall be given as to sales by all personswhose sales are required by paragraph (e) of Rule 144 to be aggregated with sales for the account of the person filing this notice.

ATTENTION:
The person for whose account the securities to which this notice relates are to be sold hereby represents by signing this notice that he does not know any material adverse information in regard to the current and prospective operations of the Issuer of the securities to be sold which has not been publicly disclosed.

____
DATE OF NOTICE

____
(SIGNATURE)

The notice shall be signed by the person for whose account the securities are to be sold. At least one copy of the notice shall be manually signed. Any copies not manually signed shall bear typed or printed signatures.

ATTENTION: Intentional misstatements or omission of facts constitute Federal Criminal Violations (See 18 U.S.C. 1001)

SEC 1147 (5-96)

Chapter 12

The Securities Regulation Laws—Tender Offers; "Going Private"; Proxy Solicitation and Contests

A. Introduction to the Securities Exchange Act of 1934

The Securities Exchange Act of 1934 (the "1934 Act") is a wide-reaching law regulating many organizations and activities. Many of its provisions do not directly affect acquisitions and divestitures. For example, the 1934 Act establishes the SEC; regulates the national securities exchanges and the NASD; requires registration of brokers and dealers and regulates their financial condition and conduct; requires registration of transfer agents and securities clearance agents and regulates their activities; sponsors development of modern, technology-oriented market systems; regulates dealers in federal, state and municipal securities; and prohibits certain payments to foreign government officials, political parties and candidates for office.

B. Registration of Securities under the 1934 Act

1. Registration of Listed Securities

Section 12(b) of the 1934 Act requires issuers to register with the SEC under the 1934 Act all securities listed for trading on a national stock exchange. Thus, securities issued to pay or to finance the purchase price of an acquisition must be registered under the 1934 Act if they will be listed on a national stock exchange.

2. Registration of Over-the-Counter Securities

Section 12(g) of the 1934 Act requires issuers of equity securities not listed on a national stock exchange to register them with the SEC under the 1934 Act if the issuer has total assets exceeding $1,000,000 and the equity securities are held of record by more than 500 persons. The SEC's Rule 12g-1 increased the assets threshold to $10,000,000. The registration requirement is linked to numerical criteria, but effectively requires registration of almost all equity securities actively traded in the over-the-counter market. The registration requirement applies, therefore, to equity securities issued to pay or to finance the purchase price of an acquisition.[1]

3. Registration Procedures

Registration under the 1934 Act is accomplished by filing a registration statement on Form 10 or Form 10-SB with the SEC. These forms call for disclosure similar to the disclosure required in a registration statement filed under the 1933 Act. Thus, much of the information can be incorporated by reference under Rule 12b-23. The registration statement becomes effective 60 days after the filing date, but the issuer can request the SEC to accelerate the effective date.

Issuers that already have securities registered under the 1934 Act can use a simpler form, Form 8-A, to register securities.

4. Periodic Reporting

Issuers with equity securities registered under the 1934 Act are subject to its disclosure requirements and periodic reporting system. The requirements include prompt disclosure of material events and filing of annual reports in Form 10-K, quarterly reports on Form 10-Q and current reports on Form 8-K.

Corporations must disclose material acquisitions and divestitures promptly to the public by announcement to media such as *The Wall Street Journal* and *Reuters* and to the stock exchange or NASDAQ market where their securities are traded. In general, mere planning or early negotiations need not, and perhaps should not, be disclosed. However, an announcement should not be usually be delayed until the acquisition contract is signed or necessarily even until an agreement in principle on the price and structure has been reached. The disclosure decision requires a balancing of the magnitude of the transaction with the probability that it will be closed. A transaction of major magnitude becomes material at an earlier stage than a small transaction, even though there may be uncertainty whether it will occur.[2]

Disclosure during negotiations becomes complicated if rumors begin to circulate and affect stock market prices. When this happens, a corporation will soon receive inquiries from the stock exchange or NASDAQ, the press and perhaps even the SEC. Under some circumstances, an initial refusal to comment may be justified.[3] However, the corporation should cooperate with the stock exchange or NASDAQ if it appears that any insider trading might be occurring. In no event should a corporation make the mistake of denying negotiations when negotiations are actually in progress. To avoid such an error, corporations should assure that public relations and shareholder relations personnel are kept aware of pending negotiations.

---

[1]The use of numerical criteria in the 1934 Act was a practical necessity because trading in the over-the-counter market occurs as a result of voluntary decisions by market makers to quote and trade equity securities.

[2]*Basic, Inc. v. Levinson*, 485 U.S. 224 (1988). See also *Weiner v. The Quaker Oates Co.*, 129 F.3d 310 (3d Cir. 1997).

[3]*Basic, Inc. v. Levinson*, supra; *SEC v. Geon Industries, Inc.*, 531 F.2d 39 (2d Cir. 1976).

Item 2 of the Current Report on Form 8-K requires the reporting of significant acquisitions or dispositions of assets. The terms *acquisition* and *disposition* are broadly defined to include events such as mergers and acquisitions or dispositions of securities that result in the control of assets. An aqcuisition or disposition involves a significant amount of assets (1) if the registrant and its subsidiaries equity in the net book value of such assets or the amount paid or received therefor exceeded 10 percent of the total assets of the registrant and such subsidiaries or (2) if it involved a business which is significant.

Item 7 of Form 8-K requires that audited financial statements of businesses' acquisitions described in answer to Item 2 be filed together with pro forma financial information and exhibits including the acquisition contracts. A manually signed accountants' report must also be provided in accordance with Rule 2-02 of Regulation S-X.

C. Listing for Trading on a Stock Exchange or for Quotation in the NASDAQ System

Securities issued to pay or finance the purchase price of an acquisition are usually listed for trading on the stock exchange where the acquiring corporation has other securities listed. If the acquiring corporation has other securities quoted in the NASDAQ System, securities issued to pay or finance an acquisition will usually be listed for quotation in that market.[4]

Listing is accomplished by filing a listing application with supporting exhibits. The application should demonstrate that the applicant meets the applicable listing criteria. A brief summary of key listing standards for common stock required of domestic issuers by the New York Stock Exchange, the American Stock Exchange and NASDAQ are presented here. Separate listing standards apply to foreign issuers.

Applicants should not assume that securities will routinely be approved for listing simply because they have been registered with the SEC or have met other regulatory requirements. The exchanges and the NASDAQ are quasi-regulatory agencies and apply their own criteria that must be met or the securities will not be listed. For example, the New York Stock Exchange has standards relating to outside directors, audit committees, voting rights and oversight of related party transactions that must be met, unless waived.[5]

When securities meet listing standards, the exchange or NASDAQ sends a letter approving them for listing or quotation upon official notice of issuance. Under appropriate circumstances, "when issued" trading has been allowed to begin before the actual issuance of securities.

[4]Acquiring corporations can issue securities that are not listed. However, persons receiving securities in acquisition and financing transactions usually negotiate contractual rights to listing in order to obtain the liquidity afforded by access to the trading market. Further, standard listing agreements typically require that all newly issued shares of a class of stock for which shares are listed must also be listed.

[5]The author once spent an entire day working with representatives of a leading accounting firm to persuade the New York Stock Exchange that "pooling of interests" accounting was appropriate for an acquisition for common stock. The SEC had not questioned use of the "pooling of interests method" and the accounting firm had determined the method to be appropriate. However, the Exchange conducted its own review.

Readers who want more information about listing standards and procedures can contact the following sources:

New York Stock Exchange, Inc.
11 Wall Street
New York, NY 10005
(212) 656-3000

The American Stock Exchange
86 Trinity Place
New York, NY 10006-1881
(212) 936-5100

National Association of Securities Dealers, Inc.
1735 K Street, N.W.
Washington, DC 20006-1500
(202) 728-8000

The NASDAQ Stock Market, Inc.
33 Whitehall Street
New York, NY 10004
(212) 858-4000

Listing Standards for Domestic Issuers

1. New York Stock Exchange (NYSE)

Assets:

Net tangible assets of $40,000,000

Earnings:

Pre-tax income of $2,500,000 in the most recent fiscal year and $2,000,000 in each of the 2 preceding fiscal years; or pre-tax income of $4,500,000 in the most recent fiscal year and $6,500,000 aggregate for the last 3 fiscal years with all 3 years profitable; or aggregate adjusted net income (i.e., operating cash flow) of $25,000,000 for the last 3 fiscal years with each year a positive amount and $500,000,000 market capitalization and $200,000,000 in revenues for the most recent year.

Market Capitalization:

$40,000,000

Public Shareholdings (Float):

1,100,000 shares and either 2,000 holders of "round lots," i.e., 100 shares, or 2,200 total shareholders and average monthly trading of at least 100,000 shares for 6 months, or 500 total shareholders and average monthly trading volume of 1,000,000 shares for 6 months.

Corporate Governance:

Two outside directors; audit committee with only outside director members; shareholder voting rights policies; internal review and oversight of related party transactions.

2. American Stock Exchange (AMEX)

Alternative One:

Stockholders Equity:

Stockholders' equity of $4,000,000

Earnings:

Pre-tax income of $750,000 in the most recent fiscal year or in 2 of the last 3 fiscal years.

Market Capitalization:

$3,000,000 based on a minimum market price of $3 per share

Public Shareholdings (Float):

500,000 shares held by 800 public shareholders, or 1,000,000 shares held by 400 public shareholders, or 500,000 shares held by 400 public shareholders and 2,000 shares average daily trading volume for 6 months if the shares are also regularly traded.

Corporate Governance:

Two outside directors; audit committee with a majority of outside directors (recommended); voting rights of common stock; scrutiny of companies engaged in gaming operations or exploration and development and companies dependent on one product or customer.

Alternative Two:

Operating History:

Three years

Stockholders' Equity:

$4,000,000

Public Shareholdings (Float):

Same as Alternative One.

Market Capitalization:

$15,000,000

Corporate Governance:

Same as Alternative One.

3. NASDAQ, National Market System

Alternative One:

Assets:

Net tangible assets of $6,000,000

Earnings:

Income before income tax of $1,000,000 in the most recent fiscal year or in 2 of the last 3 fiscal years.

Market Capitalization:

Not applicable.

Operating History:

Not applicable.

Public Shareholdings (Float):

1,100,000 shares held by 400 public shareholders (round lot holders) with a market value of $8,000,000.

Market Makers:

Three dealers acting as NASDAQ market makers and a price per share of $5.

Corporate Governance:

Voting rights and shareholders' approval policies.

Alternative Two:

Assets:

Net tangible assets of $18,000,000

Market Capitalization:

Not applicable.

Operating History:

Not applicable.

Earnings:

Two years

Public Shareholders (Float):

100,000 shares held by 400 public shareholders (round lot holders) with a market value of $18,000,000.

Market Makers:

Three dealers acting as NASDAQ market makers and price of $5 per share.

Corporate Governance:

Voting rights and shareholders' approval policies.

Alternative Three:

Assets:

Not applicable.

Market Capitalization or Total Assets and Total Revenues:

Market capitalization of $75,000,000 **or** total assets **and** total revenues of $75,000,000.

Earnings:

Not applicable.

Operating History:

Not applicable.

Public Shareholders

1,100,000 shares held by 400 public shareholders (round lot holders) with a market value of $20,000,000.

Market Makers:

Three dealers acting as NASDAQ market makers and price of $5 per share.

Corporate Governance:

Voting rights and shareholders' approval policies.

The NYSE, AMEX and NASDAQ have separate listing criteria for foreign issuers. NASDAQ also has more lenient criteria for shares traded in its Small Cap Market.

The NASD also provides an electronic OTC Bulletin Board (OTCBB) service for which it prescribes rules. See the *NASD Manual* (CCH), Rule 6500 *et seq.* The NASD also regulates the over-the-counter (OTC) market for securities quoted only in the "pink sheets" published by National Quotation Bureau, Inc. and requires that its members report transactions in OTC equity securities in its Automated Confirmation Transaction Service. See the *NASD Manual* (CCH), Rule 6600 *et seq.* There are no listing criteria for securities traded only in these markets.

An example of a Listing Application to the New York Stock Exchange, Inc. for shares issued in an acquisition transaction appears as Exhibit 12-1.

D. Tender Offers

1. How Tender Offers Are Made

A tender offer is a mechanism for acquiring shares by the stock purchase method.[6] The acquiring corporation makes an offer directly to the shareholders[7] of the corporation to be acquired, inviting them to tender their shares by delivering them to a bank depository[8] where they will be purchased if and when the conditions of the tender offer are met. Typical conditions in a tender offer include (1) the tender by shareholders of a minimum number or percentage of the outstanding shares, (2) approval or other favorable action by government agencies and (3) absence of litigation affecting the tender offer.

A tender offer is accomplished by mailing the offer to the shareholder with a form of transmittal letter for use by the shareholders in tendering their shares. Information explaining to the shareholders how they can tender shares held in "street name" and by a broker's guaranty of delivery is also included. The mailing also includes the Tender Offer Statement contained in the Schedule 14D-1 filed with the SEC, as described later in this

[6]The term *tender offer* is not defined in the 1934 Act. However, the characteristics of a public tender offer have been identified in court decisions such as *Wellman v. Dickinson*, 475 F. Supp. 783 (S.D.N.Y. 1979), aff'd 682 F.2d 355 (2nd Cir. 1982), cert. den. 460 U.S. 1069 (1983); *SEC v. Carter-Hawley Hale Stores, Inc.*, 760 F.2d 945 (9th Cir. 1985); and *Hanson Trust PLC v. SCM Corporation*, 774 F.2d 47 (2nd Cir. 1985).

[7]Tender offers are also made for debt and other securities. For brevity, this chapter describes tender offers as made for shares of common stock, except when special provisions apply to tender offers for other securities.

[8]Banks are most often selected to act as the depository, but other companies with appropriate authority and experience, such as American Stock Transfer & Trust Company and Registrar & Transfer Company, can also act as a depository.

chapter. Concurrently, a "tombstone" advertisement of the tender offer is published in *The Wall Street Journal* and other financial publications.

Upon receipt of the mailing, the shareholders read the Tender Offer Statement and consult with advisers to the extent they wish. Those shareholders who decide to accept list their stock certificates on the transmittal letter, sign the letter and obtain a signature guaranty. They send the transmittal letter with their stock certificate to the depository, which examines them for possible discrepancies. The depository then holds the tendered shares pending notice of the acquiring corporation's decision to purchase upon fulfillment of the conditions of the offer.

Tender offers usually allow a period of at least 30 days for shareholders to tender their shares. Most shareholders wait until a few days before the offer will expire to tender their shares. This allows time to see how the market reacts to the offer and whether any competitive offer is made. In practice, many shares are tendered at the "eleventh hour" by brokers' guarantees of delivery.

When the conditions to the tender offer are fulfilled, the acquiring corporation publicly announces and notifies the depository of its acceptance of the shares that it offered to purchase and pays the purchase price to the depository. The depository then pays the shareholders and delivers the shares accepted to the acquiring corporation. If the number of shares tendered exceeds the number accepted for purchase, the depository prorates the shares tendered, pays each shareholder for the shares accepted and returns to each shareholder his or her excess shares.[9]

2. Regulation of Tender Offers.

(a) Disclosure Schedules. The 1934 Act contains several provisions designed to regulate tender offers. The most important are the following disclosure requirements:

> *Schedule 13D:* Any person, or group of persons acting in concert, who acquires beneficial ownership of 5 percent or more of an issuer's equity securities registered under the 1934 Act must file a Schedule 13D with the SEC within 10 days after reaching that percentage and send copies to the issuer and each exchange where the securities are traded. The Schedule 13D must be amended and updated whenever the person or group acquires an additional 1 percent of the equity securities.
>
> *Schedule 14D-1:* No person, or group of persons, may commence a tender offer until such person or group has filed a Schedule 14D-1 with the SEC. The SEC's Rule 14d-2 states that a tender offer commences upon any announcement that identifies the target and refers to the price or number of shares to be acquired. Thus, a Schedule 14D-1 must sometimes be filed well before a tender offer is actually sent to the target's shareholders.

[9]As explained later in this chapter, the 1934 Act requires proration when the shares tendered exceed the shares purchased in a tender offer for equity securities registered under the 1934 Act.

> *Schedule 14D-9:* Management and certain other persons may not solicit or make any recommendation with respect to a tender offer unless on the date of the solicitation or recommendation they file a Schedule 14D-9 with the SEC and deliver copies to the bidder and to the exchanges where the securities are listed. Before filing a Schedule 14D-9, however, management may make a "stop, look and listen" communication in compliance with the SEC's Rule 14d-9. The typical communication states that management is evaluating the tender offer and possible alternatives and recommends that shareholders defer a decision whether to tender until management provides further information.

Schedule 13D. Persons filing a Schedule 13D must disclose (1) the equity securities acquired and their issuer; (2) their own identity and background; (3) the source and amounts of funds or other consideration used in acquiring the equity securities; (4) the purposes of their acquisition of the equity securities; (5) the number and percentage of the issuer's equity securities they beneficially own and other information; (6) any contracts, arrangements, understandings or relationship with respect to the issuer's securities; and (7) certain exhibits.[10] Whenever an amendment to Schedule 13D is filed, these disclosures must be updated.

Schedule 13D alerts the issuer's shareholders and the stock markets that someone has acquired a substantial position and a tender offer or other changes may occur. Schedule 13D also alerts the issuer, who may take some or all of the defensive actions described later in this chapter if it has not already done so.

Item 4 is the most difficult item of Schedule 13D to answer. It requires that the person or persons filing the Schedule 13D disclose any plans or proposals that would result in the acquisition of additional securities or disposition of securities of the issuer and any of a series of changes that would affect the issuer or its securities. As subsequent events develop, the issuer and others can review the disclosures in Item 4 by hindsight and contend that they show the existence of undisclosed plans. If an issuer can successfully sustain such a contention in a lawsuit to enjoin an unfriendly tender offer, the court may temporarily or permanently enjoin the tender offer or grant other remedies such as an order to divest equity securities or to nullify their voting rights.[11]

Schedule 13D and Schedule 14D-1 call for answers to several items that are similar. Thus, an acquiring corporation that wishes to announce a tender offer without waiting to acquire a 5 percent shareholding may combine the two schedules and file them as one document.

A copy of Schedule 13D appears as Exhibit 12-2.

---

[10]Certain institutional investors acquiring securities in the ordinary course of business and having no involvement with changing or influencing control of the issuer may use a simpler Schedule 13G. See Rule 13d-1.

[11]Risk arbitrageurs who file Schedules 13D provide lengthy disclosures of plans to urge the issuer to achieve shareholder values by restructuring and other means and stating that they may acquire or dispose of shares, make a tender offer or take other actions as events develop.

Schedule 14D-1. A brief summary of the items that a bidder or bidders filing a Schedule 14D-1 for a tender offer must disclose is as follows: (1) the equity securities for which the tender offer will be made, the consideration offered for them, and a 2 year trading history on their principal market; (2) the identity and background of the bidder and certain other persons; (3) past contacts, transactions or negotiations with the issuer; (4) the source and amount of funds or other consideration for purchase of the maximum number of securities for which the tender offer is made including any plans or arrangements for their repayment; (5) the purpose of the tender offer and any plans or proposals of the bidder that would result in material transactions or changes that would affect the issuer or its securities; (6) the aggregate ownership of the issuer's shares of the bidder and certain other persons; (7) contracts, arrangements or relationships with respect to the issuer's securities; (8) the persons retained, employed or to be compensated to make solicitations or recommendations and the terms of their engagement; (9) financial statements of the bidder if the bidder is other than a natural person and its financial condition is material to a decision whether to sell, tender or hold securities being sought in the tender offer; (10) additional information relating to present or proposed material contracts, arrangements, understandings or relationships between the bidder and the issuer and certain persons related to them, the applicability of regulatory requirements and material legal proceedings relating to the tender offer; and (11) exhibits including the tender offer material to be given to the securityholders and loan agreements, material contracts, tax opinions and scripts for oral solicitation of securityholders.

The requirement in item 9 for financial statements of the bidder originally arose from "David and Goliath" tender offers in which a decision to sell rather than tender may be prudent. However, financial statements of the bidder are also useful to shareholders receiving a partial tender offer in which a decision to hold may be prudent if the bidder is a strategic buyer with ample resources to enhance the issuer's business.

Issuers with securities registered under the 1934 Act may incorporate by reference their financial statements filed in reports under that Act. Issuers not subject to reporting under the 1934 Act may use unaudited financial statements if audited financial statements are unavailable.

The most important exhibit in Item 11 is the tender offer statement, a booklet describing the tender offer and containing the disclosures required by Schedule 14D-1 in readable text. The tender offer statement is mailed to the issuer's shareholders and is circulated widely in the financial community in a manner similar to a prospectus.

A copy of Schedule 14D-1 appears as Exhibit 12-3.

Schedule 14D-9. Management of the issuer (and any other persons) who file a Schedule 14D-9 for a solicitation or recommendation concerning a tender offer are required to make several disclosures similar to those in Schedules 13D and 14D-1. A copy of Schedule 14D-9 appears as Exhibit 12-4.

Item 4 is the most important item in Schedule 14D-9. It requires a statement whether management is advising securityholders to accept or reject the tender offer, or to take other action which must be described. If a recommendation is not being made, management must state whether it is either expressing no opinion and remaining neutral or is unable to take a position. Management must state the reasons for its position or inability to take a position.

Item 4 discourages "waffling" statements by management who decide to solicit or make recommendations. In addition, if management makes a recommendation and misstates the true reasons for the recommendation, they will be subject to criminal and civil penalties and to financial liabilities under the 1934 Act.

(b) Rules to Keep the "Playing Field" Level. Unlike the state legislatures and regulatory agencies, the U.S. Congress and the SEC are neutral in tender offer contests between bidders and management. A bidder may advocate realization of shareholder value, the attractiveness of its bid and any claimed shortcomings of management. Management may argue any failure of the bid to reflect full value and other events that they claim are threatened, such as "breakup" divestitures and employee layoffs. The SEC administers the 1934 Act to maintain a "level playing field" between the contestants and the shareholders make the decisions whether or not to tender their shares.

The SEC has adopted several tender offer practices rules to protect shareholders and investors and to maintain a relatively "level playing field." Brief summaries of these rules are as follows:

1. Tender offers must remain open for 20 business days. Rule 14e-1(a).
2. Upon any increase or decrease of the securities to be purchased, the price offered or the solicitation fees, the bidder must extend the tender offer at least 10 business days. Rule 14e-1(b).
3. Any extension of the length of a tender offer must be publicly announced by specific methods. Rule 14e-1(d).
4. Failure to pay the consideration offered or to return tendered securities promptly after termination of a tender offer is prohibited. Rule 14e-1(c).
5. Any person in possession of material nonpublic information relating to a tender offer may not purchase or sell the securities sought or to be sought in a tender offer until a reasonable time after the information and its source are publicly disclosed. Rule 14e-3.
6. Securities may not be tendered in response to a partial tender offer by or on behalf of persons who are "short" the securities or who are not prepared to make prompt delivery. Rules 14e-5 and 10b-4.
7. Upon receipt of a written request from a bidder, the company subject to a tender offer must either mail the bidder's tender offer materials to its securityholders or furnish to the bidder a copy of its stockholder list and securities position listings. Rule 14d-5.
8. Any person who has deposited securities in response to a tender offer has the right to withdraw them while the offer remains open. Rule 14d-7.
9. If a bidder tenders for less than all outstanding equity securities of a class and a greater number of the securities are deposited than the

bidder is bound or willing to purchase, the securities must be purchased pro rata, disregarding fractions. Rule 14d-8.

10. A tender offer must be open to all securityholders of the class for which the offer is made and, with certain exceptions, the consideration paid to each securityholder must be as high as the consideration paid to any other securityholder during the tender offer. Rule 14d-10.
11. A bidder may not purchase securities for which it has tendered, or securities convertible into them, in the market or otherwise outside its tender offer. Rule 10b-13.[12]

3. State Antitakeover Laws

Unlike the U.S. Congress and the SEC, the state legislatures and state regulatory authorities have not been neutral toward tender offers. Managements opposed to uninvited tender offers were highly successful in portraying them as a threat to local business and employment.[13] As a result, state legislatures adopted laws regulating tender offers that were thinly disguised efforts to block them entirely. These early state antitakeover laws fell by the wayside when the U.S. Supreme Court held that the Illinois Business Take-Over Act violated the "commerce clause" of the U.S. Constitution because it unduly burdened interstate commerce.[14]

The states then adopted more skillfully drafted antitakeover laws designed to avoid conflict with the "commerce clause" and conflict with the tender offer regulatory provisions of the 1934 Act. When the U.S. Supreme Court upheld the Control Share Acquisitions Chapter of the Indiana Business Corporation Law, states across the nation rapidly adopted laws designed to frustrate tender offers without overtly preventing them.[15]

The operation of the Indiana Control Share Acquisitions Chapter illustrates how many state antitakeover laws operate. If a person acquires shares that exceed certain thresholds (20 percent, $33^1/_3$ percent or 50 percent), it will be entitled to vote its shares only if the disinterested shareholders of the corporation approve. If the acquiring person does not seek approval or the shareholders do not approve, the corporation may redeem the acquiring person's shares for fair value, but is not obligated to do so.

Before the *CTS Corp.* decision, Delaware did not have an antitakeover law. However, its legislature was compelled to act or risk a management-led exodus of the many corporations chartered under its laws to states having antitakeover laws. In 1988, the legislature adopted Section 203 of the Delaware General Corporation that prohibits any bidder acquiring over 15 percent of the stock of a Delaware corporation from engaging in a business combination with the corporation for 3 years unless the bidder acquires at

---

[12]See also *Heine v. The Signal Companies,* Fed. Sec. L. Rep. (CCH) § 95,898 (S.D.N.Y. 1977); *Sunshine Mining v. Great Western United,* Fed. Sec. L. Rep (CCH) § 96,049 (D. Idaho 1977); and *Field v. Trump,* 661 F. Supp. 529 (S.D.N.Y. 1987).

[13]Hostile tender offers threaten the employment of senior management and their legal and financial advisers. Tender offers seldom threaten operating activities because they hold the values for which the offer was made. Operating activities may be divested as part of a restructuring strategy, but are typically sold to a strategic buyer who can operate the activities successfully.

[14]*Edgar v. Mite Corporation,* 45T U.S. 624, 102 S. Ct. 2629 (1982).

[15]*CTS Corp. v. Dynamics Corporation of America,* 481 U.S. 69, 107 S. Ct. 1637 (1987).

least 85 percent of its outstanding shares in the same transaction. Thus, Section 203 focuses on two-step leveraged takeovers because the bidder in those transactions needs a merger to gain access to the assets and cash flows of the target company. Section 203 excludes management shares from the 85 percent calculation, but not shares held by an employee stock ownership plan (ESOP) if the employee beneficiaries can confidentially direct the ESOP trustee to tender their shares. Section 203 has fostered the adoption of many ESOPs that acquire a minority interest to defend against a possible takeover, rather than fulfilling their traditional role as a vehicle to acquire an entire business.[16]

The New York Business Corporation Law denies the right to engage in a merger or other business combination for 5 years to any bidder that acquires 20 percent or more of the outstanding stock of a New York corporation without prior approval of the business combination by the board of directors of the target corporation.[17]

Over 40 states have adopted antitakeover laws, each creating one or more obstacles to uninvited tender offers and other methods used to change corporate control such as proxy contests. The laws can be grouped by their mechanisms as follows:

- *Control Share Laws.* Like the Indiana Control Share Acquisitions Chapter described earlier, control share laws provide that shareholders who acquire more than a specified percentage of the shares of a corporation may not vote their shares without approval of the disinterested shareholders, in other words, shareholders unaffiliated with management or with the shareholder seeking the approval. The shares subject to these restrictions are called "control shares," although the threshold percentages (10 to 30 percent) are not necessarily sufficient to confer control.
- *Business Combination Laws.* Like the Delaware and New York laws described earlier, business combination laws state that shareholders who acquire more than a specified percentage of the shares of a corporation without approval of its board of directors may not merge with the acquired corporation for a period of years. The periods range from 2 to 5 years. These laws may also impose other requirements such as payment of a "fair price" when a merger becomes permissible.
- *Fair Price Laws.* Fair price laws require that a bidder pay in a second stage merger an amount at least equal to the highest price paid during the first stage acquisitions of shares, unless a lower price is approved by the board or a high percentage of the shareholders.
- *Consideration of Nonshareholder Constituencies.* These laws expressly authorize boards of directors to consider the interests of constituencies other than the shareholders in making decisions on acquisitions and other transactions. The constituencies typically in-

[16]In 1989, Polaroid Corporation used an ESOP as part of its successful defense of a hostile tender offer. *Shamrock Holdings, Inc. v. Polaroid Corporation,* 559 Atl.2d 257 (Del. Ch. 1989)

[17]New York Business Corporation Law, § 912.

clude employees and holders of bonds that could lose their credit rating after a leveraged takeover. They may also include other creditors, customers, suppliers and communities.

- *Shareholder Rights ("Poison Pill") Plans.* These laws expressly authorize boards of directors to adopt shareholder rights ("poison pill") plans.

The foregoing laws are the most important antitakeover laws because all have been adopted in over 20 states and some in 30 states.[18] Smaller numbers of states have adopted statutes banning "greenmail" and "golden parachutes" under certain circumstances. Some states require assumption of collective bargaining agreements and may also require that severance pay be paid to employees laid off after a takeover. Like the takeover rules in the City of London, a few states require that a bidder acquiring more than a specified percentage of the outstanding shares must offer to buy the rest of the shares at a fair price.

4. Issuer Repurchases and Issuer Tender Offers

(a) Issuer Repurchases. Publicly owned corporations repurchase their own outstanding shares (and other securities) for a variety of reasons. A common reason is that the board of directors finds the shares to be undervalued in the market and a better bargain than alternative investments for corporate cash. Another reason is to deter a hostile tender offer.

In 1985, Carter Hawley Hale Stores Inc. successfully defended a hostile tender offer by The Limited through a then-controversial repurchase campaign called a "street sweep." Carter Hawley's brokers purchased very large quantities of its stock at prevailing market prices, thus absorbing shares (especially those held by arbitrageurs) likely to be tendered to The Limited. The SEC commenced a lawsuit against Carter Hawley and argued that the repurchase campaign was an unlawful tender offer. However, the federal courts held that the purchase methods used in a "street sweep" are not a tender offer. Thus, Carter Hawley was not required to comply with the SEC's issuer tender offer rules.[19]

For a more recent example, Unitrin Inc. used a stock repurchase program in resisting an uninvited merger proposal by American General Corp. American General commenced a lawsuit to enjoin the repurchase based on allegations that the repurchases were a disproportionate response that violated the fiduciary obligations of Unitrin's directors. The Delaware Chancery Court agreed and granted a preliminary injunction. However, the Delaware Supreme Court found that the Chancellor had substituted his business judgment for that of Unitrin's board and reversed the injunction and remanded the lawsuit for further proceedings.[20]

Issuer repurchases after a tender offer must be disclosed as required by the SEC's Rule 13e-1 and other disclosure regulations. The repurchases should be made in a manner that does not risk the antimanipulation prohibitions of the 1934 Act. The SEC's Rule 10b-18 is a safe harbor rule that

---

[18] *Mergers & Acquisitions* periodically publishes lists of the states that have adopted antitakeover statutes based on information supplied by the Investor Responsibility Research Center.

[19] *SEC v. Carter Hawley Stores Inc.*, 760 F.2d 945 (9th Cir. 1985).

[20] *Unitrin, Inc. v. American General Corp.*, 651 Atl.2d 1361 (Del. 1995).

establishes appropriate conditions for timing, prices and volumes of purchases. For example, purchases should be made through only one broker-dealer firm on any day, so that the firm can monitor the conduct and effects of the purchases.

(b) Issuer Tender Offers. When an issuer decides to make a self-tender offer to repurchase its shares, it must meet several disclosure requirements. If the repurchases are of equity securities in response to a tender offer, the issuer must file with the SEC both the disclosure statement required by Rule 13e-4 and an Issuer Tender Offer Statement on Schedule 13 E-4.

Rule 13e-1 prohibits an issuer from repurchasing any of its equity securities after it receives notice of the filing of a Schedule 14D-1 for a tender offer until it has filed a disclosure statement with the SEC. The statement must describe the securities and the market in which they will be purchased. The statement must also disclose the purpose of the purchases and the source and amount of funds to be used in making the purchases. The disclosure statement used to comply with Rule 13e-1 is Schedule 13E-4.

Rule 13e-4 requires that issuers making a self-tender offer file a Schedule 13E-4, a form that requires disclosure similar to that required in Schedule 14D-1 except for items not applicable to an issuer. Thereafter, Rule 13e-4 requires reporting of any material change by promptly filing an amendment to the Schedule 13E-4. Rule 13e-4 also requires that the results of the tender offer be reported by a final amendment to the Schedule 13E-4.

Rule 13e-4 also contains rules on the manner of making an issuer tender offer that parallel many of the tender offer practices rules described earlier in this chapter.

5. The Role of Management during Tender Offers

(a) Friendly Tender Offers. Transactions leading to friendly tender offers are generally negotiated by management of the company to be acquired, often together with principal shareholders who have decided to sell. Thus, management is involved in negotiating the price and terms of the tender offer.

For example, the author's first tender offer experience was a transaction in which Michigan Seamless Tube Company, an NYSE listed corporation, acquired The Standard Tube Company, an AMEX listed company. Michigan Seamless (now named Quanex Corporation) agreed to make a cash tender offer at $11 per share and Standard Tube's principal shareholder agreed to tender all of the shares it owned in response to the tender offer. Standard Tube's management cooperated with the transaction.

For another example, the management of First Maryland Bancorporation negotiated a friendly transaction in which The Allied Irish Banks Limited agreed to buy for a cash price of $40 per share originally issued shares of First Maryland, thus providing capital for its rapidly growing operations. Allied Irish also agreed to buy additional outstanding common stock through a tender offer at $35 per share, a price that was significantly above recent market prices in the $19 to $25 range. The agreement also provided for future purchases of newly issued shares providing capital infusions until Allied Irish attained ownership of between 50 and 60 percent of First Maryland's outstanding common stock. First Maryland's management recommended the tender offer favorably to its public shareholders.

In friendly tender offers, management and any participating controlling shareholders must be mindful of their fiduciary obligations to the public shareholders. However, management does not face the severe pressures that occur during a hostile tender offer and their conduct is likely to be measured by the business judgment rule described later in this chapter. However, management is likely to obtain a "fairness opinion" from an investment banking firm or other expert financial valuation analyst to use during the negotiations and to support its business judgment.[21] See the discussion of fairness opinions later in this chapter.

(b) Hostile Tender Offers. When hostile tender offers became common in the 1970s, a typical reaction by management of the target company was to undertake any actions whatsoever that might be necessary to defeat the offer. Management generally perceived the bidder as an unprincipled "raider" seeking to capture corporate values created by management's efforts and to convert them into a quick profit by tactics such as employee layoffs and breakup sales of businesses and assets.[22]

In this frame of mind, many managements sought to deter shareholders from receiving uninvited tender offers by adopting legalistic "shark repellent devices" such as the following:

- "Supermajority" voting requirements for shareholder approval of merger and other acquisition transactions, typically adopted by amendment of the certificate of incorporation.
- Staggered election of directors over a period such as 3 years, also adopted by amendment of the certificate of incorporation.
- "Golden parachute" contracts providing severance benefits to management at levels so generous that they would create burdensome obligations for the corporation in the event of a tender offer or change of control. Some companies provided "silver parachute" contracts to management beyond the top executive levels or "tin parachute" severance benefits to a wide group of employees.
- "Lock up" options to buy stock or assets granted to management allies, sometimes at bargain exercise prices. The options became exercisable in the event of a tender offer or acquisition of a significant percentage (such as 20 or 30 percent) of the outstanding shares without management approval.
- "Crown jewel" sales of valuable businesses or assets to third parties, sometimes at bargain prices. In addition to direct sales, "lock

[21]If any members of management believe that careful financial valuation is unnecessary because a bidder is offering a price that is a premium over the market price, they should be advised of the decision in *Smith v. Van Gorkom,* 488 A.2d 858 (Del. 1985). The Delaware Supreme Court held the directors of TransUnion Corporation liable for agreeing to its acquisition by Marmon Corporation for a price about 50 percent above recent market prices. Expert testimony at trial indicated that the value was substantially higher than the price accepted by management. See also *Edelman v. Fruehauf Corp.* 798 F.2d 882 (6th Cir. 1986).

[22]Some of the entrepreneurs who led hostile takeover campaigns initially saw some tactical advantage in a "buccaneer" image. Later, some sought to recast this image and to portray themselves as champions of the creation and realization of shareholder values. They also became adept at portraying management as ineffective bureaucrats seeking to entrench and enrich themselves at shareholder expense by devices such as "golden parachute" employment contracts.

up" options were sometimes granted for "crown jewel" businesses that became exercisable in the event of a tender offer or acquisition of a significant percentage (such as 20 or 30 percent) of the outstanding shares without management approval.

- "Shareholder rights" plans (also called "poison pills") with "flip in," "flip over" and/or "back-end" features that entitled shareholders to exercise rights to purchase shares or other securities of the target company, or of the bidder in the event of a merger, at bargain prices that would fatally dilute the ownership acquired by the bidder in an uninvited tender offer. An announcement of a "shareholder rights" plan appears as Exhibit 12-5.

Efforts to block the adoption of such devices on grounds that they are manipulative devices or that their mere adoption violated management's fiduciary obligations were unsuccessful.[23] However, as described later, the courts have frequently enjoined such devices in situations when management used them in a manner contrary to their fiduciary obligations to shareholders.

When uninvited tender offers were threatened or made, managements used the "shark repellent" devices as defenses. They also frequently turned to other alternatives:

- Sale of the target company to a "White Knight," in other words, a company regarded by management as friendly.
- Sale of a significant block of voting securities to a "White Squire," i.e., an investor likely to refuse a tender offer and to vote in support of management.
- Sale of the target company in a management buyout.
- Sale of a significant block of securities to an employee stock ownership plan ("ESOP").
- An issuer tender offer to absorb shares likely to be tendered or sold in response to a hostile tender offer and also intended to strengthen the market for the target company's stock.
- An issuer "street sweep" conducted in a manner that was not a tender offer in order to absorb shares likely to be tendered or sold in response to a hostile tender offer.
- An overall business and financial restructuring, usually financed by borrowing and involving any of several transactions such as a large one-time cash distribution to shareholders, an issuer tender offer or divestitures of businesses.[24]

[23]*Shreiber v. Burlington Northern,* 472 U.S. 1 (1985); *Moran v. Household International, Inc.*, 500 Atl.2d 1346 (1985).

[24]A few target companies initiated a counter tender offer, called a "PAC MAN" defense. The objective was to buy enough shares to control the bidder and then vote the shares to oust the bidder's management and elect a new management that would cancel the bidder's tender offer. The flaw in this defense is the time and difficulty involved in making the tender offer and then calling a shareholders' meeting in the face of litigation and other tactics. A tender offer by Bendix Corporation in which the target, Martin Marietta, used a "PAC MAN" defense resulted in a litigation war and eventual stalemate with the result that both companies were acquired by Allied Signal.

Bidders, sometimes joined by shareholders of the target company, fought the management defenses with considerable success. Typically, the courts were reluctant to allow management to block an attractively priced tender offer unless management could present an alternative of equal or greater benefit to the shareholders.

(c) Management's Legal Duties. Under the laws of all states, officers and directors of corporations have fiduciary duties to the corporation and its shareholders, especially to minority shareholders who are often public shareholders. When determining whether officers and directors who serve as management have performed their duties, the courts apply a presumption called the "business judgment rule" that provides important protection to responsible management members. The rule presumes that management acts on an informed basis, in good faith and in the honest belief that their actions are in the best interests of the corporation and its shareholders. An important effect of the presumption is that shareholders claiming mismanagement have the burden of proof of their claims. Another effect is that a court will not substitute its judgement for any judgment by management that can be attributed to a rational business purpose.[25]

There are decisions in which the courts found that management failed to meet the business judgment rule. When management fails to meet the business judgment standard in approving a business sale, a court may enjoin the sale.[26] A court may also hold the management personally liable for shareholder losses if the sale has been closed.[27]

Management loses the benefit of the business judgment rule when it engages in a transaction involving a conflict of interest. When management chooses to engage in a transaction in which it has a self-interest, management must bear the burden of proof that the transaction is entirely fair to the corporation and its shareholders.[28] The "entire fairness" standard is a very exacting standard.[29]

When evaluating their response to an uninvited tender offer, management does not have a conflict of interest in the typical sense. Indeed, management usually makes extensive efforts to respond to a tender offer in a manner that serves a wide range of interests including those of the corporation and its shareholders, employees, customers, suppliers and other stockholders. The task is not easy because uninvited tender offers create pervasive uncertainty. It is difficult to manage during a tender offer because competitors use the uncertainty to take away customers, employees send resumes seeking more stable employment and the target company may be perceived as a wounded animal.

Some shareholders, eager to sell for a premium price, claim that management should stand aside during tender offers. However, bidders who

---

[25] *Aronson v. Lewis*, 473 A.2d 805 (Del. 1984); *Pogostin v. Rice*, 480 A.2d 619 (Del. 1984); *Norlin Corp. v. Rooney Pace Inc.*, 733 F.2d 255 (2nd Cir. 1984); *Unocal Corp. v. Mesa Petroleum Co.*, 493 A.2d 946 (Del. 1985).

[26] *MacAndrews & Forbes Holdings, Inc. v. Revlon Inc.*, 506 A.2d 173 (Del. 1985); *Edelman v. Fruehauf Corporation*, 798 F.2d 882 (6th Cir. 1986).

[27] *Smith v. Van Gorkom*, 488 A.2d 858 (Del. 1985).

[28] *Weinberger v. UOP, Inc.*, 457 A.2d 701 (Del. 1983); *AC Acquisitions Corp v. Anderson, Clayton & Co.*, 519 A.2d 103 (Del. Ch. 1986); *Norlin Corporation v. Rooney, Pace, Inc.*, 733 F.2d 255 (2nd Cir. 1985).

[29] *AC Acquisitions Corp. v. Anderson, Clayton & Co.*, 519 A.2d 103 (Del. Ch. 1986).

make uninvited tender offers do so because they perceive that the target company has greater value than the price offered. Thus, management protects the interests of shareholders, even those who are critical, when it makes sound evaluations and recommendations during a tender offer. On many occasions, a management conclusion that a tender offer price was inadequate was rapidly verified by the bidder's decision to increase its price or the offer of an increased price by a "white knight" or another uninvited bidder. The Delaware courts have said that management should take a proactive role in evaluating tender offers and protecting the interests of shareholders invited to tender their shares.[30]

On the other hand, many uninvited tender offers are made for undervalued target companies suffering from management that has been ineffective or preoccupied with its own interests. Further, even capable managers do not welcome a change of control likely to result in loss of their positions and compensation and a diversion to the bidder of the benefits of their accomplishments and strategic plans. The Delaware Supreme Court has found that there is an "omnipresent specter" that management may be acting in its own interests in responding to an uninvited tender offer and that "enhanced scrutiny" of their conduct is appropriate before applying the business judgment rule.[31]

The Delaware courts require management to meet two tests before they can claim the benefit of the business judgment rule. First, management must show that opposition to a tender offer is a response to a threat posing a real danger to corporate policy and effectiveness, such as an inadequate or coercive tender offer. Second, management must show that its response was reasonably related to the threat. To support a reasonable basis for its actions, management must show that it acted in good faith after investigation of the danger and the alternatives for responding to it.[32] The showing is strengthened when management's decision involves participation by outside directors and the well-prepared advice of independent valuation experts.[33]

The Delaware courts have had numerous opportunities to apply the enhanced scrutiny mandated by the *Unocal* decision including the two threshold tests. In 1986, the Delaware Chancery Court found that the directors of Anderson, Clayton & Co. had failed to meet the second test when they approved a coercive partial self-tender offer at $65 per share in response to a $56 tender offer for all shares by Bear, Stearns & Co., Inc., Gruss Petroleum Corp. and Gruss Partners. Thus, the Court enjoined the self-tender offer until the original offer could be made.[34]

In 1985, the Delaware Supreme Court made a dramatic interpretation of directors' responsibilities when it found that the board of directors of

---

[30]See for example, *Paramount Communications, Inc. v. QVC Network Inc.*, 637 Atl.2d 34 (Del. 1994) at page 48.

[31]*Unocal Corp. v. Mesa Petroleum Co.*, 493 Atl. 2d 946 (Del. 1985).

[32]*Unocal Corp. v . Mesa Petroleum Co.*, supra.

[33]*Cinerama, Inc. v. Technicolor, Inc.*, CCH Red. Sec. L. Rep. (Del. (1995); *Paramount Communications, Inc. v. Time, Inc.*, 571 Atl.2d 1140 (Del. 1989); *Hanson Trust v. ML SCM Acquisition Inc.*, 781 F.2d 264 (2nd Cir. 1986); *Gelco Corp. v. Coniston Partners*, 652 F. Supp. 829 (D. Minn. 1986); aff'd 811 F.2d 414 (8th Cir. 1987).

[34]*AC Acquisitions v. Anderson, Clayton & Co.*, 519 A.2d 103 (Del. Ch. 1986). However, a partial self-tender offer was allowed in *Gelco Corp. v. Coniston Partners*, supra, and later cases.

Revlon, Inc. had "auction obligations" after it authorized the officers to negotiate a merger or sale in response to a hostile tender offer by Pantry Pride, Inc., a subsidiary of MacAndrews & Forbes Holdings, Inc.[35] Revlon's board found the initial tender offer of $47.50 per share was inadequate. However, Pantry Pride increased its offer by stages, eventually reaching $56.25 per share in cash. In the meantime, the board authorized management to negotiate with other parties and an agreement was reached with Forstmann Little & Co. providing for a "break up" sale at a price of $57.25, subject to complex terms and conditions that eventually included "lock up" provisions for sales of "crown jewel" assets, a "no shop" provision and a large cancellation fee if the agreement was not closed. Pantry Pride increased its offer to $58.00 per share conditioned, among other things, upon nullification of Revlon's shareholder rights ("poison pill") plan and an injunction of Forstmann Little's "lock up" agreements and other arrangements. The Delaware Supreme Court found that the directors had breached their fiduciary obligations in approving the arrangements with Forstmann Little. The Court also found that directors had made extra concessions to Forstmann Little in return for a commitment to support the price of Revlon notes whose holders had threatened litigation. In affirming an injunction, the Court said:

> *"The Revlon board's authorization permitting management to negotiate a merger or buyout with a third party was a recognition that the company was for sale. The duty of the board had thus changed from the preservation of Revlon as a corporate entity to the maximization of the company's value at a sale for the stockholders' benefit. This significantly altered the board's responsibilities under the Unocal standards. It no longer faced threats to corporate policy and effectiveness, or to the stockholders' interests, from a grossly inadequate bid. The whole question of defensive measures became moot. The directors' role changed from defenders of the corporate bastion to auctioneers charged with getting the best price for the stockholders at a sale of the company."*

In subsequent cases, the Delaware courts rendered further decisions enforcing the "auction obligations." In 1988, for example, the Delaware Supreme Court upheld an injunction of a "poison pill" adopted by McMillan Inc.[36] In reaching its decision, the Court found that McMillan's directors had improperly favored, disclosed confidential bid information and otherwise favored a friendly bid by Kohlberg Kravis Roberts & Co. over uninvited bids by Robert M. Bass Group Inc. and Maxwell Communications Corp. Maxwell Communications then acquired substantially all of McMillan's shares in a tender offer. Subsequently, the Delaware Chancery Court declined to enforce a "lock up" option for "crown jewel" assets that McMillan had granted to Kohlberg Kravis.

On the other hand, the Delaware courts have rendered several decisions holding that management's actions met the *Unocal* tests. In these decisions, management's defensive steps were sustained under the business judgment rule and the auction obligations were held to be inapplicable.[37]

---

[35] *Revlon, Inc. v. MacAndrews & Forbes Holdings,* 506 Atl.2d 173 (Del. 1985).

[36] *Mills Acquisition Co. v. McMillan, Inc.,* 559 Atl.2d 1261 (Del. 1988).

[37] *City Capital Associates v. Interco Inc.,* 551 Atl.2d 787 (Del. Ch. 1988); *Paramount Communications, Inc. v. Time Inc.,* 571 Atl. 2d 1140 (Del. 1990).

The courts have tended to apply the business judgment rule and not to impose auction obligations when management implemented decisions made before a hostile tender offer commenced.[38] For example, the Delaware Chancery Court declined to enjoin a restructuring plan involving a large one-time distribution to shareholders that was actively being considered by Interco before a tender offer was commenced. For another example, the Delaware Chancery Court refused to enjoin the planned establishment, for sound business reasons, of an employee stock ownership plan (ESOP) by Polaroid Corporation, although the effect was to impede a tender offer.

For still another example, the Delaware Supreme Court denied an injunction sought by Paramount Communications, Inc. against an acquisition by Time Inc. of Warner Communications, Inc. Paramount had commenced a tender offer for Time's shares. Paramount argued that Time's directors had auction obligations and should not be permitted to proceed with the Warner acquisition which would impede a sale. The Delaware Supreme Court disagreed and pointed out that Time had not authorized a break up sale such as Revlon agreed with Forstmann Little. On the contrary, Time intended to continue and expand its business by completing the Warner acquisition that was in progress when Paramount began its "eleventh hour" tender offer. Thus, the directors of Time met the tests described in the *Unocal* decision and their business judgment to remain independent was upheld.

In its decision in favor of Time, the Delaware Supreme Court offered guidance to managements confronted by an uninvited tender offer when corporate plans call for continuation in business rather than a sale. In summary, the Court held that a board of director's duty to manage includes setting a corporate course of action, including a time frame, designed to enhance corporate profitability. The board must chart a course that is in the corporation's best interests without regard to a fixed investment horizon and questions such as "long term" or "short term" are largely irrelevant. While always required to act in an informed manner, a board has no intrinsic duty to maximize shareholder value in the short term, even in the context of a takeover. In a footnote, the Court added that it is not a breach of faith for directors to determine that the present stock market price of shares is not representative of true value or that there might be several market values for any corporation's stock.[39]

The words of the Delaware Supreme Court in the *Time* case were welcome to managements hoping for justification of a simple "Just Say No" defense. However, in an ironic turnabout, Paramount, which had attempted a takeover of Time, found itself under attack only a short time later by an uninvited offer from QVC Inc. QVC's attack came in 1993 after the directors of Paramount Communications, Inc. approved an agreement for its merger into Viacom Inc. with the result that Summer Redstone, the Chairman and controlling shareholder of Viacom, would control the merged corporation. QVC Inc. then proposed a hostile tender offer and second-

---

[38] *Gelco Corp. v. Coniston Partners,* supra; *Danaher Corp. v. Chicago Pneumatic Tool,* 635 F.Supp. 246 (S.D.N.Y. 1986); *Terrydale Liquidating Trust v. Barness,* 642 F.Supp. 917 (S.D.N.Y. 1986); *City Capital Associates v. Interco Inc.,* 551 Atl.2d 787 (Del. Ch. 1988); *Shamrock Holdings Inc. v. Polaroid Corporation,* 559 Atl.2d 257 (Del. Ch. 1989); *Paramount Communications, Inc. v. Time Inc.,* 571 Atl.2d 1140 (Del. 1990).

[39] *Paramount Communications, Inc. v. Time Inc.,* 571 Atl.2d 1140 (Del. 1990).

step merger transaction at a higher price. A bidding contest followed in which Viacom also offered a tender offer and second-step merger transaction at higher prices. However, QVC's eventual offer on November 12, 1993 exceeded Viacom's offer by approximately a billion dollars. Nevertheless, Paramount's board determined that the QVC offer was not in the best interests of its stockholders. QVC sought an injunction against Paramount's defensive measures, including a "poison pill" and several provisions of the merger agreement with Viacom that included an option to purchase 19.9 pecent of Paramount's outstanding common stock. Paramount argued that auction obligations did not apply because there would be no "breakup" of its business such as occurred in the *Revlon* case. Paramount also argued that the decision of its board to merge into QVC was comparable to the acquiring of Warner Communications by merger. However, the Delaware Supreme Court ruled that auction obligations apply to a sale of control and that Paramount's directors had breached their fiduciary duties in favoring Viacom's offer. Thus, the Delaware Supreme Court affirmed the injunction granted by the Chancery Court.[40]

In 1995, the Delaware Supreme Court upheld actions by the directors of two companies that did not resort to either a "breakup" sale or a sale of control. In the first case, the directors of Unitrin, Inc. found that a hostile tender offer by American General Corp. was inadequate and authorized a stock repurchase program under which its investment banker repurchased nearly five million shares at slightly above the tender offer price. After applying *Unocal* analysis, the Delaware Supreme Court held that Unitrin's directors were entitled to the business judgment presumption and reversed a decision by the Chancery Court granting an injunction to American General.[41]

In the second case, the directors of Technicolor, Inc. authorized its sale to MacAndrews & Forbes, Inc. in a two-stage tender offer and merger transaction for $23 per share in cash. Cinerama, Inc., which had acquired 4.4 percent of Technicolor's shares, sued Technicolor's directors for breach of fiduciary duties. Cinerama alleged that some of the Technicolor directors had conflicts of interest that influenced their conduct. Applying the exacting "entire fairness" standard, the Delaware Supreme Court upheld the decision of the Chancery Court that the sale was entirely fair. In support of its decision, the Supreme Court pointed to the approval of the transaction by Technicolor's independent directors and the board's reliance on the advice of highly regarded investment banking and law firms. The investment banking firm had provided an opinion that $23 was a fair price. Perhaps most significant, the Supreme Court observed that two Technicolor directors who were significant shareholders had tendered their own shares and that no rival bidders appeared over a period of several months before the merger closed.[42]

6. Business Planning to Avoid Takeovers

(a) Introduction. Since the early 1970s, managements of publicly held corporations have had to include the possibility of a hostile takeover in their

---

[40]*Paramount Communications Inc. v. QVC Inc.*, supra.

[41]*Unitrin, Inc. v. American General Corp.*, supra.

[42]*Cinerama, Inc. v. Technicolor, Inc.*, CCH Fed. Sec. L. Rep. § 98,812 (Del. 1995).

strategic planning. Many managements placed their trust in elaborate financial restructurings developed by investment bankers and in legal devices created by law firms. They paid enormous fees, but many lost their corporate independence anyway because management, the investment bankers and the lawyers did not focus on the fundamental actions necessary to maintain independence.

Takeover bids come from financial buyers and strategic buyers. Planning to deter a bid differs for the two kinds of buyers.

(b) Preparing for Unwanted Financial Buyers. Financial buyers tend to be bargain hunters who seek to deploy their capital as effectively as possible among available acquisition opportunities. Financial buyers are attracted to a corporation that is undervalued or undermanaged. Financial buyers are also attracted to a corporation that has excess cash, unused borrowing power, excess management and administrative employees, or readily disposable assets.

Assuming that management is performing capably, undervaluation usually results either from failure to assure that shareholders benefit from corporate progress or from poor shareholder and investor communications.

Shareholders seek to profit from appreciation in the value of their shares and dividend payments. Shareholders have long recognized that management must consider other constituencies such as employees, customers and government regulators. However, if shareholders and investors perceive that management will consistently apply corporate profits to empire building or compensating themselves and their allies, the market value of the corporation's shares will decline.

Shareholders also recognize that corporations must make long-term capital investments and sponsor research and development programs that do not provide quick profit returns. Indeed, investors flock to corporations perceived to have strong capital investment and R&D programs, such as Intel and Microsoft. However, some corporations have communications programs that are either inadequate or too conservative. Thus, the market value of the corporation's shares declines because public shareholders and investors do not know about the hidden assets being accumulated.

Management can deter unwanted financial buyers by making prompt use of cash and borrowing power. If management finds that attractive internal expansion or acquisition projects are insufficient to use cash and borrowing power, management can increase dividends or repurchase shares. Either step is likely to enhance the market price of the shares and reduce the corporation's attractiveness to a financial buyer.

Management can also deter uninvited financial buyers by trimming "excess" management and administrative personnel and assuring that compensation systems and levels are not excessive. Further, management can deter financial buyers by shunning corporate airplanes, yachts, limousines, apartments and "Taj Mahal" office buildings. Excesses in these areas are a double disadvantage. They attract unwanted financial buyers who envision rapid cuts to enhance cash flow. They can also be used by an unwanted financial buyer to accuse management of waste in any tender offer or proxy contest.

As further discussed in the next section, stock ownership by management and persons friendly to management is also a significant deterrent to uninvited financial buyers.

(c) Preparing for Unwanted Strategic Buyers. During the early 1990s, many hostile tender offers were made by strategic buyers rather than the financial buyers whose offers predominated during the 1980s. Some examples were IBM's acquisition of Lotus; AT&T's acquisition of NCR; Kimberly Clark's acquisition of International Paper; Lockheed's acquisition of Loral; Union Pacific's acquisition of Southern Pacific; Wolters Kluwer's acquisition of Commerce Clearing House; Praxair's acquisition of CBI Industries; Johnson & Johnson's acquisition of Cordis Corporation; and St. Gobain's acquisition of Bird Corporation.

Uninvited bids by strategic buyers can be difficult to resist. If a strategic bidder has important synergistic objectives, the fact that shares are fully priced in the stock market may not be an important deterrent. The fact that cash and borrowing power may have been well utilized and personnel and asset expenditures have been carefully controlled may be seen as an incentive rather than a deterrent. Strategic bids by large corporations with a "war chest" firmly in place are especially hard to fight because they can overcome even state "control share," "business combination" and other antitakeover laws.

An important method to deter uninvited bids by strategic and other uninvited bidders is to place and maintain as many shares as possible in the hands of management, employees and other persons who are convinced that management will provide a better investment return than can be obtained by selling in response to a premium bid. This last element is essential because managements have often found that shares in hands thought to be "friendly" are tendered in response to a premium bid. Management must understand that institutional investors are not free to ignore an attractive bid simply because management has been competent and investor relations have been cordial. This is especially true for employee stock ownership plans (ESOPs). An ESOP was used as part of a successful campaign by Polaroid Corporation to defeat a tender offer.[43] However, ESOP trustees have fiduciary obligations to the employee-participants when deciding whether to tender shares and their decisions may be scrutinized by the U.S. Department of Labor under the principles of the Employee Retirement Income Security Act (ERISA).[44]

Another factor that can deter an uninvited bid is diversification. If a corporation has several businesses, including a "crown jewel," a potential strategic bidder that wants only the "crown jewel" may decide that the effort of acquiring and divesting the other businesses is prohibitive. However, there is some history demonstrating that the necessary divestitures can be accomplished, if not easily. For example, Dow Chemical acquired Essex Chemical on friendly terms in 1988 and divested all of its subsidiaries and divisions except those engaged in production of specialty chemicals. There have also been hostile tender offers that were settled and withdrawn when

---

[43]*Shamrock Holdings, Inc. v. Polaroid Corporation,* 559 Atl.2d 257 (Del. Ch. 1989).

[44]*Donovan v. Bierwirth,* 680 F.2d 263 (2nd Cir. 1982); cert. den. 459 U.S. 1069 (1982).

the target corporation agreed to sell a key subsidiary or division to the bidder. For example, Dainippon Ink & Chemicals withdrew a takeover campaign for Sun Chemical when Sun Chemical agreed to sell its ink manufacturing business to Dainippon. In Germany, Krupp announced in early 1997 a takeover campaign against Thyssen AG, but withdrew when Thyssen agreed to combine its steel businesses in a joint venture with Krupp.

In recent years, some companies have deterred uninvited strategic bidders by disposing of assets, altering their equity capital structure, or taking other actions that would avoid an aqcuisition accounted for by the pooling of interests method. See Chapter 9 for a description of the criteria for use of the pooling of interests method.

E. "Going Private" Transactions

1. Regulation

When the management or controlling shareholders of a corporation with publicly traded shares decide that it should "go private," the transaction typically involves conflicts of interest between them and the public shareholders. The SEC adopted Rule 13e-3 and Schedule 13E-3 to focus on the conflict of interest and fairness issues that arise in "going private" transactions.

Rule 13e-3 refers to a "going private" transaction as a "Rule 13e-3 transaction," meaning (1) an issuer repurchase of its equity securities, (2) an issuer tender offer for its equity securities, or (3) a proxy solicitation for a merger, sale of assets or restructuring transaction, if the effect is to cause any class of the issuer's equity securities to be deregistered under the 1934 Act or delisted from a stock exchange or the NASDAQ.[45] Rule 13e-3 contains several exceptions including an exception for exchanges of equity securities that have substantially the same rights and privileges as the equity securities that are the subject of the Rule 13e-3 transaction, including registration under the 1934 Act and listing on a national securities exchange or the NASDAQ.

Schedule 13E-3 calls for disclosures of many items that are similar to those required by Schedules 13D, 14D-1 and 13E-4. The most important disclosures required by Schedule 13E-3 are those in Item 8, Fairness of the Transaction and Item 9, Reports, Opinions, Appraisals and Certain Negotiations. See Rule 13e-100.

Item 8 requires the issuer to state whether it reasonably believes that the Rule 13e-3 transaction is fair or unfair to the public shareholder. Any dissent or abstention by a director from voting on the transaction must be disclosed with the director's reasons. The basis for the issuer's belief that the transaction is fair or unfair must be discussed including the weight given to financial valuation factors including market prices; book value; going-concern value; liquidation value; the purchase price of previous purchases; any valuation report, opinion or appraisal; and any firm offers within 18 months for a merger, assets acquisition, or securities acquisition that would enable

[45]Rule 13e-3 does not refer to deregistration, but to the criteria for deregistration, i.e., a class of equity securities held of record by less than 300 persons. Rule 13e-3 refers to the NASDAQ as an inter-dealer quotation system of a registered national securities association.

the acquirer to exercise control. This discussion must be in reasonable detail including all material factors and the weight assigned to each factor. Short conclusory statements are not considered sufficient disclosure.

Item 8 also requires statements whether (1) the transaction must be approved by a majority of the unaffiliated (public) shareholders; (2) the issuer's outside directors have retained an unaffiliated representative to act solely on behalf of the unaffiliated (public) shareholders to negotiate the transaction or to prepare a fairness opinion; (3) the transaction was approved by a majority of the outside directors; or (4) any firm offers have been received from competitive bidders.

Item 9(a) requires a statement whether the issuer (or an affiliate) has received any report, opinion (other than an opinion of counsel) or appraisal from an outside party that is materially related to the Section 13e-3 transaction. In effect, Item 9(a) requires disclosure of any fairness opinion whether prepared as a report, opinion or appraisal.

Item 9(b) requires disclosure about any report, opinion or appraisal from an outside party or any negotiation or report of an unaffiliated representative. The identity, qualifications and method of selection of the outside party or unaffiliated representative must be disclosed. Their material relationships and compensation must also be disclosed. If the report, opinion or appraisal relates to fairness of the consideration, disclosure must be made whether the issuer (or an affiliate) determined the amount or the outside party recommended the amount.

Any negotiation report, opinion or appraisal must be summarized including the procedures followed; the findings and recommendations; the bases for and methods of arriving at the findings and recommendations; instructions received from the issuer or affiliate; and any limitation on the scope of investigation. A statement must also be made that the report, opinion or appraisal will be made available for inspection and copying and that a copy will be transmitted to any interested shareholders (or their representatives) upon request and at their expense.

Items 8 and 9 require disclosures that are fertile ground for class action plaintiff attorneys. On a subject so complex and judgmental as the fairness of the price paid in a "going private" transaction, the plaintiff attorneys can use the disclosed information to retain experts who are known to have different views on valuation methods and who will testify that the price is not fair. Thus, even when the price is fair, the issuer may have to offer a substantial settlement to avoid the time, effort, cost and risk of litigation.[46]

2. Fairness Opinions

Fairness opinions have become so customary that firms such as Duff & Phelps LLC, Willamette Management Associates and Houlihan, Lokey, Howard & Zukin write many such opinions (or reports) per year. Still

[46]Cases in which fairness opinions or valuation reports were challenged with whole or partial success include *Weinberger v. UOP, Inc.*, Atl.2d (Del. 1982); *Edelman v. Fruehauf Corp.*, 798 F.2d 882 (6th Cir. 1986); *Grand Metropolitan v. The Pillsbury Co.*, 588 Atl.2d 1049 (Del. 1988); *Herskowitz v. Nutri-System, Inc.*, 857 Fed.2d 179 (3d Cir. 1988); *Mills Acquisition Co. v. McMillan, Inc.*, 559 Atl.2d 1261 (Del. 1988); and *CTS Corp v. Dynamic Corporation of America*, 794 F.2d 250 (7th Cir. 1986), reversed on other issues 107 S.Ct. 1637 (1987). The author participated in the defense of *Herskowitz v. Nutri-System, Inc.*

more fairness opinions are written by investment banking firms, academic experts and others. See Chapter 4 for further discussion of fairness opinions. An example of a fairness opinion appears as Exhibit 12-6.

F. Proxy Solicitation and Proxy Contests

1. State Corporation Laws

The great majority of industrial, commercial and other corporations are organized under state corporation laws. Of these corporations, a very large number are organized in Delaware because of its stable laws, modest taxes and skilled judiciary.

Requirements that annual and special meetings of shareholders be held and the related procedures are included in the state corporation laws. Additional requirements and procedures may be included in the certificate of incorporation and are included in the by-laws. State corporation laws typically require a vote of shareholders on at least the following matters: (1) election of directors; (2) amendment of the certificate of incorporation; (3) merger or consolidation; (4) sale of substantially all assets; and (5) dissolution.

Under the state corporation laws, directors are usually elected as a single slate by a plurality (i.e., a majority of a quorum) unless the certificate of incorporation or by-laws modify the procedures and requirements.[47] Other actions typically require a majority of the outstanding shares entitled to vote or a supermajority such as two-thirds of the voting shares for actions such as mergers and sales of substantially all assets.[48]

State corporation laws usually allow shareholders to attend annual or special meetings either in person or by proxy. If a shareholder will not attend in person, the shareholder signs a proxy card appointing another person who can attend as proxy (or agent) to vote at the meeting. The proxy card directs how the proxy will vote on known issues and at the proxy's discretion on other issues, although the discretionary authority may be limited if there is any concern that unplanned substantive issues may be presented.

Managements of corporations have some freedom in making arrangements for shareholder meetings. However, the freedom is not unlimited. A management that attempted to adjourn a meeting to avoid imminent defeat in an election was enjoined.[49] A management that attempted to advance a meeting date to favor incumbent directors was also enjoined.[50] The courts have also enjoined other management maneuvers.[51]

---

[47]Recently, staggered boards and classified boards have become common. In a staggered board, the directors are divided into groups and one group is elected each year for a multiple year term, thus assuring continuity of membership. In a classified board, the directors are divided into groups, each of which is nominated and elected by the holders of a class of stock.

[48]Under the state corporation laws, voting, nonvoting and limited voting shares may be issued. For each meeting, a record date is set for the determination of shareholders entitled to vote. Shareholders who acquire record ownership after the record date are not usually entitled to vote.

[49]*Aprahamian v. HBO & Co.*, 531 Atl.2d 1204 (Del. Ch. 1987).

[50]*Shoen v. Amerco*, 1994-95 Fed. Sec. L. Rep. (CCH), § 98, 461 (1996).

[51]*Blasius Industries, Inc. v. Atlas Corp.*, 564 Atl.2d 651 (Del. Ch. 1988).

2. The SEC's Proxy Rules

Section 14(a) of the 1934 Act prohibits the solicitation of any proxy, consent or authorization for securities registered under the 1934 Act in contravention of the rules and regulations of the SEC. The SEC has adopted extensive rules on the solicitation of proxies.[52] The SEC's rules require that a solicitation be accompanied by a written proxy statement containing the information specified in Schedule 14A to the rules. If a solicitation is made on behalf of the corporation and relates to an annual meeting (or consent) at which directors will be elected, the proxy statement must be accompanied or preceded by an annual report containing financial statements and other specified information.[53]

Preliminary copies of the proxy statement, form of proxy and any other solicitation material must be filed with the SEC at least 10 calendar days prior to the date when definitive copies will be sent to securityholders. That time period provides an opportunity for the SEC to furnish comments and for amended proxy materials to be filed, if necessary. Definitive copies of the proxy materials must be filed, or mailed for filing, with the SEC not later than the date when they are first sent or given to the securityholders.[54]

With some exceptions, solicitations prior to furnishing the definitive proxy statement are prohibited.[55] The SEC's rules contain detailed instructions on the methods to be used in sending proxy materials to securityholders, including those whose securities are held in "street name."[56]

Rule 14a-8 of the SEC's proxy rules requires management to include securityholder proposals in its proxy statement with a supporting statement not exceeding 500 words. For many years, John and Lewis Gilbert and institutional investors have submitted rational proposals that, although often defeated, have achieved a cumulative effect on corporate governance. Unfortunately, some environmental and other groups make nominal share purchases in order to use the shareholder proposal right to publicize their causes at corporate expense, although they are routinely defeated by the other shareholders. Proposals that obtain insignificant percentages of the votes can be omitted in future years.

The American Society of Corporate Secretaries reported that some of the most common shareholder proposals for the 12-month period from July 1, 1995 to June 30, 1996 were acquisition-related. The proposals were (1) elimination of a staggered board of directors, (2) elimination of pension benefits for nonemployee directors, (3) cumulative voting, (4) redemption of poison pills, (5) payment of directors' fees in stock, (6) elimination of "golden parachutes," and (7) a sale or merger.

The 1934 Act and the SEC's rules prohibit any false or misleading statements of material fact and omissions of material fact in a proxy statement, proxy or other communication. Any statement made in an earlier commu-

---

[52]Regulation 14A, Rules 14a-1 *et seq.*

[53]Rule 14a-3.

[54]Rule 14a-6.

[55]Rule 14a-12.

[56]Rule 14a-13; Rules 14b-1 and 14b-2

nication for the same meeting must be corrected if it becomes false or misleading.[57]

3. Solicitation for Mergers and Asset Sales

Item 14 of Schedule 14A to the SEC's proxy rules describes the information that must be included in a proxy statement if proxies will be solicited for a vote or consent on a merger, consolidation, acquisition, sale of all or a substantial part of the corporate assets, or a liquidation or dissolution of the corporation.

The proxy statement must contain extensive information about the transactions. The corporation soliciting proxies must include a description of the business of the other corporation participating in the transaction and a summary of the material features of the transaction. For example, the summary must include (1) the terms of the transaction; (2) the reasons for the transaction; (3) any material differences in the rights of the security-holders as a result of the transaction; (4) the accounting treatment of the transaction; and (5) the federal income tax consequences of the transaction. Information describing any securities to be issued must be provided. Historical and pro forma financial information and financial statements required by Regulation S-X must also be provided. A statement must be made as to whether any federal or state regulatory requirements must be complied with or approval obtained and, if so, the status of the compliance or approval. Any material report, opinion or appraisal such as a fairness opinion received from an outside party must be described. Material contracts must be described and recent market prices of securities must be shown. The proxy statement must also contain extensive information about the corporation soliciting the proxies and the other corporation involved in the transaction.

Although Item 14 requires extensive information, corporations reporting under the 1934 Act can incorporate much of the information by reference to other reports and documents filed with the SEC.

4. Proxy Contests

During the 1980s and 1990s, proxy contests and the threat of proxy contests became a significant factor in corporate governance. When shares of publicly owned corporations were owned primarily by individuals and passive institutional investors, management could use its control of the shareholder meeting and proxy solicitation process to perpetuate control. Lack of initiative and cohesion among the shareholders prevented them from taking effective action to challenge poor management performance.

---

[57]Rule 14a-9. Shareholders and investors have a private right of action to recover damages or seek an injunction if they have been or will be injured by a false or misleading proxy solicitation. *J. I. Case Co. v. Borak,* 377 U.S. 426 (1964); *Mills v. Electric Auto-Lite Co.,* 396 U.S. 375 (1970); *TSC Industries, Inc. v. Northway, Inc.,* 426 U.S. 438 (1976); *Wilson v. Great American Industries, Inc.,* 1992-1993 CCH Fed. Sec. L. Rep. § 97, 236 (2nd Cir. 1988); *Virginia Bankshares, Inc. v. Sandberg,* 111 S. Ct. 2749 (1991). Outside directors who did not participate in preparation of a proxy statement and did not know about omissions of material facts may be able to avoid liability. *Salit v. The Stanley Works,* 1992-1993 CCH Fed. Sec. L. Rep. § 97,305 (D. Conn. 1992).

During the 1980s, Drexel Burnham Lambert Incorporated (DBL) perceived the major growth of institutional investment power and sold billions of dollars of high yield securities ("junk bonds") to fund takeover campaigns led by a variety of colorful campaigners, such as Ronald Perelman and Samuel Heyman. Other investment banking firms also drew on the large resources of institutional investors to support takeover campaigns.[58] An important side effect of these takeover campaigns was that managements across the nation became far more conscious of the need to create shareholder value. Many managements implemented corporate governance reforms and business and financial restructurings.

When the "control share," "business combination" and other state antitakeover laws were upheld by the U.S. Supreme Court, the leveraged takeover lost its viability. However, institutional investors had seen the influence that they could exercise on corporate governance when their large shareholdings were combined. They foresaw that many managements would regard their success in persuading state legislatures to adopt antitakeover laws as an opportunity to deemphasize corporate governance reforms and the creation of shareholder value.

Institutional investors such as the California Public Employees Retirement System (CALPERS) increased the use of their right to make shareholder proposals under Rule 14a-8. They also kept management aware of their right to initiate a proxy contest. Other dissident shareholders also considered proxy contests when dissatisfied with management performance.

A proxy contest is a bitter battle that ebbs and flows until the votes are counted at the shareholders' meeting, because the shareholders can revoke their proxies if they decide to switch sides. Even after the meeting is held, the result remains uncertain until the end of litigation challenging the methods used by the victor. Management has major advantages in a proxy contest. Management's advantages include acquaintance with the major shareholders, ability to use corporate funds and personnel to solicit proxies and the opportunity to correct actions criticized by dissident shareholders, thus depriving them of key issues.

On the other hand, dissident shareholders must bear their own expenses which include the services of a law firm, an investment banking firm, a proxy solicitation firm, a financial printer, an investor relations consulting firm and perhaps also an accounting firm. A proxy contest can be expected to cost $1,000,000 or more and the dissident shareholder or shareholders who bear the expenses will not be reimbursed unless they are successful.[59] If the dissident shareholders acquire shares to strengthen their voting power, they must be careful not to trigger the provisions of a "control share" law that would deny voting rights to their shares or create other adverse consequences.

---

[58]The media lionized campaigners such as Carl Icahn, T. Boone Pickens, Harold Simmons and Asher Edelman and often described DBL and other investment banking firms as supporting them with funds. However, except for *Forbes*, the media seldom reported that the major funding sources were institutions such as insurers, pension funds and banks.

[59]If the dissident shareholders are successful in electing their nominees, the new board typically authorizes reimbursement of their proxy solicitation expenses on grounds that the change of management is beneficial to the corporation.

Despite these disadvantages, dissident shareholders who seek to gain control through a proxy contest have several advantages. Unlike a tender offer, there is no need to purchase all or a majority of the outstanding shares. Thus, although proxy contests are expensive, they are far less costly than a tender offer. Finally, unlike a tender offer, the shares owned by the dissident shareholders continue to be listed on a stock exchange or traded in the NASDAQ system, thus preserving the liquidity of the dissident shareholders' investment, except for the partial restrictions on sales of control shares imposed by the 1933 Act.

An example of a successful proxy contest was the 1983 contest led by Samuel Heyman to oust the board of directors of GAF Corporation and replace it with a slate of directors, including the author, that Mr. Heyman had assembled. The focus of Mr. Heyman's campaign was the performance over a period of years of GAF's chief executive officer, Dr. Jesse Werner. Mr. Heyman began the contest with only 6 percent of the outstanding shares, an unusually modest holding to use as the base for a proxy contest. Nevertheless, after a campaign costing over $1,000,000, 58 percent of the shareholders voted for the nominees proposed for the Heyman nominees at GAF's annual meeting in April 1983. After the resolution of litigation, the Heyman nominees became GAF's board of directors in December 1983 and elected Mr. Heyman as Chairman and Chief Executive Officer. Mr. Heyman then led a turnaround of GAF's businesses, resulting in an important increase of the market value of its shares.

The SEC permits contentious writing in proxy contest materials, in contrast to the bland and sometimes soporific style it has encouraged in other documents. In doing so, the SEC recognizes that dissident shareholders have little chance to oust an incumbent management if they cannot gain the attention of shareholders with sharply critical comments that overcome inertia and misplaced loyalty. Conversely, although the SEC is no friend to incumbent managements, it is aware that persons who commence proxy contests may have self-serving objectives and allows management to warn shareholders about them in blunt language. Otherwise, the SEC would risk criticism for allowing unqualified, and perhaps even unscrupulous, persons to gain control of publicly owned corporations.

The SEC's proxy rules contain several provisions designed to "level the playing field" for proxy contests so that dissident shareholders have a chance of success in spite of the advantages held by incumbent management. Rule 14a-2(b) provides a broad exemption from almost all requirements of the proxy rules, except certain filing requirements, for any solicitation made by persons other than the company when the total persons solicited is less than ten. Subject to several exceptions, a larger number of persons may be solicited by any person who does not during the solicitation seek, directly or indirectly, the power to act as a proxy or to obtain a form of revocation, abstention, consent or authorization. However, one of the exceptions prevents use of the exemption by any person required to file a Schedule 13D (i.e., a 5 percent shareholder) who has disclosed an intent to engage in a control transaction or a contested solicitation for the election of directors. Thus, the broader solicitation has limited availability in proxy contests.

Rule 14a-7 requires management to provide a shareholders' list to the dissident shareholder for use in sending its proxy materials and other solicitation materials or to mail them for the dissident shareholder at the dissident shareholder's expense. Dissident shareholders typically prefer to obtain a court order under state law requiring management to deliver a shareholders' list so that they can send their own materials without giving management advance knowledge of their plans.

Rule 14a-11 allows solicitation prior to furnishing a written proxy statement, subject to several conditions. The dissident shareholder may not furnish a form of proxy; must identify the participants in the solicitation and their interests; and must furnish a written proxy statement meeting the requirements of Regulation 14A at the earliest practical date thereafter. The dissident shareholder must also file copies of the materials with the SEC no later than the date such material is published, sent or given to any shareholder.

Rules 14a-7 and 14a-11 do not fully balance management's advantage of prior acquaintance with the shareholders. However, they allow a dissident shareholder to learn the identity of the shareholders and evaluate the feasibility of a proxy contest.

The SEC has adopted regulations to facilitate transmittal of proxy materials and other communications to shareholders. Rule 14a-13 obligates corporations soliciting proxies to inquire of record holders who are brokers, dealers, banks, associations or other entities exercising fiduciary powers and who hold shares in nominee name, about the quantities of proxy and other soliciting materials and annual reports needed for the beneficial owners of shares held by them.

The corporation can also notify them that it intends to distribute directly to non-objecting beneficial owners, or NOBOs. Rule 14b-1 requires brokers and dealers and Rule 14b-2 requires banks, associations and other fiduciaries promptly to furnish the approximate number of beneficial owners and, if the corporation intends to mail directly, the names and addresses of NOBOs. If the corporation will not mail directly, these entities must transmit materials promptly with requests for voting instructions. They must also act promptly in mailings and requests for voting instructions from objecting beneficial owners, or OBOs.

The rules allow Depository Trust Company and other clearing services to issue omnibus proxies in favor of their members. They also allow broker-dealers, banks, associations and other fiduciaries to delegate their functions to an agent. Hundreds have appointed the Independent Election Corporation of America, or IECA, to handle their mailings and requests for voting instructions. The corporation must pay specified fees per mailing and request for instructions to help defray the costs of these tasks, as provided in the rules of the stock exchanges and the NASDAQ Market.

The SEC's regulations do not fully extend the communication system to shareholders soliciting votes in a proxy contest. As mentioned earlier, sponsoring shareholders must rely on state law to obtain stockholder lists. As part of the court order, they can also obtain the list of brokers, dealers, banks and others for whom clearing services hold shares, but they can obtain a list of NOBOs only if management has obtained a list.[60] Thus, a sponsoring shareholder must rely on the experience of the proxy solicitation

[60] *Shamrock Associates v. Texas American Energy Corp.*, 517 Atl.2d 658 (Del. Ch. 1986); *RB Associates v. The Gillette Co.*, No. 9711 (Del. Ch. March 22, 1988).

firm and the rules of the exchanges and NASD to arrange effective mailings, voting instructions and direct communications.

Interested readers can obtain information from the American Society of Corporate Secretaries, Inc., 521 Fifth Avenue, New York, New York 10175, including its *Manual for the Solicitation of Proxies, Proxy Contact List and Nominee List.* Information is also published by the Depository Trust Company (CEDE & Co.) and the Independent Election Corporation of America, Lake Success, New York. A very informative newsletter is published on a quarterly basis by Registrar and Transfer Company, 10 Commerce Drive, Cranford, New Jersey 07016-3572.

G. Certain Tax Issues

1. Golden Parachutes

The threat of a hostile tender offer or proxy contest can have a serious adverse effect on the morale of employees of the target corporation, especially the senior management members who are the most likely persons to lose their employment if an acquisition or other change of control occurs. They often decide to seek other employment or receive unsolicited offers of employment. As a result, many corporations have entered into employment or other contracts with their key executives providing attractive compensation and benefit commitments in the event of a change of control. Executive compensation consultants and investment bankers have advised management that lucrative commitments in the contracts could even serve as a "shark repellant" device. This advice led to an escalation of the compensation and benefits that gave the contracts the name "golden parachutes."

In "golden parachute" contracts, a change of control is usually defined broadly to include a "hostile" tender offer and also a "friendly" acquisition or a proxy contest in which the dissident shareholders gain control. The customary definition, although its wisdom is questionable, arose because executives often lose their employment after "friendly" transactions, such as an acquisition by a "white knight."

"Golden parachute" contracts have been challenged in court with little success so far.[61] However, they attract growing criticism, especially when they result in large payments to executives who continue as executives after a change of control that they negotiated.[62]

Section 4999 of the Internal Revenue Code imposes a 20 percent excise tax on any "excess parachute payment" as defined in Section 280G of the Internal Revenue Code. Section 280G(a) denies a deduction for any excess parachute payment.

Stated briefly, Section 280G(b) defines a "parachute payment" as a payment in the nature of compensation to an officer, director or highly compensated individual if the payment is contingent on a change in (1) the

[61] *Bershad v. Hartz,* No. 6960 (Del Ch. Jan. 29, 1987); see also *Rand v. Western Airlines, Inc.,* No 8632 (Del. Ch. Feb. 25, 1994) in which the court rejected a challenge to a merger based on allegations that the officers who negotiated the merger terms could not be objective because of the financial benefits in their "golden parachute" contracts.

[62] "Have Parachutes Become More Than Security Blankets?" Bowie et al, *Mergers & Acquisitions,* November/December 1996.

ownership or effective control of the corporation or (2) the ownership of a substantial portion of the assets of the corporation, **and** the aggregate present value of the payments equal or exceeds three times a base amount which is the individual's annualized includible compensation for a 5-year base period. An "excess parachute payment" is the excess of any parachute payment over the portion of the base amount allocated to such payment.

Section 280G contains several exceptions and exemptions. For example, a parachute payment does not include any amount that the taxpayer establishes by clear and convincing evidence is reasonable compensation for personal services rendered on or after the date of the change that triggered the payment. Exemptions are provided for small business corporations and payments under qualified plans.

2. Greenmail

As hostile tender offer and proxy contests became relatively common in the 1970s and 1980s, some managements repurchased shares from shareholders who had acquired substantial holdings and were known or believed to be considering a tender offer or proxy contest. Indeed, some risk arbitrageurs obtained a reputation for acquiring shares and then seeking a repurchase at a considerable premium over prevailing market prices. Because the payment of such a premium was made under the pressure created by a hostile tender offer or proxy contest, the arrangements came to be called "greenmail."

Managements that repurchased shares at a premium from an unfriendly shareholder justified their decisions on grounds that the repurchase saved the corporation from the major costs and uncertainty of a hostile tender offer or proxy contest that could upset its business. The courts in Delaware have upheld the actions of boards of directors who authorized repurchases of shares for premium prices as a reasonable exercise of "business judgment."[63]

Section 5881 of the Internal Revenue Code imposes on any person who receives greenmail a tax equal to 50 percent of gain or other income of such person by reason of its receipt.

Under Section 5881, "greenmail" is any consideration transferred by a corporation (or a person acting in concert with such corporation) to directly or indirectly acquire stock of such corporation from any shareholder if (1) the shareholder held the stock for less than 2 years before entering into the agreement to make the transfer; (2) at some time during the 2-year period ending on the date of such acquisition the shareholder (or certain other persons) made or threatened a public tender offer for stock of the corporation; **and** (3) such acquisition is not pursuant to an offer not made on the same terms to all shareholders.

Section 5881 states that the tax applies whether or not the gain or other income is recognized. Thus, for example, if greenmail is paid in connection with a tax free reorganization or a tax free spin off, split off or split up, the 50 percent tax must nevertheless be paid.

---

[63]*Polk v. Good*, 507 A.2d 531 (1986); *Grobow v. Perot*, 539 A.2d 180 (Del. 1988); In re *General Motors Class E. Stock Buyout Securities Litigation*, 694 F. Supp. 1119 (D. Del. 1988). However, see *Heckmann v. Ahmanson*, 168 Cal App.3d 119, 204 Cal Rep. 177 (1985). Some corporations have included anti-greenmail provisions in their charters and some state antitakeover laws also prohibit "greenmail" payments.

H. "Short Form" Mergers

A corporation that owns a high percentage (such as 90 or 95 percent) of the outstanding stock of a subsidiary is allowed by the corporation laws of many states to cause a merger of the subsidiary without a vote of shareholders. The parent corporation can accomplish the merger by simply filing a certificate of merger with the Secretary of State or other appropriate corporate authority.[64] The minority shareholders typically have a statutory right to receive the appraised fair value of their shares in cash after any such merger.

Plaintiff attorneys have attempted to challenge "short form" subsidiary mergers on a variety of grounds. An attempt to impose liability on Santa Fe Industries, Inc. by characterizing a "short form" merger of its subsidiary, Kirby Lumber Corp., as a "manipulative or deceptive device or contrivance" or as a fraud prohibited by the SEC's Rule 10b-5 was rejected by the U.S. Supreme Court.[65] A later attempt to sue Santa Fe under a "blue sky law" (New York's Martin Act) was also rejected. Challenges based on allegations that the merger lacked a business purpose or violated the fiduciary obligations of the directors or the parent corporation to the minority shareholders have also generally been unsuccessful.[66] However, appraisal rights are not an exclusive remedy and a "short form" merger may be enjoined if the parent and the directors of the subsidiary breach their fiduciary duties to the minority shareholders.[67]

I. "Short Swing" Trading Liability

Section 16(a) of the 1934 Act requires persons who become officers, directors or beneficial owners of more than 10 percent of any class of equity security registered under the Act to file with the SEC an initial report of their holdings on Form 3. Thereafter, if they acquire or dispose of securities beneficially owned in a calendar month, a report on Form 4 showing the transactions must be filed within 10 days after the end of the month. *The Wall Street Journal* and other newspapers publish the contents of these reports.

Section 16(b) provides that any profit realized by a director, officer or beneficial owner of 10 percent or more of any class of equity security registered under the 1934 Act from any purchase and sale, or sale and purchase, of such equity security within any period less than 6 months shall inure to and be recoverable by the issuer. Stated more simply, directors, officers and 10 percent shareholders must pay to the corporation any profit they realize from "short swing" trading of its shares within a 6 month period. The SEC and the courts enforce Section 16(b) strictly.

---

[64]For example, see the Delaware Corporation Law, § 523 and the New York Business Corporation Law, § 905.

[65]*Santa Fe Industries, Inc. v. Green*, 530 U.S. 462 (1977); *Leogard v. Santa Fe Industries, Inc.*, 639 F. Supp. 673 (SDNY 1986).

[66]*Harnett v. Billman*, 800 F.2d 1308 (4th Cir. 1986); *Rosenblatt v. Getty Oil Co.*, 493 Atl.2d 929 (1985); *Coleman v. Taub*, 638 F.2d 628 (3d Cir. 1981); *Kalmanovitz v. G. Heileman Brewing Co.*, 595 F.Supp. 1385 (D. Del. 1984).

[67]*Sealy Mattress Co. of New Jersey v. Sealy, Inc.*, 532 Atl.2d 1324 (Del. Ch. 1987).

Prospective bidders that acquire shares (or other equity securities) of another corporation in anticipation of a possible acquisition sometimes do not complete the acquisition. This can happen, for example, if another bidder, friendly or unfriendly, acquires the corporation or if the corporation successfully uses defensive tactics such as an issuer repurchase of shares. As a result, the bidder may be faced with semivoluntary or involuntary resale of the acquired shares. If the bidder beneficially owns more than 10 percent of any class of equity securities of the corporation, a resale of the securities within 6 months of their purchase will create liability under Section 16(b).

Section 16(b) liability is one reason why prospective bidders often acquire less than 10 percent of the shares of a target corporation until they have decided whether to go forward with a tender offer or other acquisition transaction.[68]

Prospective bidders owning more than 10 percent of a class of shares can avoid liability by retaining them for 6 months. When that is not possible, an alternative is to sell first the shares in excess of 10 percent. These sales will be subject to Section 16(b) liability, but the remaining 10 percent of the shares can be sold without liability.

The SEC's Rule 16b-7 contains exemptions for acquisitions or dispositions of securities pursuant to certain mergers or consolidations in exchange for a security of a company that previously owned 85 percent or more of either (1) the equity securities of all other involved companies or (2) the combined assets of all companies involved in the merger or consolidation.

J. Insider Trading

Fulfillment of disclosure obligations during acquisition and divestiture transactions is an important and difficult task. Announcements of acquisitions and divestitures involving publicly owned corporations are commonly followed by significant increases or decreases in the market prices of their shares. Experienced corporate managers know that transactions often "crater" in the late negotiation stages. Thus, they rightly avoid premature disclosure of transactions while in early negotiation stages that may never lead to an agreement.[69]

During the negotiations, however, corporate officers and directors, their adviser professionals and other persons obtain nonpublic information about the proposed transaction that could be used to gain an unlawful advantage in the stock market over as yet uninformed public shareholders. Thus, corporations must be especially alert during acquisition and divestiture negotiations to assure that no misuse or wrongful disclosure of material nonpublic information occurs in violation of the insider trading prohibitions of the 1934 Act.

[68]For risk arbitrageurs who initially acquire shares for investment, another reason is the 10 percent limit contained in the regulation of the Federal Trade Commission exempting acquisitions of shares solely for investment from filing a Hart-Scott-Rodino notification and report. 16 C.F.R. § 802.9.

[69]The announcements may also trigger actions by customers, suppliers, government agencies, competitors and employees. However, when it becomes probable that a material acquisition will be consummated, disclosure is required. *Basic, Inc. v. Levinson*, 485 U.S. 224 (1988).

The statutory bases for the prohibition of insider trading are Sections 10(b) and 14(e) of the 1934 Act. Section 10(b) prohibits, among other things, the use of any manipulative device or contrivance in connection with the sale or purchase of a security in violation of an SEC rule. The SEC adopted Rule 10b-5 to implement Section 10(b). Section 14(e) prohibits fraudulent practices in connection with any tender offer. The SEC adopted Rule 14e-3 to implement Section 14(e).

The civil liability and civil and criminal penalties imposed by the 1934 Act on insider trading are corollaries of its disclosure obligations. Corporate management who are responsible for fulfilling disclosure obligations cannot be permitted to profit from failure to perform the obligations. Thus, they must meet a "disclose or abstain" standard. When material nonpublic information is not ready for disclosure, the corporate "insiders" must abstain from using it for trading and from disclosing it to others who use it for trading.

The persons who were originally considered to be "insiders" were officers, directors and controlling shareholders. However, the SEC and the courts have gradually added to persons who must refrain from trading when in possession of material nonpublic information.

The first noninsiders held subject to liability for trading on the basis of nonpublic information were investment bankers, financial consultants, lawyers, accountants and other professionals to whom corporate management entrusted the information in the course of their work.[70] These professionals were sometimes called "quasi insiders" or "temporary insiders" because of their working relationships with the corporate insiders.

The insider trading prohibition was soon extended to much wider groups. In November 1963, personnel of Texas Gulf Sulphur Co. tested a drill core sample taken near Timmins, Ontario and the results showed a high content of copper, zinc and silver containing ore. However, Texas Gulf postponed disclosure and later issued a conservative press release pending the results of further tests and completion of a land acquisition program. The additional tests confirmed a major ore deposit and a public announcement of discovery was made. A major increase of the price of Texas Gulf's shares followed, reaching $58 per share in May 1964. However, before the public announcement and on the day it was released, officers, directors and employees of Texas Gulf and persons (called "tippees") who learned about the drilling activities from them purchased shares at prices ranging from $17 to $34. In a landmark decision, the insiders who had furnished information to "tippees" were held liable for the purchases made by their "tippees."[71]

Unlike insiders and quasi insiders, "tippees" do not have professional responsibilities that create fiduciary obligations to a corporation and its shareholders. However, if an insider has breached his or her fiduciary duty by disclosing material nonpublic information, a "tippee" who receives the information succeeds to the insider's duty to refrain from trading.[72] If a "tippee" does not know that the insider breached his or her fiduciary lia-

---

[70]*Shapiro v. Merrill, Lynch, Pierce, Fenner & Smith, Inc.*, 495 F.2d 228 (2d Cir. 1974)

[71]*SEC v. Texas Gulf Sulphur Co.*, 258 F.Supp. 262 (S.D.N.Y. 1966), aff'd 401 F.2d 833 (2d Cir. 1968). The "tippees" had not been named as defendants.

[72]*Dirks v. Securities and Exchange Commission*, 463 U.S. 646 (1983).

bility or that the information is confidential, the "tippee" may be excused from liability.[73]

There are limits on the extent to which the courts will extend insider trading liability, especially in cases involving criminal or civil penalties. For example, the U.S. Supreme Court, in a decision on which the Justices divided 6 to 3, reversed the criminal conviction for violation of Section 10(b) and Rule 10b-5 of Vincent Chiarella, who worked as a "markup man" for a large financial printing firm. Chiarella had obtained nonpublic information about several proposed takeover bids as a part of his work on the printing of the bid announcements. He purchased stock in the target companies and resold at higher prices after the takeover offers were made public. The Supreme Court found that Chiarella was not an insider and had received no information from the corporations or their insiders. Thus, the Supreme Court found that Chiarella had no duty to disclose or refrain from trading.[74]

In a later 6 to 3 decision, the U.S. Supreme Court struck down a censure by the SEC of John Dirks, an officer of a broker-dealer firm who used his skills as an insurance stock analyst to investigate and expose a major fraudulent overstatement of assets by Equity Funding of America. Neither Dirks nor his firm owned or traded shares of Equity Funding, but Dirks told several customers and investors about his investigation and they sold their shares before the fraud was published and Equity Funding went into receivership. The Supreme Court held that Dirks was not an insider and the Equity Funding employees who cooperated with his investigation did not violate any fiduciary duty to its shareholders by providing information to Dirks. Thus, Dirks did not violate Section 10(b) and Rule 10b-5.[75]

In recent years, the SEC and plaintiff attorneys developed a "misappropriation theory" that again expanded the persons subject to insider trading liability. Under this theory, a person who receives nonpublic information in a relationship of trust and confidence and misappropriates the information by using it to trade in securities is in violation of Rule 10b-5, or Rule 14e-3 if related to a tender offer. The theory also applies to a person who misappropriates by furnishing the information to a "tippee" who uses it to trade in securities. The significance of the misappropriation theory is that a violation can exist even though the information was not received from insiders or quasi insiders of the corporation that issued the securities traded. For example, Foster Winans, a financial columnist for *The Wall Street Journal*, breached his duty to his employer when he furnished advance information about the contents of the column "Heard in the Street" to securities brokers, who used the information to trade in the securities mentioned in the column. Thus, Winans and the stockbrokers were convicted for violating Rule 10b-5.[76]

[73]*U.S. v. Chestman*, 903 F.2d 75 (2d Cir. 1990), vacated 947 F.2d 551 (2d Cir. 1991); cert. den. 112 S. Ct. 1759 (1992); *SEC v. Monarch Fund*, 608 F.2d 938 (2d Cir. 1979).

[74]*Chiarella v. Unites States*, 445 U.S. 222 (1980). Based on many years of experience working with financial printers, the author believes that the case was erroneously decided. Corporations regularly entrust valuable nonpublic information to financial printers in reliance on their integrity and assurances of confidentiality. The personnel of financial printers are selected for their intelligence, motivation and integrity and are well paid for their work.

[75]*Dirks v. Securities and Exchange Commission*, supra.

[76]*U.S. v. Carpenter*, 791 F.2d 1024 (2d Cir. 1986), affirmed in a 4 to 4 decision 44 U.S. 19 (1987)

The "misappropriation theory" was adopted by the U.S. Circuit Courts of Appeal for the Second, Third, Seventh and Ninth Circuits. However, it was rejected in the Fourth and Eighth Circuits. In the Eighth Circuit, the Court of Appeals also ruled that the SEC had exceeded its authority in adopting Rule 14e-3 by omitting any requirement of a breach of fiduciary duty.[77] However, the U.S. Supreme Court reversed the decision of the Eighth Circuit and upheld both the "misappropriation theory" and Rule 14e-3. Thus, the "misappropriation theory" has become established law.

Defendants in insider trading cases can present evidence that the nonpublic information they received was not material and its disclosure to the public was not required. They can also present evidence that their purchases or sales were motivated by information other than the nonpublic information. Depending on the timing of the purchases or sales and other factors, such evidence could be credible and persuasive. However, hindsight affects the willingness of the SEC and the courts to accept such evidence. For example, Texas Gulf presented extensive evidence that test results from a single core sample were not sufficient evidence to justify announcing the discovery of a major ore deposit. Some judges of the Court of Appeals agreed, but a majority were not persuaded. The defendants' own trading activities were a strong factor in assessing materiality and motives.[78]

In 1984, Congress adopted the Insider Trading Sanctions Act (ITSA) which authorized penalties up to three times the profit gained or loss avoided as a result of insider trading. In 1988, Congress adopted the Insider Trading and Securities Fraud Enforcement Act (ITSFEA) which, among other things, strengthened the enforcement powers of the SEC and increased the criminal penalties for insider trading violations. The ITSFEA also expressly provided that a controlling person who knows or recklessly disregards the fact that a controlled person is likely to engage in an act or acts constituting an insider trading violation and fails to take appropriate preventive steps is liable for the violation.[79]

A controlling person that is a registered broker-dealer or investment adviser is also liable if it knowingly or recklessly fails to establish, maintain or enforce a policy or procedure reasonably designed, taking into account the nature of its business, to prevent misuse of material nonpublic information. Among the policies or procedures that broker-dealers can adopt are the following:

- restriction on communication of nonpublic information by means such as a "Chinese Wall";
- monitoring dissemination of nonpublic information by means such as restraining access to files;
- continuing education programs;
- restricting or monitoring trading in securities for which the firm's employees possess nonpublic information by means such as a "restricted list";

[77]*U.S. v. O'Hagan,* 92 F.2d 612 (8th Cir. 1996); reversed 117 S.C. 2100. 65 L.W. 4650 (1977).

[78]*SEC v. Texas Gulf Sulphur Co.,* supra.

[79]The ITSFEA provides, however, that no person shall be subject to a penalty solely by reason of employing another person subject to a penalty.

- monitoring and reviewing trading for the account of the firm; and
- requiring employees to conduct trading through in-house accounts or that trading in outside accounts be reported expeditiously to the firm.

To prevent violations, many corporations require that their directors, officers and employees notify the corporate secretary or counsel before any purchase or sale of shares. By doing so, they can avoid a sale or purchase at a time when a material transaction or event is occurring or has occurred that has not yet been publicly announced. Some corporations go further to restrict sales and purchases to brief "window" periods of a few days after annual and quarterly earnings have been announced, provided that no material event is then occurring.

K. Margin Rules

The 1934 Act authorizes the Board of Governors of the Federal Reserve System (FRB) to adopt regulations governing the extension of credit for the purchase or carrying of securities. The FRB has adopted Regulation T (brokers and dealers), Regulation U (banks and other lenders) and Regulation X (borrowers). Regulation T applies to all credit extended by brokers and dealers, including inadvertent credit when customers fail to deliver securities or payments on time. Regulation U applies only to credit extended by banks and other lenders for the purpose of purchasing or carrying securities. For many years, the margin percent has been 50 percent of the value of the securities involved. The rule is met (or not met) on the date of purchase and violations cannot result from a later decline in value of the securities. **Note:** In December 1997, the FRB merged former Regulation G into Regulation U, but retained distinctions between banks and other lenders.

L. Reference Materials

1. Books

Blue Sky Law Reporter, Commerce Clearing House

Blue Sky Practice, Fass and Wittner, Clark Boardman Callaghan

Corporate Anti-Takeover Defenses: The Poison Pill Device, Simon, Clark Boardman Callaghan

Federal Securities Law Reporter, Commerce Clearing House (seven volumes)

Insider Trading: Regulation, Enforcement and Prevention, Langevoort, Clark Boardman Callaghan

Proxy Rules Handbook, Sargent and Honabach, Clark Boardman Callaghan

Section 16 of the Securities Exchange Act, Jacobs, Clark Boardman Callaghan

Securities Law Handbook, Bloomenthal Clark Boardman Callaghan

Securities Regulation, Jennings, Marsh, Coffee and Seligman, Foundation Press

Securities Regulation, Loss and Seligman, Little Brown & Co.

2. Articles

"Inside the New Insider Trading Act," Shea, *The Practical Lawyer*, Sept. 1989

M. Exhibits

12-1 Example of a Listing Application to The New York Stock Exchange

12-2 Schedule 13D

12-3 Schedule 14D-1

12-4 Schedule 14D-9

12-5 Announcement of a Shareholder Rights ("Poison Pill") Plan

12-6 Example of a Fairness Opinion

EXHIBIT 12-1

LISTING APPLICATION TO
NEW YORK STOCK EXCHANGE, INC.

C-___________
May, 1989

GUARDSMAN PRODUCTS, INC.

175,000 ADDITIONAL SHARES OF COMMON STOCK,
$1 PAR VALUE PER SHARE, AND
175,000 RIGHTS TO PURCHASE PREFERRED STOCK

IN CONNECTION WITH THE ACQUISITION OF ASSETS OF
ISIS COATINGS, INC.

Number of Shares of Common Stock Issued and Outstanding On May 1, 1989 (excluding Treasury shares):	Number of Stockholders of Record of Common Stock on May 1, 1989:
5,573,881	1,479

Date of Action by Board of Directors of Guardsman Products, Inc.:	March 29, 1989
Date of Approval by Stockholders of Guardsman Products, Inc.:	Not Required

DESCRIPTION OF TRANSACTION

GUARDSMAN PRODUCTS, INC., a Delaware corporation ("Guardsman" or the "Company"), has entered into an Asset Purchase Agreement dated May 13, 1989 (the "Agreement"), with ISIS COATINGS, INC., a Connecticut corporation ("ISIS"), and certain principal shareholders of ISIS for the acquisition of the principle assets of ISIS. The consideration for the assets will be a cash payment plus the issuance and delivery on the Closing Date (scheduled for on or before June 12, 1989), of 175,000 shares of Guardsman's common stock, $1 par value per share (the "Common Stock"). This Listing Application is for the 175,000 additional shares of the Common Stock to be transferred to ISIS under the Agreement, and for the 175,000 Preferred Stock Purchase Rights relating to that Common Stock.

ISIS is a manufacturer of chemical coatings, with manufacturing facilities in Connecticut and Missouri. The acquisition of the ISIS coatings business by Guardsman will benefit Guardsman by expanding its coatings manufacturing

10280129

capability and customer base into the northeastern United States, and by enabling Guardsman to enter certain coatings specialty-niche markets in which Guardsman does not currently operate.

No officer, director or principal stockholder of Guardsman or any of its subsidiaries has any direct or indirect beneficial interest in the assets to be purchased. The terms of the transaction were determined as a result of arm's-length negotiations. The Company decided to acquire ISIS on the basis of examination, review and analysis by its management staff and accounting personnel. Under the Agreement, the Company will acquire all inventories, machinery and equipment of ISIS, together with the patents, formulae, goodwill, the name "ISIS Coatings, Inc.," and other intangible assets relating to ISIS' coatings business for One Million Dollars ($1,000,000) in cash and 175,000 shares of ISIS' real estate, cash on deposit or accounts receivable. The cash portion of the purchase price will be adjusted, upward or downward, to the extent that ISIS' inventories exceed or are less than One Million Three Hundred Thousand Dollars ($1,300,000) on the date the transaction is consummated. In addition, Guardsman will enter into noncompetition agreements with two of ISIS' principal officers and shareholders.

No approval by the stockholders of Guardsman is required in connection with the proposed transaction because the number of authorized but unissued shares of Common Stock of Guardsman is sufficient for the proposed transaction. Approval of the Agreement by the shareholders of ISIS is required by the Connecticut Stock Corporation Act. A Special Meeting of the Shareholders of ISIS has been scheduled for June 12, 1989, for this purpose.

The acquisition of ISIS' principal assets by Guardsman will be treated as a purchase for accounting purposes. Guardsman anticipates that it will record the fair market values of the identifiable tangible and intangible assets on its statement of financial position as of the date the asset purchase transaction is consummated. The excess of the purchase price over the fair market value of the tangible assets will be recorded on the statement of financial position as goodwill and amortized over 20 years in accordance with Guardsman's accounting policy. This accounting procedure has been approved by Ernst & Whinney, the Company's independent auditors, as being in accordance with generally accepted accounting principles.

Preferred Stock Purchase Rights, which entitle the holder thereof to purchase shares of the Company's preferred stock under certain circumstances (the "Rights") have been attached to the Common Stock pursuant to the terms of a Rights

Agreement between Guardsman and Manufacturers Hanover Trust Company, as Rights Agent (the "Rights Agreement"), as described in Listing Application No. C-19137 dated February 10, 1988, as that Rights Agreement has been amended. Each share of Common Stock issued in connection with the acquisition of the assets of ISIS will have a Right attached to that share, subject to the expiration and redemption provisions of the Rights Agreement, as amended. Guardsman has previously listed Rights in connection with outstanding shares of Common Stock and shares of Common Stock reserved for issuance under Guardsman's stock option plans. This Listing Application seeks the listing of an additional 175,000 such Rights in connection with the listing of the 175,000 shares of Guardsman's Common Stock to be issued as part of Guardsman's contemplated transaction with ISIS.

A discussion of the history and business of ISIS is contained in the Prospectus and Proxy Statement of Guardsman Products, Inc., dated May 12, 1989, which is attached to this Listing Application as Exhibit A and made a part hereof. Certified year-end and interim balance sheets and income statements of ISIS are attached to this Listing Application as Exhibit B and made a part hereof.

RECENT DEVELOPMENTS

On March 31, 1989, Guardsman acquired a manufacturing facility, machinery, equipment and inventories located in Rocky Hill, Connecticut, from the Dexter Corporation. This transaction was disclosed on Guardsman's Form 8-K Current Report filed with the Securities and Exchange Commission on April 10, 1989.

AUTHORITY FOR ISSUANCE

The Agreement was approved and the issuance of shares applied for listing herein was authorized by Guardsman's Board of Directors at a meeting held on March 29, 1989. The Agreement was approved by the Board of Directors of ISIS on May 9, 1989, and will be submitted to th shareholders of ISIS for their approval on June 12, 1989.

OPINION OF COUNSEL

The counsel rendering the opinion in support of and accompanying this Listing Application is the firm of Warner, Norcross & Judd, 900 Old Kent Building, Grand Rapids, Michigan 49503-2489. The opinion states that the shares of Common Stock which are the subject of this Listing Application will be legally issued and outstanding, fully paid and nonassessable, when issued in connection with the acquisition of ISIS under the duly approved Agreement. The opinion is also to the effect that no liability will attach to the ownership of such shares of Common Stock under the laws of the State of Delaware, in which the Company is incorporated, or under the laws of the State of Michigan, where the Company maintains its principal offices.

The Company filed a Form S-4 Registration Statement (Number 33-28380) with the Securities and Exchange Commission on April 26, 1989, concerning the Common Stock which is the subject of this Listing Application. The Registration Statement was declared effective on May 11, 1989.

As required by Section 702.04 of the New York Stock Exchange Listed Company manual, please be advised that Mr. Paul K. Gaston, a director of the Company, is a partner with Warner, Norcross & Judd.

GUARDSMAN PRODUCTS, INC.

By __________________________
William P. Radcliff, Sr.
Its President

The New York Stock Exchange, Inc. hereby authorizes the listing of 175,000 additional shares of Common Stock and 175,000 Rights to purchase additional shares of Preferred Stock of Guardsman Products, Inc., in connection with the acquisition by Guardsman Products, Inc., of the assets of ISIS Coatings, Inc., making a total of 6,756,662 shares of Common Stock and related Rights authorized for listing.

David L. Domijan Senior Vice President, New Listings and Corporate Liaison	John J. Phelan, Jr. Chairman of the Board New York Stock Exchange, Inc.

EXHIBIT 12-2

OMB APPROVAL	
OMB Number:	3235-0145
Expires:	December 31, 1997
Estimated average burden hours per response. . . .14.90	

UNITED STATES
SECURITIES AND EXCHANGE COMMISSION
Washington, D.C. 20549

SCHEDULE 13D

Under the Securities Exchange Act of 1934
(Amendment No. ________)*

____
(Name of Issuer)

____
(Title of Class of Securities)

____
(CUSIP Number)

____
(Name, Address and Telephone Number of Person Authorized to Receive Notices and Communications)

____
(Date of Event which Requires Filing of this Statement)

If the filing person has previously filed a statement on Schedule 13G to report the acquisition which is the subject of this Schedule 13D, and is filing this schedule because of Rule 13d-1(b)(3) or (4), check the following box ☐.

Check the following box if a fee is being paid with the statement ☐. (A fee is not required only if the reporting person: (1) has a previous statement on file reporting beneficial ownership of more than five percent of the class of securities described in Item 1; and (2) has filed no amendment subsequent thereto reporting beneficial ownership of five percent or less of such class.) (See Rule 13d-7.)

Note: Six copies of this statement, including all exhibits, should be filed with the Commission. See Rule 13d-1(a) for other parties to whom copies are to be sent.

*The remainder of this cover page shall be filled out for a reporting person's initial filing on this form with respect to the subject class of securities, and for any subsequent amendment containing information which would alter disclosures provided in a prior cover page.

The information required on the remainder of this cover page shall not be deemed to be "filed" for the purpose of Section 18 of the Securities Exchange Act of 1934 ("Act") or otherwise subject to the liabilities of that section of the Act but shall be subject to all other provisions of the Act (however, see the Notes).

SCHEDULE 13D

CUSIP No. ____________________ **Page ________ of ________ Pages**

1	NAME OF REPORTING PERSON S.S. OR I.R.S. IDENTIFICATION NO. OF ABOVE PERSON	
2	CHECK THE APPROPRIATE BOX IF A MEMBER OF A GROUP*	(a) ☐ (b) ☐
3	SEC USE ONLY	
4	SOURCE OF FUNDS*	
5	CHECK BOX IF DISCLOSURE OF LEGAL PROCEEDINGS IS REQUIRED PURSUANT TO ITEMS 2(d) or 2(e)	☐
6	CITIZENSHIP OR PLACE OF ORGANIZATION	

NUMBER OF SHARES BENEFICIALLY OWNED BY EACH REPORTING PERSON WITH		
	7	SOLE VOTING POWER
	8	SHARED VOTING POWER
	9	SOLE DISPOSITIVE POWER
	10	SHARED DISPOSITIVE POWER

11	AGGREGATE AMOUNT BENEFICIALLY OWNED BY EACH REPORTING PERSON	
12	CHECK BOX IF THE AGGREGATE AMOUNT IN ROW (11) EXCLUDES CERTAIN SHARES*	☐
13	PERCENT OF CLASS REPRESENTED BY AMOUNT IN ROW (11)	
14	TYPE OF REPORTING PERSON*	

***SEE INSTRUCTIONS BEFORE FILLING OUT!**
INCLUDE BOTH SIDES OF THE COVER PAGE, RESPONSES TO ITEMS 1–7 (INCLUDNG EXHIBITS) OF THE SCHEDULE, AND THE SIGNATURE ATTESTATION.

INSTRUCTIONS FOR COVER PAGE

(1) *Names and Social Security Numbers of Reporting Persons* — Furnish the full legal name of each person for whom the report is filed — i.e., each person required to sign the schedule itself — including each member of a group. Do not include the name of a person required to be identified in the report but who is not a reporting person. Reporting persons are also requested to furnish their Social Security or I.R.S. identification numbers, although disclosure of such numbers is voluntary, not mandatory (see "Special Instructions for Complying with Schedule 13D" below).

(2) If any of the shares beneficially owned by a reporting person are held as a member of a group and such membership is expressly affirmed, please check row 2(a). If the membership in a group is disclaimed or the reporting person describes a relationship with other persons but does not affirm the existence of a group, please check row 2(b) [unless a joint filing pursuant to Rule 13d-1(f)(1) in which case it may not be necessary to check row 2(b)].

(3) The 3rd row is for SEC internal use; please leave blank.

(4) Classify the source of funds or other consideration used or to be used in making purchases as required to be disclosed pursuant to Item 3 of Schedule 13D and insert the appropriate symbol (or symbols if more than one is necessary in row (4):

Category of Source	Symbol
Subject Company (Company whose securities are being acquired)	SC
Bank	BK
Affiliate (of reporting person)	AF
Working Capital (of reporting person)	WC
Personal Funds (of reporting person)	PF
Other	OO

(5) If disclosure of legal proceedings or actions is required pursuant to either Items 2(d) or 2(e) of Schedule 13D, row 5 should be checked.

(6) *Citizenship or Place of Organization* — Furnish citizenship if the named reporting person is a natural person. Otherwise, furnish place of organization. (See Item 2 of Schedule 13D)

(7)-(11), (13) *Aggregate Amount Beneficially Owned by Each Reporting Person, etc.* — Rows (7) through (11) inclusive, and (13) are to be completed in accordance with the provisions of Item 5 of Schedule 13D. All percentages are to be rounded off to nearest tenth (one place after decimal point).

(12) Check if the aggregate amount reported as beneficially owned in row (11) does not include shares which the reporting person discloses in the report but as to which beneficial ownership is disclaimed pursuant to Rule 13d-4 [17 CFR 240.13d-4] under the Securities Exchange Act of 1934.

(14) *Type of Reporting Person* — Please classify each "reporting person" according to the following breakdown and place the appropriate symbol (or symbols, i.e., if more than one is applicable, insert all applicable symbols) on the form:

Category	Symbol
Broker-Dealer	BD
Bank	BK
Insurance Company	IC
Investment Company	IV
Investment Adviser	IA
Employee Benefit Plan, Pension Fund, or Endowment Fund	EP
Parent Holding Company	HC
Corporation	CO
Partnership	PN
Individual	IN
Other	OO

Notes:

Attach as many copies of the second part of the cover page as are needed, one reporting person per page.

Filing persons may, in order to avoid unnecessary duplication, answer items on the schedules (Schedule 13D, 13G or 14D-1) by appropriate cross references to an item or items on the cover page(s). This approach may only be used where the cover page item or items provide all the disclosure required by the schedule item. Moreover, such a use of a cover page item will result in the item becoming a part of the schedule and accordingly being considered as "filed" for purposes of Section 18 of the Securities Exchange Act or otherwise subject to the liabilities of that section of the Act.

Reporting persons may comply with their **cover page** filing requirements by filing either completed copies of the blank forms available from the Commission, printed or typed facsimiles, or computer printed facsimiles, provided the documents filed have identical formats to the forms prescribed in the Commission's regulations and meet existing Securities Exchange Act rules as to such matters as clarity and size (Securities Exchange Act Rule 12b-12).

SPECIAL INSTRUCTIONS FOR COMPLYING WITH SCHEDULE 13D

Under Sections 13(d) and 23 of the Securities Exchange Act of 1934 and the rules and regulations thereunder, the Commission is authorized to solicit the information required to be supplied by this schedule by certain security holders of certain issuers.

Disclosure of the information specified in this schedule is mandatory, except for Social Security or I.R.S. identification numbers, disclosure of which is voluntary. The information will be used for the primary purpose of determining and disclosing the holdings of certain beneficial owners of certain equity securities. This statement will be made a matter of public record. Therefore, any information given will be available for inspection by any member of the public.

Because of the public nature of the information, the Commission can utilize it for a variety of purposes, including referral to other governmental authorities or securities self-regulatory organizations for investigatory purposes or in connection with litigation involving the federal securities laws or other civil, criminal or regulatory statements or provisions. Social Security or I.R.S. identification numbers, if furnished, will assist the Commission in identifying security holders and, therefore in promptly processing statements of beneficial ownership of securities.

Failure to disclose the information requested by this schedule, except for Social Security or I.R.S. identification numbers may result in civil or criminal action against the persons involved for violation of the federal securities laws and rules promulgated thereunder.

General Instructions

A. The item numbers and captions of the items shall be included but the text of the items is to be omitted. The answers to the items shall be so prepared as to indicate clearly the coverage of the items without referring to the text of the items. **Answer every item.** If an item is inapplicable or the answer is in the negative, so state.

B. Information contained in exhibits to the statements may be incorporated by reference in answer or partial answer to any item or sub-item of the statement unless it would render such answer misleading, incomplete, unclear or confusing. Matter incorporated by reference shall be clearly identified in the reference by page, paragraph, caption or otherwise. An express statement that the specified matter is incorporated by reference shall be made at the particular place in the statement where the information is required. A copy of any information or a copy of the pertinent pages of a document containing such information which is incorporated by reference shall be submitted with this statement as an exhibit and shall be deemed to be filed with the Commission for all purposes of the Act.

C. If the statement is filed by a general or limited partnership, syndicate, or other group, the information called for by Items 2-6, inclusive, shall be given with respect to (i) each partner of such general partnership; (ii) each partner who is denominated as a general partner or who functions as a general partner of such limited partnership; (iii) each member of such syndicate or group; and (iv) each person controlling such partner or member. If the statement is filed by a corporation or if a person referred to in (i), (ii), (iii) or (iv) of this Instruction is a corporation, the information called for by the above mentioned items shall be given with respect to (a) each executive officer and director of such corporation; (b) each person controlling such corporation; and (c) each executive officer and director of any corporation or other person ultimately in control of such corporation.

Item 1. Security and Issuer

State the title of the class of equity securities to which this statement relates and the name and address of the principal executive offices of the issuer of such securities.

Item 2. Identity and Background

If the person filing this statement or any person enumerated in Instruction C of this statement is a corporation, general partnership, limited partnership, syndicate or other group of persons, state its name, the state or other place of its organization, its principal business, the address of its principal business, the address of its principal office and the information required by (d) and (e) of this Item. If the person filing this statement or any person enumerated in Instruction C is a natural person, provide the information specified in (a) through (f) of this Item with respect to such person(s).

(a) Name;

(b) Residence or business address;

(c) Present principal occupation or employment and the name, principal business and address of any corporation or other organization in which such employment is conducted;

(d) Whether or not, during the last five years, such person has been convicted in a criminal proceeding (excluding traffic violations or similar misdemeanors) and, if so, give the dates, nature of conviction, name and location of court, and penalty imposed, or other disposition of the case;

(e) Whether or not, during the last five years, such person was a party to a civil proceeding of a judicial or administrative body of competent jurisdiction and as a result of such proceeding was or is subject to a judgment, decree or final order enjoining future violations of, or prohibiting or mandating activities subject to, federal or state securities laws or finding any violation with respect to such laws; and, if so, identify and describe such proceedings and summarize the terms of such judgment, decree or final order; and

(f) Citizenship.

Item 3. Source and Amount of Funds or Other Consideration

State the source and the amount of funds or other consideration used or to be used in making the purchases, and if any part of the purchase price is or will be represented by funds or other consideration borrowed or otherwise obtained for the purpose of acquiring, holding, trading or voting the securities, a description of the transaction and the names of the parties thereto. Where material, such information should also be provided with respect to prior acquisitions not previously reported pursuant to this regulation. If the source of all or any part of the funds is a loan made in the ordinary course of business by a bank, as defined in Section 3(a)(6) of the Act, the name of the bank shall not be made available to the public if the person at the time of filing the statement so requests in writing and files such request, naming such bank, with the Secretary of the Commission. If the securities were acquired other than by purchase, describe the method of acquisition.

Item 4. Purpose of Transaction

State the purpose or purposes of the acquisition of securities of the issuer. Describe any plans or proposals which the reporting persons may have which relate to or would result in:

(a) The acquisition by any person of additional securities of the issuer, or the disposition of securities of the issuer;

(b) An extraordinary corporate transaction, such as a merger, reorganization or liquidation, involving the issuer or any of its subsidiaries;

(c) A sale or transfer of a material amount of assets of the issuer or any of its subsidiaries;

(d) Any change in the present board of directors or management of the issuer, including any plans or proposals to change the number of term of directors or to fill any existing vacancies on the board;

(e) Any material change in the present capitalization or dividend policy of the issuer;

(f) Any other material change in the issuer's business or corporate structure including but not limited to, if the issuer is a registered closed-end investment company, any plans or proposals to make any changes in its investment policy for which a vote is required by section 13 of the Investment Company Act of 1940;

(g) Changes in the issuer's charter, bylaws or instruments corresponding thereto or other actions which may impede the acquisition of control of the issuer by any person;

(h) Causing a class of securities of the issuer to be delisted from a national securities exchange or to cease to be authorized to be quoted in an inter-dealer quotation system of a registered national securities association;

(i) A class of equity securities of the issuer becoming eligible for termination of registration pursuant to Section 12(g)(4) of the Act; or

(j) Any action similar to any of those enumerated above.

Item 5. Interest in Securities of the Issuer

(a) State the aggregate number and percentage of the class of securities identified pursuant to Item 1 (which may be based on the number of securities outstanding as contained in the most recently available filing with the Commission by the issuer unless the filing person has reason to believe such information is not current) beneficially owned (identifying those shares which there is a right to acquire) by each person named in Item 2. The above mentioned information should also be furnished with respect to persons who, together with any of the persons named in Item 2, comprise a group within the meaning of Section 13(d)(3) of the Act;

(b) For each person named in response to paragraph (a), indicate the number of shares as to which there is sole power to vote or to direct the vote, shared power to vote or to direct the vote, sole power to dispose or to direct the disposition, or shared power to dispose or to direct the disposition. Provide the applicable information required by Item 2 with respect to each person with whom the power to vote or to direct the vote or to dispose or direct the disposition is shared;

(c) Describe any transactions in the class of securities reported on that were effected during the past sixty days or since the most recent filing on Schedule 13D (§240.13d-191), whichever is less, by the persons named in response to paragraph (a).

Instruction. The description of a transaction required by Item 5(c) shall include, but not necessarily be limited to: (1) the identity of the person covered by Item 5(c) who effected the transaction; (2) the date of the transaction; (3) the amount of securities involved; (4) the price per share or unit; and (5) where and how the transaction was effected.

(d) If any other person is known to have the right to receive or the power to direct the receipt of dividends from, or the proceeds from the sale of, such securities, a statement to that effect should be included in response to this item and, if such interest relates to more than five percent of the class, such person should be identified. A listing of the shareholders of an investment company registered under the Investment Company Act of 1940 or the beneficiaries of an employee benefit plan, pension fund or endowment fund is not required.

(e) If applicable, state the date on which the reporting person ceased to be the beneficial owner of more than five percent of the class of securities.

Instruction. For computations regarding securities which represent a right to acquire an underlying security, see Rule 13d-3(d)(1) and the note thereto.

Item 6. Contracts, Arrangements, Understandings or Relationships with Respect to Securities of the Issuer.

Describe any contracts, arrangements, understandings or relationships (legal or otherwise) among the persons named in Item 2 and between such persons and any person with respect to any securities of the issuer, including but not limited to transfer or voting of any of the securities, finder's fees, joint ventures, loan or option arrangements, put or calls, guarantees of profits, division of profits or loss, or the giving or withholding of proxies, naming the persons with whom such contracts, arrangements, understandings or relationships have been entered into. Include such information for any of the securities that are pledged or otherwise subject to a contingency the occurrence of which would give another person voting power or investment power over such securities except that disclosure of standard default and similar provisions contained in loan agreements need not be included.

Item 7. Material to Be Filed as Exhibits

The following shall be filed as exhibits: copies of written agreements relating to the filing of joint acquisition statements as required by Rule 13d-1(f) (§240.13d-1(f) and copies of all written agreements, contracts, arrangements, understandings, plans or proposals relating to (1) the borrowing of funds to finance the acquisition as disclosed in Item 3; (2) the acquisition of issuer control, liquidation, sale of assets, merger, or change in business or corporate structure or any other matter as disclosed in Item 4; and (3) the transfer or voting of the securities, finder's fees, joint ventures, options, puts, calls, guarantees of loans, guarantees against loss or of profit, or the giving or withholding of any proxy as disclosed in Item 6.

Signature

After reasonable inquiry and to the best of my knowledge and belief, I certify that the information set forth in this statement is true, complete and correct.

____________________________ ____________________________

Date Signature

____

Name/Title

The original statement shall be signed by each person on whose behalf the statement is filed or his authorized representative. If the statement is signed on behalf of a person by his authorized representative (other than an executive officer or general partner of this filing person), evidence of the representative's authority to sign on behalf of such person shall be filed with the statement, provided, however, that a power of attorney for this purpose which is already on file with the Commission may be incorporated by reference. The name and any title of each person who signs the statement shall be typed or printed beneath his signature.

Attention: Intentional misstatements or omissions of fact constitute Federal criminal violations (See 18 U.S.C. 1001)

EXHIBIT 12-3

OMB APPROVAL	
OMB Number:	3235-0102
Expires:	October 31, 1994
Estimated average burden hours per response ...	362.00

UNITED STATES
SECURITIES AND EXCHANGE COMMISSION
Washington, D.C. 20549

SCHEDULE 14D-1

Tender offer statement pursuant to section 14(d)(1) of the Securities Exchange Act of 1934.

(Amendment No.)*

____

(Name of Subject Company [Issuer])

____

(Bidder)

____

(Title of Class of Securities)

____

(CUSIP Number of Class of Securities)

____

(Name, Address and Telephone Numbers of Person Authorized to Receive Notices and Communications on Behalf of Bidder)

Calculation of Filing Fee

Transaction valuation*	Amount of filing fee

*Set forth the amount on which the filing fee is calculated and state how it was determined.

☐ Check box if any part of the fee is offset as provided by Rule 0-11(a)(2) and identify the filing with which the offsetting fee was previously paid. Identify the previous filing by registration statement number, or the Form or Schedule and the date of its filing.

Amount Previously Paid: ______________________________

Form or Registration No.: ______________________________

Filing Party: ______________________________

Date Filed: ______________________________

Note: The remainder of this cover page is only to be completed if this Schedule 14D-1 (or amendment thereto) is being filed, inter alia, to satisfy the reporting requirements of section 13(d) of the Securities Exchange Act of 1934. See General Instructions D, E and F to Schedule 14D-1.

* The remainder of this cover page shall be filled out for a reporting person's initial filing on this form with respect to the subject class of securities, and for any subsequent amendment containing information which would alter the disclosure provided in a prior cover page.

The information required in the remainder of this cover page shall not be deemed to be "filed" for the purpose of Section 18 of the Securities Exchange Age of 1934 ("Act") or otherwise subject to the liabilities of that section of the Act but shall be subject to all other provisions of the Act (however, see the Notes).

1) Name of Reporting Person ______

S.S. or I.R.S. Identification No. of Above Person ______

2) Check the Appropriate Box if a Member of a Group (See Instructions)

☐ (a) ______

☐ (b) ______

3) SEC Use Only ______

4) Sources of Funds (See Instructions) ______

5) ☐ Check if Disclosure of Legal Proceedings is Required Pursuant to Items 2(e) or 2(f).

6) Citizenship or Place of Organization ______

7) Aggregate Amount Beneficially Owned by Each Reporting Person ______

8) ☐ Check if the Aggregate Amount in Row 7 Excludes Certain Shares (See Instructions).

9) Percent of Class Represented by Amount in Row 7 ______

10) Type of Reporting Person (See Instructions) ______

OMB APPROVAL	
OMB Number:	3235-0102
Expires:	October 31, 1994
Estimated average burden hours per response ...	362.00

SCHEDULE 14D-1 INSTRUCTIONS

Instructions for Cover Page

(1) *Names and Social Security Numbers of Reporting Persons*—Furnish the full legal name of each person for whom the report is filed—i.e., each person required to sign the schedule itself—including each member of a group. Do not include the name of a person required to be identified in the report but who is not a reporting person. Reporting persons are also requested to furnish their Social Security or I.R.S. identification numbers, although disclosure of such numbers is voluntary, not mandatory (see "SPECIAL INSTRUCTIONS FOR COMPLYING WITH SCHEDULE 14D-1." below).

(2) If any of the shares beneficially owned by a reporting person are held as a member of a group and such membership is expressly affirmed, please check row 2(a). If the membership in a group is disclaimed or the reporting person describes a relationship with other persons but does not affirm the existence of a group, please check row 2(b) [unless a joint filing pursuant to Rule 13d-1(f)(1) in which case it may not be necessary to check row 2(b)].

(3) The third row is for SEC internal use, please leave blank.

(4) *Source of Funds*—Classify the source of funds or other consideration to be used in making purchases as required to be disclosed pursuant to Item 4 of the schedule and insert the appropriate symbol (or symbols if more than one is necessary) in row 4:

Category of Source	*Symbol*
Subject Company (company whose securities are being acquired)	SC
Bank	BK
Affiliate (of reporting person)	AF
Working Capital (of reporting person)	WC
Personal Funds (of reporting person)	PF
Other	OO

(5) If disclosure of legal proceedings or actions is required pursuant to either Items 2(e) or 2(f) of Schedule 14D-1, row 5 should be checked.

(6) *Citizenship or Place of Organization*—Furnish citizenship if the named reporting person is a natural person. Otherwise, furnish the place of organization. (See Item 2 of Schedule 14D-1).

(7), (9) *Aggregate Amount Beneficially Owned by Each Reporting Person, etc.*— Rows 7 and 9 are to be completed in accordance with the Instructions to Item 6 of Schedule 14D-1. All percentages are to be rounded off to nearest tenth (one place after decimal point).

(8) Check if the aggregate amount reported as beneficially owned in row 7 does not include shares as to which beneficial ownership is disclaimed.

(10) *Type of Reporting Person*—Please classify each "reporting person" according to the following breakdown and place the appropriate symbol (or symbols, i.e., if more than one is applicable, insert all applicable symbols) on the form:

Category	*Symbol*
Broker Dealer	BD
Bank	BK
Insurance Company	IC
Investment Company	IV
Investment Adviser	IA
Employee Benefit Plan, Pension Fund, or Endowment Fund	EP
Parent Holding Company	HC
Group Member	GM
Corporation	CO
Partnership	PN
Individual	IN
Other	OO

Notes:

Attach as many copies of the second part of the cover page as are needed, one reporting person per page.

Filing persons may, in order to avoid unnecessary duplication, answer items on the schedules (Schedules 13D, 13G or 14D-1) appropriate cross reference to an item or items on the cover page(s). This approach may be used only where the cover ge item or items provide all the disclosure required by the schedule item. Moreover, such a use of a cover page item will sult in the item becoming a part of the schedule and accordingly being considered as "filed" for purposes of Section 18 the Securities Exchange Act or otherwise subject to the liabilities of that section of the Act.

Reporting persons may comply with their cover page filing requirements by filing either completed copies of the blank forms ailable from the commission, printed or typed facsimiles, or computer printed facsimiles, provided the documents filed have entical formats to the forms prescribed in the Commission's regulations and meet existing Securities Exchange Act rules to such matters as clarity and size (Securities Exchange Act Rule 12b-12).

SPECIAL INSTRUCTIONS FOR COMPLYING WITH SCHEDULE 14D-1

Under Sections 14(d) and 23 of the Securities Exchange Act of 1934 and the rules and regulations thereunder, the Commis- on is authorized to solicit the information required to be supplied by this schedule by certain security holders of certain issuers.

Disclosure of the information specified in this schedule is mandatory, except for Social Security or I.R.S. identification umbers, disclosure of which is voluntary. The information will be used for the primary purpose of determining and disclosing e holdings of certain beneficial owners of certain equity securities. This statement will be made a matter of public record. herefore, any information given will be available for inspection by any member of the public.

Because of the public nature of the information, the Commission can utilize it for a variety of purposes, including referral other governmental authorities or securities self-regulatory organizations for investigatory purposes or in connection with igation involving the Federal securities laws or other civil, criminal or regulatory statutes or provisions. Social Security or R.S. identification numbers, if furnished, will assist the Commission in identifying security holders and, therefore, in promptly occssing statements of beneficial ownership of securities.

Failure to disclose the information requested by this schedule, except for Social Security or I.R.S.identification numbers, ay result in civil or criminal action against the persons involved for violation of the Federal securities laws and rules promul- ated thereunder.

Filing Instructions and Fees

Eight copies of this statement, including all exhibits, and two additional copies of this statement, including only the exhibits described in Item 11(a) of this statement, should be filed with the Commission.

This statement shall be accompanied by a fee payable to the Commission as required by §240.0-11.

eneral Instructions:

A. The item numbers and captions of the items shall be included but the text of the items is to be omitted. The answers to the items shall be so prepared as to indicate clearly the coverage of the items without referring to the text of the items. Answer every item. If an item is applicable or the answer is in the negative, so state.

B. Information in exhibits to the statement may be incorporated by reference in answer or partial answer to any item or sub-item of the statement unless it would render such answer misleading, incomplete, unclear or confusing. Material incorporated by reference shall be clearly identified in the reference by page, paragraph, caption or otherwise. An express statement that the specified matter is incorporated by reference shall be made at the particular place in the statement where the information is required. A copy of any information or a copy of the pertinent pages of a document containing such information which is incorporated by reference shall be submitted with this statement as an exhibit and shall be deemed to be filed with the Commission for all purposes of the Act.

C. If the statement is filed by a partnership, limited partnership, syndicate or other group, the information called for by Items 2-7, inclusive, shall be given with respect to: (i) each partner of such partnership; (ii) each partner who is denominated as a general partner or who functions as a general partner of such limited partnership; (iii) each member of such syndicate or group; and (iv) each person controlling such partner or member. If the statement is filed by a corporation, or if a person referred to in (i), (ii), (iii) or (iv) of this Instruction is a corporation, the information called for by the above mentioned items shall be given with respect to: (a) each executive officer and director of such corporation; (b) each person controlling such corporation; and (c) each executive officer and director of any corporation ultimately in control of such corporation. A response to an item in the statement is required with respect to the bidder and to all other persons referred to in this instruction unless such item specifies to the contrary.

D. Upon termination of the tender offer, the bidder shall promptly file a final amendment to Schedule 14D-1 [§240.14d-100] disclosing all material changes in the items of that Schedule and stating that the tender offer has terminated, the date of such termination and the results of such tender offer.

E. If the bidder, before filing this statement, has filed a Schedule 13D [§240.13d-101] with respect to the acquisition of securities of the same class referred to in Item 1(a) of this statement, the bidder shall amend such Schedule 13D [§240.13d-101] and may do so by means of this statement and amendments thereto, including the final amendment required to be filed by Instruction D: *Provided* That the bidder indicates on the cover sheet of this statement that it is amending its Schedule 13D [§240.13d-101] by means of this statement.

F. The final amendment required to be filed by Instruction D shall be deemed to satisfy the reporting requirements of section 13(d) of the Act with respect to all securities acquired by the bidder pursuant to the tender offer as reported in such final amendment.

G. For purposes of this statement, the following definitions shall apply:

(i) The term "bidder" means any person on whose behalf a tender offer is made; and

(ii) The term "subject company" means any issuer whose securities are sought by a bidder pursuant to a tender offer.

Item 1. Security and Subject Company

(a) State the name of the subject company and the address of its principal executive offices;

(b) State the exact title and the number of shares outstanding of the class of equity securities being sought (which may be based upon information contained in the most recently available filing with the Commission by the subject company unless the bidder has reason to believe such information is not current), the exact amount of such securities being sought and the consideration being offered therefor; and

(c) Identify the principal market in which such securities are traded and state the high and low sales prices for such securities in such principal market (or, in the absence thereof, the range of high and low bid quotations) for each quarterly period during the past two years.

Item 2. Identity and Background

If the person filing this statement or any person enumerated in Instruction C of this statement is a corporation, partnership, limited partnership, syndicate or other group of persons, state its name, the state or other place of its organization, its principal business, the address of its principal office and the information required by (e) and (f) of this Item. If the person filing this statement or any person enumerated in Instruction C is a natural person, provide the information specified in (a) through (g) of this Item with respect to such person(s).

(a) Name;

(b) Residence or business address;

(c) Present principal occupation or employment and the name, principal business and address of any corporation or other organization in which such employment or occupation is conducted;

(d) Material occupations, positions, offices or employments during the last 5 years, giving the starting and ending dates of each and the name, principal business and address of any business corporation or other organization in which such occupation, position, office or employment was carried on;

Instruction. If a person has held various positions with the same organization, or if a person holds comparable positions with multiple related organizations, each and every person need not be specifically disclosed.

(e) Whether or not, during the last 5 years, such person has been convicted in a criminal proceeding (excluding traffic violations or similar misdemeanors) and, if so, give the dates, nature of conviction, name and location of court, and penalty imposed or other disposition of the case;

Instruction. While a negative answer to this sub-item is required in this schedule, it need not be furnished to security holders.

(f) Whether or not, during the last 5 years, such person was a party to a civil proceeding of a judicial or administrative body of competent jurisdiction and as a result of such proceeding was or is subject to a judgment, decree or final order enjoining future violations of, or prohibiting activities subject to, federal or state securities laws or finding any violation of such laws; and, if so, identify and describe such proceeding and summarize the terms of such judgment, decree or final order; and

Instruction. While a negative answer to this sub-item is required in this schedule, it need not be furnished to security holders.

(g) Citizenship(s).

Item 3. Past Contacts, Transactions or Negotiations with the Subject Company

(a) Briefly state the nature and approximate amount (in dollars) of any transaction, other than those described in Item 3(b) of this schedule, which has occurred since the commencement of the subject company's third full fiscal year preceding the date of this schedule, between the person filing this schedule (including those persons enumerated in Instruction C of this schedule) and:

(1) the subject company or any of its affiliates which are corporations: ***Provided, However,*** That no disclosure need be made with respect to any transaction if the aggregate amount involved in such transaction was less than one percent of the subject company's consolidated revenue (which may be based upon information contained in the most recently available filing with the Commission by the subject company, unless the bidder has reason to believe otherwise) (i) for the fiscal year in which such transaction occurred or, (ii) for the portion of the current fiscal year which has occurred, if the transaction occurred in such year; and

(2) the executive officers, directors or affiliates of the subject company which are not corporations if the aggregate amount involved in such transactions or in a series of similar transactions, including all periodic installments in the case of any lease or other agreement providing for periodic payments or installments, exceeds $40,000.

(b) Describe any contacts, negotiations or transactions which have occurred since the commencement of the subject company's third full fiscal year preceding the date of this schedule between the bidder or its subsidiaries (including those persons enumerated in Instruction C of this schedule) and the subject company or its affiliates concerning: a merger, consolidation or acquisition; a tender offer or other acquisition of securities; an election of directors; or a sale or other transfer of a material amount of assets.

Item 4. Source and Amount of Funds or Other Consideration

(a) State the source and the total amount of funds or other consideration for the purchase of the maximum number of securities for which the tender offer is being made.

(b) If all or any part of such funds or other consideration are or are expected to be, directly or indirectly, borrowed for the purpose of the tender offer:

(1) Provide a summary of each loan agreement or arrangement containing the identity of the parties, the term, the collateral, the stated and effective interest rates, and other material terms or conditions relative to such loan agreement; and

(2) Briefly describe any plans or arrangements to finance or repay such borrowings, or if no such plans or arrangements have been made, make a statement to that effect.

(c) If the source of all or any part of the funds to be used in the tender offer is a loan made in the ordinary course of business by a bank as defined by section 3(a)(6) of the Act, the name of such bank shall not be made available to the public if the person filing the statement so requests in writing and files such request, naming such bank, with the Secretary of the Commission.

Item 5. Purpose of the Tender Offer and Plans or Proposals of the Bidder

State the purpose or purposes of the tender offer for the subject company's securities. Describe any plans or proposals which relate to or would result in:

(a) An extraordinary corporate transaction, such as a merger, reorganization or liquidation, involving the subject company or any of its subsidiaries;

(b) A sale or transfer of a material amount of assets of the subject company or any of its subsidiaries;

(c) Any change in the present board of directors or management of the subject company including, but not limited to, any plans or proposals to change the number or the term of directors or to fill any existing vacancies on the board;

(d) Any material change in the present capitalization or dividend policy of the subject company;

(e) Any other material change in the subject company's corporate structure of business, including, if the subject company is a registered closed-end investment company, any plans or proposals to make any changes in its investment policy for which a vote would be required by section 13 of the Investment Company Act of 1940;

(f) Causing a class of securities of the subject company to be delisted from a national securities exchange or to cease to be authorized to be quoted in an inter-dealer quotation system of a registered national securities association; or

(g) A class of equity securities of the subject company becoming eligible for termination of registration pursuant to section 12(g)(4) of the Act.

Item 6. Interest in Securities of the Subject Company

(a) State the aggregate number and percentage of the class represented by such shares (which may be based on the number of shares outstanding as contained in the most recently available filing with the Commission by the subject company unless the bidder has reason to believe such information is not current), beneficially owned (identifying those shares for which there is a right to acquire) by each person named in Item 2 of this schedule and by each associate and majority-owned subsidiary of such person giving the name and address of any such associate or subsidiary.

(b) Describe any transaction in the class of securities reported on that was effected during the past 60 days by the persons named in response to paragraph (a) of this item or by any executive officer, director or subsidiary of such person.

Instructions.

1. The description of a transaction required by Item 6(b) shall include, but not necessarily be limited to: 1) the identity of the person covered by Item 6(b) who effected the transactions; 2) the date of the transaction; 3) the amount of securities involved; 4) the price per share; and 5) where and how the transaction was effected.

2. If the information required by Item 6(b) of this schedule is available to the bidder at the time this statement is initially filed with the Commission pursuant to Rule 14d-3(a)(1) [§240.14d-3(a)(1)], such information should be included in such initial filing. However, if such information is not available to the bidder at the time of such initial filing, it shall be filed with the Commission promptly but in no event later than two business days after the date of such filing and, if material, shall be disclosed in a manner reasonably designed to inform security holders. The procedure specified by this instruction is provided for the purpose of maintaining the confidentiality of the tender offer in order to avoid possible misuse of inside information.

Item 7. Contracts, Arrangements, Understandings or Relationships with Respect to the Subject Company's Securities

Describe any contract, arrangement, understanding or relationship (whether or not legally enforceable) between the bidder (including those persons enumerated in Instruction C to this schedule) and any person with respect to any securities of the subject company, (including, but not limited to, any contract, arrangement, understanding or relationship concerning the transfer or the voting of any of such securities, joint ventures, loan or option arrangements, puts or calls, guaranties of loans, guaranties against loss, or the giving or withholding of proxies) naming the persons with whom such contracts, arrangements, understandings or relationships have been entered into and giving the material provisions thereof. Include such information for any of such securities that are pledged or otherwise subject to a contingency, the occurrence of which would give another person the power to direct the voting or disposition of such securities, except that disclosure of standard default and similar provisions contained in loan agreements need not be included.

Item 8. Persons Retained, Employed or to Be Compensated

Identify all persons and classes of persons employed, retained or to be compensated by the bidder, or by any person on the bidder's behalf, to make solicitations or recommendations in connection with the tender offer and describe briefly the terms of such employment, retainer or arrangement for compensation.

Item 9. Financial Statements of Certain Bidders

Where the bidder is other than a natural person and the bidder's financial condition is material to a decision by a security holder of the subject company whether to sell, tender or hold securities being sought in the tender offer, furnish current, adequate financial information concerning the bidder *Provided* That if the bidder is controlled by another entity which is not a natural person and has been formed for the purpose of making the tender offer, furnish current, adequate financial information concerning such parent.

Instructions.

1. The facts and circumstances concerning the tender offer, particularly the terms of the tender offer, may influence a determination as to whether disclosure of financial information is material. However, once the materiality requirement is applicable, the adequacy of the financial information will depend primarily on the nature of the bidder.

In order to provide guidance in making this determination, the following types of financial information will be deemed adequate for purposes of this item for the type of bidder specified: (a) financial statements prepared in compliance with Form 10 as amended (§249.210 of this chapter) for a domestic bidder which is otherwise eligible to use such form; and (b) Financial statements prepared in accordance with Item 17 of Form 20-F [§249.200f of this chapter] for a foreign bidder that is otherwise eligible to use such form.

2. If the bidder is subject to the periodic reporting requirements of section 13(a) or 15(d) of the Act, financial statements contained in any document filed with the Commission may be incorporated by reference in this schedule solely for the purposes of this schedule: *Provided,* That such financial statements substantially meet the requirements of this item; an express statement is made that such financial statements are incorporated by reference; the matter incorporated by reference is clearly identified by page, paragraph, caption or otherwise; and an indication is made where such information may be inspected and copies obtained. Financial statements which are required to be presented in comparative form for two or more fiscal years or periods shall not be incorporated by reference unless the material incorporated by reference includes the entire period for which the comparative data is required to be given.

3. If the bidder is not subject to the periodic reporting requirements of the Act, the financial statements required by this item need not be audited if such audited financial statements are not available or obtainable without unreasonable cost or expense and a statement is made to that effect disclosing the reasons therefor.

Item 10. Additional Information

If material to a decision by a security holder whether to sell, tender or hold securities being sought in the tender offer, furnish information as to the following:

(a) Any present or proposed material contracts, arrangements, understandings or relationships between the bidder or any of its executive officers, directors, controlling persons or subsidiaries and the subject company or any of its executive officers, directors, controlling persons or subsidiaries (other than any contract, arrangement or understanding required to be disclosed pursuant to Items 3 or 7 of this schedule);

(b) To the extent known by the bidder after reasonable investigation, the applicable regulatory requirements which must be complied with or approvals which must be obtained in connection with the tender offer;

(c) The applicability of anti-trust laws;

(d) The applicability of the margin requirements of section 7 of the Act and the regulations promulgated thereunder;

(e) Any material pending legal proceedings relating to the tender offer including the name and location of the court or agency in which the proceedings are pending, the date instituted, the principal parties thereto and a brief summary of the proceedings; and

Instruction. In connection with this sub-item, a copy of any document relating to a major development (such as pleadings, an answer, complaint, temporary restraining order, injunction, opinion, judgment or order) in a material pending legal proceeding should be promptly furnished to the Commission on a supplemental basis.

(f) Such additional material information, if any, as may be necessary to make the required statements, in light of the circumstances under which they are made, not materially misleading.

Item 11. Material to Be Filed as Exhibits

Furnish a copy of:

(a) Tender offer material which is published, sent or given to security holders by or on behalf of the bidder in connection with the tender offer;

(b) Any loan agreement referred to in Item 4 of this schedule;

Instruction. The identity of any bank which is a party to a loan agreement need not be disclosed if the person filing the statement has requested that the identity of such bank not be made available to the public pursuant to Item 4 of this schedule.

(c) Any document setting forth the terms of any contract, arrangements, understandings or relationships referred to in Item 7 or 10(a) of this schedule;

(d) Any written opinion prepared by legal counsel at the bidder's request and communicated to the bidder pertaining to the tax consequences of the tender offer;

(e) In an exchange offer where securities of the bidder have been or are to be registered under the Securities Act of 1933, the prospectus containing the information to be included therein by Rule 432 (§230.432 of this chapter) of that Act;

(f) If any oral solicitation of security holders is to be made by or on behalf of the bidder, any written instruction, form or other material which is furnished to the persons making the actual oral solicitation for their use, directly or indirectly, in connection with the tender offer.

Signature. After due inquiry and to the best of my knowledge and belief, I certify that the information set forth in this statement is true, complete and correct.

______________________ ______________________

(Date) (Signature)

____

(Name and Title)

The original statement shall be signed by each person on whose behalf the statement is filed or his authorized representative. If the statement is signed on behalf of a person by his auhorized representative (other than an executive officer or general partner of the bidder), evidence of the representative's authority to sign on behalf of such person shall be filed with the statement. The name and any title of each person who signs the statement shall be typed or printed beneath his signature.

Exhibit 12-4

OMB APPROVAL
OMB Number: 3235-0102
Expires: September 30, 1997
Estimated average burden hours per response . . 354.25

UNITED STATES
SECURITIES AND EXCHANGE COMMISSION
Washington, D.C. 20549

SCHEDULE 14D-9

Solicitation/Recommendation Statement Pursuant to Section 14(d)(4) of the Securities Exchange Act of 1934
(Amendment No. ________________)

(Name of Subject Company)

(Name of Person(s) Filing Statement)

(Title of Class of Securities)

(CUSIP Number of Class of Securities)

(Name, address and telephone number of person authorized to receive notice and communications on behalf of the person(s) filing statement)

Instructions: Eight copies of this statement, including all exhibits, should be filed with the Commission.

General Instructions:

A. The item numbers and captions of the items shall be included but the text of the items is to be omitted. The answers to the items shall be so prepared as to indicate clearly the coverage of the items without referring to the text of the items. Answer every item. If an item is inapplicable or the answer is in the negative so state.

B. Information contained in exhibits to the statement may be incorporated by reference in answer or partial answer to any item or sub-item of the statement unless it would render such answer misleading, incomplete, unclear or confusing. Material incorporated by reference shall be clearly identified in the reference by page, paragraph, caption or otherwise. An express statement that the specified matter is incorporated by reference shall be made at the particular place in the statement where the information is required. A copy of any information or a copy of the pertinent pages of a document containing such information which is incorporated by reference shall be submitted with this statement as an exhibit and shall be deemed to be filed with the Commission for all purposes of the Act.

Item 1. Security and Subject Company

State the title of the class of equity securities to which this statement relates and the name and the address of the principal executive offices of the subject company.

Item 2. Tender Offer of the Bidder

Identify the tender offer to which this statement relates, the name of the bidder and the address of its principal executive offices or, if the bidder is a natural person, the bidder's residence or business address (which may be based on the bidder's Schedule 14-D-1 [§240.14d-100] filed with the Commission).

Item 3. Identity and Background

(a) State the name and business address of the person filing this statement.

(b) If material, describe any contract, agreement, arrangement or understanding and any actual or potential conflict of interest between the person filing this statement or its affiliates and: (1) the subject company, its executive officers, directors or affiliates; or (2) the bidder, its executive officers, directors or affiliates.

Instruction: If the person filing this statement is the subject company and if the materiality requirement of Item 3(b) is applicable to any contract, agreement, arrangement or understanding between the subject company or any affiliate of the subject company and any executive officer or director of the subject company, it shall not be necessary to include a description thereof in this statement, or in any solicitation or recommendation published, sent or given to security holders if such information, or information which does not differ materially from such information, has been disclosed in any proxy statement, report or other communication sent within one year of the filing date of this statement by the subject company to the then holders of the securities and has been filed with the Commission: *Provided,* That this statement and the solicitation or recommendation published, sent or given to security holders shall contain specific reference to such proxy statement, report or other communication and that a copy of the pertinent portion(s) thereof is filed as an exhibit to this statement.

Item 4. The Solicitation or Recommendation

(a) State the nature of the solicitation or the recommendation. If this statement relates to a recommendation, state whether the person filing this statement is advising security holders of the securities being sought by the bidder to accept or reject the tender offer or to take other action with respect to the bidder to accept or reject the tender offer or to take other action with respect to the tender offer and, if so, furnish a description of such other action being recommended. If the person filing this statement is the subject company and a recommendation is not being made, state whether the subject company is either expressing no opinion and is remaining neutral toward the tender offer or is unable to take a position with respect to the tender offer.

(b) State the reason(s) for the position (including the inability to take a position) stated in (a) of this Item.

Instruction: Conclusory statements such as "The tender offer is in the best interest of shareholders," will not be considered sufficient disclosure in response to Item 4(b).

Item 5. Persons Retained, Employed or to Be Compensated

Identify any person or class of persons employed, retained or to be compensated by the person filing this statement or by any person on its behalf, to make solicitations or recommendations to security holders and describe briefly the terms of such employment, retainer or arrangement for compensation.

Item 6. Recent Transactions and Intent with Respect to Securities

(a) Describe any transaction in the securities referred to in Item 1 which was effected during the past 60 days by the person(s) named in response to Item 3(a) and by any executive officer, director, affiliate or subsidiary of such person(s).

(b) To the extent known by the person filing this statement, state whether the persons referred to in Item 6(a) presently intend to tender to the bidder, sell or hold securities of the class of securities being sought by the bidder which are held of record or beneficially owned by such persons.

Item 7. Certain Negotiations and Transactions by the Subject Company

(a) If the person filing this statement is the subject company, state whether or not any negotiation is being undertaken or is underway by the subject company in response to the tender offer which relates to or would result in:

(1) An extraordinary transaction such as a merger or reorganization, involving the subject company or any subsidiary of the subject company;

(2) A purchase, sale or transfer of a material amount of assets by the subject company or any subsidiary of the subject company;

(3) A tender offer for or other acquisition of securities by or of the subject company; or

(4) Any material change in the present capitalization or dividend policy of the subject company.

Instruction: If no agreement in principal has yet been reached, the possible terms of any transaction or the parties thereto need not be disclosed if in the opinion of the Board of Directors of the subject company such disclosure would jeopardize continuation of such negotiations. In such event, disclosure that negotiations are being undertaken or are underway and are in the preliminary stages will be sufficient.

(b) Describe any transaction, board resolution, agreement in principle, or a signed contract in response to the tender offer, other than one described pursuant to Item 3(b) of this statement, which relates to or would result in one or more of the matters referred to in Item 7(a)(1), (2), (3) or (4).

Item 8. Additional Information to Be Furnished

Furnish such additional information, if any, as may be necessary to make the required statements, in light of the circumstances under which they are made, not materially misleading.

Item 9. Material to Be Filed as Exhibits

Furnish a copy of:

(a) Any written solicitation or recommendation which is published or sent or given to security holders in connection with the solicitation or recommendation referred to in Item 4.

(b) If any oral solicitation or recommendation to security holders is to be made by or on behalf of the person filing this statement, any written instruction, or other material which is furnished to the persons making the actual oral solicitation or recommendation for their use, directly or indirectly, in connection with the solicitation or recommendation.

(c) Any contract, agreement, arrangement or understanding described in Item 3(b) or the pertinent portion(s) of any proxy statement, report or other communication referred to in Item 3(b).

Signature. After reasonable inquiry and to the best of my knowledge and belief, I certify that the information set forth in this statement is true, complete and correct.

______________________	______________________
(Date)	(Signature)
	______________________
	(Name and Title)

Instruction: The original statement shall be signed by each person on whose behalf the statement is filed or his authorized representative. If the statement is signed on behalf of a person by his authorized representative (other than an executive officer of a corporation or a general partner of a partnership), evidence of the representative's authority to sign on behalf of such person shall be filed with the statement. The name and any title of each person who signs the statement shall be typed or printed beneath the signature.

EXHIBIT 12-5

UNION CARBIDE CORPORATION 39 OLD RIDGEBURY ROAD, DANBURY, CT 06817-

ROBERT D. KENNEDY
CHAIRMAN AND CHIEF EXECUTIVE OFFICER

August 3, 1989

Dear Union Carbide Shareholder:

On July 26, 1989 the Board of Directors adopted a Share Purchase Rights Plan. The Plan, which is similar to those in place at many leading companies, is designed to deal with the serious problem of coercive takeover tactics that can deprive a company's Board and its shareholders of the chance to carefully evaluate an unsolicited takeover proposal.

No such takeover proposal has been made to Union Carbide, nor do we know of any being contemplated. But at a time when hostile bids are commonplace, your Directors believe it is prudent to ensure that we will have ample time to consider all the alternatives should Carbide become the target of a hostile takeover attempt.

Shareholders will shortly receive a brochure explaining the plan in full. Basically, it provides that if a company or individual becomes the beneficial owner of 20 percent of Carbide common stock, Union Carbide shareholders of record on August 31, 1989 and thereafter, except the acquirer, would have the right to buy stock in Carbide, or in the surviving company if Carbide is acquired, at a discount.

Issuance of the rights does not in any way affect the financial strength of the company or interfere with its business plans. The distribution of the rights will not result in any taxable income to the company or to you, will not affect the company's reported earnings per share and will not change the way in which the company's shares are traded.

Separate rights certificates will not be issued and the rights will not be traded separately from the stock until 10 days after a person or group acquires 20 percent or more of Union Carbide's common stock, or announces a tender offer that if consummated would result in 20 percent or more ownership of the common stock.

The overriding objective of your company's Board of Directors in adopting the plan is to protect the interests of the Company and its shareholders. We are very optimistic about Carbide's potential to continue growing in value, and we want to give shareholders every opportunity to reap the rewards.

Sincerely,

EXHIBIT 12-6

EXHIBIT B

Salomon Brothers Inc
Seven World Trade Center
New York, New York 10048
Telephone: (212) 783-7000

Salomon Brothers

December 2, 1997

The Board of Directors
SmarTalk TeleServices, Inc.
1640 South Sepulveda Boulevard
Suite 500
Los Angeles, CA 90025

Members of the Board:

SmarTalk TeleServices, Inc., a California corporation (the "Company"), and ConQuest Telecommunication Services Corp., a Delaware corporation ("ConQuest"), have entered into an Agreement and Plan of Reorganization (the "Transaction Agreement") whereby the Company, through a wholly-owned subsidiary, will acquire ConQuest by the merger of ConQuest with the Company's wholly owned subsidiary (the "Transaction"). As more specifically detailed in the Transaction Agreement, the consideration to be paid by the Company in the Transaction consists of 7.63 shares of the Company's Common Stock, no par value ("Common Stock"), for each share of ConQuest Common Stock outstanding at the Effective Time of the merger (as defined in the Transaction Agreement) upon the satisfaction (or waiver) of certain terms and conditions set forth in the Transaction Agreement.

You have requested our opinion as investment bankers as to the fairness, from a financial point of view, of the consideration to be paid by the Company pursuant to the Transaction Agreement.

In arriving at our opinion, we have reviewed draft Transaction Agreement dated July 30, 1997. We also have reviewed certain publicly available business and financial information relating to the Company, as well as certain other information relating to the Company and ConQuest, including financial forecasts, estimates and analyses of the Company and ConQuest, provided to us by the Company. We have discussed the past and current operations and financial condition and prospects of the Company with its senior management. We have also discussed the past and current operations and financial condition and prospects of ConQuest with its senior management. In addition, we have reviewed the nature and terms of certain recent transactions which we believe to be reasonably comparable to the Transaction or otherwise relevant to our inquiry and certain publicly available information regarding certain other companies which we believe to be comparable to the Company and Conquest and the trading markets for certain of such other companies' securities. We have also considered such other information, financial studies, analyses, investigations and financial, economic, market and trading criteria that we deemed relevant.

Salomon Brothers Inc & Worldwide Affiliates
Atlanta
Berlin
Boston
Chicago
Dallas
Frankfurt
Hong Kong
London
Los Angeles
Madrid
Melbourne
New York
San Francisco
Seoul
Singapore
Sydney
Taipei
Tokyo
Toronto
Zurich

In conducting our review and in arriving at our opinion, we have relied upon and assumed the accuracy and completeness of the financial and other information provided to us or publicly available and have not assumed any responsibility for independently verifying the same. With respect to financial forecasts, estimates and analyses, we have assumed that such data have been reasonably prepared on a basis reflecting the best currently available estimates and judgments of the Company, and we express no opinion with respect to such data or the assumptions on which they are based. We have not assumed any responsibility for making or obtaining any evaluations or appraisals of the properties, assets, liabilities or reserves of the Company or ConQuest. We have not been authorized to, and we have not, solicited or investigated alternative transactions that might be available to the Company. Our opinion as expressed herein does not address the fairness to the Company or the reasonableness of any aspect of the Transaction Agreement other than the consideration being paid by the Company thereunder and does not address the underlying business decision of the Company

Salomon Brothers

to enter into the Transaction. Our opinion necessarily is based only upon business, market, economic and other conditions as they exist and can be evaluated on the date hereof.

We have acted as financial advisor to the Board of Directors of the Company in connection with the Transaction pursuant to an engagement letter dated May 23, 1997. In addition, we have acted as lead managing underwriter for the Company's initial public offering and joint-lead managing underwriter for the Company's convertible notes offering for which we received customary fees. Salomon Brothers Inc is a full service securities firm, and in the ordinary course of our normal trading activities, we may from time to time effect transactions and hold positions in the equity securities of the Company for our own account and for the accounts of customers and, accordingly, may at any time hold a long or short position in such securities.

Based upon and subject to the foregoing, it is our opinion as investment bankers that, as of the date hereof, the consideration to be paid by the Company pursuant to the Transaction Agreement is fair, from a financial point of view, to the Company.

Very truly yours,

SALOMON BROTHERS INC

By: /s/ SALOMON BROTHERS INC

Chapter 13

OTHER LEGAL MATTERS

A. INTRODUCTION

A variety of federal, state and local laws must be considered in planning and implementing acquisition transactions. Many of these laws create governmental agencies and delegate authority to them to adopt legally enforceable regulations that must also be considered. In addition, the laws are interpreted and supplemented by numerous federal and state court decisions which must also be considered.

Under the U.S. Constitution, the federal government is a government of delegated powers with all other powers being reserved to the states and the people. The powers of the federal government have grown extensively since the 1930s, but remain limited in many ways.[1] Most important in relation to acquisition transactions, the Constitution gives the federal government the power to regulate interstate and foreign commerce and prohibits state laws that unduly burden them.[2] Many federal laws applicable to acquisition transactions are based on the commerce powers granted by the Constitution.

In general, both the federal government and the states regulate commercial transactions. However, the U.S. Congress and the President sometimes perceive a need for uniform national legislation that preempts state laws.[3] This preemption power is usually exercised when the states have shown a tendency to adopt laws that discriminate in favor of their own interests and against interstate commerce.

For many laws regulating commercial transactions, the U.S. Congress or a state legislature adopt a statute establishing a basic regulatory framework and creating a government agency to administer the statute by adoption and enforcement of regulations. Federal government agencies must publish proposed regulations in the Federal Register so the public has an opportu-

[1]The roles of federal, state and local laws and government agencies is the subject of longstanding political debate that is beyond the scope of this book.

[2]For a recent example, see *C & A Carbone, Inc. v. Town of Clarkstown,* 114 S. Ct. 1677 (1994) nullifying the "waste flow control" laws and regulations of the State of New York and its Department of Environmental Conservation.

[3]Some early antitakeover laws adopted by the states were struck down by the U.S. Supreme Court as preempted by the Securities Exchange Act of 1934 and also as an undue burden on interstate commerce. *Edgar v. Mite Corporation,* 102 S.Ct. 2629 (1982). The National Securities Markets Improvements Act of 1996 partially preempted certain nationally traded securities from regulation by state authorities. 15 U.S. C. § 77r.

nity to comment on them. The federal agencies then revise the regulations to the extent that they decide that the comments have merit and publish the final regulations in the Federal Register, usually with an explanation of the reasons for accepting or rejecting public comments. The regulations are then published as part of the Code of Federal Regulations.[4] State government agencies follow similar procedures in adopting regulations.

The federal courts may nullify a statute or regulation if it conflicts with the Constitution. The federal courts may also nullify a regulation if it conflicts with, or exceeds the authority granted by, the statute under which it is adopted.[5] The state courts exercise similar powers. However, the courts do not nullify government agency actions merely because they disagree, but only if they find an agency made a mistaken interpretation of the law, acted in an arbitrary and capricious manner, or acted without substantial evidence supporting its actions.

B. State Corporation Statutes

In the United States, business corporations are organized under state statutes, commonly called general corporation laws or business corporation laws. Few corporations are organized under federal laws, the most common exception being national banking associations organized under the National Banking Act administered by the U.S. Comptroller of the Currency.

The corporation statutes place the responsibility for the management[6] of a corporation upon its board of directors whose members are elected annually by the shareholders. The board acts only collectively, however, and its members do not necessarily become employees.[7] The board acts, typically by majority vote, to appoint officers and to adopt resolutions authorizing and approving or restricting the authority of the officers to act on behalf of the corporation.

The corporation statutes require that certain major corporate actions authorized or approved by the board of directors must also be approved by the shareholders. Some statutes require an affirmative vote of the holders of a majority of the outstanding shares entitled to vote and others require a larger fraction, such as two-thirds or three-fourths of the outstanding shares entitled to vote. Actions requiring shareholder approval include (1) an amendment of the certificate of incorporation; (2) a sale of substan-

[4]There has been much recent controversy because Congress and state legislatures have created many government agencies which have published many complex regulations. A task force recently claimed they had made extensive reductions of government regulations. However, in large part, they simply deleted the text of many helpful examples and test methods that were guides to compliance.

[5]Government agencies sometimes seek to expand their powers by adopting regulations that exceed the authority granted to them. For example, the U.S. Environmental Protection Agency frequently litigates its powers with persons, such as the Natural Resources Defense Council, who are allies and not adversaries. Some courts have allowed private industry to intervene in these lawsuits so that their interests will be represented.

[6]On this point, the corporation statutes in the United States differ from those of many other nations.

[7]A director of a corporation is not authorized in that capacity to act on behalf of the corporation. For example, a director who is not an officer is not authorized to sign a contract on behalf of the corporation.

tially all assets; (3) a merger or consolidation; or (4) a dissolution of the corporation. If the required vote for these events is obtained, shareholders who vote against the proposal are bound by the result. However, shareholders who vote against a sale of substantially all assets, merger or consolidation can, if they wish, exercise dissenters' appraisal rights to be paid the fair value of their shares in cash. If they are not satisfied with the corporation's offer of a cash value, they can commence an appraisal proceeding in court to determine the fair value.

Under the corporation statutes and court decisions, directors, officers and controlling shareholders have fiduciary obligations to the corporation and its shareholders. Performance of these obligations is usually measured by the "business judgment" rule whereby directors, officers and controlling shareholders are presumed to act reasonably and in good faith unless proven to the contrary.[8] However, if they engage in a transaction that involves a conflict of interest, they have the burden of proving the "entire fairness" of the transaction to the corporation and its shareholders.[9]

A relatively high percentage of business corporations are incorporated in the State of Delaware, even though their headquarters offices and operating facilities are located in other states. There are several reasons.[10] The Delaware General Corporation Law is clearly written and up to date. The judges in the Delaware courts are experienced in corporate matters and generally render prompt and knowledgeable decisions.[11] The fees and annual franchise taxes payable upon incorporation and annually thereafter are modest. No income tax is imposed unless the corporation does business in Delaware.

C. Disclosures and Insider Information

1. Disclosure Obligations

The directors and officers of corporations with public shareholders have important obligations for the disclosure of material information about acquisition transactions. The obligations are imposed by the federal securities laws, state corporation laws and the rules of stock exchanges and the National Association of Securities Dealers, Inc. on corporations whose shares are traded on their facilities. For example, the *Listed Company Manual* published by The New York Stock Exchange, Inc. (NYSE) contains the following statement in Section 202.05:

---

[8]*Smith v. Van Gorkom*, 488 Atl. 2d 858 (1985); *Rosenblatt v. Getty Oil Co.*, 493 Atl. 2d 929 (1985).

[9]*Weinberger v. UOP, Inc.*, 457 Atl. 701 (1983); *Revlon, Inc. v. McAndrews & Forbes Holdings, Inc.*, 506 Atl.2d 173 (1986).

[10]Some people who have limited familiarity with corporate practice believe that corporations are incorporated in Delaware because the laws there are lenient toward corporate behavior. Actually, Delaware corporation law is stricter and more extensive than the law in other states, especially in enforcing the performance of fiduciary duties of directors, officers and controlling shareholders.

[11]Corporate lawyers are relatively comfortable when rendering opinions on matters governed by the Delaware General Corporation Law because of its clarity, the availability of numerous court decisions creating precedents, and the expectation that future court decisions will be made by judges familiar with corporate law.

> Timely Disclosure of Material News Developments
>
> *A listed company is expected to release quickly to the public any news or information that might reasonably be expected to materially affect the market for its securities. This is one of the most important and fundamental purposes of the listing agreement that each company enters into with the Exchange. A corporation should also act promptly to dispel unfounded rumors that result in unusual market activity or price variations.*

The NYSE is diligent in enforcing its timely disclosure requirements. During my tenure as a senior officer of publicly owned corporations, the author received several calls from NYSE listing officers inquiring about rumors and other possible explanations for unexpected buying or selling activity. They wanted, of course, to be sure that the corporation was fulfilling its disclosure obligations. Otherwise, trading could become disorderly and persons having access to nonpublic information could use NYSE's facilities to take advantage of public shareholders.

The *Company Guide of the American Stock Exchange* (ASE) contains similar disclosure policies, as described in Sections 401 to 405 of the Guide. The NASDAQ Stock Market Inc. (NASDAQ) also has rules requiring disclosure of material information.[12] In its Rule IM 4120, the first example in the list of events that may require disclosure is a merger, acquisition or joint venture.

On the other hand, premature public statements about events that are in early planning stages and may never occur is not required and may be imprudent. A corporation that announces a new contract, a business expansion, a technology advance or an acquisition before there is a reasonable basis for concluding that the transaction is real may precipitate an increase in the price of its shares followed by losses if the event does not take place. The result may then be investigation and litigation by the Securities and Exchange Commission and the shareholders who suffered the losses.

As a practical matter, there is almost always a time period during corporate transactions when discussions, planning and evaluation are in progress, but the likelihood of occurrence is uncertain. A transaction that is making good progress may unexpectedly meet obstacles that send the participants "back to the drawing board." To avoid potential liability for a premature announcement, a corporation customarily defers announcement of a material event until its occurrence is reasonably likely, although it should not wait until all details are finalized. The text of the announcement should, of course, describe the status of the transaction and any significant conditions that may remain to be fulfilled before it will take place.

The NYSE's *Listed Company Manual* provides guidance on the internal handling of confidential corporate matters in Section 202.01:

> *Unusual market activity or a substantial price change has on occasion occurred in a company's securities shortly before the announcement of an important corporate action or development. Such incidents are extremely embarrassing and damaging to both the company and the Exchange since the public may quickly conclude that someone acted on the basis of inside information.*

---

[12] Rules IM 4120, 4310(c)(1b) and 4320(d)(15).

Negotiations leading to mergers and acquisitions, stock splits, the making of arrangements preparatory to an exchange or tender offer, changes in dividend rates or earnings, calls for redemption and new contracts, products, or discoveries are the type of developments where the risk of untimely and inadvertent disclosure of corporate plans are most likely to occur. Frequently, these matters require extensive discussion and study by corporate officials before final decisions can be made. Accordingly, extreme care must be used in order to keep the information on a confidential basis.

Where it is possible to confine formal or informal discussions to a small group of the top management of the company or companies involved, and their individual confidential advisors where adequate security can be maintained, premature public announcement may properly be avoided. In this regard, the market action of a company's securities should be closely watched at a time when consideration is being given to important corporate matters. If unusual market activity should arise, the company should be prepared to make an immediate public announcement of the matter.

At some point it usually becomes necessary to involve other persons to conduct preliminary studies or assist in other preparations for contemplated transactions, e.g., business appraisals, tentative financing arrangements, attitude of large outside holders, availability of major blocks of stock, engineering studies and market analyses and surveys. Experience has shown that maintaining security at this point is virtually impossible. Accordingly, fairness requires that the company make an immediate public announcement as soon as disclosures relating to such important matters are made to outsiders.

The extent of the disclosures will depend upon the stage of discussions, studies, or negotiations. So far as possible, public statements should be definite as to price, ratio, timing and/or any other pertinent information necessary to permit a reasonable evaluation of the matter. As a minimum, they should include those disclosures made to outsiders. Where an initial announcement cannot be specific or complete, it will need to be supplemented from time to time as more definitive or different terms are discussed or determined.

Corporate employees, as well as directors and officers, should be regularly reminded as a matter of policy that they must not disclose confidential information they may receive in the course of their duties and must not attempt to take advantage of such information themselves.

In view of the importance of this matter and the potential difficulties involved, the Exchange suggests that a periodic review be made by each company of the manner in which confidential information is being handled within its own organization. A reminder notice of the company's policy to those in sensitive areas might also be helpful.

A sound corporate disclosure policy is essential to the maintenance of a fair and orderly securities market. It should minimize the occasions where the Exchange finds it necessary to temporarily halt trading in a security due to information leaks or rumors in connection with significant corporate transactions.

While the procedures are directed primarily at situations involving two or more companies, they are equally applicable to major corporate developments involving a single company.

The NYSE's *Listed Company Manual* prescribes that releases requiring immediate publicity be given to Dow Jones & Company, Inc., Reuters Economic Services and Bloomberg Business News and encourages that releases also be distributed to Associated Press, United Press International and newspapers in New York and in other cities where the company is headquartered or has plants or other major facilities.

The *Listed Company Manual* also recommends a telephone alert to the NYSE and explains the reasons as follows:

> *Telephonic Alert to the Exchange. When the announcement of news of a material event or a statement dealing with a rumor which calls for immediate release is made shortly before the opening or during market hours (presently 9:30 A.M. to 5:00 P.M., New York time,* it is recommended that the company's Exchange representative be notified by telephone at least ten minutes prior to release of the announcement to the news media. If the Exchange receives such notification in time, it will be in a position to consider whether, in the opinion of the Exchange, trading in the security should be temporarily halted. A delay in trading after the appearance of the news on the Dow Jones, Reuters or Bloomberg news wires provides a period of calm for public evaluation of the announcement. The halt also allows customers to revise the terms of limit orders on the specialist's book in view of the news announcement. Even if limit orders are not cancelled or changed during the halt, the fact that trading is halted results in the reopening being considered a new opening, thereby enabling limit orders to participate at the new opening price regardless of the previously entered limit. A longer delay in trading may be necessary if there is an unusual influx of orders. The Exchange attempts to keep such interruptions in the continuous auction market to a minimum. However, where events transpire during market hours, the overall importance of fairness to all those participating in the market demands that these procedures be followed.*

The ASE's *Company Guide* also provides extensive guidance and describes policies and methods in a question and answer format. See §§401 to 405 of the *Guide*.

The NASDAQ also provides guidance on disclosure of material information, but the discussion in its Rule IM 4120 is much briefer than the discussion in Section 2 of the NYSE's *Listed Company Manual.*

2. Insider Information and Market Surveillance

The history of civil and criminal liability for trading by insiders, quasi-insiders, temporary insiders, tippees and persons who misappropriate nonpublic information is discussed in Chapter 12.

The NYSE's Market Surveillance and Evaluation Division uses an "on-line" computer system to monitor trading in every listed stock on a trade-to-trade basis to detect unusual price and volume changes and large influxes of buy or sell orders. If price movement exceeds a predetermined guideline, it is immediately "flagged" and review of the situation is immediately undertaken. The Division's personnel are experienced and skilled and their reviews have often led to the discovery of insider trading.

The NASDAQ's Market Surveillance Department monitors real-time trading in all NASDAQ securities for price and volume activity.

---

*Effective June 13, 1991 the New York Stock Exchange off-hours trading sessions became operational. The facility offers the opportunity to trade at NYSE closing prices after the NYSE's 4:00 P.M. close until 5:00 P.M.

D. Exchange Policies on Stockholder Approval

The NYSE requires stockholder approval as a prerequisite to listing securities to be issued in the following transactions:

1. Options granted to or special remuneration plans for directors, officers or employees.
2. Actions resulting in a change or in the control of a company.
3. The acquisition,[13] direct or indirect, of a business, a company, tangible or intangible assets or property or securities representing any such interests:
   - **(a)** From a director, officer or substantial security holder of the company (including its subsidiaries and affiliates) or from any company or party in which one of such person has a direct or indirect interest:
   - **(b)** Where the present or potential issuance of common stock or securities convertible into common stock could result in an increase in outstanding[14] common shares approximating $18\frac{1}{2}$ percent or more; or
   - **(c)** Where the present or potential issuance of common stock and any other consideration has a combined fair value approximating 20 percent or more of the market value of the outstanding[15] common shares.

When appropriate, the NYSE may agree to act on a listing application, subject to the required shareholder approval. If it does so, the listing does not become effective until the shareholder approval is obtained.

The *Company Guide* of the American Stock Exchange also requires shareholder approval as a prerequisite to approval of the applications to list additional shares to be issued as consideration for acquisitions:

- **(a)** if any individual director, officer or substantial shareholder of the listed company has a 5 percent or greater interest (or such persons collectively have a 10 percent or greater interest), directly or indirectly, in the company or assets to be acquired or in the consideration to be paid in the transaction and the present or potential issuance of common stock, or securities convertible into common stock, could result in an increase in outstanding common shares of 5 percent or more; or
- **(b)** where the present or potential issuance of common stock, or securities convertible into common stock, could result in an increase in outstanding common shares of 20 percent or more.

---

[13]A series of closely related transactions may be regarded as one transaction.

[14]Only those shares actually issued and outstanding (excluding treasury shares and shares held by a subsidiary) are used in this calculation. Shares reserved for issuance upon conversion of securities or exercise of options or warrants are not used.

[15]A series of closely related transactions may be regarded as one transaction.

The NASDAQ does not have a rule requiring shareholder approval of acquisitions as a prerequisite to listing additional shares issued as acquisition currency.

E. Sale of Corporate Control

When shareholders sell stock that constitutes a controlling interest in a corporation, they usually expect to obtain a premium price. Indeed, valuation analysts customarily assign a premium when valuing stock that represents a controlling interest.

If controlling shareholders find themselves selling for a premium to a buyer whose reputation or actions arouse suspicions, they should discuss with their counsel the decision in *Perlman v. Feldmann*.[16] In that case, shareholders holding a controlling interest of 37 percent in a steel company sold their shares to a steel user. The price was $20, a considerable premium over the market price of $12. Minority shareholders sued the selling shareholders, alleging that there was a severe steel shortage that created valuable corporate opportunities for profitable sales. The minority shareholders alleged that the majority shareholders diverted the opportunity by selling to a steel user who could use its control to sell the steel to itself without paying the full price resulting from the shortage. The Court of Appeals held that majority shareholders would be required to account to the corporation for the premium to the extent that the corporation should be harmed.

The *Perlman* decision created considerable anxiety for controlling shareholders until the same court issued its decision in *Essex Universal Corporation v. Yates*.[17] In that case, the majority shareholders sold their shares for a modest premium. They also agreed to resign and elect buyer representatives to the board of directors. The Court of Appeals distinguished its decision in the *Perlman* case by observing that these arrangements (which are customary) do not imply that any harm will be done to the corporation or the noncontrolling shareholders.

At present, the effect of the *Perlman* decision is to provide some protection to minority shareholders against a sale to a buyer that may be a looter. Sales to reputable buyers can be made without undue concern. Interested readers can find further information in "The Sale of Corporate Control" by Colin K. Harley.[18] Among other things, Mr. Harley discusses court decisions involving the exercise of "due care" by selling shareholders to determine whether a buyer may plan to divert corporate assets.

F. Intellectual Properties

Among the assets that can be acquired as part of an acquisition are intellectual properties consisting of patents, trademarks, copyrights, trade secrets, corporate names and trade names. Although these assets are sometimes very valuable, they are seldom carried at any value on the balance

[16]219 F.2d 173 (2d Cir. 1955).

[17]305 F.2d 572 (2d Cir. 1962).

[18]*Corporate Practice Series Portfolio No. 19*, Harley, Bureau of National Affairs, Inc. (1994).

sheet of the corporation or business to be acquired. The reason is that the cost of development of intellectual properties is usually treated as deductible current expense. Thus, they are treated as capital assets only when they are purchased or otherwise acquired.

An example of the value of intellectual properties is illustrated by an acquisition in which the author participated some years ago. The business offered for sale was in an urban area no longer suitable for heavy industry. The plant was old and in poor condition. The equipment was also old, although it had been kept in good condition. There was a history of difficulties with the union representing the hourly paid employees. The buyer decided against purchasing any of the fixed assets, but paid a seven figure price to acquire two registered trademarks; the trade secret formulations for production of the products sold under the two trademarks; the customer lists for the products; the customer specifications and applications data; and the right to hire key sales and technical service employees.

Key characteristics of intellectual properties are as follows:

Patents. The Patent Law [19] provides that whoever invents or discovers any new and useful process, machine, manufacture, or composition of matter, or any new and useful improvement thereof, may obtain a patent for it. Patents can also be obtained for certain hybrid plants and designs. To obtain a patent, the individual inventor or inventors must file an application with the U.S. Patent and Trademark Office (USPTO) containing a specification describing and teaching the best methods to practice the invention and one or more claims delineating the scope of the invention. Patents do not exist at common law, so inventors have no patent rights unless and until the USPTO issues the patent. Patent applications can be denied for several reasons, including prior invention by another inventor and obviousness to a person having ordinary skill in the art that is the subject of the claimed invention. Most patents are issued for a term of 20 years. However, the term of patents for certain drugs, medicinal devices, food additives or color additives may be extended because they are subject to lengthy review by the Food and Drug Administration (FDA).[20] The holder of a patent has the exclusive right (i.e., a legal monopoly) to practice the art covered by the allowed claims for the term of the patent, even against innocent persons who infringe without actual knowledge of the patent. The patentholder can either maintain the monopoly or license others in return for royalties. The patentholder can sue any person who infringes any of the patent claims to enjoin the infringement and obtain monetary damages. Employees hired to perform research or technical work usually agree to assign inventions to their employers. The public imagination has been inspired by the accomplishments of legendary inventors such as Thomas Edison, Alexander Graham Bell and Guglielmo Marconi. However, there are thousands of patents covering inventions that are less dramatic, but provide an important business advantage to their holders.

---

[19]35 U.S.C. § 1 *et seq.*

[20]The FDA requires lengthy testing of drugs and other products subject to its jurisdiction. The FDA has been criticized for its slowness, but it actually works more rapidly and scientifically than some other agencies that receive less public criticism.

Trademarks. Trademarks are symbols or devices used to distinguish products or services from each other. Trademarks are created by use in commerce and are recognized at common law. Trademarks can, but need not be, registered with the USPTO or one or more state registration offices. Most trademarks of important value are registered with the USPTO because the Trademark Laws[21] provide several advantages to holders of registered trademarks, including a right to commence infringement lawsuits in the federal courts. Registration of a trademark is evidenced by a certificate of registration, initially for a 10 year term. However, the initial term expires at the end of the sixth year unless the holder files an affidavit of continuing use. Trademarks can be renewed beyond the initial term for additional terms of 10 years each. The holder of a trademark has the exclusive right to use the trademark and can sue for infringement any person who uses the same or a confusingly similar trademark in order to obtain an injunction against infringement and monetary damages. Rights to use well-known trademarks are frequently licensed in return for royalty or other payments. The licensing of trademarks is often part of an overall franchise or distributorship agreement under which the licensor also provides other products and services including advertising, training and quality standards for products and services. Well-known franchise programs have been operated by companies such as Holiday Inns and International House of Pancakes (IHOP). Distributorship programs are operated, among others, by companies such as Ford Motor Company and Texaco.

Copyrights. The Copyright Act provides to authors exclusive rights to their original works of authorship including literary, musical, dramatic, pantomime and choreographic, pictorial, graphic and sculptural; motion picture and audiovisual; sound recording; and architectural works. However, copyright protection for an original work does not extend to any idea, procedure, process, system, method of operation, concept, principle, or discovery embodied in the work.[22] Former rights under the common law are preempted by the Copyright Act.[23] The owner of a copyright has the exclusive rights to do and authorize reproduction; preparation of derivative works; distribution of copies or phonorecords; and public performance or display of certain works.[24] A copyright owner includes an employer or other person who hires another person to prepare a work unless otherwise expressly agreed in a written instrument signed by them. Copyright protection is also subject to a variety of exceptions including an exception for "fair use" that protects persons such as literary and drama critics and authors and performers who create satires and parodies. Copyrights in works created on or after January 1, 1978 endure for the life of the author plus 50 years after the author's death.[25] Copyrights in works created before January 1, 1978 endure for various terms.[26] Owners of copyrights can sue to enjoin infringers, but often choose to license reproduction or performance by others in return for royalties. The American Society of Composers and

---

[21] 15 U.S.C. § 1051 *et seq.*

[22] 17 U.S.C. § 102

[23] 17 U.S.C. § 301

[24] 17 U.S.C. § 106

[25] 17 U.S.C. § 302

Publishers (ASCAP) is well-known for its activities in detecting infringement and requiring the infringers to pay royalties, especially to ASCAP members who could not afford to enforce their own rights.

Corporate Names. The state corporation statutes generally prohibit organization of a domestic corporation and qualification to do business by a foreign corporation with a name that is the same or confusingly similar to the name of a corporation already organized and existing or qualified in the state.[27] When a corporation has achieved significant name recognition and goodwill, its corporate name is a valuable asset. The right to the name under the corporation statutes is valuable because it is not always possible to obtain trademark rights for a corporate name. After an acquisition of substantially all the assets of a corporation, it is customary to arrange for the seller to assign its name to the buyer. The seller accomplishes the transfer by filing a name change certificate simultaneously with the filing by the buyer of a certificate of incorporation for a new subsidiary having the seller's name. When an acquisition is by merger, the surviving corporation can preserve ownership of the corporate name of the disappearing corporation by simultaneously organizing a new subsidiary with the same name.

Trade names. Many unincorporated divisions or other business operations use assumed or fictitious names that have achieved significant recognition and goodwill. The states have laws requiring registration of the use of assumed or fictitious names.[28] These assumed or fictitious names may be valuable assets.

Trade Secrets. Trade secrets are intellectual properties that are protected from misappropriation by state common law, which in several states has been codified by the adoption of a statute such as the Uniform Trade Secrets Act. The *Restatement of Torts*, § 757 defines a trade secret as any formula, pattern, device or compilation of information that is used in one's business and that gives one an opportunity to obtain an advantage over competitors who do not know or use it.[29] The Uniform Trade Secrets Act defines a trade secret as information, including a formula, pattern, compilation, program, device, method, technique, or process, that: (i) derives independent economic value, actual or potential, from not being generally known to and not being readily ascertainable by proper means by, other persons who can obtain economic value from its disclosure or use, and (ii) is the subject of efforts that are reasonable to maintain its secrecy. Arguments that the trade secret laws were preempted by the Patent Law were rejected by the U.S. Supreme Court in a famous decision in which the Court's opinion summarized the benefits of the trade secret laws.[30] Trade secrets endure only so long as they are maintained secret, but disclosures can be made under secrecy agreements with licensees, employees, customers or suppliers without loss of the trade secrets. Further, unlike

---

[26]17 U.S.C. § § 303 and 304

[27]For example, see the New York Business Corporation Law, § § 301 and 302.

[28]For example, see the New York General Business Law, § 133.

[29]The definition adds that a trade secret may be a formula for a chemical compound, a process of manufacturing, treating or preserving materials, a pattern for a machine or other device, or a list of customers.

[30]*Kewanee Oil Co. v. Bicron Corp.*, 416 U.S. 470 (1974)

patents, they can be enforced only against persons who misappropriate them by theft or breach of trust, but not against persons who develop the same information independently or through reverse engineering.

G. Bulk Transfers

When a corporation or other business entity sells its assets and receives the purchase price for them, the buyer normally assumes that the seller will wind up its affairs in an orderly manner, including performance of obligations and payment of debts not assumed by the buyer. This expectation is especially typical when the buyer has paid a fair price in cash that can readily be used by the seller to pay creditors. Unfortunately, experience has shown that some sellers will pocket the price and "stiff" their creditors. They can do so with ease when the assets sold consist of quickly movable items such as inventories of merchandise and supplies. Not surprisingly, the disappointed creditors may pursue the buyer if they cannot collect their debts from the seller.

Article 6 of the Uniform Commercial Code, a uniform law adopted by states throughout the United States, protects creditors by providing that bulk transfers of materials, supplies, merchandise or other inventories are ineffective against any creditor of the transferor unless the transferee takes prescribed steps to give advance notice of the transfer to the seller's creditors. In simpler words, as against the seller's creditors, the buyer does not obtain clear title to inventories acquired in a bulk transfer unless it follows the required procedures.

The transferee must require the transferors to furnish a list of existing creditors and must work with the seller to prepare a schedule of the property to be transferred sufficient to identify it. The list of creditors must contain detailed information including names, addresses and amounts claimed, even though disputed. The transferee must then send a notice to the creditors at least ten days before taking possession of the goods or paying for them, whichever is first. The notice must contain detailed information including the names and addresses of the transferor and transferee and whether all the transfer's debts are to be paid in full as they fall due. If the debts will not be paid as described, or if the transferee is in doubt on that point, the notice must contain further information:

(a) the location and general description of the property to be transferred and the estimated total of the transferor's debts;

(b) the address where the schedule of property and list of creditors may be inspected;

(c) whether the transfer is to pay existing debts and if so the amount of such debts and to whom owing; and

(d) whether the transfer is for new consideration and if so the amount of such consideration and the time and place of payment.

The notice must be delivered personally or sent by registered or certified mail to all the persons shown on the list of creditors furnished by the transferor and to all other persons who are known to the transferee to hold or assert claims against the transferor.

After a transferee has sent the notice in a proper manner, Article 6 imposes no further duties upon the transferee. Having received the notice, the creditors are responsible to protect their own interests. The bulk transfer is not rendered ineffective by errors or omissions in the list of creditors unless the transferee is shown to have knowledge of them.

Creditors must commence action to enforce their rights within 6 months after the date on which the transferee took possession of the goods unless the transfer was concealed. If the transfer was concealed, action may be brought or levies made within 6 months after its discovery. Creditors' actions should be to sue in equity to set aside the transfer and cannot be to seek a personal judgment against the transferor or transferee for noncompliance.[31]

In recent years, numerous states repealed Article 6, but New York and several other states have retained it. A few states revised Article 6 to simplify the notice requirements and to provide that creditors are entitled to damages rather than to treat the property transfers as ineffective.

H. Successor Liability after an Assets Acquisition

An important reason for use of the assets acquisition method is to enable the buyer to assume only those liabilities and obligations of the seller that the buyer agrees to assume. The seller remains responsible for its other liabilities and obligations and can use the purchase price and its other resources to pay and perform them.

In fact, sellers usually discharge their known liabilities and obligations, although some fail to do so. Much more important, however, some sellers have sold products or taken other actions that may result in liabilities and obligations that first arise or are discovered many years later, sometimes after the sellers are no longer available to perform them. When this happens, claimants often seek ways to impose successor liability on the buyers. The courts impose successor liability after an assets acquisition in the following circumstances:

1. Mere Restructuring. An assets buyer may be held responsible for liabilities it did not assume if the transaction was a mere shift of corporate structures, such as a transfer of assets among affiliated corporations.[32]

2. De Facto Merger. A buyer of assets may be held liable for products sold prior to the acquisition if: (1) the buyer continues the seller's business with the same management, personnel, physical location, assets and operations; (2) there is continuity of shareholders because the purchaser pays for the assets with stock; (3) the seller liquidates and dissolves as soon as legally and practically possible; and (4) the purchaser assumes those liabilities and obligations of the seller necessary for uninterrupted continuation of normal operations of the seller's business.[33]

---

[31] *Interstate Cigar Co., Inc. v. Interstate Distributors, Inc.*, 210 A.D. 2d 283, 620 N.Y.S. 2d 78 (1994).

[32] *Mozingo v. Correct Manufacturing Corp.*, 752 F.2d 168 (5th. Cir. 1985)

[33] *Shannon v. Samuel Langston Co.*, 379 F. Supp. 797 (W.D. Mich. 1974).

3. Continuation of the Enterprise. In some states, a buyer of assets may be held responsible for products sold prior to the acquisition if it continues the seller's business, even if payment in stock and other elements of a de facto merger are not present. Here, the elements are: (1) continuity of the enterprise by the buyer; (2) liquidation of the seller soon after distribution of the price; (3) the buyer's assumption of the liabilities and obligations necessary for continuation of the seller's normal business operations; and (4) the buyer holding itself out to the world as the effective continuation of the seller.[34] Several courts have rejected "enterprise" continuity as a basis for liability.[35]

4. Fraudulent Transfers. A buyer may be held liable for products sold by the seller prior to the acquisition if it acquires assets for less than fair value from a seller who is left insolvent or inadequately capitalized.[36]

Successor liability after an assets acquisition is also discussed later in this chapter under specific topics such as liability to employees; union recognition and collective bargaining agreements; product liability; environmental liability; liability under the Employee Retirement Income Security Act; liability under worker safety and health laws; and liability under the equal employment opportunity laws.

I. Parent Liability after a Stock Purchase Acquisition

When an acquisition is accomplished by a stock purchase, the buyer corporation knows that the acquired subsidiary will continue to be responsible for its preexisting liabilities and obligations. When a corporation acquires another corporation by a triangular merger, the buyer corporation will have the same expectation. However, the parent corporation does not expect that it will become directly responsible for the new subsidiary's liabilities and obligations.

If the parent corporation does not allow the subsidiary to conduct its business in a manner consistent with separate corporate status, however, the courts may "pierce the corporate veil" and hold the parent responsible for the liabilities and obligations of its subsidiary. The parent corporation is not required, of course, to grant independence to the subsidiary because a subsidiary could never be truly independent of its parent. However, if a parent bypasses the separate existence of the subsidiary and directly conducts its affairs so that it is an alter ego, the parent should not be surprised if the courts do the same.

Several leading court decisions outline the criteria used by the courts to determine when the corporate veil should be pierced.[37] In the *Jon-T Chemicals* decision, the court pointed to the following criteria:

[34] *Turner v. Bituminous Casualty Co.*, 397 Mich. 406, 244 NW2d 873 (1976).

[35] *Niccum v. Hydra Tool Corp.*, 438 NW2d 96 (Minn. 1989) and decisions cited therein.

[36] *Kelly v. American Precision Indust., Inc.*, 438 So.2d 29 (Fla. App. 1983); *McKee v. Harris-Seybold Co.*, 109 N.J. Super 555, 264 A.2d 98 (1970).

[37] *Joslyn Manufacturing Corp. v. T.L. James & Co.*, 893 F.2d 80 (5th Cir. 1990); *United States v. Jon-T Chemicals, Inc.*, 768 F.2d 686 (5th Cir. 1985); cert. den. 475 U.S. 1014 (1986).

(1) the parent and the subsidiary have common stock ownership;
(2) the parent and the subsidiary have common directors or officers;
(3) the parent and the subsidiary have common business departments;
(4) the parent and the subsidiary file consolidated financial statements and tax returns;
(5) the parent finances the subsidiary;
(6) the parent caused the incorporation of the subsidiary;
(7) the subsidiary operates with grossly inadequate capital;
(8) the parent pays the salaries and other expenses of the subsidiary;
(9) the subsidiary receives no business except that given to it by the parent;
(10) the parent uses the subsidiary's property as its own;
(11) the daily operations of the two corporations are not kept separate; and
(12) the subsidiary does not observe the basic corporate formalities, such as keeping separate books and records and holding shareholder and board meetings.

Readers concerned about potential parent corporation responsibility, especially for environmental cleanup costs, should read the discussion of environmental liabilities later in this chapter. In its discussion of evidence required to justify piercing the corporate veil, the U.S. Supreme Court provided insights in deciding *U.S. v. Best Foods* that are likely to be of precedential value outside of the environmental field.

Readers should also review the discussion later in this chapter of the liability of corporate groups for compliance with ERISA, including the funding of pension plans.

J. Employee Claims

1. Introduction

On the closing date of an assets acquisition, the seller usually terminates the employees of the business sold. The buyer makes employment offers to the terminated employees. The employees accept the offers and begin work for the buyer on the morning after the closing. If the buyer hires all the terminated employees for the same responsibilities, compensation and benefits, they may little perceive the change.

The arrangements described do not always occur. In some situations, the seller may retain employees, especially employees who worked part of their time for businesses retained by the seller. In other situations, the buyer may exclude some employees of the seller's business from its offers to hire. When this happens, the seller must decide whether to retain or terminate the excluded employees. On some occasions, the buyer's business plan may call for fundamental change of the methods used to operate the seller's business and the buyer will decide to hire all new employees rather than retain the seller's employees. When this happens, the seller may retain some employees, but would seldom be able to avoid termination of most of them.

2. Wrongful Discharge and Severance Pay

If the seller has a severance pay plan or policy, any employees who are terminated by the seller and not hired by the buyer may make claims for wrongful termination or severance pay. In general, unless an employee has an employment contract, his or her employment is "at will" and the employer is not subject to a wrongful discharge claim merely for terminating the relationship.[38] In general, a claim for severance pay depends on whether the seller has a severance pay plan or policy. If the seller has a severance plan or policy, it will make severance payments. If there is no plan, the seller will deny the claims.

The claims cannot always be resolved so simply. The courts in some states have been willing to find exceptions to the "employment at will" doctrine. The exceptions have been found in cases when employees alleged (1) the existence of an implied contract based on statements in employee handbooks or other literature or based on customary practices of the employer; (2) an implied covenant of good faith and fair dealing; (3) misrepresentation, fraud or promissory estoppel; (4) commission of a tort such as selection of an employee for termination in retaliation for labor activities or "whistle blowing"; or (5) violation of the equal employment opportunity laws.

So-called "handbook" claims arise because many corporations circulated booklets and other literature for years that described benefits imprecisely and without reserving a right to amend.[39] Handbook claims have grown in popularity because, if successful, they can recover money for whole groups of employees. Other claims may benefit only individual employees or small groups of employees.

A few sellers have been chagrined to face claims for severance pay from employees whose termination was only momentary because they were immediately hired by the buyer. Such claims are more likely to be made if the buyer provides to the employees reduced compensation, benefits or working conditions. However, some claims have been made in the absence of such cutbacks. The courts have varied in their rulings on these claims.[40]

---

[38]*Martin v. New York Life Ins. Co.*, 148 N.Y. 117, 42 N.E. 416 (1895); *Sabetay v. Sterling Drug, Inc.*, 69 N.Y. 2d 329, 506 N.E. 2d 919 (1987)

[39]*Toussaint v. Blue Cross*, 408 Mich. 479 (1980); *Weiner v. McGraw-Hill, Inc.*, 57 NY2d 458, 443 NE2d 441 (1982); *Wooley v. Hoffman-LaRoche, Inc.*, 99 NJ 284, 491 A2d 1257 (1985); *Duldulao v. St. Mary of Nazareth Health Center*, 115 Ill. 2d 482, 505 NE2d 314 (1987); *Panto v. Moore Business Forms*, 547 A2d 260 (NH 1988); *In re Question (Bankey v. Storer Broadcasting Co.)*, 443 NW 2d 112 (1989); *Foley v. Interactive Data Corp.*, 47 Cal. 3d 654, 765 P 2d 373 (1988); *Sabetay v. Sterling Drug, Inc.*, 69 NY 2d 329, 506 NE2d 919 (1987); *Finley v. Aetna Life*, 202 Conn. 190, 520 A2d 208 (1987); and *Law v. Howard Univ., Inc.*, 558 A2d 355 (DC 1989).

[40]Decisions in favor of employee claimants include *Dulan Foods, Inc. v. Ayers*, 220 Va. 502, 260 S.E. 2d 196 (1979) and *Dahl v. Brunswick Corp.*, 277 Md. 471, 356 Atl. 2d 221 (1967) and cases cited therein. Decisions in favor of employers include *Albertson v. Ralston Purina*, 586 SW2d 776 (Mo. Ct. App. 1979); *Pinto v. Zenith Radio Corp.*, 480 F.Supp. 361 (ND Ill. 1979); *Younger v. Thomas Int'l Corp.*, 275 Ark. 327, 629 SW2d 294 (1982); *Armstrong v. Diamond Shamrock Corp.*, 7 Ohio App. 3d 296, 455 NE2d 702 (1982).

Buyers who hire seller employees and then terminate them in a downsizing program may face claims for wrongful discharge and severance pay based on alleged succession to seller's benefit plans and policies. Although a buyer may clearly decline to assume any such liabilities or obligations in the acquisition contract, employees may claim that they were never notified of the contract provisions and continued to rely on seller's handbooks and other literature. Thus, even if a buyer intends to match the compensation and benefit levels provided by a seller, the buyer should notify employees of its compensation and benefits programs and clarify that the seller's plans and policies are no longer in effect.

Although the extent is not clear, ERISA has preempted state law relating to employee benefit plans since 1974. Thus, older state court decisions provide some guidance on the likely analysis that will be used by the courts, but all claims must be reconciled with the provisions of ERISA.[41] Under ERISA, severance pay is generally an employee benefit plan and the employer is its administrator and must act in accordance with fiduciary standards. In a key decision, the U.S. Supreme Court reversed an appellate court decision upholding an employer's denial of severance pay to 500 salaried employees who were immediately hired by the buyer that acquired the five plants where they were employed.[42] The Supreme Court held that the appellate court had applied the wrong standard in upholding the denial merely because it was not "arbitrary or capricious" and directed that the denial be fully reviewed again, including any conflict of interest of the plan employer as administrator.

Some states, such as Massachusetts and Pennsylvania, have antitakeover laws that provide "tin parachute" severance payments to employees terminated after a "change of control". A statute of the State of Maine requiring severance pay upon a plant closing was upheld by the U.S. Supreme Court.[43]

3. Vacation Pay

Perhaps the most common employee benefit is a period of annual paid vacation. Many vacation policies develop informally and, even when written, are far from clear.

Many vacation policies simply state that employees are entitled to a specified number of weeks of annual vacation per year employed. The policies often also provide that, with some exceptions, vacation not taken in any year will not carry over to the next year. Some vacation policies also add, but many omit, a statement determining how vacation accrues during a year and whether employees whose employment is terminated, voluntarily or involuntarily, will be paid for accrued but unused vacation.

The U.S. Department of Labor has exempted vacation from ERISA.[44] The exemption was upheld by the U.S. Supreme Court.[45] Thus, vacation

---

[41]The pre-ERISA decisions also provide insight on other issues, such as vacation pay, that are not preempted by ERISA.

[42]*Firestone Tire & Rubber Co. v. Bruck,* 489 U.S. 101, 109 S. Ct. 948, 103 L.Ed. 2d 80 (1989).

[43]*Fort Halifax Packing Co. v. Coyne,* 482 U.S. 1(1987).

[44]29 C.F.R. §2510.3-1(b)(3).

[45]*Massachusetts v. Morash,* 490 U.S. 107, 109 S. Ct. 1668 (1989).

pay issues are governed by state law. The courts have divided on issues involving claims for vacation pay by employees terminated in acquisition transactions.[46]

Even when a buyer intends to match seller's compensation and benefit programs, the author recommends that the buyer state clearly to employees that their vacation pay and other benefits are furnished under its own plans and policies and that seller's plans and policies were not adopted or continued.

4. Retiree Medical and Death Benefits

Much of the discussion of severance pay and vacation pay is also applicable to any retiree medical and death benefit programs provided by a seller for former employees of a business sold by the assets acquisition method.

For many corporations, liabilities for retiree medical and death benefits are large amounts. Some corporations first realized how large their obligations had become when they were required to value them and accrue them as a balance sheet liability by Statement of Financial Accounting Standards (SFAS) No. 106 and to amortize the liability by deductions from earnings over 20 years or the remaining average employee service period, whichever is longer.

In a series of decisions, the U.S. Circuit Court of Appeals for the Sixth Circuit held that retiree medical and death benefits fully vest (i.e., become nonchangeable) upon retirement and cannot be amended or terminated unless the right to do so was expressly reserved.[47]

K. Union Recognition and Collective Bargaining Agreements

After an assets acquisition, if the buyer hires an entire new workforce in order to change the method of operations, the buyer is not obligated to bargain with the union that represented the seller's employees.[48]

If the buyer maintains generally the same business and hires a majority of the seller's employees working in the business, the buyer must recognize and bargain with their union, even though numerous changes are made in the business.[49]

Timing is an important issue. The obligation to recognize the union is determined when the buyer has hired a "substantial and representative complement" of workers.[50] Thus, if the buyer initially hires only a few of the seller's former hourly paid employees, the union will probably wait to seek recognition. If the buyer hires at any time a majority of the former bar-

---

[46] *Petella v. NL Industries, Inc.*, 529 F. Supp. 1357 (D., N.J. 1982); *Dahl v. Brunswick Corp.*, 277 Md. 471, 356 Atl. 2d 221 (1976); *Chvatal v. United States Nat'l. Bank*, 285 Ore. 11, 589 P.2d 726 (1979).

[47] *Smith v. ABS Industries*, 890 F.2d 841 (6th Cir. 1989); *UAW v. Yard-Man, Inc.*, 716 F.2d 1476 (6th Cir. 1983); *UAW Local 91 v. Park-Ohio Industries*, 661 F. Supp. 1281 and 687 F.Supp. 338, aff. in part and rev. in part, 876 F.2d 894 (6th Cir. 1989).

[48] *Howard Johnson Co. v. Detroit Local Joint Executive Board*, 417 U.S. 249 (1974).

[49] *Fall River Dyeing & Finishing Corp. v. NLRB*, 482 U.S. 27, 107 S. Ct. 2225 (1987).

[50] *NLRB v. Jeffries Lithograph Co.*, 752 F.2d 459 (9th Cir. 1985).

gaining unit employees, the union is likely to seize the opportunity to demand recognition, even though the buyer's plans call for further hiring.

A buyer cannot deal with the hiring and timing issues by discriminating in its hiring practices on the basis of union membership. That would be unfair labor practice. If union members would have become a majority of the relevant unit except for discrimination, the National Labor Relations Board (NLRB) may order the buyer to recognize and bargain with the union.[51]

The court decisions requiring that buyers recognize and bargain with the labor union that represented seller's employees do not necessarily mean that the buyer must accept the seller's collective bargaining agreement.[52] However, having granted recognition to the union, the courts expect the union to join with the buyer in good faith bargaining toward a collective bargaining agreement. This allows the buyer to seek an agreement that is suitable for its business plans and the buyer may revise work practices and pay scales from those existing during seller's ownership. However, if a seller transfers a business to a buyer that is a mere alter ego, the buyer will be bound by the seller's collective bargaining agreement.[53]

L. Product Liability

Courts in many states throughout the United States have developed doctrines that impose liability on manufacturers and sellers of products that do not apply in other fields. For example, the courts developed a doctrine of strict product liability that could more easily be proven than traditional negligence. Most courts also eliminated the doctrine of privity and allowed persons claiming injury or damage by products to sue not only their sellers, but also persons earlier in the chain of distribution including the manufacturers and the suppliers of components and services to the manufacturers. Many courts interpreted the statutes of limitations for product liability claims to run from the date when injury or damage by the product was discovered, or became discoverable, rather than from the date of sale of the product. Many courts also permit punitive damages, once rarely awarded and only for severe wrongdoing, to be claimed routinely based on dramatic portrayals of behavior that was formerly considered negligence at most.

As a result, product liability is a serious potential liability of product manufacturers and sellers that can arise after many years. For example, a worker injured while using a machine made many years ago may sue and claim the machine was defective because it was misdesigned or because the manufacturer failed to warn about hazards involved in its use. For another example, a worker may claim injuries due to inhalation of dusts or vapors from a product and claim that the adverse effects on his

---

[51]*NLRB v. Babad*, 785 F.2d 46 (2d Cir. 1986); *NLRB v. Jarm Enterprises, Inc.*, 785 F.2d 195 (7th Cir. 1986).

[52]*William J. Burns Int'l Detective Agency, Inc. v. NLRB.*, 406 U.S. 272 (1972).

[53]*New England Mechanical, Inc. v. Local 294*, 134 LRRM (BNA) 3048 (9th Cir. 1990); *NLRB v. Amatayus, Inc.*, 817 F.2d 996 (2d Cir. 1987).

or her lungs did not manifest themselves as symptoms for many years. Some state legislatures have adopted statutes limiting product liability claims and damages, but the courts have nullified some of these reform laws by finding them to be an unconstitutional deprivation of rights that the courts created.

Because of the risk of extensive and long-enduring product liability, many buyers only agree to buy a manufacturer's business as an assets purchase and disclaim any assumption of product liability. However, as described earlier in this chapter, the courts may impose successor liability if a sale of assets is a mere restructuring, a de facto merger, a continuation of the enterprise or a fraudulent transfer.

In addition, a few courts have gone beyond the traditional grounds in product liability cases. For example, a few courts have held that a buyer of assets is responsible for products sold by the seller before the acquisition simply because the buyer continued the product line, even though the buyer did not agree in the acquisition contract to assume product liabilities.[54] A larger number of courts have refused to adopt such an extension of successor liability.[55]

In addition, a few courts have said that product liability can be imposed on a buyer of a business that continued a product line and failed to warn its customers who purchased products from the seller before the acquisition about product defects discovered by the buyer after the acquisition.[56]

M. Environmental Laws

1. Introduction

The federal and state environmental laws have a major impact on acquisition transactions and are sometimes determining factors in the feasibility of a proposed transaction. The primary federal environmental laws are the National Environmental Policy Act (NEPA), the Clean Air Act (CAA), the Clean Water Act (CWA), the Safe Drinking Water Act (SDWA), the Resource Conservation and Recovery Act (RCRA), the Emergency Planning and Community Right to Know Act (EPCRA), the Comprehensive Environmental Response, Compensation and Liability Act (CERCLA), the Toxic Substances Control Act (TSCA), the Federal Insecticide, Fungicide and Rodenticide Act (FIFRA), the Endangered Species Act (ESA), the Oil Pollution Act (OPA), the Marine Mammal Protection Act (MMPA), the Asbestos Laws, the Lead-Based Paint Laws and the Noise Control Laws.

The federal laws are, for the most part, administered by the U.S. Environmental Protection Agency (EPA), although other agencies are also in-

---

[54] *Amader v. Pittsburgh Corning Corp.*, 546 F. Supp. 1033 (E.D. Pa. 1989); *Ray v Alad Corp.*, 19 Cal. 3d 22, 560 P.2d 3, 136 Cal. Rptr. 574 (1977); *Turner v. Bituminous Casualty Co.*, 397 Mich. 406, 244 N.W.2d 873 (1976); *Ramirez v. Amsted Industries, Inc.*, 86 N.J. 332, 431 A.2d 811 (1981).

[55] *Nissin Corp. v. Miller*, 594 A.2d 564 (Md. 1991); *McCarthy v. Litton Industries*, 570 N.E. 1008 (Mass. 1991); *Niccum v. Hydra Tool Corp.*, 438 N.W. 2d 96 (Minn. 1989).

[56] *Le Fountain v. Webb Industries*, 951 F.2d 544 (3d Cir. 1991); *Floron v. Elliott Mfg.*, 867 F.2d 570 (10th Cir., 1989); 70 NY 2d 806, 517 NE 2d 1313 (1987).

volved, such as the Food and Drug Administration (FDA) whose standards are used by the EPA in some of its FIFRA regulations.

There are several other federal laws that importantly affect human health and the environment. One is the Occupational Safety and Health Act (the "OSH Act") administered by the Occupational Safety and Health Administration (OSHA) of the U.S. Department of Labor. Another is the Hazardous Materials Transportation Act (HMTA) administered by the U.S. Department of Transportation (DOT). Others include the Consumer Product Safety Act (CPSA) and the Federal Hazardous Substances Act (FHSA) administered by the Consumer Product Safety Commission (CPSC).

Some of the federal environmental laws, such as the CAA and CWA, authorize the states to assume the administration of their programs if they adopt laws and regulations at least as strict as those of the EPA. Once the EPA reviews and approves a state program, the EPA's role becomes primarily supervisory. Other federal environmental laws, such as TSCA, are administered directly by the EPA. Under RCRA, the EPA is primarily responsible for hazardous waste programs and the states are primarily responsible for nonhazardous solid waste programs.

Under some of the federal environmental laws, administration is delegated to local authorities. Some air pollution control programs under the CAA are administered by counties or districts. For example, the South Coast Air Quality Management Authority (SCAQMA) in California is known for imposing severe restrictions on air pollutants contributing to "smog." Local sewer districts operating a publicly owned treatment works (POTW) impose pretreatment requirements under the CWA on industrial dischargers so that the POTW can meet the requirements of its discharge permit.

Thus, buyer representatives performing an environmental due diligence review should investigate compliance with federal, state and local laws and regulations and with permits and orders issued under them. They should also investigate the direct and indirect costs of compliance. It is especially important to determine whether compliance has, or will have, an adverse effect on products or production capacity. For example, many companies have been required to discontinue products or to operate at less than full manufacturing capacity in order to comply with environmental requirements.

The laws that create the greatest concerns during acquisition transactions are CERCLA and state environmental laws that impose liability for cleanup costs incurred to remediate contaminated properties and other facilities. While these laws are often said to follow a "polluter pays" principle, the liabilities are imposed extensively on persons who were not polluters and did not engage in any wrongdoing, such as property owners and operators.

2. Liability for Response Costs under CERCLA

CERCLA authorizes the EPA to recover its removal and remediation costs (i.e., response costs) to clean up a property or other facility contaminated with hazardous substances from owners and operators of the property and certain persons who arranged or transported hazardous substances for disposal at the property.[57] The liability is strict and retroactive and is imposed on owners and operators, such as tenants, because of their status and without regard to whether they polluted the property. The liability is very costly because the EPA has established strict, and often unattainable, cleanup methods and standards.

Although CERCLA is silent on the point, the courts have applied a presumption that the liability is not only retroactive, but joint and several.[58] The presumption is difficult to rebut. Thus, persons potentially responsible for small volumes of hazardous substances at a site face potential liability for cleanup of the entire site if other potentially responsible parties (PRPs) do not or cannot pay. As a practical matter, liability is usually allocated among the PRPs in proportion to the volumes of hazardous substances attributed to them and many PRPs are able to pay.[59] However, there are almost always "orphan shares" of parties who do not or cannot pay and these shares are absorbed by the other PRPs.

CERCLA contains a few exclusions from liability for acts of God, acts of war and acts or omissions by a third party if the person claiming the exclusion proves that it exercised all due care and that it could not have foreseen the conduct of the third party. The last exclusion is commonly called the "innocent purchaser defense." The EPA and the courts have interpreted the "due diligence" requirements for the defense so strictly that this defense has seldom been asserted successfully.[60]

As a practical matter, liability to the EPA itself for response costs at most properties is unlikely because the EPA focuses its response actions on facilities added to the National Priority List (NPL) after evaluation under its Hazard Ranking System (HRS) results in a score of 28.5. Facilities that attain such a score are highly contaminated and usually had a history of use for industrial purposes. However, the contribution rights provisions of CERCLA add significantly to the potential liability, as explained later in this chapter.

3. Owner and Operator Liability under CERCLA

As described previously, CERCLA imposes strict, retroactive and usually joint and several liability for the EPA's removal and remediation costs on

---

[57]42 U.S.C. § 9601 *et seq.* CERCLA is also called the "Superfund Law" because it imposes an excise tax on sales of petroleum and petrochemicals that has raised a multibillion dollar fund for use by the EPA to remediate contaminated facilities. However, the EPA has made relatively little use of the Superfund, because potentially parties remediate sites on its National Priority List.

[58]*B. F. Goodrich v. Betkoski*, 99 F.3d 505 (2d Cir. 1996); *U.S. v. Olin Corp.*, 107 F.3d 1506 (11th Cir. 1997).

[59]While volumetric allocation of liability is the most common method, the courts may also consider toxicity and several other factors in apportioning liability among PRPs. *Gould, Inc. v. A&M Battery*, 1997 U.S. Dist. LEXIS 15708 (M.D. Pa. No. 3-CV-91, Sept. 4, 1997); *M&M Realty v. Eberton Terminal*, ___ F.Supp. ___ (M.D. Pa. 1997); *Pneumo Abex Corp. v. Bessemer & Lake Erie Railroad Co.*, 936 F. Supp. 1250 (E.D.Va. 1996); *U.S. v. Colorado & Eastern Railroad Co.*, 832 F. Supp. 304 (D. Colo. 1996). Liability can also be affected by contractual indemnification provisions. *Lion Oil Co., v. Tosco Corp.*, 90 F.3d 268 (8th Cir. 1996).

[60]A purchaser was excused from liability in *New York v. Lashins Aracade*, 96 F.3d 353 (2d Cir. 1996). See also *U.S. v. Pacific Hide*, 716 F. Supp. 1341 (D.C. Idaho 1989); *Town of New Windsor v. Tesa Tuck, Inc.*, 935 F. Supp. 310 (S.D.N.Y. 1996) However, the courts have usually found reasons to conclude that the purchaser was insufficiently diligent. *New York v. Shore Realty*, 759 F.2d 1032 (2d Cir. 1985); *U.S. v. A&N Launderers, Inc.*, 854 F. Supp. 229 (S.D.N.Y. 1994); *Idylwoods Ass'n v. Mader Capital, Inc.*, 915 F. Supp. 1290 (W.D.N.Y. 1996).

current owners and operators of properties and other facilities.[61] Former owners and operators are also liable if they owned or operated at the time of disposal of any hazardous substance.[62]

The EPA and the courts have interpreted the terms *owner* and *operator* broadly. For example, some courts have held that continued leaking of contaminants during the period of ownership of an interim former owner is sufficient to impose liability.[63] However, mere ownership of an easement at a property was held insufficient to impose owner liability.[64] Very broad interpretations by the courts of the term *operator* have extended liability to many persons including tenants; property managers; corporate directors, officers, employees and shareholders; and secured lenders. The liability of these persons is discussed further later in this chapter.

4. Arranger Liability under CERCLA

As described previously, CERCLA imposes strict, retroactive and usually joint and several liability for response costs incurred by the EPA on persons who arrange for disposal or treatment of hazardous substances.[65]

Claims for arranger liability are commonly made against persons who arranged with transporters or disposal contractors for disposal at offsite locations such as municipal dumps that become NPL sites or state "mini-superfund" sites. Claims for arranger liability have also frequently been made against persons who made arrangements with transporters or disposal contractors who failed to perform and unlawfully stored waste at their own facilities or disposed of waste unlawfully by methods such as "midnight dumping." Arrangers are not excused from liability because of unforseen and even criminal conduct of the transporters or disposal contractors selected by them.

At NPL sites, the EPA lists arrangers as PRPs based on very thin evidence that they made the arrangements that resulted in the presence of hazardous substances. For example, if containers are found with a manufacturer's labels, the EPA frequently names the manufacturer as a PRP, although its customers may have arranged their disposal. The EPA also makes claims against arrangers based on the presence of nonhazardous wastes that contain infinitesimal amounts of hazardous substances.[66]

---

[61]42 U.S.C. § 9607(a)(1).

[62]42 U.S.C. § 9607(a)(2). *ABB Industrial v. Prime*, 120 F.3d 351 (2d Cir. 1997).

[63]*Nurad, Inc, v, William E. Hooper & Sons Co.*, 966 F.2d 837 (4th Cir. 1992) and cases cited therein. However, several courts have held that mere passive migration of contaminants disposed of by prior owners is insufficient to impose liability on an interim owner; *U.S. v. CDMG Realty Co.*, 96 F.3d 706 (3d Cir. 1996); *U.S. v. Cordova Chemical*, 59 F.3d 584 (6th Cir. 1995); *Plaskon Electronic v. Allied-Signal, Inc.*, 904 F. Supp. 644 (N.D. Ohio 1995); *Sneidiker Developers v. Evans*, 773 F. Supp. 984 (E.D. Mich 1991); *Ecodyne Corp. v. Shalala*, 718 F. Supp. 1454 (N.D. Cal. 1989).

[64]*Acme Printing Ink Co. v. Menard, Inc.*, 904 F. Supp. 644 (N.D. Ohio 1995).

[65]42 U.S.C. § 9607(a)(3).

[66]*B.F. Goodrich Co. v. Murtha*, 958 F.2d 1192 (2d Cir. 1992); *B. F. Goodrich v. Betkoski*, 99 F.3d 505 (2d Cir. 1996). However, wastes containing very low levels of hazardous constituents may escape liability for a share of the response costs during the allocation phase if the responsible party proves that the wastes did not contribute to the release. *U.S. v Alcan Aluminum Corp.*, 990 F. 2d 711 (2d Cir. 1993); *U.S. v. Alcan Aluminum Corp.*, 964 F.2d 252 (3d Cir. 1992). In another case, a court refused to hold a responsible party liable for response costs to install an alternate water system that the EPA did not show was necessary to protect the public health. *In the Matter of Bell Petroleum Services, Inc.*, 99 F.3d 889 (5th Cir. 1993).

Arranger liability can be very serious. For example, a company which arranged for disposal of a few drums of paint, adhesive or solvent waste can be held responsible for the entire cleanup costs of a highly contaminated site if other responsible parties cannot be found or are unable to pay. As described previously, a number of PRPs are usually found for most sites and the cleanup costs, including "orphan shares," are allocated among them. The allocation can be affected by contractual indemnification provisions.[67]

5. Transporter Liability under CERCLA

Waste haulers and other persons who accept hazardous substances for transportation to disposal or treatment facilities or sites which they select are subject to liability for response costs and other costs and damages.[68]

6. Parent Corporation and Shareholder Liability under CERCLA

CERCLA does not contain any statutory provisions imposing liability for response costs, other costs or damages on parent corporations and shareholders. However, buyers who acquire corporations by the stock purchase method or by triangular merger methods must exercise care because some courts have imposed CERCLA liability on parent corporations and shareholders on grounds that go beyond those applied in other areas of the law.

Parent corporations can be subjected to CERCLA liability of their subsidiaries in areas within the jurisdiction of the U.S. Circuit Courts of Appeals for the Fifth and Sixth Circuits if they engage in conduct that supports "piercing the corporate veil," the traditional basis for parent corporation liability.[69] Other Circuits have ruled that a parent corporation is subject to CERCLA liability without need to provide evidence to support piercing the corporate veil, if the parent corporation participates in daily activities or exercises pervasive control of the activities of a subsidiary.[70] In 1998, the U.S. Supreme Court unanimously held that derivative liability under CERCLA may be imposed on a parent corporation only by piercing the corporate veil, but that "operator" liability can be imposed on a parent corporation for its own actions, if any, specifically relating to operation of a facility owned by a subsidiary.[71]

---

[67] *Taracorp, Inc. v. NL Industries, Inc.*, 73 F.3d 738 (7th Cir. 1996).

[68] 42 U.S.C. § 9607(a)(4); *Tippins v. USX Corp.*, 37 F.3d 87 (3d Cir. 1994); *B.F. Goodrich v. Betkoski*, 99 F.3d 505 (2d Cir. 1996); *Kaiser Aluminum v. Catellus Development Corp.*, 976 F.2d 1338 (9th Cir. 1992).

[69] *Joslyn Manufacturing Corp v. T. L. James & Co.*, 893 F.2d 890 (5th Cir. 1990); *U.S. v. Cordova Chemical Co.*, 113 F.3d 572 (6th Cir. 1997); vacated and remanded *U.S. v. Best Foods*, ___ U.S. ___ June 15, 1998.

[70] *John S. Boyd Co. v. Boston Gas Co.*, 992 F.2d 401 (1st Cir. 1993); *U.S. v. Kayser-Roth Corp.*, 910 F.2d 24 (1st Cir. 1990); cert. denied, 498 U.S. 1084 (1991); *Jacksonville Elec. Auth. v. Bernuth Corp.*, 996 F.2d 1107 (11th Cir. 1993); *Aluminum Co. of America v. Beazer East*, 124 F.3d 551 (3d Cir., 1997); *U.S. v. Gurley*, 43 F.3d 1188 (8th Cir. 1994), cert. denied, 116 S. Ct. 73 (1995); *Sidney S. Arst Co. v. Pipefitters Welfare Education Fund*, 25 F.3d 417 (7th Cir. 1994); *B. F. Goodrich v. Betkoski*, 99 F.3d 505 (2d Cir. 1996); 96 F.3d 706 (3d Cir. 1996); *U.S. v. Carolina Transformer Co.*, 972 F.2d 832 (4th Cir. 1992); *Kaiser Aluminum v. Catellus Development Corp.*, 976 F.2d 1338 (9th Cir. 1992).

[71] *U.S. v. Best Foods*, ___ U.S. ___, 1998 WL 292076 (U.S.). The unanimous court held that actions of dual directors and officers should not necessarily be attributed to the parent corporation and that liability cannot be based on normal parent oversight of a subsidiary's facility.

7. Lender Liability under CERCLA

The courts' rapid expansion of liability under CERCLA was soon extended to lenders who are perceived as having "deep pockets." Liability as an owner was imposed on secured lenders that acquired title by foreclosing a mortgage. Liability as an operator was imposed on lenders that exercised powers in a loan agreement during "workout" activities that involved them in the borrower's affairs. CERCLA contained a security interest exemption in Section 101(2), but court interpretations effectively nullified it.[72]

As a result, lenders reduced their willingness to provide loans to finance business and real estate transactions. Although environmentalists opposed any leniency, national concern during the recession from 1990 to 1992 led to the adoption of a lender liability rule in 1992 by the EPA that interpreted the security interest exemption to allow normal lender practices including "workout" activities and foreclosure and resale activities.[73] In an unusual alliance, Frank Kelley, the Attorney General of Michigan and the Chemical Manufacturers Association (CMA) sued to invalidate the EPA's lender liability rule.[74] They won.[75]

In 1996, the U.S. Congress adopted the Clinger-Cohen Act, which contained provisions reinstating the EPA's lender liability rule retroactively to its issuance date of April 29, 1992. Anticipating a hostile reaction, the Congress also withdrew the jurisdiction of the federal courts to review the rule.

The Clinger-Cohen Act also amended Section 101(20) of CERCLA to reinforce the secured lender exemption. A summary is as follows:

> Definition of Owner or Operator. *The definition of an owner or operator subject to strict liability under CERCLA excludes any lender that, without participating in management of a facility, holds indicia of ownership primarily to protect a security interest in the facility. Thus, liability prior to foreclosure is based solely on participation in management of the facility, as discussed later.*
>
> *The definition also excludes a lender that forecloses on a facility, if the lender did not participate in management prior to foreclosure and sells, releases or divests the facility at the earliest practicable, commercially reasonable time, on commercially reasonable terms, taking into account market conditions and legal and regulatory requirements. The lender's post-foreclosure activities may also include maintenance of business activities, winding up operations, undertaking a response action under CERCLA, or taking any other measure to preserve, protect or prepare the facility prior to sale or disposition.*
>
> Definition of a Lender. *The definition of a lender includes several specified institutions, such as depository institutions insured by the FDIC, and any person (including a successor or assignee) that makes a bona fide extension of credit to or takes or acquires a security interest from a nonaffiliated per-*

---

[72]*U.S. v. Fleet Factors*, 901 F.2d 1550 (11th Cir. 1990) and cases cited therein. Different treatment was given to municipal officials, however, when the trustees of the Port of St. Helens, Oregon were excused from lender liability in *In re Bergsoe Metal Corp.*, 910 F.2d 668 (9th Cir. 1990).

[73]40 C.F.R. §§ 330.1100 and 330.1105.

[74]The CMA reasoned that other defendants are liable under CERCLA without fault or meaningful defenses. Thus, the best course of action was to make amendments correcting the liability unfairly imposed by CERCLA, rather than amendments allowing favored persons to escape the liability.

[75]*Kelley v. E.P.A.*, 15 F.3d 1100 (D.C. Cir. 1994); cert. denied (No. 94-752, Jan. 17, 1995).

son. The definition also includes certain guarantors and title insurers who acquire a facility in the course of underwriting claims and claims settlement.

Participation in Management. *The term "participate in management" is defined in a lengthy list which describes conduct included and excluded. In general, the list allows lenders to carry on normal activities without incurring liability. For example, the definition begins with the principle that participation in management means actually participating in the management or operational affairs of a facility and not merely having the capacity to influence, or the unexercised right to control, facility operations.*

For example, while a borrower is still in possession of a facility, a lender participates in management only if it

(1) *exercises decision-making control over environmental practices, such that it undertakes responsibility for hazardous substance handling or disposal practices related to the facility, or*

(2) *exercises control at a level comparable to that of a manager of the facility, such that the lender assumes or manifests responsibility (a) for the overall management of the facility encompassing day-to-day decision-making with respect to environmental compliance or (b) over substantially all the operational functions (as distinguished from financial or administrative functions) of the facility other than environmental compliance.*

As described later in this chapter, many states have adopted a law offering limited protection to lenders.

8. Successor Liability under CERCLA

When an acquisition is accomplished by a two-party merger, the surviving corporation becomes the successor by operation of law to all the liabilities and obligations of the nonsurviving corporation, including its liabilities under CERCLA.[76]

When an acquisition is accomplished by a stock purchase or a triangular merger, the subsidiary is responsible for its liabilities under CERCLA, but the parent is not responsible for them unless it engages in conduct that makes it liable under the "veil-piercing" or "operator" doctrines described previously.

When an acquisition is accomplished by a purchase of assets without an assumption of liabilities, the buyer becomes the owner of any properties and other facilities included among the purchased assets. The buyer becomes the operator of any leased property and other facilities if the lease is a net lease that makes the tenant responsible for operations. The buyer probably also becomes the operator of any property or facilities for which it is the property manager. Because CERCLA imposes strict liability on owners and operators merely because of their status as such, the buyer becomes liable without need to analyze difficult issues of successor liability. However, the buyer can look to the indemnification and other rights, if any, provided by the seller in the acquisition contract. The buyer can also pursue contribution rights and other claims against the seller, previous owners, operators and arrangers and transporters who may be responsible for the presence of hazardous substances. Contribution rights under CERCLA are described later in this chapter.

[76] *Anspec Corporation v. Johnson Controls, Inc.*, 922 F.2d 1240 (6th Cir. 1991); *Smith Land and Improvement Corporation*, 851 F.2d 86 (3d cir. 1988); *NJDEP v. Ventron Corp.*, 94 N.J. 473, 468 Atl. 2d 150 (1983).

If a buyer assumes the seller's liabilities in an acquisition accomplished by a sale of assets, the buyer may be liable even for a plant previously sold by the seller and not included in the acquired assets.[77]

Difficult issues of successor liability arise when an acquisition is accomplished by a sale of assets without an assumption of liabilities and the following situations exist:

1. The seller arranged for disposal of hazardous substances at one or more offsite locations.
2. The seller transported hazardous substances for disposal to one or more offsite locations that it selected.
3. The seller formerly owned one or more contaminated properties or other contaminated facilities that were part of the business sold to the buyer, but were not included in the assets sold to the buyer because they had previously been sold or transferred.

In general, a buyer who does not assume the seller's liabilities should not succeed to its CERCLA liabilities for offsite locations and previously sold or transferred properties.[78]

9. Contribution Rights under CERCLA

Both at sites listed on the NPL and other sites, it has become customary for PRPs to agree to perform and pay for remediation because they fear that the EPA or other government agencies will perform remedial work at excessive cost. CERCLA entitles persons who incur response costs to recover contributions from other responsible parties.[79] The contribution rights are not limited to response costs at NPL sites. Thus, persons who clean up properties in response to orders or agreements with the EPA or state agencies or for other reasons often seek contributions from others under CERCLA. They must show that the cleanup work was done in accordance with the EPA's National Contingency Plan (NCP), but that requirement can be fulfilled with proper planning. Further, they are entitled to protection from contribution claims of other PRPs.

As a practical matter, the contribution rights provided by CERCLA extend its reach far beyond the heavily contaminated NPL sites administered by the EPA. Anyone who performs environmental cleanup work has an opportunity to plan so that it can claim CERCLA contribution rights.

10. The CERCLA Lien

Response costs incurred by the EPA and damages for which a person is liable under § 107(a) of CERCLA are a lien upon all real property that belongs to such person and is subject to, or affected by, a removal or remedial action.

---

[77] *Philadelphia Electronic Co. v. Hercules, Inc.*, 762 F.2d 303 (3d Cir. 1985).

[78] *U.S. v. Mexico Feed & Grains*, 980 F.2d 478 (8th Cir. 1992). However, some courts have imposed successor liability on an assets buyer who did not assume liabilities. In *U.S. v. Carolina Transformer Co.*, 978 F.2d 832 (4th Cir. 1992) and *B.F. Goodrich Co. v. Betkoski*, supra, , a substantial continuity test was adopted. In *Louisiana Pacific Corp. v. Asarco, Inc.*, an expanded de facto merger test was applied.

[79] 42 U.S.C. § 9613.

However, the lien arises at the later of (1) the time when costs are first incurred by the EPA or (2) the time when the person is provided written notice by certified or registered mail. As to third parties, the lien is subject to rights perfected before notice of the lien is filed in the appropriate office, as designated by state law where the property subject to the lien is located.[80]

11. Environmental Assessments

Prospective purchasers and mortgage lenders usually arrange for a phase 1 assessment of the environmental condition of a property prior to a purchase or loan. The purpose is to support a claim of the "innocent purchaser defense" and also to determine whether the value of the property may be impaired by contamination or violations of environmental laws or regulations. The American Society for Testing Materials, Inc. (ASTM) issued Standard Practice E-1527-97 defining good commercial and customary practice for conducting an environmental assessment. If a phase 1 assessment reveals possible contamination or violations, it may be followed by a phase 2 assessment in which soil, groundwater and other sampling and testing are performed to verify and quantify the conditions found in the phase 1 assessment.

Environmental assessments often lead to corrective actions by the seller or to an adjustment of the price or other terms of sale so that the buyer will assume responsibility for the corrective action. In some transactions, part of the price is placed in escrow to fund the corrective actions.

Phase 1 and phase 2 assessments are usually limited in scope to identifying recognized environmental conditions at a property such as leaking underground storage tanks, asbestos-containing materials and releases of contaminants to soil and groundwater at the property or nearby properties. They are useful primarily for office buildings, shopping centers and other commercial properties. A more extensive due diligence review is necessary to evaluate the environmental status of an operating industrial business (see Chapter 5).

12. State Property Transfer and Superlien Laws

In addition to the "mini-superfund" laws adopted by all of the states, a number of states have enacted statutes requiring that owners of industrial, commercial and perhaps other properties must disclose the presence of contamination with hazardous substances and other environmental conditions at the time of any sale or transfer. These laws typically require that an environmental assessment report or other disclosure document must be delivered to the prospective buyer or transferee and filed with the state environmental agency. Events triggering these obligations may go beyond a conventional sale or transfer to include a shutdown of operations at the property, the termination of a lease of the property, or a sale or merger of a corporation owning or operating the property.

For example, the New Jersey Industrial Site Recovery Act (ISRA) requires an owner or operator planning to close operations or to sell or trans-

[80] 42 U.S.C. § 9607(1).

fer ownership or operations of an industrial establishment classified under certain standard industrial codes to file a notice with the Department of Environmental Protection (DEP). If the property is not contaminated, the owner or operator can submit a negative declaration supported by an environmental assessment report and request approval of the negative declaration by the DEP. If the property is contaminated, an investigation must be conducted, remedial cost estimates prepared and a remediation agreement made with the DEP. A remediation funding source (such as a trust fund, letter of credit or self-guarantee by persons having satisfactory financial resources) must be provided to assure performance of the remediation agreement. The DEP will then allow a transfer of the property. A remediation workplan is then prepared, approved and performed. When the cleanup is performed in compliance with its requirements, the DEP will approve a negative declaration or issue a no further action letter.

ISRA contains several exemptions under which the cleanup obligation may be excused, deferred or limited, but almost all of them require DEP approval, which is difficult to obtain. An attempt to close operations, sell or transfer without compliance is voidable by the buyer or the DEP and punishable by fines.[81] If remediation is performed to nonresidential or alternate standards, a deed of environmental restrictions (DER) must be recorded, regardless of whether actual hazards exist.

The Connecticut Transfer Act requires the seller of an establishment where hazardous substances have been used to provide to a prospective buyer prior to a sale a declaration concerning hazardous wastes at the property on Forms I, II, III or IV with an environmental condition assessment form (ECAF). A copy must be filed with the Department of Environmental Protection within 15 days after the sale. If the property is contaminated, the buyer (or another responsible person such as the seller) must certify to the Department of Environmental Protection that it will take cleanup action in accordance with the cleanup standards of the Department. Accomplishment of the cleanup can be certified by a licensed environmental professional (LEP), subject to audit by the Department. Noncompliance renders the seller liable to the buyer and to fines.[82]

The Indiana Environmental Hazardous Disclosure and Responsible Party Transfer Law requires disclosure of environmental defects to buyers.[83] A copy of the disclosure document must be delivered to the prospective buyer, recorded with the county recorder and filed with the Indiana Department of Environmental Management. The Illinois Responsible Property Transfer Act requires delivery of a document disclosing environmental information to buyers, and copies are recorded with the county recorder's office and filed with the Illinois Environmental Protection Agency.[84]

Some state laws grant to the state environmental agency a lien or a "superlien" securing cleanup costs expended by the agency for abandoned or other hazardous waste sites. The lien or superlien may apply to the prop-

---

[81]13 New Jersey Statutes Annot. § 13:1K-6 *et seq.*

[82] 22a Conn. Gen. Stat. Annot., § 22a-134 *et seq.*

[83]13 Indiana Code § 13-7-22.5-1 *et seq.*

[84]765 ILCS, § 90/1 et seq. See also California Health and Safety Code, § 25230 and § 25359.7 and Michigan Compiled Laws Annot., § 324.20116 *et seq.*

erty where the costs were incurred and perhaps also to other properties of the owner or operator. The superlien law should be reviewed to determine the extent to which it may have priority over mortgages and security interests held by banks and other lenders, including those recorded before the inception of the superlien.[85]

Many states have adopted amendments to their "mini-superfund" laws and other cleanup laws granting limited protection to lenders. In general, the state laws follow the patterns established by the EPA's lender liability rule.[86]

13. Corrective and Remedial Actions; "Brownfields" Programs

Early in its administration of CERCLA, the EPA prohibited non-emergency remedial actions by owners, operators and other persons at NPL sites. The EPA required that all actions be taken in compliance with detailed procedures contained in the National Contingency Plan. The procedures begin with detailed site investigation and characterization of hazardous substances released, especially those in soil and groundwater. A remedial investigation/feasibility study (RI/FS) must be prepared evaluating remedial alternatives from the most extensive and costly to the least costly, such as a "no action" alternative. A record of decision (ROD) is prepared to demonstrate how the remedial method was evaluated and selected. A remedial workplan must then be prepared and approved by the EPA before work can begin. Notices and reports are sent to the public and public hearings are held. Cleanup of soil, groundwater and other receptors must be done to "background" levels or to alternate concentration levels (ACLs) approved by the EPA. Even when ACLs are approved and the EPA authorizes cleanup work to begin, the remediation usually takes many years because available technologies cannot achieve the standards required by the EPA except over a period of many years. Thus, most of the sites listed on the NPL since the early 1980s have not been remediated, although they have served as "laboratories" for environmental research and development.[87]

Most state-administered cleanup programs initially followed the EPA cleanup procedures, but then went in two directions. In some northeastern states and in California, the state agencies imposed procedures and standards far stricter than those of the EPA, thus creating technical, cost and time barriers to achieving the remediation of property. This strictness accelerated the exit of industry from states such as New Jersey where many major industrial sites that once provided thousands of jobs have become so-called "brownfields" properties with minimal or no active business operations. In other states such as Michigan, the state cleanup programs have been de-

[85]For example, see Maine Rev. Stat. Annot., Title 38, § 1371, Mass. Gen. Laws Annot., Vol. 2B, Chap. 21E, § 13 and Michigan Compiled Laws Annot., § 324.20138(1).

[86]For example, the statute in New Jersey follows closely the text of the EPA's lender liability rule. 13 N.J.S.A. § 58:10-23.11g4. For other examples, see Michigan Compiled Laws § 324.20101(a) and § 324.20126 and Ohio Rev. Code Ann. § 3746.26. Large states that have not so far adopted a special lender protection laws include New York and Pennsylvania.

[87]For example, simple pump and methods that proved ineffective for remediating groundwater contaminated with leaks of gasoline, fuel oil or dry cleaning fluid have been improved or replaced with air sparging and biooxidation methods.

signed with achievable standards in order to remediate "brownfields" properties and reactivate them as sources of employment and tax revenues.

The EPA has begun limited programs that it describes as providing incentives to remediate "brownfields" properties. For example, the EPA issued a guidance document on May 24, 1995 indicating that it will consider agreements with prospective purchasers of properties containing a qualified promise not to sue them if a variety of conditions are met. The conditions include a requirement that the continued operation or development of the site benefit the EPA in terms of cleanup or funds for cleanup, but this benefit may be reduced if there are substantial indirect benefits to the community in terms of such matters as job creation and property development. The EPA also adopted a policy on May 24, 1995 that it will not take enforcement action against owners of properties relating to the cleanup of contaminated aquifers, where hazardous substances in the aquifers resulted solely from subsurface migration in an aquifer from a source or sources outside the property. The EPA also adopted a Land Use Directive on May 25, 1995 stating its policy that it would consider future land use in assessing risks, developing cleanup plans and choosing the most appropriate cleanup methods. The EPA also established pilot program grants of up to $200,000 each for technical assistance at inner-city "brownfields" locations and has reportedly funded over 120 such grants. The General Services Administration recently announced an initiative to review over 1,000 federally owned urban properties that may be candidates for "brownfields" development.

Thus far, the EPA's "brownfields" programs have not made important progress. While there is considerable enthusiasm at the EPA, the programs continue to be strict, paperwork- and time-intensive and subject to pervasive government control. The pilot projects are devoted primarily to review and evaluation activities. Thus, the programs are not yet compatible with the needs of the entrepreneurs who develop interrelated construction, development and financing packages that cannot be held together during lengthy periods of uncertainty and delay. Further, the "brownfields" programs still do not provide clear and achievable cleanup standards that offer buyers, investors and lenders assurance that remediation for which budgeted cost projections can be developed will obtain the release from liability offered by the EPA.

N. Pension Plan Liabilities

The Internal Revenue Code (IRC) and the Employee Retirement Income Security Act (ERISA) impose several liabilities for which a buyer may become liable regardless of whether it structures an acquisition as an assets purchase, stock purchase or merger and regardless of whether it agrees to assume the liability in the acquisition contract. The reason is that the IRC and ERISA impose the liabilities not only on the employer sponsoring the plan, but also on all members of its consolidated group.

ERISA defines multiemployer plans as employee benefit plans to which more than one employer is required to contribute and which are maintained pursuant to a collective bargaining agreement. A single-employer plan is any employee benefit plan other than a multiemployer plan, even though more than one employer may contribute to it.

Accumulated Funding Deficits. Section 412 of the IRC requires that active defined benefit pension plans meet minimum funding standards on an annual basis. A plan that fails to meet the minimum funding standard at the end of a plan year has an accumulated funding deficit. The employer which is the plan sponsor and all members of its controlled group are liable for the deficiency and the related excise taxes.[88] Their properties are also subject to a lien securing payment.

Termination Liability-Single Employer Pension Plans. Upon termination of a single employer defined benefit pension plan, whether voluntary or initiated by the Pension Benefit Guaranty Corporation (PBGC), ERISA imposes on the sponsoring employer and all members of its consolidated group a termination liability equal to the total unfunded benefit liabilities on the termination date to all participants and their beneficiaries. Their properties are subject to a lien securing payment.[89]

Withdrawal Liability—Multiemployer Pension Plans. Upon withdrawal of an employer participating in a multiemployer defined benefit pension plan,[90] the Multiemployer Pension Plan Amendments Act (MEPPAA), a 1980 amendment to ERISA, imposes a withdrawal liability that requires the employer to pay a share of the unfunded vested liabilities of the plan.[91] The liability is also imposed on a partial withdrawal that includes, among other things, a 70 percent decline in contributions. Upon request, the plan administrator will furnish the amount of the liability to the participating employer. If an acquisition is accomplished by a sale of stock or a merger, no withdrawal occurs unless the buyer causes a downsizing of operations that results in a whole or partial withdrawal. However, an assets sale will be treated as a withdrawal unless the buyer is an unrelated party and procedures required by ERISA are followed.[92]

---

[88]IRC § 4971 imposes a nondeductible excise tax equal to 5% of the deficiency if there is a failure to meet the annual minimum funding standard. If the failure is not properly corrected, another excise tax equal to 100% of the deficiency is imposed.

[89]ERISA § § 4062 and 4068; 29 U.S.C. § § 1362 and 1368. Liabilities on termination may significantly exceed liabilities on an ongoing basis due to vesting of rights of employee participants.

[90]Multiemployer pension plans were developed by labor innovators such as Walter Reuther and Robert Frank of the United Automobile Aerospace and Agricultural Implement Workers Union and the mid-sized employers who supplied parts to the major automotive manufacturers. Multiemployer plans achieved pension portability for workers who moved among these employers which had fluctuating levels of work. Unfortunately, some other multiemployer plans later became seriously underfunded due to controversial administrative and investment policies. This created an incentive for employers to withdraw and Congress responded by adopting MEPPAA. The press reported that a proposal by UPS to withdraw from a multiemployer pension plan of the Teamsters Union was an important issue in the 1997 strike, even though UPS was willing to pay a large withdrawal liability.

[91]ERISA § 4201 *et seq.*; 29 U.S.C. § 1381 *et seq.*

[92]ERISA § 4204; 29 U.S.C. § 1384. The buyer must agree to make contributions substantially equal to the seller's contributions. The buyer must also provide a 5-year bond to secure payment of its contributions or the withdrawal liability if it fails to make the contributions. The seller must agree to be secondarily liable if the buyer incurs withdrawal liability within 5 years and, if it wishes to make liquidation distributions within that period, must also post a bond. *Central States v. Bell Transit Co.*, 22 F.3d 706 (7th Cir. 1994).

Excise Tax Liability on Asset Reversions. If an employee benefit plan is overfunded upon termination, any reversion of assets is subject to a 20 percent excise tax imposed by IRC § 4980. This excise tax becomes 50 percent unless the employer either establishes a qualified replacement plan or amends the terminated plan to increase the benefits. As described in Chapter 18, an employer must meet several requirements in establishing a replacement plan or increasing benefits.

Termination Liability for Evasion of ERISA. If any person or its controlled group entered into any transaction within 5 years before a termination, a principal purpose of which was to evade liability under ERISA, Section 4069(a) of ERISA imposes a termination liability on such person and its consolidated group as if such person were a contributing sponsor of the terminated plan on its termination date. Section 4069(b) goes on to impose successor liability after certain corporate reorganizations. For example, if a person ceases to exist by reason of liquidation into a parent corporation, the parent corporation is treated as the person subject to ERISA. If a person ceases to exist by reason of a merger, consolidation or division, the successor corporation is treated as the person subject to ERISA.[93]

O. Worker Adjustment and Retraining Notification Act

The Worker Adjustment and Retraining Notification Act (WARN) requires any employer having 100 or more employees to provide written notice to employees or their representatives and to state and local government agencies at least 60 days before it orders a plant closing or a mass layoff.[94]

A "plant closing" is a permanent or temporary shutdown of a single site of employment, or one or more facilities or operating units within a single site of employment, if the shutdown results in an employment loss during any 30-day period for 50 or more employees, excluding any part-time employees.

A "mass layoff" is a reduction in force that (1) is not the result of a plant closing and (2) results in an employment loss at a single site of employment during a 30-day period for (a) at least 33 percent of the employees (excluding part-time employees) and at least 50 employees (excluding part-time employees) or (b) at least 500 employees (excluding part-time employees).

"Employment loss" means (1) an employment termination, voluntary departure, or retirement, (2) a layoff exceeding 6 months, or (3) a reduction in work hours of at least 50 percent during each month of any 6 month period.

If the buyer plans to relocate or consolidate the seller's business, there is no employment loss if the buyer offers to transfer the affected employee to (1) a different site within reasonable commuting distance with no more than a 6-month break in employment or (2) a different site regardless of

---

[93]ERISA § 4069; 29 U.S.C. § 1369. *PBGC v. White Consolidated Industries, Inc.*, 998 F.2d 1192 (3d Cir. 1993); cert. den. 510 U.S. 1042. The provisions of § 4069(b) may also prevent triggering withdrawal liability in corporate reorganizations by treating the successor as the same person. However, see *Bowers v. Andrew Weir Shipping Ltd.*, 27 F.3d 800 (2d Cir. 1994) in which withdrawal liability was imposed after transfers to a joint venture.

[94]U.S.C. § 2101-2109; 20 C.F.R. Part 639.

distance with no more than a 6-month break in employment and the employee may accept within 30 days of the offer, or of the closing or layoff, whichever is later.

WARN allows reduced notice periods in several situations, including (1) faltering businesses seeking capital, (2) circumstances not reasonably foreseeable and (3) natural disasters.

When a business is sold, the seller is responsible for the notice up to and including the effective date of the sale. The purchaser is responsible thereafter. Any person who is an employee of the seller (other than a part-time employee) as of the effective date of the sale is considered an employee of the purchaser. Sellers and purchasers should coordinate their plans so as to avoid WARN liability.

P. Occupational Safety and Health

The Occupational Safety and Health Act (the "OSH Act")[95] requires that employers furnish a workplace free from recognized hazards likely to cause death or serious injury. The OSH Act is administered by the Occupational Safety and Health Administration (OSHA) of the U.S. Department of Labor.[96] The OSH Act also requires that employers comply with standards adopted by OSHA.

OSHA's original standards were based on many standards previously developed by private standards organizations such as the American National Standards Institute (ANSI) and the National Fire Protection Association (NFPA). OSHA thereafter developed numerous additional standards. Recent examples are its blood borne pathogens standard and its process safety management standard. Some OSHA standards have been challenged in court and found to be invalid.[97] OSHA has recently been developing a tuberculosis standard and a controversial ergonomics standard designed to protect workers from such injuries as carpal tunnel syndrome which results from repetitive motion stresses.[98] The ergonomics standard is controversial because it is difficult to verify the injuries and to determine whether they are work-related.

Employers who fail to comply with OSHA standards are subject to fines and penalties for violations. Fines for serious violations, willful violations and repeated violations can be quite large. The penalties for egregious willful violations sometimes total several million dollars.[99]

---

[95] 29 U.S.C. § 651 *et seq.*

[96] State agencies in 21 states have established qualified programs allowing them to administer the OSH Act rather than OSHA.

[97] For example, see *AFL v. OSHA*, 965 F.2d 962 (11th Cir. 1992) in which a court vacated standards adopted by OSHA for several hundred air contaminants.

[98] OSHA has had difficulty proving a repetitive motion violations case under the general duty clause of the OSH Act. *Pepperidge Farm*, OSHRC 89-265, April 26, 1997, 1997 W.L. 212599.

[99] OSHA's authority to propose very large fines was partially limited by a recent court decision. After a reactor producing urea exploded at a chemical plant, OSHA imposed a fine of $50,000 for each of the 87 employees to whom OSHA found the employer had breached its general duty to provide a safe workplace, or a total of $4,350,000. The court ruled that only a single violation occurred and the fine could not be multiplied by the number of workers. *Reich v. Arcadian Corp.*, 110 F.3d 1192 (5th Cir. 1997).

Buyers should recognize that OSHA has limited resources and cannot inspect every employer. Further, many inspections by OSHA focus on particular kinds of violations, especially those made in response to an accident or a complaint by a worker or labor union. Thus, a buyer should not assume that the seller is in compliance simply because a recent inspection identified only a few violations, unless it was a "wall to wall" inspection.

The OSH Act does not authorize or imply any private right of action by employees against their employers or other persons.[100]

The state workers compensation laws provide that employers must provide benefits for injuries and illnesses incurred within the scope of their employment. The benefit amounts are set by schedules and are payable regardless of fault on the part of the employer with few defenses, although intentionally self-inflicted injuries are not covered. In some states, awards to employees are increased if an injury or illness results from violations of the OSH Act. The workers compensation laws bar employees from suing their employers for workplace injuries or illnesses, except for willful or intentional injuries.

Two decades ago, some courts attempted to expand the liability of employers for willful or intentional injury to include negligence by allowing lawsuits alleging that intent to injure could be inferred from evidence of repeated violations that exposed workers to injuries or illness. Reacting to the judicial activism in the *Blankenship* decision, the Ohio legislature amended the Ohio workers compensation statutes to prevent the court's interpretation from continuing to be the law. Since then, attempts by plaintiff lawyers to bypass the workers compensation laws are occasionally successful.[101]

From a buyer's point of view, the potential liabilities of acquiring a business with a poor safety and health history are as follows:

1. Workers compensation costs will increase as injuries and illnesses occur, or manifest themselves in the case of chronic injuries and illnesses.
2. Fines and penalties will be imposed by OSHA.
3. Capital and operating costs will be required to obtain and install engineering controls, safety practices and personal protective equipment.
4. The buyer will suffer poor employee morale and labor union campaigns to improve safety and health conditions affecting their members.

Buyers in acquisitions accomplished by the assets purchase method can decline to assume liabilities for injuries and illness and for fines and penalties for violations before the closing date. However, obtaining full

---

[100] *Jeter v. St. Regis Paper Co.*, 507 F.2d 973 (5th Cir. 1975); *Byrd v. Fieldcrest Mills, Inc.*, 496 F.2d 1323 (4th Cir. 1974); *Russell v. Bartley*, 494 F.2d 334 (6th Cir. 1974).

[101] *Blankenship v. Cincinnati Milacron Chemicals, Inc.*, 433 N. E.2d 572 (Ohio 1982), cert. denied 103 S.Ct. 127; *Persinger v. Peabody Coal*, 474 S.E.2d 887 (1996); *Yocum v. Phillips Petroleum*, 612 P.2d 649 (1980); *Gardiner v. Bellotti*, 785 P.2d 362 (1990).

protection can be difficult, especially for chronic injuries and illnesses that have not manifested themselves as symptoms. Thus, it is important during a due diligence review to examine the OSHA 200 Log, workers compensation claims and loss runs and other records, and to observe the engineering controls and use of personal protective equipment in order to identify potential chronic injuries and illnesses.

Q. Directors' and Officers' Duties to Preferred Shareholders and Creditors

The fiduciary duties of directors and officers to their corporation and its shareholders are discussed in Chapter 12. The same duties of loyalty, care and fairness are owed to holders of both preferred stock and common stock. However, these duties do not prevent directors from accepting an unsolicited bid to holders of the common stock that does not include holders of preferred stock.[102]

On the other hand, the duties of directors and officers to corporate creditors are ordinarily contractual in nature and are governed by the provisions of the loan agreements or other debt instruments.[103] Under ordinary circumstances, directors and officers do not owe fiduciary duties to debtholders that create obligations beyond those to which the parties have agreed.[104] However, in the event of corporate insolvency, fiduciary duties of directors and officers to its creditors arise.[105] The directors and officers do not then cease to have obligations to the shareholders, but have duties to a community of interests consisting of the corporation and its creditors, shareholders and other stakeholders.[106]

R. Laws Against Discrimination in Employment

The U.S. Congress and the state legislatures have adopted a large number of laws prohibiting various kinds of discrimination in employment. These laws are administered by the Equal Employment Opportunity Commission (EEOC) and other government agencies. Many of the laws authorize private lawsuits for breaches of their provisions. Some of the federal laws and regulations are as follows: the Civil Rights Act of 1866;[107] the Civil Rights Act of 1871;[108] the Civil Rights Act of 1964;[109] the Equal

[102]*Dalton v. American Investment Co.*, 490 Atl. 2d 574 (Del Ch. 1985); 501 Atl.2d 1238 (1985).

[103]*Katz v. Oak Industries, Inc.*, 508 Atl. 2d 873 (Del. Ch. 1986).

[104]*Simons v. Cogan*, 549 Atl.2d 300 (Del. 1988); *Hartford Fire v. Federated Dept. Stores*, 723 F. Supp. 976 (S.D.N.Y. 1989); *Metropolitan Life v. RJR Nabisco, Inc.*, 716 F. Supp. 1504 (S.D.N.Y. 1989).

[105]*New York Credit Men's Adjustment Business, Inc. v. Weiss*, 305 N.Y.1, 110 N.E.2d 397 (1953); *Geyer v. Ingersoll Publications Co.*, 621 Atl.2d 784 (Del. Ch. 1992).

[106]*Manville Corp. v. Equity Securities Holders Committees*, 52 Bankr. Rep. 879 (S.D.N.Y. 1985); aff'd 60 Bankr. Rep. 842 (S.D.N.Y. 1985); revised 801 F.2d 60 (2d Cir. 1986).

[107]42 U.S.C. § 1981.

[108]42 U.S.C. § 1983.

[109]42 U.S.C. § 2000 *et seq.*

Pay Act;[110] the Age Discrimination in Employment Act;[111] the Rehabilitation Act of 1973;[112] the Americans with Disabilities Act of 1990;[113] the Vietnam Era Veterans Readjustment Act;[114] the Veterans' Reemployment Rights Act;[115] the Immigration Reform and Control Act of 1986;[116] Executive Orders 11141, 11246, 11375, 11478, 11935 and 12250 requiring nondiscrimination and affirmative action programs by government contractors;[117] regulations of the EEOC;[118] and regulations of the Office of Federal Contract Compliance Programs.[119]

The states have also passed numerous employment discrimination (equal opportunity) laws, some of which are stricter than the federal laws.

Buyers in acquisition transactions, regardless of the method used, should exercise care to identify and avoid succession to employment discrimination. Even more important, buyers should avoid continuing practices that lead to further violations.

Buyers should keep in mind that the requirements of the antidiscrimination laws go beyond prohibiting the overt discrimination that once was found at many companies. The EEOC and other government agencies now focus on subtle practices that many companies do not readily recognize as having discriminatory effects. Some examples of practices that are discriminatory are as follows:

1. Establishing educational requirements for a position that are not reasonably related to job performance.[120]
2. Establishing height, weight and other requirements that place women at a disadvantage and are not reasonably necessary for the job.[121]
3. Excluding women from jobs because of potential reproductive hazards.[122]
4. Requiring higher retirement plan contributions from female employees than male employees because women live longer than men.[123]
5. Maintaining a hostile or abusive environment to women or minority group employees.[124]

---

[110]29 U.S.C. § 206 *et seq.*

[111]29 U.S.C. § 621 *et seq.*

[112]29 U.S.C. § 701 *et seq.*

[113]42 U.S.C. § 12101 *et seq.*

[114]38 U.S.C. § 2011 *et seq.*

[115]38 U.S.C. § 2021 *et seq.*

[116]8 U.S.C. § 1324(a) and (b)

[117]CCH Employment Practices Guide § 221

[118]29 C.F.R. § 1601 *et seq.*

[119]41 C.F.R. § 60-1 *et seq.*

[120]*Griggs v. Duke Power Co.*, 401 U.S. 424 (1971).

[121]*Dothard v. Rawlinson*, 433 U.S. 321 (1977).

[122]*International Union, U.A.W. v. Johnson Controls, Inc.*, 499 U.S. 187, 111 S. Ct. 1196 (1991).

[123]*City of Los Angeles Department of Water and Power v. Manhart*, 435 U.S. 702 (1978).

[124]*Meritor Savings Bank v. Vinson*, 477 U.S. 57 (1986); *Harris v. Forklift Systems, Inc.*, 510 U.S. 17, 126 L. Ed. 2d 295 1993); but see *Gross v. Burggraf Const. Co.*, 53 F.3d 1531 (10th Cir. 1995) and *Crain v. Lamson & Sessions*, 49 F.3d 466 (1995).

On the other hand, the antidiscrimination laws do not protect all persons who wish to complain of discrimination. For example, complaints of conduct discriminatory to homosexuals and transsexuals were held not to be sex discrimination under Title VII of the Civil Rights Act.[125] The antidiscrimination laws also do not protect employees against nondiscriminatory harsh treatment or hardships. For example, the Age Discrimination in Employment Act did not insulate an older, highly paid employee from discharge for performance deficiencies.[126]

In 1998, the U.S. Supreme Court held that employers are responsible for the actions of supervisors who sexually harrass women without showing that the employer was negligent or otherwise at fault for the supervisor's actions. However, if a woman employee does not suffer from a tangible action (such as discharge, demotion or undesirable reassignment), the employer can assert an affirmative defense that it used reasonable care to prevent and correct sexually harrassing behavior and the employee unreasonably failed to take advantage of preventive or corrective opportunities provided by the employer or to avoid harm otherwise.[127]

During the due diligence review, buyers should review the seller's EEO-1 Forms prepared and retained in compliance with the regulations of the EEOC. Records showing compliance with the Equal Pay Act, Age Discrimination in Employment Act, Americans with Disabilities Act and other laws should also be reviewed, as well as any pending complaints. A review should be made of the methods used to comply with the EEOC's guidelines on discrimination because of sex, religion and national origin and the Uniform Guidelines on Employee Selection Procedures of EEOC and OFCCP.

Buyers should be aware that the EEOC makes important use of statistical analysis in identifying employment discrimination. A statistical imbalance may not result from prohibited discrimination, but it can place the burden of proof on the employer to justify its actions. If the seller has hiring or other employment standards, the buyer should determine whether the seller has verified that they meet the requirements for bona fide occupational qualifications ("BFOQs").

If the seller is a general contractor or subcontractor to the federal government, the due diligence review should include compliance with the OFCCP regulations on affirmative action programs, including steps to assure that these programs are conducted in a manner that avoids "reverse discrimination." Buyers should be aware that a seller that has 50 or more employees and supplies products totaling $50,000 or more in a year to a prime contractor is required to adopt an affirmative action program and comply with the OFCCP's regulations.

S. Insurance Coverage

As described earlier in this chapter, business corporations are subject to a growing number of liabilities created by the U.S. Congress, state legisla-

[125]*De Santis v. Pacific Telephone*, 608 F.2d 327 (9th Cir. 1979); *Blum v. Gulf Oil*, 597 F.2d 936 (5th Cir. 1979); *Smith v. Liberty Mutual*, 569 F.2d 325 (5th Cir. 1978). However, numerous state and municipal laws prohibit discrimination based on sexual preference.

[126]*Anderson v. Baxter Healthcare Corp.*, 13 F.3d 1120 (7th Cir. 1994).

[127]*Faragher v. City of Boca Raton* 118 S.Ct. 2275 (1998) and *Burlington Industries, Inc., v. Ellerth* 118 S.Ct 2257 (1998).

tures and the courts. They reduce their risks by purchasing liability insurance, but coverage cannot be taken for granted.

When asbestos product manufacturers were named in thousands of product liability lawsuits alleging that products sold decades ago were defective, they submitted claims to their liability insurers for defense and indemnification. However, their current insurers denied coverage on several grounds. Among other things, the insurers contended that the "occurrence" that triggered coverage was exposure to the product that took place long before their policies were issued. Insurers for earlier years also denied coverage, contending that the "occurrence" that triggered policy coverage did not take place until injury or illness resulting from exposure manifested itself.

In the asbestos product liability cases, the courts required insurers to provide defense and indemnity by finding policy coverage under "exposure," "manifestation," "triple trigger" and other theories.[128] The underlying rationale for these decisions was to further the social and economic benefits of risk spreading that led to the imposition of strict product liability. As the years passed, however, risk spreading did not work as effectively as the courts expected. A number of leading product manufacturers were forced into bankruptcy or a sellout. A number of insurers, including the legendary Lloyds of London,[129] were forced into liquidation, reorganization or a sellout.

Insurers reacted by adding clear and even blunt language to their policies excluding coverage for products, such as asbestos, that had become litigation targets. The insurers also changed to "claims made" policy forms, which require that claims for occurrences within the policy period be submitted within the same policy period, except to the extent that the insured pays premiums for late notice rights. The result was that product liability insurance became expensive, limited and difficult to obtain and old policies became valuable.

When the EPA, state environmental agencies and individual claimants began suing for cleanup costs, personal injuries and property damages against owners and operators of facilities where releases of hazardous substances had occurred, many of the owners and operators submitted claims to their liability insurers. Based on the product liability experience, the insurance industry perceived that courts might again require them to pay for a major social and economic problem that they had not planned to underwrite. The insurers added brief pollution exclusions to many policies in the late 1960s and early 1970s and added a broader, "absolute" pollution exclusion in the middle 1980s. The insurers also denied claims for cleanup costs on grounds that such costs were neither damages, nor sudden and accidental, nor unexpected and unintended, as required for policy coverage.

Some property owners and operators persuaded courts to require their insurers to provide a defense and perhaps also to provide indemnity for

---

[128]For example, see *Insurance Co. of North America v. Forty-Eight Insulations, Inc.*, 657 F.2d 814 (6th Cir. 1981), cert. den. 454 U.S. 1109 (1981); *Eagle-Picher Industries, Inc. v. Liberty Material Ins. Co.*, 682 F.2d 12 (1st Cir. 1982); cert. den. 460 U.S. 1028 (1983); *Keene Corp. v. Insurance Co. of North America*, 667 F.2d 1034 (D.C. Cir. 1981), cert. den. 455 U.S. 1007 (1982); *Lac d'Amiante du Quebec v. American Homes Inc. Co.*, 613 F. Supp. 1549 (D.C.N.J. 1985).

[129]The Corporation of Lloyds is not itself an insurer, but an insurance exchange where member syndicates underwrite risks presented by member brokers. When syndicates, such as the Merritt syndicate, sustained enormous and unexpected losses in the U.S. courts, many of the syndicate investors (called "names"), who had unlimited liability for the losses, sued Lloyds as well as the syndicate managers to avoid or recover their losses.

cleanup costs and other environmental liabilities. However, the courts have been more reluctant to compel insurers to cover environmental liabilities than they were in the product liability cases. For example, some courts have found that cleanup costs payable to the EPA and state environmental agencies are "damages" within the meaning of a liability insurance policy,[130] but one court held to the contrary.[131] The courts have also held that intentional discharges of waste effluents over a period of years are not "sudden and accidental" or are barred from coverage by the "absolute" pollution exclusion.[132] A prospective business buyer should determine whether sellee's insurance covers environmental liabilities.

T. "No Shop" and "Break Up" Fee Agreements

The fiduciary duties of directors and officers, including their "auction duties," are discussed generally in Chapter 12. Until recent years, directors and officers who properly performed their fiduciary duties through the bidding process and the negotiations and execution of an acquisition contract were then free to perform the contract.

Unfortunately, the court decisions no longer offer assurance to directors and officers that they can, without liability, decline a hostile bidder, even after an acquisition contract is executed and delivered. Thus, it is increasingly common to include a provision in acquisition contracts for the sale of a publicly owned corporation authorizing withdrawal from an acquisition contract if fiduciary obligations require its directors and officers to evaluate and accept another bid that proves to be more favorable.

Not surprisingly, buyers object strongly to such a "fiduciary out" provision, and for good reasons. First, buyers do not want to be bound when sellers are not. Second, buyers fear that sellers may use the contract price and terms to "shop" for other bidders. Third, many buyers are unwilling to incur the extensive expenses and efforts (including a due diligence review) required to negotiate and sign an acquisition contract if the seller will remain free to sell to another buyer.

Directors, officers and responsible shareholders of seller corporations generally agree with the buyers' objections. They cannot respond to the first objection because the courts have tied their hands. However, it has become common to respond to the second objection by including a "no shop" provision in acquisition contracts for publicly owned corporations. It has also become relatively common to respond to the second objection by including a "breakup" fee provision in acquisition contracts for publicly owned corporations.

---

[130]For example, see *Independent Petrochemical v. Aetna Casualty*, 944 F.2d 940 (D.C. Cir. 1991); *Outboard Marine v. Liberty Mutual*, 36 ERC 1188 (Ill. 1992) and cases cited therein.

[131]For example, see *Patrons Oxford Mutual Ins. Co. v. Marois*, 573 Atl.2d 18 (1990). However, see *Central Maine Power v. Moore*, 692 Atl. 2d 943 (Me. 1997).

[132]For example, see *Technicon v. American Home*, 74 N.Y.2d 66 (1989); *Powers Chemco v. Federal Insurance*, 74 N.Y.2d 910 (1989); *Town of Harrison v. National Union*, 89 N.Y.2d 308 (1996). However, insurer efforts to use the "absolute pollution exclusion" to avoid liability for carbon monoxide bodily injury claims were rejected by courts in Illinois and Massachusetts.

Thus far, the courts have indicated that "no shop" provisions are not per se unlawful, but they will be enjoined if they prevent the directors and officers from fulfilling their fiduciary duties.[133] "Breakup fees" are also lawful, provided that they are reasonable in relation to the size of the transaction and are not so burdensome as to deter other bidders.[134] The courts evaluate the overall effect of these devices together with other deterrents and expenses, including "lockup options" and investment bankers' fees, in determining their validity.

U. Reference Materials

1. Books

New York Stock Exchange Listed Company Manual, CCH
American Stock Exchange Company Guide, CCH
NASD Manual, CCH
Patent Law, Hildreth, Practicing Law Institute
Trademark Law, Kane, Practicing Law Institute
Trade Secrets, Perritt, Practicing Law Institute
Copyright Law, Henn, Practicing Law Institute
CCH Employment Practices Guide, (4 volumes)
CCH Occupational Safety and Health Guide
Introduction to U.S. Environmental Laws, Shea, Oceana Publishing
The Lead Regulation Handbook, Shea, Government Institutes

2. Articles

"Inside the New Insider Trading Act," Shea, *The Practicing Lawyer*, 1989
"Employment Law," Davis, *National Law Journal*, Jun 9, 1997
"Intellectual Property," Tanenbaum, *National Law Journal*, Jun 9, 1997
"Paying for a Seller's Bias After Closing," Sudbury & Towns, *Mergers & Acquisitions*, May–Jun 1997
"Does Your Deal Pass Muster with the Pension Watchdog?" Hassel & Gigot, *Mergers & Acquisitions*, May–Jun 1997
"Environmental Law," Mounter & Myers, *National Law Journal*, Sep 22, 1997
"Parent, Successor CERCLA Issues Divide the Courts," *National Law Journal*, Dec 1, 1997

[133] *Paramount Communications, Inc. v. QVC Network, Inc.*, 637 A.2d 34 (Del. 1994); *Revlon, Inc. v. MacAndrews & Forbes Holdings*, 506 A.2d 173 (Del. 1986).

[134] *Paramount Communications, Inc. v. QVC Network, Inc., supra,* wherein the termination fee was not enjoined, although a "no shop" provision and a "lock up option" were enjoined; *Cottle v. Storer Communication*, 849 F.2d 570 (11th Cir. 1988); *Samjens Partners I v. Burlington Industries, Inc.*, 663 F.Supp. 614 (S.D.N.Y. 1987); *Beebe v. Pacific Realty Trust*, 578 F.Supp. 1128 (D. Ore. 1984).

Chapter 14

LEVERAGED BUYOUTS

A. INTRODUCTION

Much criticized during the 1980s and early 1990s, the leveraged buyout (LBO) continues to be an important and widely used method to acquire businesses. To understand the reasons, it helps to review the advantages of LBOs.

As its name implies, the LBO uses debt as a major component in the financing of an acquisition. The method allows business buyers to acquire a business with a small amount of equity capital. The value of the equity capital then grows as the cash flows of the acquired businesses are used to repay the acquisition debt. When the acquisition debt is fully paid, the equity holders own the full value of the business. Their ownership is free of obligations to the lenders who provided most of the acquisition financing, except to the extent that the lenders also became equity investors.

LBOs meet important and recurring needs. Some examples are as follows:

- For sellers generally, the LBO means a larger number of potential buyers. The LBO augments the traditional market consisting of established strategic buyers by making available a method that can be used by management groups, venture capital buyers and employee stock ownership plans (ESOPs)
- For business founders nearing retirement, the LBO is an alternative to going public or finding a strategic buyer. Using LBO methods, the founder can sell to a management group or an ESOP, thus fulfilling moral obligations to managers and employees while raising funds for retirement and to pay estate, inheritance and gift taxes. The founder can also sell to a venture capital buyer that offers the right price.
- For corporations seeking to divest businesses that no longer fit their business strategies, the LBO is an alternative to finding a strategic buyer or to shutting down the business with resulting losses and legal problems. If the only interested strategic buyers are competitors who could acquire only under strict antitrust scrutiny, an LBO alternative that does not require antitrust review can be very attractive.
- For failing or bankrupt businesses, the LBO may be an alternative to liquidation. The business may be sold to a management and ven-

ture capital group with the experience, resources and discipline to achieve a turnaround.

- For buyers generally, the LBO is an opportunity to obtain financing in order to compete for larger transactions.
- For buyers generally, the LBO offers important tax advantages that enhance the cash flows needed to pay acquisition debt.
- For business managers, the LBO is an opportunity to obtain a significant ownership interest in the business and seek to earn a major reward for successful management.
- For employees of a failing business, an LBO is an alternative to a shutdown that can preserve their employment. If the buyer is an ESOP, the employees can earn "sweat equity" by trading current compensation for stock that the ESOP acquires for their accounts.
- For lenders, the LBO is an opportunity to respond to growing competition and marginal returns on conventional loans by making specialized loans on which excellent returns can be earned through high interest rates and "equity sweeteners," and risk can be minimized by skills in due diligence and loan management.
- For investment bankers, lawyers, accountants, valuation professionals and other consultants, the LBO is an opportunity to apply special skills to sensitive transactions and earn fees reflecting the value of those skills.

B. A Brief History of LBO Acquisitions

By design, LBOs are transactions that involve risk because a typical financial structure with 70 to 90 percent debt and only 10 to 30 percent equity means there are only limited resources to finance opportunities or absorb losses. When LBOs were developed during the 1970s and early 1980s, the risk was low because businesses could be bought cheaply after a decade of "stagflation".[1] The low price paid by the buyer to the seller served as a substitute for equity capital that would have been necessary if the price were higher. As a result, many acquisitions were highly successful and acquisition debt was repaid or reduced to conventional levels within 2 or 3 years.

The early successful LBO acquisitions included such highly publicized transactions as Gibson Greeting Cards, Inc. and Revlon Inc. The acquisition of Weirton Steel by an ESOP received wide attention because it saved a major employer that was facing a shutdown. Less publicized successes included Gordon Cain's founding of Vista Chemicals and Sterling Chemical.

As economic policies adopted by a new presidential administration in 1982 gradually took effect, the values of companies traded on the stock exchanges and the over-the-counter market rose dramatically and with them the values of privately owned companies. The success of the early LBOs

[1] During the late 1970s and early 1980s, the shares of many sound companies traded on the stock exchanges and in the over-the-counter market at six to eight times earnings.

led many new entrants into the M&A market. Drexel Burham Lambert Incorporated and other firms adapted LBO methods to large leveraged takeovers, often accomplished by a hostile tender offer financed by high yielding debt securities, called "junk bonds."

By the late 1980s, the growing competition for deals drove prices upward and the equity supplement that once came from bargain prices became a hidden equity deficit. The euphoria from earlier successes and the inexperience of new entrants reduced the careful due diligence that is a key element in LOB planning. Indeed, for hostile takeovers, extensive due diligence was impossible. Companies that became targets, or potential targets, for hostile takeovers mounted political, legal and publicity campaigns against them with considerable success.

Congress amended the Internal Revenue Code repeatedly from 1986 to 1989 to withdraw tax benefits from M&A transactions and especially from LBOs. As described in Chapter 11, the U.S. Supreme court upheld in 1987 the validity of Indiana's "control share" law designed to impede hostile tender offers supported by leveraged financing. Other states, including Delaware, also adopted laws designed to impede leveraged hostile takeovers. Civil and criminal proceedings were commenced against a number of firms and individuals who had played leading roles in leveraged hostile takeovers, including Drexel Burnham Lambert Incorporated and its outstanding innovator, Michael Milken.

Warning signs began to appear, although too slowly for immediate widespread recognition. Businesses acquired in LBO transactions found that cash flow projections had been overly optimistic and actual cash flows were insufficient to meet the heavy obligations to service acquisition debt. Eventually, the debt burdens overcame the buyers of several well-known businesses and they filed for bankruptcy reorganization including Macy's, Revco Drug Stores, Dart Drug Stores and Campeau Corporation which had acquired the Allied, Federated and Bloomingdale department stores. Asbestos litigation forced Hillsborough Corporation into bankruptcy after its acquisition of Jim Walter Corporation.

More strains appeared during and after the hostile battle for control of RJR Nabisco in 1989 in which an originally high acquisition price was driven up by competitive bids. Almost a decade later, RJR Nabisco has survived, but additional capital of $1.9 billion was reportedly infused by Kohlberg, Kravis, Roberts & Co. In 1989, potential lenders reportedly withdrew from the proposed LBO acquisition of UAL Corporation and the transaction could not be completed as planned.

After these events, some expected that the LBO method might cease to be used. However, that did not happen. By late 1990, *Forbes* published an article titled "The takeover game isn't dead, it's just gone private."[2] The LBO acquisition had returned to its natural habitat—the privately negotiated transaction where careful due diligence and business, financial, tax and legal planning can achieve successful results for everyone involved.

[2]Pouschine, Berman and Grover, *Forbes*, Oct. 1, 1990, p. 63. The article includes an inset describing the importance of the SEC's Rule 144A in recognizing two-tier capital markets, one being the traditional public markets and the other a private market for restricted securities.

C. Developments during the 1990s

During the 1990s, important LBO developments have included the following:

- Increased emphasis on "exit strategies" during initial planning and subsequent operations.
- Growth of "leveraged buildups" in which an initial LBO acquisition of an "anchor" business is followed by a series of additional LBO acquisitions in the same field to build an overall business that can stand on its own feet as a significant competitor in its industry.
- Growth of private LBO equity investment funds managed by LBO deal makers.
- Growing involvement by managers of LBO venture capital funds in the opportunities and problems of acquired businesses. Many LBO firms have associations with skilled managers who help to select and evaluate acquisition candidates and can manage them, either on a permanent basis or on an interim basis, to pursue special opportunities or solve special problems. The "downsizing" campaigns of many large companies during the 1990s created a supply of executives willing to do this work in return for potentially important financial rewards and an opportunity to control their own destinies.
- Growth of "reverse LBOs," meaning initial public offerings (IPOs) by companies acquired in LBO transactions. Recent examples of successful "reverse LBOs" include Dominick's Supermarkets, Essex International and Gulfstream Aerospace.
- The adoption of Section 197 of the Internal Revenue Code assuring purchasers in taxable transactions of amortization deductions over a 15-year period for intangible assets such as goodwill, going-concern value and noncompetition commitments.
- The adoption of tax rates applicable to long term capital gains that are lower than the rates applicable to ordinary income by the Taxpayer Relief Act of 1997.

Readers interested in the current status of LBO acquisitions will find a special section on them in *Mergers & Acquisitions*, Nov-Dec 1997, consisting of statistics for the past decade and several articles on subjects of current interest.

D. Selecting Candidates for LBO Acquisitions

Experience has shown that candidate businesses should have several characteristics in order to offer a good change for success after an LBO acquisition:

Standalone Capability. An LBO acquisition candidate should have standalone capability. For example, a large corporation may offer to divest a division or operation that has attractive products and good sales history and prospects, but the business may not be viable if it depends heavily on the seller for key raw materials or essential services. For another example, a business founded and managed by a dominant and entrepreneurial owner may be unable to operate successfully without the founder.

Critical Mass. In addition to standalone capability, an LBO acquisition candidate should have "critical mass," meaning all of the operations essential to offer competitive "full service" expected by the customers who buy profitable products or services and are themselves viable and competitive businesses. For example, a business in an industry built around research, development and marketing can survive for some time with existing products and skilled sales personnel, but will eventually wither and die without support for them. At times, the first acquisitions in a leveraged build-up sequence need not have all the operations to make up critical mass, especially if they serve protected niche markets. However, the acquisition planners should be confident that the leveraged build-up will eventually achieve the critical mass.

Experienced Management. An LBO acquisition candidate should have experienced management, either in place or hired from outside, and who are a "good fit" for the future of the acquired business. The acquisition planners should review the existing management, not only for its ability to handle daily operations, but also for the ability to develop and implement overall strategic objectives and to maintain the disciplines needed to provide cash flows to pay the acquisition debt. Many executives perform capably in large organizations or as entrepreneurs in their own businesses, but do not have the combination of skills necessary for successful management of a highly leveraged business. When acquisition planners are not fully confident about the existing management, a common alternative is to hire an outside executive with a "track record" for successful performance. However, it is very important to assure that the outside executive will achieve the respect of the existing management and employees so that they will be motivated to perform well.[3]

Stable Business and Cash Flows. An LBO acquisition candidate should have both a stable business and stable cash flows. Characteristics of a stable business include diversified products, a broad customer base and modest cyclical fluctuations. A business can be stable in terms of gross sales and market shares, but be unsuccessful as an LBO business unless it can also generate stable cash flows. If cash flows are short, lenders can be asked for covenant restriction waivers, but only occasionally. Thus, LBO business managers must trim costs quickly during cyclical downturns. On the other hand, the business itself must also be maintained as stable because it will provide the present and future cash flows and the eventual "exit" event. Thus, cost cutting to maintain cash flows must not sacrifice the fundamental strengths of the business.

[3]Human relations managers and executive search firms use the word "chemistry" in describing management relationships. The word "respect" assuming it is genuine, is probably closer to the right word to describe the most important relationship of a successful LBO manager. A highly leveraged business must be managed for the benefit of its lenders and equity owners to a much greater degree than established, conservatively capitalized businesses. Thus, the executives must combine toughness and practicality with other skills.

Sound Business Plan and "Exit Strategy." An LBO acquisition candidate should have a sound business plan, which may be a plan for the "turnaround" of a business that has been unsuccessful. The plan should include maintenance of the existing business and the cash flows required to meet the principal and interest payments on acquisition debt. The plan should also include development and growth of the business, phased for implementation as acquisition debt is reduced. During the early years after the acquisition, business development and discretionary capital expenditures must usually be deferred, except for opportunities with a very fast payback. However, the business plan should contain a schedule for resumption of development and growth that will make the business an attractive candidate for an initial public offering or a resale to a strategic buyer within a time horizon of about 5 years.

Well-Maintained and Competitive Facilities. An LBO acquisition candidate should have well-maintained machinery and equipment and other physical assets. This is important because such facilities provide valuable loan collateral and their tax bases can be stepped up to provide significant accelerated cost recovery deductions. The facilities should also be modern and competitive. It is not essential for the facilities to be at a "state-of-the-art" level. Indeed, facilities that are too advanced or unique may not have good collateral value.

Freedom from Serious Contingent Liabilities. An LBO acquisition candidate should be free of serious contingent liabilities unless it has clearly adequate insurance or indemnification arrangements to protect the business against them.

Some lists of desirable characteristics of LBO acquisition candidates include minimal existing debt or assets that can be sold to repay acquisition debt. In the author's experience, these characteristics are sometimes helpful, but not always. If a business has existing debt, it can usually be prepaid or assumed and the effects considered in the acquisition planning and negotiations. Extraneous assets that may have salable value are helpful if the seller "throws them in" for a modest price and the buyer does not include their resale in its cash flow projections for a time sooner or a price higher than can realistically be achieved.

"People" and Technology Businesses. Finally, "people" businesses and businesses built on technology (i.e., intellectual properties) are difficult candidates for LBO financing. However, some "people" and technology businesses have very stable cash flows. Their intellectual properties may conclude assets such as film, music or book libraries that are prized and readily salable. If other characteristics are strong, these businesses should also be good LBO acquisition candidates.

E. How LBO Buyers Became Competitive Bidders

When LBOs were new, sellers were hesitant to negotiate with LBO buyers, whether management groups or venture capital groups. Sellers feared that LBO buyers would make a deal and then fail to raise the financing, or that LBO buyers would delay and renegotiate the deal in order to meet lender requirements. Sellers also feared that venture capital buyers would be "asset strippers" and would not continue the business and its employees. LBO buyers had to overcome these seller concerns in order to gain credibility.

Most LBO venture capital buyers established relationships with capital providers of senior debt, mezzanine debt and equity. Through these relationships, LBO buyers could negotiate credibly with sellers because they were familiar with the criteria that the capital providers would require. During negotiations, they could obtain preliminary reactions from key personnel with the capital providers. They could also obtain bridge funds to close transactions.

Many LBO venture capital buyers established private LBO investment funds from which they could draw equity capital as acquisitions were negotiated and closed. These funds were raised by private placements, sometimes wholly or partially overseas.[4] The private placement memoranda generally described the "track record" of the managers and the criteria[5] to be used in making acquisitions, including "exit strategies" that usually call for a resale or IPO within a time horizon of about 3 to 7 years. While operating within the criteria, the fund managers had "blank check" authority to draw funds. Needless to say, control of these private LBO investment funds greatly enhanced the credibility of LBO buyers in negotiations with sellers and lenders.

LBO venture capital buyers also learned to reassure sellers about their intentions for the future of the acquired business. For most acquisitions, the reassurances do not interfere with sound planning. Indeed, much reassurance comes during the due diligence review when post-acquisition business plans are discussed. The future managers soon learn that venture capital buyers want to minimize financial structure risk by careful business planning that identifies, preserves and develops the values purchased. If the proposed acquisition includes a failing or misfit business, the business planning may lead to a turnaround plan or a divestiture plan, but the decision will be businesslike.[6]

Especially in management buyouts, venture capital buyers usually agree, and even insist, that key managers have employment contracts and some amount of equity investment in the acquired business. The employment contracts provide employment security and incentives to the managers. However, they also protect the LBO buyer with confidentiality and

---

[4]It was necessary to structure and manage private LBO investment funds carefully so that registration of securities under the Securities Act of 1933 and registration of the fund as an investment company under the Investment Company Act of 1940 would not be required. The Investment Company Amendments Act of 1996 was adopted, in part, to ease these concerns. The amendments exempt funds from registration under the Investment Company Act if they are owned exclusively by persons who, at the time of investment, meet qualified purchaser criteria.

[5]The private placement memoranda typically contained acquisition criteria such as the industry, size of the businesses to be acquired, amount of investment in each acquisition, a leverage ratio limit for each acquisition, a policy on gaining and maintaining control of acquired businesses, and "exit" strategy" policies including distribution of the proceeds of resold businesses.

[6]True LBO venture capital buyers have goals that far exceed the profits that can be achieved by "asset stripping." In general, they are quite conservative about maintaining the values in which they have invested. Thus, they divest or close operations only in a few situations. For example, if a seller insists on including a misfit operation in a sale, it will probably be divested. An operation that cannot meet its business plan after diligent effort will probably also be divested or shut down to prevent it from becoming a "millstone" for the whole business.

noncompetition provision commitments that benefit the acquired business and all those who provide capital for the acquisition. The managers' equity investment provides an incentive for successful performance and a risk of loss for poor performance.

While most planning for LBO acquisitions calls for tight operating and capital budgets, there are LBO transactions in which management compensation can be higher than the levels that a strategic buyer would be willing to accept. The reason is that LBO planners do not need to reconcile compensation with an existing compensation structure. Strategic buyers usually have an existing compensation structure and cannot readily depart from it.

In the early years of LBO acquisitions, venture capital buyers had little capability to respond to a loss or failure of performance by the initial management team. They sometimes had resources to furnish additional capital, but could not supply management direction and strategy. However, as venture capital funds repeatedly encountered a need for "hands-on" participation, the better firms developed that capability. The author recommends that any investor in an LBO acquisition fund inquire whether the firm has successful experience in responding to unforeseen crises at the companies acquired.

F. Basic Corporate Structures and Methods

LBO acquisitions can be structured in many different ways. However, some structures are used more commonly than others.

Most structures consist of a parent holding company and one or more subsidiaries. The parent company negotiates the acquisitions and arranges the financing. The subsidiaries are used as acquiring or acquired corporations and, after the acquisition, operate the acquired businesses.

The acquisition can be accomplished by any of the three basic methods—an assets purchase, a stock purchase or a merger. The choice is dictated by balancing legal, financial, tax and accounting advantages and disadvantages. For example, the assets purchase method is often suitable for small and middle-sized transactions because the method allows selection or rejection of assets and liabilities and leads directly to the price allocation and stepped-up asset values that are part of the tax and accounting aspects of the transaction.

The stock purchase method can be and is used in LBO transactions. However, the stock purchase method requires careful planning to meet legal, financial, tax and accounting objectives and requirements. For example, the stock purchase method cannot be used if one or more minority shareholders refuse to sell. If the stock purchase method is used, a second-step merger is usually necessary in order to make the acquired subsidiary's assets available as collateral for the acquisition debt and its cash flows available for repayment of the acquisition debt. The consequences of an election under Section 338 of the Internal Revenue Code must also be considered, as discussed later in this chapter.

Triangular mergers are methods commonly used to accomplish LBO acquisitions, especially larger transactions. The merger allows a "freeze-out" of any opposing minority shareholders, subject to dissenters' appraisal rights. The merger also provides access by the buyer to the assets and cash flows of the acquired business to secure and repay the buyer's acquisition debt.

The triangular merger technique, whether forward or reverse, results in a subsidiary responsible for its own obligations and liabilities and avoids the succession by operation of law to obligations and liabilities that results from a two-party merger. In addition, as described later, the buyer can use a forward triangular merger, if it wishes federal tax treatment as an assets acquisition. The buyer can use a reverse triangular merger if it wishes federal tax treatment as a stock purchase.

To accomplish a triangular merger, a parent holding company organizes a "shell" subsidiary to which the parent contributes the purchase price on the closing date for payment to the seller or its shareholder(s). The acquired corporation is then merged into the subsidiary, if the objective is a forward merger equivalent to an assets purchase. The subsidiary, called a transitory subsidiary, is merged into the acquired corporation if the objective is a reverse merger equivalent to a stock purchase. In either event, the purchase price is distributed to the shareholders of the acquired corporation and their shares are canceled. Shares of the corporation surviving the merger are issued to the parent holding company.

Acquisition planners should keep in mind that the structures and methods used to accomplish LBO acquisitions will be recognized by government agencies and the courts when they accomplish the purposes for which the law intended them. If the structures and methods are used to accomplish purposes that deprive creditors, shareholders or other persons of their rights, a court may recast the transaction to reflect its substance rather than its form. For example, the courts may combine several steps and treat them as a single transaction.[7]

G. Financial Structuring

The financial structuring for an LBO acquisition can best be described in two categories: asset-based financing and cash flow-based financing.

1. Asset-Based Financing

Small and medium-sized LBO acquisition transactions are often financed by loans that are asset-based. In making these loans, the lender reviews the projected cash flows, but relies primarily on the realizable collateral values of the assets to be acquired. At the closing, the lender obtains mortgages and security interests of the acquired assets to hold as collateral. Heller Financial, Inc. and the CIT Group are examples of lenders that have made many asset-based loans to finance LBO acquisitions.

Asset-based financing is usually provided by a single lender in the form of two loans, a term loan and a revolving credit loan, that may be

[7] *Wieboldt Stores, Inc., v. Schottenstein*, 94 B.R. 488 (N.D. Del. 1988).

combined in a single loan agreement. The loan agreement may also include provisions to borrow for capital expenditures.

The amounts that can be borrowed depend on the realizable collateral values of the assets to be acquired. The lender will require that they be appraised by a qualified valuation firm that will provide a written report to the lender.

The term loans may be 60 to 80 percent of the value of property, plant and equipment acquired, depending on the lender's confidence that the appraised values can be realized if foreclosures should become necessary.

The revolving credit loan may authorize borrowing of 70 to 80 percent of the value of eligible accounts receivable. To be eligible, the accounts receivable must meet several requirements, including a sound credit history of the customer and reasonable aging of the receivables. Accounts receivable unpaid for a period such as 90 days will be excluded. The revolving credit agreement may authorize borrowing of 40 to 60 percent of the value of eligible inventories. To be eligible, the inventories must meet several requirements to determine their salability. Finished product and raw material inventories will usually be eligible if they are not excessive, obsolete or slow-moving. Work-in-process inventories may be excluded. Inventories of small parts and tools may also be excluded. Such factors as turnaround rate, the business standing of the customers and market trends in the industry will be considered in determining the value of inventories for loan purposes.

When an LBO acquisition is financed by asset-based loans, the balance of the purchase price must come from seller financing and equity financing. If the seller is willing to receive payment of part of the purchase price over a period of time, the seller must also be willing to subordinate its payment rights to those of the primary lender. The seller must also recognize that the primary lender will have first priority mortgages and security interests covering all of the borrower's assets. The seller can, however, have second mortgages and security interests in the assets.

Asset-based loans are expensive. The costs for appraisals, legal fees, mortgage recording fees and numerous lender's fees add substantially to the overall financing costs. Further, the lender may want to collect the receivables and charge for its services to do so unless the borrower demonstrates its experience and reliability in collection activities. In addition, the lender may want an "equity sweetener" such as an option to buy for a nominal price as much as 5 to 15 percent of the stock of LBO buyer corporation.[8]

2. Cash Flow–Based Financing

Large and middle-sized LBO acquisitions are often financed by loans that are cash flow–based. In making these loans, the lenders rely primarily on the borrower's projected cash flows in making credit decisions, although they will review asset values as well. At the closing, the senior lenders may obtain mortgages and security interests in the borrower's assets. However, some lenders may agree to accept "negative pledge" commitments from

[8]Whether the value of such an option should be treated as original issue discount under the Internal Revenue Code should be considered.

the borrower to maintain its assets free from all mortgages, security interests, liens and other encumbrances except for those specifically identified and agreed.

Because cash flow–based loans are usually used to finance larger, higher-priced acquisitions, the loan financing is likely to include "mezzanine" lenders who will purchase notes subordinated to the senior debt. Mezzanine financing provides a "cushion" for the senior lenders in addition to the equity investment provided by the stockholders. A hypothetical financing structure is as follows:

Senior debt	50%	Insurance companies and banks
Subordinated debt	25%	Venture capital investors
Common stock	25%	Venture capital investors and management

Conservatively financed companies commonly have equity (including retained earnings) that amounts to over half of their capital structure. Thus, the example shows that the mezzanine financing (i.e., the subordinated debt) serves to replace part of the financial structure that commonly consists of equity obtained by sales of common stock and retention of earnings.

The key to cash flow–based financing is evaluation of the soundness of the borrower's projected cash flows and matching them with scheduled payments of principal and interest on the acquisition debt and other debt payments and fixed charges. The cash flows should have a significant coverage margin over the payment requirements for debt fixed charges. These margins can be included as covenants in the loan agreements.

The projections and credit facilities should include expected fluctuations in accounts receivable and inventories. They should also include foreseeable necessary capital expenditures to maintain plant and equipment in good condition.

Caution should be used when including the proceeds of sales of assets in cash flow projections, especially if they are going business operations. Among the reasons for the failures of LBO acquisitions in the late 1980s was the inclusion of cash projections of the anticipated proceeds from sales of major business operations that could not be accomplished at the prices and within the times projected.

3. Characteristics of Mezzanine Debt

From the viewpoint of the borrower, the economic value of mezzanine debt in an LBO acquisition resides primarily in the tax deductibility of the interest payments and in the support that the subordination provides for senior debt in a capital structure that has only a modest amount of equity.

In negotiating and drafting the agreements for mezzanine debt, it is important that its characteristics assure the tax deductibility of the interest payments. (See the following Section.)

It is also important that the subordination and other provisions of the mezzanine debt be mutually satisfactory to the persons who will purchase both the senior debt and the mezzanine debt. The negotiated provisions are then set forth in the debt instruments and often also in an intercreditor agreement between the senior lenders and the mezzanine lenders. The provisions are quite intricate when negotiated between sophisticated lenders and their counsel and state in detail their relative rights during normal conditions and during various default conditions including bankruptcy.

For example, senior lenders want mezzanine lenders to schedule their principal payments so that they will not be paid faster than the senior debt and perhaps not until the entire senior debt is paid. Senior lenders want the subordination provisions of mezzanine debt to bar payment of principal and interest to the mezzanine lenders, not only upon bankruptcy or defaults in payments to the senior lenders, but also during any default in financial ratio and other covenants in the senior debt instruments. The senior lenders may also want the subordination provisions to apply to additional advances and refinancings of the senior debt, although they may agree to a "cap" on the amounts. The senior lenders want the subordination provisions to apply to fees, expenses, premiums and indemnity payments payable under their debt instruments. The senior lenders also want the mezzanine lenders to agree to turn over any payments they may receive when the subordination provisions are in effect. Senior lenders may also want mezzanine debtholders to forego their enforcement remedies, including the right to foreclose second priority mortgages and security interests, during defaults under the senior debt instruments. Prospective mezzanine lenders will resist, and seek to limit, many of the senior lenders' subordination requests.

To protect themselves from further risk, mezzanine lenders negotiate with the borrower for contractual protections in their debt instruments. They request the borrower to accept (1) restrictions on incurring additional senior debt and additional mezzanine debt that is *pari passu* with the mezzanine debt; (2) requirements to maintain financial ratios such as current assets to current liabilities and cash flows (measured as EBIT or EBITDA) to total interest or total fixed charges; (3) restrictions on dividend payments and other distributions to shareholders; (4) restrictions on mergers, asset sales and transactions with related parties; (5) requirements to furnish financial statements and other periodic information; and (6) an obligation to prepay the full amount of the principal and interest upon a "change of control." If the mezzanine lenders are successful in persuading the borrower to agree to prepayment upon a "change of control," the senior lenders will require that the prepayment be subordinated to the payment of the senior debt.

High-yielding securities, also known as "junk bonds," are a securitized form of mezzanine debt. Historically, the securitization of mezzanine debt is generally credited to Michael Milken and Drexel Burnham Lambert Incorporated, who accurately foresaw that the subordination risks of such debt could be importantly balanced by high interest rates and an active market. Mr. Milken and his firm made very active markets in high-yielding securities during the 1980s, thus allowing holders who found the risk unacceptable, perhaps after a decline in price, to sell them to other investors who found the risk acceptable based on the increased yield resulting from the lower price. Although high-yielding securities were sold to raise capital for many purposes, they became controversial during the 1980s because of their frequent use to raise financing for leveraged takeovers. Indeed, corporations resisting the takeovers relished and spread the nickname "junk bonds." An important factor that contributed to the risk of high-yielding securities during the 1980s was that the market depended heavily on the trading skills and strength of Mr. Milken and his firm, and as they experienced legal and financial difficulties the market weakened. During the 1990s, many other firms have entered or increased their activities in the markets for high-yielding securities and these securities have largely ceased to be controversial.

Because mezzanine debt has greater risk than senior debt, mezzanine lenders typically bargain for extra compensation in the form of higher interest and rights to convert their loans to common stock. In lieu of conversion rights, mezzanine lenders may negotiate for separate or detachable options or warrants that are somewhat more attractive.

H. Taxation

In general, LBO acquisitions are structured for tax purposes to be taxable acquisitions. Thus, the discussion of taxable acquisitions in Chapter 6 is generally applicable to LBO acquisitions. The purpose of the discussion in this chapter is to summarize the applicable tax principles and discuss how they relate to financial, legal, accounting and other factors that affect LBO structures.

Two features of the Internal Revenue Code (IRC) are essential to the economics of LBO acquisitions. One is the deductibility of interest on debt.[9] The other is the step-up of the bases of the purchased assets from the bases on the seller's tax records to new bases on the buyer's tax records by allocating the acquisition price among the purchased assets[10] in order to obtain increased depreciation and amortization deductions.[11] Because debt is a major element of LBO acquisition financing, the acquisition price is usually much higher than the seller's adjusted basis in the assets sold. Most LBO buyers have no taxable income under the IRC for several years after the acquisition. The resulting deferral of federal income taxes, except for any applicable alternative minimum tax, importantly increases the cash flows available to repay acquisition debt.[12]

In the usual situation when the purchase price is higher than the seller's bases in its assets, an LBO buyer has an incentive to negotiate for a purchase of assets or for a forward triangular merger that may be treated as an assets purchase.[13] In the unusual situation when the purchase price is lower than the seller's bases in its assets, an LBO buyer has an incentive to negotiate for a stock purchase or for a reverse triangular merger that may

[9]IRC § 163.

[10]IRC §§338 and 1060. See also IRS Form 8594.

[11]IRC § 167.

[12]During the 1980s, political advocates claimed that tax deductions were subsidizing hostile leveraged takeovers and causing important losses of tax revenues by the U.S. Treasury. These claims were incorrect. Lenders realize income from interest received as borrowers deduct interest payments. Sellers realize income from sales of assets long before the buyers can claim depreciation and amortization deductions. See also "Effects of LBOs on Tax Revenues of the U.S. Treasury," Jensen *et al.*, *Tax Notes*, Feb. 6, 1989.

[13]Rev. Rul. 69-6, 1969-1 Cum. Bull. 104.

be treated as a stock purchase.[14] In these negotiations, the seller must consider the effects of depreciation recaptures before agreeing to a sale of assets or a triangular merger that is treated as a sale of assets.[15]

As described in Chapter 6, an LBO buyer that purchases stock can obtain a stepped-up basis for the assets of the acquired subsidiary by arranging a Section 338 election. Such an election would ordinarily be disadvantageous because of the tax that would be payable with respect to the "deemed sale" of the assets by the subsidiary. However, if ample net operating loss (NOL) carryforwards are available or a Section 338(h)(10) election can be made, a stock purchase or reverse triangular merger may be appropriate. When considering the use of NOL carryforwards, tax planners must consider the limitations imposed by Section 382(b) of the IRC after a "substantial ownership change" and the potential loss of the NOLs if the business continuity requirements are not met.

It is common to use a holding company and subsidiary structure to accomplish LBO acquisitions for reasons that are not entirely tax-motivated. One reason is that the parent holding company can make further acquisitions through other subsidiaries. Another reason is that, if the acquisition loans are made at the subsidiary level, the lenders will require a guaranty and pledge of the subsidiary's stock by the parent holding company, but need not require a pledge of the parent's stock. If the loans are made at the parent level, the parent and subsidiary can file a consolidated income tax return so that interest on the parent's acquisition debt can be used to reduce the income of the acquired subsidiary.[16]

When designing and structuring mezzanine debt, tax planners in an LBO acquisition should review the several IRC sections that deny a deduction for interest paid on some kinds of debt. This review is specially important if any mezzanine debt will be held by stockholders. As described in further detail in Chapter 6, the IRC sections include (1) Section 279 that denies a deduction of interest paid on "acquisition indebtedness" meeting three narrow conditions; (2) Section 163(e) that partially denies a deduction of interest paid on certain "high yield obligations"; (3) Section 172(h) that reduces NOLs by interest resulting from corporate equity reduction transactions; (4) Section 384 that limits the use of preacquisition losses to offset built-in gains; and (5) Section 385 that authorizes the IRS to recharacterize debt as equity or equity as debt. Tax planners should also review the original issue discount provisions of Sections 163(e) and 1271 to 1275.

Corporations have been the customary legal entity used to accomplish LBO acquisitions. It has always been permissible to use partnerships or limited partnerships in LBO acquisitions, but they have not been widely used for legal reasons that include potential liability. Subchapter S corporations can also be used in LBO acquisitions, but they are subject to several restrictions imposed by the IRC that make their use generally unsuitable.

---

[14]Rev. Rul. 73-427, 1973-2 Cum. Bull. 301; Rev. Rul 79-273, 1979-2 Cum. Bull. 125. This assumes that the source of the cash paid to the shareholders of the corporation sold is the buyer, rather than its transitory subsidiary.

[15]IRC §§1245 and 1250.

[16]IRC, § 1502.

During the 1990s the limited liability company (LLC), a new entity, was created by statutes adopted by many states throughout the United States. The legislative purpose was to create an entity that would provide limited liability to its owners, called "members," and that could elect to be operated and taxed as a partnership without the restrictions imposed on Subchapter S corporations by the IRC. Initially, the IRS indicated that it would not allow an LLC to be taxed as a partnership unless it met at least minimal partnership characteristics. However, in early 1997, the IRS adopted "Check the Box" regulations that allow LLCs to elect whether they wish to be taxed as a corporation or a partnership. Thus, LLCs are being organized with growing frequency and will probably be used in some LBO transactions.

I. Rights of Creditors Other Than Acquisition Lenders

For existing lenders and trade creditors, an LBO acquisition can be a shock. They may have extended credit to a corporation with a conservative financial structure, modest obligatory demands upon its cash flows, and few encumbrances on its assets. Their debt may even have been rated favorably by Moody's or Standard & Poor's. On short notice, they learn that their borrower or customer has undertaken a large amount of debt and has usually also committed all of its assets as collateral to secure the debt. Further, the proceeds of the new debt have not been used to acquire new assets or otherwise enhance the business, but have been paid to acquire the business from its owners. One U.S. Circuit Court of Appeals described the effect briefly as follows:

> *"The effect of an LBO is that a corporation's shareholders are replaced by secured creditors. Put simply, stockholders' equity is supplanted by debt. The level of risk facing the newly structured corporation rises significantly due to the increased debt-to-equity ratio. This added risk is borne primarily by the unsecured creditors, those who will most likely not be paid in the event of insolvency."*[17]

If an LBO acquisition leads to a successful new business that pays its debts as they mature, the existing lenders and the trade creditors will relax because they have suffered no enduring harm. However, if these creditors are not paid, they will explore their legal rights and remedies. Their legal counsel will advise them that several laws may be applicable.

There are laws that allow unpaid creditors to seek to set aside fraudulent transfers of assets (including grants of mortgages and security interests) to the acquisition lenders and also fraudulently incurred obligations to the acquisition lenders. Most states have adopted the Uniform Fraudulent Transfer Act (UFTA), although a few states still have the earlier Uniform Fraudulent Conveyance Act (UFCA).[18] If bankruptcy proceedings have been filed, the trustee in bankruptcy can take similar actions under Sections 544, 548 and 550 of the Bankruptcy Code.

---

[17] *Mellon Bank, N.A. v. Metro Communications, Inc.*, 945 F.2d 635 (3d Cir. 1991).

[18] Jurisdictions still having the UFCA as of recent date were Maryland, Michigan, New York, Tennessee, the Virgin Islands and Wyoming.

Sections 4(a) and 5(a) of the UFTA read as follows:

> *§ 4. Transfers Fraudulent as to Present and Future Creditors.—(a) A transfer made or obligation incurred by a debtor is fraudulent as to a creditor, whether the creditor's claim arose before or after the transfer was made or the obligation was incurred, if the debtor made the transfer or incurred the obligation:*
>
> *(1) with actual intent to hinder, delay, or defraud any creditor of the debtor; or*
>
> *(2) without receiving a reasonably equivalent value in exchange for the transfer or obligation, and the debtor:*
>
> *(i) was engaged or was about to engage in a business or a transaction for which the remaining assets of the debtor were unreasonably small in relation to the business or transaction; or*
>
> *(ii) intended to incur, or believed or reasonably should have believed that he [or she] would incur, debts beyond his [or her] ability to pay as they became due.*
>
> *§ 5. Transfers Fraudulent as to Present Creditors.—(a) A transfer made or obligation incurred by a debtor is fraudulent as to a creditor whose claim arose before the transfer was made or the obligation was incurred if the debtor made the transfer or incurred the obligation without receiving a reasonably equivalent value in exchange for the transfer or obligation and the debtor was insolvent at that time or the debtor became insolvent as a result of the transfer or obligation.*

Thus, the UFTA and the UFCA allow creditors to seek a court order nullifying asset transfers and obligations actually made to defraud creditors, such as a sham sale to a dummy corporation. Of greater concern to LBO transactions, these laws allow creditors to seek nullification of the financing arrangements and to recapture the purchase price payments without proof of actual fraud if the debtor received less than reasonably equivalent value (UFTA) or fair consideration (UFTA) if (1) the debtor's assets were unreasonably small in relation to the business; (2) the debtor believed, or reasonably should have believed, that it was incurring debts beyond its ability to pay as they became due; or (3) the debtor was insolvent at the time, or became insolvent as a result, of the transfer or obligation.

In an LBO acquisition, however structured, the proceeds of loans are not received and used for the benefit of the debtor corporation, but are paid as purchase price to its owners. Thus, the debtor never receives reasonably equivalent value or fair consideration.[19] Thus, the validity of LBO acquisitions depends on whether the borrower has reasonably adequate remaining assets, is able to pay present and future debts as they become due and is solvent on the closing date after the debt obligations are incurred and the assets are transferred.

If the debtor is in bankruptcy proceedings, the trustee can use Section 544 of the Bankruptcy Code to avoid any transfer that is voidable under the UFTA or UFCA. Under Section 550, the trustee can recover the assets transferred, or their value, from the transferees with certain exceptions. In addition, the trustee can act to avoid fraudulent transfers and obligations under Section 548 which reads, in part as follows:

---

[19]For example, see *In re O'Day Corp.* 126 B.R. 370 (D. Mass. 1991).

§ 548. Fraudulent transfers and obligations

(a) The trustee may avoid any transfer of an interest of the debtor in property, or any obligation incurred by the debtor, that was made or incurred on or within one year before the date of the filing of the petition, if the debtor voluntarily or involuntarily—

(1) made such transfer or incurred such obligation with actual intent to hinder, delay, or defraud any entity to which the debtor was or became, on or after the date that such transfer was made or such obligation was incurred, indebted; or

(2)(A) received less than a reasonably equivalent value in exchange for such transfer or obligation; and

(B)(i) was insolvent on the date that such transfer was made or such obligation was incurred, or became insolvent as a result of such transfer or obligation;

(ii) was engaged in business or a transaction, or was about to engage in business or a transaction, for which any property remaining with the debtor was an unreasonably small capital; or

(iii) intended to incur, or believed that the debtor would incur, debts that would be beyond the debtor's ability to pay as such debts matured.

The reader should observe that the principles stated in Section 548 of the Bankruptcy Code are quite similar to those in the UFTA.

The practical effect of the UFTA, the UFCA and the applicable provisions of the Bankruptcy Code are that the lenders that provide the acquisition financing must satisfy themselves not only that the borrower can pay their debt, but also that the borrower has assets and reasonably projected cash flows sufficient to fulfill the rights of creditors protected by those laws. Otherwise, they risk nullification of their debt obligations and the mortgages and security interests that are collateral for them. The persons who receive the purchase price should also satisfy themselves about the buyer's debt obligations, remaining assets and projected cash flows or they risk losing the purchase price.

The need for careful planning to meet the standards of the UFTA, UFCA and Bankruptcy Code is serious because there has been extensive litigation under these laws after failures of LBO acquisitions. In the early lawsuits, the courts ruled several times in favor of the creditors who challenged the asset transfers and obligations.[20]

Lenders and sellers use various methods to satisfy themselves about the creditors' rights issues, including a careful due diligence review. One method is to require the borrower to deliver a "solvency letter" prepared by a person skilled in financial planning and analysis. For example, solvency letters have been prepared by firms such as Duff & Phelps and Houlihan, Lokey, Howard & Zukin. For several years, some accounting firms prepared solvency letters, but the American Institute of Certified Public Accountants (AICPA) issued an interpretation in 1988 prohibiting

[20]*U.S. v. Tabor Court Realty Corp.*, 803 F.2d 1288 (3d Cir. 1986), cert. den. sub nom. *McLellan Realty v. U.S.*, 107 S.Ct. 3229 (1987); *Wells Fargo Bank v. Dessert View Building Supplies*, 475 F.Supp. 693 (D.C.Nev. 1978); *In the Matter of Process-Manz Press, Inc.*, 236 F.Supp. 333 (N.D. Ill. 1964).

its members from writing such letters because of concern about risk and possible effects on audit independence. However, the AICPA allows "agreed upon procedures" letters, written in accordance with several requirements and other services helpful to lenders and sellers in satisfying themselves about solvency and capital adequacy.[21]

The date for determining solvency and capital adequacy of an LBO acquisition is typically the closing date on which the loan obligations are incurred and the asset transfers are made at a simultaneous closing. However, the courts will examine a company's capital throughout a reasonable period of time surrounding the precise date of a challenged transfer in order to make a realistic assessment of the impact of the transfer on its ability to conducts its affairs.[22] Some courts have indicated that solvency and capital adequacy may also be required on the dates when payments are made on the acquisition debt.

The UFTA, the UFCA and Section 548 of the Bankruptcy Code do not make clear the valuation methods that should be used in determining solvency and capital adequacy. The courts may begin by reviewing the debtor's balance prepared in accordance with generally accepted accounting principles (GAAP) but should conclude that book value is not controlling.[23] The courts then go into greater depth to apply "fair valuation" of assets as required by Section 2 of the UFTA and Section 101(31) of the Bankruptcy Code. Some courts have used orderly liquidation value in determining the values of assets.[24] Other courts have applied going business valuation methods including discounted cash flow valuation.[25] The valuation may include the values of indirect benefits, although the benefits are not sufficient to be "reasonably equivalent value" under the UFTA or "fair consideration" under the UFCA.[26] The existence of a "balloon" payment required to eventually pay the acquisition debt does not necessarily demonstrate inability to meet debts if there is adequate time for it to be refinanced.[27]

The courts also review business developments after an LBO acquisition to determine whether a subsequent failure resulted from events foreordained on the closing date or from unforeseen subsequent business reverses. If a court finds that the failure resulted from significant unforeseen adverse developments, it will not conclude that the asset transfers and obligations incurred were fraudulent, even though management errors

---

[21]AICPA Codification of Statements on Auditing Standards, CCH, ATI § 100.33-100.44. AICPA Statement of Auditing Standards No. 75 effective April 30, 1996.

[22]*Barrett v. Continental Illinois*, 882 F.2d 1 (1st Cir. 1989).

[23]*In re O'Day Corp.*, 126 B.R. 370 (D. Mass. 1991).

[24]*In re Ohio Corrugating Co.*, 91 B.R. 430 (N.D. Ohio 1988); *Wieboldt Stores, Inc. v. Schottenstein*, 94 B.R. 488 (N.D. Ill. 1988).

[25]*MFS/Sun Life Trust v. Van Dusen Airport Services*, 910 F.Supp. 913 (S.D.N.Y. 1995); *Moody v. Security Pacific Credit*, 971 F.2d 1056 (3d Cir. 1992); *In re Vadnais Lumber*, 100 B.R. 127 (D. Mass. 1989); *Kupetz v. Continental Illinois*, 77 B.R. 754 (C.D. Cal. 1987) *Credit Managers Ass'n v. Federal Co.*, 629 F.Supp. 175 (C.D. Cal. 1985).

[26]*MFS/Sun Life Trust v. Van Dusen Airport Services*, supra; *Moody v. Security Pacific Credit*, supra.

[27]*MFS/Sun Life Trust v. Van Dusen Airport Services*, supra.

[28]*MFS/Sun Life trust v. Van Dusen Airport Services*, supra; *Moody v. Security Pacific Credit*, supra;

contributed to the failure.[28] If a court finds that the debtor's finances fell apart soon after the closing for foreseeable reasons, it will probably conclude that the assets transfers and obligations were fraudulent.[29]

Creditors seeking remedies against acquisition lenders after LBO acquisitions may also seek equitable subordination of their debt under Section 510(c) of the Bankruptcy Code.[30]

If the LBO acquisition was accomplished by methods that involve a distribution by the debtor corporation to its shareholders, creditors may also seek to recapture the distribution by alleging a violation of the provisions of state corporation laws restricting the sources from which dividends and distributions may be paid. For example, Section 160 of the Delaware General Corporation Law allows dividends to be paid only (1) from surplus (including paid-in surplus in excess of par value shares) or (2) if there is no surplus, out of net profits of the current year or preceding fiscal years. Section 160 of the Delaware General Corporation Law prohibits a corporation from repurchasing or redeeming its shares if its capital is impaired or would become impaired by the repurchase or redemption. However, directors are not bound by a balance sheet that shows a capital deficit in accordance with generally accepted accounting principles and may evaluate assets and liabilities in good faith to determine whether there is a surplus or a capital impairment.[31]

Finally, creditors can challenge the validity of intercorporate guarantees, especially "upstream" guarantees given by subsidiaries of debt of parent corporations. However, the corporation laws of key states have specific provisions authorizing intercorporate guarantees.[32] Guarantees, and especially "upstream" guarantees, can also be challenged as fraudulent obligations and transfers.

J. Conflicts of Interest

At an early point in the planning of an LBO acquisition, it is important to identify the conflicting interests that will exist. Procedures for disclosure of the conflicting interests should be adopted. Procedures for independent review of transactions involving the conflicts of interest should be adopted in order to insure their entire fairness.

Some examples of conflicts of interest are as follows:

- In a management buyout, some of the directors and officers of the seller corporation will be founders of the buyer corporation. They have a duty to the seller corporation to seek a high price and other terms favorable to the seller. Those duties potentially conflict with their duties to the buyer corporation and its shareholders to seek a low price and other terms favorable to the buyer.

[29]*In re Oxford Homes, Inc.*, 180 B.R. 1 (D. Me. 1995).

[30]*In re O'Day Corp.*, 126 B.R. 370 (D. Mass. 1991).

[31]*Klang v. Smith's Food*, Del. Sup. Ct., No. 210, Nov. 7, 1997.

[32]For example, see Delaware General Corporation law, § 122(13) and New York Business Corporation Law, § 908; see also Matter of *Ollag Construction Equipment*, 578 F.2d 904 (2nd Cir. 1978).

- Whenever a corporation or its business is being sold, its directors and officers may have an incentive to favor a management buyout because the buyer is likely to want to continue their positions. They have an incentive to oppose outside buyers who may not need them. These incentives conflict with their duties to obtain the best price and terms for the seller corporation and its shareholders.
- In many LBO acquisitions, officers of the seller corporation hold positions as administrators of pension, project sharing, 401(b), stock option, ESOP and other employee plans having interests different from those of the corporation and its shareholders and those of the buyer and its debt and equity holders.
- In management buyouts, the professional advisers also have potential conflicts of interest. For example, a law firm or investment banking firm that has long provided services to the corporation will probably be approached at an early stage in the transaction and asked for advice. The firm may then continue to advise both the corporation and the management group and rationalize that everyone is working toward the same goal. However, the interests of the corporation and the management group conflict.

For large corporations with publicly traded shares, the conflict of interest issues have been the subject of famous court decisions described in Chapter 12. Officers and directors of medium-sized and small companies may believe that such issues do not apply to them because they are not business celebrities contesting for control of giant corporations. However, the conflict of interest issues apply regardless of the size of the transaction.

Officers and directors who ignore conflicts of interest generally do so because nobody is complaining at present and they believe the transaction is a good deal for everyone involved. However, if discord develops, they will bear the burden of proving the entire fairness of the transaction, probably several years afterward. While their decisions should be judged as of the time of the transaction,[33] it is difficult to avoid hindsight. For example, if the business sold in a management buyout prospered after the acquisition, minority shareholders will be inclined to believe that the officers and directors should have obtained a higher price. The result can be an unpleasant and prolonged lawsuit.

It is not necessary for directors and officers to resign from their positions during a management buyout. Such a step could be harmful to the corporation and its business. However, the management group seeking to buy the corporation or its business should carefully refrain from participating in, or influencing, the decisions of the corporation relating to the sale. The decisions should be made by a committee of independent directors who are advised by independent legal counsel and financial advisors. The committee should obtain a "fairness opinion" from an independent valuation expert and review it carefully to satisfy themselves that the expert had all relevant information and used appropriate assumptions. The

[33]*Herskowitz v. Nutri/System, Inc.*, 857 F.2d 179 (3d Cir. 1988). The author and his firm participated in the defense of Nutri/System, Inc. and some of its officers and directors in this case.

committee should also assure that the expert has no relationships and will receive no incentive compensation that would cause the expert to favor the management buyout.

K. Reference Materials

"Accountants' Group Bans the Sending of Solvency Letters," Berton, *The Wall Street Journal*, Feb. 26, 1988.

"The Accountant's Substitute for LBO Solvency Letters," Maher et al., *Mergers & Acquisitions*, Sep–Oct 1988.

"The Eclectic Mix of Leveraged Ventures in the 1990s," Callaghan et al., *Mergers & Acquisitions*, Nov–Dec 1997

"Effects of LBOs on Tax Revenues of the U.S. Treasury," Jensen et al., *Tax Notes*, Feb. 6, 1989

"Enlisting On-Call Experts in the Buyout Process," Thorpe, *Mergers & Acquisitions*, Nov-Dec 1997.

"Historical Trends in LBOs," *Mergers & Acquisitions*, Nov–Dec 1997.

"King Henry," Laderman, *Business Week*, Nov. 14, 1988."

"Reverse LBOs—1996–1997," *Mergers & Acquisitions*, Nov–Dec 1997.

"The Right Mind-Set for Repairing a Troubled LBO," Marks, *Mergers & Acquisitions*, Nov-Dec 1997.

"The sweet sound of leverage," Upbin, *Forbes*, Nov. 20, 1995.

"The takeover game isn't dead, it's just gone private," Pouschine et al., *Forbes*, Oct. 1, 1990

"The Twin Towers of a Successful Build-Up Project," Griffith, *Mergers & Acquisitions*, Nov–Dec 1997.

"When Power Investors Call the Shots," Spragins et al., *Business Week*, June 20, 1988

Chapter 15

Employee Stock Ownership Plan (ESOP) Acquisitions

A. Introduction

1. Purposes of ESOPs

The employee stock ownership plan (ESOP) is an employee benefit plan widely used to finance acquisitions of corporations by their employees. A sponsoring corporation adopts an ESOP for the benefit of its employees and commits to make periodic contributions to a trust which it adopts to implement the ESOP. The corporation can make its contributions in stock or in cash to be used to acquire stock. The ESOP trust holds the stock for the benefit of the employees and eventually distributes the stock to them upon retirement or in other events.

Some ESOPs provide for gradual accumulations of stock that may remain a minority interest in the sponsoring corporation. However, the acquisition of stock can be expedited by arranging for the ESOP trust to borrow the price, either from the sponsoring corporation or from a lending institution. An ESOP that obtains acquisition loans is called a "leveraged ESOP."

An ESOP can also be used as part of a defensive restructuring plan by a company anticipating a possible hostile tender offer for its publicly traded shares. In a defensive restructuring, the ESOP does not finance a buyout, but rather the acquisition of a minority position sufficient to block a tender offer when combined with the effects of a state antitakeover law.

2. Advantages and Disadvantages of Leveraged ESOP Acquisitions

Major financial advantages of leveraged ESOP acquisitions include the following:

- Improved cash flows resulting from tax deductibility of the sponsoring corporation's contributions and dividends used to pay the principal and interest installments on acquisition loans.
- Favorable acquisition prices because sellers who can defer income tax by investing in qualified replacement property and may obtain other tax and nontax benefits often find that a price offered by an ESOP is more favorable than higher prices offered by other potential buyers.

- An opportunity to develop motivated owner-employees. Employee participation in the business after ESOP-financed acquisitions has varied. ESOP-acquired businesses have prospered when employees have a meaningful role in making recommendations and decisions on matters familiar to them.
- An opportunity to deal more effectively with government agencies, customers, suppliers and others. For example, an employee-owned company can present its positions on environmental issues more effectively than can large corporations owned by private individuals or public shareholders.

Some important obligations and risks of leveraged ESOP-financed transactions are as follows:

- Complex structure and high organizational and operating costs for the ESOP due to strict regulation that requires specialized financial, legal and accounting services including annual valuation of shares by an independent appraiser.
- Need to adapt to a new management and shareholder control structure.
- Cash flow obligations of the sponsoring corporation to fulfill its commitment to contribute to the ESOP amounts sufficient to make acquisition loan payments.
- Cash flow obligations of the sponsoring corporation to fulfill its commitment to repurchase shares from employees who exercise "put" options. The commitment is mandatory unless the shares are readily tradable in an established securities market.
- Leveraged capital structure with relatively small equity base unless venture capital investors are invited to contribute cash capital, for which they may seek an equity share proportionately higher than that of management investors and the ESOP.

3. A Leveraged ESOP Acquisition Diagram

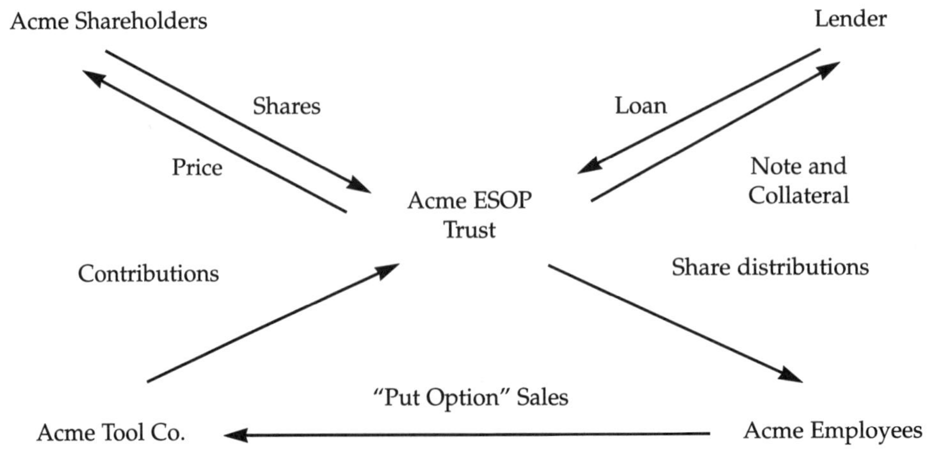

In the transaction diagram, Acme Tool Co. adopts an ESOP and signs a trust agreement, usually with the corporate trust department of a bank. The ESOP trustee agrees to buy shares of Acme from its shareholders and to borrow the price from a lending institution. The lender delivers the loan proceeds to the ESOP trustee. The ESOP trustee uses the loan proceeds to buy the shares from the Acme shareholders. The ESOP trustee delivers to the lender a promissory note and collateral including a pledge of the purchased shares and Acme's guaranty of the loan. Acme then makes periodic tax deductible cash contributions and perhaps also pays tax deductible cash dividends to the ESOP trustee which uses them to repay the lender. As the loan is paid, the pledged shares are released and allocated to employee accounts maintained by the ESOP Trustee. As the employees retire, die or leave employment, the ESOP trustee distributes the shares in their accounts to the employees, who may defer income tax by arranging for transfers of the shares to IRA accounts. If the shares are publicly traded, the employees may sell them in the market. If the shares are not readily tradable, the employees may exercise the "put" option to resell the shares to Acme.

B. Internal Revenue Code Provisions

1. Qualified Plan; Tax Exempt Trust

The ESOP is one of a group of plans entitled to special tax treatment if they qualify under Section 401 of the Internal Revenue Code (IRC or the Code). The common features of these plans are contributions by an employer to a trust that meets the requirements for tax exempt organization status under Section 501 of the Code. The contributions are credited to individual accounts maintained for each participating employee on the books of the trust. The trustee, usually a bank or trust company, invests the trust funds collectively and credits earnings and debits losses and expenses to the accounts. Upon an employee's retirement, and sometimes in other circumstances, the amount credited to the account is distributed to the employee in periodic payments, as a lump sum, or in some other form such as a purchased annuity.

An ESOP is a stock bonus plan that is qualified, or a stock bonus and a money purchase plan, both of which are qualified, under Section 401(a) of the Code, and is designed to invest primarily in qualifying employer securities.[1] Thus, an ESOP is generally subject to the same requirements and entitled to the same benefits as the plans named in its definition. For example, the following requirements apply:

- Minimum employee participation—IRC § 410(a) and (b)
- Nondiscrimination of contributions or benefits in favor of highly compensated employees—IRC § 414(g)
- Minimum vesting—IRC § 411(a)
- Restrictions on benefit cutbacks—IRC § 411(d)
- Nonassignment of benefits—IRC § 401(a)(13)

[1] IRC section 4975(e)(7).

- Operation for the exclusive benefit of the participants and their beneficiaries—IRC § 401(a)(2)
- Restrictions on "top heavy" plans—IRC § 401(l)(10)

2. Employer Contributions

Section 404 of the Code allows deductions to employers for contributions to an ESOP, subject to the following limits:

- For a stock bonus ESOP, up to 15 percent of the compensation otherwise paid or accrued to the beneficiaries.[2]
- For a stock bonus ESOP combined with one or more other defined contribution and defined benefit plans, up to 25 percent of the compensation otherwise paid or accrued to the beneficiaries, subject to various limits.[3]
- For a leveraged ESOP, up to 25 percent of compensation otherwise paid or accrued to the beneficiaries and used to pay the principal of a loan used to buy employer securities, plus an unlimited amount to pay the loan interest. [4]

The deductions are allowable whether the contributions are made in cash or stock. When the contributions are made in stock, the amount deductible is the value of the stock on the contribution date.

3. Employee Contributions

Employee contributions to an ESOP are not generally deductible, but are permissible if they do not result in prohibited discrimination and if the amounts are reasonable. Mandatory contributions up to 6 percent will be presumed not to be discriminatory. Voluntary contributions up to 10 percent are deemed reasonable.[5] If an ESOP meets the requirements of a Section 401(k) plan, employees can obtain salary deferral deductions, but the amount deductible by more highly compensated employees is restricted under antidiscrimination provisions to percentages based on the contributions of lower-paid employees.[6]

4. Employer Dividends on Stock Issued to an ESOP

In addition, Section 404(k) of the Code allows a deduction to an employer for dividends paid in cash on stock held by an ESOP if (1) the dividend is paid in cash to the participants or distributed in cash to their beneficiaries not later than 90 days after the close of the plan year in which the dividend is paid, or (2) the dividend is used to make payments on a loan incurred

---

[2]IRC section 404(a)(3).

[3]IRC section 404(a)(7).

[4]IRC section 404(a)(9).

[5]See RR 80-307, 1980-2 C.B 136 and RR 59-185, 1959-1 C.B. 86.

[6]IRC section 1.401(k)(3).

for the purpose of acquiring the qualifying employer securities on which the dividend was paid.

5. Allocation of Contributions and Income

Employee contributions are allocated directly to the account of each contributing employee on the trust records. Employer contributions are allocated to the employees' accounts, usually in the proportion that the compensation of each employee bears to the total compensation of all participating employees. The IRC specifically authorizes this method.[7] Other formulae can be used that grant credit for length of service, age and possibly other factors, but only if the formula does not discriminate in operation in favor of officers, stockholders, or highly compensated employees.

Trust income is allocated on the basis of account balances.

6. Loans

Until 1996, banks, insurance companies, corporations actively engaged in lending money and regulated investment companies were entitled to exclude from gross income an amount equal to 50 percent of the interest received with respect to a "securities acquisition loan" to an ESOP, provided that the ESOP owned more then 50 percent of each class of stock and of the value of all outstanding stock of the sponsoring corporation and other conditions prescribed in Section 133 of the Code were met. Section 133 was repealed in 1996.

Section 4975(d)(3) of the Code and IRS Reg. Section 54.4975-7 exempt loans and loan guarantees by "disqualified persons" to leveraged ESOPs from the excise taxes imposed on prohibited transactions if the loan meets several requirements. Among other things, the terms must be at least as favorable as a comparable loan between independent parties. The loan must be without recourse against the ESOP. However, it can be guaranteed by anyone, including a disqualified person, and the guarantee can be secured. The interest rate must be reasonable and can be variable. The loan must be for a specific term not exceeding 15 years and cannot be payable on demand except in the event of default. The loan proceeds must be used only to purchase qualifying employer securities or to repay the current or a previous exempt loan. Collateral can consist only of qualifying employer securities acquired with the proceeds of the loan or that were collateral for a loan repaid with the current loan.

Lenders can make loans directly to an ESOP. However, planning related to creditors' rights laws often dictates that they lend to the sponsoring corporation, which then extends a "mirror" loan to the ESOP.

7. Purchases of Employer Shares by an ESOP

An ESOP must provide that it is designed primarily to invest in qualifying employer securities that include only (1) readily tradable common stock, if

[7] IRC section 401(a)(5). However, shares held by a leveraged ESOP are regarded as unallocated so long as they are pledged as collateral for securities acquisition loans. As the loans are amortized, the shares are released for allocation free of the collateral restrictions. See subsection 8.

the employer or a member of its controlled group has common stock that is readily tradable in an established securities market; (2) nontraded common stock with the greatest combination of voting and dividend rights of any class of common stock if neither the employer nor any member of its controlled group has a readily tradable common stock; or (3) noncallable preferred stock convertible at any time into readily tradable or nontraded common stock at a reasonable conversion price.[8]

Section 401(a)(28)(C) requires that valuations of securities not readily tradable on an established securities market be performed by an independent appraiser meeting requirements of the Internal Revenue Service (IRS) regulations under IRC Section 170(a)(1).

Certain persons who sell "qualified securities" to an ESOP that owns at least 30 percent of the amount or value of the outstanding employer securities at the time of sale are entitled to a tax-free "rollover" of the purchase price, provided that they have held the securities for at least 3 years. Gain will not be recognized if the seller purchases qualified replacement property with a specified time period. "Qualified replacement property" means any security issued by a domestic operating corporation that does not have passive investment income for the tax year in which the security was issued exceeding 25 percent of its gross receipts.[9] To obtain nonrecognition, the seller must file with the IRS an election and a written statement from the employer sponsor of the ESOP consenting to the imposition of an excise tax under IRC Sections 4978 and 4979A if the securities are disposed of within 3 years.

8. Allocation of Shares

When the employer contributes shares of stock or the ESOP purchases and pays in full for shares, they are allocated by the same methods as are used to allocate employer contributions.[10] When a leveraged ESOP purchases shares with an exempt loan, the shares are held in a suspense account and are allocated to the participants' accounts as the loan is paid. This practice must be followed even if the lender has not required a pledge of the shares as collateral.[11] Either of two methods, a fractional method or a principal only method, can be used in determining the shares released for allocation when loan payments are made.[12]

9. Voting of Stock

An ESOP must pass through to its participants all voting rights of stock allocated to their accounts.[13] Any convertible preferred stock issued to the ESOP must have voting rights equivalent to those of the stock into which it is convertible. However, if the employer's stock is closely held and the ESOP lender does not use the interest exclusion provided by IRC Section

[8]IRC section 4975(e)(7) and 409(1).

[9]IRC section 1042 and 1362(d)(3)(D).

[10]IRS Reg. section 54.4975-11(d)(1).

[11]IRS Reg. section 54.4975(c).

[12]IRS Reg. sections 54.4975-7(b)(8) and 54.4971-11.

[13]IRC sections 409(c) and (1), 401(a)(22), and 4975(c)(7).

133, the vote pass-through is required only with respect to the approval of any corporate merger or consolidation, recapitalization, liquidation, reclassification, or sale of substantially all assets.

The IRC and ERISA do not prescribe methods for voting unallocated shares held in a suspense account pending full payment. When a leveraged ESOP first completes an acquisition, the number of shares held in suspense is usually large. The ESOP is not required to pass on the right to vote these suspense account shares to the participants except when a one-person, one-vote method is used.[14] Although the trustee could vote the shares, voting by a committee appointed by the employer has been common. To ease compliance with the fiduciary requirements of ERISA, the ESOP may require that shares held in suspense be voted in proportion to the votes of shares held by the participants. Voting rights can have a bearing on employee motivation.[15]

10. Distributions

Distributions may be made in stock or in cash. However, an ESOP must provide a right for participants to demand stock.

When stock is distributed, the ESOP must provide a "put" option in favor of the participant to require that the employer (not the ESOP) repurchase the stock at fair value unless the stock is readily tradable on an established securities market.[16] The employer or the ESOP, or both, can impose a 14-day right of first refusal to purchase stock from the participant if the stock was acquired with the proceeds of an exempt loan and is not publicly traded.[17]

With some exceptions, participants receiving distributions from an ESOP are taxed under Section 401 of the Code in a manner similar to participants who receive distributions from other qualified plans. Of special interest, however, is that a participant who receives a lump-sum distribution of stock need not include in income any unrealized appreciation.[18] If distributed by periodic payments or some other method, the participant need not include in income any net unrealized appreciation attributable to employee contributions.[19]

Dividends on qualifying employer securities held by an ESOP trust may be distributed at any time.[20]

Participants entitled to receive "qualifying rollover distributions" from an ESOP may exclude them from income if they are transferred in a timely and proper manner to an individual retirement account (IRA) or certain other eligible retirement plans.[21] "Qualified total distributions" include

---

[14]IRC section 409(e).

[15]See "How Dan River's ESOP Missed the Boat," *Industry Week*, Oct. 26, 1987.

[16]IRC sections 409(h), 4975(e)(7), and 401(a)(23). An independent appraiser is required by IRC section 401(a)(28)(C) to value securities not readily tradable on an established securities market.

[17]IRS Reg. section 54.4975-7(b)(9).

[18]IRC section 402(d)(4)(j).

[19]IRC section 402(a)(1).

[20]IRS Reg. section 54.4975-11(f).

[21]IRC section 402(a)(5).

lump-sum distributions and certain partial distributions that are not periodic payments.

11. Conversion of Other Plans

ESOPs can be created by converting other qualified defined contribution benefit plans.[22] The 20 percent excise tax imposed by Section 4980 of the Code on reversions of assets from such plans does not apply if the assets are transferred to an ESOP, provided that the ESOP meets requirements prescribed in Section 4980.

C. ERISA PROVISIONS

1. Obligations of Fiduciaries

ESOPs are subject to those provisions of the Employee Retirement Income Security Act (ERISA) applicable to defined contribution (individual account) plans. For example, ERISA imposes extensive obligations on persons within the definition of a "fiduciary" in ERISA Section 3(21). The definition includes not only the person designated as the "named fiduciary" in the ESOP pursuant to ERISA Section 405(c), but also those who have or exercise certain discretionary or investment advisory functions with respect to the plan. ERISA Section 404 requires that a fiduciary act solely in the interests of the participants and for the exclusive purpose of providing benefits to them and defraying reasonable expenses of administering the plan. ERISA Section 409 imposes liability for breach of fiduciary duty. ERISA Section 410 declares void any exculpatory provisions in plan documents but permits the purchase of insurance to cover such liability and other risks.

Because an ESOP is an eligible individual account plan as defined in ERISA Section 407(d)(3), its fiduciaries are not subject to the 10 percent limitation on the acquisition and holding of qualifying employer securities.[23] While an ESOP must comply with the diversification requirements of IRC Section 401(a)(28), its fiduciaries do not violate the diversification and prudence requirements of ERISA Section 404(a)(1) solely because of the acquisition or retention of qualifying employer securities.[24]

An ESOP can also purchase employer stock that pays no dividend or only a small dividend.[25]

2. Prohibited Transactions

ERISA Section 406 prohibits certain transactions between a plan and a "party in interest," a term that as defined in ERISA Section 3(14) includes any fiduciary, counsel, or employee of the ESOP; any person providing services to the ESOP; and the employer, any employee organization whose members

[22]IRS Reg. section 4975-11(a)(6).

[23]ERISA section 407(b)(1); 29 U.S.C. § 1107(b)(1).

[24]ERISA section 404(a)(2); 29 U.S.C. § 1104(a)(2). For information on the diversification requirements of IRC section 401(a)(28), see IRS Notice 88-56, 1988-1 C.B. 540

[25]IRC Rev. Ruling 69-65, 1969-1, C.B. 114.

are covered by the ESOP, and certain categories of persons related to them, including officers, directors and 10-percent shareholders of the employer.

3. Exemptions

ERISA Section 408(e) provides an exemption from ERISA Sections 406 and 407 for sales and exchanges of employer securities between parties in interest and individual account plans, including ESOPs, if (1) the security is a qualifying employer security, (2) no more than adequate consideration is paid and (3) no commission is charged with respect to the acquisition or sale. For this purpose, a "qualifying employer security" means a security acquired from the employer or a member of its controlled group that is stock or obligations meeting certain tests.[26] This same definition was used in IRC Section 4975(e)(8) prior to the Technical Corrections Act of 1979.

ERISA Section 408(b)(3) provides an exemption from Section 406 for loans by a party in interest to an ESOP. The exemption applies to the party in interest in that capacity and also in any fiduciary capacity.[27]

4. Court Decisions

Leading court decisions interpreting the obligations of ESOP fiduciaries include *Eaves v. Penn*, 587 F.2d 453 (10th Cir. 1977), *Donovan v. Cunningham*, 716 F.2d 1455 (5th Cir. 1983) and *Eyler v. Commissioner*, 69 TCM (CCH) 1995-123 (1995). See also the letter dated February 23, 1989 from the U.S. Department of Labor relating to the Polaroid Corporation ESOP.

D. Accounting Aspects

Part of the essential planning for an ESOP is the appropriate accounting treatment under generally accepted accounting principles (GAAP).

A basic document applying GAAP to ESOPs is AICPA Statement of Position (SOP) 76-3. SOP 76-3 established such basic principles as a requirement that ESOP debt be reflected as a liability in the balance sheet of the sponsoring corporation if it guaranteed the ESOP loan obligations or to make contributions to the ESOP in amounts sufficient to pay such obligations. The AICPA made important revisions to SOP 76-3 when it adopted SOP 93-6 applicable to ESOPs newly established after January 1, 1993. Accounting Series Release (ASR) No. 268, July 27, 1979, of the Securities and Exchange Commission required special treatment in the sponsoring corporation's balance sheet of shares subject to repurchase upon exercise of "put" options.

During 1989, the Emerging Issues Task Force (EITF) of the Financial Accounting Standards Board (FASB) provided guidance on several issues. For example, EITF Issue 89-8 provided guidance on expense recognition. EITF Issue 89-11 provided further guidance on balance sheet treatment of shares

[26]ERISA section 407(c)(1); 29 U.S.C. § 1107(c)(1).

[27]See ERISA Reg. section 2550.408b-3 on loans to ESOPs and the comparable IRC Reg. section 54.4975-7.

subject to "put" options. EITF Issue 89-12 provided guidance on several issues relating to the issuance of convertible preferred stock to an ESOP.

In 1989, the Securities and Exchange commission announced disclosures that should be made concerning ESOPs adopted by sponsoring corporations with shares registered under the Securities Exchange Act of 1934. They include: (1) a plan description, (2) the amount of cost for the fiscal period, (3) the method of expense recognition, (4) interest incurred on the ESOP debt during the fiscal period, (5) the cash contributed to the ESOP trust and (6) the amount of any dividends paid on unallocated shares used to pay debt of the ESOP trust. The management's discussion and analysis (MD&A) requirements of Regulation S-K, Item 303 require disclosure of the potential effect of obligations of and to leveraged ESOPs on results of operations and liquidity. The MD&A requirements would call for discussion, among other things, of any share repurchase obligations.

After considering different concepts for several years, the FASB adopted SFAS 109 in 1992 stating that the income tax benefits resulting from the deductibility of dividends paid on unallocated shares held by an ESOP trust should be recorded as a credit to retained earnings. The tax benefits with respect to dividends paid on unallocated shares held by an ESOP trust should be recorded as a credit to retained earnings. The tax benefits with respect to dividends paid on allocated shares should be recorded as a reduction of current income tax expense. Under EITF Issue 92-3, the tax benefits related to unallocated common shares cannot be used as the basis for an adjustment to earnings available to common stock.

E. Valuation of Equity Securities in Esop Transactions

1. Transactions Requiring Valuation

ESOPs engage in several kinds of transactions that require valuation:

- Contribution of shares by a corporation to an ESOP followed by an income tax deduction of their value.
- Purchase of shares by an ESOP from the sponsoring corporation or any of its shareholders who are "parties in interest."
- Repurchase of shares from employees by the corporation of the ESOP upon exercise of a "put" option or by other arrangements.
- Allocation of equity prior to a leveraged buyout among a multi-investor group including an ESOP, management and outside investors such as lenders receiving equity participation.

The least complex of these situations is the contribution of shares to an ESOP. The corporation must support its deduction of their fair market value. The financial analyst will follow the principles outlined in Revenue Rulings 59-60, 65-192, 65-193, 77-287 and 80-213.[28] Common issues include

[28]1959-1 CB 237, 1965-2 CB 27, 1965-2 237, 1977-2 CB 319, and 1980-2 CB 101.

determination of an appropriate discount for lack of marketability, minority status and limited voting rights.[29]

More requirements apply to a purchase of shares by an ESOP from the sponsoring corporation or another party in interest, which includes a director, officer, or 10-percent shareholder of the sponsoring corporation and others.[30]

2. Adequate Consideration

ERISA permits an ESOP to acquire qualifying employer securities from a party in interest for "adequate consideration."[31] The term "adequate consideration" means the price of the security on a national securities exchange or, if it is not so traded, the offering price for the security established by current bid and asked prices quoted by persons independent of the issuer and any party in interest; or in the case of an asset other than a security for which there is a generally recognized market, the fair market value of the asset as determined in good faith by the trustee or named fiduciary pursuant to the terms of the ESOP and the regulations promulgated by the Department of Labor (DOL).[32]

On May 17, 1988, the DOL published a notice of proposed rulemaking describing a proposed new ERISA regulation—Section 2510.3-18 defining "adequate consideration." The DOL withdrew the proposed rulemaking without official comment on May 8, 1995.[33]

3. Valuation Methods

The IRC requires that ESOPs obtain appraisals by an independent appraiser of employer securities that are not publicly traded.[34]

An appraisal for an ESOP need not (and should not) be inconsistent with skillfully prepared valuations using modern valuation methods. It is not necessary to follow Revenue Ruling 59-60 "jot and tittle." However, the appraiser's report should consider the criteria in Revenue Ruling 59-60 in a format that will permit the DOL, a court and others to verify that they support the range of values determined. For example, nothing in ERISA or Revenue Ruling 59-60 requires that a control premium be applied when it is not justified, but it is best to demonstrate that conclusion in the report.[35]

In valuing shares for ESOP transactions, several factors require special attention:

---

[29] *Hooker Industries v Commissioner*, 44 TCM (CCH) 259 (1982); *Las Vegas Dodge, Inc. v. United States*, 85-2 USTC, 9546 (1985).

[30] ERISA 3(14).

[31] ERISA 408(e); 29 U.S.C. § 1108(e).

[32] ERISA 3(18)(B); 29 U.S.C. § 1002(18).

[33] 53 Fed. Reg. 17632, 5/17/88; 60 Fed. Reg. 23559, 5/8/95.

[34] IRC 401(a)(28); see also IRC 170(a)(1). Neither the IRC nor ERISA require that ESOP fiduciaries be independent, although valuations and other actions approved by non-independent fiduciaries are subject to special scrutiny. *Donovan v. Bierwirth*, 680 F.2d 263 (2d Cir. 1982), cert. den. 459 U.S. 1069 (1982).

[35] *Foltz v. News & World Report, Inc.*, 865 F.2d 364 (D.C. Cir. 1989); *Sommers Drug Stores Co. v. Corrigan Enterprises Inc.* 793 F.2d 1456 (5th Cir. 1986).

- Effects of ESOP obligations on the corporation because of periodic cash contributions required to meet principal and interest requirements of the loan used to make a leveraged acquisition.[36]
- Discount for lack of marketability as affected by "put" rights and ability of the corporation to meet them as they mature in light of other demands on cash flow.[37]
- Control premium as affected by enforceable rights to obtain and maintain control.[38]
- Discount for minority status if the ESOP will be a minority shareholder.[39]
- Dilution resulting from the issuance of additional shares.[40]
- Possible special knowledge of ESOP fiduciaries about the business being valued.[41]

A well-written illustration by Christopher Bower and Jay Abrams showing use of the discounted cash flow method to value shares for ESOP transactions is provided in Chapter 8 of *Employee Stock Ownership Plans.*[42] The chapter explains each valuation component including the methods used to determine a discount rate and residual value. In valuation reports, such explanation is important because, although the courts accept discounted cash flow valuation as a generally accepted valuation method, they have difficulty weighing complex valuations based on that method.[43]

4. Allocation of Equity Ownership

A difficult and sometimes controversial financial structuring task arises when an ESOP participates in a leveraged buyout of a business with other investors. A typical multi-investor group includes the proposed management, venture capital funds or individual investors and senior and mezzanine lenders receiving options, convertible securities or other rights to buy shares. Equity investors providing up-front cash commonly believe that their risk should entitle them to a more generous percentage allocation of equity than other investors, such as the ESOP.

On the other hand, the DOL has contended that an ESOP may not receive adequate consideration if its nonrecourse note is denied recognition

---

[36]*Donovan v. Cunningham*, 716 F.2d 1455 (5th Cir. 1983); *Eaves v. Penn*, 587 F.2d 453 (10th Cir. 1978); *Eyler v. Commissioner*, supra.

[37]Formerly Proposed ERISA Regulation 2510-3-18(b)(4)(H); *Eyler v. Commissioner*, supra.

[38]Formerly proposed ERISA Regulation 2510.3-18(b)(4)1); but see *Foltz v. U.S. News & World Report, Inc.*, supra. See also *Reich v. Valley National Bank*, 837 F. Supp. 1289(S.D.N.Y. 1993).

[39]*Donovan v. Cunningham*, supra note 9.

[40]*Hooker Industries v. Commissioner*, supra note 2.

[41]DOL Notice of Proposed Rulemaking, supra note 1; but see *Foltz. v. U.S. News & World Report Inc.*, supra note 8.

[42]*Employee Stock Ownership Plans*, Robert W. Smiley, Jr. and Ronald J. Gilbert, (Prentice Hall, 1989).

[43]*Weinberger v. UOP Inc.*, 426 A.2d 1333 (Del. Ch. 1983) reversed 457 A.2d 701 (Del. 1983); *Kahn v. United States Sugar Co.*, 11 Del. J. Corp. L. 908 (1985).

at face value in the allocation of equity among a multi-investor group planning a leveraged buyout financed by an ESOP.

In 1985, the DOL issued a preliminary interpretation that Citizens & Southern National Bank, the trustee of the Scott and Fetzer Company ESOP, would breach its fiduciary duty if it participated in a leveraged buyout in which 29 percent of the equity was allocated to management and Kelso & Co. for an investment described as $9 million while the ESOP was to receive 41 percent for its $182 million nonrecourse note. The preliminary interpretation, based on dilution reflecting full exercise of options and warranties, effectively blocked the leveraged buyout of Scott and Fetzer Company. Since then, the ruling has been a deterrent to the use of an ESOP in multi-investor leveraged buyouts.

The deterrence was reinforced when the U.S. Department of Labor filed a lawsuit in 1989 against Valley National Bank, the Trustee of the Kroy Inc. ESOP. Among other things, the Department of Labor alleged that the Trustee failed to make an adequate investigation of the transaction; relied on a valuation which it should have known was deficient; acquired the shares of Kroy for the ESOP at a price that was more than fair market value; and consented to an allocation of Kroy shares between the ESOP and other investors which was not substantially fair to the ESOP in light of the equity contributions made by the ESOP and the other investors. See *Reich v. Valley National Bank*, 837 F. Supp. 1259 (S.D.N.Y. 1993). The lawsuit was reportedly settled for $20,000,000.

Among the various viewpoints argued, the DOL points to the important tax and cash flow benefits resulting from an ESOP and to the congressional policy to increase employee stock ownership. Investment bankers and other financial planners respond that the nonrecourse note issued by an ESOP usually contains terms that the market can justifiably value at a considerable discount. In addition, use of the ESOP creates preferential demands on corporate cash flow to pay the nonrecourse note and honor "put" option rights of employees. They also observe that multi-investor groups enable ESOPs to participate in buying potentially successful, higher-priced businesses rather than the "turnaround" situations that were often sold to ESOPs in the early years of their use. Thus, they urge that the DOL allow allocation issues to be determined by market forces rather than by regulation requiring that value be recognized when it may not exist.

Issuance to the ESOP of a specially designed class of preferred stock can help to provide an answer to the allocation issues. The preferred stock is typically entitled to an attractive and firmly committed dividend. The preferred stock is also entitled to a liquidation preference that provides some protection for the worker beneficiaries of the ESOP. The preferred stock is also convertible, a feature that will presumably not be exercised unless and until a pattern of success is well established.

The attractive features of the convertible preferred stock issued to the ESOP provide support for its valuation at a level higher than could be justified for the number of shares of common stock into which the preferred stock is convertible. The deductibility of the dividend payments makes the preferred stock attractive to the corporation.

Chapter 16

ACQUISITION CONTRACTS

A. INTRODUCTION

Acquisitions and divestitures are complex transactions. Not surprisingly, therefore, contracts for acquisitions and divestitures are lengthy and detailed. An acquisition contract must cover every significant business, financial, technical and legal aspect of the transaction. If it does not, there will be risk of disputes and of harm to the seller and the buyer and also to others such as customers, suppliers and employees.

Business managers and professionals know that some contracts are based on standard forms. Standard form contracts can be useful and adequate for simple transactions that are performed repeatedly in essentially the same manner. However, acquisitions and divestitures are too complex for standard contracts. For example, acquisition contracts may provide for such diverse subjects as government approvals, arrangements to finance the purchase price, hiring of managers and employees, reporting of the acquisition for accounting and tax purposes, and registration and listing of securities. Thus, acquisition contracts must be custom-designed to identify the significant aspects of the transaction and to state clearly and fully the agreement negotiated for each of them.

Lawyers drafting an acquisition contract should have a full, clear and practical understanding of all aspects of the acquisition. If the lawyers have limited information or do not understand the transaction, their clients may suffer business, financial and opportunity losses ranging from small amounts to many millions of dollars.

Some business executives assume that lawyers do not understand the intricacies of business, finance or technology. That assumption may be true for lawyers having limited experience in the acquisition and divestiture field. However, lawyers experienced in acquisition and divestiture transactions learn very rapidly, even when the business, financial and technical aspects are quite difficult. The lawyers combine their experience with the newly gained knowledge to provide practical advice to their clients. It is not unusual for senior lawyers to make recommendations of considerable value, not only on legal points but on business, financial and technical points, based on their experience in prior transactions.

When the seller, the buyer or both are enthusiastic about the transaction, they may propose an unrealistic time schedule for preparation of an acquisition contract. Acquisition contracts are customarily and properly prepared over a time period of a few weeks. The contract preparation begins with a preliminary, nonbinding letter of intent summarizing the mutual understanding on selected major issues. The contract preparation then continues as seller and buyer conduct due diligence reviews during which they identify numerous issues and negotiate agreements on the issues that are included in the acquisition contract.

An acquisition contract is customarily prepared as an integrated document. Indeed, an acquisition contract usually contains a provision stating that it includes all of the terms and conditions of the transaction and supersedes any other written or verbal agreements. An integrated acquisition contract reassures both seller and buyer that they will not face claims contending that bits and pieces from the multiplicity of communications during the negotiations should be treated as binding commitments. However, it is also a reason to prepare the acquisition contract carefully because the seller and the buyer will not be free to claim that there were commitments in addition to, or different from, those stated in the acquisition contract.

Although acquisition contracts are necessarily lengthy and detailed, lawyers skilled in the field prepare contracts that are remarkably well-organized and concise. Well-organized and well-written acquisition contracts cover numerous business, financial, technical and legal subjects, each written in concise, straightforward language that is easily read and understood. Lawyers who prepare acquisition contracts in this manner provide valuable service to their clients by enabling them to move forward confidently without needless misunderstandings and disputes.

B. Confidentiality Agreements

The first agreement between a seller and buyer is usually a confidentiality agreement for the protection of the seller's trade secret information furnished for evaluation by the potential buyer.

Throughout the United States, state laws protect trade secret information.[1] Trade secret information need not have the degree of novelty required to obtain a patent. However, trade secret information must be confidential and proprietary. Trade secret information can consist of any useful improvement and is not limited to technical information. For example, customer lists and business opportunities are classic examples of trade secret information.[2] However, information that is in the public domain is not a trade secret because it is not confidential and proprietary.

The protection afforded to trade secrets does not provide a monopoly such as that provided for patents by the Patent Law. Patents can be enforced even against innocent persons who make, use or sell the invention without knowledge of the existence of a patent. Trade secrets can be enforced only against persons who steal or misappropriate them. Thus, they must be disclosed only to persons having fiduciary or contractual obligations to maintain their confidential and proprietary nature. Trade secrets become unenforceable if they cease to be confidential and proprietary because of unrestricted disclosure. That is the reason why it is important for a seller to require a potential buyer to sign a confidentiality agreement.

[1] *Kewanee Oil v. Bicron Corporation*, 416 U.S. 470 (1974).

[2] *Town & Country House & Home Service, Inc. v. Newbury*, 3 N.Y.2d (1958).

A potential buyer who is asked to sign a confidentiality agreement should review it carefully. The agreement should not require the buyer to concede that all information furnished by the seller is confidential and proprietary because much of the information will be routine information that has neither characteristic. The buyer will wish to reserve several exceptions to its obligations for: (1) information that is not confidential and proprietary; (2) information already known by the potential buyer when received from the seller; (3) information in the public domain when it is received from the seller; (4) information entering the public domain after it is received from the seller, but through no fault of the potential buyer; (5) information obtained by the potential buyer from a third party not having nondisclosure obligations to the seller; and perhaps also (6) information independently developed by the potential buyer through the efforts of personnel who did not have access to seller's information

The burden of proof of exceptions 2 through 6 should be upon the potential buyer. The potential buyer should also be required to be responsible for the conduct of the employees directors, professionals, consultants and agents to whom it furnishes the information. Many confidentiality agreements also require that a potential buyer identify each person to whom any of seller's information will be furnished and that each person sign a similar confidentiality commitment. It is also common to require that the potential buyer return all copies of documents received from the seller if the transaction does not go forward.

Many potential buyers request a termination date in a confidentiality agreement. Such a request creates a problem because the seller's trade secrets should not lose their proprietary status and be used or disclosed by the potential buyer because a time period passes.[3] On the other hand, potential buyers do not want to maintain old confidentiality agreements with responsibilities lingering for many years. Most sellers and potential buyers compromise by agreeing to a termination date that has sufficient duration to protect the trade secrets, but is not excessive. If a compromise is necessary, the author recommends a period of 5 to 10 years, depending on the extent and nature of the trade secrets protected.

A form of a confidentiality agreement appears as Exhibit 16-1.

C. Letters of Intent

1. Reasons for Using Letters of Intent

In the early stages of acquisition discussions, the seller and the buyer want to determine as soon as possible whether the time-consuming and costly efforts required to investigate, evaluate and negotiate an acquisition contract have a meaningful chance of success. They focus on the price and other issues that are readily identifiable as important to determine whether they are "on the same wavelength" or "in the same ballpark." They also want to know whether the other party is serious as an organization and willing to devote resources to the transaction.

[3]The effect would be similar to the operation of an escheat statute.

A letter of intent is a useful mechanism to provide the comfort needed to justify further time and effort and to serve as a convenient checklist to guide the work. The letter summarizes in brief business and financial language the major terms and conditions identified at the time of its preparation. The letter should state that it is not legally binding, except for any expense reimbursement or confidentiality provisions that may be included, and that no binding obligations will arise until a formal written acquisition contract is negotiated, signed and approved by proper corporate procedures. Both the seller and the buyer know that the letter of intent is not enforceable, but they welcome the confirmation that they are thinking along the same lines. They also know that corporate officers will rarely sign a letter of intent without review by counsel and at least informal discussions with key persons whose approval will later be requested, such as a chief executive officer and board members.

A letter of intent also has other practical uses. Since it is recognized as a serious, although nonbinding, document, it can be used to support the filing of a notification and report with the Federal Trade Commission and the U.S. Department of Justice under the Hart-Scott-Rodino Federal Trade Commission Improvements Act. A letter of intent can usually also be used to request a review by other government agencies and by lenders and investors who would be reluctant to devote time and resources based on verbal discussions. A letter of intent can also be used as a basis for the fulfillment of disclosure obligations under the securities regulation laws.

2. Legal Concerns about Letters of Intent and Other Preliminary Communications

During over 30 years of acquisition experience, the author has never met a business owner, manager or lawyer who seriously thought that a business could or should be sold by a letter of intent, preliminary agreement or exchange of correspondence. However, sore losers often sue when they are unable to close a deal. Thus, corporate representatives negotiating acquisitions and divestitures should be careful about the wording of letters of intent, preliminary agreements, correspondence and even press releases.

However unrealistic, the courts have sometimes held that a binding contract for the sale of even a large, complex business can be made by brief written agreements and even by an exchange of correspondence if their language and other circumstances show an intention to make a binding agreement.[4] The courts will consider (1) the language of the agreement, (2) the context of the negotiations, (3) the existence of open terms, (4) partial performance, and (5) the necessity of putting the agreement in final form.[5] Since few judges have significant business experience, the language factor is usually the most important.[6]

---

[4]For example, a binding agreement to sell a business was found in an exchange of letters in *V'-Soske v. Barwick*, 404 F.2d 495 (2nd Cir. 1968). The Court perceived the function of the acquisition contract that was never completed as merely memorializing the agreement made by the letters.

[5]*Teachers Insurance v. Tribune Co.*, 670 F.Supp. 491 (S.D.N.Y., 1987).

[6]*Arcadian Phosphates, Inc. v. Arcadian Corp.*, 884 F.2d 69 (2d Cir. 1989).

For years, corporate lawyers have advised sellers and buyers to include language in letters of intent, preliminary agreements, correspondence and press releases that clearly indicates there is no intent to make a binding contract. The challenge is to find language that the courts will recognize as effective, notwithstanding arguments by plaintiff attorneys that judges should reinterpret or nullify the language.

Sellers and buyers commonly use several provisions to state that they do not intend to make a binding contract. They state expressly that the letter of intent, preliminary agreement or other communication is not a binding contract. They state that any subsequent binding contract is subject to the negotiation and execution of a formal written acquisition contract. They also state that any subsequent contract must be approved by their board of directors and, if necessary, by their shareholders.

Many court decisions have held that such provisions are sufficient to clarify that a letter of intent or preliminary agreement was not binding and enforceable.[7] However, some courts have found that such provisions do not necessarily prevent a preliminary agreement from being binding and enforceable.[8]

Plaintiff attorneys have argued that the letter of intent or preliminary agreement was the real agreement and that any subsequent acquisition contract was a mere formality to itemize "details" of the transactions.[9] They have also argued that the letter of intent or preliminary agreement bound the seller and buyer to negotiate in good faith to reach an acquisition contract.[10] They have also argued that partial performance by one party accepted by the other party is evidence that a binding contract was intended.[11]

The uncertainty created by the court decisions forewarns sellers and buyers to take precautions in drafting a letter of intent. The following suggestions will be helpful in avoiding a premature acquisition contract:

1. Use a letter of intent rather than a preliminary agreement because the former is less likely to be mistaken for an acquisition contract.
2. State the acquisition terms in the letter of intent in summary outline style. Do not include numerous, lengthy and detailed provisions that could be mistaken for an acquisition contract.

---

[7]For example, see *Empro Manufacturing Co. v. Ball-Co Manufacturing*, Inc., 870 F.2d 423 (7th Cir. 1989); *Budget Marketing v. Centronics*, 927 F.2d 421 (8th Cir. 1991); *Reprosystem, B.V. v. SCM Corp.*, 727 F.2d 257 (2d Cir. 1984); *Doll v. Grand Union*, 925 F.2d 1363 (11th Cir. 1991); *Anderson Chemical v. Portals Water Treatment*, 768 F. Supp. 1568 (M.D. Ga. 1991).

[8]For example, see *Arnold Palmer Golf Co. v. Fuqua Industries*, 541 F.2d 584 (6th Cir. 1976); *Texaco, Inc. v. Pennzoil Co.*, 729 S.W.2d 768 (Tex. App. 1987); cert. den. 485 U.S. 994 (1988); and *Shann v. Dunk*, 84 F.3d 73 (2d Cir. 1996).

[9]Anyone who has participated in the long days of hard bargaining required to prepare acquisition contracts and experienced the death or near-death of transactions as issues are identified and negotiated through the final hours before execution knows that such an argument is far from reality. However, the argument was successful in *Arnold Palmer Golf Co. v. Fuqua Industries*, supra, *Texaco, Inc. v. Pennzoil Co.*, supra.; and *Shann v. Dunk*, supra.

[10]*Itek Corp. v. Chicago Aerial Indus.*, 248 A.2d 625 (Del. 1968) applying Illinois law; *Teachers Inc. and Annuity Assoc. of America v. Tribune Co.*, 670 F.Supp 491 (SDNY 1987).

[11]*R. G. Group, Inc. v. Horn & Hardart Co.*, 751 F.2d 69 (2d Cir. 1984).

3. Avoid any statements indicating that the letter of intent covers the "important" terms of the deal or that the remaining terms will be "details" or will consist of "standard" terms. **Note:** When a letter of intent is signed, the seller and buyer have seldom identified, much less agreed on, many of the important issues because they have not completed the due diligence work.
4. State plainly in the letter of intent that it is not a binding contract, except for those few provisions, if any, intended to be binding.
5. State plainly in the letter of intent that no binding contract will exist unless and until the seller and the buyer agree on all terms and conditions and all such terms and conditions are expressed in a definitive acquisition contract signed by seller and buyer.
6. State plainly that each party is free to negotiate in its own best interests and to withdraw from the negotiations at any time before the definitive acquisition contract is signed by both the seller and the buyer.
7. State plainly in correspondence that any proposal or counterproposal is not a binding commitment and no binding commitment will exist until a definitive agreement is negotiated and signed.
8. Draft press releases carefully to avoid any implication that an agreement exists.
9. Avoid the words *offer* and *accept,* which the courts tend to associate with the formation of a contract.
10. Do not rely only on a statement that the letter of intent is "subject to" a definitive agreement or to approval by the board of directors. Some courts have said that these words are only a condition subsequent and are insufficient alone to show that a binding contract was not intended.
11. Do not allow the other party to commence performance, unless there is no other alternative and the arrangements are made under carefully drafted agreements.

An example of a letter of intent appears as Exhibit 16-2.

D. Option Agreements, Rights of First Refusal and Standstill Agreements

1. Option Agreements

Option agreements are occasionally, but not frequently, used in acquisition and divestiture transactions. Both corporations and shareholders are understandably reluctant to grant an option, which is a one-sided commitment, to acquire or divest a business because the transaction is too important to be left uncertain for one party.

One example of the use of options is in agreements among the shareholders of privately owned corporations in order to maintain continuity of ownership and management. A shareholders' agreement often provides that, upon the death, disability or termination of employment of a shareholder, the corporation or the other shareholders will have an option to buy his or her shares. The price is usually determined either by a formula or by an appraisal performed by one or more valuation professionals.

For another example, a buyer seeking to acquire the shares of a corporation owned by a diverse group of shareholders may pay one or more shareholders for an option to purchase their shares in order to gain a foothold to use in bargaining with the remaining shareholders.

In takeover contests during the 1980s, "lockup" options and "crown jewel" options were used with some frequency because they were fairly effective in opposing time sensitive hostile leveraged takeovers. However, lockup and crown jewel options were often challenged in court as breaches of management's fiduciary duties and were enjoined in some cases. When the takeover wars using leveraged financing subsided, the motivations for lockup and crown jewel options declined because neither is likely to be a "show stopper" for the well-planned, well-financed tender offers made in the 1990s.

To make a purchase option enforceable, the option agreement should describe each step necessary for its exercise and for the purchase of the security or other property subject to the option. The reason is that optionholders typically exercise when conditions favor them and disfavor the person who granted the option. Thus, the person who granted the option may seek to avoid the sale if steps to accomplish the sale are not clearly stated.[12]

2. Rights of First Refusal

Rights of first refusal are used most commonly in agreements among the shareholders of privately owned corporations in order to maintain continuity of ownership and management. They are also sometimes used for the same purposes by joint or common owners of commercial or industrial property.

A right of first refusal is a more flexible arrangement than a sale commitment or an option. In a typical arrangement, a shareholder agrees only to offer his or her shares for sale to the corporation or the other shareholders if the shareholder proposes to sell the shares to an outsider. The corporation or other shareholders are usually entitled to exercise the right of first refusal only if they are willing to match the price and terms offered by the outsider. Thus, a right of first refusal may not be triggered for many years, if ever. Further, even if triggered, the right might not be exercised.

A make a right of first refusal enforceable, the agreement should describe each step necessary for its exercise and for the purchase of the shares (or property) subject to the right of first refusal.

3. Standstill Agreements

A standstill agreement is an agreement to refrain from taking steps toward an acquisition such as a purchase of shares in the market or purchases privately negotiated with shareholders.

---

[12]Persons familiar with options traded in securities markets may believe that options can be stated in brief and simple terms. However, market-traded options are backed by regulations and customs that are not available for privately negotiated options.

Standstill provisions are usually included as part of a settlement of a proxy contest or hostile tender offer. For example, the agreement describes terms of the settlement, such as board membership for an insurgent shareholder, and prohibits further purchases of shares by the insurgent shareholder for a period such as five years.

Standstill provisions are sometimes included in confidentiality agreements made in contemplation of a due diligence review by one or more potential buyers. The provisions prohibit the potential buyers from "jumping the gun" by purchasing shares based on favorable information obtained during the due diligence review rather than waiting to negotiate a fair overall acquisition price.[13]

E. Provisions Common to Acquisition Contracts

1. Basic Contract Structures

Acquisition contracts can be classified according to the three basic acquisition structures: stock purchase, assets purchase and merger. They can also be classified by other characteristics: (1) the consideration paid, i.e., cash, debt or stock; (2) the tax treatment, i.e., a taxable transaction or a tax free reorganization; (3) the accounting treatment, i.e., a purchase or a pooling of interests; or (4) the methods used to accomplish the acquisition, i.e., a tender offer or a leveraged buyout.

In general, acquisition contracts are drafted as stock purchase agreements, asset purchase agreements and merger agreements. Other characteristics are then included in the structure selected. For example, an assets purchase for cash and debt may be titled "Installment Purchase of Assets Agreement." A tax free reorganization accomplished by a statutory merger pursuant to Section 368(a)(1)(A) of the Internal Revenue Code may be titled "Merger Agreement and Plan of Reorganization."

Despite these numerous structural and other differences, a number of important provisions are common to all properly drafted acquisition contracts. The provisions include the parties; recitals of the background and objectives; definitions of important terms; statements of the transaction including the price; representations and warranties; covenants, both affirmative and negative; conditions to the obligations of the parties; closing procedures, documents and payments; indemnities; default and termination provisions; general provisions; signatures; and exhibits and schedules.

From contract to contract, the subjects may be presented in a different order under different titles. For example, some lawyers prefer to place definitions near the end of an agreement or to define terms throughout the contract rather than in a separate article. Some lawyers include closing procedures, documents and payments under covenants or conditions. These differences result from the drafting preferences of the lawyers and the negotiations of the parties. Differences in style are acceptable so long as all essential subjects are clearly stated somewhere in the acquisition contract.

[13]See *Biechele v. Cedar Point, Inc.*, 747 F.2d 209 (6th Cir. 1984); *Marshall Field & Co. v. Icahn*, 537 F. Supp. 714 (S.D.N.Y. March 26, 1982); and *General Portland, Inc. v. La Farge Copper S.A.*, Fed. Sec. L. Rep. (CCH) §99, 148 (N.D. Tex. Aug. 28, 1981).

Parties to the Contract. The first paragraph of an acquisition contract identifies the parties. They include the seller or sellers and the buyer or buyers or the parties to a merger. In addition, the parties may include a corporate parent corporation or other shareholders whose vote or guaranty is necessary to the acquisition. At times a person who will provide financing is named as a party, although acquisition financing is usually provided under separate agreements and their performance is made a condition to the obligations of the parties to the acquisition contract.

Recitals. Recitals state the background and objectives of the acquisition contract in a brief and general manner. They are used to help readers to understand the subsequent detailed provisions of the acquisition contract. Some lawyers omit recitals or treat them as "boilerplate." The author believes that recitals are potentially valuable, especially if disputes arise, and that they should be written with care.

Definitions. Acquisition contracts use some terms repeatedly throughout one or more articles or sections. If the terms are lengthy or complex, a lawyer skilled at drafting acquisition contracts will develop definitions that can be used consistently throughout the contract. For example, financial statements consisting of balance sheets, income statements, cash flow statements and statements of changes in capital for several years may be defined as the "Financial Statements." A purchase price composed of a package of cash, notes and stock may be defined as the "Purchase Price."

Statement of the Transaction. An acquisition contract should state the sale and purchase or merger commitments of the parties, preferably in an early article. A stock purchase agreement should identify the shares to be sold (both in numbers of shares and as a percentage of the authorized and outstanding capital stock) and the price to be paid for them. An assets purchase agreement should identify the assets to be sold (and any excluded assets) and the price to be paid for them. The price should include the liabilities and obligations to be assumed by the purchaser and retained by the seller. A merger agreement should state how the merger will be accomplished, including the board and shareholder approvals and other steps to accomplish the merger and to pay the price to the shareholders of the acquired corporation.

The statement of the transaction should identify the price in detail (i.e., cash, debt, stock or a combination of them) and how and when it will be paid. If part of the price is contingent, the statement of the transaction should state in detail how it will be determined. The statement of the transaction should also include any provisions for withholding part of the price in escrow. In an assets purchase agreement, the statement of the transaction should also include an allocation of the purchase price among the assets sold.

In order to keep the statement of transaction concise and readable, it is customary to refer to exhibits which explain in detail any contingent price, escrow or price allocation provisions that may apply.

Representations and Warranties. Acquisition contracts customarily contain a detailed series of provisions making representations and warranties about the ownership, financial condition and many other aspects of the seller's business. If these representations and warranties are untrue or are breached, the buyer will have a variety of remedies including termination of the agreement, rescission of a completed transaction, or monetary damages.

Buyers negotiate the representations and warranties in order to assure that they receive the business values for which they pay the purchase price. Buyers usually demand and sellers fairly readily provide full and enduring protection about subjects which are and should be certain, such as corporate authorization and ownership of the shares or assets being sold. Protection limited in scope and time is usually given for less certain items, such as the salability of inventories and collectibility of inventories. Little protection, if any, is usually given for items which are uncertain in nature and potentially affected by the buyer's activities after the acquisition, such as retention of customers and employees.

An acquisition contract usually requires that the representations and warranties be true, accurate and complete on the contract date and the closing date. However, representations and warranties as to financial statements are keyed to the balance sheet dates or the ends of the periods for which earnings and cash flow statements were prepared. The contract usually provides for survival of the representations and warranties after the closing of the acquisition for agreed time periods which customarily are lengthy for matters relating to title and relatively brief for financial matters and condition of facilities and equipment. The survival provisions should be coordinated with the indemnity provisions in the acquisition contract.

The buyer customarily also provides representations and warranties. If an acquisition is for cash, they may be quite brief and consist primarily of matters relating to corporate authorization and the availability of financing. If the buyer will pay the price in installments over a period of time or will issue stock or securities, the representations and warranties will be more numerous and detailed and may correspond in some situations to the protection provided by the seller.

Covenants, Affirmative and Negative. Acquisition contracts contain a number of affirmative and negative covenants by the seller and buyer to take, or refrain from, certain actions. Some are to be accomplished by the closing and others apply after the closing. For example, the seller or buyer or both may agree to apply for government clearances. The seller may agree to seek consents from lenders, customers or suppliers to assign their contracts. The buyer may agree to assume and continue seller's pension, insurance and other employee benefit programs. The seller and its directors, officers and shareholders may agree not to compete for some time period after the closing. Both the seller and the buyer may agree to share tax records after the closing in the event of audits by federal or state tax authorities.

Conditions. In an acquisition contract, conditions are provisions excusing performance by buyer or seller or both, if certain events occur or do not occur. For example, both buyer and seller will usually be excused if government agencies decline essential clearances. The seller, and usually also the buyer, will be excused if the buyer does not obtain financing commitments within the time allowed. The buyer will be excused if a material misrepresentation by seller is discovered or a material adverse change in seller's business occurs prior to the closing. Either party will be excused if the other party fails to deliver all required closing documents and payments.

Closing Documents and Payments. Acquisition contracts specify a closing place and date and state in detail each step to be taken at the closing. The acquisition contract lists documents to be delivered and payments to be made including the medium and means of transmittal of payments such as cash wire transfers. To prevent last minute controversies, acquisition contracts that require opinions of counsel and "agreed upon procedures" letters from accountants will attach a previously agreed text of the opinions and letters.

Indemnities. Under basic principles of contract law, the parties to an acquisition contract have rights and remedies if a misrepresentation or breach of warranty is discovered, a covenant is breached, or a condition is not fulfilled. However, simple contract rights and remedies are not always adequate to provide full protection. Thus, acquisition contracts frequently contain an article providing indemnities that afford more extensive protection, subject to various conditions that must be fulfilled to obtain the protection.

In a typical indemnification provision, a seller or buyer commits to indemnify, defend and hold harmless the other party against all loss, liability, cost and expense arising from any misrepresentation or breach of warranty, breach of covenant, or unexcused failure to fulfill a condition in the acquisition contract. Some provisions do not include defense, but agree to reimburse reasonable attorney's fees and disbursements as they are incurred. Under a defense provision, a seller who failed to disclose a product liability or environmental claim would be liable to the buyer not only for damages if the buyer should have to pay the claim, but would be required to step forward and defend or settle the claim at no cost to the buyer. The defense obligation is valuable because attorneys fees and other legal costs to defend claims are high.

A typical indemnification provision requires the person indemnified to give prompt notice of its own claims and claims of third parties. The indemnified person must also cooperate in the defense of third party claims, usually at the expense of the person providing the indemnity.

Default and Termination. Most acquisition contracts contain provisions defining a default and prescribing the steps required to declare a default and to terminate the contract for default. A typical provision includes a requirement of notice of default and a right to cure. It can provide for remedies such as specific performance and liquidated damages and can also limit remedies in time, scope and amount. It can include a final date at which the contract will terminate if it has not been closed, even if no default has occurred.

General Provisions. An acquisition contract customarily includes a final article containing miscellaneous provisions of a legal nature. Common examples are amendment procedures, notice procedures, assignment restrictions and procedures, governing law, consents to jurisdiction, and an acknowledgment that the contract is the entire agreement. The general provisions may also include provisions on finder's fees, transaction costs, survival of representations and warranties and future cooperation.

Signatures. The signature page in an acquisition contract usually requires only the corporate signatures of the buyer and seller. However, it can become more complex, especially when stock is being sold by a large number of shareholders. For example, signatures by joint owners or owners by the entireties may be necessary. Signatures by agents, executors, administrators or others acting in a representative capacity may be necessary together with powers of attorney, trust agreements, court orders or other evidence of their authority to act.

Exhibits. The exhibits are vital elements of an acquisition contract. They include the documents evidencing the condition of the business, as stated in the article on representations and warranties, such as asset lists, financial statements, descriptions or copies of major contracts, and disclosures of lawsuits, claims and other contingent liabilities. They also include agreed forms of contracts to be signed at the closing such as customer and supply contracts and employment contracts. They may also include special schedules such as a chart allocating the purchase price or a real estate survey showing parcels of land being sold and retained by seller.

F. Stock Purchase Agreements

Negotiators and drafters of stock purchase agreements should keep in mind several basic principles:

1. The essential parties are the selling shareholders and the buyer. Participation by management is not essential, although it is usually desirable to have management participate. The selling shareholders customarily agree to take, or cause the corporation to take, all actions that are necessary to accomplish the transaction.
2. No vote of the board of directors or shareholders is necessary. Each shareholder makes his or her own decision whether to sell.
3. The sale is accomplished by transferring the certificates for the shares. The buyer should require the selling shareholders to represent and warrant that they own and are entitled to transfer their shares free and clear of pledges, security interests, liens, claims and transfer restrictions.[14]
4. The business, assets and liabilities of the corporation continue unchanged after the sale unless steps are taken to change them. For example, if the selling shareholders and the buyer agree, assets or liabilities can be transferred ("stripped") from the corporation before the sale.
5. The buyer does not succeed to the liabilities and obligations of the corporation as in a two-party merger or, under some circumstances, a sale of assets. However, the buyer will bear indirectly the economic effects of the liabilities and obligations of the corporation. Thus, the buyer should require the selling shareholders to provide representations, warranties and indemnities to protect the buyer's investment in the corporation.
6. The representations and warranties, covenants and indemnities are given by the selling shareholders, although shareholders who do

not work closely with the corporation may be reluctant to do so.[15] If given by the corporation, representations and warranties, covenants and indemnities would have no economic value to the buyer who will own the corporation after the sale.

If a corporate selling shareholder and the buyer agree to treat the sale of stock as a sale of assets pursuant to Section 338 (h)(10) of the Internal Revenue Code, the stock purchase agreement should contain provisions relating to the election and to the allocation of the purchase price among the assets. (See Chapter 6.)

If a corporate buyer will pay the price with its voting common stock in a tax free reorganization pursuant to Section 368(a)(1)(B) of the Internal Revenue Code, the agreement should have a title such as "Agreement and Plan of Reorganization." The agreement should contain provisions clearly requiring and demonstrating compliance with the requirements of the Code. (See Chapter 7.) If the transaction is also intended to qualify for "pooling of interests" treatment, the agreement should clearly require and demonstrate compliance with APB 16 and other applicable accounting requirements of the Financial Accounting Standards Board and the Securities and Exchange Commission. (See Chapter 9.)

An example of a Stock Purchase Agreement appears as Exhibit 16-3.

G. Assets Purchase Agreements

Negotiators and drafters of assets purchase agreements should keep in mind several basic principles:

1. The essential parties are the corporation owning the assets and the buyer.
2. If the assets to be sold are a material part of the selling corporation's assets, the agreement should require a favorable vote of the board of directors. If the assets to be sold are substantially all of the selling corporation's assets, the agreement should also require a favorable vote of the shareholders. When practicable, it is helpful to arrange for a major shareholder or shareholders to become a party to the agreement and to agree to vote for the sale.
3. The agreement should carefully identify the assets being sold and the assets being retained by the selling corporation, including intangible assets such as contracts, permits and intellectual proper-

---

[14]Stock certificates are negotiable instruments and investment securities under the Uniform Commercial Code. A creditor who wishes to perfect a pledge or security interest must take possession of the stock certificates. A restriction on transfer must be endorsed as a legend on the stock certificates to give notice to potential buyers or lenders. Thus, a buyer who receives legend-free stock certificates at a closing in good faith and without notice of any rights of third parties should acquire clear title to the shares.

[15]The author has seen several transactions in which a major selling shareholder, who was also the chief executive officer, alone gave the representations and warranties and indemnities concerning the corporation's business and financial condition. Minority shareholders who had not worked for the corporation gave representations and indemnities only as to the shares sold by each of them.

ties. The seller should assure that the agreement requires the buyer to assume at least the future obligations under seller's contracts and permits. The agreement should also contain covenants and conditions relating to necessary consents of third parties to the assignment of contracts and permits.

4. The agreement should carefully identify the selling corporation's liabilities that will be transferred to the buyer and those that will be retained by the selling corporation. The seller should assure that the agreement requires the buyer to assume and to pay or otherwise discharge the transferred liabilities.
5. The sale is accomplished by transferring the assets and liabilities individually or in groups. For example, a deed for each real property should be executed and recorded. Tangible personal properties are usually transferred by a master bill of sale and assignment document, but some, such as motor vehicles, must be transferred individually and the title certificates sent for registration to government authorities. Intangible properties such as inventories, receivables and some intellectual properties can be transferred by a master bill of sale and assignment document. However, patents and trademarks should be assigned separately and the instruments filed with the U.S. Patent and Trademark Office. Copyrights should be assigned separately and the instruments filed with the Copyright Office. Contracts, licenses and permits, including sales orders and purchase orders, that contain no assignment restrictions can be assigned by a master bill of sale and assignment document. However, contracts, licenses and permits that cannot be assigned without the consent of a third party may require separate assignment documents.
6. If the sale is a taxable transaction, the agreement should contain provisions allocating the price pursuant to Section 1060 of the Internal Revenue Code with close attention to any Section 197 intangibles. (See Chapter 6.)
7. If a corporate buyer will pay the price with voting common stock in a tax free reorganization pursuant to Section 368(a)(1)(C) of the Internal Revenue Code, the agreement should have a title such as "Agreement and Plan of Reorganization." The agreement should also contain provisions clearly requiring and demonstrating compliance with the Code. They should include the liquidation of the seller corporation and distribution of the buyer's shares to the shareholders of the selling corporation.
8. The agreement should contain provisions either requiring compliance with the bulk transfer provisions of the Uniform Commercial Code or waiving compliance. (See Chapter 13.) To the extent applicable, the agreement should also contain provisions for compliance with the bulk sales provisions of state tax authorities.
9. The agreement should contain provisions to protect the buyer from unintended successor liability upon liquidation of the selling corporation and distribution of the price to its shareholders. These steps can, of course, negate the value of the selling corporation's representations and warranties, covenants and indemnities be-

cause the seller corporation will no longer have the resources to full its commitments. The buyer can request that the shareholders who will receive liquidation distributions provide indemnities, but may find some or all of them unwilling to do so. Compromise methods to protect the buyer include (a) a requirement that the selling corporation maintain a minimum net worth in undistributed liquid assets for an agreed time period or (b) retention of part of the purchase price in escrow for an agreed time period.

10. The agreement should contain provisions carefully allocating liabilities and obligations that involve, or arguably may involve, events before and after the closing date. All too often, sellers and buyers think the allocation can be stated simply on the basis of an occurrence before or after the closing date. However, further clarification is needed for liabilities based on events that take place over a period of years. For example, product liability and environmental claims are often based on exposures that take place over many years and manifest their effects as bodily injuries or property damage after still more years.
11. The agreement should contain provisions relating to the dissenters' appraisal rights of shareholders of the selling corporation, if they are applicable to the transaction. It is customary to include a condition that excuses the obligation of the buyer to close if the exercise of dissenters' appraisal rights exceeds an agreed maximum number of shares. Such a provision is especially important in a tax free reorganization in which exercises of dissenters' appraisal rights might adversely affect tax free treatment.

An example of an Assets Purchase Agreement appears as Exhibit 16-4. An example of an Escrow Agreement used with the Assets Purchase Agreement appears as Exhibit 16-5.

H. Merger Agreements

The discussion of merger agreements focuses on triangular mergers rather than the once common two-party mergers. The ever-growing tendency of the courts to impose liability, including successor liability, on anyone perceived as having "deep pockets," has greatly reduced the use of two-party mergers.

Negotiators and drafters of merger agreements should keep in mind several basic principles:

1. The essential parties are the acquiring corporation, the acquiring corporation's acquisition subsidiary, and the corporation to be acquired. This is true whether the subsidiary will survive a forward merger or is a transitory subsidiary that will disappear in a reverse merger.

2. The agreement should require a favorable vote of the board of directors and the shareholders of the corporation to be acquired. The agreement should also provide for appropriate actions by the board and the parent shareholder of the acquisition subsidiary, but they may be able to act by written consent. The agreement should also require approval of the transaction by the board of the acquiring corporation, including its contribution of the purchase price to the acquisition subsidiary. The agreement should also provide for the execution and filing of certificates of merger.
3. The agreement should provide for distribution of the price to the former shareholders of the acquired corporation and for the surrender for cancellation of their stock certificates.
4. Whether the transaction is a forward merger or a reverse merger, the business, assets and liabilities of the acquired corporation will continue unchanged after the merger unless steps are taken to change them. If the acquired corporation and the acquiring corporation agree, assets or liabilities can be transferred ("stripped") from the acquired corporation before the merger.
5. In a triangular merger, the acquiring corporation does not succeed by operation of law to the liabilities and obligations of the acquired corporation as it would in a two-party merger. However, since the acquired corporation will be a subsidiary of the acquiring corporation after the merger, the acquiring corporation will bear indirectly the economic effects of the liabilities and obligations of its new subsidiary. Thus, the acquiring corporation should require representations, warranties and indemnities to protect the acquiring corporation's investment in its new subsidiary.
6. The agreement should contain provisions that preserve the value after the merger of the representations, warranties, covenants and indemnities relating to the business and the financial condition of the acquired corporation. The agreement could require that the shareholders of the acquired corporation commit to the representations, warranties, covenants and indemnities. If some or all of them are unwilling to make such a commitment, the usual compromise is to retain part of the purchase price in escrow for an agreed time period.
7. The agreement should contain provisions relating to the exercise of dissenters' appraisal rights. It is customary to include provisions excusing the obligation to close if exercises of dissenters' appraisal rights exceed an agreed maximum number of shares. This is especially important if the merger will be part of a tax free reorganization in which excessive cash payments to dissenters might spoil tax free treatment.

If the acquired corporation is a member of a consolidated or affiliated group for federal income tax purposes, and its parent corporation and the acquiring corporation agree to treat the acquisition as a sale of assets pursuant to Section 338(h)(10) of the Internal Revenue Code, the agreement should provide for the election and for allocation of the purchase price among the assets. (See Chapter 6.)

If a buyer corporation will pay the price with its voting common stock in a tax free reorganization pursuant to Section 368(a)(1)(A), (B) or (C) of the Internal Revenue Code, the agreement should have a title such as "Agreement and Plan of Reorganization." The agreement should contain provisions requiring and demonstrating compliance with the requirements of the Code. (See Chapter 9.) If the transaction is also intended to qualify for "pooling of interests" treatment, the agreement should require and demonstrate compliance with APB 16 and other applicable accounting requirements of the Financial Accounting Standards Board and the Securities and Exchange Commission.

An example of a merger agreement providing for a "cash-out" of all shareholders of the acquired corporation appears as Exhibit 16-6. Shareholders who vote for the merger receive the merger price in cash. Any shareholders who vote unsuccessfully against the merger can demand dissenting shareholders' appraisal rights, but they are bound by the vote of the majority shareholders in the absence of fraud.

An example of the key provisions of an agreement and plan of reorganization using a reverse triangular merger to accomplish a tax free reorganization pursuant to Section 368 of the Internal Revenue Code appears as Exhibit 16-7.

I. Drafting Contingent Price Provisions

A contingent price provision is sometimes a useful method to compromise a difference of opinion during price negotiations. For example, a seller may seek a premium price based on a recent earnings increase and projections of further growth. The buyer may be reluctant to pay the premium price because the earnings increase may have been a temporary upturn rather than a growth indicator.

The seller and the buyer can resolve the issue by agreeing to a price consisting of two components. The initial price payable at the closing will be based on conservative earnings assumptions. Thereafter, a contingent price will be payable if the business achieves the seller's projections.

A contingent price is usually based on earnings (or cash flows) of the business in excess of the conservative assumptions used in negotiating the initial price. The contingent price is payable for a period such as 2 years. If the earnings exceed the conservative assumptions, there is a "win–win" result. The buyer reaps extra earnings, but shares part of them with the seller.

A contingent price can be difficult to negotiate. For example, a seller will be reluctant to agree to a contingent price if it doubts that the buyer will operate the business in a manner that enhances earnings and will report the earnings fairly in its financial statements. A buyer will be reluctant to agree to a contingent price if it plans to make important improvements of the business from its own resources, so that the seller would obtain a "windfall" payment from factors only minimally resulting from the business sold.

When negotiating a contingent price provision, the seller and buyer should agree on the operating and accounting policies that will have a foreseeable affect on the contingent price. The provision should identify the fiscal years or other periods which will be used in determining the contingent price. The provision should also state that earnings will be reported in accordance with generally accepted accounting principles (GAAP) and that the report will be accompanied by an unqualified opinion or review of the buyer's independent accountants. However, these basic requirements should be supplemented by additional points.

GAAP allows the use of a numerous accounting policies that can significantly affect reported income, especially for brief periods. Thus, the seller will want the buyer to use accounting principles and policies that are consistent with those used for the business before the acquisition, except for specifically agreed changes. To avoid future controversies, it is best to recite the significant accounting policies likely to affect the operating results of the particular business.

Some examples of accounting policies that should be stated are as follows: (1) revenue and expense recognition policies; (2) depreciation methods and lives; (3) inventory methods; (4) receivables methods; (5) allocation of corporate interest expense; (6) allocation of tax expense; (7) allocation of corporate revenues from investment; (8) contingent liability accrual policies and credits for recoveries of related insurance proceeds; (9) credits and debits for extraordinary (nonrecurring) items and any related insurance proceeds; (10) discretionary expenses; (11) expenses for cash bonuses and for noncash compensation such as stock options; (12) accrual of expenses for any employee terminations; (13) allocations of income and expense items shared with buyer's other businesses; and (14) related-party transactions.

J. Drafting Indemnification Provisions

As described earlier in this chapter, indemnification provisions are commonly included in acquisition contracts. The author has observed that many otherwise skilled acquisition attorneys treat indemnification provisions as "boilerplate." They include detailed provisions on notices of claims and lawsuits, but overlook more serious issues. The result can be a failure to provide meaningful protection of client rights.

The most common failure is to provide defense for the indemnified person or to provide "pay as incurred" expense reimbursement if the indemnified person will provide its own defense. For example, many indemnification provisions simply require a seller to indemnify a buyer (and usually also its officers, directors and shareholders) against liability, cost and expense (including reasonable attorneys' fees and disbursements) arising from specified events prior to the closing date of the acquisition. Such a provision does not adequately cover the issues related to responsibility for defense and the related costs.

Experienced lawyers know that large numbers of nuisance and semi-nuisance lawsuits are commenced in the United States. If the persons named as defendants in these lawsuits cannot afford a vigorous defense by qualified counsel, they will be forced to settle and may even lose.

Using the example of a seller indemnification, a threshold question is whether the buyer wants the seller to provide defense or the buyer wants to defend itself with defense costs being reimbursed by the seller. If the seller has the resources and motivation to provide an effective defense, the buyer may be glad to turn over defense to the seller and be free of its burdens. However, it is prudent to require the seller to keep the buyer informed about the status of the lawsuit and to reserve a right, if necessary, for the buyer to participate in the defense at the buyer's own expense.

If the seller has a potential conflicting interest, limited resources or little motivation to defend effectively, the buyer should undertake its own defense and provide for the seller to reimburse the costs. It is important to state expressly that defense costs will be paid currently as they are incurred. Otherwise,the seller is likely to reserve its rights until the lawsuit is finally decided or settled, so that it can question whether any liability falls within exceptions to its indemnification obligations and whether the defense costs were reasonable. In the meantime, the buyer must pay the defense costs out of its own pocket.

Indemnification provisions usually contain language that clearly covers liability to third parties. They do not always state whether the indemnification will cover such items as losses, punitive damages, fines and penalties. A person who is willing to indemnify against liability to third parties may, nevertheless, be reluctant to indemnify against losses because losses may be unpredictably large and can result from multiple contributing causes. Such a person may also be reluctant to indemnify against punitive damages, fines and penalties because they may also be unpredictably large and can be affected by the conduct of the indemnified person. Indeed, indemnification provisions sometimes contain exceptions if the person indemnified is found to have engaged in willful misconduct or gross negligence. These coverage issues are potentially significant and should be identified and discussed, so that the seller and buyer can evaluate the risks and make knowledgeable decisions.

Indemnification provisions for product liability, environmental and other "long tail" liabilities can be difficult to negotiate and to draft. For example, health problems attributed to a product can result from exposure over a period of years and then gradually grow without being recognized for further years until the problems finally manifest themselves in symptoms long after the first exposure. For another example, an old underground storage tank can silently leak hazardous substances into soil and groundwater over a period of many years without detection until the hazardous substances finally migrate into nearby wells, streams or rivers.

For product liability, indemnification is usually linked to the date of sale of the product alleged to have caused illness or injury. Another trigger for indemnification can be the commencement of the alleged period of exposure to the product.

For environmental liability, the indemnification is usually linked to the commencement of a release of hazardous substance, contaminants or pollutants, although the time of commencement can be difficult to identify.

Lawyers drafting indemnification provisions sometimes link the indemnification to "violations" of the environmental laws and regulations. Such a provision does not provide enough protection. The major liabilities for cleanup and other costs under the federal and state environmental laws are imposed without fault on persons who own or operate facilities as well as certain other persons who arranged or transported hazardous substances for disposal. In many situations, none of the persons held responsible has violated any law or regulation.

Lawyers drafting environmental indemnities should also be aware that useful products sometimes considered to be hazardous are not listed as hazardous under some environmental laws or, if listed, may not be a subject of mandatory abatement. For example, petroleum is not a hazardous substance under CERCLA. Asbestos-containing materials in commercial and industrial buildings need not be removed or otherwise abated unless renovation, demolition or certain other activities are undertaken. The same is true of lead-based paint in commercial and industrial buildings. Dielectric fluids containing low levels of polychlorinated biphenyls (PCBs) can continue to be used in transformers and capacities if they are properly labeled and maintained. There is no universal requirement that underground storage tanks be removed. If a buyer wants a seller to remove or remediate asbestos-containing materials, lead-based paint, PCB fluids or equipment, or underground storage tanks, specific contractual provisions should be drafted.

Finally, special attention should be given to provisions indemnifying against liabilities relating to intellectual properties, i.e., patents, trademarks, trade secrets and copyrights. Some lawyers unfamiliar with intellectual property law assume that patents cover only products and machines. However, an indemnification against patent infringement should apply to compositions of matter (products), processes, and apparatus (machines). Some lawyers believe that trade secrets must be scientific or technical in nature. However, the law of trade secrets covers a broad range of confidential, proprietary business information including customer lists and business opportunities. The indemnification should be broad enough to protect against claims of wrongful disclosure or use of the full range of protectible trade secrets.

K. Drafting Securities Registration Provisions

An example of contractual provisions for registration with the Securities and Exchange Commission of securities restricted from public sale because they were issued in a private placement appears as an exhibit to Chapter 11. An example of the legend used to implement the restrictions appears as an exhibit to the same chapter.

L. Drafting Noncompetition Provisions

Noncompetition provisions given in connection with the sale of a business have long been a recognized exception to the federal and state antitrust laws. However, the courts generally require, as a condition of enforcement, that they be restricted to a reasonable scope, territory and duration.

For example, a buyer in the grommet business that acquires a widget business can insist that the seller agree not to compete in the widget business. However, if the buyer also requires that the seller agree not to compete in the grommet business, a court may find that the scope is excessive.

For another example, a buyer that acquires a business actively selling throughout the New England states can insist that the seller agree not to compete in New England. However, if the buyer requires the seller not to compete anywhere in the eastern United States, a court may find that the territory is excessive.

Finally, a buyer can usually insist that the seller agree not to compete for a period up to 5 years, depending on the circumstances. If the buyer requires the seller not to compete for a period such as 10 years, a court may find that the duration is excessive.

Some states, such as California, have statutes or court decisions that place further restrictions on the validity and enforcement of noncompetition provisions.

M. Reference Materials

Model Stock Purchase Agreement with Commentary, Section of Business Law, American Bar Association, 1995

Mergers and Acquisitions in the 90s, Goldberg, Practicing Law Institute, 1996

"Read Very Carefully Before Signing Pre-Deal Documents," McCarthy, *Mergers & Acquisitions,* 1997

Acquisitions, Mergers, Sales, Buyouts & Takeovers, 4th Ed., Scharf, Shea and Beck, Prentice Hall, 1991

N. Exhibits

16-1: Confidentiality Agreement

16-2: Letter of Intent

16-3: Stock Purchase Agreement

16-4: Assets Purchase Agreement

16-5: Escrow Agreement

16-6: Merger Agreement (Cash Out Merger)

16-7: Merger Agreement and Plan of Reorganization (Tax Free Reorganization)

Exhibit 16-1

CONFIDENTIALITY AGREEMENT

THIS CONFIDENTIALITY AGREEMENT is made as of this ___ day of ________, 1997 by PRIME PLASTICS, INC. ("PRIME"), 1234 Main Street, Mountainview, New York 10099 and MODERN MATERIALS, INC. ("MODERN"), 5678 High Street, Industryville, New York 10211.

RECITALS:

A. Prime and Modern are engaged in discussions about a possible acquisition of Prime by Modern.

B. Prime is willing to furnish information to Modern relating to Prime's business and financial condition to enable Modern to evaluate whether to acquire Prime or its assets, but only subject to the terms of this Agreement.

AGREEMENTS:

In consideration of the mutual benefits to be derived from their business relationship, the parties agree as follows:

1. The Information. The information ("Information") covered by this Agreement shall include all information furnished by Prime to Modern relating in any way to the business of Prime and its subsidiaries including, without limitation, manufacturing processes and equipment, product formulations and specifications, sales and marketing plans, customers, business opportunities, and financial and other data.

2. Maintenance of Confidentiality. Modern agrees to maintain all Information obtained from Prime in strict confidence and separate from its other records and shall not disclose, or allow disclosure of, any of such Information to any third party or use any of such Information for any purpose other than for evaluation of the acquisition of Prime. However, such obligations shall not apply to any Information which Modern can show (a) was known to it before it was received from Prime; (b) is now or hereafter in the public domain other than as a result of disclosure for which Modern is responsible; (c) was obtained by Modern from a third party lawfully entitled to disclose such Information without restriction; or (d) was developed independently by Modern solely through the efforts of persons who had no access to the Information.

3. Legally Required Disclosure. Section 2 shall not apply to the extent that Modern is required by applicable law, regulation or legal process to disclose any of the Information. Prior to any such disclosure, however, Modern shall notify Prime promptly so that it may seek a protective order or other appropriate remedy or, in Prime's sole discretion, waive in writing compliance with the terms of this Agreement. In any event, Modern will furnish only that portion of the Information which it is legally required to disclose and will exercise all reasonable efforts to obtain reliable assurances that confidential treatment will be accorded to the Information. Modern agrees that it will consult with counsel to Prime, at Prime's cost, in each instance when disclosure of Information is required to be made or requested of it.

4. Return of Information. Upon completion of its evaluation or at any time upon the request of Prime, Modern will promptly return all copies of the written or recorded Information received from Prime in whatever form received or currently stored, including, without limitation, computer memory or other electronic, magnetic or laser archival system, in Modern's possession. Modern will also return or destroy any memoranda or notes in which it has recorded any of the Information. Any oral Information will continue to be subject to the terms of this Agreement.

5. No Solicitation of Employees. Modern agrees not to solicit, directly or indirectly, any person now employed with Prime for employment, consultation or any similar role for two years after the date of this Agreement.

6. Standstill Obligation. Modern agrees that any acquisition proposal will be presented to Prime's management and will be for an acquisition of Prime or substantially all of its assets in a single transaction, whether by stock purchase, assets purchase or merger. Modern agrees to refrain from purchasing any shares of Prime, either in the public stock markets or by private negotiations, for two years from the date of this Agreement without the prior written consent of Prime.

7. Reservations of Rights. Prime and Modern each reserve full freedom to or discontinue their negotiations toward an acquisition at any time for any reason without any liability for doing so. Without limitation, the foregoing reservations mean that Modern shall have no obligation to make a proposal or negotiate to acquire Prime and Prime shall have no obligation to accept or negotiate with respect to any proposal that Modern may make. Further, any binding acquisition agreement shall be made only when a definitive acquisition agreement covering all terms and conditions has been signed by Prime and Modern and approved by their boards of directors.

EXHIBIT 16-1 (*CONT.*)

8. Remedies. Modern acknowledges that remedies at law may be inadequate to protect Prime against any actual or threatened breach of this Agreement and, without prejudice to any other rights and remedies otherwise available to Prime, Modern agrees to the granting of injunctive relief without proof of actual damages. In the event of litigation relating to this Agreement, if a court of competent jurisdiction determines in a final, nonappealable order that this Agreement has been breached by Modern, then Modern will reimburse Prime for all costs and expenses (including, without limitation, legal fees and expenses) incurred in connection with all such litigation. Modern shall be responsible for compliance by its employees including any who leave employment after receiving information hereunder.

9. Waivers. Modern agrees that no failure or delay by Prime in exercising any right, power or privilege hereunder will operate as a waiver, nor will any single or partial exercise preclude any other or further exercise of any right, power or privilege hereunder.

10. Governing Law. The validity, interpretation, performance and enforcement of this agreement shall be governed by the laws of the State of New York without regard to any conflict of laws principles that might cause the law of some other jurisdiction to apply.

11. Entire Agreement. This Agreement contains the entire agreement between the parties hereto concerning the confidentiality of the Information. No modifications of this Agreement or waiver of its terms and conditions will be binding upon any party unless approved in writing by such party.

12. Survival. The confidentiality obligations of this Agreement shall continue to bind Modern for seven years after the date of this Agreement.

13. Benefits of Agreement. This Agreement shall be binding upon and inure to the benefit of the parties hereto and their respective successors and permitted assignees. This Agreement may be signed in one or more counterparts, each of which shall constitute an original but all of which shall constitute one and the same instrument.

PRIME PLASTICS, INC.	MODERN MATERIALS, INC.
By ____________________	By ____________________
President	Executive Vice President

Exhibit 16-2

MODERN MATERIALS, INC.
5678 High Street
Industryville, New York 10211

____________ __, 1997

Dr. Leo Bakelite, President
Prime Plastics, Inc.
1234 Main Street
Mountainview, New York 10099

Dear Dr. Bakelite:

Based on the information you have furnished to date, this letter is written to confirm our mutual present intention that Prime Plastics, Inc. be acquired by Modern Materials, Inc. on the following terms and conditions:

1. Modern will purchase all of the assets of Prime for $15,500,000, of which $14,000,000 will be paid in cash on the closing date and the balance of $1,500,000 will be held in escrow for two years after the closing date as security for possible claims.
2. You will retire on the closing date and will act as a consultant to Prime and Modern under a consulting agreement for three years after the closing date for $240,000 per year payable in equal monthly installments of $20,000 each. I will be pleased to nominate you for election to our board of directors at our next annual shareholders meeting.
3. Modern will make employment offers on the closing date to all of Prime's employees and will offer two year employment contracts at their present compensation to Prime's officers listed in Exhibit A to this letter. Modern will arrange for Prime's employees to participate in Modern's employee benefit plans for which each of them meets the general requirements for participation.
4. Modern will not assume any of Prime's liabilities or obligations except the industrial revenue bonds issued to finance the construction of Prime's pollution control facilities at Mountainview, New York and obligations first incurred after the closing date under Prime's permits, licenses and customer and supplier contracts. Prime will pay, settle or otherwise discharge all its other liabilities with reasonable promptness on and after the closing date.
5. Modern plans to conduct a due diligence review of Prime's business and financial affairs as soon as practicable after this letter is signed. Prime will cooperate with the due diligence review. The review will include an environmental assessment by Green Environmental, Inc.
6. Modern also plans to arrange a review of Prime's financial statements for 1996 and 1997 and subsequent unaudited quarterly periods by Deloitte, Coopers & Waterhouse. Prime will cooperate with the review. Prime agrees to arrange for the reviewers to have access to the workpapers of its auditors, Andersen, Young & Mitchell.
7. Prime understands that the assets purchase agreement between Prime and Modern will contain representations and warranties, covenants, conditions, indemnities and other provisions including an agreed allocation of the price among the assets sold pursuant to Section 1060 of the Internal Revenue Code.
8. Prime and Modern will each pay its own legal, financial, accounting and other expenses related to the transaction, whether it is closed or not. For example, Prime shall pay any and all amounts that may be payable to its investment banking firm, Merrill Lehman Salomon, Inc. for financial, finder and other services.

The provisions of this letter of intent are a preliminary outline of plans being made by Prime and Modern and are not intended to be binding or enforceable except for the expense provisions of Section 8. Prime and Modern each reserve full freedom to discontinue their negotiations toward an acquisition at any time for any reason without liability for doing so. A binding contract between Prime and Modern shall come into existence only when a definitive assets purchase agreement containing all terms and conditions has been executed by both companies and approved by both boards of directors.

If this letter of intent conforms to your understanding, please sign and return the enclosed copy of this letter.

MODERN MATERIALS, INC.

By ____________________
Paul E. Carbonate

Chairman and CEO

EXHIBIT 16-3

STOCK PURCHASE AGREEMENT
Index

STOCK PURCHASE AGREEMENT

This Agreement is made on __________, 199__ between MULTISTATE BAKERIES, INC., a Delaware corporation (the "Seller") and BAKERY HOLDINGS, INC., a Delaware corporation (the "Purchaser").

RECITALS:

(A) As part of a restructuring of its businesses, Seller wishes to divest its wholly-owned subsidiary, Mama's Old Fashioned Cookies Corporation (the "Corporation").

(B) Purchaser is a corporation organized and owned by key members of the management of the Corporation and venture capital investors who plan to provide financing for Purchaser's acquisition of the Corporation.

(C) Seller owns 500 shares of common stock of the Corporation, which shares are all of its issued and outstanding capital stock.

(D) Seller wishes to sell, and Purchaser wishes to purchase, all of the outstanding stock of the Corporation on the terms and conditions contained in this Agreement.

AGREEMENTS:

On consideration of their mutual promises, Seller and Purchaser agree as follows:

1. THE STOCK PURCHASE

1.1 Sale and Purchase. Seller agrees to sell to Purchaser, and Purchaser agrees to purchase from Seller, all of the 500 outstanding shares of Common Stock of the Corporation for the purchase price provided in Section 1.2.

1.2 The Price. (A) The purchase price for the shares of Common Stock described in Section 1.1 shall be $8,500,000 plus or minus the accounting review adjustments described in Section 1.3.

1.3 Pre-Closing Accountants' Review. (A) Before the Closing and within 20 days after the execution of this Agreement, Purchaser's accountants, Touche, Whinney & Mitchell ("TW&M") will perform a review of the Corporation's financial statements for its fiscal years ended December 31, 1996 and 1997 and the subsequent unaudited eight months ended August 31, 1998 attached as Exhibit A. If TW&M shall find any discrepancies in the Corporation's financial statements, it shall provide its finding to Purchaser in a written report within 30 days after the date of this Agreement. Within 10 days after receipt of the report, Purchaser shall be entitled to furnish written notice to Seller requesting adjustments of the purchase price based on TW&M's report, a copy of which shall be delivered to Seller with such notice.

(B) Seller shall be entitled to review with its auditors, Deloitte & Ernst ("D&E") the requested price adjustments and TW&M's report. Within 15 days after receipt of the price adjustment requests and TW&M's report, Seller shall furnish written notice to Purchaser stating whether it accepts or rejects the requested price adjustments and its reasons therefor. Within 7 days thereafter, Seller and Purchaser shall meet and negotiate in good faith to settle the requested price adjustments. If they shall fail to reach a settlement within the 30 day period thereafter, TW&M and D&E shall within 10 days after the expiration of such 30 day period jointly appoint a third accounting firm to review the price adjustment requests, the TW&M report and other relevant materials which it may request and the parties may elect to present. Both Seller and Purchaser shall cooperate with the requests for information by the appointed accounting firm. The decision of the appointed accounting firm shall be provided in writing within 30 days after its appointment and shall be final and binding on both Seller and Purchaser.

1.4 The Closing. The closing ("Closing") of this Agreement shall be held at the offices of Dewey & Cromwell, 200 Wall Street, New York, N.Y. 10001 on _______, 199__ (the "Closing Date") or at such other time and place as the parties may agree in writing. The obligation of each party to close is subject to its respective conditions stated in Article IV. If the Closing shall not take place on or before the Closing Date, either party may thereafter terminate this Agreement by written notice to the other party. Any such termination shall not release any rights or obligations that accrued before termination or any right to sue for breach of this Agreement.

2. REPRESENTATIONS AND WARRANTIES

2.1 Seller's Representations and Warranties. Seller represents and warrants to the Purchaser as follows:

(a) Incorporation and Good Standing. Seller and the Corporation are each a corporation duly organized and existing in good standing under the laws of the State of Delaware and each is qualified to do business with full power, corporate and otherwise, to carry on its business and own its properties. Accurate and complete copies of the Certificates of Incorporation and By-Laws of Seller and the Corporation, including all amendments, are attached as Exhibits B and C. Seller and the Corporation are each qualified to do business and in good standing in all jurisdictions where the nature of its activities or ownership of properties requires such qualification and each has properly prepared and filed all franchise and other tax returns required to be filed by the laws of such jurisdictions and each has paid all taxes shown to be due and payable in such returns.

(b) Authorization of the Agreement. The execution, delivery and performance of this Agreement has been duly authorized by all requisite corporate action on the part of the Seller. The Seller has all necessary power and authority to enter into and perform this Agreement which does not conflict with any law, regulation, restriction or agreement to which it is subject.

(c) Equity Capital Structure of the Corporation. The equity capitalization of the Corporation is accurately and completely set forth in Exhibit D. All outstanding capital stock of the Corporation is validly issued, fully paid and non-assessable. Except as set forth in Exhibit D, the Corporation does not have any authorized, issued or outstanding securities convertible into or exchangeable for capital stock, nor does any person hold any option or right to purchase or otherwise acquire any shares of capital stock or any securities convertible into or exchangeable for such capital stock. The Corporation has not declared, and has no outstanding commitment to pay, any dividend or to make any distribution or transfer of assets to its shareholders or persons affiliated with them. The Corporation has not adopted or committed to any change in its equity capitalization.

(d) Ownership of the Corporation. The Seller owns all 500 outstanding shares of Common Stock of the Corporation free and clear of all pledges, liens, encumbrances, security interests, mortgages, deeds of trust and claims whatsoever and of all restrictions on its right to sell them to Purchaser hereunder. Without limitation, neither the Seller nor the Corporation are parties to any existing agreement restricting sale or transfer of the shares or granting any person a right to buy them.

(e) Subsidiaries of the Corporation. The Corporation has no subsidiaries except those listed in Exhibit E. Except as set forth in Exhibit E, the Corporation owns all of the authorized and outstanding stock of each of its subsidiaries free and clear of all pledges, liens, encumbrances, security interests, mortgages, deeds of trust, claims or restrictions on the change of control contemplated herein.

(f) Financial Statements. (i) The audited financial statements of the Corporation for its fiscal years ended December 31, 1996 and 1997 and its unaudited interim financial statements for the eight month period ended August 31, 1998 attached as Exhibit A reflect fairly the financial condition of the Corporation at such dates and its results of operations, cash flows, retained earnings and changes in financial position for the fiscal years and the eight month period then ended in accordance with generally accepted accounting principles consistently applied. All material liabilities and obligations, existing and contingent, of the Corporation at August 31, 1998 are fairly reflected or disclosed and described in its financial statements and the notes thereto. Since August 31, 1998, the Corporation has conducted its activities only in the ordinary course and no material change in its financial condition, results of operations, cash flows or retained earnings occurred during such period.

(ii) All inventories reflected in the Corporation's balance sheet at December 31, 1997 are fully usable and salable and all receivables reflected in such balance sheet are collectible except to the extent of the reserves shown therein. The Corporation's fixed assets are in good repair and able to operate at full capacity on a day to day basis, normal wear and tear excepted.

(g) Tax Returns. Seller has included the Corporation in its consolidated federal, state and local tax returns for each of the five years ended December 31, 1997. Such returns and the information contained therein were properly and accurately compiled and completed and reflected the tax liabilities of the Seller, including the Corporation, for such years. The Corporation has paid or made adequate provision for the payment of all taxes which have become or may become due in respect of operations during the periods to which such returns relate.

(h) Lawsuits, Governmental Proceedings, Investigations and Claims. Except as described in Exhibit F, there is no governmental proceeding or investigation, or claim pending or threatened against the Corporation or the Seller or the Corporation's properties or business which might materially and adversely affect its financial condition, business or operations, or against or relating to the transactions contemplated by this Agreement.

(i) Properties, Contracts and Material Information. Exhibit G is an accurate and complete list as of the date of this Agreement of (i) all real property and all significant items of machinery and equipment presently owned or leased by the Corporation with a brief description of each property and its use and copies of title instruments and leases, and details relating to any liens, encumbrances or claims thereto and any direct or indirect interest therein of any of the Corporation's directors or officers, (ii) all patents, trademarks, trade names, copyrights, including all registration thereof and applications therefor presently owned in whole or in party by the Corporation, and all patent, trademark or copyright licenses to which the Corporation is a party, (iii) all bonds debentures, notes, stock or other securities other than stock of subsidiaries already listed in Exhibit E, and all accounts receivable other than trade accounts receivable which are not more than 90 days old, held or owned by the Corporation; (iv) all policies of insurance in force covering or owned by the Corporation; (v) all loan agreements or bank credit agreements in effect, setting forth the amount of the original loan, the unpaid balance, the interest rate and payments, the maturity date, any prepayment penalties and the name of the lender; (vi) all material agreements to which the Corporation is a party except that the Corporation may omit agreements made in the ordinary course of business which are terminable by the Corporation by notice of not more than 90 days without penalty or which do not obligate the Corporation in amounts in excess of $25,000 in the aggregate per agreement; (vii) all employment contracts with any officers or employees of the Corporation and the names and current salary rates of all such officers and employees whose current annual salary rate is U.S. $100,000 or more, together with a description of all incentive, compensation, bonus, profit sharing retirement, pension or other similar plans or arrangements for any of such officers or employees and (viii) all agents, consultants and independent contractors retained by the Corporation, with a brief description of the arrangement for compensation, and all persons, if any, holding a power of attorney, to act on its behalf (ix) all agreements and transactions entered into and in force with any officer, director or stockholder of the Corporation or any person related to any of them, except for agreements which are terminable by the Corporation within 90 days without penalty or which do not obligate the Corporation in amounts in excess of $25,000 in the aggregate per agreement. Complete and correct copies of all agreements, instruments or other documents relating to the items referred to above have been delivered or made available to the Purchaser. The Corporation is not in material default on any obligation to be performed by it under any loan, plan or agreement referred to in Exhibit G. or in material violation of any law, ordinance, regulation, order or decree applicable to it.

(j) Compliance with Laws, Regulations, etc. The Corporation has all required permits and is in compliance with all laws, regulations, permits and orders applicable to its business and assets. The Corporation has not, and is not, infringing any patent, trademark or copyright or using or disclosing without authorization any trade secret of third parties.

(k) Labor Relations and Equal Employment Opportunity. Since January 1, 1998, the Corporation has not experienced any strike, work interruption, organization or other concerted action by its employees and has not received any complaint of failure to comply with equal employment opportunity laws.

(l) Employee Benefit Plans. All employee benefit plans, as defined in the Employee Retirement Income Security Act, covering present and former employees of the Corporation have been fully disclosed to the Purchaser including, without limitation, all commitments to provide employee benefits. Any plans intended to be qualified plans and trusts intended to be exempt organizations under the Internal Revenue Code are qualified and exempt and the Corporation has determination letters evidencing such status. There has been, and is, no reportable event, accumulated funding deficiency, termination liability, withdrawal liability or prohibited transaction in connection with such plans. The Corporation has no obligation to provide post-retirement health, medical, death or other welfare benefits. All group health plans have been maintained in compliance with the Internal Revenue Code. All vacation, severance and similar plans or policies of the Corporation have been fully and accurately disclosed to the Purchaser.

(m) Environmental, Safety and Product Liability. Without limitation of other representations and warranties herein, the Corporation and its business and assets are in compliance with, and are not subject to, any liability under federal, state and local environmental laws. The Corporation is not aware of any reason why it will not continue to be able to comply with all its permits or to renew any permit expiring within one year after the date of this Agreement without imposition of standards materially stricter than those now, in effect. The Corporation is not subject to any liability, existing or contingent, with respect to a release or disposal of hazardous waste, hazardous substances, constituents or pollutants at its present or former properties or any offsite locations. The Corporation is not subject to any liability with respect to defective products regardless of whether such liability results from breach of express or implied warranties or strict liability imposed by reason of misdesign, mismanufacture or failure to warn.

2.2 Purchaser's Representations and Warranties. The Purchaser represents and warrants to the Seller as follow:

(a) Purchaser is a corporation duly authorized and existing in good standing under the laws of Delaware with full corporate power and authority to carry out the transactions contemplated by this Agreement.

(b) The execution, delivery and performance by Purchaser of this Agreement and all other agreements and transactions contemplated herein have been authorized on the part of Purchaser by all requisite corporate actions and will not violate or conflict with its certificate of incorporation or by-laws or with any law, regulation, judgement, order, restriction or agreement to which Purchaser is a party or to which it is subject.

(c) The shares of Common Stock of the Corporation are being acquired by Purchaser for investment and without any view to, or for resale in connection with, any distribution of such shares within the meaning of the Securities Act of 1933.

(d) No consent, approval, permit, registration, filing or notice to or with any governmental agency or third party is required on the part of Purchaser for the execution, delivery and performance of this Agreement except as expressly provided herein.

(e) There is no litigation or governmental proceeding pending or, to the best of Purchaser's knowledge, threatened against Purchaser that questions the validity or challenges the performance of this Agreement or any action to be taken by Purchaser pursuant to this Agreement.

3. COVENANTS

3.1 Cooperation with Continuing Due Diligence. Until the Closing, Seller shall consult with Purchaser on the operation of its business and shall afford access to Purchaser and its representatives during normal business hours to all records of its business and Assets and to its employees, accountants, customers and suppliers. However, no investigation by Purchaser shall limit responsibility of Seller for the representations, warranties and agreements herein. Seller shall maintain its assets in good order and repair, but no material alterations or improvements shall be made except with the written approval of Purchaser.

3.2 Conduct of Business in the Ordinary Course. Pending the Closing, Seller shall cause the Corporation to conduct its business only in the ordinary course. Without limitation of the foregoing, the Seller shall cause the Corporation to (A) use its best efforts to preserve intact its business and its assets; (B) maintain its assets in good repair and operating condition except for fire, flood or other Acts of God; (C) continue in full all existing insurance coverage, (D) not enter into any material contract or other transaction without prior written approval of Purchaser; (E) use its best efforts to retain employees, customers and suppliers; (F) refrain from any increase in the compensation or benefits of employees or any commitment for an increase; (G) not engage in any inter-company transaction with any of its affiliates except for continuation of transactions in the normal course of business fully disclosed in exhibits to this Agreement; (H) refrain from any sale or transfer or commitment to sell or transfer any of its assets except for sales of products in the ordinary course of business and the transfers provided in Section 3.4, (I) refrain from any action or omission which will subject its assets to any lien, encumbrance, or security interest; (J) refrain, without Purchaser's consent, from any material modification of any of its assets or commitment for any capital expenditure in excess of $.

3.3 Title to Real Properties. Prior to the Closing Date, Seller shall at its expense furnish to Purchaser a title report and commitment from a title insurer acceptable to Purchaser for the issuance of ALTA title insurance policy insuring that title to all real property owned and to be owned by the Corporation on the Closing Date conforms in all respects to the representations and warranties contained in Section 2.1. Such commitment and policy shall contain no exceptions other than the standard printed exceptions contained in all ALTA policies issued for industrial properties by the insurer. The Seller shall concurrently deliver to Purchaser a current ALTA survey of the real property by a registered land surveyor showing the locations of all buildings, improvements, easements, rights of way and encroachments. Purchaser shall have 10 days after receipt to notify Seller of any objections to title. If Purchaser shall elect to purchase a final policy, Purchaser shall notify Seller at least three business days prior to the Closing Date and shall pay the premium therefor.

3.4 Transfers of Certain Properties. At or prior to the Closing, Seller shall transfer to the Corporation, and the Corporation shall transfer to Seller, the respective assets listed in Exhibit H.

3.5 Future Cooperation. After the Closing, Seller and Purchaser shall cooperate in transition of ownership of the Corporation from Seller to Purchaser. Without limitation, if Seller shall receive any assets of the Corporation after the Closing, it shall promptly deliver such assets to the Corporation. If the Seller, the Corporation or the Purchaser shall need any information for the preparation of tax returns, the other parties shall furnish such information upon reasonable prior notice.

3.6 Protection of Trade Secrets. All technical and business information furnished by the Seller or the Corporation to the Purchaser in connection with the transactions contemplated by this Agreement shall be maintained in confidence an shall not be disclosed to third parties or used except for the purposes of this Agreement. The foregoing obligations shall not apply to information which Purchaser can show that (a) the information was previously known to it at the time of receipt, (b) was in the public domain at the time of receipt or thereafter entered the public domain without fault of the Purchaser, (c) corresponds to information which was furnished to Purchaser by a third party lawfully entitled to do so, (d) was developed independently by personnel of the Purchaser who had no access to the information or (e) is required to be disclosed in legal proceedings. If this Agreement shall not be closed, Purchaser shall return to Seller all documents concerning the Corporation obtained by Purchaser from Seller.

3.7 Noncompetition. Seller agrees not to compete, directly or indirectly, with the Corporation in its cookie manufacturing and distribution business anywhere in the States of Illinois, Indiana, Iowa, Michigan, Ohio and Wisconsin for a period of five years after the Closing Date.

3.8 Finder's and Other fees. Seller represents to Purchaser, and Purchaser represents to Seller, that it has not retained any finder, broker or agent or agreed to pay a fee or commission to any such person. Each of them agrees to defend and indemnify the other party against all loss, liability, cost and expense (including reasonable attorneys fees) in connection with any claim or claims which may be made against the other party by reason of alleged agreements, understandings or arrangement for such a fee or commission made or alleged to have been made by it.

3.9 Section 338(h)(10) Election. (A) Seller and Purchaser agree to file with the Internal Revenue Service an election under section 338(h) (10) of the Internal Revenue Code on Forms 8023 that the transactions herein be treated as a sale of the assets of the Corporation by the consolidated group of which Seller and the Corporation are members.

(B) Seller and Purchaser agree that the purchase price shall be allocated among the assets of the Corporation as provided in Exhibit I.

4. CONDITIONS PRECEDENT TO THE OBLIGATIONS OF THE PARTIES

4.1 Conditions to Purchaser's Obligations. Purchaser's obligation to close this Agreement is, at its option, subject to the following conditions

(a) Seller's representations and warranties shall continue to be accurate in all respects as though made on the Closing Date, subject to changes occurring in the ordinary course of business and not materially adverse in nature, and Seller shall have performed all covenants and other obligations under this Agreement required to be performed by it at or before the Closing Date.

(b) There shall have been no material adverse change in the business, assets, financial condition, results of operations or cash flows of the Corporation.

(c) Seller shall have delivered at the Closing all of the documents described in Section 5.1 of Article 5.

4.2 Conditions to Seller's Obligations. Seller's obligation to close this Agreement is, at its option, subject to the following conditions:

(a) Purchaser's representations and warranties shall continue to be materially accurate in all respects as though made on the Closing Date and Purchaser shall have performed all covenants and other agreements herein required to be performed by it on or before the Closing Date.

(b) Purchaser shall have delivered at the Closing the payments and documents described in Section 5.2 of Article 5.

4.3 Failure of Fulfillment of Conditions; Remedies. The parties each agree to make all reasonable efforts to fulfill their respective conditions and to cooperate with the other party in fulfillment of its conditions. If any party fails or refuses to perform this Agreement, the other party or parties shall be entitled to specific performance of this Agreement and to damages and such other remedies as may be granted in equity or law by a court of competent jurisdiction.

5. DOCUMENTS TO BE DELIVERED AT THE CLOSING

5.1 Documents to be Delivered by Seller. At the Closing, the Seller shall deliver to the Purchaser the following documents:

(a) Such evidence of corporate existence, qualification, good standing, incumbency of officers adoption of resolutions and evidence of other corporate procedures and authority as may reasonably be requested by counsel for the Purchaser.

(b) Evidence that the property transfers described in Section 3.4 have been made.

(c) A certificate signed by the Seller updating and reaffirming the representations and warranties set forth in Section 2.1 as though made on the Closing Date and confirming performance of all the covenants set forth in Article 3 to the extent they are to be performed by Seller and the Corporation on or before the Closing Date.

(d) An "agreed upon procedures" letter from Deloitte & Ernst, dated the Closing date, in the form attached as Exhibit J.

(e) A written opinion of Seller's counsel, dated the Closing Date, in the form attached as Exhibit K.

(f) A release signed by Seller in the form attached as Exhibit L.

(g) The certificate representing the 500 shares of Common Stock of the Corporation held by the Seller together with a stock power endorsed in blank by the Seller.

5.2 Documents to be Delivered by Purchaser. At the Closing and upon fulfillment of the conditions described at Section 5.1 by the Seller, the Purchaser shall deliver documents and make payments as follows:

(a) such evidence of corporate existence, qualification, good standing, incumbency of officers, adoption of resolutions and evidence of other corporate procedures and authority as may reasonably be requested by counsel for the Seller.

(b) A certificate signed by an officer of the Purchaser updating and reaffirming its representations and warranties set forth in Section 2.2 as though made on the Closing Date and confirming performance of all the covenants set forth in Article III to the extent they are to be performed by the Purchaser on or before the Closing Date.

(c) A written opinion of Purchaser's counsel, dated the Closing Date, in the form attached as Exhibit M.

(d) A wire transfer of the purchase price to Seller.

5.3 Simultaneous Delivery. All documents delivered at the Closing shall be deemed to have been delivered simultaneously.

6. GENERAL PROVISIONS

6.1 Survival; Indemnities. All representations, warranties and agreements of the parties shall survive the Closing, notwithstanding investigations made by the parties. Seller shall indemnify and defend the Purchaser, and Purchaser shall indemnify and defend Seller, against all loss, liability, damage and expense resulting from untruth, inaccuracy or incompleteness of the information contained in their respective representations and warranties or any failure to perform their respective agreements.

6.2 Further Actions. The parties agree to execute and deliver from time to time hereafter any and all such further documents and to take such further actions as shall be reasonably necessary to carry out the transactions contemplated by this Agreement.

6.3 Nonassignability. Neither this Agreement nor any rights thereunder may be assigned or otherwise transferred directly or indirectly by any party without the prior written consent of the other parties and any attempt to do so shall be null and void.

6.4 Entire Agreement. In entering into and closing this Agreement, no party has relied or shall rely upon any promises, representations and warranties not expressed herein, and this Agreement expresses their entire agreement on the subject matter.

6.5 Amendment and Waiver. Neither this Agreement nor any provision or provisions herein may be amended or waived except by a written amendment or new agreement executed by the parties.

6.6 Governing Law. The validity, interpretation, performance and enforcement of this Agreement shall be governed by the laws of the State of New York. Each of the parties consents to the jurisdiction of the federal and state courts in New York in all matters relating to this Agreement. Seller and Purchaser hereby appoint ____________ as the agent of each of them to receive process in any legal action or proceeding.

6.7 Notices. All notices or other communications hereunder shall be given in writing and shall be deemed to be, if duly given if delivered or mailed, first class postage prepaid, to the following addresses:

6.8 Expenses. The Seller shall pay all costs and expenses incurred by it (including, without limitation, the payment of all fees and expenses of their counsel) and any tax on the sale or transfer of its shares and the Purchaser shall pay all costs and expenses incurred by it (including, without limitation, all fees and expenses of its counsel) in carrying out its obligations under this Agreement and the transactions contemplated herein.

IN WITNESS WHEREOF, the parties have executed and delivered this Agreement as of the day of ________ 199_.

MULTISTATE BAKERIES, INC. "SELLER"	BAKERY HOLDINGS, INC. "Purchaser"
By________________________	By________________________ President

EXHIBIT 16-4

ASSETS PURCHASE AGREEMENT

Index

EXHIBITS

A. List of Assets—§1.1
B. Purchase Price Adjustments—§1.2
C. List of Accounting Methods and Policies for Determination of the Contingent Purchase Price—§1.3
D. Allocation of the Purchase Price—§1.4
E. Financial Statements—§2.1(c)
F. List of Inventories—§2.1(e)
G. List of Contracts, Leases, Licenses, Permits, Registrations—§2.1(g)
H. List of Environmental and Safety Matters—§2.1(h)
I. List of Customers and Suppliers—§2.1(i)
J. List of Insurance Policies—§2.1(j)
K. List of Patents, Trademarks, Etc.—§2.1(k)
L. List of Lawsuits, Administrative Proceedings, Investigations and Claims Pending or Threatened—§2.1(l)
M. List of Facilities and Equipment Needing Repair—§2.1(m)
N. List of Personnel and Labor Matters—§2.1(n)
O. List of Approvals, Ratings or Certifications by Independent Testing Organizations and Customers—§2.1(o)
P. List of Distributors, Agents and Off-Site Warehouses—§2.1(p)
Q. List of Transactions with Affiliated Persons—§2.1(q)
R. List of Toxic and Hazardous Substances—§2.1(r)
S. List of Employee Benefit Plans—§2.1(s)

ASSETS PURCHASE AGREEMENT

This Agreement is made on ____________, 1998 between PRIME PLASTICS, INC., a Delaware corporation ("Seller") and MODERN MATERIALS, INC., a Delaware corporation ("Purchaser").

RECITALS:

A. Seller's business includes a Division engaged in the formulation, development, manufacture and sale of engineering plastic materials for special applications (the "Business"). Seller owns assets used in the Business consisting, among other things, of land and manufacturing, laboratory and office facilities of the Division located at Mountainview, New York and of machinery and equipment, patents and trade secrets, and other tangible and intangible property (the "Assets") of the Division more particularly described hereinafter.

B. Seller desires to sell, and Purchaser desires to purchase, the Assets on the terms and conditions contained in this Agreement.

AGREEMENTS:

1. THE TERMS OF THE SALE AND PURCHASE

1.1 <u>Agreements to Sell and Purchase</u>. Subject to the conditions contained herein, Seller agrees to sell, and Purchaser agrees to purchase, the Assets, wherever located, used by Seller in the Business and further described in Exhibit A.

1.2 <u>The Base Purchase Price and the Escrow Deposit</u>

(A) The base purchase price for the Assets shall be a cash price of $15,500,000, subject to the following adjustments:

(i) the price shall be increased or decreased by the amount to which the book value as of the Closing Date, of raw material, work-in process and finished product inventories (excluding inventories which are obsolete or off-specification) is more or less than $3,300,000. Such book value shall be determined as described in Exhibit B,

(ii) the price shall be increased or decreased by the amount by which the book value of accounts receivable as of the Closing Date, excluding receivables past due over 120 days and items owing for unauthorized customer deductions, is more or less than $3,100,000. Such book value shall be determined as described in Exhibit B.

(B) To secure and to provide a source of payment for Seller's indemnification obligations in Section 1.6, Purchaser shall withhold $1,500,000 of the purchase price payable at the Closing and shall deposit such amount in escrow with Industryville National Bank, as Escrow Agent, pursuant to the Escrow Agreement attached as <u>Annex I</u> to this Agreement.

1.3 <u>The Contingent Purchase Price</u>.

(A) In addition to the base purchase price, Seller agrees to pay to the Purchaser a contingent purchase price equal to ____% of the net operating earnings of the Business in excess of $_______ in each of the first two years after the Closing Date. For this purpose, net operating earnings shall mean net income before any charges for interest, income taxes and general corporate overhead, determined in accordance with generally accepted accounting principles applied consistently with those used by the Seller for the Business prior to the Closing Date, except for the increased depreciation deductions resulting from Seller's stepped-up bases in the Assets resulting from their purchase hereunder. In determining net operating earnings, Seller shall use the accounting methods and policies described in Exhibit C.

(B) Purchaser shall determine the contingent purchase price within 120 days after the end of each of two years described in Subsection (A) of this Section. Purchaser shall within that time pay such price to the Seller and shall concurrently deliver to Seller the financial statements of the Business for the applicable year together with its determination, explained in reasonable detail, of the net operating earnings and the amount of the contingent purchase price payment.

(C) Within 30 days after receipt of the documents described in Subsection (b), Seller shall be entitled to furnish written notice to Purchaser that Seller wishes to review the contingent purchase price payment. Upon receipt of such notice, Purchaser shall promptly make available during reasonable business hours to Seller and its accountants and other representatives such financial and other records as they shall reasonably request in order to perform the review. During the review, Purchaser shall cause its personnel to cooperate with the review in a reasonable manner.

(D) If Seller should decide, based on its review, that Purchaser's determination of the contingent purchase price payment was less than the correct amount, Seller shall promptly furnish written notice to the Purchaser describing in reasonable detail such proposed adjustments to the net operating earnings of the Business and/or such adjustments to the calculation of the contingent purchase price as Seller believes are appropriate. Seller and Purchaser and their accountants shall meet within ten days thereafter and shall attempt in good faith to resolve their differences as to the determination of the contingent purchase price. If Seller and Purchaser shall fail to resolve their differences within thirty days after Seller's written notice of proposed adjustments, the accounting firms for Seller and Purchaser shall within ten days appoint a third accounting firm which shall make a final determination of the contingent purchase price payment that shall be binding on both Seller and Purchaser. Both Seller and Purchaser and their accounting firms shall cooperate and furnish documents to the third accounting firm in order to facilitate its final determination of the contingent purchase price payment.

(E) During the first two years after the Closing Date, Purchaser shall operate the Business in a manner that is sufficiently ditinguishable from its other businesses to allow a clear determination of the contingent price provided in this Section.

1.4 Price Allocation for Tax Purposes. Seller and Purchaser agree to allocate the purchase price among the Assets for federal, state and local income tax purposes as provided in Exhibit D and to file with their federal income tax returns a Form 8594 consistent with such allocation. Seller and Purchaser agree that any contingent purchase price payments shall be treated by both of them as paid for Section 197 intangibles as defined in the Internal Revenue Code.

1.5 Liabilities and Obligations.

(A) Purchaser shall not assume or otherwise be liable for any liabilities or obligations, fixed or contingent, known or unknown, first incurred by Seller or to which its business or assets first became subject prior to the Closing Date, except that Purchaser shall assume the unpaid balance of the industrial revenue bonds secured by Seller's manufacturing facilities at Mountainview, New York. Nevertheless, Purchaser shall assume the performance from and after the Closing Date of those contracts, leases, licenses, permits, registrations and other obligations continuing by their terms after the Closing Date which Seller has fully and accurately disclosed in the exhibits described in Section 2.1.

(B) Seller shall be responsible for product liability with respect to all products sold on or before the Closing and all products included in the finished product inventories sold to Purchaser except to the extent that liability arises from any express recommendation by Purchaser of the use of products for unsuitable applications, failure by Purchaser to label or furnish material safety data sheets to customers, or any damage to such products during their storage or handling prior to shipment by Purchaser. Purchaser shall be responsible for any product liability for Products manufactured after the Closing Date.

1.6 Indemnification.

(A) Seller shall defend and indemnify Purchaser and its shareholders, directors and officers against all loss, liability, cost and expense (including reasonable attorneys' fees) related to (a) any misrepresentation made in or pursuant to this Agreement and any breach of a warranty or agreement herein, (b) all liabilities and obligations relating to the Business or the Assets, whether fixed or contingent, existing on the Closing Date and not expressly assumed by Purchaser.

(B) Purchaser shall defend and indemnify Seller against all loss, liability, cost and expense (including reasonable attorneys' fees) related to the performance after the Closing Date of the contracts, leases, licenses, permits, registrations, covenants and other liabilities and continuing contractual obligations expressly assumed by Purchaser.

1.7 Proration of Certain Items. Seller and Purchaser shall prorate as of the Closing Date all rents, royalties, real and personal property taxes, prepaid items and deposits and shall credit or debit the net amount as appropriate. Proration of property taxes shall be calculated in accordance with local custom as confirmed by the title insurer.

1.8 Transfer Taxes and Fees. Seller shall pay, or reimburse Purchaser for, any sales, use, transfer or other taxes and fees imposed on the transfer of the Assets by Seller to Purchaser and upon registration or recording of any instruments effecting such transfer. Purchaser shall pay the cost of the title insurance policy described in Section 3.10.

1.9 The Closing. Subject to the conditions stated in Article V, the closing (the "Closing") of this Agreement shall take place at the offices of Cravath & Davis, 100 Broad Street, New York, N.Y. 10004 at 10:00 A.M. on ____________, 1998 (the "Closing Date"). The Closing shall be deemed effective at the close of the business on the Closing Date.

2. REPRESENTATIONS AND WARRANTIES

2.1 Seller's Representations and Warranties. Seller represents, warrants and agrees as follows:

(a) Incorporation and Good Standing. Seller is a corporation duly organized and existing in good standing under the laws of Delaware; is duly qualified to do business and in good standing in the State of Delaware; has properly prepared and filed all tax returns and paid all franchise, income and real personal property taxes and assessments to such jurisdictions as affect its right to sell or its title to the properties covered by this Agreement except taxes not yet due and payable; and has all requisite power to enter into and perform this Agreement.

(b) Corporate Authorization. Seller has taken all requisite action, corporate and otherwise, to authorize the execution and performance of this Agreement including the approval of its board of directors. No approval by Seller's stockholders is required. The execution and performance of this Agreement will not violate any provision of Seller's Certificate of Incorporation or By-Laws, or any agreement to which it is a party or to which Seller or the Business or Assets is subject, or of any law or regulation or any order in any action or proceeding to which it is a party or which affects its business or properties.

(c) Financial Statements. The financial statements of the Business consisting of certain balance sheet items for the years ended December 31, 1996 and 1997 and the six-month period ended June 30, 1998, and statements of operating earnings (before tax) for the years and period then ended are attached as Exhibit E. Except as explained in footnotes thereto, such financial data fairly present the results of operations of the Business in accordance with generally accepted accounting principles consistently applied. There has been no material change in the Business or Assets since June 30, 1998.

(d) The Assets. The Assets listed in Exhibit A are all of the properties of every kind located at the Plant or which have been used primarily in the Business since December 31, 1997 except for properties sold or disposed of in the ordinary course of business. Except as described in Exhibit A, Seller owns good and marketable title to all the Assets, free and clear of all other claims of ownership, leases, licenses, easements, mortgages, liens, encumbrances, charges, security interests, conditions and restrictions except for rights-of-way of utilities, public roadways and railroad rights-of-way passing over or through its real property, and matters of record which do not affect marketability, and the lien of property taxes not yet due and payable. There are no existing violations of zoning ordinances and restrictions and no encroachments either on Seller's real property or by Seller on any adjoining property except as set forth in Exhibit A. None of the Assets is subject to any agreement or commitment for sale or disposition, or has been disposed of, except for (i) inventories being sold in the ordinary course of business and (ii) dispositions of properties for depreciation or obsolescence in the ordinary course of business.

(e) Inventories. A complete and accurate list of the places where all inventories are located, including estimates of the types and quantities of inventories at each location, is attached as Exhibit F. All raw material, work-in-process and finished goods inventories sold to Purchaser on the Closing Date will be free of defects, meet applicable specifications and be salable to customers in the ordinary course of business.

(f) Receivables. All receivables (net of reserves) on Seller's books as of the Closing Date will be collectible in full within 90 days after the Closing Date.

(g) Contracts, Leases, Licenses, Permits, Registration's and other Continuing Contractual Obligations. An accurate and complete list of all contracts, leases, licenses and other contractual obligations relating to the Business or the Assets is attached as Exhibit G. In preparing Exhibit G, Seller may omit each purchase order for the purchase of goods or services if the aggregate amount to be sold or purchased over the term of the purchase order is less than $20,000. Seller may also omit any office equipment lease calling for rental payments less than $15,000 over the term of the lease. Seller does not know of any existing failure or refusal by the other party to any of such contracts, leases, licenses or contractual obligations to perform any of them or plan to terminate or modify any of them.

(h) Environmental and Safety Matters. (i) Except as disclosed in Exhibit H, the Business and Assets are in compliance with, and are not subject to any liability under, any and all applicable federal, state and local environmental and safety laws, regulations and codes ("Environmental Laws") other than liabilities which are not in the aggregate material to the Business or the Assets. Without limitation, except as so disclosed, (A) Seller holds all permits and registrations required by the Environmental Laws and is in compliance with each of them; (B) Seller has properly prepared and maintained all records and filed all notices and reports required by the Environmental Laws; (C) none of Seller's properties or facilities contains any asbestos-containing material, polychlorinated biphenyl dielectric fluid or underground storage tank or is contaminated with any hazardous substance, pollutant or contaminant regardless of whether its presence originated prior to Seller's ownership or operation or was caused by outside sources such as migration from another property or a spill by a common carrier, supplier, customer or tenant; (D) Seller has not incurred any liability, existing or contingent, for offsite releases or disposal of hazardous wastes, hazardous substances, pollutants or contaminants and has not received any notice that it has or may be named as a party potentially responsible for any such release or disposal and (E) Seller is in compliance with all occupational safety and health standards required by the Environmental Laws and has not received notice of any work-related illness or injury among its employees except accidents and illnesses accurately reported in its OSHA 200 log.

(ii) Except as disclosed in Exhibit H, to the best of Seller's knowledge, each of Seller's permits and registrations can be transferred or reissued, if necessary, to Purchaser without any interruption of the Business and without material modification, and Seller knows of no reason why any of them cannot be renewed upon expiration of their current term without imposition of materially stricter conditions if such expiration will occur within one year from the date of this Agreement.

(iii) Except as disclosed in Exhibit H, to the best of Seller's knowledge, none of the products, raw materials, components, catalysts, intermediates, by-products or other substances used in the Business is the subject of any study, investigation or proceeding conducted or sponsored by any governmental agency under the Environmental Laws.

(i) Customer and Suppliers List. An accurate and complete list of each customer who purchased products during 1997 and the first six month period of 1998 and each supplier who furnished raw materials or services in an aggregate amount exceeding $20,000 during such year and period is attached as Exhibit I and includes the products purchased, unit volume and dollar volume for each customer. No customer or supplier has advised Seller since January 1, 1997 that it expects to discontinue or materially reduce its purchases or its supply of raw materials or services except as described in Exhibit H.

(j) Insurance Policies. An accurate and complete list of all insurance policies held by Seller, including all liability policies held during the 20 year period preceding the Closing Date, with respect to the Business or Assets is attached as Exhibit J. Such list shall contain the name and address of the insurer and broker, the policy number and a brief description of the coverage and the extent to which aggregate limits of coverage have been exhausted by claim payments. Seller shall maintain all its insurance in effect through the Closing. If any of the Assets shall be the subject of any loss or damage covered by such insurance and Purchaser shall elect to close, Seller shall assign to Purchaser the right to receive the insurance proceeds.

(k) Intellectual Property. An accurate and complete list of all patents and trademarks and applications therefor used in the Business is included in Exhibit K. Seller has not licensed or otherwise authorized anyone to use such patents, trademarks or applications or any trade secrets of the Business including, but not limited to, customer lists and business opportunities, except as fully described in Exhibit K. Seller has not received any claim that any of its products, processes or equipment infringes any patent, trademark or trade secret of any third party except as described in Exhibit K. Seller holds all licenses necessary to use its existing processes and equipment and to manufacture and sell its Products without infringement or violation of any patent, trademark copyright or trade secret rights of any third party.

(l) Litigation, Administrative Proceedings, etc. An accurate and complete list describing all lawsuits, administrative proceedings, investigations and claims pending or threatened with respect to the Business or the Assets is attached as Exhibit L. Seller has and is conducting the Business and operating the Assets in compliance with all applicable federal, state and local laws and regulations except as described in Exhibit L.

(m) Condition of Facilities and Equipment. Except as disclosed in Exhibit M, all facilities and equipment at the Mountainview Plant are in good condition and repair (fair wear and tear excepted), and have received customary maintenance (including planned overhauls and annual maintenance turnarounds) through the date of this Agreement.

(n) Personnel and Labor Matters. An accurate and complete list of all employees who are employed full-time in the Plastics Business and their duties, compensation and benefits is attached as Exhibit N. Seller has not increased, or promised to increase, the compensation or benefits of any employee since January 1, 1997 except as described in Exhibit N. Seller has no agreement or understanding with any of such employees with respect to their duties, compensation or benefits except as described in Exhibit N. Seller is a party to a written agreement with respect to ownership and assignment of inventions and ownership, nonuse and nondisclosure of trade secrets with all of such employees and all employees whose employment terminated within the past two years except as described in Exhibit N. Seller has not experienced any strike, work stoppage or other concerted work action at the Mountainview Plant since January 1, 1997. To the best of its knowledge, Seller is and has been in compliance with all equal employment opportunity laws. Seller does not know of any organization campaign or plan of any labor union to seek representation of any employees at the Mountainview Plant except as described in Exhibit N.

(o) Approvals, Test Ratings, Etc. An accurate and complete list of all approvals, ratings or certifications by independent testing organizations and customers of its products which are part of the Business is attached as Exhibit O. Seller has received no notice that any of them has or will be withdrawn for any reason.

(p) Distributors, Agents and Warehouses. An accurate and complete list of all distributors, agents and off-site warehouses used in connection with the Business is attached as Exhibit P.

(q) List of Transactions with Affiliated Persons. An accurate and complete list of all transactions since January 1, 1997 relating to the Business between the Seller and any of its officers, directors, or stockholders or any person related to them, is attached as Exhibit Q.

(r) Toxic and Hazardous Substances. A complete and accurate list of all materials used at the Mountainview Plant by Seller, which are listed as toxic or hazardous substances or materials in the regulations of the Occupational Safety and Health Administration, 29 CFR, §1910.1000 *et seq.*, the regulations of the U.S. Department of Transportation, 49 C.F.R. §171 *et seq.*, or the regulations of the U.S. Environmental Protection Agency under the Emergency Planning and Community Right to Know Act, 40 CFR § 11001 et seq. is attached as Exhibit R.

(s) Employee Benefit Plans. All employee benefit plans (as defined in Section 3(3) of ERISA) covering former and current employees of the Business under which Seller has any obligation or liability with respect to employees of the Business are listed and identified as "Benefit Plans" in Exhibit S. Seller does not contribute to or have any obligation or liability with respect to any multiemployer plan (as defined in Section 3(37)) of ERISA) to provide pension, medical or other benefits to present or former employees of the Business.

The Benefit Plans are and have been administered in compliance with their terms and the applicable requirements prescribed by ERISA, the applicable provisions of the Code, and any other applicable Regulation. None of the Benefit Plans which are "employee welfare plans" as defined in Section 3(1) of ERISA are funded through a trust. The transactions contemplated by this Agreement will not result in liability of Purchasee for severance pay to the Seller's employees.

There are no pending or, to the best of Seller's knowledge, threatened claims by or on behalf of the Benefit Plans or by any employee or beneficiary thereof alleging a breach of fiduciary duty or violation of other applicable federal or state law which could result in any liability under ERISA or any other law.

Each Benefit Plan which is an employee pension benefit plan, as defined in Section 3(2) of ERISA (collectively, the "Pension Plans") which is intended to be "qualified " under Section 401(a) of the Code is so qualified and has received a favorable determination letter from the IRS as to its qualified status. To the best of Seller's knowledge, nothing has occurred since the respective dates of such letters that would adversely affect such qualification.

None of the Pension Plans (or any pension plan maintained by a trade or business under common control with the Seller within the meaning of Section 414(b) or (c) of the Code) which are subject to Title IV of ERISA have completely terminated or been the subject of a "reportable event" as defined in Section 4043 of ERISA. None of the Pension Plans has been partially terminated or incurred a complete discontinuance of contributions. Neither Seller nor any entity which would be considered a single employer with the Seller under Section 414(b), (c), (m) or (o) of the Code has incurred any liability under Sections 412 or 4971 of the Code and no lien has been imposed on the assets of the Subsidiary or its affiliates pursuant to Section 412 of the Code. No Pension Plan has incurred an "accumulated funding deficiency" (whether or not waived) within the meaning of Section 412 of the Code. No amendment has been made to a Pension Plan with respect to which security is required under Section 401 (a)(29) of the Code. There has been no prohibited transaction (as such term is defined in Section 4975 of the Code or in Part 4 of the Title I of ERISA) with respect to any Benefit Plan, and no penalty or tax under Section 501(i) of ERISA or Section 4975 of the Code has been imposed upon the Company or the Subsidiary that could subject Purchaser to a tax or penalty on prohibited transactions.

None of the Pension Plans has "unfunded benefit liabilities" within the meaning of Section 4001(a)(18) of ERISA. Using the actuarial assumptions used for funding purposes for the 1997 plan year, the fair market value of the assets of each Pension Plan will exceed the "projected benefit obligations" (within the meaning of Statement of Financial Accounting Standards No. 87) of such Plan as of the date hereof and the Closing. None of the Pension Plans hold any shares of stock or other securities of the Company or any of its affiliates.

The Seller has delivered to Purchaser correct and complete copies of (a) the Benefit Plans and Pension Plans and all trust agreements and other funding vehicles relating thereto, (b) the most recent IRS determination letter relating to each Pension Plan for which a letter of determination was obtained, (c) to the extent required to be filed, the most recent Annual Report (Form 5500 Series) and accompanying schedules of each Benefit or Pension Plan, as filed with the Internal Revenue Service, (d) if available, any summary plan description relating to the Benefit or Pension Plans, (e) if available, the most recent certified financial statements of each Benefit or Pension Plan and (f) the most recent actuarial valuation report for each Pension Plan.

All group health plans (as defined in Section 1 62(i) of the Code) covering the present and former employees of the Business, and any trade or businesses which would be treated as a single employer with the Subsidiary under Section 414(b), (c), (m) or (o) of the Code, have been maintained in compliance with the continuation coverage requirements of Section 4980B of the Code and Part 6 of Title I or ERISA.

2.2 Purchaser's Representations and Warranties. Purchaser represents and warrants as follows:

(a) Corporate Standing. Purchaser is a corporation duly organized and existing in good standing under the laws of the State of New York; is duly qualified and in good standing in the State of New Jersey; has paid all franchise and other taxes to each jurisdiction which affect its right to enter into and perform this Agreement and has all requisite power to enter into and perform this Agreement.

(b) Corporate Authorization. Purchaser has taken all requisite action, corporate and otherwise, to authorize the execution and performance of this Agreement and the matters contemplated hereto, including the approval of its board of directors. No approval by Purchaser's stockholders is required. The execution and performance of this Agreement will not violate any provision of Purchaser's Certificate of Incorporation or By-Laws, or any agreement to which it is a party or to which it is subject, or any order in any action or proceedings to which it is a party or which affects its business or properties.

(c) Consents, etc. No consent, approval, permit, registration, filing or notice to or with any governmental agency or third party is required on the part of Purchaser for the execution, delivery and performance of this Agreement except as expressly provided herein.

(d) Litigation, etc. There is no litigation or governmental proceeding pending or, to the best of Purchaser's knowledge, threatened against Purchaser that questions the validity or challenges the performance of this Agreement or any action to be taken by Purchaser pursuant to this Agreement.

3. COVENANTS

3.1 Antitrust Clearance.

(A) Each party agrees to prepare properly and file promptly after the date of this Agreement a notification and report pursuant to the Hart-Scott-Rodino Federal Trade Commission Improvements Act (the "HSR Act") with the U.S. Department of Justice (DOJ) and Federal Trade Commission (FTC). If either party shall require information possessed by the other party in order to prepare its notification and report, the party having the information shall furnish it to counsel for the requesting party but may require that counsel refrain from disclosing such information to the requesting party.

(B) Each party shall furnish to the DOJ or FTC such further information as it may reasonably request to evaluate the sale of the Assets and shall exercise reasonable diligence to obtain termination of the waiting period under the HSR Act without any adverse action by the applicable agency. Such obligation to exercise diligence shall not require either party to agree to any modification of this Agreement or to agree to divest or restrict the Business or the Assets or any other business or assets of the Seller or the Purchaser.

3.2 Conduct of Business Until Closing. Pending the Closing, Seller shall conduct the Business only in the ordinary course. Without limitation of the foregoing, Seller shall, with respect to the Business, (A) use its best efforts to preserve intact the Business and the Assets; (B) maintain the Assets in good repair and operating condition except for fire, flood or other acts of God; (C) continue in full all existing insurance coverage; (D) not enter into any material contract or other transaction without prior written approval of Buyer; (E) use its best efforts to retain employees, customers and suppliers; (F) refrain from any increase in the compensation or benefits of employees or commitment for any increase; (G) not engage in any inter-company transaction with Seller or any of its affiliates except for continuation of support services and other transactions which have been in the normal course of business. (H) refrain from any transfer or commitment to transfer any of the Assets except for sales of Products in the ordinary course of business or to subject the Assets to any lien, encumbrance or security interest; (I) refrain, without Purchaser's consent, from any material modification of any of the Assets or commitment for any capital expenditure in excess of $20,000 and (J) refrain, without Purchaser's consent, from entering into any contract for the sale of Products or purchase of raw materials for any aggregate amount in excess of $100,000 or a period longer than 90 days.

3.3 Continuing Due Diligence and Cooperation. Until the Closing, Seller shall consult with Purchaser on the operation of the Business and shall afford access to Purchaser during normal business hours to all records of the Business and Assets and to its employees, accountants, customers and suppliers. However, no investigation by Purchaser shall limit responsibility of Seller for the representations, warranties and agreements herein. Seller shall maintain the Assets in good order and repair, but no alterations shall be made except with the written approval of Purchaser. No Assets shall be purchased or sold or transferred to other plant locations except for the sale of Products and purchase of raw materials or suppliers in the ordinary course of business.

3.4 Future Cooperation in Sharing Records. Within 30 days after the Closing, Seller shall transfer to Purchaser all business records and historical information pertaining specifically to the Business, except that Seller shall retain copies of (a) documents pertaining to its disposal or shipment of wastes from the Mountainview Plant and (b) its personnel records pertaining to employees at the Mountainview Plant. Both Purchaser and Seller shall retain their respective records pertaining to the Business for no less than six years. Each party shall furnish from time to time, as requested by the other party, such records or information (other than confidential trade secrets) pertaining to the Business as required for the requesting party to conduct its operations or fulfill its legal obligations. After the expiration of this six year retention period, neither party shall discard or dispose of any such records or information without thirty days prior written notice to the other party, advising the other of the materials to be discarded or disposed of and offering the other the opportunity to retrieve such materials for retention at its own facilities.

3.5 Cooperation After the Closing.

(A) If Seller is unable to assign any supply or sale contracts, leases, licenses or permits to be transferred to Purchaser under this Agreement and Purchaser nevertheless elects to close this Agreement, Seller shall continue to perform such contracts, lease, licenses or permits for the account of Purchaser, but Purchaser shall reimburse Seller's actual out-of-pocket costs. After the Closing, Seller shall execute and deliver from time to time such further assignments and other documents as Purchaser shall reasonably request to effect or evidence the assignments and transfers of title contemplated by this Agreement.

(B) If Seller shall (i) discover in its possession or control after the Closing any Assets which were not delivered at the Closing or (ii) shall receive payment of any receivable transferred hereunder, Seller shall promptly notify Purchaser and shall deliver the same to Purchaser. Should Seller receive or learn of any business opportunity or other benefit pertaining to the Business or Assets, Seller shall use best faith efforts promptly to notify Purchaser thereof or to refer same to Purchaser.

(C) Seller shall at its expense arrange for the proper disposal prior to the Closing of all waste stored at the Mountainview Plant. Seller shall further at its expense arrange for the proper disposal promptly after the Closing of all inventories found during the physical inventory pursuant to Section 1.5 to be obsolete or off-specification. Such disposal may include the sale of such inventory, but any sale shall not be made without first offering to Purchaser's right of first refusal.

3.6 Confidential Information.

(A) Prior to the Closing, all technical and business information furnished by either party to the other party in connection with the transactions contemplated by this Agreement shall be maintained in confidence and shall not be disclosed to third parties or used except where the recipient can show that (a) the information was previously known to it at the time of receipt, (b) was in the public domain at the time of receipt or thereafter entered the public domain without fault of the recipient, (c) corresponds to information which was furnished to the recipient by a third party lawfully entitled to do so or (d) was developed independently by personnel of the recipient who had no access to the information. If this Agreement shall not be closed, Purchaser shall return to Seller all documents concerning the Business or Assets obtained by Purchaser from Seller and shall continue to be bound by its obligations under this subsection.

(B) After the Closing, Seller shall neither disclose nor use any technical or business information related to the Business and shall take appropriate action to require its employees to refrain from any such disclosure or use. After the Closing, Purchaser shall neither disclose nor use any technical or business information of Seller not related to the Business, but obtained by Purchaser through its due diligence activities prior to the Closing or through its hiring of Seller's employees.

3.7 Bulk Transfer Law. The parties waive compliance with the bulk transfer provisions of Section 6 of the Uniform Commercial Code as in effect in New York and Seller hereby agrees to indemnify and defend Purchaser against all loss, liability, cost and expense which may result from such noncompliance.

3.8 Consulting Agreement and Personnel Arrangements.

(A) Dr. Leo Bakelite, President and founder of Seller, will retire on the Closing Date, but agrees to consult with Purchaser for three years after the Closing Date. Purchaser shall pay $240,000 per year to Dr. Bakelite for such services in equal, monthly installments of $20,000 each. Purchaser agrees to nominate Dr. Bakelite, and Dr. Bakelite agrees to serve, as a member of Purchaser's board of directors during such three year period, if elected.

(B) Purchaser agrees to make offers for employment after the Closing to those employees of Seller who are identified in Exhibit N and Seller consents to such offers of employment. Seller agrees to make reasonable efforts to persuade such employees to accept employment with Purchaser. For a period of two years after the Closing Date, Seller shall not solicit or rehire any of such employees who accept employment with Purchaser without the prior written consent of Purchaser. This Section shall not imply any obligation of Purchaser to retain any employees in employment for any time period or limit its freedom to change their responsibilities or compensation after the Closing.

(C) Purchaser will not assume or continue any of the existing pension or other employee benefit plans of Seller. Seller agrees to provide vested rights as of the Closing Date under its existing defined benefit pension plan to each of the salaried employees participating therein on the date of this Agreement. As soon as reasonably practicable, Seller shall cause the administrator or trustee of such plan to distribute in cash or in fully paid annuities an amount equal to the present value of accrued benefits of each such participant on the Closing Date. Seller shall defend and indemnify Purchaser against all loss, liability, cost or expense related to Seller's employee benefit plans.

3.9 Non-Competition. Seller and its subsidiaries shall not compete with Purchaser in the manufacture or sale of the products which are part of the Business anywhere in New York, Connecticut, Delaware, Maryland, Massachusetts, New Jersey, Pennsylvania and Rhode Island for a period of five years after the Closing Date. Seller shall require any person to whom any significant part of its retained businesses or to whom any subsidiary or the business of any subsidiary is sold or transferred to assume the obligations of this Section.

3.10 Real Property Title Matters. Within ten days after the execution of this Agreement, Seller shall at its expense furnish to Purchaser a title report and commitment from a title insurer acceptable to Purchaser for the issuance of an American Land Title Association ("ALTA") form title insurance policy insuring that title to all real property to be acquired by Purchaser at the Closing conforms in all respects to the representations and warranties contained in Section 2.1(d). Such commitment and policy shall contain no exceptions other than the standard printed exceptions contained in all ALTA policies issued for industrial properties by the insurer. Purchaser shall have 10 days after receipt to notify Seller of any objections to title. If Purchaser so objects, Seller shall have 10 days to clear title to meet such objections and shall use its best efforts to do so, but shall not be obligated to commence a lawsuit against anyone as part of such efforts. If Purchaser has no objection or if Seller clears all title objections, Seller shall arrange at its expense for the title insurer to issue a title policy conforming to the commitment at the Closing.

3.11 Environmental Property Remediation Act.

(A) Seller shall promptly take such steps as shall be required by the New York Environmental Property Remediation Act to notify the New York State Department of Environmental Conservation (NYSDEC) of the proposed sale and either to (A) file a negative declaration with the NYSDEC or (B) seek either a memorandum of understanding (MOU) an administrative consent order (ACO) with the NYSDEC under which Seller shall develop and carry out a remediation work plan for its Mountainview Plant at its expense including, without limitation, the provision of a trust fund, letter of credit or other remediation funding source in an amount and kind acceptable to NYSDEC.

(B) If Seller shall file a negative declaration which is not approved within 45 days by NYSDEC, Seller shall seek a MOU or ACO and carry out and perform a remediation work plan as provided above.

(C) Seller shall hire at its expense such environmental consultants and contractors (reasonably satisfactory to Purchaser) as shall be necessary to perform the cleanup plan with reasonable promptness and efficiency. Purchaser shall afford access after the Closing to Seller and its consultants and contractors to perform all necessary investigation and the remediation work plan. Seller shall assure that the cleanup is performed in a manner which does not significantly interfere with Purchaser's operations.

(D) Seller shall be entitled to terminate this Agreement if it cannot within _____ days after the date of this Agreement obtain an ACO or MOU authorizing a remediation work plan which can be performed for a cost reasonably estimated to cost no more than $___________.

(E) Purchaser shall be entitled to terminate this Agreement if Seller cannot within days after the date of this Agreement obtain an ACO or MOU which can be performed without substantial interruption or interference with operations at the Mountainview Plant.

NOTE TO READERS: New York does not have an environmental law that requires disclosure of releases of hazardous substances and other environmental conditions upon a direct or indirect transfer of real estate. However, other states (such as Connecticut, Illinois, Indiana and New Jersey) have such laws. Thus, Section 3.11 was included to illustrate steps taken to comply with a hypothetical law).

3.12 Finder's Fees or Commissions. (A) Seller agrees to pay the finder's fee or commission owed to its investment banking firm, Merrill Lehman Salomon Inc. Seller further agrees to defend and indemnify the Purchaser against all liability, cost and expense (including reasonable attorneys' fees) in connection with any claim or claims which may be made against the Purchaser by reason of agreements, understandings or arrangements for a finder's fee or commission made by Seller.

(B) Purchaser agrees to defend and indemnify the Seller against all liability, cost and expense (including reasonable attorneys fees) in connection with any claim or claims which may be made against the Seller by reason of agreements, understandings or arrangements for a finder's fee or commission made by the Purchaser.

3.13 Labels, Business Forms, Packaging, Signs, Literature and Other Materials. Seller has retained and the Assets do not include any trademarks or tradenames containing the name "Prime Plastics." Notwithstanding such retention, Purchaser shall not be required to remove such tradenames or trademarks from existing labels, containers and printed material or matter used in the Business, provided, however, that, commencing as promptly as possible after the Closing Date, Products shipped by Purchaser shall have affixed thereto a stamp, sticker or other evidence of the fact that the Business has been sold to Purchaser. Purchaser shall further exercise diligent efforts to remove or modify all labels, business forms, packaging, signs, literature and other materials which use such names as soon as reasonably practicable after the Closing Date in the ordinary course of business, but in no event later than six months after the Closing Date.

4. CONDITIONS PRECEDENT TO THE OBLIGATIONS OF SELLER AND PURCHASER

4.1 Conditions to the Obligations of Purchaser. The obligation of Purchaser to close this Agreement is, at its option, subject to the following conditions:

(a) The representations and warranties of Seller shall continue to be accurate in all respects as though made on the Closing Date, except for changes in the ordinary course of business and not materially adverse in nature, and Seller shall have performed all the agreements required to be performed by it on or before the Closing Date.

(b) There shall have been no material adverse change in the Business or Assets and have no material loss, destruction or damage to the plants or major items of equipment to be sold by fire, flood, windstorm or other Act of God. The risk of such loss, destruction or damage to property shall remain with Seller until the Closing.

(c) Seller shall have delivered at the Closing all of the documents described in Section 5.1.

(d) No governmental agency shall have commenced or advised that it plans any lawsuit or administrative proceeding to prevent or restrict the transactions contemplated by this Agreement or to require any later divestiture of all or any part of the Business or Assets.

(e) Such other documents as counsel for the Purchaser may reasonably request.

4.2 Conditions to the Obligations of Seller. The obligation of Seller to close this Agreement is, at its option, subject to the following conditions:

(a) Representations and Warranties. The representations and warranties of Purchaser shall continue to be accurate in all respects on the Closing Date and Purchaser shall have performed all agreements herein required to be performed by it on or before the Closing Date.

(b) Purchaser shall have delivered at the Closing the payments and documents described in Section 5.2.

(c) Such other documents as counsel for the Purchaser may reasonably request.

4.3 Failure of Fulfillment of Conditions; Remedies. Seller and Purchaser agree to make reasonable efforts to fulfill their respective conditions and to cooperate with the other party in fulfillment of such conditions. If this Agreement shall be terminated prior to the Closing Date for inability of either party, after reasonable efforts, to fulfill its conditions, the parties shall each bear their own expenses and shall have no liability to the other party for damages or expenses. If either party fails to use reasonable efforts to fulfill its conditions or otherwise fails or refuses to perform this Agreement, the other party shall be entitled to specific performance of this Agreement and to damages and such other remedies as may be granted in equity or by law by a court of competent jurisdiction.

5. DOCUMENTS TO BE DELIVERED AT THE CLOSING

5.1 Documents of Seller. At the closing, Seller shall deliver to Purchaser the following documents:

(a) Incorporation and Good Standing. Copies of Seller's Certificate of Incorporation and all amendments, certified by the Secretary of State of New York, and a good standing certificate including payment of taxes.

(b) Secretary's Certificate. A Secretary's Certificate as to the resolutions adopted by Seller's board of directors and as to its By-Laws and the incumbency of its officers.

(c) Officer's Certificate. An Officers Certificate reaffirming as though made on the Closing Date the representations and warranties in Section 4.1, signed by its President or a Vice President.

(d) "Agreed Upon Procedures" Letter. An "agreed upon procedures" letter from Seller's accountants in form and substance reasonably satisfactory to the Purchaser.

(e) Deeds for Real Property. A special warranty deed to the real property described in Exhibit A, subject only to exceptions permitted by this Agreement, together with a commitment for a title insurance policy described in Section 3.10.

(f) General Bill of Sale. A general bill of sale conveying the Assets (tangible and intangible) of the Business subject only to exceptions permitted by this Agreement.

(g) Specific Assignments of Contracts, Etc. Specific assignments of all contracts, leases and other continuing contractual obligations described in Exhibit G together with all necessary consents which may be required to validly assign the same.

(h) Specific Assignments of Environmental Permits. Specific assignments or other arrangements for transfer of environmental permits listed in Exhibit H together with evidence of the consent of each applicable environmental agency to the transfer of such permits without substantive modifications.

(i) Specific Assignments of Patents and Trademarks. Specific assignments of all patents, trademarks and applications therefor in form satisfactory for recording with the patent office or registries of the nations where the same are held.

(j) Specific Assignment of Motor Vehicles. Specific assignments of Seller's motor vehicle title certificates or registrations.

(k) Pollution Control Bonds. Specific assignments of the Trust Indenture and other agreements related to the Columbia County 6% Industrial Revenue Bonds secured by the Assets and the written consent of Mohawk Trust Company, as Indenture Trustee.

(l) Antitrust. A letter from the DOJ or FTC or other evidence that the waiting period under the HSR Act has expired or been terminated.

(m) Termination of Shareholders Agreement. A copy of an agreement effectively terminating the Shareholders Agreement dated November 1, 1963 between Seller and its shareholders.

(n) Environmental. A copy of an approved negative declaration, ACO or MOU signed by Seller and approved by the NYSDEC pursuant to Section 3.11.

(o) Consulting Agreement. A Consulting Agreement, dated on the Closing Date, signed by Dr. Leo Bakelite containing terms mutually satisfactory to Dr. Bakelite and the Purchaser.

(p) Employment Agreements. Employment Agreements, dated on the Closing Date, signed by each of the officers and managers of Seller identified in a letter dated _____, 1998 from Purchaser to Seller on terms consistent with such letter.

(q) Evidence of Payment of Finder's Fees. A letter from Merrill Lehman Salomon Inc. acknowledging payment of all amounts owed to it for finder's fees or commissions.

(r) Affidavit. A non-foreign person affidavit, signed by Seller.

(s) Escrow. The Escrow Agreement, signed by Seller.

(t) Legal Opinion. Legal opinion of Prime's counsel, Carter & Milbank, in form and substance reasonably satisfactory to the Purchaser, but Purchaser acknowledges that such opinion will not include title to the assets.

(u) Receipt. Receipt of the Seller for the basic purchase price, including an acknowledgement that it was correctly calculated pursuant to Section 1.2 herein, less the $1,500,000 delivered to Industryville National Bank, as Escrow Agent.

5.2 Documents of Purchaser. Purchaser shall deliver at the Closing:

(a) Incorporation and Good Standing. Copies of Purchaser's Certificate of Incorporation and all amendments, certified by the Secretary of State of New York, and a good standing certificate including payment of taxes.

(b) Secretary's Certificate. A Secretary's Certificate as to resolutions adopted by Purchaser's board of directors and as to its By-Laws and the incumbency of its officers signing documents at the Closing.

(c) Officer's Certificate. An Officer's Certificate reaffirming Purchaser's representations in Section 4.1 hereof, signed by its President or a Vice President.

(d) Assumption Agreements. Assumption agreements evidencing the assumption by Purchaser of the contracts, leases and other continuing contractual obligations provided in Section 1.3(B).

(e) Consulting Agreement. A Consulting Agreement, dated on the Closing Date, signed by the Purchaser containing terms mutually satisfactory to Dr. Leo Bakelite and the Purchaser.

(f) Employment Agreements. Employment Agreements, dated on the Closing Date, between Prime and each of the officers and managers of Seller identified in a letter dated ______, 1998 from Purchaser to Seller on terms consistent with such letter and signed by Purchaser.

(g) Escrow Agreement. The Escrow Agreement executed by Purchaser and the Escrow Agreement.

(h) Legal Opinion. Legal opinion of Purchaser's counsel, Cravath & Davis, in form and substance reasonably satisfactory to Seller.

(i) Purchase Price Payment. A wire transfer of the basic purchase price, as adjusted pursuant to Section 1.2 hereof, and an acknowledgement that the amount paid was correctly calculated under Section 1.2.

(j) Escrow Payment. Evidence of payment of $1,500,000 to Industryville National Bank, as Escrow Agreement, pursuant to Section 1.2 hereof.

6. GENERAL PROVISIONS

6.1 Successors and Assigns. This Agreement shall be binding upon and shall inure to the benefit of Seller and Purchaser and their respective successors and assigns, but any attempt by either party to assign this Agreement shall be null and void without prior written consent of the other party. Nevertheless, Purchaser may assign this Agreement to a wholly owned subsidiary or a purchaser of substantially all of its materials businesses, provided that the assignee assumes in writing all of the assignor's obligations hereunder.

6.2 Strict Compliance. Failure of any party hereto to insist upon strict observance of or compliance with all of the provisions of this Agreement in any one or more instances shall not be deemed to be a waiver of its right to insist upon such observance or compliance with such provisions in the future or with any other provisions of this Agreement.

6.3 Entire Agreement. This Agreement, including the attached Exhibits, constitutes the entire agreement between the parties as to its subject matter and there are no other agreements or warranties, express or implied, made by Seller or Purchaser with respect thereto.

6.4 Notices. All notices pursuant to this Agreement shall be given in writing either by prepaid telefax, air express, courier or express mail addressed as follows:

If to Seller:

If to Purchaser:

6.5 Amendment: This Agreement may be amended only by a written document stating expressly that it is intended to be an amendment of this Agreement and that is signed by an officer of both Seller and Purchaser.

6.6 Survival of Representations and Warranties. The representations, warranties and agreements made herein shall survive and shall not be terminated or otherwise extinguished by the Closing under this Agreement on the Closing Date.

6.7 Governing Law. The validity, interpretation, performance and enforcement of this Agreement shall be governed by the laws of the State of New York, without regard to any conflict of laws principles which may result in application of the law of any other state or jurisdiction.

6.8 Severability. If any provision or provisions of this Agreement shall be found to be invalid or unenforceable, the remaining provisions shall be deemed independent and shall continue in full force and effect.

6.9 Public Communications. Seller and Purchaser agree not to issue any press releases or other communications in relation to the transactions contemplated by this Agreement without prior consultation of the other party.

IN WITNESS WHEREOF, the parties have caused this instrument to be signed by their duly authorized officers, as of the day and year first hereinabove written.

PRIME PLASTICS, INC.

By______________________________

MODERN MATERIALS, INC.

By______________________________

____

Dr. Leo Bakelite, Individually
as to Section 3.8

EXHIBIT 16-5

ESCROW AGREEMENT

This Escrow Agreement is made on , 199_ between PRIME PLASTICS, INC., a Delaware Corporation ("Seller") and MODERN MATERIALS, INC., a New York corporation ("Purchaser") and INDUSTRYVILLE NATIONAL BANK, a national banking association ("Escrow Agent").

RECITALS:

A. Pursuant to an Assets Purchase Agreement dated _______, 199_ (the "Assets Purchase Agreement"), Seller has agreed to sell its business and assets to Purchaser for a price of $15,500,000.

B. Section 1.4(A) of the Purchase Agreement provides that Seller shall indemnify and defend Purchaser against all loss, liability, cost and expense related to any breaches by Seller of the representations, warranties and covenants contained in the Purchase Agreement.

C. Seller has agreed to secure and provide a source for payment of its indemnification and defense obligations by a deposit of $1,500,000 of the price in escrow on the terms and conditions of this Agreement.

AGREEMENTS:

In consideration of the mutual promises herein contained, the parties agree as follows:

1. APPOINTMENT OF ESCROW AGENT.

Seller and Purchaser hereby appoint the Escrow Agent, and the Escrow Agent hereby accepts such appointment, to serve until the termination of this Agreement as provided in Section 4 or as otherwise provided in Section 7. Purchaser agrees to pay the fees and expenses of Escrow Agent set forth in Exhibit A.

2. DEPOSITS IN THE ESCROW FUND

To secure and provide a source for payment of the indemnification and defense provisions of the Assets Purchase Agreement, Seller hereby deposits $1,500,000 in cash in escrow with the Escrow Agent which hereby acknowledges its receipt. Such amount, plus interest and other income, is called the "Escrow Fund."

3. CLAIMS AGAINST THE ESCROW FUND

(A) During the term of this Agreement, the Purchaser may deliver written notice (a "Claim Notice") to the Escrow Agent and the Seller of claims under the indemnification and defense provisions of the Purchase Agreement specifying the known facts relating to each claim and the amount or estimated amount thereof.

(B) The Seller shall have 10 business days from the delivery of any Claim Notice to deliver a notice (a "Dispute Notice") indicating any dispute as to liability for, or the amount of, the claim or claims therein together with the facts alleged to support such dispute.

(C) If the Purchaser asserts a claim in the manner specified in this Section and the Seller accepts such claim or fails to dispute such claim by a Dispute Notice given within the time permitted, Escrow Agent shall pay from the Escrow Fund to Purchaser the amount of the claim as specified in the Claim Notice plus interest from the Closing Date to the date of payment.

(D) If the Seller shall properly deliver a Dispute Notice with respect to any claim described in a Claim Notice, Escrow Agent shall reserve an amount from the Escrow Fund equal to the amount or estimated amount of the disputed claim alleged in the Claim Notice and shall hold such amount plus interest attributable thereto until it shall receive either (i) written notice, signed by both Seller and Purchaser, furnishing agreed instructions with regard to payment or nonpayment of the claim or (ii) a final order from a federal or state court in New York from which there is no further right of appeal directing payment or nonpayment of the claim.

(E) Whenever any amount is paid from the Escrow Fund, interest earned thereon from the effective date to the date of such payment shall be calculated and distributed by the Escrow Agent to the person or persons receiving the payment. The Seller and Purchaser agree to cooperate in the calculation of interest hereunder.

4. TERMINATION.

(A) All Claim Notices must be served by Purchaser within 18 months after the Closing Date, as defined in the Purchase Agreement. If no Claim Notices are delivered within such time period, or if all claims alleged in Claim Notices delivered during such period have been paid or withdrawn, Escrow Agent shall promptly thereafter pay the Escrow Fund to the Seller.

(B) If any Claim Notice has been delivered and remains unresolved at the end of 18 months after the Closing Date, Escrow Agent shall continue to hold such amount of the Escrow Fund as shall relate to the subject matter of each unresolved Claim Notice until it has been resolved. The balance of the Escrow Fund shall be distributed to the Seller. Within 10 days after the resolution of all Claim Notices and payment of all amounts owed to Purchaser, Escrow Agent shall release from escrow and deliver to the Seller any then remaining balance of the Escrow Fund, at which time this Agreement shall terminate.

(C) If any Claim Notice remains unresolved two years after the Closing Date as defined in the Purchase Agreement, at its discretion, Escrow Agent may commence in a court of competent jurisdiction an interpleader action seeking a declaration of the rights of the parties. Escrow Agent may also, at its discretion, deposit the Escrow Fund with such court and shall thereupon be discharged of any and all further duties and liability under this Agreement.

5. NONALIENATION OF INTERESTS IN THE ESCROW FUND.

The rights of Seller in the Escrow Fund shall be nonassignable except by operation of law and any attempt to assign its interest shall be null and void. Such right shall not be evidenced by any formal certificate.

6. INVESTMENT OF ESCROW FUNDS.

(A) Escrow Agent shall invest the cash deposited with it pursuant to this Agreement in such manner as Purchaser from time to time may direct, provided that all of such investments shall be either (i) obligations of or guaranteed by the United States of America, or (ii) certificates of deposit in commercial banks with capital exceeding $1,000,000,000 (collectively, "Permitted Investments") or (iii) money market funds which are invested solely in Permitted Investments; provided, further, that the maturities of Permitted Investments shall be such as to permit Escrow Agent to make prompt payment of the Escrow Fund to persons entitled thereto. To the extent that Permitted Investments must be sold in order to make payments pursuant to this Agreement, the Escrow Agent shall have the power and duty to do so and shall be reimbursed by Purchaser for the related costs including, without limitation, any applicable "breakup" fees.

(B) Escrow Agent shall not be responsible for, and Purchaser shall replace, any monies lost through any investment made at Purchaser's direction pursuant to Section 6(A) hereof.

7. DUTIES AND LIABILITIES OF ESCROW AGENT; EXPENSES; RESIGNATION.

(A) Escrow Agent shall have no duties or obligations as Escrow Agent hereunder except the ministerial duties and obligations specifically set forth herein which shall be determined solely by the express provisions hereof. In performing any of its duties under this Agreement, Escrow Agent shall not incur any liability to anyone for damages, losses or expenses, except for Escrow Agent's willful default, gross negligence or breach of trust. Accordingly, Escrow Agent shall not incur any such liability for (1) any action that is taken or omitted in good faith upon advice of its counsel given regarding any question relating to the duties and responsibilities of Escrow Agent under this Agreement or (2) any action taken or omitted in reliance upon any instrument, including any notice, written statement or receipt given pursuant to this Agreement, that Escrow Agent shall in good faith believe to be genuine, to have been signed or delivered by a proper person or persons and to conform to the provisions of this Agreement.

(B) Seller and Purchaser jointly and severally shall defend, indemnify and hold harmless Escrow Agent against any losses, claims, damages, liabilities and expenses, including reasonable costs of investigation and counsel fees and disbursements that may be imposed on Escrow Agent or incurred by Escrow Agent in connection with its acceptance of appointment of the performance of its duties under this Agreement, including any litigation arising from this Agreement or involving the subject matter hereof, unless any such loss, claim, damage, liability or expense shall be the result of Escrow Agent's gross negligence, willful default or breach of trust.

(C) Escrow Agent shall be entitled to resign by written notice to each of other parts to this Agreement. Such resignation, however, shall not be effective until the later of the following events: (i) Seller and Purchaser have agreed upon and appointed a successor which has agreed in writing to act as Escrow Agent thereunder, (ii) a successor has been judicially appointed and agreed in writing to act hereunder or (iii) 120 days from the date the written notice of resignation is given to Seller and Purchaser. The foregoing provision shall not limit the rights of Escrow Agent under subsection (B) of this Section.

(D) Escrow Agent shall furnish to the parties monthly reports of income earned and receipts and disbursements. Upon resignation or other termination of its duties hereunder, Escrow Agent shall deliver copies of canceled checks, Claim Notices, Dispute Notices and other records to the successor Escrow Agent, if any, and otherwise to Purchaser. Seller shall be entitled to a copy of such records.

8. COOPERATION.

Subject to the terms and conditions of this Agreement, each party shall use its best efforts to carry out the transactions contemplated by this Agreement.

9. PARTIES IN INTEREST; ASSIGNMENT.

This Agreement shall inure to the benefit of and be binding on the parties and their respective successors and assigns. Except when expressly permitted by this Agreement or approved by each party, any assignment of this Agreement by any party without the prior written consent of the other parties shall be void. Nothing in this Agreement is intended to confer any rights or remedies on anyone other than a party to this Agreement or the holder of a valid assignment of rights under this Agreement.

10. GOVERNING LAW.

The validity, interpretation, performance and enforcement of this Agreement shall be governed in all respects by the laws of the State of New York without regard to any conflict of interests principles that may apply the law of any other state. Any action or proceeding by or against the Escrow Agent shall be brought in the Supreme Court for New York County, New York or the U.S. District Court sitting in New York County, New York and each of the parties hereto hereby submits to and accepts generally and unconditionally the jurisdiction of those courts with respect to its respective person and property in any such action.

11. AMENDMENTS OR SUPPLEMENTS TO AGREEMENT.

This Agreement may not be amended or supplemented except by a written instrument duly executed by each party.

12. ENTIRE AGREEMENT.

This Agreement, and any documents delivered under this Agreement, sets forth the entire agreement among the parties with respect to its subject matter and supersedes all prior agreements or understandings among the parties regarding those matters.

13. NOTICES.

All notices, requests, demands and other communications under this Agreement shall be in writing and shall be deemed to have been duly given if either delivered personally or sent by telefax or Federal Express or by certified or registered mail, return receipt requested, with postage prepaid to the parties at their respective addresses set forth below:

If to Seller:

If to Purchaser:

If to Escrow Agent:

14. COUNTERPARTS.

This Agreement may be executed in two or more counterparts, each of which is an original, all of which together shall be deemed to be one and the same instrument.

IN WITNESS WHEREOF; this Escrow Agreement has been executed as of the day and year first above written.

PRIME PLASTICS, INC.
"Seller"

By____________________________

MODERN MATERIALS, INC.
"Purchaser"

By____________________________

INDUSTRYVILLE NATIONAL BANK
"Escrow Agent"

By____________________________

EXHIBIT 16-6

MERGER AGREEMENT

TABLE OF CONTENTS

MERGER AGREEMENT

THIS MERGER AGREEMENT (the "Agreement") is made on ______, 1998 among INTERNATIONAL MACHINE TOOLS, INC., a Delaware corporation ("Buyer"), INTERMAC, INC., a Delaware corporation that is a wholly-owned subsidiary of Buyer ("Intermac"), and CAD EQUIPMENT, INC., a Delaware corporation (the "Company").

Buyer wishes to acquire the Company by having Intermac merge with and into the Company (the "Merger"), as the result of which the Company will be the surviving corporate entity and a wholly-owned subsidiary of Buyer. The Merger shall be upon the terms and subject to the conditions set forth herein. The Boards of Directors of Buyer, Intermac, and the Company have each duly approved this Agreement. Capitalized terms used herein shall have the meanings given to them or referred to in Section 1.5 of this Agreement.

In consideration of the the mutual representations, warranties, and agreements contained herein, Buyer, Intermac and the Company agree as follows:

ARTICLE 1 MERGER; CLOSING; EFFECTIVE TIME; DEFINITIONS

1.1 The Merger. Subject to the terms and conditions of this Agreement, the Company and Intermac shall consummate the Merger in which (i) Intermac shall be merged with and into the Company and the separate corporate existence of Intermac shall thereupon cease and all the rights, privileges, powers, franchises, properties and assets of Intermac shall be vested in the Company, (ii) the Company shall be the surviving corporation of the Merger and shall become a wholly-owned subsidiary of Buyer, and (iii) the Company shall continue to be governed by the laws of the State of Delaware and the name, identity and existence of the Company and all its rights, privileges, powers, and franchises shall continue unaffected and unimpaired by the Merger. The Merger shall have the effects set forth in Section 259 of the General Corporation Law of the State of Delaware ("DGCL") . The Company after the Merger is sometimes referred to herein as the "Surviving Corporation."

1.2 Closing: Effective Time. The Closing shall occur at the offices of Taft, Wardwell & Marx, in New York, New York, at 10:00 a.m., local time (the "Closing Date"), on the later of:

(i) ____ __, 1998, provided that all of the conditions set forth in Article 6 have been satisfied or waived; or

(ii) the business date that is no more than five business days after the satisfaction or waiver of all the conditions set forth in Article 6, but no event later ______, 1998.

The Merger shall become effective in accordance with the DGCL upon the filing, on the Closing Date, of a certificate of merger by the Surviving Corporation as provided in the DGCL, or at such time thereafter as Buyer and the Company may agree upon in writing to provide in such certificate of merger (the "Effective Time") .

1.3 Articles of Incorporation: By-Laws. At the Effective Time (a) the Certificate of Incorporation of the Company as in effect immediately prior to the Effective Time shall become the Certificate of Incorporation of the Surviving Corporation, and (b) and the By-Laws of Intermac as in effect immediately prior to the Effective Time shall become the By-Laws of the Surviving Corporation.

1.4 Directors and Officers; Further Assurances. The directors of Intermac immediately prior to the Effective Time and the individuals identified on Schedule 1.4 hereto to be officers of the Surviving Corporation, from and after the Effective Time shall be the directors and officers, respectively, of the Surviving Corporation until their successors have been duly elected or appointed in accordance with the By-Laws of the Surviving Corporation (and Buyer, as the then sole shareholder of the Surviving Corporation, and the Surviving Corporation shall take such actions as may be appropriate to elect or appoint such persons as directors and officers of the Surviving Corporation).

1.5 Definitions. In addition to capitalized terms otherwise defined herein, as used in this Agreement, the following capitalized terms shall have the meanings provided in this Section 1.5:

"Affiliate" of, or a person "Affiliated" with, a specific Person is a Person that directly or indirectly, through one or more intermediaries, controls, or is controlled by, or is under common control with, the Person specified.

"Benefit Plan" shall mean a defined benefit plan as defined in Section 3(35) of ERISA (other than a Multiemployer Plan) in respect of which the Company, any subsidiary or any ERISA Affiliate is, or within the immediately preceding six (6) years was, an "employer" as defined in Section 3(5) of ERISA.

"CERCLA" shall mean the Comprehensive Environmental Response, Compensation and Liability Act, 42 U.S.C. §§ 9601 *et seq.*, any amendments thereto, any successor statutes, and any regulations or guidance promulgated thereunder.

"Contaminant" shall mean any waste, pollutant, contaminant, pollutant, hazardous substance, hazardous waste, petroleum or petroleum derived substance or waste, radioactive material, named as such in CERCLA or the regulations of the U.S. Environmental Protection Agency ("EPA") thereunder or in any other Environmental, Health or Safety Law.

"DGCL" means Delaware General Corporation Law.

"Effective Time" shall have the meaning given to such term in Section 1.2 hereof.

"Environmental, Health or Safety Law" shall mean any federal, state or local law, ordinance, rule, regulation, permit, license or other determination of any Governmental Authority relating to, imposing liability or standards concerning, or otherwise addressing the environment, health and/or safety, including but not limited to the Clean Air Act, the Clean Water Act, RCRA, CERCLA, any so-called "Superfund", "Minisuperfund" or "Superlien" law, the Toxic Substances Control Act and the OSH Act, each as from time to time hereafter in effect.

"Environmental Lien" shall mean a Lien in favor of any Governmental Authority for any (i) liabilities under any Environmental, Health or Safety Requirements of Law, or (ii) damages arising from, or costs incurred by such Governmental Authority in response to, a Release or threatened Release of a Contaminant into the environment.

"ERISA" means the Employee Retirement Income Security Act of 1974, as amended.

"ERISA Affiliate" shall mean any (i) corporation which is a member of the same controlled group of corporations (within the meaning of Section 414 (b) of the IRC) as the Company or any subsidiary, (ii) partnership or other trade or business (whether or not incorporated) under common control (within the meaning of Section 414(c) of the IRC) with the Company or any subsidiary, (iii) member of the same affiliated service group (within the meaning of Section 414 (m) of the IRC) as the Company or any subsidiary, any corporation described in clause (i) above or any partnership or trade or business described in clause (ii) above, or (iv) any entities required to be aggregated with the Company or any subsidiary under IRC Section 414(o).

"Escrow Agent" means a bank or trust company mutually agreeable to the parties that serves as escrow agent under the Escrow Agreement.

"Escrow Agreement" means the Escrow Agreement in substantially the form attached hereto as Exhibit A.

"Escrow Fund" means the amount of $1.7†million deposited with the Escrow Agent pursuant to Section 2.2(a) hereof.

"Force Majeure" shall mean an act of God, fire, flood, storm, strike or labor difficulties, riot, insurrection, act of war (whether declared or otherwise), act of governmental authority or other supervening event, in each case beyond the reasonable control of the party claiming Force Majeure.

"Full Compliance with ISRA" means conducting all site assessment, site investigation, remedial investigation, and remedial workplan preparation and implementation activities and such other actions that may be required by the New Jersey Department of Environmental Protection (NJDEP) pursuant to ISRA until such time as the New Jersey Department of Environmental Protection approves in writing a negative declaration or delivers a no further action letter containing no qualifications other than its standard reopener provisions and the exceptions allowed by the Section 5.8 of this Agreement.

"GAAP" means United States generally accepted accounting principles consistently applied.

"Governmental Approval" shall mean any authorization, consent, approval, waiver, exception, variance, franchise, permission, permit, exception, filing, publication, declaration, license or other form of required permission from, of or with any governmental authority, and shall include, without limitation, each building, occupancy, environmental and operating permit and license that is required for the ownership, use and operation of any facility owned or leased by the Company and any of its subsidiaries.

"HSR Act" means the Hart-Scott-Rodino Antitrust Improvements Act of 1976, as amended, and the regulations adopted thereunder.

"Indemnifiable Losses" means all claims, demands, liabilities, obligations, losses, fines, penalties, costs, royalties, proceedings, lawsuits, judgments, awards, deficiencies, assessments, or damages (whether or not absolute, contingent, accrued, conditional or otherwise, and whether or not resulting from third party claims or governmental actions), including without limitation out-of-pocket expenses and reasonable attorneys' and accountants' fees and expenses.

"Intellectual Property Rights" means the rights described and defined in Section 3.10.

"ISRA" means the New Jersey Industrial Site Recovery Act, N.J.S.A. § 13:1K-6 *et seq.*, as amended , and regulations promulgated thereunder.

"Key Employee" means any of the individuals listed on Schedule 1.5 hereto.

"Lien" shall mean any mortgage, pledge, deed of trust, assignment, lien, charge, encumbrance or security interst of any kind, or the interest of a vendor or lessor under any conditional sale agreement, capital lease or other title retention agreement, but excluding easements, rights of way or similar encumbrances on real property which are in the ordinary course and which do not materially affect the value, use, marketability and insurability of title of such real property.

"Material Contract" shall have the meaning given to such term in Section 3.19.

"Merger Price" means the price defined in Section 2.1.

"Multiemployer Plan" shall mean a "multiemployer plan" as defined in Section 4001(a)(3) of ERISA which is, or within the immediately preceding six (6) years was, contributed to by the Borrower, the Company or an ERISA Affiliate.

"The OSH Act" shall mean the Occupational Safety and Health Act, 29 U.S.C. §§ 651 *et seq.*, any amendments thereto, and any successor statutes, and all regulations promulgated thereunder.

"Permitted Liens" shall mean:

(i) Liens for taxes on property if the same shall not be due and payable, or are being diligently contested in good faith and by appropriate proceedings and for which the Company shall have set aside reserves on its books as required by GAAP;

(ii) Liens imposed by law, such as carrier's, warehousemen's and mechanic's liens and other similar liens, which arise in the ordinary course of business with respect to obligations not yet due or being contested in good faith by appropriate proceedings and for which the Company shall have set aside reserves on its books as required by GAAP;

(iii) Liens arising out of pledges or deposits under workmen's compensation laws, unemployment insurance, old age pensions, or other social security benefits other than any Lien imposed by ERISA;

(iv) Liens incurred or deposits made in the ordinary course of business to secure surety bonds provided that such Liens shall extend only to cash collateral for such surety bonds:

(v) Liens for purchase money debt incurred to acquire assets owned by the subsidiaries and used in their respective businesses; and

(vi) Standard encumbrances of record on property of the Company or any subsidiary which do not materially impair the value or marketability of such Property and do not materially interfere with the continued use or operation of the Property as currently operated and used.

"Plan" shall have the meaning given in ERISA § 3(3) (other than a Multiemployer Plan) in respect of which the Company, any subsidiary or any ERISA Affiliate is, or within the immediately preceding six (6) years was, an "employer" as defined in Section 3(5) of ERISA.

"RCRA" shall mean the Resource Conservation and Recovery Act, 42 U.S.C. §§6901 *et seq.*, any amendments thereto or any successor statutes, and any regulations promulgated thereunder.

"Release" shall mean any release, spill, emission, leaking, pumping, injection, deposit, disposal, discharge, dispersal, leaching or migration into the indoor or outdoor environment or into or out of any property, including the movement of Contaminants through or in the air, soil, surface water, groundwater or property.

"Remedial Action" shall mean actions to (i) clean up, remove, treat or in any other way address Contaminants in the indoor or outdoor environment; (ii) prevent the Release or threat of Release or prevent or minimize the further Release of Contaminants; or (iii) perform pre-remedial studies and investigations and post-remedial monitoring and care.

"Reportable Event" shall mean any reportable event as defined in Section 4043 of ERISA.

"Services Agreements" means the agreements defined as such on Section 3.14(c).

"Shareholders' Agents" shall have the meaning given to such term in Section 8.5.

"Shareholders Agreement" shall mean the Shareholders Agreement dated ________ __, 1992 among the Company and its shareholders.

"ERISA Event" shall mean (i) a Reportable Event with respect to any Benefit Plan; (ii) the withdrawal of the Company, any subsidiary or any ERISA Affiliate from a Benefit Plan during a plan year in which the Company, any subsidiary or such ERISA Affiliate was a "substantial employer" as defined in Section 4001(a)(2) of ERISA; (iii) the imposition of an obligation on the Company, any subsidiary or any ERISA Affiliate under Section 4041 of ERISA to provide affected parties written notice of intent to terminate a Benefit Plan in a distress termination described in Section 4041(c) of ERISA; (iv) the institution by the Pension Benefit Guaranty Corporation of proceedings to terminate a Benefit Plan; (v) any event or condition which might constitute grounds under Section 4042 of ERISA for the termination of, or the appointment of a trustee to administer, any Benefit Plan; or (v) the partial or complete withdrawal of the Company, any subsidiary or any ERISA Affiliate from a Multiemployer Plan.

ARTICLE 2 MERGER PRICE; CONVERSION OF SHARES

2.1 Terms of Merger. Upon the Merger becoming effective:

(a) Subject to the terms and conditions of this Agreement, each of the 850,000 outstanding shares of Common Stock (other than any treasury shares) of the Company that is outstanding immediately prior to the Effective Time shall at the Effective Time shall be converted into the right to receive $20 cash (the "Merger Price"). Thus, the aggregate Merger Price shall be $17,000,000, subject to the provisions relating to dissenter's appraisal rights.

(b) Certificates representing outstanding Common Stock of the Company shall, after the Effective Time, represent only the right to receive from Buyer the Merger Price applicable to such shares, subject to the terms hereof. Until presented and surrendered to Buyer in accordance with the terms hereof, each certificate which represented issued and outstanding Common Stock of the Company shall be deemed for all purposes to evidence ownership of the Merger Price for such shares. No interest shall accrue or be payable with respect to the Merger Price except as otherwise provided in the Escrow Agreement.

(c) Each treasury share of its Common Stock held by the Company shall be canceled and retired and no part of the Merger Price or any other payment shall be made therefor.

(d) Each share of common stock of Intermac issued and outstanding at the Effective Time shall, automatically and without any action on the part of its holder, be converted into one share of the common stock of the Surviving Corporation (the "Surviving Corporation Common Stock"). Outstanding certificates representing shares of common stock of Intermac shall be deemed to represent an identical number of shares of Surviving Corporation Common Stock. Promptly after the Effective Time, the Surviving Corporation shall issue to the Buyer a stock certificate or certificates representing 1,000 shares of Surviving Corporation Common Stock in exchange for the certificate or certificates which formerly represented shares of Intermac common stock, which shall be cancelled.

(e) Notwithstanding anything in this Agreement to the contrary, outstanding shares of Common Stock held by shareholders of the Company who have effectively dissented from the Merger and demanded their appraisal rights in accordance with the provisions of Section 262 of the DGCL (the "Dissenting Shares"), shall not be converted into or exchangeable for the right to receive the Merger Price, but the holders thereof shall be entitled to payment from the Surviving Corporation of the appraised value of such shares in accordance with the provisions of Section 262 of the DGCL; provided, however, that if any such holder shall fail to perfect such appraisal rights or shall effectively withdraw or lose such rights, the shares of such holders thereupon be converted, as of the Effective Time, into the Merger Price, to be paid in the manner set forth in this Agreement and without any interest thereon.

2.2 Payment for Common Stock.

(a) Subject to the requirements of Section 2.2(b), at the Closing, the Buyer shall pay the Merger Price to each holder of Common Stock less such shareholder's pro rata share of the Escrow Fund. At the Closing, the Buyer shall also pay the Escrow Fund of $1,700,000 to the Escrow Agent.

(b) Upon surrender by such shareholder to Buyer of such shareholder's certificate(s) together with a Letter of Transmittal, duly executed and completed, Buyer shall promptly cause to be paid to the shareholders entitled thereto, by wire transfer for amounts in excess of $250,000 and otherwise by a check, the amount payable to such shareholder under Section 2.2(a), after giving effect to any required tax withholdings. If any payment is to be made with respect to shares of Common Stock to a person other than the registered holder of the certificate surrendered, it shall be a condition of such payment that the certificate surrendered shall be properly endorsed or otherwise in proper form for transfer and that the person requesting such payment shall pay any transfer or other taxes required by reason of the payment to a person other than the registered holder of the certificate surrendered or shall establish to the reasonable satisfaction of Buyer that such tax has been paid or is not applicable.

(c) Promptly after the termination of the Escrow Agreement, Buyer shall cause the Escrow Agent to disburse to the shareholders, in accordance with the terms of the Escrow Agreement, any funds that have not been disbursed to Buyer, including any interest earned thereon. Buyer shall pay all charges and expenses, including those of the Escrow Agent, in connection with the payment of the Merger Price.

(d) If any certificate representing Common Stock of the Company shall have been lost, stolen, or destroyed, Buyer shall deliver in exchange for such lost, stolen, or destroyed certificate, upon the making of an affidavit of that fact by the holder thereof, such payment as may be required pursuant to this Section; provided, however, that the Buyer may, in its discretion and as a condition precedent to any such payment, require the owner of such lost, stolen, or destroyed certificate to deliver a bond in such sum as it may reasonably direct as indemnity against any claim that may be made against the Surviving Corporation, Buyer, or any other party with respect to the certificate alleged to have been lost, stolen, or destroyed.

2.3 Closing of Company Transfer Books. At the Effective Time, the stock transfer books of the Company shall be closed and no transfer of its Common Stock shall thereafter be made. If, after the Effective Time, certificates formerly representing shares of Common Stock are presented to Buyer or the Surviving Corporation, they shall be canceled and exchanged for the Merger Price into which such shares are convertible under Section 2.1, without any interest thereon.

2.4 Transfer Taxes. The Surviving Corporation shall bear and pay all applicable sales, transfer, stamp, documentary, and other similar taxes (other than any taxes based on income) and governmental fees that are due or payable as a result of the transactions contemplated by this Agreement, except the transfer taxes described in Section 2.1(b).

ARTICLE 3 REPRESENTATIONS AND WARRANTIES OF THE COMPANY

The Company represents and warrants to Buyer and Intermac as follows:

3.1 Incorporation; Qualification; Powers; etc.

(a) The Company and each of its subsidiaries (i) is a corporation duly incorporated and validly existing in good standing under the laws of the state of its incorporation is qualified to do business in every jurisdiction where such qualification is necessary, except where the failure to qualify would not have a material adverse effect on the Company's financial condition or operations.

(b) The Company and each of its subsidiaries has the power and authority to own its properties and to carry on its business as now conducted.

(c) Accurate and complete copies of Certificate of Incorporation and By-Laws of the Company and each of its subsidiaries have been delivered to Buyer. The minute books of the Company and each subsidiary, which have been made available for review by Buyer, contain a true, complete and correct record in all material respects of all corporate actions taken on or prior to the date hereof at all the meetings of their boards of directors, shareholders and committees. The stock certificate books and ledgers of the Company and each subsidiary, which have been made available for review by Buyer, are true, correct and complete, and accurately reflect, at the date hereof, the ownership of the issued and outstanding capital stock of the Company and each subsidiary.

3.2 Authorization by the Company. The Company has all necessary power and authority to execute and deliver this Agreement and to consummate the transactions contemplated hereby. The execution, delivery and performance of this Agreement by the Company:

(a) has been duly and validly authorized by the Company's board of directors;

(b) does not violate (A) any provision of applicable law, (B) the Certificate of Incorporation or By-Laws of the Company or any subsidiary, or (C) any applicable order of any court or other governmental authority, or (ii) except as listed on Schedule 3.2, does not conflict with, result in a breach of or constitute (with due notice or lapse of time or both) a default under any indenture, agreement for borrowed money, bond, note or other similar instrument or any other material agreement to which the Company or any subsidiary is a party or by which the Company or such subsidiary or any of the Company's, or such subsidiary's, property is bound;

(c) does not result in the creation or imposition of any Lien of any nature whatsoever upon any property or assets of the Company or any subsidiary;

(d) constitutes the legal, valid and binding obligation of the Company enforceable against the Company in accordance with its terms; and

(e) does not, as of the date of execution hereof, require any governmental approval or the consent of any third party except (i) the filing of the certificate of merger contemplated by Section 1.2, (ii) the approval of this Agreement by the shareholders of the Company, (iii) the requirements of ISRA, (iv) the applicable requirements of the HSR Act, and (v) the other consents set forth in Schedule 3.2.

3.3 Capitalization; Title to Shares.

(a) The authorized capital stock of the Company consists of 1,000,000 shares of Common Stock, par value $0.01 per share, of which 850,000 shares are outstanding and are validly issued, fully paid, and nonassessable and free of preemptive rights. No other shares of Common Stock are issued or outstanding. There are no outstanding options, warrants, convertible or other rights in or with respect to the unissued or any treasury shares of Common Stock, and the Company is not obligated to issue any additional shares of Common Stock or any options, warrants, or other rights in or with respect to the unissued or any treasury shares of Common Stock or any other securities convertible into Common Stock. The Company has no stock option plan or stock purchase plan for its employees. There are no obligations (contingent or otherwise) of the Company to repurchase, redeem, or otherwise acquire any shares of its Common Stock.

(b) Schedule 3.3 contains a true, accurate, and complete list of the names of the shareholders of record of the Company and the number and class of shares held of record by each of them as of the date hereof. All outstanding capital stock of the Company is owned of record by such shareholders and each of them has good marketable title to such shares free and clear of any liens, encumbrances, security agreements, claims, equities, charges, restrictions, voting agreements, proxies, options, rights of first refusal, calls, contractual rights or other interests, other than the restrictions contained in the Shareholders Agreement which shall be terminated immediately prior to the Effective Time.

(c) The Company owns all of the outstanding capital stock of each of its subsidiaries. There are no outstanding options, warrants, or other rights in or with respect to the unissued shares of common stock of the subsidiaries nor any securities convertible into such stock and no subsidiary is obligated to issue any additional shares of its common stock or any additional options, warrants, or other rights in or with respect to the unissued shares of its common stock or any other securities convertible into such common stock.

(d) Except for the Shareholders Agreement, a true, accurate, and complete copy of which has been delivered by the Company to Buyer, the Company does not have any agreements with any of its shareholders with respect to its Common Stock.

(e) Except for its subsidiaries, the Company does not own or hold or have the right to acquire any equity interest in any person, directly or indirectly.

3.4 Financial Statements. The audited consolidated and consolidating balance sheets of the Company and its subsidiaries as of December 31, 1997 and the related consolidated and consolidating audited statements of income, retained earnings and cash flows of the Company and its subsidiaries for the fiscal year then ended, accompanied by an opinion of its independent public accountants, and the unaudited consolidated and consolidating balance sheets of the Company and its subsidiaries as of June 30, 1998 and the consolidated and consolidating statements of income, retained earnings and cash flows of the Company and its subsidiaries for the six months then ended (collectively, the "Financial Statements"), copies of which have been furnished to the Buyer, are true and correct in all material respects and fairly present the financial condition of the Company and its subsidiaries on a consolidated and consolidating basis as of such dates and the results of the operations of the Company and its subsidiaries for the periods ended on such dates, subject to normal year-end adjustments with respect to the unaudited financial statements, all in accordance with GAAP applied and maintained consistently by the Company throughout the periods therein. Since June 30, 1998, except as disclosed on Schedule 3.4, there have been no material adverse changes in the financial condition or operations of the Company and its subsidiaries on a consolidated basis.

3.5 Litigation. Except as set forth on Schedule 3.5, there are no actions, suits or proceedings at law or in equity or by or before any governmental authority or other agency now pending or, to the knowledge of the Company, threatened against or affecting the Company or any subsidiary, or their respective directors, officers or employees, relating to the Company or any subsidiary or any property or rights of the Company or any subsidiary, or which seeks to enjoin or prohibit or otherwise questions the validity of, any action taken or to be taken in connection with this Agreement. Except as set forth in Schedule 3.5, neither the Company nor any subsidiary has received any notice or other correspondence indicating that any of its respective insurers may be reserving its rights to disclaim coverage at a later time or is presently disclaiming coverage with respect to any actual or potential claims or litigation.

3.6 Tax Returns.

(a) The Company and each subsidiary has filed all federal, state and local tax returns which are required to be filed and has paid all taxes shown on such returns or on any assessment received by any of them to the extent that such taxes have become due, and all other taxes that may be due, except to the extent that the amount, applicability or validity of any taxes are being contested in good faith by appropriate proceedings. All such tax returns are complete and correct in all material respects. Except as set forth in Schedule 3.6, neither the Company nor any subsidiary (a) is or has been a member of any consolidated, combined, unitary or similar group for tax purposes, (b) is bound by any tax sharing, allocation or similar agreement, (c) has at any time filed a consent under Section 341(f) of the IRC, (d) is or has been a "United States real property holding corporation" (as defined in Section 897(c)(2) of the IRC) during the applicable period specified in section 897(C)(1)(A)(ii) of the IRC, or (e) will as a result of the transactions contemplated by this Agreement make or become obligated to make any parachute payment as defined in Section 280G of the IRC.

(b) The Company has established in its consolidated financial statements reserves that are adequate for the payment of any taxes that are accrued, but are not yet due and payable, except for taxes contested in good faith and by appropriate proceedings. No deficiency for any taxes has been proposed, asserted or assessed against the Company or any subsidiary which has not been resolved and paid in full and, to the knowledge of the Company, there is no basis for any such claim for unpaid taxes not fully reserved. No waiver or comparable consent given by the Company or any subsidiary regarding the application of the statute of limitations with respect to any taxes is outstanding, nor is any request for any such waiver or consent pending. No federal, state, local or foreign audit or administrative proceeding or court proceeding is presently pending with regard to any taxes and neither the Company nor any subsidiary has received written notice of commencement of any such audit.

3.7 No Defaults; Conflicts. Neither the Company nor any of its subsidiaries is in default (and no event has occurred that with due notice or lapse of time or both would result in a default): (i) with respect to any judgment, writ, injunction, decree, rule or regulation of any governmental authority, or (ii) in the performance, observance or fulfillment of any of the obligations, covenants or conditions contained in any contract.

3.8 Properties. (a) The Company and its subsidiaries has good and marketable title to all its assets, free and clear of all Liens of any nature whatsoever, except Permitted Liens. All utility services, means of transportation, facilities and other materials and services necessary for the operation of the facilities owned or operated by the subsidiaries at their respective capacity levels are available to such facilities and arrangements have been made on commercially reasonable terms for them.

(b) Schedule 3.8(b) contains a list of all real property owned or leased by the Company and its subsidiaries. Title to such real property is insurable by nationally-recognized title insurance companies under customary terms and exceptions. The Company has delivered to the Buyer, or will deliver prior to Closing, true and correct copies of all title insurance policies and surveys in the Company's or any subsidiary's possession relating to each parcel of real property owned by the Company and its subsidiaries. The improvements upon each such parcel of real property conform in all material respects to all restrictive covenants, conditions, easements, building, subdivision and similar codes and Applicable Laws and neither the Company nor any subsidiary has received any written notice of any violation of any such restrictive covenant, condition or easement or any building, subdivision or similar code or any Applicable Law. The improvements on the real property are in reasonably good working condition and repair, excepting ordinary wear and tear.

(c) Schedule 3.8(c) contains a complete and correct list of all real property leases to which the Company or any subsidiary is a party together with any amendments. The improvements upon each parcel of real property leased by the Company or any subsidiary, as the case may be, and the current use and operation of such real property conform in all material respects to all restrictive covenants, conditions, easements, building, subdivision and similar codes and Applicable Laws and neither the Company nor any subsidiary has received any written notice of any violation of any such restrictive covenant, condition or easement, or any building, subdivision or similar code or any Applicable Law. The improvements on the real property premises which are the subject of the real property Leases are in reasonably good working condition and repair, ordinary wear and tear excepted. Each real property lease is legal, valid and binding, enforceable and, to the knowledge of the Company or a subsidiary, in full force and effect. None of the Company, any subsidiary, or to the knowledge of the Company or a subsidiary, any other party is in default, violation or breach under any real property lease.

(d) The warehouse facilities disclosed on Schedule 3.8(d) are the only real property used or occupied by the Company or any subsidiary other than the real property and the real property leases listed in Schedule 3.8(b).

(e) Except as set forth in Schedule 3.8(e), neither the Company nor any subsidiary has any knowledge or has received written notice of any pending, threatened or contemplated action to take by eminent domain or otherwise to condemn any portion of its real property or any portion of any premises which are the subject of its real property leases. The Company has provided Buyer with copies of all correspondence, notices and other documents relating to matters disclosed in Schedule 3.8(e).

3.9 Governmental Approvals. The Company and each of its subsidiaries has obtained all Governmental Approvals which are necessary and appropriate for the operation of its respective facilities and businesses and which are correctly listed in Schedule 3.9. All Governmental Approvals set forth in Schedule 3.9 have been duly obtained and are in full force and effect unless otherwise indicated in Schedule 3.9. There is no circumstance or proceeding pending or, to the best knowledge of the Company, threatened which seeks, or which may be expected, to result in rescission, termination, modification, condition, suspension, non-renewal or other alteration of any Governmental Approval. The Governmental Approvals are free from conditions and requirements which materially and adversely affect, or which may so affect, the operation of the Business or financial condition of the Company or either of the subsidiaries. There has been no violation, cancellation, suspension, revocation or default of any Governmental Approval or any notice of violation, cancellation, suspension, revocation, default or dispute affecting any Governmental Approval, except for any such violation, cancellation, suspension, revocation, default or dispute which would not have a material adverse effect on the Company's business. To the knowledge of the Company and each subsidiary, no reasonable basis exists for any action referred to in the immediately preceding sentence, including, without limitation, as a result of the consummation of the transactions contemplated by this Agreement.

3.10 Intellectual Property.

(a) The Company and each of its subsidiaries owns or licenses or otherwise has the right to use all patents, patent applications, trademarks, trademark applications, service marks, trade names, trade secrets, copyrights, copyright applications, franchises, licenses and other intellectual property rights that are necessary for the operation of its businesses, without infringement upon or in conflict with the rights of any other person. All such intellectual property rights (other than trade secrets) are correctly listed or described in Schedule 3.10 (the "Intellectual Property Rights").

(b) Neither the Company nor any of its subsidiaries has received any written charge, complaint, claim, demand, or notice alleging any infringement, misappropriation or violation of any intellectual property owned by another entity including any claims that the Company or any subsidiary must license or refrain from making, selling, offering for sale, importing, or using any intellectual property owned by another entity. To their knowledge, neither the Company nor any subsidiary has interfered with, infringed upon, misappropriated, or otherwise come into conflict with any intellectual property owned by another entity.

(c) The Intellectual Property Rights include all intellectual property (other than trade secrets) used in, held for use in or necessary to the business of the Company and each subsidiary as presently conducted. Neither the Company nor any subsidiary has sold or otherwise disposed of any of the Intellectual Property Rights to any person and neither the Company nor any subsidiary has agreed to indemnify any person for any patent, trademark, trade secret or copyright infringement.

3.11 Compliance With Laws; Environmental Matters. Except as set forth on Schedule 3.11:

(a) Neither the Company nor any subsidiary is (nor has been in the past five years) in conflict with or in violation or breach of any applicable law (including, without limitation, any applicable Environmental, Health or Safety Requirements of Law), and neither the Company nor any subsidiary has received any written notice alleging any conflict with or violation or breach of any applicable law.

(b) Neither of the Company nor any subsidiary nor any of their respective properties or operations, nor to the best of the Company's knowledge, their past property or operations, is subject to any investigation, judicial or administrative proceeding, order, judgment, decree, settlement or other agreement respecting (i) any Environmental, Health or Safety Requirements of Law, (ii) any Remedial Action or (iii) any claims or liabilities and costs arising from the Release or threatened Release of a Contaminant.

(c) Neither the Company nor any of its subsidiaries has filed, or has failed if required to file, any:

(i) notice under CERCLA, 42 U.S.C. § 9603(a), the Clean Water Act, 33 U.S.C. § 1321(b)(5), or any state equivalent, reporting a Release of a Contaminant during the past five years);

(ii) notice under CERCLA, 42 U.S.C. § 9603(c), or any provision of RCRA or any state equivalent indicating past or present treatment, storage or disposal of a hazardous waste, as that term is defined under 40 C.F.R. Part 261 or any state equivalent, or seeking a permit either under RCRA, Part A or Part B; or

(iii) report of a violation of any applicable Environmental, Health or Safety Requirement of Law during the past five years;

(d) Neither the Company's nor any subsidiary's present property nor, to the best knowledge of the Company, any property formerly owned or operated by any of them, is listed or proposed for listing on the National Priorities List ("NPL") pursuant to CERCLA or on the Comprehensive Environmental Response Compensation Liability Information System List ("CERCLIS") or, to the best knowledge of the Company, any similar state list of sites requiring investigation or Remedial Action.

(e) Neither the Company nor any of its subsidiaries has sent or arranged for the transport of any waste or Contaminant to any site listed or proposed for listing on the NPL or on any state list of sites requiring investigation or Remedial Action.

(f) There is not now, nor has there ever been on or in any property now or formerly owned or operated during the period of the Company's or its subsidiaries' ownership thereof:

(i) any treatment, recycling, storage or disposal of any hazardous waste, as that term is defined under 40 C.F.R. Part 261 or any state equivalent, requiring a permit by a governmental authority;

(ii) any landfill, waste pile, underground storage tank or surface impoundment, septic system, lagoon or drywell;

(iii) any polychlorinated biphenyls (PCBS) used in hydraulic oils or as dielectric fluid in electrical transformers or other equipment; or

(iv) any designation of "interim status" or submission of any "Part A" or "Part B" permit application under RCRA.

(g) Neither the Company nor any of its subsidiaries has received any written notice or claim to the effect that such entity is or may be liable to any person as a result of the Release or threatened Release of a contaminant into the environment;

(h) No Environmental Lien has attached to any property of the Company or any of its subsidiaries;

(i) All asbestos containing material which is on or part of the property now owned by the Company or its subsidiaries is nonfriable and does not violate any applicable Environmental, Health or Safety Requirement of Law; and

(j) None of the products that the Company or any subsidiary manufactures, distributes or sells, or that the Company or either subsidiary ever has manufactured, distributed or sold, contains any detectable amount of asbestos, PCB's, radioactive material or chlorodioxins.

(k) Except as set forth in Schedule 3.11, no condition or Release has occurred or Contaminant exists on any property now or formerly owned or operated by the Company or any of its subsidiaries, and no business activities have taken place, that can reasonably be expected to give rise to any material liability or obligation under Environmental, Health or Safety Requirements of Law.

(l) The Company has identified to the Buyer the location of all sites to which the Company or any of its subsidiaries has arranged transportation for disposal; destruction; treatment; storage; regeneration; recycling or tolling.

(m) The Company has supplied to the Buyer the environmental reports itemized on Schedule 3.11. The Company has also supplied to the Buyer all sampling data, environmental compliance assessments and any other material information available to the Company relating to actual or possible contamination of its property and compliance with requirements of and obligations under Environmental, Health or Safety Requirements of Law in connection with or arising from the operation of its business or ownership or use of any business property.

3.12 <u>ERISA</u>.

(a) Neither the Company nor any of its subsidiaries maintains, contributes to, or is obligated to contribute to any other than a Plan listed on Schedule 3.12 hereto, and no ERISA Affiliate maintains, contributes to or is obligated to contribute to any employee benefit plan, as defined in ERISA (hereinafter a "Plan"), or any other plan, program, or arrangement (whether or not it is a Plan), other than the Plans listed on Schedule 3.12 hereto.

(b) Each Plan which is intended to be qualified under Section 401(a) of the Internal Revenue Code has been determined by the Internal Revenue Service to be so qualified, and each trust related to any such Plan has been determined to be exempt from federal income tax under Section 501(a) of the Internal Revenue Code. Each such plan has received a favorable determination letter from the Internal Revenue Service which covers amendments to the Plan that needed to be made to comply with the Tax Reform Act of 1986. The Company has no knowledge of any facts or circumstances that would cause any Plan not to be qualified or its trust to lose its tax exempt status. Except as disclosed on Schedule 3.12, neither of the subsidiaries, nor the Company nor any ERISA Affiliate maintains or contributes to any employee welfare benefit plan within the meaning of Section 3(l) of ERISA which provides benefits to employees after termination of employment other than health care contribution coverage as required by Section 601 of ERISA.

(c) The Company and all its ERISA Affiliates are in compliance in all material respects with the requirements, obligations, and duties imposed by ERISA and the Internal Revenue Code or regulations promulgated thereunder with respect to any Plan. No Plan has incurred any accumulated funding deficiency (as defined in Section 302(a)(2) of ERISA and Section 412(a) of the Internal Revenue Code), whether waived or not waived. Neither the Company nor any ERISA Affiliate nor any fiduciary of any Plan which is not a Multiemployer Plan (i) has engaged in a nonexempt "prohibited transaction" described in Section 406 of ERISA or Section 4975 of the IRC or (ii) has taken or failed to take any action which would constitute or result in an ERISA Event. Neither of the subsidiaries, nor the Company nor any ERISA Affiliate has incurred any liability to the Pension Benefit Guaranty Corporation which remains outstanding other than the payment of premiums, and there are no premium payments which have become due which are unpaid. Schedule B to the most recent annual report filed with the IRS with respect to each Plan is complete and accurate. Since the date of each such Schedule B, there has been no adverse change in the funding status or financial condition of the Plan relating to such Schedule B.

(d) Neither the Company nor any ERISA Affiliate has (i) failed to make a required contribution or payment to a Multiemployer Plan or (ii) made a complete or partial withdrawal under Sections 4203 or 4205 of ERISA from a Multiemployer Plan. Neither the Company nor any ERISA Affiliate has failed to make a required installment or any other required payment under Section 412 of the IRC on or before the due date for such installment or other payment. Neither the Company nor any ERISA Affiliate is required to provide security to a Plan under Section 401(a)(29) of the IRC due to a Plan amendment that results in an increase in current liability for the plan year.

(e) Except as set forth in Schedule 3.12, there is no pending or threatened litigation with respect to any Plan.

3.13 Insurance. Schedule 3.13 contains a description of all insurance which the Company and its subsidiaries maintain with respect to their respective businesses. All of such insurance is in full force and effect. The insurance is in such amounts, types, and forms as are, in the opinion of management of the Company, appropriate for the Company's and each subsidiary's business, operations, properties, and assets. No notice of termination or premium increase has been received under any such insurance policy except as disclosed in Schedule 3.13.

3.14 Labor Matters. (a) Except as disclosed in Schedule 3.14, neither the Company nor any of its subsidiaries is a party to any collective bargaining agreement, and there are no strikes or other labor disputes pending or, to the Company's knowledge, threatened. Hours worked and payments made to employees have not been in violation of any applicable law dealing with such matters. All payments for which any claim may be made on account of wages and employee health and welfare insurance and other benefits have been paid or accrued as a liability on the books of such subsidiary. Except as disclosed in Schedule 3.14, there are no employment agreements covering the employees of the Company or any of its subsidiaries. Since January 1, 1998, there has not occurred any strike, slowdown, picketing, work stoppage, concerted refusal to work overtime or similar labor activity with respect to any employees or former employees of either subsidiary. There are no labor disputes currently subject to any grievance procedure, arbitration or litigation.

(b) The Company and each of its subsidiaries have each complied in all material respects with all applicable laws pertaining to the employment or termination of employment of its respective employees, including, without limitation, all such applicable laws relating to labor relations, equal employment opportunities, fair employment practices, prohibited discrimination and other similar employment activities.

(c) Schedule 3.14 contains a true and complete list of all employment, consulting and other service or compensatory plans, contracts and arrangements, other than any such plan, contract or arrangement (a) which may be terminated upon no more than 30 days' notice without any liability or obligation of the Company or any subsidiary or (b) which provides for annual payments not exceeding $50,000 in the aggregate (the "Services Agreements"). Except pursuant to the terms of a Services Agreement listed on Schedule 3.14, there are no plans, contracts, agreements or other arrangements which provide for the accrual or payment of any compensation or benefit to or in respect of any person in the form of phantom stock or units convertible into or exchangeable for any equity security of the Company or either subsidiary or otherwise measure or base the compensation or benefits paid, payable or accrued by any person with reference to the equity value or equity securities of the Company or any of its subsidiaries. True and complete copies of all Services Agreements have been provided to the Buyer.

3.15 Force Majeure. No event of Force Majeure has occurred and is continuing.

3.16 Books and Records. The books and records of the Company and each of its subsidiaries truly and accurately reflect in all material respects its business and affairs and have been maintained in accordance with sound and customary business practices.

3.17 Accounts Receivable; Inventories.

(a) All accounts receivable that are reflected on the Financial Statements of the Company and its subsidiaries at June 30, 1998 represent valid obligations arising from sales actually made or services actually performed. Subject to the reserves for doubtful accounts maintained in such Financial Statements, the accounts receivable either have been or will be collected in full, without any set off, within ninety days after the day on which they first become due and payable, except as listed on Schedule 3.17.

(b) All inventories (including, raw material, work-in-process and finished goods) reflected in the Financial Statements of the Company and its subsidiaries at June 30, 1998 consist of a quality and quantity usable and/or salable in the ordinary course of business. Such inventories have been priced at the lower of cost or market on a first in, first out basis. Obsolete items and items of below-standard quality have been written off or written down to net realizable value.

3.18 Brokers' Compensation; Sale Bonuses. Except for the Company's agreement with Duff & Houlihan, Inc., the Company is not a party to any agreement or has any obligation to any broker, finder, or investment banker relating to the transactions contemplated hereby.

3.19 Material Contracts.

Schedule 3.19 sets forth all the following agreements to which the Company or its subsidiaries is a party:

(i) any agreement permitting the Company or any subsidiary to borrow money, any letter of credit, any pledge, any security agreement, any lease, any guarantee, and any subordination agreement or other similar or related type of contract (including, without limitation, loan agreements) as to which the Company or any of its subsidiaries is a debtor, pledgor, lessee, or obligor;

(ii) any agreement (A) for the sale of its assets in excess of $50,000 outside of the ordinary course of business, or (B) for the grant of any preferential right to purchase any of its assets, properties, or rights in excess of $50,000;

(iii) any agreement dealing with advertising, brokerage, distributorship, licensing, consulting, dealership, representative, or agency relationships in excess of $50,000 per annum or which can not be terminated by its terms upon thirty days notice;

(iv) any agreement pursuant to which any person is or will become entitled to any benefit upon a change in control of the Company or any of its subsidiaries;

(v) any agreement for a period in excess of one year, which has a value in excess of $100,000, to purchase, sell, or provide services, materials, supplies, merchandise, facilities, or equipment and which is not terminable without penalty by the Company or any subsidiary on not more than 30 days' notice;

(vi) any agreement for one capital expenditure or a series of related capital expenditures, the aggregate amount of which is in excess of $100,000;

(vii) any agreement for the hiring of any director, officer, employee or consultant including any employee manual or policy or practice providing for severance benefits;

(viii) any agreement involving payment or receipt by the Company or any subsidiary of $100,000 or more which would be terminable by its express terms by any party other than the Company or any subsidiary as a result of the consummation of the transactions contemplated by this Agreement;

(ix) any lease, rental or occupancy agreement, license, installment, conditional sale agreement, warehousing agreement, or other agreement affecting the ownership of, leasing of, title to, use of, or any leasehold or other interest in, any property (except personal property leases and installment or conditional sale agreements having a value per item or aggregate payments of less than $100,000 and with terms of less than one year);

(x) any agreement not otherwise disclosed pursuant to this Section 3.19 which involves the payment or receipt by the Company or any subsidiary of more than $100,000, except for those incurred in the ordinary course of business, and except for intercompany payments between the Company and any subsidiary, payroll, benefit plan payments, and tax payments and deposits;

(xi) any joint venture, partnership, or other agreement (however named) involving a sharing of profits, losses, costs, of liabilities by the Company or any subsidiary with any other person;

(xii) any agreement containing covenants that in any way purport to restrict the business activity of the Company or any subsidiary or limit the freedom of either to engage in any line of business or compete with any person;

(xiii) any agreement providing for payments to or by any person based on sales' purchase, or profits, other than direct payment for goods; and

(xiv) any power of attorney granted by any subsidiary or the Company that is currently effective;

The documents identified in Schedule 3.19 are collectively referred to herein as the "Material Contracts, and individually as a "Material Contract." Each Material Contract is valid, in full force and effect, binding and enforceable by the Company or the subsidiary that is a party to such Material Contract in accordance with its respective terms. The Company and its subsidiaries have complied in all material respects with the terms of all Material Contracts and are not in default under any Material Contract. True and correct copies of all documents identified in Schedule 3.19 have been delivered to Buyer prior to the date hereof.

3.20 Bank Accounts. Schedule 3.20 contains a true and complete list showing the name of each bank or financial institution in which the Company or any of its subsidiaries has an account or safe deposit box and the names of all persons authorized to draw thereon or to have access thereto.

3.21 Suppliers. Except as set forth in Schedule 3.21, no supplier of materials or services to the Company or any of its subsidiaries in an amount in excess of $100,000 per year has during the last 12 months decreased materially or, to the knowledge of the Company, threatened to decrease or limit materially, its provision of such services or supplies. There has been no termination, cancellation, or limitation of, or any material modification or change in, during the last 12 months, the business relationships of the Company or any of its subsidiaries with any supplier of materials or services in an amount in excess of $100,000 per year.

3.22 Customers. Schedule 3.22 sets forth a list of the ten largest customers of the Company and its subsidiaries in terms of sales during the fiscal year ended December 31, 1997. Except as set forth in Schedule 3.22, there has not been any material adverse change in the business relationships of the Company or any of its subsidiaries with any customer identified on such schedule. Neither the Company nor any of its subsidiaries has received any notice that any customer has materially reduced, or will materially reduce, purchases of the products of the Company or any of its subsidiaries. To the actual knowledge of the Company, no such customer has experienced any material adverse change in its financial condition that would threaten its viability as an ongoing concern.

3.23 No Material Misstatements. No representation contained herein contains any material misstatement of fact or omits to state any material fact necessary to make the statements therein not materially misleading.

3.24 Transactions with Affiliates. Except as set forth in Schedule 3.24, (a) no Affiliate of the Company or any of its subsidiaries (i) owns any assets used, held for use or necessary to the business of the Company or a subsidiary as presently conducted, (ii) possesses, directly or indirectly, any financial interest in or is a partner, director, officer, or employee of any partnership, corporation, firm, association or business organization which is a client, supplier, customer, lessor, lessee or competitor of the Company or any subsidiary, or (iii) is a party to any Material Contract (other than employment agreements disclosed pursuant to this Agreement) and (b) no payments are due and owing under any Material Contract with any Affiliate.

3.25 Absence of any Material Adverse Change. Except as disclosed in Schedule 3.25 or as expressly permitted by this Agreement, there has not been any material adverse change affecting the Company and its subsidiaries taken as a whole since December 31, 1997.

ARTICLE 4 REPRESENTATIONS AND WARRANTIES OF BUYER

Buyer hereby represents and warrants to the Company as follows:

4.1 Organization, Standing and Power. Buyer is duly incorporated and existing in good standing under the laws of the State of Delaware and has all requisite corporate power and authority to own, lease, and operate its properties and assets and to carry on its business as presently conducted and to consummate the transactions contemplated hereby. Intermac is duly organized and existing as a corporation under the laws of the State of Delaware and has all requisite corporate power and authority to enter into this Agreement and to consummate the transactions contemplated hereby. Intermac does not own, lease, or operate any properties or assets and has not carried on any business activities since its inception. Intermac is a wholly-owned subsidiary of Buyer.

4.2 Authority of Buyer; No Violation.

(a) Buyer and Intermac each have all requisite corporate power and authority to enter into this Agreement and to consummate the Merger and the transactions contemplated hereby. The execution and delivery by Buyer and Intermac of this Agreement and the consummation of the transactions contemplated hereby have been duly and validly authorized by all necessary corporate action on the part of Buyer and Intermac, and this Agreement has been duly executed and delivered by Buyer and Intermac and is a valid and binding obligation of Buyer and Intermac, enforceable in accordance with its terms.

(b) Neither the execution and delivery by Buyer or Intermac of this Agreement, the consummation of the transactions contemplated herein, nor compliance by Buyer and Intermac with any of the provisions hereof, will: (i) conflict with or result in a breach of any provision of their respective Articles or Certificate of Incorporation or By-Laws (ii) constitute a breach of or result in a default, or give rise to any rights of termination, cancellation, or acceleration under any of the terms, conditions or provisions of any note, bond, mortgage, indenture, franchise, license, permit, agreement, or other instrument or obligation to which Buyer or Intermac is a party, or by which Buyer or Intermac or any of their respective properties or assets is bound; or (iii) violate any order, writ, injunction, decree, statute, rule, or regulation applicable to Buyer or Intermac or any of their respective properties or assets. No consent of, approval of, notice to, or filing with any governmental authority having jurisdiction over any aspect of the business or assets of Buyer or Intermac, and no consent of, approval of, or notice to or filing with any other person, is required in connection with the execution and delivery by Buyer and Intermac of this Agreement or the consummation by Buyer and Intermac of the transactions contemplated hereby, except the filing of the certificate of merger contemplated by Section 1.2 and except as required by the HSR Act and ISRA.

4.3 Litigation. There is no private or governmental suit, claim, action, or proceeding pending or, to Buyer's knowledge, threatened, against Buyer, its subsidiaries or against any of their directors or officers that would impair the ability of Buyer or Intermac to perform its obligations hereunder.

4.4 Necessary Financing. Buyer has the funds necessary to consummate the Merger and to carry out its obligations under this Agreement.

4.5 Brokers or Finders. Buyer has not incurred any obligation or liability, contingent or otherwise, for brokerage or finders fees, agents commissions, or any similar payment in connection with this Agreement.

ARTICLE 5 ADDITIONAL COVENANTS AND AGREEMENTS

5.1 Access to Information. Between the date of this Agreement and the Effective Time, the Company will afford to the officers, accountants, attorneys, and authorized representatives of Buyer reasonable access during normal business hours to the premises, personnel, advisors, consultants, properties, contracts, commitments, and books and records of the Company and each subsidiary. The Company shall furnish Buyer with all its books and records (financial and otherwise), documents or copies thereof, and other information concerning the business and affairs of the Company and each subsidiary as Buyer shall, from time to time, reasonably request. The Company further agrees to use its best efforts to cause its accountants, attorneys, employees and agents to fully cooperate with Buyer and its representatives in connection with the right of access granted herein.

5.2 Conduct of Business by the Company. Between the date of this Agreement and the Effective Time, the Company and its subsidiaries shall operate their respective businesses in the ordinary course and consistent with past practices. The Company will use all reasonable efforts to preserve intact the present business organizations of the Company and each subsidiary and maintain in effect all licenses, permits, and approvals of governmental authorities and agencies necessary for the conduct of such businesses. Without limitation, neither the Company nor any of its subsidiaries shall:

(a) amend its Certificate of Incorporation or By-Laws or issue, sell, purchase, or redeem, or agree or commit to issue, sell, purchase, or redeem any shares of its capital stock; or grant, issue or create any options, warrants or rights to purchase shares of its capital stock; or issue, sell, or authorize the issuance or sale of securities of any kind convertible into or exchangeable for shares of its capital stock; split, combine or reclassify any shares of any class of its capital stock; or declare, set aside, or pay any dividend or make any distribution in respect of its capital stock;

(b) make any general or unusual increase in compensation or rate of compensation payable or to become payable to hourly, salaried, or commissioned employees or officers, except for those which are normal and consistent with past practices or as provided for by contracts in existence as of the date hereof, or make any increase in compensation or rate of compensation payable to employees who are parties to separation, severance, or employment agreements with the Company or any subsidiary except for those which are normal and consistent with past practices, or enter into any separation, severance, or "change in control" agreements, or enter into any written or oral employment agreement which by its terms cannot be terminated on thirty days notice or less without penalty;

(c) accrue, set aside, or pay to any shareholder, director, consultant, officer or employee any bonus, profit-sharing, severance, retirement, insurance, death, fringe benefit, or other extraordinary compensation (except pursuant to a Company Plan presently in effect and in accordance with past practices).

(d) make any unbudgeted capital expenditure or any series of related capital expenditures (other than emergency repairs and replacements, the amount or aggregate amount of which is in excess of $100,000;

(f) create or incur any liabilities in excess of $100,000 other than liabilities incurred in the ordinary course of business consistent with past practice or as specifically permitted by or in connection with this Agreement and the consummation of the Merger; or

(g) make any payment whatsoever to any shareholder except continued compensation payments to shareholders who are directors and/or employees in the ordinary course of business consistent with past practice, and continued reimbursement of their ordinary and customary business expenses consistent with past practice.

5.3 Regulatory Matters. Buyer and the Company will cooperate with each other and use their best efforts to prepare as expeditiously as possible all necessary documentation, to effect any necessary filings, and to obtain at the earliest practicable date any necessary permits, consents, approvals, authorizations, and clearances of all third parties and governmental bodies necessary to consummate the transactions contemplated by this Agreement.

5.4 Shareholder Approval. The Company will take all steps necessary to duly call and hold a meeting of its shareholders as soon as practicable to obtain shareholder approval of this Agreement and the Merger or to obtain such approval by written consent of its shareholders.

5.5 Updated Financial Information. As soon as reasonably available, the Company shall deliver to Buyer complete copies of any internal unaudited monthly statements of earnings and balance sheets requested by Buyer. The Company covenants that, except for normal interim and year-end and audit adjustments, such financial statements shall be prepared in accordance with GAAP and (except for changes required by GAAP) consistently applied, and shall fairly present in all material respects the consolidated financial condition and results of operations of the Company and each subsidiary as of the dates indicated and for the periods ended on such dates.

5.6 Further Assurances. Subject to the terms and conditions herein provided, each of the parties hereto agrees to use its best efforts to take, or cause to be taken, all action necessary, proper, or advisable under applicable laws and regulations to consummate and make effective the transactions contemplated by this Agreement. If any time after the Effective Time any further action is necessary or desirable to carry out the purposes of this Agreement, the officers and directors of each party to this Agreement shall take such necessary action.

5.7 Release and Indemnification of Directors. The Buyer shall deliver a release at the Closing of those individuals who currently serve, or in the past have served, as directors of the Company and each of its subsidiaries from any liability of the Company and each subsidiary arising in connection with the acts or omissions of such individuals in their capacity as directors prior to the Closing. After the Closing, the Buyer shall defend and indemnify the former directors of the Company and each subsidiary from any claim asserted by any third party for any liability or obligation of the Company or any of its subsidiaries or fines or penalties resulting therefrom to the greatest extent allowed under the Company's Certificate of Incorporation, By-Laws and DGCL; provided that nothing in this Section or in the release contemplated hereby shall (i) relieve or be deemed to limit the provisions of Article 8 of this Agreement, (ii) release or indemnify such directors for fraud, willful misconduct or gross negligence or other matters not defense or indemnifiable under the DGCL, or (iii) provide indemnification in connection with any disputes or claims between any current or former directors of the Company or its current or former shareholders.

5.8 ISRA Compliance. The Seller, at its expense, comply or cause the Company to comply with all provisions of ISRA required to consummate the transactions contemplated hereby including, without limitation:

(a) the filing of all necessary notices, investigation reports, remedial cost estimates, applications for a remediation agreement and remediation funding sources within the times provided by ISRA; and

(b) the taking of such further actions as may be necessary to obtain from the NJDEP an approved negative declaration, an approved remediation agreement or and any other necessary written approvals to proceed with the transaction.

If remediation of any of the Company's property is required pursuant to ISRA, the Seller shall, at its expense, take all necessary actions to achieve Full Compliance with ISRA. However, Seller shall be required to meet only the nonresidential criteria of the NJDEP. The Buyer agrees to record, if required by the NJDEP, a deed of environmental restrictions from use of the property for residential purposes and cooperate with any groundwater classification exception area that may be required or authorized by the NJDEP. Seller shall bear cost, if any, of any engineering and institutional controls and monitoring that the NJDEP may require as a condition of a negative declaration or no further action letter.

5.9 No Solicitation of a Competing Transaction. The Company agrees that, during the term of this Agreement, it shall not, and shall not authorize or permit any of its subsidiaries or their directors, officers, employees, agents or representatives, directly or indirectly, to solicit, initiate, encourage or facilitate any inquiries or the making of any proposal with respect to any merger, consolidation or other business combination involving the Company or any subsidiary, or acquisition of any capital stock or any material portion of the assets of the Company or any subsidiary, or any combination of the foregoing (a "Competing Transaction"), or negotiate, explore or otherwise engage in discussions with any Person with respect to any Competing Transaction; provided, however, that if the Company receives any unsolicited written proposal from any third party relating to a Competing Transaction that the board of directors of the Company determines in good faith, upon advice of its outside legal counsel, it is obligated by principles of fiduciary duty to consider, the Company, without violating any provisions of this Agreement, may furnish or disclose non-public information to, and may enter into discussions and negotiations with, such third party. The Company shall deliver written notice of this Agreement to any such third party and shall notify Buyer prior to entering into discussions and negotiations with such third party. If the Company executes any agreement for a Competing Transaction, the Company shall thereupon immediately pay $1,500,000 cash to the Buyer.

ARTICLE 6 CONDITIONS

6.1 Conditions to Obligations of Buyer. The obligations of Buyer to consummate the transactions provided for by this Agreement are subject to the satisfaction at or prior to the Closing of each of the following conditions, any one or more of which may, to the extent waivable, be waived (but only in writing) by Buyer in its sole discretion:

(a) Representations and Warranties of the Company. (i) All of the Company's representations and warranties in this Agreement (considered collectively) and each of those representations and warranties (considered individually) that are qualified as to materiality must have been true and correct in all respects as of the date of this Agreement and must be true and correct in all respects as of the Closing Date as if made at the Closing Date, and the representations and warranties of the Company contained in this Agreement that are not so qualified must have been true and correct in all material respects as of the date of this Agreement and must be true and correct in all material respects as of the Closing Date as if made at the Closing, (ii) the Company shall have performed all agreements and covenants required by this Agreement to be performed by it; and (iii) with respect to (i) and (ii), at the Closing there shall be delivered to Buyer a certificate signed by the Chief Executive Officer of the Company to the foregoing effect and to the effect that there has been no material adverse change after December 31, 1997.

(b) Shareholder Approval. This Agreement, and the Merger and all other transactions contemplated hereby, shall have been either approved by the Company's shareholders by written consent or at a meeting duly called and held at which a majority of such shareholders are present and vote affirmatively, in person or by proxy.

(c) Escrow Agreement. The Company, the Shareholders' Agents, and the Escrow Agent shall have executed and delivered the Escrow Agreement in the form attached as Exhibit A.

(d) Non-Competition Agreements. Each of the directors of the Company and each of its officers other than those listed in Schedule 1.4 as expected to continue as officers of the surviving corporation shall have executed and delivered to Buyer a Non-Competition Agreement in the form attached as Exhibit B.

(e) Opinion of Counsel. Buyer shall have received the opinion of Taft, Plimpton & Marx, counsel to the Company, in the form and content attached as Exhibit C hereto.

(f) No Litigation. None of Buyer, Intermac, or the Company shall be subject to any order, decree, ruling, or injunction (either preliminary or permanent) of a court or agency of competent jurisdiction which seeks to enjoin or prohibit the consummation of the Merger or the transactions contemplated hereby or seeks to impose material limitations on the ability of the Buyer to exercise full rights of ownership of any of the material assets or business of the Company or its subsidiaries or seeks material damages from the Buyer in connection with such ownership.

(g) Resignations. Buyer shall have received, in form reasonably satisfactory to Buyer, the resignations, effective as of the Effective Time, of all directors of the Company and each subsidiary and the resignations of all officers thereof other than officers identified in Schedule 1.4 as expected to continue as officers of the Surviving Corporation after the Effective Date.

(h) Loan Agreements. With respect to the debt obligations of the Company and its subsidiaries under its term loan agreements with Security Life Insurance Company and First National Bank:

(i) to the extent Buyer repays such debt at the Closing, the lenders shall have terminated their respective loan agreements and executed and delivered to Buyer security interest termination statements, mortgage releases or other appropriate executed forms of release to evidence the repayment in full of all such indebtedness and the discharge of any existing liens related thereto; and

(ii) To the extent Buyer does not repay such debt at the Closing, the lenders shall have provided any necessary consents to the transactions contemplated by this Agreement without requiring the payment of any penalty, premium or other fees and charges by the Company or the Buyer.

(i) Shareholders Agreement; Agreements with Affiliates. The Shareholders Agreement and any agreements between the Company or any subsidiary and any Affiliate shall have been terminated, except for those employee agreements and consulting agreements set forth in Schedule 3.14.

(j) HSR Act. The requirements of the HSR Act applicable to the Merger, including any applicable filing requirements and expiration or termination of the waiting period required thereby, shall have been satisfied.

(k) Dissenters. The Company shall not have received notice from the holder or holders of more than 5% of the outstanding Common Stock that such holder or holders have demanded or intend to demand its or their appraisal rights under Section 262 of the DGCL.

(l) Estoppel Certificate. The Company shall have used its best efforts to obtain an executed estoppel certificate from each landlord under its real property leases in a form reasonably acceptable to Buyer.

(m) Tax Certificate. The Buyer shall have received a certificate from the Company dated the Closing Date and sworn to under penalty of perjury, to the effect that it is not a "United States real property holding corporation" within the meaning of Section 897(c)(2) of the IRC.

(n) ISRA Compliance. All requirements of ISRA necessary to consummate the transactions contemplated by this Agreement (including, without limitation, Section 5.8) shall have been met and any orders, or conditions to consummation imposed by NJDEP pursuant to ISRA shall not require remediation or other expenditures or activities that may reasonably be anticipated to result in a material adverse change of the financial condition or operations of the Company.

(o) Title Insurance. Any title insurance that the Buyer may have elected to obtain with respect to the Company's property shall demonstrate that such property is free and clear of all liens and encumbrances other than

(i) Liens for taxes on property if the same shall not be due and payable, or are being diligently contested in good faith and by appropriate proceedings and for which the Company shall have set aside reserves on its books as required by GAAP; and

(ii) Standard encumbrances of record on property of the Company or any subsidiary which do not materially impair the value or marketability of such property and do not materially interfere with the continued use or operation of the property as currently operated and used.

(p) Corporate Documents of the Company and each subsidiary certified by Secretary of State. For the Company and each subsidiary, Buyer shall have received from the Company (i) a certified copy of the certificate or articles of incorporation, as the case may be, (ii) a certified copy of the By-Laws and (iii) a certificate of good standing, each of which shall be certified within five business days of Closing by the Secretary of State of the state in which such entity is incorporated and (iv) a certified copy of any certificates of good standing or other comparable certificate evidencing the qualification of such entity to do business in each foreign jurisdiction where it does business or owns property so as to require qualification, certified within five (5) business days of Closing by the Secretary of State of such foreign jurisdiction.

6.2 <u>Conditions to Obligations of the Company</u>. The obligations of the Company to consummate the transactions provided for by this Agreement are subject to the satisfaction at or prior to the Closing of each of the following conditions, any one or more of which may be waived by the Company (but only in writing), to the extent waivable:

(a) Representations and Warranties of Buyer. All of Buyer's representations and warranties in this Agreement (considered collectively) and each of those representations and warranties (considered individually) must have been true and correct in all material respects as of the date of this Agreement and must be true and correct in all material respects as of the Closing Date as if made at the Closing Date, (ii) Buyer shall have performed all agreements and covenants required by this Agreement to be performed by it; and (iii) with respect to (i) and (ii), at the Closing there shall be delivered to the Company a certificate signed by an Executive Officer of Buyer to the foregoing effect.

(b) No Litigation. None of Buyer, Intermac, or the Company shall be subject to any order, decree, or injunction of a court or agency of competent jurisdiction which enjoins or prohibits the consummation of the Merger or the transactions contemplated hereby.

(c) Opinion of Counsel. The Company shall have received the opinion of Simpson & Paul counsel to Buyer, in form and content of that attached as Exhibit D.

(d) Escrow Agreement. Buyer and the Escrow Agent shall have executed and delivered the Escrow Agreement.

(e) Merger Price. At the Closing, Buyer or the Intermac shall first pay the Escrow Funds to the Escrow Agent. The Buyer or Intermac shall then pay the balance of the Merger Price to the shareholders who have delivered their certificate(s) and letters of transmittal to the Buyer as described in Section 2.2. To the extent that the shareholders have not delivered their certificates and letters of transmittal, Buyer or Intermac shall pay the unpaid amounts to a separate bank account to be distributed in accordance with Section 2.2.

(f) HSR Act. The requirements of the HSR Act applicable to the Merger, including any applicable filing requirements and expiration or termination of the waiting period required thereby.

(g) ISRA Compliance. Any orders or conditions to compliance with ISRA imposed by the NJDEP shall not require remediation or other expenditures that may reasonably be expected to exceed $________ or require the provision of a remediation funding source in excess of that amount.

ARTICLE 7 TERMINATION

7.1 Termination. By notice given prior to the Closing, this Agreement may be terminated and the transactions contemplated hereby may be abandoned:

(a) by the Company, if any of the conditions for the benefit of the Company in Section 6.2 have not been satisfied as of _____ __, 1998 or if the Buyer or Intermac shall have materially breached any of their respective covenants herein;

(b) by the Buyer, if any of the conditions for the benefit of the Buyer in Section 6.1 have not been satisfied as of _____ __, 1998 or if the Company shall have materially breached any of its covenants herein;

(c) by either the Buyer or the Company if the Merger shall not have been consummated (other than through the failure of the party seeking termination to comply fully with its obligations under this Agreement) by _______, 1998, or such later date as the parties may agree upon; or if the waiting period (and any extension thereof) applicable to the consummation of the Merger under the HSR Act shall not have expired or been terminated prior to _______, 1998; or if the requirements of ISRA necessary to consummate the transactions contemplated by this Agreement shall not have been met prior to _____, 1998; or

(d) by either the Buyer or the Company if any court of competent jurisdiction or other governmental agency of competent jurisdiction shall have issued an order, decree or ruling or taken any other action restraining, enjoining or otherwise prohibiting the Merger.

7.2 Effect of Termination. (a) If this Agreement is terminated as provided in Section 7.1, no party hereto shall have any liability or further obligation to any other party to this Agreement except (i) that any termination shall be without prejudice to the rights of any party hereto arising out of a breach by any other party of any covenant or agreement contained in this Agreement; (ii) that the provisions of Sections 9.6(c), 9.7 and the Confidentiality Agreement shall survive such termination; and (iii) that if this Agreement is terminated by any party hereto other than as permitted under Section 7.1(d), or 7.1(e) hereof, then the following shall apply:

(i) if this Agreement is terminated under Section 7.1(b), then Buyer shall immediately upon such termination pay to the $1,500,000 as liquidated damages on account of the Company's expenses and the effects of the failure to close this transaction.

(ii) if this Agreement is terminated under Section 7.1(d), then the Company shall immediately upon such termination pay to Buyer One Million Dollars $1,500,000 as liquidated damages on account of the Buyer's expenses and the effects of the failure to close this transaction.

7.3 No Release. No termination of this Agreement under this Article 7 or for any other reason shall release either party from its obligations under Section 9.7 hereof or under the Confidentiality Agreement.

ARTICLE 8 SURVIVAL; INDEMNIFICATION; ESCROW FUND

8.1 Survival of Representations and Warranties. The representations, warranties and covenants contained in this Agreement shall survive the Closing and continue in effect for two years thereafter except that the representations and warranties contained in Section 3.3 hereof shall survive the Closing and continue in effect indefinitely. Any investigation by or on behalf of any party hereto shall not constitute a waiver as to enforcement of any representation, warranty or covenant.

8.2 Indemnification by Certain Shareholders of the Company.

(a) Notwithstanding the Closing and subject to the provisions set forth in subsection (c) below, the shareholders of the Company named at the end of this Agreement as the "Indemnifying Shareholders" covenant and agree to defend, indemnify and hold harmless the Buyer and its Affiliates and their officers, directors, employees, agents, advisers and representatives (collectively, the "Buyer Indemnitees") from and against, and to pay or reimburse each such person for, Indemnifiable Losses resulting from or arising out of (i) any breach of any covenant or agreement made by the Company under this Agreement, (ii) any breach or inaccuracy of any representation or warranty of the Company under this Agreement. The exclusive remedy of the Buyer Indemnitees to recover Indemnifiable Losses shall be the Escrow Fund as provided in Section 8.3.

(b) Notwithstanding the Closing, Buyer shall defend, indemnify and hold harmless all shareholders of the Company and their respective agents and Affiliates and the officers, directors, employees, agents, advisers and representatives of each such person (collectively, the "Shareholder Indemnitees") from and against, and pay or reimburse each such Person for, Indemnifiable Losses arising out of, based upon, or resulting from (i) any breach of any covenant or agreement made by the Buyer under this Agreement or (ii) any breach or inaccuracy of any representation or warranty of the Buyer under this Agreement and Buyer shall reimburse such Shareholder Indemnitees for any and all such Indemnifiable Losses.

(c) All payments from the Escrow Fund for indemnification of or reimbursement to Buyer required pursuant to this Agreement shall be made net of any income tax benefit attributable to the deductibility of any Indemnifiable Losses giving rise to such indemnification or reimbursement payment, as mutually agreed to by Buyer and the Shareholders' Agents in good faith in the manner described below. If any claim for indemnification asserted hereunder by Buyer is, or may be, the subject of the Company's insurance, Buyer agrees that it shall cause the applicable insurance carrier promptly to be notified of any such claim or loss and tender defense thereof to such carrier. Further, Buyer agrees to take reasonable steps to pursue such claims and to reasonably cooperate with each applicable insurance carrier for a period of ninety days after the making of a claim for coverage. Buyer may make a claim under this Agreement and the Escrow Agreement subject to the outcome of the insurance claim. If such insurance carrier shall deny coverage, or if no resolution of an insurance claim shall occur with ninety days after a claim has been made, Buyer may proceed further against the Escrow Fund and the Shareholders' Agents shall be subrogated to the rights of Buyer or the Company against such insurance carrier. If Buyer or the Company shall receive insurance benefits from an insurance policy with respect to any event or circumstance for which Buyer shall receive indemnification hereunder out of the Escrow Fund, such monies shall be deposited (less expenses incurred by Buyer to receive or collect such insurance benefits) in the Escrow Fund and disbursed as provided therein.

8.3 <u>Limitation on Indemnity Obligation</u>.

If any Buyer Indemnitee shall be entitled to indemnification for any Losses under Section 8.2(a)(i) and 8.2(a)(ii) hereof at any time prior to the expiration of the term of the Escrow Agreement, the Buyer shall make a claim only on the Escrow Fund in accordance with the provisions of the Escrow Agreement and neither the Shareholders' Agent nor any Shareholder shall be personally liable to make payment of such indemnity obligation. Neither the Shareholders' Agent nor any Shareholder shall have any indemnification obligation under this Article 8 at any time after expiration of the term of the Escrow Agreement, except for breaches of the representations and warranties of the Company contained in Section 3.3(b) hereof.

8.4 <u>Procedure for Indemnification of Buyer or Intermac with Respect to Third-Party Claims</u>.

(a) If the Buyer or Intermac determines to seek indemnification under this Article with respect to claims for Indemnifiable Losses resulting from the assertion of liability by third parties, it shall give notice to the Shareholders' Agents within 30 days of it becoming aware of any such claim and the facts upon which any such claim for Indemnifiable Losses will be based; the notice shall set forth such information with respect thereto as is then reasonably available to the Buyer or Intermac. If any such liability is asserted against the Buyer or Intermac, and the Buyer or Intermac notifies the Shareholders' Agents thereof, the Shareholders' Agents will be entitled, if they so elect by written notice delivered to the Buyer or Intermac within 30 days after receiving the Buyer or Intermac's notice, to assume the defense thereof with counsel reasonably satisfactory to the Buyer or Intermac.

(b) If the Shareholders' Agents, within 30 days after receipt of the aforesaid notice of a claim for Indemnifiable Losses, fail to assume the defense of the Buyer or Intermac against such claim, the Buyer or Intermac shall have the right to undertake the defense, compromise or settlement of such action on behalf of and for the account and risk of the Shareholders.

8.5 <u>Procedure For Indemnification with Respect to Non-Third-Party Claims</u>. If the Buyer or Intermac asserts the existence of a claim for Indemnifiable Losses (but excluding claims resulting from the assertion of liability by third parties), it shall give written notice to the Shareholders' Agents specifying the nature and amount of the claim asserted. If the Shareholders' Agents, within 30 days or such greater time as may be necessary for the Shareholders' Agents to investigate such claim for Indemnifiable Losses not to exceed 90 days, after receiving the notice from the Buyer or Intermac, shall not give written notice to the Buyer or Intermac announcing their intent to contest such assertion of the Buyer or Intermac, such assertion shall be deemed accepted and the amount of such claim shall be deemed a valid claim for Indemnifiable Losses. During the time period set forth in the preceding sentence, the Buyer or Intermac shall cooperate fully with the Shareholders' Agents in respect of such claim for Indemnifiable Losses. In the event, however, that the Shareholders' Agents contest the assertion of a claim by giving such written notice to the Buyer or Intermac within said period, then if the parties hereto, acting in good faith, cannot reach agreement with respect to such claim within ten days after such notice, the contested assertion of a claim shall be referred to arbitration in accordance with the Escrow Agreement.

8.6 <u>Escrow Fund</u>. Pursuant to Section 2.2(a) hereof, Buyer shall deposit into escrow with the Escrow Agent, as security for and as a source of money for claims that may be made by Buyer under Section 8.2, the Escrow Fund which shall be invested, reinvested and administered pursuant to the terms of the Escrow Agreement. The terms and conditions on which the

Escrow Fund shall be held, invested, and distributed and the manner of resolving disputes pertaining to claims made on the Escrow Fund by the Buyer shall be as set forth in this Article 8 and in the Escrow Agreement.

8.7 Shareholders' Agents. By their vote or written consent for this Agreement and the Merger and other transactions contemplated hereby, the shareholders of the Company shall be deemed to have irrevocably appointed the individuals specified as Shareholders' Agents in the Escrow Agreement (the "Shareholders' Agents") as their agents and attorneys-in-fact for purposes of executing and entering into the Escrow Agreement and exercising all rights and privileges of such shareholders under the Escrow Agreement, this Agreement, or otherwise with respect to the claims by Buyer against the Escrow Fund. The shareholders have the right to remove and replace one or more of the Shareholders' Agents, and such action shall be taken only by written notice to Buyer and the Surviving Corporation signed by shareholders who, at the Effective Time, held not less than a majority of the total number of the then outstanding shares of Common Stock. Until Buyer receives such notice, Buyer and the Surviving Corporation shall have the right to rely on the decisions made and actions taken unanimously by the then acting Shareholders' Agents. The grant of such power by the Shareholders is coupled with an interest and is irrevocable and is granted by each of the Shareholders as a durable power of attorney.

ARTICLE 9 GENERAL

9.1 Notices. All notices and other communications hereunder shall be in writing and shall be deemed given upon receipt if delivered personally, sent by telefax (confirmed by regular mail), sent by overnight courier, or mailed by registered or certified mail, postage prepaid, return receipt requested (such mailed notice to be effective on the date such receipt is acknowledged or refused) as follows:

If to Seller or Intermac, addressed to:
International Machine Tools, Inc.
50 Industrial Highway
Mechanicsville, New York 10123
Attention: General Counsel

If to the Corporation or the Shareholders, addressed to:
CAD Equipment, Inc.
Designers Street
Hightown, New York 12121
Attention: President

or to such other place and with such other copies as either party may designate as to itself by written notice to the others.

9.2 Extension; Waiver. At any time prior to the Closing, parties hereto may (a) extend the time for the performance of any of the obligations or other acts of the other party hereto, (b) waive any inaccuracies in the representations and warranties of the other party contained herein or in any document delivered pursuant hereto and (c) waive compliance by the other party with any of the agreements or conditions contained herein. Any agreement on the part of a party hereto to any such extension or waiver shall be valid if set forth in an instrument in writing signed on behalf of such party by a senior officer of the waiving party, provided that after the Merger has been approved by the Shareholders, the Board of Directors of the Company shall not have any authority to change the form or amount of consideration to be paid in the Merger without the approval of such changes by the Shareholders in accordance with applicable legal requirements.

9.3 Choice of Law; Venue. (a) This Agreement shall be governed by, construed, interpreted, and the rights of the parties determined in accordance with the internal laws of the State of Delaware including, without limitation, the DGCL.

(b) Any litigation concerning disputes or controversies under this Agreement shall be commenced only in the federal or state courts of competent jurisdiction sitting in the State of New York or the State of Delaware. The Company, the Buyer and Intermac hereby consent to the jurisdiction of the federal and state courts sitting in those states.

9.4 Amendment; Integrated Agreement. This Agreement may not be amended except by an instrument in writing signed on behalf of each of the parties hereto. This Agreement, together with the attachments and the schedules hereto, and the Confidentiality Agreement constitute the entire Agreement between the parties pertaining to the subject matter hereof and supersede all prior and contemporaneous agreements, understandings, negotiations, and discussions, whether oral or written, of the parties.

9.5 Counterparts; Headings. This Agreement may be executed in one or more counterparts, each of which shall be deemed an original, but all of which together shall constitute one and the same instrument. The headings of the several Articles and Sections herein are inserted for convenience of reference only and are not intended to be part of or to affect the meaning or interpretation of this Agreement.

9.6 Expenses. The Buyer and the shareholders of the Company shall bear all fees and costs of counsel and other costs and expenses incurred by them in connection with the transactions contemplated by the Agreement. To the extent that the Company shall advance any such costs and expenses prior to the Closing, such shareholders shall reimburse the amounts so advanced on the Closing Date.

9.7 Publicity. All announcements, press releases, and communications regarding this Agreement and the transactions contemplated hereby shall be made by a party only with the prior approval of the other party hereto, which shall not be unreasonably withheld, except as otherwise required by law or legal process.

9.8 Severability. If any term, provision, covenant, or restriction of this Agreement, other than any term, provision, covenant or restriction that reduces the price payable hereunder to Shareholders, is held by a court of competent jurisdiction or other authority to be invalid, void, unenforceable, or against its regulatory policy, the remainder of the terms, provisions, covenants, and restrictions of this Agreement shall remain in full force and effect and shall in no way be affected, impaired or invalidated.

9.9 Assignment. Neither this Agreement nor any of the rights, interests, or obligations of the parties hereto may be assigned by any party hereto, whether by operation of law or otherwise, without the prior written consent of the other parties hereto and any attempt to do so shall be null and void. Subject to the foregoing, this Agreement shall be binding on and inure to the benefit of and be enforceable by the parties and their respective successors and assigns.

IN WITNESS WHEREOF, Buyer, Intermac, and the Company have each caused this Agreement to be executed by their respective officers as of the date first above written.

International Machine Tools, Inc.

By ______________________________
Name:
Title:

Intermac, Inc.

By ______________________________
Name:
Title:

CAD Equipment, Inc.

By ______________________________
Name:
Title:

The Indemnifying Shareholders:

____

____

Exhibit 16-7

DISCLOSURE SCHEDULES

TO THE

MERGER AGREEMENT

BETWEEN

INTERNATIONAL MACHINE TOOLS, INC., AS BUYER,

INTERMAC, INC., AS INTERMAC

AND

CAD EQUIPMENT, INC., AS THE COMPANY

DATED AS OF __, 1998

THE DISCLOSURE SCHEDULES ATTACHED HERETO ARE SUBJECT TO THE FOLLOWING TERMS AND CONDITIONS:

1. THE INTRODUCTORY LANGUAGE AND HEADINGS TO EACH OF THE PARTS TO THESE DISCLOSURE SCHEDULES ARE INSERTED FOR CONVENIENCE ONLY AND SHALL NOT CREATE A DIFFERENT STANDARD FOR DISCLOSURE THAN THE LANGUAGE SET FORTH IN THE AGREEMENT AND PLAN OF REORGANIZATION.

2. THE INCLUSION OF ANY ITEM ON A PART, WHICH PART REQUIRES A LISTING OF A "MATERIAL" ITEM OR AN ACTION "NOT IN THE ORDINARY COURSE OF BUSINESS" IS NOT DEEMED TO BE AN ADMISSION OR REPRESENTATION THAT THE INCLUDED ITEM IS "MATERIAL" OR IS "NOT IN THE ORDINARY COURSE OF BUSINESS."

3. ALL CAPITALIZED TERMS USED HEREIN AND NOT OTHERWISE DEFINED SHALL HAVE THE MEANING GIVEN TO SUCH TERMS IN THE AGREEMENT AND PLAN OF REORGANIZATION.

MERGER AGREEMENT AND PLAN OF REORGANIZATION

This Merger Agreement and Plan of Reorganization is made on ________, 1998 between NATIONAL PAPER INDUSTRIES, INC., a Delaware corporation ("National"), NPI SUBSIDIARY, INC., a Delaware corporation ("NPI"), and PAPER RECYCLING CORPORATION OF AMERICA, INC., a New York corporation ("Recycling").

RECITALS:

A. National is a basic manufacturer of paper and packaging products throughout the United States including the management and restoration of forests used in its business. NPI is a wholly owned subsidiary of National organized to participate in the triangular merger contemplated by this Agreement.

B. Recycling is a leading manufacturer of tissue paper products throughout the eastern United States and owns valuable technology for the recycling of municipal waste paper to produce tissue paper products and other useful coproducts.

C. National wishes to acquire Recycling by a reverse triangular merger of NPI into Recycling in a transaction that will qualify as a reorganization pursuant to Section 368(a)(1) of the Internal Revenue Code (the "Code"). The reorganization will result in an exchange of 1.5 shares of National's Common Stock for each of the outstanding shares of Recycling's Common Stock.

AGREEMENTS:

In consideration of their mutual promises, National, NPI and Recycling agree as follows:

I. THE MERGER TRANSACTIONS

1.1 Corporate Approval. On or before the Closing Date hereinafter defined, National, NPI and Recycling shall take all appropriate actions to obtain the approval of this Agreement and the merger and exchange of shares contemplated herein by their respective boards of directors, shareholders and any necessary third parties.

1.2 Contribution of National Common Stock. On or before the Effective Time, National shall make a capital contribution to NPI of such number of shares of National's Common Stock, par value $1.00 per share (the "Merger Shares"), as shall be required to make the conversions described in Section 1.5.

1.3 The Merger. The constituent corporations to the merger shall be NPI and Recycling. Subject to the fulfillment of the conditions in this Agreement, NPI and Recycling shall file on the Closing Date a Certificate of Merger with the Secretary of State of Delaware pursuant to Section 251 of the Delaware General Corporation Law ("DGCL") with tax clearance certificates and other appropriate supporting documents. Unless otherwise provided in the Certificate of Merger, the merger shall become effective at 5:00 P.M., Eastern Standard Time, on the Closing Date (the "Effective Time"). At the Effective Time, the separate existence of NPI shall cease and Recycling shall continue as the surviving corporation with the effects provided in Section 259 of the DGCL. The certificate of incorporation, by-laws, board of directors and officers of Recycling, as in effect immediately before the merger, shall continue to be those of the surviving corporation.

1.4 Conversion of Shares of NPI. At the Effective Time, each of the 100 shares of Common Stock, $.50 par value, of NPI shall automatically, and without any action by National, become a share of Common Stock, $.50 par value, of Recycling, the surviving corporation, and shall continue to be owned by National so that Recycling shall thereupon be a wholly owned subsidiary of National.

1.5 Conversion of Shares of Recycling. At the Effective Time, each of the 800,000 outstanding shares of the Common Stock, $.10 par value, of Recycling (the "Recycling Common Stock") shall be cancelled by operation of law and without any action by their holders and, except for shares of Recycling Common Stock held by dissenting shareholders, each shall be converted into 1.5 Merger Shares. However, no fractional Merger Shares shall become issuable, and all fractional shares automatically be converted into a right to receive cash equal to the corresponding fraction of the closing price per share of National's Common Stock on The New York Stock Exchange on the Closing Date.

1.6 Exchange of Stock Certificates. (A) On the Closing Date, NPI shall furnish to Second National Bank (the "Exchange Agent") certificates representing Merger Shares sufficient to make the exchanges described in Section 1.5 together with cash sufficient to make cash payments in lieu of the issuance of fractional Merger Shares. Certificates for the Merger Shares shall be dated the Closing Date and shall be deemed issued at the Effective Time.

(B) The Exchange Agent shall mail as soon as practicable after the Effective Time to each person who held of record shares of Recycling's Common Stock immediately before the Effective Time a form of letter of transmittal with instructions for surrender of his, her or its certificates in exchange for Merger Shares or cash in lieu of fractional Merger Shares, or both, as applicable. Upon receipt of properly executed transmittal letters with the proper certificates for Recycling's Common Stock, the Exchange Agent shall transmit to such holders the certificate or certificates for the Merger Shares or cash in lieu of Merger Shares, or both, as applicable. The certificates for Recycling's Common Stock surrendered shall be cancelled.

(C) The Merger Shares issuable pursuant to the conversion provided in Section 1.5 shall be treated as outstanding of record as of the Effective Time. However, until the holders of record of Recycling's Common Stock properly surrender their certificates for cancellation, they shall not be entitled to receive their certificates for the Merger Shares or any cash in lieu of fractional Merger Shares or any dividends upon the Merger Shares. They shall also not be entitled to vote their Merger Shares.

(D) The stock transfer records of Recycling shall be closed as of the Effective Time and no transfers of Recycling's Common Stock shall be made thereafter. Stock certificates for Recycling's Common Stock received after the Effective Time by Recycling or its transfer agent shall be forwarded to the Exchange Agent for cancellation and exchange as provided heretofore.

(E) Notwithstanding the foregoing, each holder of Recycling's Common Stock who does not vote in favor of the merger and who takes the necessary steps under Section 262 of the DBCL to demand dissenter's appraisal rights shall not be entitled to receive Merger Shares or cash in lieu of fractional Merger Shares pursuant to Section 1.5 unless and until such holder shall fail to perfect, or shall withdraw or lose, such dissenter's appraisal rights. Such dissenting holders shall be entitled to receive only the amount to which they are entitled under Section 262 of the DGCL.

1.7 Substitution of Stock Options. On or before the Closing Date, National shall arrange to grant to each person holding options granted under Recycling's Incentive Stock Option Plan such number of options as will entitle them to purchase 1.5 shares of National's Common Stock under National's Management Incentive Stock Option Plan at the same exercise prices and for the same remaining time periods as the options to purchase Recycling's Common Stock held by them at the Effective Time. As a condition precedent to such grants, each such employee shall be required to sign a written consent to the cancellation of the options issued by Recycling.

Chapter 17

Acquisition Closings

A. Introduction

Acquisition closings are formal meetings during which documents are exchanged to demonstrate that all required conditions in the acquisition contract have been fulfilled and to accomplish the sale or merger. The closings are arranged and conducted by the law firms representing the seller, the buyer and any other participants. It is generally agreed that all events at the closing will be treated as interdependent and as occurring simultaneously. Thus, all conditions must be met and all obligations performed or the sale or merger will not take place.

Acquisition closings are paperwork-intensive and often take several hours to complete. However, closings provide important protection against risk for sellers, buyers and others. Thus, a seller need not deliver stock or assets and risk a later failure by the buyer to pay for them. A buyer need not pay the price and risk a failure by the seller to deliver the stock or assets. Neither the buyer nor the seller must perform their obligations and risk a later refusal by a government agency, a lender or a customer to provide a necessary consent. Of course, the seller or buyer can agree to exceptions, but the closing provides an opportunity to evaluate and negotiate any such exceptions.

Acquisition closings are often combined with closings of related transactions. For example, a buyer may concurrently close a loan agreement or a private placement of stock to obtain funds to pay the acquisition price. A seller may close an agreement to prepay an existing term loan in order to obtain releases of security interests and mortgages necessary to allow the buyer to close its loans. In addition, employment agreements may be signed; brokers or finders may be paid; an escrow deposit may be made; and a variety of other transactions may take place.

B. Setting a Closing Date

Acquisition closings are usually set in the acquisition contract for a date when the parties estimate that the contract conditions can be fulfilled. The most important and time-consuming conditions are usually arrangements for financing and government clearances.

For example, a buyer may obtain a commitment letter from a bank to finance the acquisition price, but the letter will typically be subject to a "due diligence" review and other steps that can take several weeks to perform and evaluate. Thus, the buyer will negotiate a financing condition that allows ample time to allow the bank to evaluate the loan. Ample time must also be allowed to apply for and obtain tax rulings, securities registration and listing, and other important conditions.

In many acquisition contracts, the seller and the buyer set an ambitious closing date. They do so to assure that all participants move promptly through the closing preparations. The steps required to accomplish an acquisition can be complex and costly. They usually become more complex and costly with the passage of time. Thus, experience has shown that a closing is most likely to proceed smoothly when the work is done in a brief, well-coordinated campaign given high priority by all participants.

In many transactions, the parties extend the contract closing date because lenders, government agencies and others do not act within the expected time periods. However, the parties may also set a "drop dead" date that will not be extended. The reason is that acquisition transactions that remain open too long can become subject to problems such as competitor raids on customers and employees.

At times, a seller and buyer engage in lengthy negotiations and continue to exchange drafts of the acquisition contract through a time when all conditions to close have been fulfilled. When this happens, they may set a date at which all remaining issues will be negotiated and the acquisition contract will be signed and closed on the same date. This technique can be useful in international and other transactions when distance prevents early resolution of contract issues.

Closings are likely to proceed best when held on a Tuesday, Wednesday or Thursday. Monday is a poor choice because out-of-town participants may have to travel on Sunday and a pre-closing will be difficult to arrange. Friday is a poor choice because any flaws that cannot be resolved on the closing date will remain unresolved for the weekend. Participants who would stay over for one night cannot be expected to stay for a weekend or be free of commitments on the next Monday. The wire transfer concerns described later in this chapter become especially difficult when a closing is held on Friday.

C. Factors Affecting the Closing Procedures

Important factors affecting closing procedures and documents are as follows:

- **i.** The structure of the transaction, i.e., a stock purchase, assets purchase or merger.
- **ii.** The acquisition currency, i.e., cash, debt or stock.
- **iii.** The ownership of the seller or buyer by private or public shareholders.
- **iv.** The extent of approvals or clearances required from government agencies and other third parties.

D. Documents Needed for Most Closings

There are several basic documents that are necessary or useful at most acquisition closings, regardless of their structure as a stock or assets purchase or as a merger:

1. Certificates of state governmental officials as to the certificates of incorporation of the corporate parties, including all amendments.
2. Certificates of state governmental officials evidencing that the corporations were duly incorporated and are existing in good standing and have paid all necessary franchise taxes.
3. Certificates of the corporate secretaries of the corporate parties as to their by-laws and all amendments; the adoption of enabling resolutions by their boards of directors and, if necessary, by their shareholders; and the incumbency and specimen signatures of their corporate officers who will sign closing documents.
4. "Agreed-upon procedures" letters of accounting firms.
5. Approvals or clearances by government agencies.
6. Consents of lenders, landlords and other private third parties.
7. Legal opinions.
8. Instructions for deliveries of payments including wire transfers.
9. Receipts for payments.
10. Announcements to employees, customers and suppliers, and the public.

Several other documents are frequently provided at closings, regardless of the structure of the transaction, if they are applicable:

1. Tax rulings by the Internal Revenue Service and state agencies or opinions of counsel on tax issues.
2. Opinions of accounting firms on the applicability of "pooling of interests" accounting treatment or other issues under GAAP.
3. Evidence from the U.S. Department of Justice or the Federal Trade Commission that the Hart-Scott-Rodino waiting period has expired.
4. Orders of the Securities and Exchange Commission declaring the registration statement effective for any securities to be issued to public shareholders in the transaction.
5. Letters from a stock exchange or the NASD Stock Market, Inc. listing securities for trading on the exchange or for quotation in the NASDAQ System.
6. Escrow agreements to secure obligations under representations, warranties, covenants and indemnities.
7. Fairness opinions of valuation experts.
8. Solvency opinions delivered for leveraged buyout transactions by firms expert in financial analysis, but not including accounting

firms because they have been prohibited from issuing such opinions by the American Institute of Certified Public Accountants (AICPA).

Counsel for the seller and buyer usually prepare a draft closing memorandum and document checklists for use in preparing for the closing. The brief memorandums and checklists then serve to memorialize the closing events and documents. An example of a Closing Memorandum and Document Checklist appears as Exhibit 17-1.

E. Stock Purchase Transactions (Closely Held Corporations)

The simplest basic closing procedures are those necessary for the acquisition of a privately held corporation by the stock purchase method. The transfer is accomplished by assigning and delivering the stock certificates evidencing ownership of the stock of the corporation in exchange for payment of the purchase price.

The assignment of the stock certificates is made by either of two methods. Certificates issued to a registered holder should be endorsed by the holder and delivered to the buyer together with a signature guarantee by a bank or brokerage firm or at least a verification by a notary public.[1] Certificates, if any, issued to "bearer" can simply be delivered by the holder to the buyer.[2] Review of the certificate of incorporation, minute books and stock books will enable counsel for the buyer to determine that the stock transfers are in good order or to identify potential problems.

Several problems may arise at stock purchase closings. Some shareholders may have lost their stock certificates. Some shareholders may have pledged and delivered their stock certificates to a bank or other lender as security for a loan. Some shareholders may have made gifts of shares, but never recorded the transfer. Some shareholders may have died, leaving certificates registered in their names, but no probate proceedings may have been held to determine the person entitled to the shares.

When stock certificates are lost, the buyer should require the shareholder to obtain a lost certificate bond from a surety company. When stock has been pledged, arrangements can usually be made with the lender to allow delivery of the certificates at the closing against payment to the lender of a portion of the acquisition price to repay the debt for which the stock was pledged. When unrecorded gifts have been made, the donor should surrender the certificates for transfer to the donee. If a shareholder of record has died, it may be necessary for the persons interested in the shareholder's estate to commence probate proceedings in order to obtain authority to sell the stock and to determine the persons entitled to the sale proceeds. If the decedent was a joint owner and the other joint owner has survived, the task is simpler and may only require delivery of a death certificate and a death tax waiver letter, if applicable.

When counsel for a buyer finds that the seller's stock books are not in good order, the author recommends that the buyer and its counsel be cour-

---

[1]A separate stock assignment form can be used rather than endorsing the certificate itself.

[2]"Bearer" certificates are seldom issued by closely held companies in the United States.

teous but strict, and remain somewhat aloof from the corrective actions. Otherwise, the buyer may be drawn into disputes outstanding for years among the seller's shareholders. The buyer may be asked to support one side or the other with insufficient evidence about the merits of the disputes. The buyer should avoid involvement because acquisitions present enough risk without adding uncertainty whether selling shareholders can deliver title to their shares.

F. Stock Purchase Transactions (Publicly Held Corporations)

The acquisition of a publicly held corporation by the stock purchase method requires complex procedures because the shares are typically held by numerous shareholders located throughout the United States and perhaps in other nations.

When a buyer acquires the shares of a publicly held corporation for cash, the transaction is called a tender offer. When the buyer uses its own debt securities or stock as the acquisition currency, the transaction is called an exchange offer.

For both a tender offer and an exchange offer, the buyer hires a bank or trust company to serve as a depository. The buyer arranges to mail the tender offer statement or the exchange offer prospectus to the shareholders of the corporation to be acquired as they appear of record on its stockholders' list.[3]

The offering material includes a form of transmittal letter to be used by the shareholders to submit their stock certificates, if they choose to do so. The shareholders list their certificates on the letter of transmittal, sign it, obtain a signature guarantee, and mail it with their certificates to the depository. The depository personnel examine the transmittal letter and the certificates, which may total many millions of shares, to determine whether they are in good order. When defects are identified, depository personnel contact the shareholders to correct them, if possible.

Because many shares of publicly held corporations are held in "street name," the distribution of the offering materials is a complex task. When shares are held by a brokerage firm (or at a clearing corporation such as Depository Trust Company), the buyer must offer to reimburse the expenses of the brokerage firms for distributing the offering materials and obtaining the instructions of their customers whether to submit their shares or not. If the instructions are received shortly before the offer will expire, a brokerage firm submits a guaranty of delivery to the depository in order to gain time to make a formal submission of the shares.

When all conditions of the tender offer or exchange offer are met, the buyer delivers the price to the depository. If the shares submitted exceed the number for which the offer was made, the depository determines the

[3]When the offer is friendly, the buyer can obtain the stockholders' list without difficulty. Indeed, the transfer agent for the corporation to be acquired may mail the offer to the shareholders. When the offer is hostile, the buyer may have to sue to obtain the stockholders' list pursuant to state corporation law and SEC Rule 14d-5.

shares to be accepted on a pro rata basis.[4] The depository delivers the shares accepted to the buyer. The depository then transmits the price for the shares accepted to the shareholders together with certificates for any shares not accepted because of the proration.

When a tender offer or exchange offer is friendly, an acquisition contract has usually been made between the buyer and the corporation to be acquired or its principal shareholders. Thus, a formal closing will be held on the date when the shares are accepted. However, when a tender offer is hostile, there will probably not be a closing.

G. Assets Purchase Transactions

The closing of assets purchase transactions is necessarily complex because numerous assets must be transferred in groups or individually. To the extent that liabilities are assumed, they must also be transferred in groups or individually. As a practical matter, the tasks involved require so much effort and time that the assets purchase method is generally used only to acquire small and middle-sized companies. When an asset-intensive large company is to be acquired, the buyer and the seller may use a forward triangular merger or a stock purchase accompanied by an election under Section 338(h)(10) of the Internal Revenue Code.

The documents used to transfer assets consist of (1) deeds to transfer real property; (2) general bills of sale to transfer inventories, machinery and equipment and miscellaneous assets; and (3) specific bills of sale or similar instruments to transfer personal property to be filed or recorded; (4) general assignments of contracts, leases, purchase orders, accounts receivable, permits, licenses, registrations and other continuing rights of a contractual or regulatory nature; and (5) specific assignments of contacts, permits and other rights of a contractual or regulatory nature that require consent of a third party or a filing or recording.

The documents used to transfer liabilities consist of general assignment and assumption agreements for liabilities and obligations such as contracts, leases, purchase orders, accounts payable, permits, licenses and registrations that will continue after the closing. Specific assignment and assumption agreements will be used to transfer liabilities and obligations if the consent of a third party or a filing or recording is required. The agreements often include both assumption and indemnification provisions.

Many assets (such as contracts, leases and permits) involve a combination of property and contract rights, liabilities and obligations. For such assets, it is customary to combine the transfers in a single document under a title such as "Bill of Sale, Assignment, Assumption and Indemnity Agreement." Such a document is especially useful when a third party consent, filing or recording is needed. The document can cover fully the arrangements for the transfer of a specific contract, lease or permit without involving the third party, a government agency or the public in other aspects of the acquisition transaction.

---

[4]For example, if a tender offer is for 4,000,000 shares and 5,000,000 shares are submitted, the depository accepts 80 percent of the shares submitted by each shareholder and returns the remaining 20 percent.

In assets purchase transactions it is important and customary to hire service companies and title insurers to search the public records to determine whether the assets are encumbered by (1) security interests; (2) mortgages or deeds of trust; (3) tax, mechanics, judgment or other liens; or (4) conflicting claims of ownership. For example, a search firm examines the records of the secretary of state (and county records, if applicable) and reports any financing statements on Form UCC-1 that have been filed to perfect security interests in the assets. A title insurer examines the county records where real properties are located and provides a title report and a commitment to issue a title insurance policy, subject to various requirements and exceptions. The title report and commitment include such items as outstanding mortgages, liens of unpaid taxes, easements, any recorded leases and rights of way, and applicable zoning and other use restrictions. The requirements also include a current survey by a licensed surveyor including such items as a metes and bounds description and the locations of improvements, easements, rights of way and encroachments.

Especially when an assets purchase transaction is closed simultaneously with a secured loan transaction, it is important to time the closing so that titles can be transferred, mortgages and security interests terminated of record, and new mortgages and security interests recorded on a timely basis. The title insurer's representative should deliver copies of the "marked up" title commitment evidencing fulfillment of requirements and removal of exceptions to counsel for the seller, buyer and lender for later comparison when the final title policies are issued.

An important but sometimes neglected part of the closing of an assets purchase transaction is the payment of transfer taxes, recording fees and any sales taxes applicable to the assets transfers. Of similar importance is the proration of current real and personal property taxes, rents, royalties, deposits, and fuel and water charges. The assets purchase agreement usually contains provisions stating whether the seller or the buyer will be responsible for each item of taxes and fees and how the prorations will be calculated. However, many assets purchase agreements omit one or more items because they are perceived as minor at the time the agreement is negotiated and signed. The author recommends that lawyers preparing for a closing identify and resolve these items, preferably in writing, before the closing. Otherwise, they may become a source of disagreements and friction that can spoil the atmosphere of an otherwise cooperative closing.[5]

The author recommends that a pre-closing be held on the day before the closing of an assets purchase transaction. At the pre-closing, counsel can identify potential problems while a day still remains to solve them.

H. Merger Transactions

At closings of merger transactions, the exchanges of closing documents must be accomplished in time to allow the filing on the closing date of the certificates of merger with the secretary of state (or other corporate au-

[5]Proration of annual property taxes can be a difficult matter. For example, some states and counties treat property taxes as payable in advance and others treat them as payable in arrears. If proration is based on local law and custom, the seller or buyer may be surprised to find the proration payable by the party who expected to receive a payment.

thority) in the state capitals where the merger parties are incorporated. To accomplish timely filings, it is customary for officers of the parties to pre-sign the certificates of merger and entrust them to counsel who have them sent by corporate service firms to the appropriate state capitals. The service firms hold the certificates of merger at their offices awaiting calls from counsel authorizing their filing when all preconditions have been fulfilled.

When a merger takes effect, the assets and liabilities and the rights and obligations of the disappearing corporation are transferred by operation of law to the surviving corporation. In theory, there is no need for deeds, bills of sale, assignments and other transfer instruments to be signed and delivered such as is done at the closing of an assets purchase transaction. However, as a practical matter, it is advisable to prepare, sign and deliver confirmatory documents that can be recorded to clarify title records and to deliver to third parties who want evidence of a transfer but do not want to review the complex merger agreements. For example, if they are properly executed, it may be possible to record the certificates of merger with county clerks as part of the land title records.

In theory, there is also no need to transfer the certificates of the shareholders of the disappearing corporation. Their shares are canceled automatically. However, stock certificates are negotiable instruments and it is wise not to leave them outstanding. Thus, as shown in Chapter 16, it is customary to include provisions in a merger agreement requiring the shareholders of the disappearing corporation to surrender their certificates for cancellation of record as a condition to receipt of their share of the merger price. This task is usually accomplished by a depository or exchange agent and is not completed until after the closing.

The author recommends that a pre-closing be held on the day before the closing of a merger transaction. At the pre-closing, counsel can identify and solve problems that might delay the closing and the timely filing of the certificates of merger on the closing date.

I. Fulfilling the Closing Conditions

When fulfilling the conditions of an acquisition contract, some tasks are routine but others are major projects. However, even a minor task can become important if failure to fulfill it creates an excuse from performance or an opportunity to negotiate for a better bargain.

1. Incorporation and Good Standing

A task that should be routine is obtaining evidence that the corporations participating in the closing are duly incorporated; are existing in good standing in their states of incorporation; have corporate power and authority to execute and perform the acquisition contract and related agreements; and are duly qualified and in good standing in all other states where the nature of their business activities or ownership of property requires such qualifications.

Incorporation and good standing are customarily evidenced by a certificate of the secretary of state (or other agency) responsible for administering the corporation law in the state of incorporation. The "long form" certificate is preferable and should include a copy of the certificate of incorporation and all amendments so that counsel can determine whether they contain any problem provisions. Good standing certificates should cover the payment of franchise taxes necessary to maintain corporate existence in the state of incorporation and qualification to do business in other states. These certificates are important because state laws frequently provide that contracts of corporations that fail to maintain corporate existence or qualification to do business are unenforceable.

Unfortunately, the task is not always routine. Many corporations, especially privately held corporations, forget to file annual franchise tax returns and lose their good standing and eventually their existence. Further, many corporations do not apply for qualification to do business in states other than their state of incorporation, although their activities or properties in those states require qualification. Thus, counsel should begin to assemble documents early enough to take corrective actions when discrepancies are discovered.

2. Due Authorization by Corporate Proceedings

Another task that should be routine is providing evidence that the acquisition contract and other agreements and actions at the closing were duly authorized by all necessary corporate proceedings. These requirements are customarily evidenced by a Secretary's Certificate as to the enabling resolutions adopted by the board of directors and, if applicable, the shareholders of the corporation. The Certificate should state that the resolutions remain unmodified and in full force and effect on the closing date.

The Secretary's Certificate should also include the by-laws and all amendments to evidence that corporate proceedings were held in compliance with their requirements. The Secretary's Certificate also usually verifies the incumbency of officers who will sign documents at the closing and the genuineness of specimens of their signatures.

Counsel for other major participants in the closing will have reviewed the necessary corporate actions during the "due diligence" review of the corporate minute books and stock books. They may have their own ideas about the proper wording of authorizing resolutions and certificates evidencing their adoption. To avoid disagreements, it is customary to preclear the resolutions with counsel for the other major participants. Otherwise, there may be disputes that delay and frustrate the closing.

General practitioners should be patient when counsel for other parties are large firm lawyers who limit their practice to particular fields. They often believe that resolutions and other closing documents can only be prepared their way. They are frequently quite insistent, even about minor matters. If there will be no harm to client best interests, it is often better to go along with their views than to spend time debating language preferences.

When a closely held corporation (or its assets) is being acquired or merged, an important step is to terminate and release rights under any existing shareholders' agreement between all or some of its shareholders. Under state corporation law, a shareholders' agreement can modify the normal provisions of the corporation law under certain circumstances. Shareholders' agreements often contain voting restrictions, rights of first refusal to purchase shares and other rights and obligations that could prevent the performance of the acquisition contract. The closing documents should evidence that all rights under shareholders' agreements have been fulfilled, terminated or released.

An example of a Secretary's Certificate appears as Exhibit 17-2.

3. Officer's Certificate Reaffirming Representations and Warranties

When time passes between the signing of an acquisition contract and the closing, events may occur that render obsolete the representations and warranties made in the acquisition contract. Because the representations and warranties are the basis of the bargain struck between the seller and the buyer, it is customary to require that a senior officer sign and deliver an Officer's Certificate at the closing in order to reaffirm that the representations and warranties continue to be accurate and complete. If the Officer's Certificate is not true, the party to whom it is delivered will have legal remedies as of the date when the transaction was consummated. An example of an Officer's Certificate appears as Exhibit 17-3.

4. Transfer Documents

As previously described, shares of stock, assets and liabilities are transferred by a variety of documents. The most common are deeds, bills of sale, and assignments and assumptions of liabilities and obligations.

Real estate deeds must follow the requirements of state and local law, which differ considerably throughout the United States. It is necessary to use forms that meet these requirements.

Personal property, tangible or intangible, is usually transferred by a general bill of sale with language broad enough to include fixtures that might be real property, contractual rights and governmentally granted rights such as permits. An example of a General Bill of Sale, Conveyance and Assignment appears at the end of this Chapter as Exhibit 17-4.

Contracts, leases, permits and similar assets that involve not only rights, but also obligations and perhaps liabilities, are usually transferred by a two-party assignment and assumption agreement. An example of a General Assignment and Assumption Agreement appears at the end of this chapter as Exhibit 17-5.

As described earlier, it is necessary or advisable to make specific transfers of some assets in order to fulfill the requirements of third parties such as government agencies, lenders, customers, suppliers and landlords. For example, separate assignments of patents, trademarks and copyrights should be made so that they can be filed with the U.S. Patent and Trademark Office and the Register of Copyrights.

5. Tax Certificates

Section 1145 of the Internal Revenue Code, which was adopted by the Foreign Investment in Real Property Tax Act ("FIRPTA"), requires that a transferee of a U.S. property interest withhold tax if the transferor is a foreign person, but excuses the transferee from liability if it fulfills any of several requirements.

One permissible method for a transferee to be excused from withholding tax liability is to obtain a certificate from the transferor that it is not a foreign person. An example of a non–foreign person FIRPTA Certificate appears at the end of this Chapter as Exhibit 17-6.

Another permissible method for a transferee to be excused from withholding tax liability is to obtain a certificate from stockholders or other owners of interests in a corporation or other entity that it is not, and has not been, a United States real property holding corporation as defined in Section 897(c)(2) of the Code during the period specified in Section 897(c)(1)(A)(ii) of the Code.

6. Wire Transfers

When the author began handling acquisitions, payment of a cash price was typically made by delivery of a certified or official bank check. Alert sellers would often specify that the bank certifying or issuing the check meet specified requirements designed to assure prompt availability of funds, such as membership in the New York Clearing House. Otherwise, several days might be needed to clear the check and transfer the funds.

For many years, however, it has been customary to arrange for payment of a cash purchase price and any other significant cash amounts by wire transfer. If arranged properly, wire transfers move funds much more rapidly than checks.

Wire transfers are accomplished by using the automated clearing house (ACH) facilities sponsored by the Federal Reserve System. The buyer should furnish payment instructions that identify its bank and the bank's ABA number. The instructions should also provide the seller's corporate account number to which the bank should credit funds received from the buyer.

If the seller's bank is a local state bank that is not a member of the Federal Reserve System, an extra step will be necessary. The local bank will typically have an account with a larger bank that has an account with a Federal Reserve Bank. The transfer can be routed through the correspondent bank to the local bank.

The seller should discuss with its bank the arrangements for wire transfer of the funds and when it will receive final credit for the funds so that they can be drawn upon for transfer to interest-bearing investments or for other purposes.

One reason the author recommends against closing acquisition transactions on Friday is experience with mysterious temporary losses of wire transfers made on Friday afternoons. Transfers should be initiated before 3:00 P.M. However, there can be problems with any transfers initiated after noon on Fridays. Banks that must meet capital adequacy requirements over a weekend may not always act as diligently as possible in making wire transfers. The author recommends that contact persons be identified at the transferring and receiving banks so that funds can be traced.

7. Legal Opinions

Acquisition contracts customarily require that opinion letters of counsel for the seller and the buyer be delivered at the closing. The opinion letters typically cover (1) due incorporation, existence and good standing; (2) adequacy of corporate powers; (3) due authorization of the execution, delivery and performance of the acquisition contract and related agreements and documents by all necessary corporate and other actions; (4) absence of any conflict between the acquisition contract and its performance and any other corporate documents or agreements; and (5) the validity and enforceability of the acquisition contract and related agreements and other documents. The opinion on enforceability typically contains exceptions for the bankruptcy and insolvency laws and general equitable principles that limit enforcement.

Legal opinions may also advise whether a business being sold has all necessary government permits, registrations and approvals. They may also advise on the registration of securities with the Securities and Exchange Commission or the availability of an exemption from registration. They may also advise that all necessary government clearances have been obtained, such as the termination of the Hart-Scott-Rodino waiting period.

Legal opinions may also cover title matters. For example, counsel for the selling stockholders in a stock purchase transaction may opine that the purchaser will obtain title to the shares free and clear of pledges, security interests, mortgages, liens, encumbrances and conflicting ownership claims. Traditionally, counsel rendered opinions on title to real estate and other property. However, that task has largely passed to title insurers. Many law firms decline, as a matter of policy, to render opinions on title to real estate. They explain to clients that their remedies against a reputable and financially sound title insurer are far more valuable than a fault-based claim against a law firm.

Legal opinions sometimes cover tax aspects of the acquisition transaction, such as eligibility for tax free reorganization treatment or withholding obligations. Tax opinions are typically provided in lengthy, detailed letters that are separate from the opinions on corporate and contractual matters. Before agreeing to render a tax opinion, a law firm discusses with its client the alternative of seeking a ruling from the Internal Revenue Service or applicable state tax authorities.

On many occasions, a seller or buyer relies on its accounting firm for advice on tax matters. If so, the seller or buyer may request a written opinion that may be delivered privately and not become part of the closing documents. Law firms are often pleased with this result, which relieves them from a serious responsibility where the potential liability could far exceed the fee for the tax opinion. The law firm may, however, offer tax ideas for consideration by the client and its tax accountants.

When a seller or buyer is considering whether to request an opinion from a law firm or an accounting firm, the author recommends consideration of some differences between the two professions. In providing tax advice, accounting firms analyze the law and regulations, but tend to emphasize their extensive practical experience in preparing tax returns and participating in tax audits. Law firms use their experience in preparing or advising on the preparation of tax returns and participating in audits, but tend to emphasize their skills in analyzing the language and intent of the law. When a tax return is challenged, the author's experience indicates that accounting firms are more inclined to compromise and law firms are more inclined to fight to uphold the advice they have given.

An example of a legal opinion for an assets purchase transaction appears at the end of this Chapter as Exhibit 17-7.

8. Comfort and Agreed-Upon Procedures Letters

The price and other terms of an acquisition contract are often negotiated in reliance upon the seller's audited financial statements for recent fiscal years and usually also in reliance upon unaudited financial statements for a period of months since the last fiscal year. As a step to verify the financial statements, it was formerly common for buyers to require that a "comfort letter" be delivered at the closing by the independent accounting firm that audited the seller's financial statements.

Statement on Auditing Standards (SAS) No. 72, as modified by SAS No. 76, of the American Institute of Certified Public Accountants (AICPA) provides guidance to accountants limiting the availability of comfort letters to underwriters of securities offerings and certain other persons involved in securities transactions. For acquisition transactions, accountants may issue a comfort letter if the transaction involves an exchange of stock such as a typical Form S-4 or merger proxy transaction. However, an accountant's report for a preliminary investigation in connection with a proposed acquisition should be an agreed-upon procedures letter rather than a comfort letter.

In transactions for which a comfort letter is appropriate, the person or persons requesting the comfort letter should do so by a formal written representation letter addressed to the accountants. The representation letter should state that review will be consistent (or substantially consistent) with the due diligence review process under the Securities Act of 1933 (the "1933 Act"). The requesting person should also identify the procedures that the accountants are to undertake and the form of comfort letter it wishes.

A typical comfort letter conforming to SAS Nos. 72 and 76 includes:

- **a.** A statement on the accountants' independence.
- **b.** An opinion whether the audited financial statements and schedules included in the registration statement comply as to form in all material respects with the applicable accounting requirements of the 1933 Act and related published rules and regulations.
- **c.** Negative assurance on whether
  1. The unaudited condensed interim financial information included in the registration statement complies as to form in all material respects with the applicable accounting requirements of the 1933 Act and the related published rules and regulations.
  2. Any material modifications should be made to the unaudited condensed consolidated financial statements included in the registration statement for them to be in conformity with generally accepted accounting principles (GAAP).
  3. During a specified period following the date of the latest financial statements in the registration statement and prospectus, there has been any change in capital stock, increase in long term debt or any decrease in other financial statement items.

Negative assurance, as a general concept, consists of a statement by accountants that, as a result of performing specified procedures, nothing came to their attention that caused them to believe that specified matters do not meet a specified standard.

SAS No. 75 provides guidance to accountants on agreed-upon procedures letters including those requested in connection with acquisition transactions. These letters report on engagements to apply agreed-upon procedures to specified items, accounts or items of a financial statement. In SAS No. 75, the term "accountant" means a person possessing the professional qualifications to perform as an independent auditor.

The nature of the engagement is one in which an accountant is retained by a client to issue a report of findings based on specific procedures applied to specific subjects. For example, during the due diligence review for an acquisition, a seller may engage its independent accountants to assist the buyer in evaluating the specific subjects because the buyer requires that findings be independently derived. The buyer and the accountants must agree on the procedures to be performed by the accountants. The buyer must assume responsibility for the sufficiency of the procedures since the buyer best understands its own needs. In such an engagement, the accountant does not perform an audit and does not provide an opinion or negative assurance. Instead, the report is in the form of procedures and findings.

An example of an agreed-upon procedures report in connection with a proposed acquisition, taken from SAS No. 75, appears at the end of this chapter as Exhibit 17-8.

9. Evidence of Antitrust Clearances

If an acquisition is subject to the Hart-Scott-Rodino prenotification and reporting requirements, the acquisition contract usually requires that a copy of the letter from the Department of Justice or the Federal Trade Commission terminating the waiting period be delivered at the closing. Although reopening a review is unlikely, cautious lawyers may inquire to verify that the letter is still in effect if a significant time period passes between the issuance of the letter and the closing date. If the Department of Justice or the Federal Trade Commission raised issues that were resolved by a consent order to hold separate or to divest any businesses or assets, copies of the consent order and any related documents should be included in the closing documents.

When the Hart-Scott-Rodino requirements do not apply, sellers and buyers rarely risk contacting the Department of Justice or the Federal Trade Commission to preclear an acquisition. First, there is the problem that two federal government entities have jurisdiction as well as one or more state attorneys general. Second, any clearance would be limited to the facts furnished as a basis for the clearance. However, economic facts relating to an acquisition are often complex and uncertain. Any brief simplified presentation of the facts could lead to extensive requests for more information and resulting delays. However, a detailed worst-case presentation could lead to a refusal to clear the acquisition. Thus, sellers and buyers that are not subject to the Hart-Scott-Rodino requirements usually make their own assessment of the risk.

If the seller and the buyer seek a state antitrust law clearance under procedures established by the National Association of Attorneys General, the clearance letter should also be a closing document.

10. Evidence of Securities Registrations or Exemptions

If the "acquisition currency" consists, wholly or partially, of stock or other securities, the closing documents should include evidence of registration with the Securities and Exchange Commission (SEC) and any applicable state securities authorities or evidence of applicable exemptions.

Registration of securities with the SEC includes registration under the Securities Act of 1933 and the Securities Exchange Act of 1934. Evidence of registration under the 1933 Act is the SEC's order accelerating the effective date of the registration statement. Evidence of registration under the 1934 Act can be provided by a receipt for the filing, because registration statements become effective automatically under the 1934 Act.

Evidence of the availability of an exemption from registration under the 1933 Act is usually provided by an opinion of counsel. If there are unusual circumstances, a request for a "no further action" letter can be submitted to the SEC, but it is rarely necessary to do so.

Since the adoption of the Capital Markets Efficiency Act of 1996, the states are preempted from regulating offerings of securities listed on the major stock exchanges or traded in the National Association of Securities Dealers Automated Quotation (NASDAQ), National Market System (NMS). For other securities, registration may be necessary under the applicable state securities (Blue Sky) laws unless an exemption is available. Compliance with the Blue Sky laws is usually summarized in a Blue Sky Survey prepared by the law firm handling the compliance work. The Blue Sky Survey contains a chart or lists showing the compliance status for each state where the securities will be offered. Counsel preparing a Blue Sky Survey customarily discloses that they are not admitted to practice in most of the states whose requirements are described in the Survey, but have relied on the *CCH Blue Sky Reporter* and other secondary sources. The Surveys are accepted because it is well known that counsel is in close contact with the staff of the state regulatory authorities and knows their requirements.

11. Evidence of Listing of Securities for Trading

When additional authorized but unissued shares of common stock (or other securities) are used as "acquisition currency," the acquisition contract usually requires that the buyer apply to list the additional shares or securities for trading on a stock exchange or for quotation in the NASDAQ System together with shares that the buyer has previously issued for trading.

Counsel for the buyer prepares a preliminary Listing Application for signature by the buyer and sends it to the stock exchange or NASDAQ for review and any comments. The Listing Application may be modified in response to comments. When the exchange or NASDAQ are ready to approve, the approval is communicated by letter.

12. Fairness Opinions

During some acquisition transactions, the board of directors of the seller obtains a fairness opinion from an investment banking firm or another firm or person expert in financial analysis for use in evaluating the fairness of the price and terms offered by the buyer. Fairness opinions are discussed in greater detail in Chapter 12. Depending on the terms of the acquisition contract, the fairness opinion may or may not be a closing document. An example of a fairness opinion appears as an exhibit to Chapter 12.

13. Escrow Agreements

The negotiation of an escrow agreement and its implementation at the closing can be routine, but is sometimes very difficult and controversial. Counsel should recommend that arrangements be made to obtain an escrow agent and to review the proposed escrow agreement well before the closing date to identify and resolve possible issues that could otherwise create delay and friction at the closing.

Sellers and buyers often assume that obtaining an escrow agent will be easy. They sometimes assume that one of their law firms will readily agree to serve as the escrow agent because they know that some law firms are willing to hold funds in escrow to facilitate real estate closings. However, the two situations are quite different. Escrow deposits for real estate closings are usually short-term and are typically seen by both seller and buyer as a routine precaution during a transaction that both are eager to perform. Thus, claims are relatively rare. By contrast, escrow agreements securing the representations and warranties, covenants and indemnities in an acquisition contract are typically made for terms of 1 or 2 years and claims are likely. Many law firms are concerned that a role as an escrow agent will involve them in controversies, including assertions that such a role may disqualify them from representing their client in claims or lawsuits arising from the acquisition contract.

Many banks are also reluctant to serve as an escrow agent. They often find that the seller and buyer perceive the services as routine and worth only modest fees. However, they know from experience that, if claims are made and disputed, efforts may be made to pressure them and to second-guess their decisions. However, banks will often agree to serve as an escrow agent to accommodate customer relationships, which should, of course, be disclosed to all parties.

When a bank (or other person) has agreed to serve as an escrow agent, counsel for the escrow agent focuses on the dispute resolution mechanisms, the provisions for investment of the escrow funds, the exculpatory provisions, and the fee and expense reimbursement provisions in the escrow agreement.

The dispute resolution provisions should obligate the buyer and seller (and any other parties) to resolve their own disputes so that the escrow agent will pay funds only if it receives either (1) clear, undisputed written instructions or (2) a clear and final court order. The provisions for investment of the escrow funds should usually authorize and instruct the escrow agent to invest the escrow funds in conservative, near-cash securities with maturities keyed to the term of the escrow agreement. Typical investments include U.S. Treasury bills and notes and bank certificates of deposit. Many escrow agreements expressly authorize a bank serving as an escrow agent to invest in its own certificates of deposit. The exculpatory provisions should, among other things, protect the escrow agent from liability except for willful misconduct or gross negligence. The fee and reimbursement provisions should authorize the escrow agent to reimburse itself from the moneys or other assets in the escrow fund if the person obligated to pay them fails to do so. The right to reimbursement should include reasonable fees and disbursements of counsel for the escrow agent.

J. Cordiality

For the law firms, investment banking firms and other outside professionals, a closing is the end of an activity to which they have typically devoted intense effort over a period of weeks or months. Thoughtful clients often express appreciation for the skills and hard work of the outside professionals.

For a seller, the closing is also an end, wholly or partially, of business and personal relationships that may have endured for decades. For some or all of the seller's personnel, the closing may be the commencement of new relationships that will bring important changes into their lives, for better or worse.

For a buyer, the closing is a beginning. The buyer has taken the risk of a major investment. The buyer now has the opportunity to work with the personnel, customers, suppliers and others in the seller's organization to achieve success. Success cannot be measured on the closing date, but only after several years.

The author recommends that lawyers and other participants make every effort to identify and resolve significant controversial issues before the closing. If properly planned, closings should be cordial ceremonies where only occasional issues are resolved in a courteous and low-key manner. This will permit all participants to attend the customary lunch or dinner where they can relax and enjoy their accomplishments and look forward to future working relationships.

J. Exhibits

17-1 Closing Memorandum and Document Checklist

17-2 Secretary's Certificate

17-3 Officer's Certificate

17-4 General Bill of Sale, Convergence and Assignment

17-5 General Assignment and Assumption Agreement

17-6 FIRPTA Certificate

17-7 Legal Opinion

17-8 Agreed-Upon Procedures Letter

EXHIBIT 17-1

ACQUISITION OF ASSETS
OF
PRIME PLASTICS, INC.
BY
MODERN MATERIALS, INC.

Closing Memorandum and Document Checklists

I. TIME, PLACE AND PERSONS PRESENT

The closing of the Assets Purchase Agreement stated ______, 1997 providing for the acquisition of the assets of Prime Plastics, Inc. ("Prime") by Modern Materials Inc. ("Modern") was held at the offices of Cravath & Davis, 100 Broad Street, New York, N.Y. at 10:00 A.M. on _______, 1997.

A list of the persons present at the closing is attached as Exhibit A.

II. ACTIONS BEFORE THE CLOSING

Before the closing, Prime and Modern took the following actions:

1. A Confidentiality Agreement dated _____, 1997 was signed by Prime and Modern.
2. A preliminary "due diligence" review of documents furnished by Prime was made by Modern.
3. A letter of intent dated ______, 1997 was signed by Prime and Modern.
4. A joint press release announcing the proposed acquisition was issued by Prime and Modern on _____, 1997.
5. Prime and Modern each filed a notification and report pursuant to the Hart-Scott-Rodino Act with the Federal Trade Commission and the U.S. Department of Justice on ________, 1997.
6. Modern filed a Current Report on Form 8-K disclosing the proposed acquisition with the Securities and Exchange Commission on ______, 1997.
7. A "due diligence" review of the business and assets of Prime was performed by Modern from _____, 1997 to ______, 1997.
8. A phase 1 environmental assessment of Prime's plant at Mountainview, New York was performed by Green Environmental, Inc.
9. Prime's Board of Directors approved the final form of the Assets Purchase Agreement and Escrow Agreement on ______, 1997.
10. Modern's Board of Directors approved the final form of the Assets Purchase Agreement on _______, 1997.
11. Officers of Prime and Modern signed the Assets Purchase Agreement on _____, 1997.
12. Prime's shareholders approved the Assets Purchase Agreement and the form of Escrow Agreement at a meeting on ______, 1997.
13. Modern filed a Current Report on Form 8-K, including the Assets Purchase Agreement and the form of Escrow Agreement, with the Securities and Exchange Commission on ______, 1997.
14. Modern obtained a commitment letter from the United Bank to provide first mortgage debt financing to the Purchaser to finance the acquisition of the assets of Prime on ____, 1997.
15. United Bank performed a "due diligence" review of Prime's business and assets.
16. Realty Title Insurance Co. delivered commitments for lender's and owner's title insurance policies on ______, 1997.
17. The Federal Trade Commission notified Prime and Modern of early termination of the waiting period under the Hart-Scott-Rodino Act on ______, 1997.
18. Acme Corporation, a major customer of Prime, signed a consent to the assignment of its three year purchase contract on _____, 1997.
19. Prime and its shareholders signed on agreement terminating the Shareholders Agreement dated November 1, 1963 between them including, without limitation, all rights of first refusal to purchase the Seller's shares. The termination was made contingent on the closing of the Assets purchase Agreement.

20. Prime and the New York Department of Environmental Conservation (NYSDEC) signed are administrative consent order providing for the removal of an underground gasoline storage truck at Prime's property, including the remediation of soil and groundwater contamination.
21. Mohawk Trust Company, as Indenture Trustee for the Columbia County 6% Pollution Control Bonds secured by the pollution control equipment at Prime's property in Mountainview, New York agreed to their assignment to Modern.
22. On the day before the closing, Modern and Prime and their accountants reviewed Prime's inventories and accounts receivable to determine the purchase price adjustments prescribed in Section 1.2 of the Assets Purchase Agreement.

III. DESCRIPTION OF THE CLOSINGS

Closings of two agreements took place on the closing date:

1. The Loan Agreement between the Modern and United Bank.
2. The Assets Purchase Agreement between Prime and Modern.

Except as otherwise stated, all actions at the two closings were deemed to take place simultaneously.

IV. LOAN AGREEMENT BETWEEN PURCHASER AND UNITED BANK

At the closing of the Loan Agreement, Modern delivered the following documents to United Bank in order to obtain acquisition financing secured by the business and assets being acquired from Prime other than its pollution control facilities:

1. Copies of Modern's Certificate of Incorporation and all amendments, certified by the Security of State of New York, and a good standing certificate including the payment of taxes.
2. A Secretary's Certificate as to resolutions adopted by Modern's Board of Director and as to its By-Laws, as amended , and the incumbency of its officers.
3. An Officer's Certificate reaffirming Modern's representations and warranties in the Loan Agreement.
4. A "Agreed-upon Procedures Letter" from Modern's independent accountants.
5. Releases of mortgage and security interests in the property of Mountainview, New York.
6. Mortgage and Security Interest Agreement between Modern and United Bank with respect to the business and assets at Mountainview, New York.
7. Intercreditor Agreement signed by United Bank, Mohawk Trust Company, as Indenture Trustee for the Columbia County 6% Pollution Control Bonds, and Modern.
8. Marked up commitments of Realty Title Insurance Corporation to issue a lender's title insurance policy to United Bank for the property at Mountainview, New York.
9. Promissory Note signed by Modern.
10. Mortgage of the Mountainview property, signed by Modern.
11. Financing Statements on Form UCC-1 signed by Modern.
12. Owner's Affidavit signed by Modern.
13. Survey and Survey Affidavit and Indemnity signed by Modern.
14. Collateral assignments of certain contact rights, signed by Modern.
15. Collateral assignments of patent and trademark rights, signed by Modern.
16. Collateral assignments of motor vehicle titles, signed by Modern.
17. Loss payable endorsement in favor of United Bank to the insurance policies covering the property and operations at Mountainview, New York.
18. Payout letter signed by Modern instructing United Bank about disbursements of the loan proceeds.
19. Opinion of Modern's counsel, Cravath & Davis.
20. Receipt for the loan proceeds, signed by Modern.

V. THE ASSETS PURCHASE AGREEMENT

A. At the closing of the Assets Purchase Agreement, Prime delivered to Modern the following documents:

1. Copies of Prime's Certificate of Incorporation and all amendments, certified by the Secretary of the State of New York, and a good standing certificate including confirmation of payment of taxes.

EXHIBIT 17-1 (CONT.)

2. A Secretary's Certificate as to resolutions adopted by Prime's board of directors and shareholders and as to its By-Laws and the incumbency of its officers.
3. An Officers Certificate reaffirming Prime's representations and warranties in the Assets Purchase Agreement.
4. An "Agreed-upon procedures letter" from Prime's independent accountants.
5. A Special Warranty Deed for Prime's property at Mountainview, New York.
6. A General Bill of Sale, Conveyance and Assignment transferring Prime's business and assets and certain liabilities and obligations to Modern.
7. A specific assignment of Prime's contract with its major customer, Acme Corporation, accompanied by Acme's written consent to such assignment.
8. Specific assignments of Prime's environmental permits.
9. Specific assignments of Prime's patents and trademarks in form acceptable for filing with the U.S. Patent and Trademark office.
10. Specific assignments of Prime's motor vehicle title certificates.
11. Specific assignments of the Trust Indenture and other agreements related to the Columbia County 6% Pollution Control Bonds and the written consent of Mohawk Trust Company, as Indenture Trustee.
12. Copy of the letter of the Federal Trade Commission granting early termination of the waiting period under the Hart-Scott-Rodino Act.
13. A copy of the agreement terminating the Shareholders Agreement dated November 1, 1963 between Prime and its shareholders.
14. A copy of the Administrative Consent Order signed by Prime and the NYSDEC providing for removal of an underground storage tank at Prime'sMountainview property including remediation of soil and groundwater contamination.
15. Consulting Agreement signed by Dr. Leo Bakelite
16. Employment agreements between Modern and certain former officers and managers of Prime, signed by such officers and managers.
17. Letter from Merrill Lehman Salomon Inc., acknowledging payment of all amounts owed for finder's fees or commissions.
18. Non-Foreign Person Affidavit, signed by Prime.
19. The Escrow Agreement, signed by Prime.
20. Legal opinion of Prime's counsel, Carter & Milbank.
21. Receipt for the base purchase price including an acknowledgment that it was correctly calculated pursuant to Section 1.2 of the Assets Purchase Agreement, less $1,500,000 delivered to Industryville National Bank, as Escrow Agent.

B. At the closing of the Assets Purchase Agreement, Modern delivered to Prime the following documents.

1. Copies of Modern's Certificate of Incorporation and all amendments, certified by the Secretary of State of New York, and a good standing certificate including confirmation of taxes.
2. A Secretary's Certificate as to resolutions adopted by Modern's board of directors and as to its By-Laws and the incumbency of its officers.
3. An Officer's Certificate reaffirming Prime's representations and warranties in the Assets Purchase Agreement.
4. General Assignment and Assumption Agreement confirming the assignment to and assumption of certain of Prime's liabilities and obligations by Modern.
5. Consulting Agreement for Dr. Leo Bakelite, signed by Modern, and a copy of his nomination for election to Modern's board directors.
6. Employment Agreements for certain former officers and director of Prime, signed by Modern.
7. The Escrow Agreement, signed by Modern and the Escrow Agent.
8. Legal opinion of Modern's counsel, Cravath & Davis.
9. A wire transfer of the base purchase price, as adjusted pursuant to Section 1.2 of the Assets Purchase Agreement, and an acknowledgment that it was correctly calculated pursuant to Section 1.2 of the Assets Purchase Agreement.
10. Evidence of payment of $1,500,000 to Industryville National Bank, as Escrow Agent, pursuant to Section 1.2 of the Assets Purchase Agreement.

EXHIBIT 17-2

SECRETARY'S CERTIFICATE

Pursuant to the Assets Purchase Agreement dated ________________, 1997 between Prime Plastic Inc. (the "Seller") and Modern Materials, Inc. (the "Purchaser"), the undersigned does hereby certify as follows:

1. An accurate and complete copy of Seller's Certificate of Incorporation and all amendments through the date hereof is attached as Annex A.
2. An accurate and complete copy of Seller's By-Laws and all amendments through the date hereof is attached as Annex B.

3. Complete copies of resolutions adopted on __________, 1997 by the board of directors and shareholders of Prime Plastics are attached as Annex C.

4. The following named individuals are duly elected, incumbent and acting officers of Seller holding the positions set forth opposite their respective names. The signatures appearing opposite their respective names and titles are true and genuine specimens of their signatures.

NAME	TITLE	SIGNATURES
Leo Bakelite	Chairman of the Board	______________________
James Weizmann	President	______________________
Grace Hopewell	Treasurer	______________________
Enrico Fabriani	Secretary	______________________

IN WITNESS WHEREOF, I have hereunto set my hand and seal of the Company to be affixed on ___________, 1997.

____
Enrico Fabriani
Secretary

The undersigned, Leo Bakelite, in his capacity as President of the Seller, does hereby certify that Enrico Fabriani has been duly elected and now holds the office of Secretary of the Seller and that the signature set forth opposite his name is his true and genuine signature.

________________, 1997

____
Leo Bakelite, President

EXHIBIT 17-3

OFFICER'S CERTIFICATE

Leo Bakelite, President of Prime Plastics, Inc., a Delaware corporation ("Seller") does hereby certify to Modern Materials, Inc., a Delaware corporation ("Purchaser"), as follows:

1. Each of the representations and warranties made by Seller in Section 2.1 of the Assets Purchase Agreement dated ____, 1997 between Seller and Purchaser (the "Agreement") continues to be true and complete as though made on the date hereof.

2. The Seller has performed all of the agreements and obligations which it is required by the Agreement to perform on or before the Closing Date, as such term is defined in the Agreement.

This Certificate is delivered pursuant to Section 5.1 of the Agreement

Dated: _________, 1997

____
Leo Bakelite, President
Prime Plastics, Inc.

EXHIBIT 17-4

GENERAL BILL OF SALE, CONVEYANCE AND ASSIGNMENT

THIS GENERAL BILL OF SALE, CONVEYANCE AND ASSIGNMENT dated __________, is made by Prime Plastics, Inc., a Delaware corporation ("Purchaser"), pursuant to that certain Assets Purchase Agreement dated __________, 1997 between Seller and Purchaser, (the "Agreement"), providing for the purchase and sale of certain of the Business and Assets of Seller identified in the Agreement. Capitalized terms used but not defined in this General Bill of Sale, Conveyance and Assignment shall have the respective meanings ascribed to them in the Agreement.

KNOW ALL MEN BY THESE PRESENTS THAT, pursuant to the terms and conditions of the Agreement and for the consideration set forth therein, the receipt and sufficiency of which is hereby acknowledged by Seller, Seller hereby sells, transfers, conveys, assigns and delivers the Business and the Assets to Purchaser, subject to the terms and conditions set forth in the Agreement.

TO HAVE AND TO HOLD the same unto Purchaser, its successors and assigns forever.

Seller, for itself and its successors and assigns, covenants and agrees that it will at any time and from time to time, at the request of Purchaser, its successors and assigns, do, execute and deliver, or cause to be done, executed or delivered, all such further acts, transfers, assignments and conveyances as buyer, its successors or assigns shall reasonably require to assure, convey and confirm unto Purchaser, its successors and assigns, full right, title, interest and benefit in and to the Business and the Assets.

This General Bill of Sale, Conveyance and Assignment shall be binding upon Seller, its successors and assigns and shall insure to the benefit of the Purchaser, its successors and assigns.

EXCEPT AS MAY BE EXPRESSLY PROVIDED IN THE AGREEMENT, SELLER MAKES NO WARRANTY AS TO THE CONDITION OF THE BUSINESS AND THE ASSETS INCLUDING, WITHOUT LIMITATION, ANY WARRANTY OF MERCHANTABILITY OR FITNESS FOR A PARTICULAR PURPOSE WHETHER EXPRESS OR IMPLIED.

IN WITNESS WHEREOF, Seller has caused this instrument to be signed in its name by its officer thereunto duly authorized, on the date first above written.

PRIME PLASTICS, INC.

By ____
President

EXHIBIT 17-5

GENERAL ASSIGNMENT AND ASSUMPTION AGREEMENT

This GENERAL ASSIGNMENT AND ASSUMPTION AGREEMENT is made on ______, 1997 (the "Closing Date") between Prime Plastics, Inc., a Delaware corporation ("Seller") and Modern Materials, Inc., a Delaware corporation ("Purchaser").

RECITALS:

A. Seller and Purchaser entered into an Assets Purchase Agreement dated ________, 1997 (the "Agreement") providing, among other things, for the sale by Seller to Purchaser of the Business and Assets of Seller identified in the agreement in consideration of the payment by Purchaser to Seller of a cash purchase price in accordance with Sections 1.2 and 1.3 of the Agreement and the assumption by Purchaser of certain of liabilities and obligations of Seller in accordance with Section 1.5 of the Agreement; and

B. This General Assignment and Assumption Agreement is executed and delivered in order to evidence the assumption by Purchaser of certain liabilities and obligations of Seller as provided in Section 1.5 of the Agreement;

AGREEMENTS:

1. Pursuant to the Agreement and in consideration of the sale, conveyance, assignment, and transfer of the Business and Assets pursuant to a General Bill of Sale, Conveyance and Assignment, and other instruments of sale and transfer executed and delivered on the date hereof, Seller hereby assigns and transfers to Purchaser, and Purchaser hereby assumes and agrees to discharge:
   (a) Seller's liabilities or debts under unpaid purchase orders for materials and supplies ordered in the ordinary course of business and undelivered as of the Closing Date;
   (b) Seller's obligations under the contracts, leases, licenses, permits, registrations and other obligations described in Exhibit G to the Agreement; and
   (c) All agreements, indentures, mortgages, security agreements and other obligations relating to the Columbia County 6% Pollution Control bonds issued by Seller to finance pollution control facilities at its plant at Mountainview, New York as further evidenced by specific agreements delivered on the date hereof by Seller to Mohawk Trust Company, the Indenture Trustee for the aforesaid Bonds.
2. Except as provided in Section 1, Purchaser does not assume any liability, obligation, debt, charge or expense of Seller of any kind, description, or character, whether accrued, absolute, contingent, or otherwise. Nothing contained in this General Assignment and Assumption Agreement shall require Purchaser to pay, perform, or discharge any debts, liabilities, obligations, or commitments assumed hereunder so long as it shall in good faith actively contest or cause to be actively contested the amount or validity thereof in a court of competent jurisdiction or other appropriate forum.
3. Purchaser shall, subject to the terms and conditions of the Agreement, indemnify and defend Seller against all loss, liability, cost and expense any failure by Purchaser to discharge the liabilities and perform the obligations assumed hereunder.
4. This General Assignment and Assumption Agreement shall be construed in accordance with and governed by the laws of the State of New York.

IN WITNESS WHEREOF, the parties hereto have caused this Assignment and Assumption Agreement to be signed by their respective officers thereunto duly authorized on _______, 1997.

PRIME PLASTICS, INC.

By: ________________________________
President

MODERN MATERIALS, INC.

By: ________________________________
Vice President

EXHIBIT 17-6

FIRPTA CERTIFICATE

Section 1445 of the Internal Revenue Code provides that a transferee of a U.S. property interest must withhold tax if the transferor is a foreign person. To inform the transferee that withholding of tax is not required upon the sale of a U.S. real property interest of even date herewith (the "Property") by Prime Plastics, Inc., a Delaware corporation (the "Seller"), and Modern Materials, Inc. (the "Purchaser"), the undersigned hereby certifies the following on behalf of the Corporation.

1. The Seller is not a foreign corporation, foreign partnership, foreign trust, or foreign estate (as those terms are defined in the Internal Revenue Code and Income Tax Regulations);
2. The U.S. tax identification number of the Seller is ____________.
3. The office address of the Seller is 1234 Main Street, Mountainview, New York 10099.

The Seller understands that this certification may be disclosed to the Internal Revenue Service by the Purchaser and that any false statement made herein could be punished by fine, imprisonment, or both.

The undersigned additionally states that, to the best of his knowledge and belief, no information or documentation of any kind regarding the Property has been given to either the attorneys for the Seller or the attorneys for the Purchaser of the Property which would tend to conflict with or controvert any statement made hereby.

Under penalties of perjury, the undersigned declares that he has examined this certificate and to the best of his knowledge and belief it is true, correct, and complete, and does further declare that he has authority to sign this document.

Dated: ___________, 1997

PRIME PLASTICS, INC.

By ____
Leo Bakelite, President
Prime Plastics, Inc.

EXHIBIT 17-7

CARTER & MILBANK
1300 Madison Avenue
New York, New York 12579

Modern Materials, Inc.
5678 High Street
Industryville, NY 10211

Dear Sirs/Madams:

We have acted as counsel to Prime Plastics, Inc., a Delaware corporation ("Seller"), in connection with the Assets Purchase Agreement dated _________, 1997 (the "Agreement"), between Seller and Modern Materials, Inc., a Delaware corporation ("Purchaser").

This opinion is delivered to you pursuant to Section 5.1 of the Agreement. All capitalized terms used herein and not otherwise defined herein shall have the meanings ascribed to them in the Agreement.

In connection with the foregoing, we have examined the Certificate of Incorporation and By-Laws of Seller, and resolutions adopted by the board of directors and shareholders of Seller. We have also examined the Agreement and documents delivered to or to be delivered pursuant thereto. We have also reviewed such other documents and matters as we have deemed necessary in the circumstances.

Based upon and subject to the foregoing and subject to the qualifications set forth below, we are of the following opinions:

EXHIBIT 17-7 (CONT.)

1. Seller is a corporation duly organized and existing in good standing under the laws of the State of Delaware.
2. Seller has qualified as a foreign corporation, and is in good standing, under the laws of the State of New York and any other state where the nature of its business and ownership of property requires such qualification and the failure to so qualify would have a material adverse effect on the business of Seller or the validity and enforceability of the Agreement and the agreements attached thereto as exhibits. Seller has all requisite corporate powers to enter into and perform the Agreement.
3. Seller has full corporate power and authority to conduct the Business as it is now being conducted and to enter into and perform the Agreement. The execution and delivery of the Agreement by Seller and the performance by Seller of all of its obligations under the Agreement have been duly authorized and approved prior to the date hereof by Seller's board of directors and shareholders.
4. To the best of our knowledge, no consent of any governmental authority or other person is required for the execution and delivery of the Agreement and the consummation by Seller of any of the transactions contemplated by the Agreement.
5. Neither the execution nor the delivery of the Agreement by Seller, nor the consummation by Seller of the transactions therein contemplated, will conflict with or result in a breach of any of the terms, conditions or provisions of Seller's Certificate of Incorporation or By-laws or any statute or administrative regulation or, to the best of our knowledge, any order, writ, injunction, judgment or decree of any court or governmental authority or of any arbitration award or any agreement, indenture, mortgage, debenture, note or other instrument binding on Seller or its assets.
6. The Agreement and the Escrow Agreement are each legal, valid and enforceable obligations of Seller, except to the extent that each such agreement is subject to applicable bankruptcy, insolvency, moratorium or similar laws affecting the enforcement of creditors' rights generally or limited by overriding considerations of public policy of the forum in which a particular remedy is sought or limited by general equitable principles regardless of whether enforcement is sought at law or in equity.

The opinions set forth above are subject to the following qualifications:

(a) We have assumed the genuineness of all signatures, the authenticity of all documents submitted to us as originals, the conformity to the originals of all documents submitted to us as copies, and the authenticity of the originals of all such latter documents. We have also assumed the accuracy of the factual matters contained in the documents we have examined.

(b) We have assumed the due execution and delivery for value of the Agreement and the other documents (including, without limitation, the Escrow Agreement) delivered in connection therewith by Purchaser.

(c) We have relied as to matters of fact upon statements and/or certificates furnished by the officers of Seller and governmental officials. We have no reason to believe that such reliance is not justified or that such statements are not accurate.

(d) Our opinions are limited to matters expressly set forth herein and no opinion is to be implied or inferred beyond the matters expressly so stated.

(e) We are qualified to practice law in the State of New York and we do not purport to be experts in, and we have not made a special examination of, any law other than the law of the State of New York and the federal law of the United States and the corporate law of the State of Delaware. Accordingly, and in connection with rendering this opinion, we express no opinion as to laws of any state, or as to any matter subject to such laws, other than the laws of the State of New York and the corporate law of the State of Delaware. We also do not render any opinion as to whether any state would uphold the choice of law provisions in the Agreement or any other agreement or document delivered pursuant thereto.

The opinions expressed herein are furnished by us solely for your benefit and they may not be relied upon, quoted from, or delivered to, any person other than your legal counsel in this matter without our express, prior written consent.

Very truly yours,

CARTER & MILBANK

EXHIBIT 17-8

Report in Connection With a Proposed Acquisition

Independent Accountant's Report on Applying Agreed-Upon Procedures

To the Board of Directors and Management of X Company:

We have performed the procedures enumerated below, which were agreed to by the Board of Directors and Management of X Company, solely to assist you in connection with the proposed acquisition of Y Company as of December 31, 19XX. This engagement to apply agreed-upon procedures was performed in accordance with standards established by the American Institute of Certified Public Accountants. The sufficiency of these procedures is solely the responsibility of the Board of Directors and Management of X Company. Consequently, we make no representation regarding the sufficiency of the procedures described below either for the purpose for which this report has been requested or for any other purpose.

The procedures and the associated findings are as follows:

Cash

1. We obtained confirmation of the cash on deposit from the following banks, and we agreed the confirmed balance to the amount shown on the bank reconciliations maintained by Y Company. We mathematically checked the bank reconciliations and compared the resultant cash balances per book to the respective general ledger account balances.

Bank	General Ledger Account Balances as of December 31, 19XX
ABC National Bank	$ 5,000
DEF State Bank	13,776
XYZ Trust Company—regular account	86,912
XYZ Trust Company—payroll account	5,000
	$110,688

We found no exceptions as a result of the procedures.

Accounts Receivable

2. We added the individual customer account balances shown in an aged trial balance of accounts receivable (identified as exhibit A) and compared the resultant total with the balance in the general ledger account.

   We found no difference.

3. We compared the individual customer account balances shown in the aged trial balance of accounts receivable (exhibit A) as of December 31, 19XX, to the balances shown in the accounts receivable subsidiary ledger.

   We found no exceptions as a result of the comparisons.

4. We traced the aging (according to invoice dates) for 50 customer account balances shown in exhibit A to the details of outstanding invoices in the accounts receivable subsidiary ledger. The balances selected for tracing were determined by starting at the eighth item and selecting every fifteenth item thereafter.

   We found no exceptions in the aging of the amounts of the 50 customer account balances selected. The sample size traced was 9.8 percent of the aggregate amount of the customer account balances.

5. We mailed confirmations directly to the customers representing the 150 largest customer account balances selected from the accounts receivable trial balance, and we received responses as indicated below. We also traced the items constituting the outstanding customer account balance to invoices and supporting shipping documents for customers from which there was no reply. As agreed, any individual differences in a customer account balance of less than $300 were to be considered minor, and no further procedures were performed.

   Of the 150 customer balances confirmed, we received responses from 140 customers; 10 customers did not reply. No exceptions were identified in 120 of the confirmations received. The differences disclosed in the remaining 20 confirmation replies were either minor in amount (as defined above) or were reconciled to the customer account balance without proposed adjustment thereto. A summary of the confirmation results according to the respective aging categories is as follows:

EXHIBIT 17-8 (CONT.)

Accounts Receivable
December 31, 19XX

	Customer Account Balances	Confirmations Requested	Confirmation Replies Requested
Aging Categories			
Current	$156,000	$ 76,000	$ 65,000
Past due:			
Less than one month	60,000	30,000	19,000
One to three months	36,000	18,000	10,000
Over three months	48,000	48,000	8,000
	$300,000	$172,000	$102,000

We were not engaged to, and did not, perform an audit, the objective of which would be the expression of an opinion on the specified elements, accounts, or items. Accordingly, we do not express such an opinion. Had we performed additional procedures, other matters might have come to our attention that would have been reported to you.

This report is intended solely for the use of the Board of Directors and Management of X company and should not be used by those who have not agreed to the procedures and taken responsibility for the sufficiency of the procedures for their purposes.

Chapter 18

POST-CLOSING INTEGRATION AND OTHER ACTIVITIES

A. INTRODUCTION

Post-closing activities can be grouped in two categories. One category comprises the important steps to achieve the strategic objectives of the acquisition. The other category includes numerous financial, accounting, tax, legal, administrative and other steps required to complete the acquisition transaction because it is never possible to accomplish everything by the closing date. A checklist of these steps appears in Section F of this chapter.

B. ACHIEVING ACQUISITION OBJECTIVES

1. The "Window of Opportunity"

Experienced executives and M&A experts agree that the post-closing period is the time when the most important steps can be taken to achieve a successful acquisition.

As described in Chapter 17, the success or failure of an acquisition cannot be determined on the closing date. Persons who describe an acquisition as successful at such an early date mean only that the price and other terms are favorable and there appears to be strong synergistic potential.

During the early weeks and months after an acquisition is closed, a "window of opportunity" exists to set strategic objectives for the buyer and seller organizations and start down the roads that lead to their achievement.

After the closing, the buyer should move rapidly but cautiously to complete the evaluation made during the due diligence review and to implement its strategic plans. Unnecessary delay wastes a unique time period when changes are expected and are likely to be supported by employees seeking opportunities in the combined business. If changes are deferred, buyer and seller personnel will return to their daily activities and may resist later changes.

The integration of an acquired business is sometimes delayed and may even fail because management does not invite a sufficient range of officers, managers and key employees to participate in the integration process. This often happens when an acquisition is handled by a chief executive officer, a small management team, and outside investment bankers, accountants and lawyers. Preoccupied with the negotiations and the financial and other arrangements, the chief executive officer and the management team may seek participation in strategic and integration planning by intermediate levels of management only after the acquisition is closed. The result is likely to be uncertainty, poor communication, and perhaps even a development of rivalries between seller and buyer personnel.

2. Downsizing

Downsizing is a painful but necessary step after some acquisitions. Some cost reductions can be accomplished easily and may be well received by the seller organization. If a buyer eliminates boats, luxury vehicles or other perquisites of former owners, everyone will be glad to be rid of their costs. If the buyer eliminates a layer of former owner management to facilitate direct communication between operating personnel and the buyer's senior management, the operating personnel may welcome the opportunity to perform more effectively.

The situation is different when a serious downsizing of one or more of the seller's businesses is necessary. Downsizing should be implemented as soon as the plans can be evaluated and the steps taken in a lawful and courteous manner. Downsizing is a difficult task, both for those who give and those who receive the bad news. However, delay creates painful uncertainty that can spawn rumors and impair the effectiveness of a whole organization, even when only a small number of employees will eventually be terminated. Most organizations and employees prefer to know their status as soon as practicable so that they can plan for the future. Employees in support services (such as administrative, financial and legal departments) are seldom naive about the likelihood that their ranks will be thinned to eliminate duplication. They may prefer a termination at the time of the acquisition rather than later when the termination may appear to reflect on their competence.

Downsizing and other cost-cutting steps gain time and save cash, but time and savings alone do not achieve success. The time and cash are valuable only if used effectively to build for the future. Growth strategies usually require more extensive and longer evaluation than cost reduction strategies. The extra effort is justified because growth strategies are usually more complex and have more important long-term effects than cost reductions. However, there is one, usually modest growth plan that should not be delayed—a recovery plan for any business activity that will be downsized but continued in operation.

When a business is downsized, its managers and employees wonder whether the buyer's strategy is to achieve a turnaround or to use the business as a "cash cow" until it is eventually sold or shut down. The answer is important, especially to those who must assume additional duties after the downsizing. If the buyer wishes to achieve a turnaround, it is important to give back part of the cost savings to make improvements of the downsized businesses and to compensate employees who accept additional duties. A common strategy is to provide a modest increase of fixed compensation and larger bonuses based on achievement of the turnaround objectives.

Practical examples are not difficult to provide. If a buyer terminates 20 percent of the employees of one of seller's business operations without affirmative programs, the adverse effect on morale may be drastic, even if the cost savings return the business to profitability. However, if the layoff is accompanied by a purchase of long-needed modern equipment to make "state of the art" products, and key managers are included in a bonus plan based on improved revenues or cash flows, the effect on morale can be strongly positive.

Downsizing should be done in a manner that meets the multitude of applicable laws, regulations and court decisions. Special attention must be given to possible claims by persons who may assert that they were victims of discrimination. In recent years, special interest groups have successfully pressured the U.S. Congress and state legislatures to expand the antidiscrimination laws far beyond the classic prohibitions against discrimination on the basis of race, religion, national origin, sex and age. Under present law, plaintiff attorneys can state a claim that almost any employee's failure to perform is arguably protected by the antidiscrimination laws because even serious matters such as alcoholism and violent antisocial behavior may be associated with a disability. (See Chapter 13.)

3. Methods for Achieving Long-Term Improvements

Alfred Rappaport, the well-known business developer, professor and author, said in an article that the several potential sources of value due to postmerger improvements in operations could be classified in three broad categories: (1) economies of scale, (2) technical and managerial skill transfer, and (3) asset restructuring.[1] A somewhat expanded list of methods for achieving acquisition synergies is as follows:

1. Establishment of effective communications between buyer and seller personnel at operating levels.
2. Exchange of information relating to marketing, products and customers, manufacturing processes and equipment, raw materials and suppliers, and research and development.
3. Expansion into new markets.
4. Provision of broader product lines to sales representatives, agents and distributors to make "one-stop shopping" available to customers.
5. Improvement of the overall product mix to emphasize products with higher profit margins and longer commercial lives.
6. Utilization of unused production capacity.
7. Use of increased production volumes to obtain price discounts from raw material, transportation and other suppliers.
8. Consolidation of functions to eliminate unnecessary duplication of costs, especially for corporate services.
9. Elimination of layers of intermediate managerial personnel whose roles may once have provided valuable experience or technical

[1] "Converting Merger Benefits to Shareholder Value," Rappaport, *Mergers & Acquisitions*, Mar-Apr 1987.

know-how, but have become obsolete, ceremonial or counterproductive.

10. Investment in facilities, equipment and other resources with "state of the art" capacities and performance characteristics at a scale larger than would have been feasible before the acquisition.
11. Divestiture of business operations that have salable value, but are not part of the strategic business plan.
12. Financial restructuring to substitute lower-cost debt capital for equity capital.
13. Planning to save or defer taxes.

4. Examples of Postclosing Integration Methods

To illustrate successful integration methods, the following examples are provided:

Sales Integration. Buyer's due diligence review revealed that seller's products had been sold for years through a system of distributors. The distributors purchased at considerable discounts from retail price levels under contracts that had been renewed annually since they were negotiated many years earlier by the seller's founder and chief executive officer. Seller's sales representatives sold to the distributors and a few "national' customers that were end users. In recent years, sales had been flat and market share was lost to competitors offering upgraded and somewhat more complex products with technical support provided directly to end user customers. Seller's distributors declined to undertake the effort and cost to provide technical support to their end user customers. Instead, the distributors complained that the seller had failed to provide sufficient national advertising and marketing programs, leaving the distributors dependent on their own local advertising campaigns. As a positive factor, the buyer learned that seller's southeastern division had begun to offer upgraded products and technical service directly to "national" accounts located in that area. The buyer combined the seller's sales department with its own larger department and initiated a program to make direct sales of upgraded products with technical service. The seller's southeastern sales and technical service managers were given leadership responsibilities to train sales and technical personnel in other areas. The nationwide offering of upgraded products was supported by national advertising and marketing programs developed by buyer's advertising and marketing managers. The distributors contracts were renegotiated to apply only to sales of the traditional products to customers with whom the distributors had special relationships.

Manufacturing Integration. The seller and the buyer each had a plant manufacturing polymers for the coatings industry and the plastics industry located in a midwestern state. The buyer dedicated one plant to polymers for coatings and the other to polymers for plastics. These steps enabled each plant to buy larger volumes of raw materials at discounted prices and to arrange for their delivery in jumbo tankcars at reduced freight rates. In return for the larger volumes, suppliers also agreed to provide "just in time" deliveries, thus saving buyer costs for storing and financing raw material inventories. These efficiencies and economics enabled the buyer to apply operating cash to product development and technical service needed to improve product mix and to seek sales to larger customers that were willing to pay for value-added products.

Strategic Divestiture. After a stock purchase acquisition, the buyer evaluated one of seller's businesses that had been a developmental project sponsored by the former owner and chief executive. The strengths were a talented group of research scientists and product development technicians who were also performing the marketing and sales functions. However, the products were manufactured using small, used equipment at one manufacturing plant. Although the products had achieved a good reputation for performance and quality, they were priced higher than most competitive products and had achieved less than 2 percent market share. Due to the small volume sold, the business could not obtain raw material and transportation discounts or achieve incremental savings by allocating fixed costs to a large volume of units sold. The buyer considered the cost of adding marketing and sales personnel and installing full-scale production facilities for the business, which was outside of its core businesses. After some debate, the buyer decided that the effort and cost would be excessive. After a frank discussion with the key personnel, who were not prepared to undertake a management buyout, the buyer negotiated a divestiture of the business to a large manufacturer in the same field. The large manufacturer had been seeking to upgrade its products, which were primarily commodities. It welcomed the opportunity to acquire some "added value" product lines and an in-place research and technical organization that could relate well to its existing marketing and sales personnel.

Strategic "Buildup" Acquisitions. A buyer made an acquisition of a small business to gain entry to a segment of its industry that produces established but specialized products that earn premium profit margins in return for superior performance in customer applications. Keys to the superior performance were carefully guarded product formulations and proprietary manufacturing processes. After studying the seller's business to gain an understanding of the technology and verify its evaluation of market trends, the buyer embarked on a series of acquisitions and internal expansion projects in order to build the business to a "critical mass" that could support skilled management, "state of the art" production facilities and equipment, aggressive marketing and sales personnel, and other resources necessary to become a leader in the market segment.

Secondary Recovery of Useful Materials. In seller's state, environmental regulations gradually closed or greatly increased the cost of traditional methods used to dispose of waste materials. Old landfill and incinerator facilities were closed and new facilities met years of delay and opposition from government agencies and environmental activists. High "tipping fees" were charged by the operators of the remaining landfills and incinerators as their regulatory compliance costs increased and they realized that the declining availability of facilities had reduced the need to compete. Sewer charges also multiplied. The buyer analyzed the components of the seller's process streams and found some components that were potentially valuable raw materials if they were extracted from the streams and trace contaminants were removed. The buyer also found that these raw materials could be combined with components of process streams from its previously owned plants to make useful commercial products. Most of the products were commodities, but they could be sold at very competitive prices because the buyer's primary objective was to save disposal costs that would be incurred if the materials were allowed to become effluent or waste. Thus, the buyer converted activities that were a severe cash drain to a modest source of cash inflows.

Blending Diverse Cultures. Established business organizations develop a "culture," shared and strongly held viewpoints about the fundamental ways to do business. Cultural differences are sometimes found in acquisitions in the same industry and locality and are frequently found in international or interregional acquisitions. For example, an aggressive, fast-moving New York company that acquires a company headquartered in Atlanta or St. Louis may find that New York methods are politely and steadily resisted by acquired company personnel who are accustomed to a slower and steadier pace. Buyers should move quickly to evaluate and then either accept or resolve these cultural differences so they do not impair acquisition objectives.

In a perceptive article titled "A job I never wanted,"[2] John Rutledge described how he helped to persuade buyer and seller personnel, who had continued preacquisition competitive hostility, to work together. Among other steps, he established a penalty for any use of the names of the former companies except in the past tense. Each offender had to contribute a dollar immediately to the office fund used to provide snacks. The penalties were accepted with good humor, especially when combined with real efforts to install a "bottom up" rather than a "top down" management style.

Differences that can be resolved by the good-humored and modest methods described by Mr. Rutledge are very common, but do not run deep. Buyers should be cautious about demanding changes of deeply held beliefs. As one step, the author recommends that the buyer determine whether its own methods can be adapted to accommodate the differences. Visible accommodations by buyer personnel may result in accommodations by seller personnel.

If other methods do not succeed and the business plan is being seriously impaired, the buyer may have no choice but to make personnel changes. The reason is that orders or pressures to change deeply held views may be nominally accepted, but then not implemented because people do not easily change fundamental beliefs. If changes become necessary, they represent a partial loss of the values acquired in the acquisition. However, decisive action to install personnel who can perform effectively as part of the buyer's team can avoid a long period of stagnation.

Before making changes in seller's management, the buyer should perform a survey to assure that the replacements will be able to perform effectively within the culture of the overall seller organization and its customer and supplier network. Otherwise, the buyer may find that it has only killed the messengers because the replacements are unable to achieve their objectives.

---

[2] *Forbes*, July 28, 1997.

If cultural differences run very deep, they can break the seller organization and sometimes even the buyer organization into fragments, resulting in losses of key personnel and customers. Before this happens, a buyer should recognize the problem and, if necessary, arrange a divestiture that could include a tax-free split-off or a management buyout.

5. Perils of "Quick Fix Integration

Postacquisition integration can do more harm than good if it consists of "quick fix" steps that create a brief appearance of success followed by a downward spiral. Some examples of steps that can be serious errors are as follows:

1. Reduction of normal advertising of retail products.
2. Reduction of operating and capital expenditures needed to maintain facilities and equipment in good condition and to comply with safety and health laws.
3. Reduction of sales and technical services and customer-responsive, short-term research projects.
4. Installation of strict credit and collection policies without a campaign to win the understanding and cooperation of customers.
5. Termination of employees respected in the seller organization for diligent and effective work while retaining less capable "office politicians" skilled at making favorable initial impressions.
6. Reduction of employee compensation without installing incentive programs that will share the rewards of a successful "turnaround."

C. Avoiding Loss of Insurance Coverage

Buyers should plan to take steps before and after the closing to avoid loss of the seller's preacquisition insurance coverage, including any coverage of the seller's predecessors, that can be identified and preserved. It is important that this coverage continue after the closing.

Since the early 1960s, judges have reinterpreted the tort liability of private industry in several important ways:

1. Buyers claiming product defects were allowed to sue not only the sellers of the products but also their manufacturers and other persons who supplied components and services.
2. Product sellers, manufacturers and suppliers were subjected to court-developed strict liability, a doctrine that sharply reduced their defenses against product liability.
3. Buyers were allowed to sue for personal injury and property damage allegedly caused by products sold many years ago under court-developed interpretations that statutes of limitations begin to run only when injury or damage is discovered or should have been discovered.

4. Plaintiff attorneys were allowed broad authority to demand production of large volumes of current and historical internal records of sellers, manufacturers and suppliers in order to seek evidence that could be used against them.
5. Buyers of businesses were held responsible for the liabilities of acquired businesses under several court-developed theories including successor, enterprise and "veil piercing" liability.[3]

The courts found that these expansions of product liability were popular with the communications media and brought prosperity to the legal profession. However, many companies did not have enough financial resources to pay for them. Thus, the courts developed interpretations of insurance policy provisions that expanded the coverage available to product sellers, manufacturers and suppliers. Most important, the courts limited the effects of coverage exclusions and held that policies could afford coverage for claims made many years after their terms expired.

The courts also expanded the liability of private industry in other fields, such as employment and environmental liability, and some courts also interpreted insurance policy coverage so as to provide funds to companies to pay for the expanded liability.

Perceiving the trend, insurers have in recent years ceased to offer policies covering some risks. They have also drafted coverage provisions and exclusions in their policies to speak so plainly that the courts can no longer easily find an interpretation that obligates the insurers to pay claims they did not intend to insure. The practical result is that older policies with simpler provisions have become valuable assets.

Reasons why old liability policies are valuable are as follows:

1. Old policies typically afford coverage based on an "occurrence" within the policy term. Many courts have found that they provide coverage if a claimant suffered exposure to a product or the continuing effects of such exposure during the policy term, even though injury or damage did not manifest itself until years later. Many courts have also found that the "occurrence" policies in effect at the time of manifestation also provided coverage. Thus, some old policies may cover a claim for a slowly developing chronic illness or slow leakage of hazardous substances from an underground storage tank into soil and groundwater.
2. Old policies do not contain "claims made" provisions limiting coverage to claims made within the policy terms for occurrences also within the term, except to the extent that the insured may purchase the right to give "late notice" after the policy period.
3. Some old policies contain obligations to defend the insured that are separate from the obligation to indemnify the insured against liability. The defense obligations may also be free of any aggregate limits.
4. Some old policies do not contain a pollution exclusion and others contain a pollution exclusion found by some courts to be ineffective to prevent coverage of some kinds of environmental claims.

[3]These court-developed changes of the law are also discussed in Chapter 13.

5. Old policies contain modest deductible provisions rather than the large deductible or self-insured retention provisions found in many recent policies.
6. Some old policies contain liability limits applicable to each occurrence, but no aggregate limits, so they cover large numbers of claims.
7. Some old policies contain separate limits of liability for bodily injury and property damage.

After an acquisition, the buyer's risk manager often switches the seller's insurance to the buyer's broker. Both the risk manager and the broker advise management that they will save premium cost by changing insurers. From that point, the seller's insurers view their coverage of the seller as an historical obligation to be fulfilled as economically as possible.

As time passes, the former broker and the former insurers also discard the seller's old policies and the related records. If plaintiff attorneys develop lawsuits based on old occurrences, the buyer must be able to produce its policies, or other convincing evidence of coverage. If it does not, the insurers will deny coverage. The need to reconstruct old insurance coverage has led to the new field of insurance archaeology practiced by professionals such as IAG Incorporated in New York, New York and R. M. Fields & Co. Ltd. in Philadelphia and London. They have found evidence of coverage in remote places, including the attics of abandoned factories and the records of the slips signed by underwriting syndicates at Lloyds.

When lawsuits are being defended by a former insurer, the usual tendency to minimize investigation and defense costs and settle within deductible limits grows. In product liability litigation, this tendency can become seriously harmful because plaintiff attorneys who obtain easy settlements will find more plaintiffs. Eventually, the reputation of the product can be harmed. The author recommends that a buyer retain its own counsel to monitor defense of lawsuits by a former insurer in order to assure proper defense and settlements.

The risk manager and broker who set such a sequence in motion usually suffer no consequences. They blame a variety of scapegoats, including the seller and the courts.

D. Continuing, Modifying or Terminating Pension Plans

1. Introduction

After an acquisition, a buyer may continue, modify or terminate the employee benefits afforded to the seller's employees and to former employees if the seller has retirees receiving benefits. The tasks must be performed carefully because employee benefit plans are regulated by the Employee Retirement Income Security Act (ERISA) and perhaps other laws.

The task is especially complex for pension plans because they are regulated by the Internal Revenue Service (IRS), the Department of Labor (DOL) and the Pension Benefit Guaranty Corporation (PBGC). In addition, both ERISA and the Internal Revenue Code (IRC) contain special provisions applicable to pension plans.

2. Continuation, Modification or Termination

Effects of the Acquisition Structure. After a stock purchase acquisition, the pension plan or plans of the newly acquired subsidiary continue without significant change unless the buyer takes action to change them. After an acquisition by merger, the surviving corporation automatically succeeds to the rights and obligations of the corporation whose existence terminates, so its pension plan or plans are automatically continued without significant change unless the surviving corporation takes action to change them. However, after an assets purchase acquisition, the buyer must take several actions if the seller's pension plans will continue, beginning with hiring all or part of the seller's employees and then either (1) adopting all or part of the seller's pension plans or (2) adopting and merging all or part of the seller's pension plans into its own plans.

Readers should read the discussion under "Termination" later in this chapter to see how provisions of ERISA nullify the usual protection that parent corporations have from claims that they are responsible for the obligations and liabilities of their subsidiaries.

When making structural changes, the buyer should keep in mind that the PBGC regulations list as a reportable event any change of the contributing sponsor if a plan has unfunded vested benefits of $1,000,000 or more.[4]

Compliance with Participation, Coverage and Other Requirements. After a stock purchase transaction, a buyer cannot assume that it will be in compliance with the IRC and ERISA merely by allowing the seller's pension plan to continue without change. The buyer should determine whether it will meet applicable minimum participation, nondiscriminatory coverage, funding and other requirements of the IRC and ERISA if the seller's plan is continued without change. If not, amendments must be made to achieve compliance.

After a merger transaction, a buyer should also review group compliance with applicable minimum participation, antidiscrimination, funding and other requirements of the IRC and ERISA as described in the preceding paragraph. If not, the necessary amendments must be made.

After assets transaction, a buyer should make the review recommended in the preceding two paragraphs whether it agrees or declines to hire seller's employees and adopt its pension plan or plans. Whatever actions are taken or not taken, the end result must achieve group compliance with the IRC and ERISA.

A buyer that continues seller's plans without change after an acquisition has until the end of the first plan year beginning after the acquisition date to achieve compliance with the participation and coverage requirements.[5]

Deciding Whether to Continue Seller's Plan. Buyers do not always wish to continue a seller's pension plan, especially after an assets acquisition.

---

[4] 29 CFR § 2615.23.

[5] IRC §401(a)(26)(F) and IRS Reg. §1.401(a)(26)-1(b)(5); IRC §410(b)(c) and IRS Reg. §1.410(b)-2(F); and IRC §414(r) and IRS Reg. § 1.414(r)-1(d)(4). See also the minimum standards rules of the U.S. Department of Labor in 29 CFR Part 2530.

After hiring all or part of the seller's employees, many buyers prefer that the new employees have the same benefits as their own previous employees, even though those benefits may be more or less generous. Further, if a buyer will succeed to a seller's plan, the buyer will want to know that the seller provided adequate funding to pay accrued benefits up to the acquisition date and that those funds will be available as the benefits come due. If the seller's plan is underfunded, a buyer should either negotiate to require the seller to provide additional funds or decline to assume the plan.

Sellers do not always wish to have a buyer succeed to their pension obligations. For example, a "deep pocket" seller divesting a subsidiary, division or other business unit to a small buyer may fear that the buyer will not meet its funding obligations and its former employees will then claim that the seller is responsible. Such an employer may decide to freeze and continue its plan, as described later. If so, employees hired by the buyer will receive two checks when they retire, one from the trustee of the seller's plan for their years of employment with the seller and one from the trustee for the buyer's plan for their years of employment with the buyer.

Adoption of Seller's Plan. When a buyer adopts a seller's pension plan after an assets purchase acquisition, either of two methods can be used:

1. If the buyer will assume the entire plan, the seller can assign the plan and the related trust, group annuity contract or other funding vehicle. The buyer can adopt them as its own plan and funding vehicle.
2. If the buyer will assume part of seller's plan and part of its assets and liabilities, the buyer can adopt a plan that has essentially the same provisions as the seller's plan. The buyer can also establish its own funding vehicle which may or may not receive funds from the seller's funding vehicle.

Continuation of Part of Seller's Plans. When a buyer acquires an unincorporated division, subsidiary or other business unit of a seller, the seller can split the value of the assets of its pension plan into assets allocable to the employees of the business being sold and assets allocable to its retained employees. For defined contribution plans, the split is based on the actuarial values credited to the accounts of the employee-participants. For defined benefit plans, the allocation is more complex and requires analysis of the provisions of the plan and calculations by its actuarial firm to determine the split. Once the allocable amount is known, the appropriate amount of assets can be transferred to the trust under the buyer's plan.

Based on experience, the author recommends that the buyer contact the trustee well before any transfer of assets will take place. Otherwise, the trustee will presume a cash transfer and will liquidate assets to raise cash, thus incurring broker's commissions and perhaps investment losses because the sales may be untimely from an investment viewpoint. The buyer should arrange for a transfer of the assets in kind unless investment strategy favors their liquidation. The seller and the trustee transferring the assets may request, and the buyer can provide, an indemnity of reasonable scope.

After the transfer of assets, each participant must be entitled immediately after the transfer to a benefit that would, if the buyer's plan were then terminated, be equal to or greater than the benefit that such participant would have been entitled to receive immediately before the transfer if the seller's plan were then terminated.[6]

Merger of Pension Plans. After a merger or stock purchase acquisition and sometimes after an assets acquisition, a buyer may decide to merge the seller's pension plan and its assets with its own pension plan and assets. The steps involve amending the seller's plan, prospectively or retroactively, to become identical to the buyer's plans and making corresponding amendments to the annuity contracts or trust agreements used to fund the plans.

After a merger of defined contribution plans, the balance in the individual account of each participant in the merged plan must be the same as it was in the predecessor plan immediately before the merger.[7]

A merger of defined benefit plans involves complex actuarial calculations because each participant must be entitled to a benefit immediately after the companies' merger that is at least equal to the benefit the participant had been terminated immediately before the merger. The sufficiency of the plan assets to meet these requirements can be evidenced by preparing a schedule of benefits or retaining sufficient data for 5 years to permit preparation of such a schedule. A buyer does not usually wish to merge pension plans that are considerably different in benefits or funding sufficiency, except perhaps prospectively.[8]

Freezing a Pension Plan. An employer can "freeze" a defined benefit pension plan by amending its benefit provisions to eliminate benefits accruing on and after the amendment date. Benefits accrued before the amendment date cannot be reduced by such an amendment.[9] A 15-day notice must be given to all plan participants and beneficiaries and to the unions representing them.[10]

Freezing a plan can provide important financial relief to an employer, but does not eliminate all continuing costs. Administration and reporting requirements must continue to be met. Premiums must continue to be paid to the PBGC.[11] Contributions must continue to be made to fund benefits committed before the amendment date, including any amounts owed for deficiencies.

If there is a complete discontinuance of contributions, the rights of all participating employees to accrued benefits, to the extent then funded, must become vested.[12]

---

[6]IRC, §§414(1) and 411(d)(6); IRS Regulation §1.414(1)-1(m); ERISA §4044; IRS Revenue Rulings 86-47 and 86-48.

[7]IRS Regulation §1.414(1)-1(m).

[8]IRS Regulation §1.414(1)-1(n).

[9]IRC, §411(d)(6).

[10]ERISA §204(g) and (h); 29 USC §1054(g) and (h).

[11]ERISA §4007(a); 29 USC §1307(a).

[12]IRC §411(d)(3) and IRS Regulation §1.411(d)-2.

On the other hand, an employer that freezes and continues a plan can benefit from favorable actuarial experience, such as employee turnover and investment appreciation. In addition, individuals designated by the employer can continue to act as plan administrator, investment manager and trustee. These advantages should be compared to ongoing costs including PBGC premium. Any plan, including a frozen defined benefit plan, must cover at least 50 employees or, if less, 40 percent of all the employees of the employer.[13] A frozen plan that initially meets this requirement may lose its qualification over a period of years unless it is terminated or merged into another plan.

Curtailment of Benefits. A buyer can curtail benefits under a seller's plan by amending its provisions to reduce benefits accruing after the date of the amendment, but consideration should be given to whether a partial termination may result.[14]

Termination. A buyer can voluntarily terminate a defined benefit pension plan that it has assumed or is otherwise responsible for only by meeting the criteria for a standard termination or a distress termination. Both methods of termination require that notice be sent to the PBGC, all participants and beneficiaries, and any union or other person representing them. A voluntary termination may not proceed if it would violate an existing collective bargaining agreement.[15] The PBGC regulations contain procedures for challenges of both a distress termination and a standard termination under a collective bargaining agreement.[16]

ERISA Section 4069(a) imposes termination liability on any person and its controlled group (determined as of the termination date) if such entities entered into any transaction within the preceding 5 years before the termination, a principal purpose of which was to evade their liability under ERISA. This provision creates potential seller liability whether a merger, stock sale or assets sale is made. There may be risk of use of ERISA Section 4069(a) to impose seller liability after leveraged buyout transactions if the buyer terminates a plan within 5 years. The courts will presumably examine the capital adequacy and cash flow projections in determining whether there was a purpose to evade.

From the point of view of the buyer, a stock purchase does not provide its usual insulation for direct liability for obligations of an acquired subsidiary, because ERISA Section 4062 imposes termination liability on all members of a controlled group. Further, an acquired subsidiary may have contingent liability if it was a member of a controlled group sponsoring a pension plan before the sale. Thus, the buyer must carefully review not only the pension obligations of the subsidiary but also those of affiliates, and must obtain indemnification or other protection against them.

From the point of view of the buyer, any liability in an assets purchase should arise only if a plan is assumed in the acquisition contract. The lan-

[13]IRC §401(a)(26).

[14]IRS Regulation §1.411(d)-2.

[15]ERISA §4041; 29 USC §1341; see also PBGC Regulations at 29 CFR Parts 2616 and 2617.

[16]PBGC Regulations at 29 C.F.R. §§2616.5 and 2717.5.

guage of ERISA Section 4069(a) does not appear to apply to a buyer if the buyer does not assume a plan. Nevertheless, claims based on such theories as successor liability and the practical merger doctrine are possible, so the buyer should inquire how the seller plans to meet any termination liability if a plan is not assumed. It should also obtain indemnification or other protection against such liability.

If an employee benefit plan is overfunded upon termination, any reversion of assets is subject to a 20 percent excise tax imposed by IRC §4980. This excise tax becomes 50 percent unless the employer either establishes a qualified replacement plan, or amends the terminated plan to increase the benefits. To establish a qualified replacement plan, an employer must meet several requirements including a direct transfer of assets equal to 25 percent of the maximum value of the reversion to the replacement plan. If the employer decides to make benefit increases, they are also subject to several requirements including a minimum present value equal to at least 20 percent of the maximum reversion.

E. Postclosing Claims

After an acquisition, there are always a number of adjustments and claims because it is never possible to foresee and complete every step by the closing date.

1. Shared Assets and Services

A common postclosing issue is the ownership and use of assets that an acquired business has shared with other persons. For example, when a large corporation divests a division or subsidiary, the business sold often has shared the use of property, buildings, equipment and services with other divisions and subsidiaries. The acquisition contract typically resolves the major items, but some significant items may be overlooked. For example, will the seller allow the buyer part-time use of lift trucks at an off-site warehouse? Will electricians hired by the buyer continue to perform repairs of equipment retained by the seller at an adjoining facility? Should the seller and the buyer continue to combine their purchases of some supplies and services in order to obtain favorable pricing?

For another example, when a family-owned business is sold, there has often been personal use of corporate assets without compensation, counterbalanced by uncompensated contributions of long hours of service and perhaps property from the owners to the corporation. Here again, the acquisition contract typically resolves the major items, but some significant items may be overlooked. The issues are especially important if family members will continue to participate in management.

The author recommends that these issues be resolved by give-and-take methods as harmoniously as possible. Headquarters management should allow minor issues to be resolved by local management if they can do so.

2. Purchase Price Adjustments

Some acquisition contracts contain provisions for adjustment of the purchase price based on inventory count and valuation as of the closing date. The acquisition contract typically prescribes the methods to be used, such as performance during a weekend or a temporary interruption of operations; identification and valuation of off-specification products; treatment of items in transit; and the times to be allowed for objections to count and valuation. If the acquisition contract is silent or too brief, it is best for the financial representatives of the seller and buyer to prepare in advance a memorandum outlining mutually agreed procedures.

3. Breaches of Representations, Warranties and Covenants

Claims for breaches of representations, warranties and covenants usually consist of relatively minor items such as uncollected receivables modestly exceeding an amount warranted. However, the claims may consist of more serious items such as undisclosed liabilities that were known to some seller personnel but not communicated to its accountants. On relatively rare occasions, the claims may be for major items, such as an undisclosed imminent loss of a major customer or manipulation of earnings to make the seller's business appear more successful than its actual operating results.

Most acquisition contracts impose a time limit on the right to make claims for breaches of representations, warranties and covenants. Financial and legal personnel should identify and document all potential claims well before the deadline so that they can be evaluated by management, including the officers who participated in negotiating the acquisition contract.

Most claims for breaches of representations, warranties and covenants are to recover losses or potential losses and related costs and expenses. However, a buyer can seek the equitable remedy of rescission to set aside the acquisition contract and reverse the sale, if the breaches are important and the damages are irreparable by money. Rescission is a drastic remedy and courts will not order it lightly. However, if the business is disintegrating, the buyer should seek rescission, but should be prepared to rebut countercharges by the seller that the deterioration is exaggerated, resulted from risks known to the buyer, or resulted from postacquisition events such as poor management by the buyer.

If an acquired business is deteriorating badly, a resale to some or all of the previous owners or to its management may be a prudent decision by a buyer. For example, some businesses are best operated by talented, "hands on," fast-moving entrepreneurs and do not fare well as part of a large, structured organization in which decisions are planned and made at a central corporate headquarters. A resale or management buyout can cut the buyer's losses, save employment, and provide a good opportunity for a new buyer to achieve a "turnaround."

F. A Checklist of Steps to Complete Acquisition Transactions

A checklist of postclosing steps that may be needed to complete the acquisition transactions is as follows:

1. File Forms 1099 with the Internal Revenue Service (IRS) for funds paid.
2. File a Foreign Investment in Real Property Tax Act (FIRPTA) affidavit with the IRS.
3. File a Current Report on Form 8-K with the Securities and Exchange Commission (SEC) if the buyer is publicly owned and the acquisition was material.
4. File Forms BE-12 and BE-13 with the U.S. Department of Commerce if the buyer is foreign owned, directly or indirectly.
5. Obtain Forms W-2 for new employees.
6. Complete recording of title transfer documents not recorded on the closing date and the issuance of title insurance policies.
7. Allocate the purchase price in assets purchase transactions among the assets purchased for accounting purposes as described in Chapter 9, and for tax purposes as described in Chapter 6, and record the assets at "stepped-up" values.
8. File federal and state tax forms to make elections such as a Section 338(h)(10) election or to report required information by Section 1.368-3 of the IRS Income Tax Regulations.
9. Arrange to continue, discontinue or modify the seller's casualty, liability, workers compensation, fidelity and other insurance policies so as to preserve coverage.
10. Change the seller's bank accounts, if appropriate, and the persons authorized to draw upon the accounts.
11. Send notices to customers and other interested persons of any change of the corporate name and of lockboxes or other places where payments of invoices should be sent.
12. Communicate to new employees the changes, if any, in their employee benefit programs, including life, health and disability insurance and their retirement benefits, including any defined benefit pensions and any defined contribution benefits under 401(K) or similar plans.
13. If the seller or any of its affiliates will beneficially own 5 percent or more of the buyer's equity securities, verity that they have filed a Schedule 13-D with the SEC.
14. If any owners, directors or officers of the seller will become directors, officers or 10 percent beneficial shareholders of the buyer, alert them to file Forms 3 and 4 with the SEC.

G. Reference Materials

"Does Your Deal Pass Muster with the Pension Watchdog?" Hassel and Gigot, *Merger & Acquisitions*, May–Jun 1997

"Extricating a Division from Its Parent," Doran et al., *Merger & Acquisitions*, Jul–Aug 1997

"Getting the Biggest Marketing Bang from the Merger," Clemente and Greenspan, *Merger & Acquisitions*, Jul–Aug 1996

"Revisiting the Merger Syndrome: Crisis Management" Marks and Mirvis, *Merger & Acquisitions*, Jul–Aug 1997

"Seizing the Moment to Capture Value in a Strategic Deal," Smith and Quella, *Merger & Acquisitions*, Jan–Feb 1995

Chapter 19

Some Aspects of International Acquisitions

A. Introduction

The international M&A market is very active and growing. For 1996, *Mergers & Acquisitions* reported 970 overseas acquisitions by U.S. companies with a total value of $60.4 billion. These totals represent a major increase from 183 overseas acquisitions by U.S. companies with a total value of $7.1 billion in 1987. For 1996, *Mergers & Acquisitions* reported that U.S. buyers made numerous and sizable acquisitions in the United Kingdom, Canada, France, Germany, Australia, Argentina and Brazil.

For 1996, *Mergers & Acquisitions* reported 628 foreign acquisitions of U.S. companies by foreign companies with a total value of $69.9 billion. These totals represent a significant increase from 373 acquisitions of U.S. companies by foreign companies with a total value of $59.1 billion in 1987. For 1996, *Mergers and Acquisitions* reported that the most active foreign acquirers in the United States were companies from the United Kingdom, Canada, Germany, France, the Netherlands, Japan and Switzerland.

There are several reasons for international acquisitions. Companies that have established export markets for their products realize that they must eventually manufacture the products in the export market nations, either by "grass roots" expansion or by acquisition, or they will lose those markets to local competitors and to other factors such as transportation costs and changes in currency values. Companies that have products with well-known trademarks and wide public acceptance realize that they must commence manufacture in other nations or risk the growth of competitive, "me too," products sold at lower prices and perhaps also under confusingly similar trademarks. An important incentive for acquisitions by U.S. companies in other nations has been the rapid growth of unpredictable and rapidly changing environmental regulation in the United States, leading to investment in (1) developed countries where environmental standards are also strict, but clear, and (2) developing countries where environmental regulations are lenient. U.S. companies also frequently acquire interests in ventures in other nations as part of development projects for which they provide product and process technology.

An important incentive for "grassroots" expansion or acquisitions by foreign companies in the United States is that the United States is remarkably open to foreign investment and provides a very large market where goods and service move freely from state to state. Another incentive for investment in the United States is the recurrence of unstable conditions in some other nations that causes capital to flee from time to time.

This chapter discusses some aspects of acquisitions by U.S. companies in foreign nations and acquisitions in the United States by foreign companies.

B. Acquisitions by U.S. Companies in Foreign Nations

1. Due Diligence Reviews

The due diligence review for an acquisition in a foreign nation is more difficult than the review for a domestic acquisition. It is also very important.

To be effective, the reviewers must accommodate differences in language; laws and regulations; financial and accounting methods; and business, political and social customs. They must also skillfully manage travel schedules and available time. However, participants to international transactions usually make extra efforts to be cooperative and helpful, so the challenges can be met.

Due diligence reviews are discussed generally in Chapter 5. The author recommends that the review for an acquisition in a foreign nation focus especially on the following matters:

- Any laws that may prohibit or limit the right of a U.S. company (or any foreign company) to acquire the business.
- The extent of dependency of the business on relationships between the present owners and major customers, suppliers and other persons essential to the business.
- The accounting system used for the business (such as international generally accepted accounting principles), the differences from U.S. generally accepted accounting principles, and the effort and cost of making the systems compatible.
- Subsidies and tax incentives offered by the national or local government authorities.
- Withholding taxes on distributions of profits to U.S. investors and available tax treaty benefits.
- Legal restrictions on foreign-owned businesses and the persons who manage them including the right to repatriate earnings by payments of dividends, royalties and service fees.
- Political risks such as war, revolution, civil strife and expropriation.
- Currency risks such as inconvertibility of currency, refusal to transfer converted currency and devaluation.
- Adequacy of legal protection for property and contract rights. For example, do the courts effectively enforce patent, trade secret and other intellectual property rights?
- Existence of practices that are inconsistent with ownership by a corporation subject to U.S. law, such as payments to foreign government officials to obtain or maintain business or cooperation with international boycotts. **Note:** See the discussion of those subjects later in this chapter.

- Laws making termination of distributors, agents and employees difficult and costly.

2. Organizing Business Entities in Foreign Nations

When making an acquisition in another nation, it is often advantageous to organize a local business entity to make the acquisition. The most important advantage is usually limited liability.

Like the United States, foreign nations offer a choice of business entities. Some entities have characteristics like corporations and others like partnerships, limited partnerships or limited liability companies. The characteristics have some similarities but are not identical to the characteristics of business entities in the United States.

Examples of foreign business entities include the Societe Anonyme (SA) and the Société a Responsabilitée Limitée (SARL) in France; the Aktiengesellschaft (AG) and the Gesellschaft mit beschränkter Haftung (GmbH) in Germany; and the Sociedad Anonima (SA) and the Sociedad de Responsabilidad Limitada (SRL) in Spain.

The management structure and the authority of managers of foreign business entities also follow concepts different from those in the United States. Persons having authority to sign for a business entity typically must be named in the commercial register. For example, in addition to the Vorstand who manage an AG in Germany, one or more Prokurist may be named in the commercial register as having authority to sign. It is common to require two signatures.

Unlike the United States, where corporations and other business entities can be organized overnight, the organization of business entities in most foreign nations is a tedious and time-consuming task. Part or all of the documentation must be handled by a notary, who is a politically powerful and ceremonious official. The notary may take weeks and even months for the copying and registration of documents. It is wise to allow plenty of time to work with local counsel when organizing a business entity in foreign nations.

3. Political and Currency Risks

Acquisitions in foreign nations, especially in developing nations, present political risks as well as business risks. The risks include war, revolution, civil strife and expropriation, as well as inconvertibility, nontransferability or devaluation of currency. They also include regulatory restrictions that may be confiscatory, such as restrictions on repatriation of earnings by dividend and royalty payments and payments for services.

A company making an acquisition in a foreign nation may be able to purchase political and currency risk insurance for its lenders and perhaps also for itself. In the United States, political and currency risk insurance (excluding devaluation) is offered by the U.S. Overseas Private Investment Corporation (OPIC). During the past decade, political and currency risk insurance has also been offered by the Multilateral Investment Guarantee Agency (MIGA) of the World Bank. Some host nations also offer political and currency risk insurance. Political and currency risk insurance is also available in the private markets, including the underwriters at Lloyds and other London insurers. Protection from political and currency risk is also provided as part of the loan guaranty programs of organizations such as the International Bank for Reconstruction and Development, known as "IBRD" or as the "World Bank," and the International Development Association, known as the "IDA."

Foreign currency translation gains and losses are reported in financial statements prepared in accordance with generally accepted accounting principles as prescribed in Statement No. 52 of the Financial Accounting Standards Board as a separate component of stockholders' equity rather than by inclusion in net income.

Before making an acquisition in a foreign nation, the planners should determine whether a bilateral investment treaty exists between the United States and the nation where the acquisition will be made. If so, the treaty may contain provisions that alleviate some concerns about political risk. For example, the treaty may provide for "most favored nation" treatment or at least treatment as favorable as nationals of the host nation receive. When applied to expropriation, treatment on the same basis as nationals is called the "Calvo Doctrine."

In the author's experience, the greatest political risk is that of "creeping expropriation." In some nations, the government discriminates against foreign companies in ways that can eventually confiscate their investment. For example, foreign companies may be required to pay excessive prices for raw materials, components and services. They may be required to hire large numbers of unnecessary employees and to promote them to positions for which they lack qualifications. Thus, the business may be condemned to years of unprofitable operation that renders the investment worthless. For example, India maintained policies for years that deprived foreign companies of any meaningful role in managing and repatriating earnings from subsidiaries and joint venture entities. The results were foreign investment losses, reluctance to invest in India, and the tragedy at Bhopal, where Indian government policies required that Union Carbide Corporation turn over plant management to local employees some years before the fatal emission of methyl isocyanate. In recent years, India has adopted policies that reportedly allow more realistic treatment of foreign investment.

4. U.S. Export Controls and Licensing

Companies considering an acquisition in another nation should be familiar with the federal laws and regulations that control the export of goods and technology or software from the United States. This section briefly summarizes the controls, because integration of domestic and foreign operations may depend on qualification for necessary export licenses.

The Bureau of Export Administration (BEA) of the U.S. Department of Commerce maintains Export Administration Regulations.[1] The regulations were originally adopted to implement the Export Administration Act of

[1]15 C.F.R. Parts 730 to 774.

[2]50 U.S.C. §1701; Executive Order 12924 dated Aug. 19, 1994 (59 Fed. Reg. 43437); Notice of President dated Aug. 17, 1995 (60 Fed. Reg. 42767); and Executive Order 12981 dated Dec. 5, 1995 (60 Fed. Reg. 62981); and former 50 U.S.C. App. §§2401 *et seq.* See also The Trading with the Enemy Act, 50 U.S.C. App. §1 *et seq.* and 12 U.S.C. §95a.

1979, which expired on August 20, 1994. However, the regulations have continued in effect under executive orders of the President issued under his statutory authority to deal with an unusual and extraordinary threat with respect to a declared national emergency.[2]

The BXA's regulations apply to goods and technology or software originating in the U.S. and certain other goods and technology or software. For example, they control the initial export transaction and also any reexport from one foreign nation to another nation. They also control foreign made direct products of U.S. origin technology or software. The regulations apply regardless of the nationality of the exporter. The regulations also apply to any informal export of technology by such means as a demonstration or an oral briefing of a foreign national during a visit to the United States.

The BXA's regulations are imposed to protect national security, implement foreign policy and conserve short supplies. Thus, goods and technology or software may be exported and reexported unless a license is required by the regulations.

The regulations provide three primary tools for use in determining whether a license is required: (1) a list of ten general prohibitions in Part 736, (2) a Commodity Control List (CCL) in Part 774, Supplement No. 1, and (3) a Country Chart in Part 738, Supplement No. 1. The regulations prescribe steps for determining whether a license is required. First, an exporter should determine whether the goods, technology or software are subject to the regulations. Second, the exporter should determine whether its item or activity requires a license under one or more of the ten general prohibitions. If general prohibitions one, two or three are applicable, the exporter should review the CCL to determine whether and how its item may be classified. The exporter then uses the Country Chart to determine whether a license is required based on the classification. However, for certain prohibitions, a license may be required for some exports not covered by the Country Chart. For example, a license is generally required for exports to embargoed nations such as Cuba, Iran, Iraq, Libya and North Korea. License requirements beyond those shown in the Country Chart apply for Angola, Bosnia-Herzegovina, Croatia, Rwanda, Serbia and Montenegro.

If an initial determination is made that a license is required, the exporter should review the Part 740 license exceptions that are available for some prohibitions. The exporter must also take additional steps such as determining whether its transferee, ultimate end-user, any intermediate consignee, or any other party to a transaction is a person denied export privileges and whether any end use or end user is prohibited.

While the BXA's regulatory procedures are very detailed, a relatively small percentage of exports and reexports subject to the regulations require a license. Many items are not on the CCL or, if on the CCL, require a license to export to only a limited number of countries. Other transactions may be covered by the license exceptions. Thus, most exports can be made without a license except to embargoed nations. Special licenses may also be available.

If a license is required, an application is submitted to the BXA on Multipurpose Application Form BXA-748 P with supporting documents that may include an Import and End-User Certificate and Statement by Ultimate Consignee and Purchaser (BXA-711).[3] Delivery verification may be

[3]15 C.F.R. Part 748.

required for some transactions. Shippers' export declarations are also required.[4] Special licenses may be available for certain exports.[5]

If an item subject to the regulations is available in fact in a controlled or noncontrolled country from a non-U.S. source in sufficient quantity to render the regulations ineffective, the BXA may license an export transaction otherwise prohibited.[6]

Other federal government departments and agencies also control export transactions involving their areas of regulatory authority. They include the Department of State, Drug Enforcement Administration, Food and Drug Administration, Department of the Interior, Department of theTreasury, Department of Energy, Nuclear Regulatory Commission, Federal Maritime Commission, Patent and Trademark Office, Department of Transportation and Maritime Administration.[7]

Based on the author's experience, exporters seeking a license should provide a helpful response to the application questions calling for a description of the goods or the technology and its end use or users. Most important, technology should be distinguished from any near-related sensitive information. The application should also demonstrate that the technology does not have a dual use, one of which is inimical to U.S. interests.

For example, the export of technology for manufacture of commercial grades of fiberglass should present no licensing problems. However, the BXA and other federal government agencies may wish to be sure the manufacturing technology or equipment does not include manufacture of special grades which can be used for strategic applications. An applicant can save time by anticipating such concerns and demonstrating to the BXA and other interested agencies that strategic technology is not involved.

5. Restrictive Trade Practices and Boycotts

The Bureau of Export Administration (BEA) administers the antiboycott provisions of the Export Administration Act.[8] The BXA has adopted regulations prohibiting certain restrictive trade practices or boycotts and imposing reporting requirements.[9]

The Act and the BXA's regulations were adopted in reaction to the boycott imposed by many Arab nations against Israel. The boycott imposed by these nations is not only a primary boycott, but seeks to impose a secondary boycott by requiring firms in nations such as the U.S. to refuse to do business with Israel, nationals or residents of Israel, or persons engaged in activities that support Israel, by compliance with the so-called Arab "black list" and other conditions.

United States persons are responsible for transactions by foreign subsidiaries, affiliates and other permanent foreign establishments that they control in fact. *Control in fact* means authority or ability of a domestic con-

---

[4]15 C.F.R. Part 758.

[5]15 C.F.R. Part 752.

[6]15 C.F.R. Part 768.

[7]15 C.F.R. Part 730, Supp. 3.

[8]50 U.S.C. App. §2401 *et seq.*; 50 U.S.C. §1701 *et seq.*

[9]15 C.F.R. Part 760.

cern to establish general policies or to control day-to-day operations. The regulations presume control in fact, subject to rebuttal, if a domestic concern has specified percentages of voting stock, a majority of the governing board, or certain contractual powers of exclusive management or to appoint the chief operating officer or a majority of the governing board.

The BXA's regulations prohibit U.S. persons from refusing to do business with or in a boycotted country or with business concerns, nationals or residents of a boycotted country. U.S. persons are also prohibited from agreeing to such a refusal and from requiring or agreeing to require other persons to refuse. An agreement to comply generally with the laws of a boycotting country is not itself a refusal. However, a refusal can be shown by a course or pattern of conduct.

The BXA regulations also prohibit discrimination against any individual who is a U.S. person on the basis of race, religion, sex or national origin. The regulations also prohibit discrimination against any corporation or other organization which is a U.S. person on the basis of the race. This provision was included because some boycott officials in Arab nations sought to require foreign companies to refuse to do business in their own nations with companies whose directors and officers were active in supporting Israel.

The BXA's regulations also prohibit U.S. persons from cooperating with secondary boycott pressures such as requirements to furnish information about the race, religion, sex or national origin of any U.S. person or about business relations with boycotted countries or blacklisted persons or with charitable and fraternal organizations that support a boycotted country. For example, U.S. persons may not furnish information about persons who contribute to the United Jewish Appeal.

The BXA's regulations also contain prohibitions against implementing letters of credit containing prohibited conditions or requirements. No U.S. person may pay, honor, confirm or otherwise implement a letter of credit which contains a condition or requirement compliance with which is prohibited, nor shall any U.S. person, as a result of the application of the BXA's regulations be obligated to pay, honor or otherwise implement such a letter of credit. Compliance with the BXA's regulations is an absolute defense in any action brought to compel payment of, honoring of, or other implementation of a letter of credit, or for damages resulting from failure to do so. However, a U.S. person is not prohibited from advising a beneficiary of the existence of a letter of credit in its favor or from taking ministerial actions to dispose of a letter of credit which it is prohibited from implementing.

The BXA's regulations contain exceptions which allow U.S. persons to comply with primary boycott requirements. For example, a U.S. person supplying goods or services to a boycotting country or a national or resident of a boycotting country may comply with its requirements which prohibit the import of goods or services from the boycotted country. A U.S. person shipping goods to a boycotting country may comply with requirements prohibiting shipment of goods on a carrier of the boycotted country or by a route other than that prescribed by the boycotting country or the recipient of the shipment. A U.S. individual may comply with the immigration, passport, visa or employment requirements of a boycotting country, but only by furnishing information about himself or herself and members of his or her own family and not about others. A U.S. person may proceed with a project in a boycotting country even if some of its employees are denied entry, but may not preselect employees to comply with a boycott. The exceptions do not justify any across-the-board refusal to do business with a boycotted country or a national or resident of a boycotted country. The exceptions also do not authorize a U.S. person to furnish prohibited information or excuse compliance with the import and shipping document requirements.

The BXA's regulations require that a U.S. person who receives a request to take any action which has the effect of furthering or supporting a restrictive trade practice or boycott must report the request to the Department of Commerce. The reports must be submitted in duplicate to the Report Processing Staff, Office of Antiboycott Compliance, U.S. Department of Commerce, Room 6099C, Washington, D.C. 20230. The reports can be made on a single transaction form, 621P, or a multiple transaction form, BXA-6051P. The reporting requirements contain several exceptions for requests to comply with requirements allowed by the regulations.

Section 999 of the Internal Revenue Code requires any person to file an international boycott report on Form 5713 with the Internal Revenue Service (IRS) if the person, or a member of a controlled group that includes that person, has operations, in or related to, (A) a country on the list of boycotting countries maintained by the IRS, or (B) any other country known to require participation in or cooperation with an international boycott as a condition of doing business with such country or its nationals or residents. The report must describe any such participation or cooperation at any time during the taxable year and any requests for such participation or cooperation. However, U.S.–approved boycotts need not be reported.

In addition, the Internal Revenue Code may deny taxpayers who participate in or cooperate with an international boycott a portion of several tax benefits:

- The foreign tax credit (section 908(a));
- Deferral of taxation of earnings of a controlled foreign corporation (section 952(a)(3));
- Deferral of taxation of DISC income (section 995(b)(1)(F)(ii));
- Exemption of foreign trade income of a foreign sales corporation (FSC) (Section 927(e)(2)).

6. Federal Taxation

Taxation under the Internal Revenue Code (the "Code") of companies acquired overseas is an extensive and complex subject that is beyond detailed discussion in this chapter. However, before making an acquisition, the buyer's tax planners should consider, at minimum, the application of several provisions of the Code:

- *Consolidated Returns.* A foreign corporation generally cannot be included in the consolidated return of a U.S. corporation. Code §1504(b).
- *Information Returns.* U.S. shareholders and U.S. citizens who are directors or officers of certain foreign corporations, including controlled foreign corporations, must file Form 5471, Information Re-

turn of U.S. Persons with Respect to Certain Foreign Corporations, with their federal income tax returns. Code §§898 and 6038. Special rules apply for failure to comply with this information reporting requirement.

- *U.S. Trade or Business.* In general, foreign corporations are not subject to federal income taxation in the U.S. However, if a foreign corporation is engaged in a trade or business in the U.S., it is subject to federal income taxation on income (including foreign source income) effectively connected with the conduct of such trade or business. Code §882. It is also subject to a branch profits tax. Code §884.
- *Income from Sources within the U.S.* A foreign corporation that is not engaged in a U.S. trade or business is subject to federal income taxation on certain pasive income items (other than portfolio interest) treated as income from sources within the U.S. The tax rate is 30 percent unless reduced by treaty. Code §881. See also Code §§861 and 862. Certain items of income (and deductions) may be allocated or apportioned to sources within or without the U.S. Code §863.
- *Controlled Foreign Corporations.* In general, U.S. shareholders are not subject to federal income taxation upon the income of foreign corporations until the income is repatriated as dividend income. However, U.S. shareholders of a controlled foreign corporation are subject to federal income taxation on its Subpart F income. In general, a U.S. shareholder is a U.S. person who owns, directly or by attribution, 10 percent or more of the voting stock of a foreign corporation. In general, a foreign corporation is a controlled foreign corporation if more than 50 percent of the voting power and value of its stock is owned by U.S. shareholders. Stated briefly, Subpart F income includes certain captive insurer and other insurance income; certain tax haven and other foreign base company income; certain international boycott income; and certain payments illegal under the Foreign Corrupt Practices Act. Foreign base company income includes, among other things, foreign personal holding company income. Code §§951-964.
- *Foreign Tax Credits.* Foreign corporations are allowed certain credits against federal income taxation for taxes paid or accrued to a foreign country or U.S. possession on income effectively connected with its U.S. trade or business. Code §906(a). U.S citizens, residents, certain nonresidents and domestic corporations are also allowed a credit against federal income tax for taxes of a foreign country or U.S. possession, including certain taxes paid by controlled foreign corporations. Code §§78, 901, 902, 960 and 962.
- *Transfer Pricing.* Whenever two or more organizations, trades or businesses are owned or controlled directly or indirectly by the same interests, the Internal Revenue Service ("IRS") may distribute, apportion or allocate gross income, deductions, credits or allowances between or among them in order to clearly reflect their income. Code §482. The IRS has adopted under §482 extensive intercompany transfer pricing regulations in order to prevent, among other things, shifting of income through such devices as bargain

pricing or overpricing of products in intercompany transactions. Income Tax Regulation §1.482-1 *et seq.* In addition, if property is imported into the U.S. in a transaction between related persons, the amount of any costs taken into account in computing its basis or inventory cost by the purchaser and also in computing its customs value shall not be greater than the costs taken into account in computing the customs value. See Code §1059A.

- *Sales or Liquidations of Controlled Foreign Corporations.* If U.S. stockholders (who own 10 percent or more of the voting stock) of a foreign corporation sell or liquidate the corporation, gain on the sale or liquidation is treated as ordinary income to the extent that its earnings and profits were not previously taxed as actual dividends or as Subpart F income. Code §948.
- *Treaties.* The provisions of the Code are often modified or superseded by a treaty (tax convention) between the U.S. and another nation. Thus, the provisions of any applicable treaty must be reviewed as well as the Code and the regulations and court decisions thereunder.
- *Tax Free Reorganizations and Transfer of Property to Foreign Corporations.* See Chapter 7 for a discussion of Section 367 of the Code which governs tax free reorganizations involving foreign corporations and transfers of property to foreign corporations.

7. The Foreign Corrupt Practices Act

Any domestic company planning an overseas acquisition must plan for compliance with the accounting and antibribery provisions of the Foreign Corrupt Practices Act ("FCPA").[10]

Companies which have issued securities registered under the Securities Exchange Act of 1934 (the "1934 Act") will already be familiar with the accounting provisions of the FCPA. These provisions require that the issuers keep books, records and accounts in reasonable detail that accurately and fairly represent its transactions and dispositions of its assets. The provisions also require that the issuers maintain a system of internal accounting controls reasonably assuring that (1) transactions occur in accordance with the authorization of management, (2) transactions are recorded as necessary to permit preparation of financial statements in accordance with generally accepted accounting principles, and (3) recorded assets are compared with existing assets at reasonable intervals and appropriate action is taken with respect to any differences.

Upon closing of an acquisition, the accounting provisions of the FCPA apply to the acquired company, even though it is incorporated under the laws of a foreign nation. However, if the issuer holds 50 percent or less of the voting power of a foreign company, its obligation is only to make a good faith effort to cause the foreign company to maintain a system of internal accounting controls in compliance with the FCPA. Since the extent of effort required to show good faith is uncertain, the author recommends

---

[10] 15 U.S.C. §§§78a, 78m, 78dd-1 and 2. These provisions are part of the Securities Exchange Act of 1934.

that, when possible, issuers make compliance with the accounting provisions of the FCPA a contractual requirement in joint venture agreements.

The antibribery provisions of the FCPA apply to any issuer with securities registered under the 1934 Act and also to any "domestic concern." A "domestic concern" includes any U.S. citizen and any corporation, partnership or association incorporated in the United States. Thus, individual U.S. citizens are required to comply with the antibribery provisions.

The FCPA prohibits issuers and domestic concerns from using the mails or any instrumentality of interstate commerce corruptly in furtherance of an offer, payment, promise to pay or authorization of payment of any money or anything of value to a foreign official, foreign political party or candidate for foreign political office for the purpose of influencing any act or decision in his, her or its official capacity, or inducing such foreign official, political party or candidate to do or omit any act in violation of his, her or its lawful duty, in order to assist such issuer or domestic concern in obtaining or retaining business. The FCPA also prohibits such use corruptly in furtherance of an offer, payment, promise to pay, or authorization of payment to any other person while *knowing* that all or a portion of the money or thing of value will be offered, given or promised, directly or indirectly, to a foreign official, political party or candidate for political office for the purposes described.[11]

The FCPA contains an exception for payments intended to facilitate or expedite routine government activities. This exception allows, for example, payment of "tips" to government dock workers to unload cargo promptly. Cargo unloading is a nondiscretionary task that the workers must perform in any event and the tips only assure that they do so with reasonable care and speed. The FCPA also contains affirmative defenses that a payment was lawful under written laws and regulations of the foreign country or is a reasonable and bona fide expenditure, such as travel expenses, directly related to the promotion, demonstration, or explanation of products or services or the execution or performance of a foreign government contract. For example, these affirmative defenses would allow a company to take a foreign governmental official for a demonstration flight in a new aircraft offered for sale to a foreign nation.

Liability under the FCPA requires proof of a corrupt purpose. If payments are made by a foreign subsidiary or agent, proof is required that the issuer or domestic concern "authorized" the payment, but knowing acquiescence might be equated to authorization. If the payment is made to a third party, proof is required that the issuer or domestic concern knew that the third party would corruptly give the payment to a foreign official, political party or candidate for public office, but conscious disregard or deliberate ignorance may be equated to knowledge.

In some foreign nations, especially developing countries, it is difficult to determine who may be a government official, political party or candidate for office because their governmental systems differ from our own. In some nations, members of a relatively small educated community serve both in the government and in industry from time to time.[12] Connections

[11]15 U.S.C. §78dd-1(a)

[12]In 1988, the FCPA was amended to delete the words "having reason to know" because those words imposed duties beyond practical ability to comply.

may be familial, religious or military. Decision makers may have no visible connection to a transaction. Considerable care is needed to comply with the FCPA in these nations.

No trade or business expense deduction is allowed by the Internal Revenue Code for payments that are unlawful under the FCPA.[13] Payments unlawful under the FCPA are also included in Subpart F income of controlled foreign corporations that is taxable to their U.S. shareholders.[14]

The United States is no longer alone in prohibiting payments that may be bribes to foreign government officials. For example, the Organization for Economic Cooperation and Development (OECD) announced in November 1997 that 29 nation members had agreed to a treaty outlawing bribes to foreign government officials, although the definitions in the treaty are reported to be narrower than those in the FCPA and the enforcement remedies will depend importantly on decisions to be made upon implementation by the member nations.

8. Antitrust Laws

For many years, antitrust laws outside the United States were not perceived as significant barriers to mergers and acquisitions. However, foreign antitrust officials have recently been taking stronger positions.

For example, the European Commission reviews acquisitions under powers granted by Articles 85 through 88 of the Treaty of Rome. The Commission has adopted a merger regulation on the control of concentrations between undertakings, Regulation 4064/89, OJ 1990 L 257/13, amended by Regulation 1310/97, OJ 1997 L 180/1, corrected at OJ 1997 L199/69.

Mergers are reviewed by the Commission if global turnover of the merging companies (undertakings) exceeds 2,500 million European Currency Units (ECU), currently about U.S.$2,725 million; the aggregate turnover of each of at least two of the merging companies throughout the European Community (EC) exceeds 100 million ECU, currently about U.S.$109 million; the aggregate turnover of all the merging companies in each at least three member nations exceeds $100 million ECU, currently about U.S.$109 million; and the aggregate turnover of at least two of the merging companies in each of at least three member nations exceeds 25 million ECU, currently about U.S.$27 million, unless all of the merging companies derive over two-thirds of their EC turnover in one and the same EC member nation. See Regulation 1310/97, OJ 1997 L180/1 as corrected at OJ 1997 L199/69. If these criteria are not met, applications for clearance must be made to the antitrust authorities of the member nations.

Like analysis under the U.S. Clayton Act, the Commission begins its evaluation by determining the relevant market and the market shares of the undertakings. However, the Commission must find that a merger creates or strengthens a "dominant" position in the relevant market. Thus, the Commission looks for combined market shares of 40 percent or more, a

[13]Code §162(c).

[14]Code §952(a)(4).

level much higher than the triggers associated with the Herfindahl-Hirschman Index used by the U.S. Department of Justice and the Federal Trade Commission.

Acting under the Merger Rule, the Commission approved the acquisition of McDonnell Douglas Corporation (MDC) by the Boeing Company only after Boeing agreed to several conditions. For example, Boeing agreed not to make any further exclusive supplier contracts with customers such as American Airlines, Continental Airlines and Delta Airlines.

Recently, a proposed merger of Ernst & Young and KPMG Peat Marwick was withdrawn because, among other reasons, of objections by the European Commission and antitrust regulators in other world areas. The merger would have created the world's largest accounting firm which would have had over 40 percent of the market in the European Community.

Another proposed merger between the accounting firms of Coopers & Lybrand and Price Waterhouse is awaiting approval by the Commission. These firms are also very large and reportedly have important shares of the market for auditing services in the European Community and other nations. However, their combined market shares of the market in the European Community are much less than those of Ernst & Young and KPMG Peat Marwick. Thus, the firms are optimistic that the Commission will approve their merger.

Readers considering foreign acquisitions should also be familiar with the Antitrust Guidelines for International Operations issued by the U.S. Department of Justice. If a foreign acquisition may have a significant adverse effect on competition in the U.S., the Department of Justice may challenge the acquisition under the Clayton Act.

9. Reporting of U.S. Direct Investment Abroad

The Bureau of Economic Analysis (BEA) of the U.S. Department of Commerce maintains statistics on investments by U.S. persons in foreign corporations or businesses. A benchmark survey is conducted every 5 years. The BEA's last benchmark survey was conducted for 1994 and required the filing of a Form BE-10 by any person that had direct or indirect ownership or control of at least 10 percent of the voting stock of an incorporated foreign business enterprise (or an equivalent interest in an unincorporated foreign business enterprise) at the end of 1994, unless an exemption applied. See 15 C.F.R. Part 806.

Thereafter, annual reports on Form BE-133 or BE-11 must be filed by persons for each foreign affiliate exceeding an exemption level of $10,000,000 and on Form B-11 for larger foreign affiliates, unless an exemption applies. Quarterly reports on Form BE-577 are required for each affiliate exceeding an exemption level of $20,000,000. The exemption levels are exceeded if any one of total assets, net sales or gross operating revenues less sales taxes, or net income after income taxes exceeds the specified amount.

The BEA's regulations also requires other reports including a Form BE-507 Industry Classification Questionnaire. Surveys of service providers are governed by 15 C.F.R. Part 801.

C. Acquisitions in the United States by Foreign Companies

1. Few Restrictions on Investment in the United States

The United States has traditionally welcomed foreign investment, except in a few industries that involve national defense or other vital national interests. Profits can freely be repatriated to foreign nations as dividends or as royalty or compensation payments. Conversion of U.S. dollars into foreign currency is not restricted. Except for the industries discussed in the next paragraph, foreign companies and individual investors can acquire businesses in the United States and can operate them under laws and regulations that do not distinguish between them and domestic companies and investors, although domestic companies may be able to comply more easily with the laws and regulations than foreign companies.

Examples of restrictions on foreign ownership or participation by foreign persons in the management or operations of certain industries are as follows:

Air Transportation. The U.S. maintains sovereignty over its air space. Navigation of U.S. air space by foreign civil aircraft is allowed, but only with the authorization of the Federal Aviation Administration (FAA) or the U.S. Department of Transportation. The basic statutory provisions for general, temporary, charter and all cargo certificates of convenience and necessity prescribe that they be issued to citizens of the United States. Thus, foreign air carriers must apply for permits under separate provisions. Foreign air carriers and persons controlling them, may not acquire control of U.S. domestic carriers. Registration of aircraft is restricted to aircraft owned by U.S. citizens, aliens admitted for permanent residence in the U.S., or domestic corporations if the aircraft is based and primarily used in the U.S.[15]

Banking. A majority of the directors of a national bank must be U.S. citizens. Foreign banks are not eligible for membership in the Federal Reserve System.[16] However, under the International Banking Act and the Bank Holding Company Act, foreign banks and their subsidiaries, branches, agencies and representative offices are allowed many of the same rights and privileges of domestic banks including some benefits of membership in the Federal Reserve System. Deposit insurance can be obtained by subsidiaries of foreign banks.

Intercoastal Maritime Activities. Restrictions are imposed on foreign participation in coastal shipping; towing and salvage operations; fishing; dredging; and vessel documentation and operations.[17]

Government Subsidies and Loans. The Maritime Administration administers programs providing cost-differential subsidies to U.S. citizens (including shipyards) for the construction and operation of vessels used in

[15]49 U.S.C. §§40103, 41102, 41103, 41108, 41302, 41703 and 44102. A corporation is a citizen of the United States if it is organized under the laws of the U.S. in one of its states, territories, or possessions; two-thirds of its board and other managing officers are U.S. citizens; and 75 percent of the voting interest is owned or controlled by U.S. citizens.

[16]12 U.S.C. §§72 and 321.

[17]46 U.S.C. §§292, 251, 292, 316, 802, 835, 885, 12102 and 12110.

foreign commerce.[18] Loans by the Secretary of the Interior to purchase, construct, equip, maintain, repair or operate new or used commercial fishing vessels or gear may be made only to a U.S. citizen or national.[19] The Department of Transportation is authorized to have vessels constructed for essential trade routes that cannot be successfully maintained under private operation by U.S. citizens using U.S. registered vessels and to charter them to American-flag operators for use on such routes.[20] With various exceptions, government officers and employees are required to travel on U.S. flag vessels and exports of cargoes procured, furnished or financed by the U.S. government are required to be shipped on U.S. flag vessels.[21]

Radio, Television and Comsat. A radio or television communication license may not be granted to or held by (1) a foreign government; (2) any alien; (3) any corporation organized under the laws of a foreign government; (4) any corporation of which more than one-fifth of the capital stock is owned of record or voted by aliens, a foreign government or foreign corporation; or (5) any corporation directly or indirectly controlled by another corporation of which more than one-fourth of the capital stock is owned of record or voted by aliens, a foreign government or foreign corporation if the Federal Communications Commission finds that refusal or revocation of such a license will serve the public interest. Restrictions also apply to persons who are representatives of a foreign government or alien.[22] Alien ownership of the Communications Satellite Corporation is limited to 20 percent of the voting stock held by holders other than authorized carriers.[23]

Nuclear and Other Energy Programs. Atomic energy licenses may be granted by the Nuclear Regulatory Commission only to persons for activities under and within U.S. jurisdiction and may not be granted to any corporation or entity owned, controlled or dominated by an alien, foreign corporation or foreign government.[24] The Department of the Interior may grant geothermal energy licenses only to U.S. citizens, associations of U.S. citizens, domestic corporations and domestic governmental units including municipalities.[25] The geothermal energy reservoir insurance program is also limited to persons (including corporations and other entities) which are U.S. citizens.[26]

Government Leasing of Natural Resources. Federal government leases and other dispositions of coal, phosphate, sodium, potassium, oil, oil shale, gilsonite, gas, and lands containing such deposits are restricted to U.S. citizens, associations of U.S. citizens, and domestic corporations. Citizens of another country whose laws, customs or regulations deny similar privileges to U.S. citizens or corporations may not by stock ownership, holding or control own any interest in such a lease.[27]

[18]46 U.S.C. §§1151 and 1171.

[19]16 U.S.C. §742c.

[20]46 U.S.C., App. §1204.[21]46 U.S.C., App. §1241.

[22]47 U.S.C. §310.

[23]47 U.S.C. §734.

[24]42 U.S.C. §§2131 to 2134.

[25]30 U.S.C. §1015.

[26]30 U.S.C. §1522.

[27]30 U.S.C. §§181 and 352. See also the regulations of the Interior Department's Bureaus of Land Management and Minerals Management in Titles 30 and 43 of the Code of Federal Regulations.

Government Contracting. There is no general prohibition or restriction on the right of foreign corporations to engage in government contracting. However, domestic miners, producers and manufacturers are granted preferences by the Buy American Act.[28] No entity controlled by a foreign government may merge with, acquire, or take over a company (1) performing a Department of Defense (DoD) or Department of Energy (DoE) contract under a national security program that cannot be performed satisfactorily unless it is given access to proscribed information, or (2) during the previous fiscal year was awarded (A) DoD prime contracts in excess of \$500,000,000, or (B) DoE prime contracts under national security programs in excess of \$500,000,000.[29] However, the foregoing provision does not apply if a merger, acquisition or takeover is not suspended by the President after specified review procedures.[30]

There is also no general prohibition against foreign and foreign-owned corporations engaging in defense contracting. However, no DoD contract under a national security program may be awarded to an entity controlled by a foreign government that has repeatedly supported acts of international terrorism or if that entity requires proscribed information to perform the contract.[31] Foreign and foreign-owned corporations that qualify to perform defense contracts and their personnel must also comply with the DoD's personnel Security Program Regulation and its Defense Industrial Personnel Security Clearance Program.[32]

State Laws. A few states impose restrictions on ownership of some kinds of land by foreign persons.

2. Exon-Florio Review of Acquisitions by Foreign Persons

The Office of International Investment of the U.S. Department of Treasury has regulations providing for a review of mergers, acquisitions and takeovers of U.S. firms by foreign persons[33] by a Committee on Foreign Investment in the United States (CFIUS). An acquisition includes an acquisition of control by means such as a proxy contest.

Under the regulations, notification to the CFIUS and cooperation with its review are voluntary. However, if no notice is given, the CFIUS can initiate an investigation. However, clearance by the CFIUS makes it unlikely that the President would seek to block or nullify the cleared acquisition.[34] Thus, many foreign companies have provided the notice.

---

[28] 10 U.S.C. §10a *et seq.*; 48 C.F.R., Ch. 2, Subparts 225.1 and 225.2.

[29] 50 U.S.C. App. §2170a. This sectionis part of the National Defense Authorization Act for Fiscal Year 1993 and not the Defense Production Act of 1950 that has expired except for certain provisions continued in effect by Presidential Executive Orders.

[30] 50 U.S.C. App. 2170.

[31] 10 U.S.C. §§2327(b) and 2536(a); 48 C.F.R., Ch. 2, §§225.702, 209.104-1(g)(ii) and §252.209-7002.

[32] 32 C.F.R. Ch. 1, Parts 154 and 155.

[33] 31 C.F.R. Part 800. The regulations were adopted pursuant to a provision of the Defense Production Act of 1950 that was kept alive by the "Exon-Florio" Amendment when the rest of the Act lapsed in 1990. See 50 U.S.C. App. 2170.

[34] For example, the President can seek to block acquisitions of defense contractors under 50 U.S.C. App. 2170a.

3. Corporate Structures for Foreign Acquisitions in the United States

Except for the few industries for which restrictions exist, a foreign corporation is entitled to acquire a business in the U.S. and to own and operate it directly. However, few foreign corporations wish to subject their non–U.S. assets to the uncertainties of litigation in the U.S. court system. Thus, foreign corporations typically organize or acquire subsidiaries which own and operate the businesses.

When a foreign corporation acquires a business using its own internal funds or funds raised by borrowing in its home nation, the foreign corporation may decide to acquire directly by the stock purchase method or organize a domestic corporation to acquire by the merger method or assets purchase method. In either event, the acquired business will be owned and operated by a domestic subsidiary of the foreign corporation.

If a foreign corporation plans to finance an acquisition or acquisitions in the United States using the proceeds of loans raised in the U.S., the foreign corporation is likely to organize a holding company in the U.S. to make the acquisitions. A domestic holding company provides an extra layer of insulation from the U.S. court system. Further, the holding company can file a consolidated federal tax return for a group including itself and the acquired domestic subsidiaries, provided that the holding company owns at least 80 percent of the total voting power and value of the stock of each subsidiary.[35] In the consolidated return, the holding company can deduct the interest on the debt it incurred to acquire its subsidiaries from the income of those subsidiaries.

4. Federal Taxation

A foreign corporation is subject to taxation based on taxable income effectively connected with its conduct of a trade or business in the U.S.[36] Its deductions, credits and rates are generally the same as those for domestic corporations. However, the deductions and credits must be allocated and apportioned.[37] In addition, a foreign corporation is subject to a branch profits tax equal to 30 percent of its "dividend equivalent income." This tax is another reason why foreign corporations usually organize a subsidiary to conduct business in the United States.

Foreign corporations receiving income from sources within the United States not effectively connected with the conduct of a trade or business within the U.S. are subject to a flat 30 percent tax,[38] unless reduced by treaty, on the following items:

1. Interest (other than OID), dividends, rents, salaries, wages, premiums, annuities, compensations, remunerations, emoluments, and other fixed or determinable annual or periodical gains, profits and income;

---

[35]Code §§ 1501 and 1504.

[36]Code § 882(a).

[37]Code § 882(b).

[38]Code § 881. The 30 percent tax is also a withholding tax. It is modified by tax treaties with some foreign nations. See Code § 894.

[39]Code §881(c).

2. Gains from certain timber, coal and iron interests;
3. Certain income from OID obligations; and
4. Certain gains from the sale or exchange of patents and other intellectual properties.

However, the 30 percent tax does not apply to "portfolio interest" received by a foreign corporation from sources within the United States which does not include contingent interest.[39]

Gain or loss of a foreign corporation from the disposition of a U.S. real property interest is treated as effectively connected with a trade or business in the U.S. under the Foreign Investment in Real Property Tax (FIRPTA)[40]

Income from sources within the U.S. includes the following items: (1) interest from the U.S. or from interest bearing obligations of noncorporate residents or domestic corporations except interest from resident alien individuals and domestic corporations earning at least 80 percent of their income from the active conduct of a foreign trade or business, including interest from deposits with the foreign branches of U.S. commercial banks; (2) dividends from domestic corporations and certain foreign corporations including foreign corporations whose income treated as effectively connected with the conduct of a trade or business in the U.S. is 25 percent or more of its income from all sources; (3) compensation from labor or personal services performed in the U.S. with certain exceptions; (4) rents and royalties from property located in the U.S.; (5) gains, profits and income from the disposition of U.S. real property; (6) gains, profits and income from the purchase of inventory property without the U.S. and its sale or exchange within the U.S.; (7) amounts received as underwriting income of any insurance or annuity contract; and (8) social security benefits.[41]

The Code also contains provisions defining income not effectively connected with the conduct of a trade or business in the U.S. In general, the definition excludes income of a foreign corporation from sources without the U.S. that is not attributable to its U.S. business. However, income will be treated as effectively connected income if it is attributable to an office or other fixed place of business in the U.S. and the income consists of (1) rents and royalties for the use of intangible property derived in the active conduct of its U.S. trade or business; (2) dividends or interest derived from the active conduct of a banking, financing or similar business within the U.S. or received by a corporation whose principal business is trading stocks or securities for its own account; or (3) gain or sale from the sale or exchange (outside the U.S.) through such office of personal property unless the property is sold or exchanged for use, consumption or disposition outside the U.S. and an office or fixed place of business of the taxpayer in a foreign country participated materially in the sale.[42]

The foregoing provisions do not apply to Subpart F income or to dividends, interest or royalties paid by a foreign corporation to a taxpayer

[40]Code § 897. FIRPTA also imposes withholding tax requirements.

[41]Code § 861(a). Income from sources without the U.S. is defined in Code § 862(a) primarily as a "mirror" of the definition of income from sources within the U.S.

[42]Code § 864(c)(4)(B).

who owns more than 50 percent of the voting power of the stock of the corporation.[43]

Tax planners should always recall that tax treaties (conventions) between the U.S. and foreign nations frequently modify the tax provisions otherwise applicable. For example, the tax convention between the U.S. and Germany exempts royalty income from source taxation. However, the FIRPTA tax applies regardless of treaties.

A 25 percent foreign-owned U.S. corporation or a foreign corporation engaged in a U.S. trade or business is required to file annually with the IRS an information return or Form 5472 describing transactions between the corporation and foreign-related parties. Code § 6038A and C.

5. Product Liability

Product liability is a far greater risk in the United States than in other nations. Even in the European Community, which has a Strict Liability Directive, product liability risk is modest compared to the United States.

The differences are attributable to the judges and plaintiff attorneys who play leading roles in expanding liability law in the U.S. through the common law process of judicial interpretation. For example, the courts have discovery procedures allowing broad reviews of the records of product manufacturers and lengthy depositions of their personnel. The courts also allow plaintiff attorneys to seek punitive damages in very large amounts, subject to only modest standards. See Chapter 13 for further discussion of product liability in the United States.

6. Reporting of Foreign Investment in the United States

The Bureau of Economic Analysis (BEA) of the U.S. Department of Commerce conducts every 5 years a survey of foreign direct investment in the United States. The BEA has announced its 1997 benchmark survey which will require foreign investors to file Form BE-12 based on the new North American Industry Classification System (NAICS) that will replace the U.S. Standard Industrial Classification (SIC) system. See 15 C.F.R. Part 806.

The survey is mandatory and is required for each U.S. affiliate in which a foreign person owned or controlled, directly or indirectly, 10 percent or of the voting securities of a foreign corporation (or an equivalent interest in an unincorporated business) at the end of 1997. Beneficial, not record, ownership is the basis of the reporting criteria. A short form can be used for small investments. A separate form is used for banks.

An annual report on Form B-15 is required for each U.S. affiliate with total assets, sales, gross operating revenues excluding sales taxes or net income after U.S. income taxes exceeding an exemption level of $10,000,000. If any of the three exemption factors exceed $50,000,000, a long form report is required. A quarterly report on Form BE-605 is required for each U.S. affiliate exceeding an exemption level of $20,000,000.

Other reports may also be required including a Form 607, Industry Classification Questionnaire. A broker or other person who assists or in-

[43]Code § 864(c)(4)(D).

tervenes in the acquisition of a U.S. business enterprise and any person who enters into a joint venture with a foreign person must file a Form B-14 unless an exemption applies.

INDEX

About the Author

Edward E. Shea is a partner concentrating on acquisitions and mergers with the law firm of Windels, Marx, Davies & Ives in the City of New York. He is also an Adjunct Professor teaching courses in mergers and acquisitions and securities offerings at the Graduate School of Business of Pace University, and he also teaches similar courses at the New York Institute of Finance. Mr. Shea previously served as Chairman of the Board of Reichhold Chemicals Inc. for over nine years and as Senior Vice President, General Counsel and a director of GAF Corporation for several years.

Mr. Shea has been an author and editor of several previous books including *Acquisitions, Mergers, Sales, Buyouts & Takeovers* (Prentice-Hall), and the *Acquisitions Yearbooks—1991, 1992* and *1993* (New York Institute of Finance). He has also written numerous articles for professional publications including *Mergers & Acquisitions, Standard & Poor's Review of Financial Services Regulation*, the *American Bar Association Journal*, the *National Law Journal, The New York Law Journal* and *The Practical Lawyer*. He is a graduate of the University of Michigan Law School.